D0672522

TREE MAINTENANCE

The author is examining the leaves of a magnificent century-old London planetree (*Platanus acerifolia*) on the grounds of The New York Botanical Garden, Bronx Park, New York. The tree, 90 feet tall, has a trunk circumference of 13 feet and a branch spread of 100 feet.

Tree Maintenance

Fifth Edition

P. P. Pirone

New York
Oxford University Press
1978

Copyright © 1978 by Oxford University Press, Inc.

Originally published in 1941 as *Maintenance of Shade and Ornamental Trees*, and revised in 1948 and 1972; copyright 1941, 1948, 1959, and 1972 by Oxford University Press, Inc.

Library of Congress Cataloging in Publication Data

Pirone, Pascal Pompey, 1907–
    Tree maintenance.

    First-2d ed. published under title: Maintenance
of shade and ornamental trees.
    Includes bibliographical references and index.
    1. Ornamental trees—Diseases and pests.
2. Trees, Care of. I. Title.
SB761.P6 1978   635.9'77   77–23786
ISBN 0–19–502321–8

9 8 7 6   Printed in the United States of America

To Loretta

Foreword to Original Edition

The care of trees is a never ending obligation, more insistent each year because appreciation of them is increasing. The owner of the tree carries the responsibility of his own account and he then naturally extends his concern to trees that stand on public property and need the interest of citizens.

One's responsibility is met only when one recognizes the cause of injury and disease and is informed on the remedies and proper procedures. Even if one has been taught these subjects in school he nevertheless needs to be informed on the newest difficulties and the latest approved practices. The difficulties increase. Thus it comes that new and authoritative books are always needed.

Therefore I am glad to see this book on Maintenance of Shade and Ornamental Trees by Dr. P. P. Pirone, whose work I have known for many years. He is investigator and teacher. He has an eye to the immediately practical, as evidenced by the simplicity of the writing, clearness of the directions, and the significant pictures. It is an important presentation of the subject.

L. H. BAILEY

Ithaca, N.Y.
March 1, 1941.

Preface

Six years have passed since I prepared the fourth edition of this book on tree maintenance. In that brief period enough changes have occurred in the field of arboriculture to justify the preparation of a new edition.

The words in the foreword by L. H. Bailey, one of America's all-time greats in botany and horticulture, in the first edition of this book more than a third of a century ago, remain true today. Interest in the planting and care of trees is at an unprecedented high in this country.

Arbor Day is observed annually in most states. Block associations in many large cities sponsor the planting and maintenance of trees. Only recently, 50,000 new trees were planted along New York City's streets, parkways, and in parks. Other cities all over America have or are planning extensive tree-planting programs.

The present edition differs considerably from earlier ones, particularly as to the kinds and uses of pesticides.

The Environmental Protection Agency has banned the use of Aldrin, Dieldrin, and DDT and in late December 1975, citing a cancer risk to humans, banned most uses of chlordane and heptachlor. Wherever there is a choice, the pesticides least harmful to people, animals, and fish life are recommended in this edition. The relative toxicity for most pesticides is given in Chapters 11 and 13. Although some pesticides have been used improperly or excessively in the past, the fact remains that there is a place for their continued use. This is especially true for trees and other ornamental plants.

New information in this edition includes the following:

The latest innovations in transplanting and tree feeding equipment, which are described and illustrated.

Data on the ability of trees to withstand prolonged flooding of the soil in which they are growing.

A new and more accurate method of estimating the fertilizer requirements of trees growing in wide, open spaces, as suggested by Professor Russell M. Bettes of Temple University.

New concepts on the effectiveness of tree wound paints and on treating cavities in trees, based on the research of Dr. A. L. Shigo, Chief Plant Pathologist of the U.S. Department of Agriculture Forest Service.

Latest research results on the effect of natural gas to trees, based largely on the researches of Dutch scientist Dr. J. Hoeks and

Dr. J. H. B. Garner of the Environmental Protection Agency at the National Environmental Research Center in North Carolina.

Diagnosis and treatment for the lethal yellowing disease that has killed thousands of coconut palms in Florida in the past few years.

Newest injection treatments for protecting—and in some instances, curing—elm trees against the highly fatal Dutch elm disease.

The bibliography at the end of each chapter has been greatly expanded to include all the more important research work on tree maintenance reported up to mid-1977.

Earlier editions consistently advocated the burning of diseased or insect-infested branches, or entire trees. Now, with present restrictions on open burning of such materials, that easy way of disposing of them is unavailable. Some of the material can be buried; most of the remainder can be placed in the trash can to be carted away. Hence, the frequent use of "destroy" or "discard" when dealing with the situation.

As in earlier editions, I tried to incorporate my experiences with tree maintenance problems—experiences involving personal examinations of literally thousands of trees. Helping me to locate and diagnose some of the tree problems were several highly trained and experienced arborists, including Jack Cutler of Stamford, Conn., Robert Mullane of Alpine Tree Care, Inc., White Plains, N.Y., and R. W. Doherty of Sleepy Hollow Restorations, Tarrytown, N.Y.

I also chose to follow a course midway between the technical and the popular. That is, I have tried to be not too technical for the beginner in tree maintenance work, and not too elementary for the professional arborist, nurseryman, landscape architect, and the college student enrolled in a course on tree maintenance. I trust I will satisfy most of my readers.

Many persons have lent a hand in the preparation of this edition. First, as in all earlier editions, is my dear wife, Loretta. Despite poor health for the past five years, she has been a constant source of encouragement to enable me to complete the present edition.

Others who helped in preparing this edition are Thomas Corell, cooperative Extension, Suffolk County, N.Y.; Ellen Hayes, my former secretary, and Bernice Winkler, secretary of the Harding Research Laboratory, New York Botanical Garden; Dr. Clark Rogerson, mycologist; my son, Dr. Thomas Pirone, University of Kentucky; my daughter, Mary Pirone; Dr. Louis Vasvary, Entomologist at Rutgers University; and Alfred G. Wheeler, Jr., Entomologist for the Bureau of Plant Industry, Pennsylvania Department of Agriculture.

I wish now to pay my respects to two fine persons who had much to do with earlier editions of this book and who are no longer with us:

First is Mrs. Herminie B. Kitchen, Specialist Emeritus in Agricultural Information at Rutgers University, who helped edit this book from its inception in 1941 through to its fourth edition.

My long-time friend, Edward Scanlon, is the second great loss to arboriculture. His love for trees, his quest for new and better kinds, his ability to raise new and better ones, and his publication of the magazine, *Trees*, devoted entirely to trees and their care, will be difficult to replace.

In all probability, this will be my final edition of *Tree Maintenance*. After all, when one passes the proverbial "three-score year and ten" he is entitled to rest and to reminisce.

My association with Oxford University Press (whose 500th Anniversary will be celebrated this year) has been a pleasant, productive and profitable one, starting with its Trade Editor, Philip Vaudrin in 1940 and continuing until now with its vice-president, Sheldon Meyer, Leona Capeless, managing editor, and Annabel Tyrrell.

I also want to express my gratitude to the many professional arborists and agricultural scientists whose publications are listed in the bibliographies. Without their contributions, a book like this could not have been written. I wish to single out, particularly, the *Journal of Arboriculture*, published by the International Society of Arboriculture, for its excellent articles on all phases of tree care.

Finally, I wish to thank the following persons and organizations for the use of illustrations:

Asplundh Tree Expert Co., Chalfont, Pennsylvania: Fig. 5-9.

Bartlett Tree Expert Co., Stamford, Connecticut: Fig. 4-4, 10-12, 12-2, 14-2, 14-6, 15-4, and 17-5.

Dr. Dominick Basile, Lehman College, New York City: Frontispiece and Fig. 8-12.

John Bean Div., Food Machinery Corp., Tipton, Indiana: Fig. 12-5.

Dr. J. C. Carter, Illinois Natural History Survey, Urbana, Illinois: Figs. 9-2, 15-22, and 17-9.

R. A. Cool, Lansing, Michigan: Figs. 3-4 and 3-5.

Thomas Corell, Cooperative Extension Association of Suffolk County, New York: Fig. 17-15.

Ross Daniels, West Des Moines, Iowa: Figs. 3-13, 4-4, 4-5 and 4-6.

R. W. Doherty, Sleepy Hollow Restorations, Tarrytown, New York: Fig. 6-16.

T. H. Everett, New York Botanical Gardens: Figs. 3-2, 3-3, 5-10, 5-11, 5-12, 6-3, 6-4, 8-2, 8-3, 8-5, 8-6, 8-10, 15-3 and 17-19.

Geigy Co., Ardsley, New York: Fig. 10-15.

E. F. Guba, Massachusetts Agricultural Experiment Station: Fig. 17-4.

Dr. George Hepting, Asheville, North Carolina: Fig. 14-3.

Homelite Div., Textron, Charlotte, North Carolina: Fig. 5-2.

H. D. Hudson Mfg. Co., Chicago, Illinois: Fig. 12-4.

Niels Hvass, Sitas Skovveg 56, 2750 Ballerup, Denmark: Fig. 6-6.

Gary H. Maier, Des Moines, Iowa: Figs. 4-3 and 9-3.

Mobile Aerial Towers, Fort Wayne, Indiana: Fig. 5-3.

Nassau County Co-op extension Association, Garden City, New York: Fig. 16-42.

New Jersey Federation of Shade Tree Commissions, New Brunswick, New Jersey: Fig. 3-12.

William A. Rae, Frost and Higgins Co., Burlington, Massachusetts: Fig. 3-8.

Edward Scanlon Associates, Olmsted Falls, Ohio: Figs. 8-1, 8-4, 8-7, 8-9, and 8-11.

Dr. John C. Schread, Connecticut Agricultural Experiment Station, New Haven, Connecticut: Figs. 15-18, 15-19, 15-24, 17-1, 17-20, 17-22, 17-23, 17-25 and 17-86.

Dr. A. L. Shigo, USDA, Forest Service, Northeastern Forest Experiment Station, Durham, New Hampshire: Fig. 6-5.

Siebenthaler Co., Dayton, Ohio: Fig. 8-8.

C. Powers Taylor, Rosedale Nurseries, Eastview, New York: Figs. 3-9 and 3-11.

Alfred G. Wheeler, Jr., Bureau of Plant Industry, Pennsylvania Dept. of Agriculture, Harrisburg: Figs. 16-21 and 16-22.

P. P. PIRONE

New York,
September 1977

Contents

to fill a cavity. Filling the cavity. Specifications for a good filler. Filling materials. Advice to tree owners.

II. Specific Abnormalities of Trees

16. *Diseases and Insect Pests of Tall-growing Trees* 379

Contents

17. Diseases and Insect Pests of Evergreen Trees

TREE MAINTENANCE

I

General Maintenance Practices

1

The Normal Tree

Almost everyone likes trees for one reason or another. Some like them for the cool shade they provide during hot summer days. Others like them because they add to the beauty or to the value of a property. Still others like them for sentimental reasons—perhaps because grandpa planted the trees when he and grandma moved into the neighborhood many years ago. No matter what the reason, whether aesthetic, financial, or sentimental, a tree is a sound investment. A house surrounded by large trees is worth more money than a house without them. A house with no trees near it looks hot in summer, appears unbalanced, and suggests, however unjustly, a lack of interest on the part of those who live in it.

Old residential areas are usually more inviting and more restful than most brand-new housing developments for one important reason: they are well supplied with large trees.

Trees have other beneficial effects. They help supply oxygen we need to breathe. Each year an acre of trees can produce enough oxygen to keep 18 persons alive. They also help to keep our air supply fresh by using up some of the carbon dioxide that we exhale and that factories and engines emit.

Trees cut noise pollution by acting as barriers to sound. Each 100-foot width of trees can absorb about 6 to 8 decibels of sound intensity.

Trees may be effectively used to keep a house cooler in summer and warmer in winter. Deciduous trees planted to the south of the house allow most of the winter sun's rays to reach the house, thus providing some warmth. In summer, the same trees will shade the house and thus make the rooms on that side much cooler. Evergreen trees planted on the north side will help to shield the house from cold winds.

It has been shown that with an air temperature of 84°F. (29°C.), the surface temperature is 108°F. (42°C.). But on a street lined with trees, with an air temperature of 84°F., the surface temperature is just 88°F. (31°C.) because heat rays are reflected off the surface of leaves, thus making it more comfortable for pedestrians and travelers in automobiles.

The character of a city is changed by an abundance or a dearth of trees. Cities that spend liberal amounts of money to maintain their old trees and to plant new ones are generally considered nicer places in which to live.

Trees planted along streets and parkways of towns and cities represent a considerable financial investment. The number planted along city streets alone in the United States has been estimated at more than 32 million. States having more than 2 million trees along city streets include New York with 2,825,000, Pennsylvania with 2,540,000, and Ohio with 2,172,000. States with more than a million street trees are California, Illinois, Massachusetts, Michigan, New Jersey, and Texas.

New York City, usually considered a place of steel and concrete, has upwards of two million trees within its borders. Of these, more than 250,000 grow along city streets and in parks and are under the jurisdiction of its Department of Parks, Recreation and Cultural Affairs. Under the Department of Parks and Public Property, Cleveland has 130,000 trees, most of which are planted along city streets. The Department of Parks and Recreation in Los Angeles takes care of some 380,000 trees.

Among the cities with most trees per unit of population are Greenwich, Connecticut and Whittier, California, each with 0.7 people for each street tree, and Santa Ana, California, with 1 person for each tree. Brooklyn, New York reported the fewest trees on a population basis, or 20 persons for each tree.

The number of persons per street tree in cities of different sizes has been estimated as follows:

Size of City	Average Number of Persons per Street Tree
Less than 25,000	1.6
25,000 to 50,000	2.0
50,000 to 100,000	2.6
100,000 to 250,000	4.2
250,000 to 500,000	5.4
1,000,000 or over	10.0

Because shade and ornamental trees represent such a great investment, it behooves all Americans to do what they can to keep the trees in good health. There are many ways, as this book shows, to increase the beauty, usefulness, longevity, and value of trees.

Value of Individual Trees

Occasionally it becomes necessary to appraise the value of a tree. This may be needed to establish a casualty loss to determine the damages one must pay for injuring or killing someone else's tree. Or an insurance company may want to know the value of an insured tree that died. Or the homeowner may want to know how much to deduct from his income tax for a tree damaged or destroyed by hurricane, ice-storm, lightning, or fire.

Highly qualified members of the International Society of Arboriculture prepared an excellent booklet on how to appraise the value of a tree. The latest (1975) edition was edited by Dr. Dan Neely of Urbana, Illinois.*

The basic factors of this particular evaluation system are the kind of tree, its size, and its condition. The diameter at breast height (DBH)—which is about 4½ feet above ground level—determines the tree's size. This is translated by means of a conversion table into a measurement of the cross section of the tree. A basic valuation of $10 per square inch of trunk cross section has been established as a fair price. This figure is then taken at 100, 80, 60, 40, or 20 per cent, depending on the kind of tree involved. An oak tree or a dogwood obviously is worth much more than a silver maple or an ailanthus. Finally, this adjusted figure is taken at 100, 80, 60, 40, or 20 per cent, depending on the condition of the tree as determined by a competent arborist or forester. A tree with an extensive trunk cavity is certainly far less valuable than a sound, uninfected one.

A little common sense is also needed in adjusting a local situation to this guide. Obviously a 12-inch DBH white oak growing on the front lawn of a $50,000 house is worth more than the same kind of tree growing in a wooded, isolated plot of ground.

What Is a Normal Tree?

Before anyone can successfully maintain old trees or plant new ones, he must understand the anatomy and functions of a normal, healthy tree. Without such knowledge it is difficult to diagnose accurately the

* Copies of the booklet 'A Guide to the Professional Evaluation of Landscape Trees, Specimen Shrubs, and Evergreens' can be purchased from the International Society of Arboriculture, P. O. Box 71, Urbana, Illinois, 61801.

many abnormalities that commonly occur in trees or to appreciate various practices undertaken to maintain or restore their vigor.

Normality in any living organism is so vague and relative it almost defies definition. Perhaps a scientifically accurate definition might be derived by applying to the tree something of the psychologists' concept of the normal human being. By their rule, the normal tree would fall within certain limits of health and vigor that include the majority of trees in a specified range.

For our purposes, however, we cannot go far astray if we are guided in our evaluation of a healthy tree by the desirable external appearances with which we are all familiar. Since a tree is most admired when it has a symmetrical branch system and abundant, attractive foliage, we may include these two characteristics among our standards of perfection. Healthy roots must also be included, for without them proper branch and foliage growth cannot continue.

To gain a working knowledge of the proper care of trees, we must know something of the structure of each of the different parts that constitute a normal shade tree, the functions these parts perform in the growth process, and the relation between the parts.

Parts of a Tree

The tree is divided into three major parts or organs: the stem, the leaves, and the roots. Each of these has its important and specific functions to perform, and each by its peculiar structure is remarkably well adapted to the performance of these functions.

Structure of the Stem. Tree trunks and their branches are constituted to endure the strains placed upon them by the varying conditions of their environment. The largest part of the stem or trunk is composed of a wood cylinder made up of tissues called *xylem.* The xylem is composed chiefly of long, thick-walled tubes or ducts, through which water containing nutrient salts is conducted from the roots to the leaves, and wood fibers, which lend tensile strength to the tree. Xylem makes up the greater part of the stem and in trees is commonly known as wood. Wood, then, is that part of a tree that gives it strength and stability. The inner central portion, called *heartwood,* is entirely composed of dead cells and does not conduct water or nutrients. The outer portion of the wood cylinder, the *sapwood,* has many living cells and is the region in which upward conduction of water and nutrient takes place.

In the center of every tree is a region known as *pith,* small in most trees, relatively large in the alders. The pith is composed of the remnants of the soft, cellular tissues of the growing tip. It has no specific function and is frequently so crowded by growth pressure that in older stems it is entirely lost.

Inspection of the cross section of any tree trunk (Fig. 1-1) reveals numerous concentric lines, the *annual rings,* which are plainly visible because of the alternating large and small cells. These rings represent the annual increase in the diameter of the tree. The large cells are formed by rapid growth in the spring; the smaller, by slower growth in the summer. As the season progresses, the new cells become smaller and smaller, until growth stops altogether in the fall. This compact region of small cells, known as *summer wood,* makes the annual ring. It is in sharp contrast to the large cells, or *spring wood,* formed by rapid growth during the spring.

Across the annual rings many radial lines are visible, running from the outer edge of the wood cylinder toward the center. These lines, called *medullary rays,* are groups of cells extending through the many cylinders of woods that provide for radial transfer of water and food.

Immediately outside the xylem is a narrow band of cells known as the *cambium.* During the growing season, the cells of the cambium are stimulated, perhaps by certain natural hormones, to active and continu-

Fig. 1-1. Cross section of a tree trunk, showing A, the heartwood, composed of dead cells; B, the sapwood, which has many living cells that conduct water and nutrients upward; c, the annual rings composed of summer and spring wood; D, the medullary rays, which transfer water and food radially; E, the cambium, from which are formed xylem cells on the inside and phloem tissue on the outside; F, the phloem cells, which conduct elaborated food downward; G, the cork cambium, which produces cork cells to form the outer bark, H.

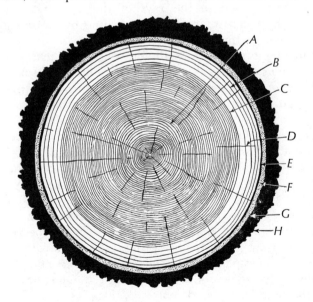

ous division, giving rise to xylem tissue on the interior, and *phloem* tissue on the exterior. The phloem tissue is mainly conductive in function, but, unlike the xylem, which conducts water and nutrients upward, it chiefly conducts the elaborated food material from the leaves to the growing region in a downward direction. Outside of the phloem lies another type of cambium, the *cork cambium,* which gives rise to cork cells, the *outer bark.* The bark serves the very important function of preventing loss of moisture from the inner tissues. It also provides some protection from mechanical injuries, from the claws and teeth of animals, and from insects. Rapid growth of the inner, woody cylinder frequently causes the bark to crack. In some trees the outer layers of corky tissues soon become detached from the stem, leaving the surface of the bark smooth and relatively thin, as in buttonwood. Trees such as oak and elm, on the other hand, may retain the cork layers for many years, forming a thick furrowed bark. The outer bark of some trees has such unusual config- uration that the species can be identified from the bark alone.

Function of the Stem. The functions of the stem, or trunk, of a tree are structural support, the conduction of water, food, and nutrients, and the storage of elaborated food materials.

One of the chief services rendered by the much-branched stem or trunk of a tree is support of the leaves in such a manner that they may derive maximum benefit from the direct action of the sun's rays. The importance of this role will become more apparent when the functions of the leaf itself are discussed. Let us remember for the present, however, that it is essential to the growth of the tree that as many leaves as possible be exposed to the rays of the sun. This exposure is accomplished by means of multiple branching of the tree trunk into limbs, branches, and finally twigs.

The trunk and its subdivisions, the branches, are the connecting links between the roots, where water and soil nutrients are absorbed, and the leaves, where food is manufactured. It is the function of these connect- ing links first to transport the water and inorganic salts in water solution from the roots to the leaves; and second, to distribute to every growing part of the tree, including every twig and root tip, the elaborated food products built up from raw materials.

In all deciduous trees, food materials manufactured in the leaves are gradually conducted to the twigs. These foods are partially assimilated for immediate growth. The surplus is stored in the twigs, in the trunks, and in the roots. Late in the season, when the leaves become less active in the manufacture of food, part of this surplus is reabsorbed for assimila- tion by the growing parts. In the spring, too, the initial twig and root growth—which takes place before the leaves are expanded and active— and frequently blossom production are entirely dependent upon food stored in the twigs, stems, and roots.

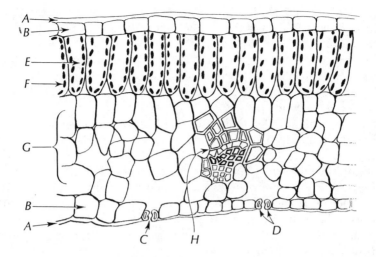

Fig. 1-2. Diagrammatic cross section of a leaf, showing A, the cuticle; B, the epidermis; C, the stomata; D, the guard cells; E, the palisade cells; F, the chloroplasts; G, the spongy parenchyma; and H, the veinal tissues.

During a severe drought the trunks of tree can shrink so much that their diameters are smaller than they were before the growing season started.

Structure of Leaves. If we look at the cross section of a leaf (Fig.1-2) under a microscope, we see that the outer walls of the surface cells, or *epidermis,* are coated with a waxy covering or *cuticle.* This covering was once thought to be continuous except for the areas perforated with thousands of minute openings called *stomata* (singular *stoma*). Recent research has revealed, however, that instead of being a continuous coating over the surface, the cuticle is interspersed with pectin-like substances (Fig. 4-7). The cuticle and the epidermis help to prevent rapid drying out of the moist inner cells. Each stoma is surrounded by two kidney-shaped, movable cells, the *guard cells.* Through these pores moisture evaporates* from the leaf, thus allowing additional water and nutrients to be drawn from the roots. The stomata also allow free interchanges of gases from within the leaf to the atmosphere surrounding it, and vice versa. The guard cells are very sensitive to light, opening

---

* The forces primarily responsible for the upward movement of fluids operate mainly in the leaf. Evaporation from the leaves sets up a pull on the countless columns of water in the xylem tissues. The tensile strength of the water itself holds these columns intact from the root to the leaf, thus aiding an influx of soil water at the roots proportional to the amount of moisture lost by evaporation.

in light and partially closing in the dark. Thus the loss of water and the gaseous exchange through the stomata are much greater during the day than at night.

Stomata are often about 10 to 20 microns long. In scarlet oak (*Quercus coccinea*) there may be as many as 100 stomata per square centimeter. Despite their great numbers, they occupy only 1 to 2 per cent of the leaf surface when they are fully open.

As a rule stomata are open in bright light and closed at night. Adverse conditions, especially when water is deficient, can also result in their closing.

Beneath the epidermis are one or more layers of long, cylindrical cells, the *palisade cells*. These contain many minute bodies known as *chloroplasts*, which in turn contain the green substance known as *chlorophyll*. Chlorophyll absorbs the light energy from the sun and transforms it into chemical energy, which acts upon water from the soil and carbon dioxide from the air to form sugars.

Numerous large, loosely arranged cells (the spongy *parenchyma*) lie between the palisade cells and the lower epidermis. The spaces between these cells facilitate the diffusion of gases between the stomata and the palisade cells.

Function of Leaves. The primary function of the leaf is the manufacture of sugars, the basic food materials used directly or after combination with other elements in various cells of the tree for root growth, maturation of woody tissues, formation of fruits and seeds, and storage. Green leaves, therefore, represent factories upon which the tree depends for its entire food supply. The foods used by trees for growth are the same carbohydrates, proteins, and fats used by animals, but green plants have the power to make their own food, whereas every other living thing is dependent upon green plants for its food, shelter, clothing, and fuel.

The process of food manufacture, *photosynthesis* (photo = light; synthesis = manufacture), is highly complicated and need be discussed here only in its essential details.

Food cannot be manufactured when a plant wilts and the stomata are nearly closed. But in a normal tree, carbon dioxide enters through the stomata of the leaf into the intercellular spaces, surrounds the cells, and is absorbed by the water solution there. Having passed through the cell walls into the chloroplasts, the carbon dioxide and the water split up into their separate constituents. These recombine chemically to form a series of intermediate products, resulting eventually in sugars and starches, known collectively as carbohydrates. By the addition of nitrogen, small quantities of the element sulfur, and in some cases phosphorus also, these carbohydrates become proteins. Sugars may also be transformed into cellulose, lignin, fats, and oils.

During photosynthesis, oxygen is given off. Thus the process resolves itself into one of taking carbon dioxide from the atmosphere and returning oxygen to it. Animals bring about the reverse process (respiration) by utilizing the oxygen and returning carbon dioxide to the atmosphere. This is one of the interesting partnerships between plants and animals in which each helps contribute the elements necessary for the other's existence.

The leaves function somewhat differently when suitable plant foods are sprayed on them. The pectinlike substances previously mentioned have a high capacity for absorbing and releasing water and nutrients. They provide a direct connection between the outside atmosphere and the interior of the leaf via so-called *plasmodesma*. Hence, by spraying a balanced plant food on the leaves, one can supply nitrogen, phosphate, and potash, and certain minor elements to the plant. Most of these nutrients formerly were applied to the soil. More details on this method of supplying raw food elements to the trees are presented in the chapter on tree fertilization.

Structure of Roots. There are two principal types of roots, *tap* and *surface*, named according to their shape and depth of penetration. Examples of tap-rooted trees are hickory, walnut, tulip, and many oaks. Elm, spruce, and maple are surface-rooted species. Some trees have a combination of both types of root systems.

The root system of some trees is enormous. It may comprise one third to one half of the entire volume of the tree. The total length of all roots of a large, spreading oak runs into hundreds of miles.

At the point of attachment to the trunk, the roots are relatively few and large. They then divide and redivide, becoming progressively smaller in diameter until they become extremely fine rootlets at some distance from the trunk. The smallest of these strands are the absorption rootlets, which are covered a short distance back from the tips with numerous, very fine outgrowths of thin-walled individual cells, called the *root hairs.* Through these root hairs nearly all the water and nutrient salts are absorbed. As these minute appendages are very delicate, no single invididual lives very long. The older ones are constantly dying, but new ones are continually being formed behind the growing tip. On certain rootlets more than 10,000 root hairs to a square inch have been found.

In advance of the root-hair region of rootlets is a section where primary elongation of the root takes place. This growing point is just behind the root tip and is protected from injury by a group of cells known as the *root cap.* The growing point is composed of a small group of rapidly dividing cells, which push the tip through the soil and lay down in their wake new tissues of the root.

Function of Roots. The functions of roots are primarily four: storage of elaborated foods, conduction, absorption, and anchorage. Tree roots, like those of other plants, store elaborated food materials, as do stems and twigs. The conducting tissues of the roots are, in form and function, essentially like those in the stem. Absorption and anchorage are so intimately associated with the medium in which roots grow—the soil— that they will be discussed in considerable detail in the following chapter.

Selected Bibliography

Allen, S. W. 1938. *An introduction to American forestry.* McGraw-Hill Book Co., New York, 402 p.

Anonymous. 1976. 'Tree evaluation for tax purposes.' *Shade Tree Digest.* January, 1976.

Bingham, Charlotte A. 1968. 'Tree preservation and protection on private property.' *Proc. Forty-fourth International Shade Tree Conference.* p. 234–46.

Butcher, Devereaux. (ed.) 1974. *Knowing your trees,* 5th Tree Edition. American Forestry Assoc., Washington, D.C. 105 p.

Chopowick, R. E. 1971. 'Trees and the urban microclimate.' *Garden Journal.* New York Botanical Garden. Vol. 22 (No. 6). p. 176–78.

Elias, Thomas (Ed). 1976. *Trees and the community.* The Cary Arboretum, New York Botanical Garden. 32 p.

Federer, C. A. 1976. 'Trees modify the urban microclimate.' *Jour. Arboriculture.* Vol. 2 (No. 7). p. 121–27.

Fritts, H. C. 1966. 'Growth-rings of trees: their correlation with climate.' *Science.* Vol. 154. p. 973–79. Nov. 25, 1966.

Gibbs, R. D. 1939. 'Studies in tree physiology.' I. General Introduction. Water contents of certain Canadian trees. *Canad. Jour. Res.* Vol. 17. p. 460–82.

Haller, J. M. 1954. *Tree care.* Macmillan, New York. 224 p.

Hemming, E. S. 1966. 'Trees do grow fast." *Am. Hort. Magazine.* Vol. 45 (No. 21). p. 257–60.

Hutchins, R. E. 1964. *This is a tree.* Dodd, Mead, New York. 159 p.

Kielbaso, J. J. 1975. 'Economic values of trees in the urban locale.' *Trees Magazine.* Vol. 34 (No. 1). p. 9–13.

Kiernan, John. 1954. *An introduction to trees.* Hanover House, Garden City, N.Y. 224 p.

King, G. C. 1977. 'Plant material evaluation.' *Jour. Arboriculture.* Vol. 3 (No. 4). p. 61–64.

Kozlowski, T. T. 1968. 'Water balance in shade trees.' *Proc. Forty-fourth International Shade Tree Conference,* p. 29–42.

Kramer, P. J. and T. T. Kozlowski. 1960. *Physiology of trees.* McGraw-Hill Book Co., New York. 642 p.

Lewis, C. L. (ed.) 1970. *Shade tree evaluation.* International Shade Tree Conference. Urbana, Ill. 44 p.

McKensie, M. A. 1970. 'The role of shade trees in urban forestry.' *Arborist's News.* Vol. 35 (No. 3). p. 21–24. March 1970.

Miller, E. C. 1939. *Plant physiology.* McGraw-Hill Book Co., New York. 900 p.

Muller, Katherine K. 1965. 'Trees as a community asset.' *Arborist's News.* Vol. 30 (No. 7). p. 49–54.

Murphy, R. C. and W. E. Meyer. 1969. *The care and feeding of trees.* Crown Publishers, New York. 164 p.

Neel, P. L. 1969. 'Growth factors in trunk development of young trees.' *Proc. Forty-fifth International Shade Tree Conference.* p. 46–59.

Neely, Dan. (ed.) 1975. *A guide to the professional evaluation of landscape trees, specimen shrubs, and evergreens.* International Society Arboriculture. Urbana, Ill. 18 p. Revision III. July 1975.

Pack, C. L. 1922. *School book of forestry.* American Tree Assoc., Washington, D.C. p. 159.

Pirone, P. P. 1972. 'Tree maintenance.' *Garden Journal.* New York Botanical Garden. Vol. 22 (No. 1) p. 12–15.

———. 1972. *Tree maintenance.* 4th ed. Oxford Univ. Press, New York. 574 p.

Platt, Rutherford. 1952. *American trees.* Dodd, Mead, New York. 256 p.

Priestley, J. H. 1935. 'Radial growth and expansion growth in the tree.' *Forestry* (Gt. Brit.) Vol. 9 (No. 2). p. 84–95.

Purcell, C. R. 1956. 'The realty value of trees.' *Proc. Thirty-second National Shade Tree Conference.* p. 128–36.

Reisch, K. W. and C. E. Hull. 1970. 'Characteristics and adaptability of species and cultivars of shade and ornamental trees with emphasis on street and highway landscape use.' *Arborist's News.* Vol. 35 (No. 3). p. 24–27. March 1970.

Sachs, R. M. 1969. 'Growth control in trees—anatomical and physiological aspects.' *Proc. Forty-fifth International Shade Tree Conference* (Oregon). p. 60–77.

Steele, Fletcher. 1946. 'Tree values shift.' *Proc. Twenty-second National Shade Tree Conference.* p. 79–93.

Stevenson, Tom. 1970. 'A healthy tree is a precious thing.' *Am. Hort. Magazine.* 103–10. Summer 1970.

Stout, B. B. 1967. Root systems of deciduous trees.' *Proc. Forty-third International Shade Tree Conference.* p. 30–36.

Wikle, Jack. 1970. 'Appreciation of trees.' *Arborist's News.* Vol. 35 (No. 10). p. 105–6.

2

The Soil and Its Relation to Trees

No book on the maintenance of shade and ornamental trees would be complete without some discussion of that important natural body, the soil. Usually considered by the layman to be an inert mass, soil is actually a dynamic entity in which physical, chemical, and biological changes are constantly occurring. A detailed treatment of these changes is beyond the scope of this book, but a brief presentation of the more important ones, particularly as they relate to trees, is essential.

Soil serves as a storehouse for plant nutrients, a habitat for microorganisms, and a reservoir of water for the tree's growth. It also provides anchorage for the tree.

Soil Components

The soil is composed of three distinct parts or phases: gaseous, the soil air; liquid, the soil water; and solid, the soil minerals and organic matter. These parts are interrelated very closely.

The Soil Air. The pore space in soils amounts to 30 to 50 per cent of the volume. The quantity of air contained in the soil is governed primarily by the extent to which this pore space is filled with moisture. Ordinarily, air comprises about 20 per cent of the volume of a well-tilled soil.

Oxygen, one of the most important components of soil air, is used in the oxidation of toxins that otherwise would accumulate in the soil. It also supports the activity of numerous beneficial microorganisms. Nitrogen, another component of the soil air, is used as a raw material by nitrogen-fixing bacteria to manufacture protein materials, which later decompose to yield nitrates that nourish the tree.

All three roots and soil microorganisms respire,* that is, they continuously consume oxygen and give off carbon dioxide. In poorly aerated soil, where gaseous exchange between the soil air and the atmosphere is retarded, the oxygen supply decreases, whereas the quantity of carbon dioxide increases. This unfavorable oxygen-carbon dioxide balance may retard or, in extreme cases, completely check root growth. Roots do not thrive in such areas. This, in fact, explains why the more active roots of city trees are often confined to the soil areas between the curb and the sidewalk, and to nearby lawn areas.

Although oxygen is absolutely necessary for a healthy root system, an insufficiency of this element for relatively short periods will not result in serious damage. Studies by Cornell University scientists revealed that the oxygen content of orchard soils in spring sometimes falls from the normal 21 per cent at the surface to as low as 1 or 2 percent at a depth of 3 to 5 feet. The carbon dioxide content of the same soil increases to 2 to 3 per cent at the 1-foot level, and occasionally exceeds 12 per cent at 5 feet.

Flooding of soil in winter when roots are dormant is not so serious as it is during summer when the roots are making most active growth. Roots of apple trees can grow slowly with as little as 3 per cent oxygen, but they require at least 10 per cent for good growth.

Because the concentration of carbon dioxide must be very high, over 20 per cent, to cause direct injury to tree roots, lack of oxygen probably is the more common cause for restricted growth or death of roots.

Capillary and gravitational movements of water and the daily changes in temperature and barometric pressure are responsible for the aeration of soils. The oxygen supply is often renewed too rapidly in sandy soils and too slowly in heavy clay soils. In either case, the situation is improved by adding organic matter or by mixing the two classes of soil. Aeration of soils is also increased by structural changes caused by the use of lime and certain fertilizer salts. The channels remaining after the roots of plants decay and those caused by the burrowing of earthworms also aid in ventilating the soil.

Some trees can thrive under conditions of relatively poor soil aeration. Willows, for example, will grow along streams and ponds where the oxygen supply is relatively low. Some scientists believe that in willows oxygen produced by photosynthesis in the leaves is transferred internally to the root cells. The roots of one species of willow, *Salix nigra*, were found to be capable of growing and absorbing nutrients in almost complete absence of oxygen. Cypress grows naturally in swamps where

---

* Actually, all living cells in the trunk and leaves also respire. Respiration, however, is of the utmost concern in roots, inasmuch as it is most often hindered in them.

the soil is flooded for long periods. The roots of this tree have pyramid-shaped protuberances called 'knees,' which extend as high as 10 feet into the air. The 'knees' are composed of light, soft, spongy wood and bark which permit air to reach the roots during the weeks and even months when the swamps are covered with water.

On the other hand, plants like yew and cherry thrive in soils that are well drained and well aerated. Such trees are killed or severely damaged if the soil is waterlogged for only a few days during the growing season.

Some trees can survive prolonged periods of soil flooding; others cannot. New York State nurseryman Philip M. White observed the response of trees whose roots were flooded in from 4 to 15 inches of standing water for 10 days as the aftermath of hurricane Agnes in western New York State in 1972. Listed among the survivors were:

Acer rubrum	Red Maple
Cornus mas	Cornelian Cherry
Fraxinus americana	White Ash
Gleditsia triacanthos inermis	Thornless Honey Locust
Juglans nigra	Black Walnut
Juniperus chinensis 'Pfitzeriana'	Pfitzer Juniper
Juniperus virginiana	Red Cedar
Malus dolgo	Dolgo Crabapple
Morus alba	Mulberry
Platanus occidentalis	Sycamore
Populus deltoides	Cottonwood
Salix alba	White Willow
Salix discolor	Pussy Willow
Tilia cordata	European Littleleaf Linden

Trees that did not survive the prolonged flooding were:

Acer saccharum	Sugar Maple
Acer platanoides	Norway Maple
Betula papyrifera	White Birch
Betula populifolia	Gray Birch
Cercis canadensis	Redbud
Cladrastis lutea	Yellowwood
Cornus florida	White Flowering Dogwood
Cornus florida 'Rubra'	Red Flowering Dogwood
Cornus florida 'Cloud 9'	'Cherokee Chief' Dogwood
Crataegus phaenopyrum	Washington Hawthorn
Crataegus lavallei	Lavalle Hawthorn
Magnolia soulangiana	Saucer Magnolia
Malus spp. 'Hopa,' 'Lodi,' 'McIntosh,' 'Radiant'	Apple and Crabapple
Picea abies	Norway Spruce
Picea pungens	Colorado Spruce
Picea pungens 'Glauca'	Colorado Blue Spruce
Prunus persica	Flowering Peach

Prunus serotina	Black Cherry
Prunus subhirtella 'Pendula'	Weeping Cherry
Quercus borealis	Red Oak
Robinia pseudoacacia	Black Locust
Sorbus aucuparia	European Mountain-Ash
Taxus cuspidata	Upright Yew
Taxus cuspidata 'Expansa'	Spreading Yew
Taxus media 'Hicksi'	Hick's Yew
Thuja occidentalis	American Arborvitae
Tsuga canadensis	Canadian Hemlock

Inadequate aeration of the soil may affect the roots in an indirect manner. It may change the kind of organisms in the soil flora and make the roots more susceptible to attack by parasitic fungi. For example, the fungus *Phytophthora cinnamomi* may become so abundant in a poorly drained soil as to cause severe damage to tree roots.

Then, too, certain organisms thrive under conditions of little to no oxygen. These produce compounds such as hydrogen sulfide and nitrites which may harm the roots.

Aside from direct injury to the roots, poor aeration also prevents the roots from absorbing water and minerals. A deficiency of oxygen and an excess of carbon dioxide reduce the permeability of the roots to water. They also prevent the roots from absorbing minerals from the soil solution.

Poor aeration of the soil results in development of roots near the soil surface. Such a shallow root system makes the tree more susceptible to toppling by winds and to droughts during the summer.

According to C. Powers Taylor, nationally known nurseryman and plantsman, *'The single most critical factor in the success or failure of tree planting is soil drainage and aeration.* There is nothing that kills trees more often than poor soil drainage. We can modify this a little in selecting species more tolerant of poor soil drainage but no tree grows best in a totally saturated soil.'

Soil Water. Trees depend on the water contained in the pore space of the soil in which they are growing. The roots absorb the water and pass it on to the leaves, where it functions both as a nutrient and in the absorption of carbon dioxide from the air. Water is an essential part of the protoplasm, or living matter, of every cell. It also functions in the soil as a solvent of the necessary mineral nutrients and as a medium by which they enter the plant. Further, water transports other raw materials and elaborated food from one part of the tree to another.

Water may exist in any soil in the *hygroscopic, capillary,* or *free water* state. *Hygroscopic water* occurs in the form of a very thin film over the soil particles where the moisture in the soil is in equilibrium with that in the air. It acts both as a lubricant and as an attractant for *capillary water.* The latter exists as a thicker film, which is attracted to the particle by its own surface tension. This tension is stronger than the pull of gravity. When two soil particles are in contact, and one has a thinner film of capillary water than the other, the drier surface has a greater attraction for the water. As a result, the water moves from the wetter to the drier surface, until both particles are surrounded by films of equal thickness. When a film of capillary water reaches the maximum thickness that can be maintained by surface tension, any additional water responds to the pull of gravity and flows downward into the soil to become *free water*. Free water occupies the spaces between the moist soil particles, just as the air does when only hygroscopic and capillary water are present. When free water occupies all the pore spaces in the soil or any horizon of the soil, its upper surface is known as the water table. Because of lack of air, roots cannot survive long in such a water-saturated zone (Fig. 2-1).

When soil water comes in contact with the complex organic compounds that comprise the cell walls of the root hairs, it is absorbed by *imbibition*. From this point the water now passes on, by a process known as *osmosis*, through the plasma membrane lining the cell walls and becomes part of the cell sap. The concentration of soluble substances in the cell sap is usually greater than that in the soil solution. The movement of water into the cell tends to equalize the concentrations on both sides of the cell wall. The pull exerted by the water lost from the leaves during transpiration further aids the movement of water from cell to cell and the influx of water from the soil into the root hairs.

When the soil surrounding the root hairs becomes very dry, as during a drought, the concentration of the solution in the soil may be greater than that within the cell. Then the reverse process takes place. Water moves out of the root hairs and plant cells, causing their collapse, and the continuous water column from roots to leaves cannot be maintained. Consequently, the plant wilts. Wilting also occurs if the quantity of water lost from the leaves is greater than that gained by the roots. Such reverses are often evident in shade trees during June, July, and August.

Trees vary with respect to their moisture requirements. Red maple, pin oak, sweetgum, and most species of willow prefer soils with a high moisture content, whereas red oak, chestnut oak, ash, and poplar grow best in soils containing smaller amounts of water. Spruces can tolerate wetter soils than can most other species of conifers.

A change in the water table often seriously affects a tree's health. Although not evident at the surface, a rise in the water table may cause drowning of the deeper roots. This happened to London planetrees planted in Battery Park at the lower tip of Manhattan Island and to Hyssop crabapple trees planted in New York City's Stuyvesant Town many years ago.

Fig. 2-1. These trees died because the high water table excluded air from the roots.

The Soil Minerals. The solid body of the soil consists of varying proportions of coarse grains (sand), medium-sized grains (silt), and fine particles (clay), all of which are mineral particles originating from the disintegration of rocks. In addition, it contains varying amounts of humus substances formed in the bacterial decomposition of plant remains.

The smaller-sized particles of the clay portion of the soil are known collectively as colloidal clay. These particles aid greatly in the retention of water and plant nutrients in the soil. The working qualities of a soil depend largely on its content of colloidal clay and the condition in which this exists.

Chemically, colloidal clay consists mainly of iron and aluminum silicates and oxides. The silicates are the seat of retentive or 'exchange' processes in soils. Surrounding each tiny fragment of the exchange mineral is a layer of adsorbed water containing both cations and anions.* The cations consist chiefly of hydrogen (H), calcium (Ca), magnesium (Mg), potassium (K), and sodium (Na); while the anions are hydroxyl (OH), phosphate (PO_4), nitrate (NO_3), sulfate (SO_4), and chloride (Cl) ions. Most of these ions are plant nutrients.

As a root hair enters the zone of adsorbed water, an exchange of ions takes place between this water layer and the root hairs. As a result, the mineral nutrients of the soil solution move into the plant, and the carbonic acid of the plant is excreted into the soil.

Soil Organic Matter. The second solid component of soil is usually concentrated in the upper layers. This organic matter is essential for the maintenance of soil microorganisms. It also serves to make the soil porous and friable, to increase its water-holding capacity, and to improve its aeration. In its decay, organic matter yields up mineral nutrients and nitrogen for the use of the currently growing plants. In addition, organic matter has a high 'exchange capacity,' and acts much like the exchange minerals in colloidal clay.

Soil Reaction

Soils are acid, neutral, or alkaline in reaction. The degrees of acidity or alkalinity are expressed in terms of pH values, very much as temperatures are expressed in degrees centigrade or Fahrenheit. Temperature scales center on the freezing point of water, whereas the acidity-alkalinity scale centers on a neutral point (pH 7). The latter scale is divided into 14 major units. Values between pH 7 and 14 are alkaline, and those from pH 7 to 0 acid. The intensity of the alkalinity increases

---

* Soluble soil nutrients dissociate in water to form electrically charged particles known as cations and anions. Cations are positively charged (+), and anions are negatively charged (−).

tenfold with each unit increase in pH. For example, the alkalinity of pH 8 is 10 times as great as that of pH 7. Likewise, the acidity increases 10 times for each unit decrease in the pH scale. Thus the acidity at pH 6 is 10 times as great at that of pH 7, and at pH 5 it is 10 times as great as that at 6 and 100 times as great as that at pH 7.

The pH scale refers not to the total amount of acid or alkaline constituents in the soil, but to those portions of the acid and alkali that are in a free or dissociated state. A pH reading gives an indication of the relative number of free *acid* (H+) and *alkaline* (OH−) particles in the soil, and not of the combined or undissociated acid particles.

Most tree soils are acid in reaction, because a large portion of the alkaline exchange cations (Ca, Mg, K, and Na) have either been absorbed by the trees or lost through leaching, leaving acid exchange minerals behind. In addition, the continued use of acid-forming fertilizers and sprays (especially those containing sulfur) tends to increase acidity. In cities, certain gases, such as ammonia and sulfur dioxide, which are carried down by the rain water, further tend to increase the acidity of the soil. The pH values of most eastern tree soils lie between 5 and 6.5. They are seldom higher than 7, unless their content of limestone is naturally high or large quantities of lime have been added to them.

Although soil acidity is not the only factor governing the availability of nutrients, it nevertheless plays an important part. For example, an increase in acidity beyond certain limits means a decrease in the supply of certain plant nutrients, the hydrogen having taken the place of the basic cations in the exchange complex. The exchanged cations may have been removed by the trees, or may have been carried away by the drainage water. At the other extreme, as the alkalinity increases, the roots are less able to absorb iron, manganese, zinc, copper, and boron, because these minerals are insoluble under such conditions. A good case in point is that of the availability of iron salts, which are absorbed by the plant at a pH of 6.7 or below. If the tree is growing in an alkaline soil (above pH 7), there is a strong possibility that it will suffer from iron deficiency and that the leaves will become chlorotic (see Chlorosis, p. 236).

In general, most plants grow best on soils having a slightly acid reaction. A pH value between 5.5 and 7 seems most favorable for nearly all trees. Growth is best when the soils in which trees are planted and grown are maintained within the pH range to which they are adapted. Relatively few trees seem to prefer a distinctly acid soil. Among those that do are silverbell (*Halesia*), sourwood (*Oxydendrum*), yellowwood (*Cladrastis*), and Franklin-tree (*Franklinia*).

Some form of lime is usually recommended to sweeten excessively acid soils, and the use of aluminum sulfate and sulfur is suggested for overcoming alkalinity in soils. But sulfur should not be added to a soil that is wet and well supplied with organic matter in its deeper layers. In such a soil, it will form hydrogen sulfide, a chemical that is extremely toxic to roots.

Table 2-1 indicates the amount of ground limestone needed to increase the alkalinity of different types of soil to a 6-inch depth.

Table 2-1. Lime requirement to raise alkalinity of different soil types of same reaction

		Pounds of Agricultural Ground Limestone Needed per 1000 sq. ft.				
		Sandy Loam Soils		Silt Loam Soils		Silty-Clay Loam Soils
Present pH of Soil		to pH 6.0	to pH 6.5	to pH 6.0	to pH 6.5	to pH 6.0	to pH 6.5
6.0		none	23	none	41	none	58
5.5		23	46	41	83	55	115
5.0		46	69	83	124	115	173
4.8		55	78	97	138	138	196

Table 2-2 indicates the approximate number of pounds of sulfur or aluminum sulfate per 100 square feet of area that are required to increase the acidity of a silt loam soil to a 6-inch depth.

Table 2-2. Sulfur or aluminum sulfate requirements to increase acidity of silt loam soil

			Pounds needed per 100 sq. ft.			
		Sulfur	Aluminum Sulfate		Sulfur	Aluminum Sulfate
pH	8.0 to 7.0 . . . .2.0		4.5	pH	7.0 to 6.5 . . . .1.5	2.5
	8.0 to 6.5 . . . .3.0		7.0		7.0 to 6.0 . . . .2.0	5.5
	8.0 to 6.0 . . . .4.0		10.0		7.0 to 5.5 . . . .3.5	9.0
	8.0 to 5.5 . . . .5.5		13.5		7.0 to 5.0 . . . .5.0	13.0
	8.0 to 5.0 . . . .7.0		17.5		6.5 to 6.0 . . . .1.5	3.0
	7.5 to 7.0 . . . .1.75		3.5		6.5 to 5.5 . . . .2.5	6.5
	7.5 to 6.5 . . . .2.0		5.0		6.5 to 5.0 . . . .4.0	10.5
	7.5 to 6.0 . . . .3.5		7.5		6.0 to 5.5 . . . .1.5	3.5
	7.5 to 5.5 . . . .5.0		11.5		6.0 to 5.0 . . . .3.0	7.5
	7.5 to 5.0 . . . .6.5		15.5		5.5 to 5.0 . . . .1.5	4.0

County agricultural agents, agricultural experiment station chemists, and field representatives of agricultural chemical companies offer soil-testing services and supply information as to the amount of lime or sulfur or aluminum sulfate that must be added to produce the desired change in pH on a specific soil. If preferred, inexpensive soil-testing kits can be purchased for individual use.

The listing of the most favorable pH range of most shade and ornamental trees will be found at the end of this chapter (Table 2-3).

Soil Temperatures

Old, well-established trees, as well as recently transplanted ones, are adversely affected by extremes in soil temperatures. Low soil temperatures retard or even prevent water and mineral absorption by the roots. If, at the same time, the air temperature is high enough to allow loss of water from the leaves and twigs, serious injury may result. The winter loss, by the leaves of more moisture than can be replaced through the roots often results in drying and browning of both narrow- and broad-leaved evergreens (see Winter Drying of Evergreens, p. 213).

As soil temperatures normally drop slowly with the approach of fall and winter, heat can be conserved for a long period by early fall mulching. This practice prevents deep freezing of the soil and reduces the amount of winter drying of the trees. The mulching materials should be removed early the following spring; otherwise they will screen out the warm rays of the sun.

The Soil as an Anchor

By embedding themselves in the soil, the roots are able to hold the tree erect. Trees tend to develop anchorage where it is most needed. The tendency of isolated trees is to develop anchorage rather equally all around, with perhaps a slightly stronger development on the side toward the prevailing strong winds. The more a tree is protected from winds, the less is its dependence upon secure anchorage and the less it seems to provide for such anchorage.

The factors that are important to a tree from the standpoint of anchorage are the depth and the texture of the soil, the relative abundance of such mechanical allies as stones, and the roots of other trees and shrubs. Sufficient room for the roots to spread horizontally must also be available.

Trees growing in wet soils are more easily blown over during wind storms than are trees growing in well-aerated soils. One reason is that the lubricating action of the wet soil particles lowers the trees' resistance. Another is the absence of deep anchor roots, which are unable to develop because of lack of air in the deeper layers. In wet soils most of the tree roots are confined to the upper 18 inches; in well-aerated soils the roots may pentrate much deeper.

Soil Improvement for Trees

Probably the best way to improve the physical condition of the soil is to incorporate large amounts of organic matter (Fig. 2-2). Such material not only improves the structure of the soil but increases its water-holding capacity as well. Disappointing or unprofitable results may ensue,

Fig. 2-2. Effect of peat moss on root development of dogwood. **Left:** Tree grown in soil without the addition of peat moss. Notice the few scraggly roots. **Right:** Tree grown in soil to which peat moss has been added. Notice the heavy mass of fibrous roots.

however, if the organic matter is added to infertile, very wet, or extremely acid soils. Such adverse conditions must be rectified before much benefit from the organic matter can be expected. Wet soils, for instance, may be improved by the insertion of drain tiles to draw off the excess water, thus increasing the aeration. Shallow soils, likewise, will respond better to organic matter incorporations if any underlying hardpan or impervious subsoil is first broken up by the use of special digging tools or by blasting with dynamite. Incorporating ground limestone into the subsoil also markedly improves the physical condition of the soil, especially where the subsoil is very acid.

Of the many sources of organic matter, those most commonly used for shade and ornamental trees are stable manure and two distinct types of peat—peat moss and sedge peat. Manure that is to be placed in transplanting holes or at any considerable depth in the soil around established trees should be well rotted or past the stage of most rapid decay; otherwise, it may injure the tree. Peat, on the other hand, appears to decompose without the formation of harmful effects when mixed to considerable depths in well-aerated and well-drained soils.

Peat moss, also known as sphagnum peat or peat, is very acid in reaction (pH 3.0 to 4.5) and is used principally for acid-loving plants, such as rhododendrons and azaleas, hemlocks, pines, and spruces. It is also used in back fill for almost all trees. It is fibrous in nature, light brown in color, low in nitrogen content (around 1 per cent on a dry basis), and has a high water-absorbing capacity. It should never be applied in the form in which it is purchased, but must be thoroughly soaked beforehand. This may take several days. When large quantities of this type of peat are used, some nitrogen in the form of nitrate salts should be applied from time to time throughout the following summer, to supply both the trees and the bacteria that decompose the peat. This practice will compensate for the leaching due to the frequent watering necessary for transplanted trees, and for the consumption by the bacteria.

Sedge peat, also known as reed peat or humus, may, in time, have more extensive use than peat moss. Large deposits of this type of peat are available for exploitation. As offered for sale, sedge peat is dark brown to black and relatively high in nitrogen (2.0 to 3.5 per cent). It is less acid in reaction (pH 4.5 to 6.8) and has a lower water-absorbing capacity than peat moss. It can be safely used around most trees.

Mycorrhiza

The roots of many trees are so intimately associated with strands of fungus tissue as to form compound organs known as mycorrhiza. There are several types of mycorrhiza, distinguished mainly by the location of fungus development on and in the root. The fungi on beech, elm, spruce, hickory, birch, oak, and red and white pine develop between the root cells, whereas the fungi on ash, maple, red cedar, sweetgum, and ericaceous plants develop within the individual root cells. The former are known as ectotrophic and the latter as endotrophic mycorrhiza.

The function of mycorrhiza is not clearly understood. In some instances, the intimate association between the root and the fungus is believed to be beneficial to the tree. In others, it is said to be harmful. The ectotrophic mycorrhiza are believed to play an important role in salt absorption in soils of low nutrient level. Among the endotrophic kinds a direct transfer of nutrients to the host takes place through the dissolution of the fungus strands.

The failure of some trees, especially beech, when moved away from their natural soil environment in the woods is attributed to the lack of mycorrhizal development around their roots in the new locality. Success in the transplanting of such trees has been reported by several tree specialists when woods soil (containing the fungi) has been mixed with the soil in the new location. The greatest danger of such a practice lies in the possibility of introducing harmful species of fungi with the desirable ones.

Table 2-3. Soil reaction adaptations of some trees

Common Name	Botanical Name	Most Favorable pH Range
Acacia	Acacia	6.5 to 7.5
Alder	Alnus, named spp.	6.5 to 7.5
Almond, Flowering	Prunus glandulosa	6.5 to 7.5
Apple	Malus spp.	6.5 to 7.5
Arborvitae	Thuja spp.	6.5 to 7.5
Ash	Fraxinus spp.	6.0 to 7.5
Bald Cypress, Common	Taxodium distichum	6.5 to 7.5
Beech	Fagus, named spp. & var.	6.5 to 7.5
Birch, Sweet	Betula lenta	4.0 to 5.0
Box, Common	Buxus sempervirens	6.5 to 7.5
Buckeye, Ohio	Aesculus glabra	6.5 to 7.5
Buckeye, Red	Aesculus pavia	6.0 to 6.5
Catalpa	Catalpa, named spp.	6.5 to 7.5
Cherry	Prunus spp.	6.5 to 7.5
Cherry, Choke	Prunus virginiana	6.5 to 7.5
Chestnut, American	Castanea dentata	4.0 to 6.0
Chinquapin	Castanea pumila	4.0 to 6.5
Cypress	Chamaecyparis, named spp. & var.	4.0 to 7.5
Dockmackie	Viburnum acerifolium	4.0 to 5.5
Dogwood, Flowering	Cornus florida	5.0 to 6.5
Douglas-Fir	Pseudotsuga taxifolia	6.0 to 6.5
Elm	Ulmus spp.	6.5 to 7.5
Eucalyptus	Eucalyptus spp.	6.5 to 7.5
Fir	Abies, named spp.	4.0 to 6.5
Franklin-Tree	Franklinia alatamaha	4.0 to 6.0
Fringe-Tree	Chionanthus virginica	4.0 to 6.0
Hackberry	Celtis spp.	6.5 to 7.5
Hawthorn	Crataegus spp.	6.0 to 7.5
Hemlock, Canada	Tsuga canadensis	4.0 to 6.5
Hemlock, Carolina	Tsuga caroliniana	4.0 to 5.0
Hickory, Shagbark	Hicoria ovata	6.0 to 6.5
Holly, American	Ilex opaca	4.0 to 6.0

Table 2-3. Soil reaction adaptations of some trees   *Continued*

Common Name	Botanical Name	Most Favorable pH Range
Hop-Hornbeam, American	*Ostrya virginiana*	6.0 to 6.5
Hornbeam	*Carpinus,* named spp.	6.5 to 7.5
Horsechestnut	*Aesculus hippocastanum*	6.0 to 7.0
Juniper	*Juniperus,* many spp.	6.5 to 7.5
Juniper, Common	*Juniperus communis* & var.	6.0 to 6.5
Juniper, Creeping	*Juniperus horizontalis*	4.0 to 6.0
Juniper, Mountain	*Juniperus communis saxatilis*	4.0 to 5.0
Kentucky Coffe Tree	*Gymnocladus dioicus*	6.5 to 7.5
Larch	*Larix,* named spp.	6.5 to 7.5
Linden	*Tilia* spp.	6.5 to 7.5
Loblolly Bay	*Gordonia Lasianthus*	4.0 to 6.0
Locust, Black	*Robinia pseudo-acacia*	5.0 to 7.5
Locust, Honey	*Gleditsia,* named spp.	6.5 to 7.5
Maidenhair Tree	*Ginkgo biloba*	6.0 to 6.5
Magnolia	*Magnolia* spp.	4.0 to 7.0
Maple	*Acer,* many spp.	6.5 to 7.5
Maple, Mountain	*Acer spicatum*	4.0 to 5.0
Maple, Red	*Acer rubrum*	4.5 to 7.5
Maple, Striped	*Acer pennsylvanicum*	4.0 to 5.0
Mock-Orange	*Philadelphus* spp.	6.0 to 7.5
Mountain-Ash, American	*Sorbus americana*	5.0 to 7.0
Mountain-Ash, European	*Sorbus aucuparia*	6.5 to 7.5
Mountain Laurel	*Kalmia latifolia*	4.0 to 6.5
Mulberry	*Morus,* named spp. & var.	6.5 to 7.5
Oak, Black	*Quercus velutina*	6.0 to 6.5
Oak, Blackjack	*Quercus marilandica*	4.0 to 5.0
Oak, Chestnut	*Quercus prinus*	6.0 to 6.5
Oak, English	*Quercus robur* & var.	6.5 to 7.5
Oak, European Turkey	*Quercus cerris*	6.5 to 7.5
Oak, Overcup	*Quercus macrocarpa*	4.0 to 5.0
Oak, Pin	*Quercus palustris*	5.5 to 6.5
Oak, Post	*Quercus stellata*	4.0 to 6.5
Oak, Red	*Quercus borealis maxima*	4.5 to 6.0
Oak, Sand Blackjack	*Quercus catesbaei*	4.0 to 5.0
Oak, Scarlet	*Quercus coccinea*	6.0 to 6.5
Oak, Shingle	*Quercus imbricaria*	4.0 to 5.0
Oak, Shrub	*Quercus ilicifolia*	5.0 to 6.0
Oak, Southern Red	*Quercus falcata*	4.0 to 5.0
Oak, Swamp White	*Quercus bicolor*	6.5 to 7.5
Oak, White	*Quercus alba*	6.5 to 7.5
Oak, Willow	*Quercus phellos*	4.0 to 6.5
Oak, Yellow	*Quercus Muhlenbergii*	4.0 to 5.0
Paulownia, Royal	*Paulownia tomentosa*	6.5 to 7.5
Peach	*Prunus persica*	6.5 to 7.5

Table 2-3. Soil reaction adaptations of some trees   *Continued*

Common Name	Botanical Name	Most Favorable pH Range
Pear	*Pyrus* spp.	6.5 to 7.5
Pine	*Pinus,* many spp.	4.0 to 6.5
Planetree	*Platanus,* named spp.	6.5 to 7.5
Plum, American	*Prunus americana*	6.5 to 7.5
Plum, Beach	*Prunus maritima*	6.5 to 7.5
Plum, Common	*Prunus domestica*	6.5 to 7.5
Plum, Purple-leaf	*Prunus cerasifera pissardi*	6.5 to 7.5
Poplar	*Populus,* named spp.	6.5 to 7.5
Quince, Flowering	*Chaenomeles japonica* & var.	6.5 to 7.5
Redbud	*Cercis* spp.	6.5 to 7.5
Red Cedar	*Juniperus virginiana* & var.	6.0 to 6.5
Savin	*Juniperus sabina* & var.	6.0 to 6.5
Serviceberry	*Amelanchier* spp.	6.0 to 6.5
Silverbell	*Halesia tetraptera*	4.0 to 6.0
Sourgum	*Nyssa sylvatica*	5.0 to 6.0
Sourwood	*Oxydendrum arboreum*	4.0 to 6.0
Spruce	*Picea* spp.	4.0 to 6.5
Spruce, Colorado	*Picea pungens* & var.	6.0 to 6.5
Stewartia	*Stewartia Malacodendron*	4.0 to 6.0
Storax	*Styrax americana*	4.0 to 6.0
Sweetgum	*Liquidambar styraciflua*	6.0 to 6.5
Sweetleaf, Horse Sugar	*Symplocos tinctoria*	4.0 to 6.0
Tree-of-heaven	*Ailanthus altissima*	6.5 to 7.5
Tuliptree	*Liriodendron tulipifera*	6.0 to 6.5
Walnut	*Juglans,* many spp.	6.5 to 7.5
White Cedar	*Chamaecyparis thyoides*	4.0 to 5.5
Willow	*Salix,* many spp.	6.5 to 7.5
Willow, Creeping	*Salix repens*	4.0 to 5.0
Yew	*Taxus* spp.	6.0 to 6.5

Selected Bibliography

Anonymous. 1964. 'Peats and other soil conditioners. *Consumers Report.* Mount Vernon, New York, p. 442–44. Sept. 1964.

Baver, L. D. 1940. *Soil physics.* Wiley, New York. 370 p.

Bear, F. E. 1965. *Soils in relation to crop growth.* Rheinhold Publ. Co., New York. 297 p.

—— 1966. 'Soils.' *Horticulture.* Apr. 1966. p. 40, 41, 51, 53.

—— 1967. 'What does a soil analysis mean?' *Horticulture.* March 1967. p. 26–27.

Berger, K. C. 1965. *Introductory soils.* Macmillan, New York. 371 p.

Boynton, D. and D. C. Compton. 1944. 'Normal seasonal changes of oxygen and carbon dioxide percentages in gas from the larger pores of three orchard soils.' *Soil Science.* Vol. 57. p. 107–17.

Burges, A. 1936. 'On the significance of mycorrhiza.' *New Phytol.* Vol. 35. p. 117–31.

Bushey, D. J. 1937. 'Root extension of shade trees.' *Proc. Thirteenth National Shade Tree Conference.* p. 22–30.

Cannon, W. A. 1925. *Physiological features of roots, with special reference to the relation of roots to aeration of soil.* Carnegie Inst. Publ. 368. Washington, D.C.

Chadwick, L. C. 1934. 'Soil acidity and plant growth.' *Proc. Tenth National Shade Tree Conference.* p. 14–25.

Doll, C. C. 1950. 'Soil structure and treatment for plant growth.' *Arborist's News.* Vol. 23 (No. 10). p. 73–77.

Hacskaylo, Edward and J. G. Palmer. 1955. 'Mycorrhizae in relation to tree nutrition.' *Arborist's News.* Vol. 20 (No. 11). p. 81–85.

Hatch, A. B. 1936. 'The role of mycorrhizae in afforestation.' *Jour. Forestry.* Vol. 34. p. 22–29.

Heinicke, A. J. 1932. 'The effect of submerging roots of apple trees at different seasons of the year.' *Proc. Amer. Hort. Soc.* Vol. 29. p. 205–7.

Jacobs, H. L. 1939. 'The influence of root environment on shade tree vitality.' *Proc. Fifteenth National Shade Tree Conference.* p. 51–65.

Kozlowski, T. T. 1968. 'Water balance in shade trees.' *Proc. Forty-fourth International Shade Tree Conference.* p. 29–42.

Kramer, P. J. 1949. *Plant and soil water relationships.* McGraw-Hill Book Co., New York. 347 p.

Martin, W. P. 1968. 'Soil structure—its importance to tree root growth.' *Proc. Forty-fourth International Shade Tree Conference.* p. 42–50.

Millar, C. E., L. M. Turk, and H. D. Foth. 1965. *Fundamentals of soil science.* 4th ed. Wiley, New York. 491 p.

Mitcheltree, W. A. 1961. 'Soil management.' *Trees Magazine.* Sept.-Oct. 1961. p. 10, 12–14.

Parker, J. 1950. 'The effects of flooding on the transporation and survival of some southeastern forest-tree species.' *Plant Physiology.* Vol. 25. p. 453–60.

Salter, R. M., 1940. 'Some soil factors affecting tree growth.' *Science* n. s. Vol. 91. p. 2365.

Slowik, K. W. and N. A. Willits. 1962. 'Study effect of soil type on tree root distribution.' *New Jersey Agriculture.* May-June 1962. p. 8–12.

Stout, B. F. 1968. 'Root systems of deciduous trees.' *American Nurseyman.* Jan. 1, 1968. p. 13, 120–22.

Tanner, J. W. 1968. 'Roots.' *Horticulture.* May 1968. p. 26, 27, 46, 56.

White, P. M. 1972. 'Plant tolerance for standing water: an assessment.' *The Cornell Plantations.* Vol. 28 (No. 3). p. 50–52. Cornell University, Ithaca, N.Y.

Wikle, Jack. 1969. 'Soil and root growth of trees.' *Arborist's News.* Vol. 34 (No. 8). p. 1–6.

Yeager, A. F. 1935. 'Root systems of certain trees and shrubs grown on prairie soils.' *Jour. Agr. Res.* Vol. 51. p. 1085–92.

Yelenosky, George. 1964. 'Tolerance of trees to deficiencies of soil aeration.' *Proc. Fortieth International Shade Tree Conference.* p. 127–46.

Young, H. C. 1929. 'The aeration of tree roots.' *Proc. Fifth National Shade Tree Conference.* p. 28–34.

3

Transplanting Trees

Transplanting is the moving of a tree from one location to another in such a manner that it will continue to grow. Success, however, should be measured not in terms of whether the tree merely lives or dies, but on the amount of shock to the tree and its subsequent ability to continue growth and development with the least possible interruption. Transplanting involves three distinct operations—digging or 'lifting' moving to the new site, and replanting.

Importance of Good Transplanting

Except where trees are transported for long distances or where large trees are involved, the whole process of transplanting usually can be completed in a few hours or within several days. In any case, the time required is only a small fraction of the anticipated life span of the tree, which may vary from 30 to 300 years. Yet the future of the tree—its health, its resistance to insects and diseases, its beauty, and the cost of maintenance—can be greatly influenced by the methods used in digging, transporting, and planting. Faulty transplanting can cause considerable trouble and even the death of the tree, despite the use of good soil and a fine specimen.

A good transplanting job takes only a little more time, thought, and money than does a crude job and is always well worth the difference. Most of the trouble resulting from poor transplanting originates from the operator's thinking in terms of minimum requirements, that is, what the tree will tolerate rather than what it needs.

Before digging operations are begun, one must consider several points that will greatly influence not only the success of transplanting but also the future vigor, or thriftiness, of the tree.

Selection of the Tree

The selection of the tree is governed by soil type, exposure, elevation, and climate. A study of the relation of these factors to the future health of the tree requires considerable technical information not readily available to most individuals. Probably the most dependable criterion of what to plant in any locality, therefore, is *the selection of species that are already well established and thriving in that locality.* Any woodlot near the site picked for the new tree will reveal more pertinent information on the most suitable species than will the best scientific knowledge of the specific requirements of the tree. Trees in such areas are thriving because all the factors that combine to produce good growth are favorable.

Different tree species vary greatly in their reactions to being moved. As a rule, trees with compact, fibrous root systems are moved with greater ease and less shock than are those with large taproots or long scraggly root systems. Among the trees that are most easily moved and that appear to suffer least shock are ash, elm, ginkgo, linden, maple, pin oak, poplar, and willow. Trees moved with greater difficulty are apple, buckeye, dogwood, hemlock, and spruce. Those moved with most difficulty are beech, birch, hawthorn, hickory, magnolia, sourgum, sweetgum, tuliptree, and many species of oak, particularly the willow oak.

A 4-foot DBH valley oak (*Quercus lobata*), 50 feet tall, with a branch spread of 50 feet, and estimated to be 300 years old was successfully moved a half mile in California in 1968.

Season for Transplanting

Although no blanket recommendation can be made for the best season to move all trees, most arborists agree that deciduous trees are best moved in the spring, fall, or winter. In northern states, however, it is sometimes difficult to move trees in winter, especially when the ground is frozen deeply, and some arborists now guarantee successful transplanting of fairly good-sized trees even during the summer. Extraordinary precautions are necessary in the latter case to reduce the shock of cessation of growth and food storage due to water loss and root injury. Some trees with fleshy root systems, such as dogwood, magnolia, tuliptree, willow oak, and yellowwood, are more successfully moved in the spring than in the fall. Among other trees that are also moved more successfully in the spring are: American hornbeam, hickory, pecan, white fringe-tree, beech, butternut, goldenrain-tree, sweetgum, tupelo, sassafras, and walnut.

A dry fall followed by a cold winter may result in the death of a high percentage of fall-transplanted trees. Because of this, many municipal tree men prefer to plant street trees in the spring.

When a tree is dug in midsummer the soil in the ball of earth should be near its maximum water-holding capacity. This can be assured by trenching and watering the tree prior to the actual digging.

With care, evergreens can be moved at any season of the year. Best success, however, follows their transplanting during August and early September. When evergreens are to be exposed to high winds, spring transplanting is better than fall. Among evergreen trees that are more successfully moved in the spring are: fir, American holly, and hemlock. Greatest success in transplanting evergreens is attained when the soil is warm and root growth continues immediately. Such conditions prevail in most parts of the country in early fall and late spring.

In general, evergreen trees as a group are best moved earlier in the fall and later in the spring than deciduous trees. The roots of evergreen trees cease to grow, or at least make very little growth, during dry summer periods. With the advent of late summer or early fall rains, the roots begin to grow again.

The roots of deciduous trees are capable of growing even when the soil temperature drops to as low as $45°F$ ($7°C$.). This means that deciduous trees transplanted before the soil gets cold can make some root growth in the fall and even during some of the winter months.

Preparing Trees for Transplanting

Nursery-grown Trees. Young trees develop few roots. These do not branch readily but spread through relatively large areas of soil and are thin and scraggly. Unless the growth of such roots is regulated by pruning, the trees can be dug and transplanted only with great difficulty. Properly grown nursery trees are root-pruned every few years, not only to confine the greater part of the root system within a small area but also to encourage the roots to branch and to develop a greater abuandance of small roots and rootlets. Trees that have been properly root-pruned can be transplanted most efficiently and with maximum chances of success.

Collected or Wilding Trees. Many trees growing naturally in fields or woods without previous cultivation are transplanted to new sites to provide shade or ornament. These trees have fewer roots, many of which are long and scraggly. Trees growing in medium heavy or clay soil and in open areas are preferable as subjects for transplanting to those growing in sandy soil or in heavily wooded areas. A tree growing in the woods whose top has been protected by other trees and whose roots are shallow because of the protection by shade and mulch is more apt to do poorly when moved out into the open and exposed to full sunlight and drying winds.

As a rule, very small collected trees are not root-pruned. Large trees, on the other hand, can be root-pruned to stimulate the formation of a compact root system and a greater number of fibrous roots. Best results are obtained when such trees are root-pruned, as shown in Figure 3-1, for two successive years before the actual moving operation. In the spring or fall a circular area around the tree at some distance from the trunk* is marked off. Three ditches, covering half the area of the circle, are dug with a spade and all the exposed roots are severed. A year later, the remaining area is dug and the roots are treated similarly. The soil excavated each time should be mixed with manure, leaf mold, or a commercial fertilizer (p. 60) before it is replaced in the open trenches. The tree is ready for moving one year after the second series of trenches are dug and refilled. Trenching and root-pruning in this manner encourage greater root development within the cut area. They also spread the shock to the tree over a 3-year period rather than concentrating it in one severe shock, as is the case when trenching and moving are done at one time.

In commercial arboricultural practice, however, root-pruning a year or two in advance of moving is rare, principally because the client usually demands immediate delivery of the tree.

Digging Deciduous Trees and Evergreens

Proper digging includes the conservation of as much of the root system as possible, particularly of the smaller roots and finer rootlets. Any appreciable reduction in such roots, which are the most active in absorbing water and nutrients, results in a considerable checking of the tree's growth and reduces the speed of reestablishment.

Deciduous trees may be moved with bare roots or with balls of soil adhering to the roots (Fig. 3-2). The former method leads to greater transplanting shock and slower reestablishment; on the other hand, less equipment is required. Evergreens are always more safely moved with a soil ball than with bare roots (Fig. 3-3).

Before any digging begins it is advisable to tie in the tree's branches with heavy twine or quarter-inch rope. This will reduce the chances of damage or breakage to the branches.

---

* The distance varies with the type and size of the tree. For deciduous trees the radial distance from the trunk should be about 5 inches for each inch in trunk diameter. For example, the radial distance from the trunk to the point where the ditch is dug on a tree 4 inches in diameter at breast height should be about 20 inches.

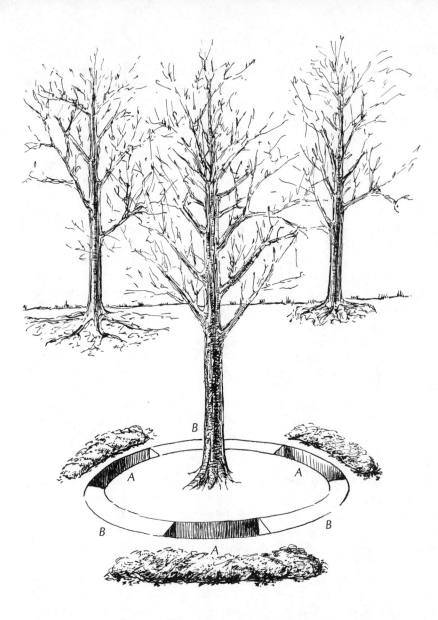

Fig. 3-1. Method of root-pruning a wildling tree before it is moved. The soil is dug at sectors A, and exposed roots are pruned, and the soil is replaced after having been improved by fertilizing or manuring. One year later the same procedure is followed in sectors B. The tree should be moved a year after the pruning at sectors B. **Upper left:** Sketch shows the extent of the roots before root pruning. **Upper right:** After root pruning.

Fig. 3-2. Close-up showing a balled and burlapped deciduous tree ready for transplanting

Fig. 3-3. Balled and burlapped evergreen ready for transplanting.

Bare Root. In preparing trees to be moved free of soil, a trench is dug around the tree to a depth just below the greater part of the root system. With most trees this depth is 2 or 3 feet. The circumference of the trench should be just beyond the last root-pruning zone for well-grown nursery trees, or just outside the root-pruning trenches for collected stock. If no previous root-pruning has been done, as is the case with most trees, the trench should be dug at a radial distance from the trunk of approximately 5 inches for each inch in trunk diameter. The roots are then combed by inserting a spading fork into the exposed face of the trench and pulling the upper end of the fork toward the operator. After the smaller roots are exposed, the combing is continued until the larger roots are cleared of soil to within a foot or so of the trunk. One part of the root system should be uncovered and freed of soil completely before another area is attacked.

As the roots are completely uncovered, they should be wrapped in wet burlap to prevent drying and mechanical injury. Each part of the root system should be uncovered and wrapped separately. If the soil is left intact close to the tree, sufficient anchorage is maintained to hold the tree erect until most of the roots have been uncovered and wrapped.

The tree is then bent over carefully to raise the roots, and the entire root system is tied in a large ball with wet burlap and rope. If the roots are to remain wrapped for several days, wet sphagnum or peat moss should be placed around them before they are enclosed to the burlap.

Soil Ball. Whenever possible, deciduous trees over 3 or 3½ inches in diameter should be moved with the soil adhering to the roots, the circumference and depth of the soil ball depending largely on the type of soil, the root habit and the type of tree, and several other factors. As a rule, trees with shallow roots require a flat ball, while those with deeply penetrating roots require a deeper ball with a smaller circumference. The main objective governing the size of the earth ball is the protection of the greatest number of roots in the smallest soil mass.

The soil ball for deciduous trees is usually 9 to 12 inches in diameter for each inch diameter of the trunk. As a rule, evergreens require a ball of smaller circumference.

Since most soils weigh about 110 pounds a cubic foot, no more soil than is absolutely necessary should be allowed to remain around the ball. A rapid method for computing the weight of a soil ball is to square the diameter of the ball in feet, multiply this figure by the depth in feet, then take two thirds of this total and multiply by 110. The resulting figure will give the approximate weight of the soil in pounds.

Digging should not be attempted unless the soil is moist. If the soil is dry it should be watered thoroughly at least two days before digging. Unless this is done the soil ball will break and the roots will be completely separated from the soil. Such a tree will have much less chance of surviving in its new location. If considerable time is to elapse before evergreens are to be replanted, they should be placed in shaded areas and the soil balls watered frequently.

Table 3-1. The recommended minimum diameter and depth in inches of soil balls for deciduous trees of various sizes

Trunk Diameter in Inches of Tree 1 Foot above Ground	Diameter of Ball	Depth of Ball
1¼–1½	18	14
1½–1¾	20	15
1¾–2	22	16
2–2½	24	17
2½–3	28	18
3–3½	33	20
3½–4	38	23
4–4½	43	26
4½–5	48	30
5–5½	53	31
5½–6	58	33
6–7	65	35

The preliminary preparations for moving a tree with a soil ball are similar to those for bare-root trees. The trench is dug and the roots are combed out and then severed, both around and underneath, at approximately the predetermined size of the ball. The ball of earth is then held in place by wrapping it with a large piece of burlap or tarpaulin and securely tying this with rope. A tree thus prepared is known in nurserymen's catalogues as a balled and burlapped (B & B) tree. Because the soil ball is easily broken and the root system injured, only an experienced person should be entrusted with this task.

In recent years, the increased costs in preparing balled and burlapped trees have forced some nurserymen to prepare so-called 'soft' or 'homemade' balls. These are merely bare-root trees wrapped in soil and burlap. The chances of their successful establishment are not much better than trees planted bare root.

Where large numbers of trees are to be planted it appears to be more economical to use a Vermeer TS-44T Tree Spade (Figs. 3-4, 3-5) rather than to plant the trees bare root or balled and burlapped.

Tests conducted by the Forestry Division of the city of Lansing, Michigan, revealed that the mortality rate for streetside trees planted bare root was 28 per cent, whereas only one per cent of the trees planted with a Vermeer TS-44T Tree Spade died.

Several other methods of preparing and conserving the ball are used in different sections of the country. Where the soil is sandy and crumbles easily, the so-called box method is commonly employed. After a square

Fig. 3-4. The Vermeer Tree Spade (TS-447) digging a tree in a nursery.

trench is dug around the tree, four pieces of board are nailed together to form the sides of a box. The soil underneath the root stystem is dug out, and additional boards are slid under and fastened in place to complete the box.

Arborists interested in obtaining a detailed description of additional balling, wrapping, and roping methods are referred to the excellent treatment of this subject in *Tree Preservation Bulletin Number* 1, of the United States Department of the Interior, National Park Service. This

Fig. 3-5. The Tree Spade planting a tree along a city street.

publication is obtainable from the Superintendent of Documents, U.S. Government Printing Office, Washington, D.C. 20402, for a small charge.

Container-grown Trees

In recent years another technique for handling trees and shrubs has proved popular with home gardeners and profitable for nurserymen. Trees are grown in containers for some time before being put up for sale. The practice, referred to as 'can culture,' originated in California, where the sandy soil in which trees and shrubs are grown does not lend itself to 'ball and burlap' handling because it breaks away from the roots.

The can culture method of growing and selling trees has several advantages over the ball and burlap method. First, it extends the planting season. Even in June and July a gardener can plant a shrub or tree grown in a can. It is much like planting a pot-grown geranium or fuchsia in midsummer.

A can-grown tree suffers far less transplanting shock than a field-grown balled and burlapped one. Few if any roots are lost from the former. Container-grown plants need not be planted immediately, as do bare-root or even balled and burlapped plants.

A nurseryman finds container-grown plants profitable because his selling season is extended, he can display more plants in a given space, his watering problem is less complex, and he can hold any surplus over for another season with less extra cost.

As with all other innovations, can culture has certain disadvantages. First, the size of tree is limited. Very large trees cannot be grown in cans, at least under present methods. For trees more than 10 feet high the cans would be too heavy and awkward to handle. Second, can-grown trees and shrubs held too long in their containers tend to become pot-bound. Unless such pot-bound plants are handled properly, they may not make satisfactory growth after they are removed from their containers and set into the garden. The roots of pot-bound trees should be spread out at planting time to reduce the possibility of girdling roots (p. 219) later on.

The metal containers used today are a great improvement over the ones originally used. They are so constructed that the gardener merely taps the edge of the can on a firm surface to release the plant. Both plant and soil then slide out as a unit.

Transporting

Small trees are transported very easily. Large trees usually require special types of transportation equipment. A sled with wooden runners can be used where the trees are to be transported for relatively short distances.

A number of well-designed and efficient tree-moving machines are now on the market. These are used mainly by commercial arborists, park superintendents, and other persons who move large trees. The machines are of two distinctly different types—trailer and automotive. The trailer types have 2, 6, or 8 wheels, and are drawn by trucks or tractors. Many of the trailer types of tree movers are designed to carry most of the weight on the rear wheels, the soil ball of the tree resting on a cradle just ahead of these wheels. The front wheels balance and guide the trailer. The automotive types of tree movers are mounted on trucks. At least five different types are in common use, one of which is illustrated in Figure 3-6.

Large tree movers are made by Vermeer Manufacturing Co. of Pella, Iowa. Its model TM-700T Tree Mover is a self-propelled, truck-mounted machine which will dig, transport, and plant trees up to 7 to 8 inches DBH. Vermeer tree movers are equipped with two hydraulically operated 'cutting' cups that scoop out in minutes the soil ball surround-

Fig. 3-6. A modern tree-moving machine ready to place a large evergreen tree in the transplanting hole.

ing the tree. The tree and surrounding soil are lifted out of the hole, moved to the new site, and set into a previously dug receiving hole (Fig. 3-7). Vermeer also makes several other models for lifting and moving trees up to 4 inches DBH. Another large tree mover is illustrated in Figure 3-8.

Ideal Crane, Division of Bert Parkhurst and Co., Tulsa, Oklahoma 74116, also manufactures a one-man-operated tree mover.

The Beseler Tree Moving Equipment Company of Minneapolis, Minnesota, manufactures a versatile tree mover as well as tree slings. When the slings are used, there is less need for undercutting and extensive lacing. They are quickly attached and easily removed.

The Big John Tree Transplanter is capable of moving trees up to 10

Fig. 3-7. The Vermeer Tree Mover in action.

Fig. 3-8. Loading a large, old, multi-stemmed Japanese maple, 22 feet high and 24 feet in width, with a 9½ foot root ball, at a Long Island, New York, nursery.

inches DBH and with a root ball weighting 7000 pounds. The manufacturer, Big John Tree Transplanter Co. Inc., Heber Springs, Arkansas, claims it is the 'world's largest patented tree spade.'

The limit to the size of tree that can be moved is governed by the amount of road clearance over which the tree is to be transported and the weight the roads and bridges will stand. The number of men needed for moving trees varies with the size of the specimens. As a rule, 3 to 7 men are needed for trees ranging from 8 to 24 inches in diameter.

Considerable injury may occur during the moving of large trees unless the following precautions are taken:

Pad unprotected areas with burlap, canvas, or some other material to avoid bruising and slipping the bark of the trunk and branches.

Carefully tie in all loose ends with a soft rope to avoid twig and branch breakage.

Keep the earth ball moist or cover bare roots with wet burlap or moist sphagnum moss.

Avoid excessive drying of the tops, especially of evergreens, while the trees are in transit by covering them with canvas or wet burlap or spraying them with an anti-transpirant such as Wilt-Pruf NCF (p. 52).

Planting

Preparation of the New Site. It has often been said that if a person has $10 to spend on a tree, he should spend $2 for the tree and $8 to prepare the planting hole. This advice may be slightly exaggerated but the fact remains that the care taken in the preparation of the new site is the major factor ensuring ultimate success in transplanting.

The hole should be dug sufficiently deep and wide to accommodate the full root system of the tree. In especially poor soils, it should be larger and deeper. As the hole is dug, the soil from the upper layers, which is richer, should be kept separated from the subsoil. The latter should be discarded and replaced with good topsoil, or improved by incorporating liberal quantities of well-rotted manure or peat moss.

Trees planted in heavy or poorly drained soils will not thrive unless some precauations are taken prior to planting. Properly installed 3-inch agricultural tile will help. But only a person skilled in the mechanics of laying tile drains and with a knowledge of subsoil conditions should be entrusted to a job of this sort. Another practice is to blast the holes with dynamite after all digging is completed. This fractures the deeper, more impervious layers and thus not only improves the drainage but allows deeper root penetration later.

Setting the Tree. The depth of planting must be close to the original as measured by the distance from the soil-stained ring at the base of the trunk to the base of the root bundle. Experienced arborists have found that if a tree is set a bit higher in its new location than in its former one, the chances of continued good growth are increased. It is a well-known fact that trees set too deeply will not thrive and may even die within a few years. Flowering dogwood, American beech, and narrow-leaved evergreens are especially sensitive to too-deep planting.

The soil to be placed around the roots should be neither too dry nor too wet. These extremes can be avoided by adding water if the soil is too dry and peat moss if too wet.

Do not set the tree until the hole depth has been adjusted by adding or removing the soil and until the soil to be worked around the roots is in proper condition.

Because the roots of trees grow downward at a slight angle from the horizontal, it is wise to make a cone-shaped mound of soil at the bottom of the hole when planting bare-root trees. The root crown can then be set on this mound and the roots spread over and down the sides, thus assuring close contact with the soil along their entire length. The soil should be added gradually. Work the first lot in firmly at the base of the roots. Then add more soil and work it under and around the lower roots. The tree may be gently raised and lowered during the filling process to eliminate air pockets and bring the roots in close contact with the soil. Some water can be added also to eliminate air pockets. When the roots are covered, tamp the entire area firmly with the feet. Heavy soils should not be tamped too firmly around the roots; otherwise, oxygen and water cannot reach the roots.

Balled evergreen and deciduous trees require somewhat different handling. After they are set at the proper level in the hole, the rope holding the burlap in place should always be removed and the burlap loosened. If there is no danger of breaking the ball, the burlap should also be removed, or it may be loosened from the sides and left in the soil to decay. Soil is then added to half fill the remaining hole space and is firmly tamped. Water should be added to settle the soil further and to eliminate air pockets. When the water has drained off, the remainder of the hole is filled with soil.

The final level around any type of tree should be a few inches below the surface of the surrounding ground to form a shallow basin for catching and preventing run-off of water. The circumference of the basin should be smaller than the circumference of the soil ball. The ground should be leveled off, however, before winter sets in, since water collected in the basin may freeze and injure the trunk (Fig. 3-9).

Supporting. Newly planted trees need some artifical support to prevent excessive swaying in the wind, which would disturb the roots and hinder their normal functioning and development.

For trees up to 20 feet in height, 1 or 2 strong stakes or poles, 6 to 8 feet in length, can be driven 2 feet or so into the ground and 6 to 12 inches from the trunk. A short length of old garden hose with a wire run through it is then placed around the trunk to protect the bark, and the wire is twisted around the stake in the form of a figure 8 to complete the support (Fig. 3-10). A wide cloth tape may be substituted for the wired hose. This is wound around the tree and the loose ends nailed to the supporting stake.

A patented brace, Paul's Tree Brace, is available from Colonial Gardens, Delaware, Ohio. Another, Cinch-Tie, made of flexible vinyl, is long-lasting, attractive, and reusable.

The Montreal Shade Tree Service has developed the S.F.M. Saddle for supporting young, newly transplanted trees. The saddle is quickly installed, is waterproof, attractive, and comes in four sizes: 2, 2½, 3, and 3½ inches in diameter.

Another product used for tying, guying, and supporting trees is known as Tree-minder. It will not damage trees (as do wires), adjusts automatically as the trunk grows, and fits all sizes of transplanted trees. Tree-minder is made by Product Design and Manufacturing Corp., Willoughby, Ohio 44094.

Also available for supporting newly planted trees are Chainlock Tree Ties. These are adjustable, quickly applied, and require a mere twist to lock them in place. They are available from Good-Prod Sales, Kenilworth, New Jersey.

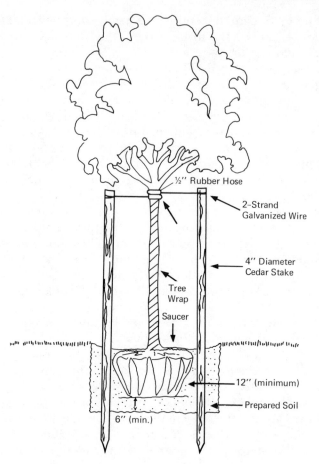

½" Rubber Hose

2-Strand
Galvanized Wire

4" Diameter
Cedar Stake

Tree
Wrap

Saucer

12" (minimum)

Prepared Soil

6" (min.)

Fig. 3-9. Details of planting and supporting a tree.

Guy wires or cables must be used to support larger trees. They should slope from about halfway up the trunk to the ground at an angle of about 45 degrees. The upper ends of the wires are attached with lag screws or by encircling the trunk with a loop encased in a piece of garden hose or other protective cover. The lower ends of the wires are anchored to stakes driven deeply into the soil. From one to four wires or cables are usually placed around a large tree (Fig. 3-11).

Guy wires or cables are rarely placed around trees set along the city streets or in public parks. Unless protected or plainly marked so as to be readily visible, especially at night, they are a constant source of danger to passersby.

Fig. 3-10. Wire run through a piece of garden hose and twisted around the trunk and the supporting stake in the form of the figure 8.

Pruning. The tops of transplanted trees are pruned to compensate for the loss of roots and thus maintain a more natural balance between the two parts. Pruning should be heavier on collected than on nursery-grown trees. The amount of pruning* depends not only on the condition of the tree at transplanting time but also on the care the tree is to receive while it is becoming firmly reestablished. Less pruning is needed when most of the roots have been conserved during digging and when adequate water and aftercare are assured.

Pruning should be confined to the secondary branches in order to maintain the natural shape of the tree. The growing tip of single-stemmed shade trees should not be cut back. Twigs and buds along the branches and upper part of the trunk should not be removed until the tree is well established, for these tissues manufacture much-needed food and, by providing shade, help to reduce scalding of the trunk and branches.

Little or no pruning of balled evergreens is needed except to remove broken or severely injured branches. If the leading shoot is broken during moving, one of two practices may be followed: (1) one of the next nearest lateral branches may be bent upward and held in place by tying it with raffia to a small piece of wood; or (2) all the nearest laterals but one may be removed. The lone lateral will tend to grow upright and will soon replace the broken leader.

Watering. The soil around the tree must be watered thoroughly after the tree is set in place. Additional water must be applied from time to

* Some municipal tree men prune transplants drastically. For example, all branches except the leader on a tree 2 to 2½ inches in diameter are pruned, so that only stubs ranging from 4 to 12 inches remain on the bole. In general, as much as 30 to 40 per cent of the leaf-bearing wood may be removed.

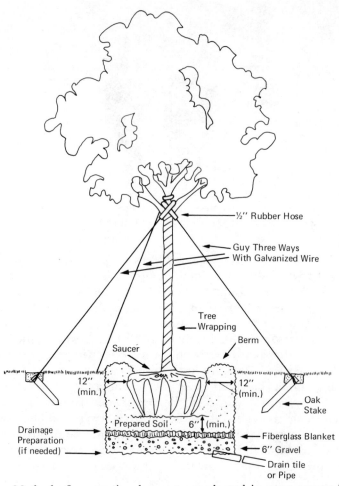

Fig. 3-11. Method of supporting larger trees planted in open areas with guy wires.

time until the tree is firmly established. The frequency of watering depends on the type of soil, the size of the tree, and the amount of rainfall. Deciduous trees moved during late fall or winter require very little water, at least until new leaves emerge the following spring.

The water must be allowed to soak into the ground slowly until the soil is moistened down to the roots. This can best be determined with a soil auger or by digging with a narrow spade. The tree benefits little from frequent light waterings which moisten the soil to a depth of only a few inches. If water must be applied with a pail, it is best to pour it on 2 or 3 pailfuls at a time and allow it to soak in completely before more is added.

One common error of inexperienced gardeners is to overwater the soil around the newly transplanted tree. This drives out the oxygen from the soil, an element that is essential to normal root development, and it also favors the development of root-decaying fungi. The soil around newly planted trees should be kept relatively dry in spring until root growth starts and the leaves begin to emerge.

The soil ball around a large newly transplanted tree, however, can dry out in a surprisingly short time. Summer showers cannot be depended upon to supply sufficient moisture to keep the soil ball moist. Hence an occasional good soaking with the garden hose is necessary. To get good penetration into the ball itself, it may be necessary to punch holes into the ball with a crowbar or to bore holes with a soil auger at varying depths before applying the water.

Frequent syringing of the leaves of newly planted evergreens on cloudy days helps to cut down water loss by the leaves, and in some cases washes off spider mites and soot.

Mr. Edgar Rex, former secretary of the New Jersey Federation of Shade Tree Commissions, and Mr. C. N. Keyser of the Bartlett Tree Expert Company devised a method for facilitating the watering of newly planted shade trees. It involves the establishment of two vertical porous cores containing ½- to 1-inch mesh dolomitic limestone or crushed stone. Through these cores rainwater or applied water can more easily reach the critical root zone. Details of installing the Rex-Keyser method of subsurface irrigation are illustrated in Figure 3-12.

Another product that facilitates watering of newly planted trees and reduces water runoff is known as the Water Hole. This is a 12-inch-long H. D. polyethylene tube with a 3¼-inch opening at the top and 24 holes on the sides. It is inserted into the soil so that its top is flush with the soil surface. At least two Water Holes are needed for each tree.

Surfactants or wetting agents are being used more and more by nurserymen and landscape planters. These materials, sold under the name Aqua-gro and Aqua-T, make water 'wetter.' That is to say, they enable water to penetrate soil more quickly and more uniformly. They break up air-filled spaces between soil particles and allow water to pass more freely among them. Water containing the surfactant readily wets the sides of the soil particles and is quickly absorbed by them.

Mulching. With particularly valuable trees, especially evergreens planted in the fall, a good practice is to mulch the area above the roots with straw, leaf mold, or well-rotted manure. Such mulches prevent wide fluctuations in soil temperaure, keep the soil warmer, and help to conserve moisture. They are usually left on over winter and either removed or worked into the soil in spring. A newly planted deciduous tree collected from the woods should be mulched to a depth about equal to that of the mulch in its former location.

Sand is sometimes used as a mulch in the depressed area around small newly planted trees along streets. Water is thus absorbed more rapidly and is held longer. The sand also keeps the area free of weeds and is said to increase the chances of the tree's survival.

Wrapping. The trunk and larger branches of a transplanted tree should be wrapped with burlap, specially prepared crepe paper, or some other material to prevent sunscald and drying of the bark and to reduce the possibility of borer infestation. A protective covering is especially desirable on trees collected from shaded woods, since the bark of such trees is extremely susceptible to sunscalding. The covering should be securely fastened in place with cord and left on two years or until it falls off.

Wrapping the trunk of a newly transplanted tree has one disadvantage. In rainy seasons the trunk is kept unduly wet beneath the wrapping, a condition which fosters the development of fungus cankers. The author has found that pin oaks are especially sensitive to such cankers: Perhaps a coating of some fungicide on the trunk before wrapping might help to reduce such infections.

Any wires that hold labels should be loosened or removed so that they do not girdle the trunk or branch as it increases in girth.

To protect young dogwood, flowering crabapple, and other susceptible trees from rabbit and mice feeding, wrap some hardware cloth or old fly screening around the base of the tree in late fall.

An improved, recently introduced tree wrap is the Ross TreeGARD, a simple, easy-to-handle plastic snap-on tube that expands to fit any young tree. It protects the trunk from sun scald (yet allows proper ventilation) and damage from lawn mowers, rabbits, and rodents. Ross TreeGARD is available from Ross Daniels, Inc., West Des Moines, Iowa (Fig. 3-13).

Fertilizing. A a rule, dry commercial fertilizer should not be applied until new roots are formed and can absorb it. It is best to wait until the end of the first growing season before applying dry fertilizer. However, a dilute solution of a completely balanced chemical fertilizer can be added to the soil the first summer after transplanting, for by that time the tree will have formed sufficient roots to absorb the nutrient solution. A more immediate response to nutrients can be obtained by spraying the leaves with a plant food such as Ra-pid-gro, which is formulated especially for foliar applications. Start as soon as the leaves are half grown and repeat 4 or 5 times at 10-day intervals.

Anti-transpirants

Loss of water from evergreen trees or deciduous trees in leaf can be partly overcome by spraying with an anti-transpirant (also known as an anti-desiccant) such as Wilt-Pruf NCF just before the trees are moved.

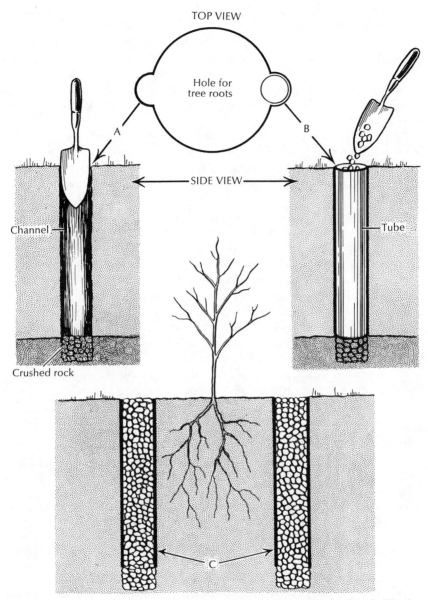

TOP VIEW

Hole for
tree roots

A

B

← SIDE VIEW →

Channel

Tube

Crushed rock

C

Fig. 3-12. Diagrammatic sketch showing Rex-Keyser method for facilitating watering of newly planted trees: After the hole is dug, semi-circular areas are cut into the sides of the hole. Cylindrical cardboard tubes approximately 18″ × 3″ × .070″ are inserted above a few inches of crushed rock or dolomitic limestone, with the upper ends flush with the soil surface. The tubes are filled with crushed stone and the top of the tubes are covered until the tree is planted in the normal manner. The lower sketch presents a cross section of the completed installation.

This product is a liquid plastic which is diluted in water and then applied over the leaves and stems with a pressure sprayer. It dries in about 20 minutes to form a film that permits the exchange of gases but inhibits the passage of water vapor, thus reducing the loss of water from the leaves.

Trees sprayed with Wilt-Pruf NCF must still be watered in their new location, although perhaps not so frequently as untreated trees. Treated trees become established in their new locations more quickly than untreated ones.

For use on evergreen and deciduous trees, one part of Wilt-Pruf NCF is mixed in 4 to 6 parts of water. The diluted mixture is then applied as a fine spray at air temperatures above freezing. According to the manufacturer, the material needs to be applied to the upper surfaces of the leaves only.

According to the manufacturer, Wilt-Pruf NCF has not been known to injure humans or pets. Nor is it likely to cause foliage burn when used as directed. Many professional arborists and nurserymen now use Wilt-Pruf NCF whenever they move trees out of season. They find that it largely eliminates the gamble of moving large trees in leaf.

Although the use of this product assures more successful transplanting of trees, it should not be considered a substitute for good gardening practices. Carelessly handled trees and those with poor root systems will not survive transplanting shock nearly so well as those that are properly handled and have an adequate root system.

Among other anti-transpirants on the market are: Geon Vinal Latex, Foligard, Folicote, Plantgard, and Vapor Gard.

Selected Bibliography

Anonymous. 1943. 'Transplanting of trees and shrubs in the northeastern and north central states.' *Proc. Nineteenth National Shade Tree Conference.* p. 74–146.

———. 1958. *Transplanting of trees and shrubs in the northeastern and north central states.* National Shade Tree Conference and National Arborist Assoc. Revision of 1958. Wooster, Ohio. 73 p.

———. 1972. *Transplanting ornamental trees and shrubs.* USDA, Home and Garden Bull. 192. 12 p.

Bailey, L. H. 1934. *The nursery manual.* Macmillan, New York. 450 p.

———. 1947. *Standard cyclopedia of horticulture.* Macmillan, New York, 3639 p.

Baumgardt, J. B. 1975. 'When, how to water your trees.' *Grounds Maintenance.* Vol. 11 (No. 6). p. 11, 12, 14, 17. Intertec Publ. Co. Overland Park, Kansas 66212.

Carter, J. C. 1966. *Illinois trees: selection, planting, and care.* Illinois Natural History Survey Circ. 51. 123 p.

Chester, K. S., H. J. Harper, R. O. Monosmith, and F. A. Fenton. 1938. *A program for shade trees in Oklahoma.* Oklahoma Agr. Exp. Sta. Bul. 234. 45 p.

Fig. 3-13. Protecting a young tree with a Ross TreeGARD, a durable, weather-resistant vinyl coil that is easily twisted onto the trunk. The coil can be expanded to fit any size young tree.

Cool, R. A. 1976. 'Tree spade vs. bare root planting.' *Jour. Arboriculture*. Vol. 2 (No. 5). p. 92–95.

Coplen, M. G. 1962. 'Mechanics of moving big trees.' *American Nurseryman*. Vol. 76. p. 9–11. Nov. 1, 1962.

Cox, L. D. 1916. *A street tree system for New York City*. N. Y. State Col. of Forestry Bul. 8. 89 p.

Davis, J. E. 1940. *Planting and care of shade trees*. Illinois Natural History Survey. Circ. 36. Urbana, Illinois. 23 p.

Fernow, B. E. 1910. *The care of trees in lawn, street and park*. Holt, New York. 392 p.

Flemer, W. F. III. 1967. 'Is bare-root transplanting a dying art?' *American Nurseryman*. July 1, 1967. p. 24, 25, 185–93.

———. 1968. 'Safe out-of-season digging.' *American Nurseryman*. May 1, 1968. p. 7, 107–13.

———. 1969. 'Plant with nature.' *American Nurseryman*. Dec. 15, 1969. p. 26, 27, 30, 32–36.

Ford, D. H. and L. E. Foote. 1973. 'Large tree moving.' *Weeds, Trees, and Turf*. Vol. 12 (No. 6). p. 10–11, 20–21, 44–45, 54.

Franke, W. A. 1937. 'Big tree moving.' *Proc. Thirteenth National Shade Tree Conference*. p. 118–30.

Harris, R. W. 1976. 'Early care of trees in the landscape.' *American Nurseryman*. Sept. 15, 1976. p. 12, 114–132.

Hayes, G. L., and J. H. Buell. 1955. *Trees also need water at the right time and place*. Yearbook Agr. 1955, p. 219–28. U.S. Dept. Agr., Washington, D.C.

Hottes, A. C. 1932. *The book of trees*. A. T. De La Mare Co., New York. 440 p.

Irish, E. E. 1976. 'Transplanting large trees.' *Journ. Arboriculture*. Vol. 2 (No. 9). p. 173–75.

Jacobs, H. L. 1938. 'Shifting small trees and shrubs.' *The Arboriculturist*. Vol. 4. p. 5–12. Davey Tree Company, Kent, Ohio.

Marsh, A. W. 1963. 'Watering a street tree.' *Arborist's News*. Vol. 28 (No. 6). p. 41–44. June 1963.

Martin, F. E. 1968. 'Large tree moving by frozen ball method.' *Proc. Forty-fourth International Shade Tree Conference*. p. 97–99.

Mulford, F. L. 1929. *Transplanting trees and shrubs*. USDA Farmer's Bul. 1591. 34 p.

———. 1930. 'Transplanting.' *Proc. Sixth National Shade Tree Conference*. p. 43–46.

———. 1938. *Planting the roadside*. USDA Farmer's Bul. 1481. 37 p.

Paul, A. F. 1946. 'How to transplant trees.' *Brooklyn Botanic Garden Record*. Plants and Gardens. Vol. 2. p. 44–47. Spring 1946.

Peirson, H. B. and R. W. Nash. 1936. *The planting and care of shade trees*. Maine Forest Service Bul. 10. 28 p.

Rae, W. A. 1968. 'Large tree moving by frozen root balls.' *Proc. Forty-fourth International Shade Tree Conference*. p. 100–104.

———. 1976. 'Tree transplanting.' *Jour. Arboriculture*. Vol. 2 (No. 7). p. 133–35.

Shield, V. I. 1938. 'Tree moving practices of Shield shade tree specialists.' *Proc. Fourteenth National Shade Tree Conference*. p. 45–51.

Speer, Low. 1969. 'Kaspar Burgi, successful with massive tree transplant.' *Weeds, Trees, and Turf*. Jan. 1969. p. 18–21, 41.

Stephenson, K. Q., J. C. Sager, and D. O. Norman. 1974. 'New machine for digging balled plants.' *Grounds Maintenance.* Vol. 10 (No. 3). p. 102–3. Intertec Publ. Co., Overland Park, Kansas.

Tilford, P. E. 1938. 'Effect of some synthetic growth substances on root development of transplanted trees.' *Proc. Fourteenth National Shade Tree Conference.* p. 51–59.

Thompson, A. R. 1954. *Transplanting trees and other woody plants.* Tree Preservation Bul. No. 1. Rev. of 1954. Supt. of Documents, Washington, D.C.

Van Wormer, H. M. 1954. 'Tree moving practices and problems.' *Proc. Thirtieth National Shade Tree Conference.* p. 76–81.

———. 1968. 'Large tree moving by frozen ball.' *Proc. Forty-fourth International Shade Tree Conference.* p. 105–7.

4

Fertilizers and Their Use

Many abnormalities in trees are closely associated with plant-food deficiencies. Professional arborists recognize the benefits trees derive from periodic feeding and for this reason they always stress the importance of such a practice. They also appreciate that although fertilization does not constitute the whole of soil improvement, it is an important part of any successful tree maintenance program.

Many laymen are unaware that trees should be fed in much the same manner as smaller plants and vegetables. Woodland trees thrive despite the absence of artificial feeding, but many of our shade and ornamental trees do not grow in such a favorable environment. Their leaves are gathered and discarded in the fall, thus destroying an important food source. Concrete or other impervious pavements usually cover a considerable area that otherwise might be good hunting ground for hungry roots. Water often becomes a limiting factor for good growth, even where trees are growing on open lawns. The heavy sod uses much of the available water and food that might otherwise be utilized by the trees. Moreover, lawns inhibit good soil aeration.

The effects of undernourishment are usually evident in the gradual decline in the vigor of the tree. This decline, which at times may be very rapid, is hastened by the more serious effects of fungus and insect attack.

Until recently the problem of feeding shade and ornamental trees was not so clearly understood as was the fertilizing of fruit trees and farm crops, principally because less research had been done. Within the last 35 years, however, agricultural experiment station workers and some of the larger tree companies have investigated the problem more carefully, with the result that general recommendations on shade and ornamental tree fertilization can now be made. Nevertheless, many questions are still unanswered, and considerable work has yet to be done.

The application of fertilizers improves the appearance and condition of trees and in some cases enables the trees better to withstand future attacks by parasites. Recovery from mild cases of Verticillium wilt in maples (see p. 301), in which the fungus invades the vascular tissues, has been repeatedly observed following liberal applications of high nitrogenous fertilizers. It should be clearly understood, however, that fertilization exercises no 'cures' upon trees affected by fungus leaf spots, heartwood rots, or bark and cambium diseases.

Not all trees respond to fertilizer to the same degree; oak, elm, walnut, and basswood are among those which usually show the quickest response.

How Fertilizers Act. Contrary to general belief, tree roots do not obtain food for growth directly from the fertilizers added to the soil. The food for any part of the tree is obtained from the leaves. Fertilizing materials supply elements necessary for the maintenance of the bodies that constitute the green coloration in leaves. As discussed in Chapter 1, these green bodies (chloroplasts) have the ability to change the light energy from the sun into the chemical energy of foods. Obviously, a dark-green leaf can manufacture and store more food than a yellow one or one attacked by fungus or insect pests.

To cope with the problem of feeding trees, it is necessary to understand not only the fundamental requirements of plants but also the influence of the various elements upon the development of plant tissues. With such knowledge one can better adapt the fertilizer recommendations to the soil and other environmental conditions in which the particular tree is growing.

The Essential Elements for Food Manufacture

Plant foods and tissue-building compounds of plants are manufactured from the following raw materials: carbon, oxygen, hydrogen, nitrogen, phosphorus, sulfur, potassium, calcium, magnesium, iron, and several so-called trace elements, such as boron, copper, manganese, molybdenum, vanadium, and zinc. Of these, only carbon, oxygen, and hydrogen are essential in the first step of food manufacture. As already discussed in the first chapter, carbon and oxygen are provided by the carbon dioxide in the atmosphere, which enters the leaves through the stomata or breathing pores. Hydrogen is obtained from water absorbed through the roots and carried to the leaves through the water-conducting system. These three elements are then united by means of energy obtained from the sun by the chloroplasts in the leaf. The results of this reaction are expressed in the simple equation:

$$6 \ H_2O + 6 \ CO_2 = C_6H_{12}O_6 + 6 \ O_2$$

6 parts water plus 6 of carbon dioxide give 1 part sugar and 6 of oxygen

This equation represents mainly the gaseous exchange involved, and not the complex nature of the process.

Nitrogen is taken out of the air and fixed or assimilated by certain kinds of soil bacteria. Trees in turn obtain nitrogen from decaying organic and inorganic nitrogen in the soil.

All other elements required by trees are taken from the soil. These are absorbed by the roots only in solution in the manner already described in Chapter 2. Obviously plants will absorb many elements from the soil solution that are not used for food manufacture and tissue formation.

From the standpoint of their relative value as raw materials for plant food, the elements in the soil may be divided into three classes: nonessential; essential and abundant; and essential and critical.

The nonessential elements include silicon (Si), aluminum (Al), sodium (Na), and some of the rarer elements. These elements are believed to have no role in the nutrition of plants.

The second group includes iron, calcium, magnesium, and sulfur, all essential to plant growth and usually present in soils in ample amounts. One or more of these elements may occasionally be deficient, however. For example, pin oaks in alkaline soils often develop yellow or chlorotic leaves because of a deficiency of iron or the inability to absorb it. Such a condition can be corrected by the addition to the soil of iron salts and sulfur or by injections of certain iron salts into the trunk and by the use of iron chelates.

The third class includes nitrogen, phosphorus, and potassium, and in some cases magnesium, managnese, and boron. These elements, which are essential for plant growth, are usually present in the soil in only small quantities and are often the limiting factor in plant growth. This is especially true of nitrogen. Nitrates, the source of nitrogen, are soluble in water and are readily leached by drainage water. During very rainy seasons considerable nitrogen (as nitrates) is lost in this manner, whereas in dry seasons this material accumulates. All commercial fertilizers have as their main constituents the first three elements in this important group. The percentage of these elements in any commercial fertilizer is expressed by formulas such as 12-8-6, 6-8-4, or 10-8-6, the first number denoting the percentage of nitrogen; the second, the phosphoric acid; and the third, the potash. Recently many fertilizer companies have added small amounts of the rarer but essential elements such as boron, magnesium, and manganese to their standard formulas. These are then sold as complete fertilizers with 'minor elements' added. Only an expert is capable of diagnosing troubles due to deficiencies of the minor elements. Descriptions of some of the deficiency symptoms are available in experiment station publications to persons interested in pursuing this subject further.

The Influence of Essential Elements on Growth. The essential elements exert various influences on plant growth. Some of these influences are not clearly understood, and others are difficult to detect, but the knowledge available will give some basis for fertilizer recommendations and some indication of what may be expected from these applications. Only the main functions of the various elements will be considered here.

Carbon, hydrogen, and *oxygen* are constituents of all sugars and starches. They, of course, are not added in fertilizers but are obtained from the air or through the soil.

Nitrogen is a constituent of all proteins that are active chemical parts of protoplasm. Lack of nitrogen results in small yellow foliage. This element is the principal fertilizer constituent involved in the production and maintenance of the green color in leaves. If in proper balance with other nutrients, it will produce abundant twig as well as leaf growth. Overdoses of nitrogen may damage roots, especially when the soil is rather dry.

Nitrogen is obtained from sodium nitrate, calcium nitrate, ammonium sulfate, and such organic materials as cottonseed meal, tankage, dried blood, and activated sludge. The organic fertilizers can supply nitrogen only after they are decomposed by the soil organisms (principally bacteria), and for this reason they are the more slowly available but longer lasting sources of nitrogen. The ureaform nitrogens also supply nitrogen at a very slow rate.

Orchard soils do not usually show a great shortage of nitrogen, since cultivation and turning under of cover crops tend to increase the supply. In contrast, nitrogen is usually deficient in the conditions under which shade and ornamental trees grow. Nitrates are present in the surface layers of the soil, but only if there is no competition from the sod or small shallow-rooted plants. Lawn clippings should be left where cut, since they supply some food to trees growing in lawns.

Phosphorus has a less obvious role than nitrogen. It stimulates root growth, hastens the maturation of tissues, stimulates flower and seed production, and is an active part of certain proteins. In addition, it helps to make stored carbohydrates, such as starch, available for plant growth in spring. Phosphorus, as used by plants, is in the form of phosphates, which penetrate into the soil very slowly when applied to the surface. Consequently fertilizing materials containing phosphates should be worked into the soil or inserted into the zone occupied by the roots. Phosphorus is most readily available from soils containing abundant amounts of organic matter. It becomes less available in highly acid or highly alkaline soils.

Potassium or potash must be present for the manufacture of sugars and starches and for the reactions that are necessary before these materials can move from one part of the tree to another. It helps to overcome succulence and brittleness, hastens maturity of the plant, and intensifies the color of flowers.

Calcium exerts an influence both in the plant cells and in soil. In the plant it is essential for growth and cell divisions. In the soil it overcomes harmful effects of excessive amounts of aluminum and iron salts. In addition, it favors development of beneficial bacteria and aids in the liberation of nitrogen, phosphorus, and potassium.

Magnesium aids in the transportation of phosphorus and is a chemical constituent of chlorophyll. Without it, leaves become yellow.

Iron is essential to the formation of the all-important chlorophyll. Though this element is not a constituent of chlorophyll, as is magnesium, plants lacking it have yellowed foliage.

Sulfur is a constituent of plant proteins.

Molybdenum acts as a catalyst in enzyme systems that function in reducing nitrate to ammonium in preparation for the synthesis of amino acids and proteins.

Vanadium is the latest element to be found essential for normal leaf growth.

Fertilizing Materials and Formulas

One of the best materials for small trees is well-rotted stable manure. This is not used extensively, however, because its application is limited to open areas and because it is not available in large quantities. Commercial fertilizers are more readily available and can be used under most conditions.

No general agreement exists among scientists or commercial arborists as to the best formula for tree fertilizer. Some claim a tree cannot be overfertilized, whereas others claim that severe injury may result from too much fertilizer. Virtually all agree on one point, however, that a complete mix, containing the three critical elements, nitrogen, phosphorus, and potassium, should be used.

There is much disagreement on the amount and source of nitrogen. Some workers maintain that one third to one half of the nitrogen must be derived from organic sources, such as cottonseed meal, tankage, or dried blood. Others claim this is unnecessary, that the nitrogen can come entirely from inorganic sources, such as ammonium sulfate, nitrate of soda, or calcium nitrate.

Most of the recent research on shade-tree fertilization indicates that fertilizers with the approximate analysis 5-10-5, which are commonly used for vegetable and other commercial crops, are not entirely suitable for shade trees. These investigations reveal that formulas with higher amounts of nitrogen—for example, 10-8-6 or 10-6-4—are more effective. Some of the larger tree companies have especially prepared formulas which they feel are most effective.

It should be borne in mind that most ornamental trees grow naturally in an acid soil. For this reason, commercial fertilizers tending to leave an alkaline residue should not be used. If the soil reaction needs a change toward the alkaline side, this can best be accomplished by adding lime.

Table 4-1. A suggested formula for mixing a ton of 10-8-6 fertilizer

Materials	Amount Required (lbs.)	Nitrogen (lbs.)	Phos-phoric Acid (lbs.)	Potash (lbs.)
Nitrate of Soda, 16% N	600	96	..	..
Sulfate of Ammonia, 20.5% N	280	57.4	..	..
Urea, 48% N	40	19.2	..	..
Tankage 6% N, 2% P_2O_5	470	28.2	9.4	..
Superphosphate 42%	360	..	151.2	..
Muriate of Potash, 48%	250	..	..	120
Total	2,000	200.8	160.6	120
Analysis	..	10	8	6

The mere insertion of fertilizer into the soil around the tree is no guarantee that the tree will benefit. The fertilizer must be placed where the tree's roots can use it. The reason is that the various components of fertilizers do not move readily through the soil. Unless they are placed in the immediate vicinity of roots, they will do little or no good. Nitrate nitrogen is perhaps the only ingredient in a complete fertilizer that will move to areas beyond its application. The other major essential nutrients such as calcium, magnesium, phosphorus, and potassium are absorbed on the surface of the soil particles, and the plant roots must come in close contact with these particles before the nutrients can become available.

Rates of Application

Opinions differ on how much commercial fertilizer should be applied. Recommendations range from 1 to 8 pounds for each inch in diameter of the trunk at breast height. Probably a figure about midway between those extremes is the best general recommendation. With that quantity, there will be no danger of root injury, and if it does not produce the desired results, an additional application can be made in a year or two.

A safe method to follow, then, is to use about 2 to 4 pounds of complete fertilizer for each inch in diameter of the tree trunk at breast height.* Small trees (less than 6 inches in diameter) should have half this dosage. For example, a tree 10 inches in diameter should receive 20 to 40 pounds (2 to 4 pounds per inch diameter) of commercial fertilizer, whereas a tree 4 inches in diameter should receive 4 to 8 pounds (1 to 2 pounds per inch). When grade changes or building operations have restricted the feeding area, most arborists recommend slightly larger amounts. For large trees, as much as 4 to 5 pounds of 10-6-4 per inch in trunk diameter may be used.

Recently Professor Russell M. Bettes of Temple University has questioned the adequacy of applying a fixed number of pounds of fertilizer per inch of trunk diameter. A more logical method of estimating the fertilizer requirements, he believes, is based on the root area involved rather than on the diameter at breast height (DBH). He suggests squaring the DBH and then dividing the result by 3. This gives the number of pounds of fertilizer needed, using a formula with 10 per cent available nitrogen.

Professor Bettes clarifies his contention as follows: Two trees are growing in a good lawn with no interference to root pasturage. One tree has a 6-inch DBH and the other a 12-inch DBH. Under the present system of calculating the amount of fertilizer needed, the 12-inch tree should receive twice as much food as the 6-inch tree. According to Professor Bettes's method, the 12-inch tree requires four times as much. The smaller tree requires 12 pounds of fertilizer and the second requires 48 ($12 \times 12 = 144 \div 3 = 48$).

In determining the amount of fertilizer to apply, one should consider the age of the tree and what one desires to achieve. If the tree is young and the owner wants it to grow as rapidly as possible, then extra food is called for. On the other hand, relatively less fertilizer would be applied to an older tree that must be kept in good vigor but with further growth restricted.

Fertilizing Narrow-leaved Evergreens

At one time commercial fertilizers were not generally applied to evergreens because they were thought to be extremely toxic. It is now known that good growth responses can be obtained with these materials. The only precaution necessary is to avoid excessive applications.

---

* American beech and crabapple are more sensitive to fertilizer than most trees. Hence the dosage should be reduced by one half.

Since small evergreens may be occasionally injured by commercial fertilizers, it is probably safer to apply nitrogen in some organic carrier at first. For small narrow-leaved evergreens, about 5 pounds of tankage or cottonseed meal should be applied to each 100 square feet of bed area in the spring. The fertilizer should be hoed or watered in, so as to mix readily.

For large narrow-leaved evergreens, commercial fertilizers can be used with safety. From 2 to 4 pounds of 10-6-4 fertilizer should be applied to every 100 square feet of bed area if the trees are in a group. For large evergreens standing in open areas, about 2 pounds of this fertilizer can be applied for each inch in diameter of the trunk.

Fertilizing Broad-leaved Evergreens

The problem of fertilizing broad-leaved evergreens is more complex. Such plants as azalea, rhododendron, laurel, and leucothoe require a distinctly acid soil. For this reason fertilizing materials that tend to sweeten the soil should be avoided. Greatest success with broad-leaved evergreens is obtained when liberal quantities of humus are incorporated in the soil and applied as mulch. Acid peat moss and rotted oak-leaf mold are two of the best materials. As a rule they provide enough nutrients and at the same time help to keep the soil acid. In poor soils, where additional nitrogen fertilization is necessary, cottonseed meal or tankage may be added at the rate of 5 pounds per 100 square feet of bed area. An excellent formula for broad-leaved evergreens, developed by Dr. R. P. White, is made up as follows:

	lbs.
Tankage or Cottonseed Meal (6% N)	650
Sulfate of Ammonia	200
Ammoniated Superphosphate (1.88–17.5%)	800
Muriate of Potash	200
Magnesium Sulfate or Magnesium Oxide	150
Total	2,000

This should be applied at the rate of 1,000 pounds an acre for large plantings or 1 pound to 50 square feet for small plantings. It contains all the ingredients required by broad-leaved evergreens and has an acid reaction. The magnesium sulfate (epsom salts) in this formula aids in the production of deep-green leaves.

Fresh manure, lime, or wood ashes should not be used to fertilize rhododendron, azalea, or related plants, since these materials will neutralize or sweeten the soil.

64

Methods of Applying Fertilizers to Trees

Obviously the area to be fertilized is governed by the location of the feeding roots. In this respect there is considerable variation among species of trees and in different soil types. But the feeding roots usually occupy the outer band of a circular area whose circumference lies just beyond the spread of the outermost branches. The width of this band is equal to about two thirds of the radius of the circle. With most trees, few feeding roots lie within the center third of the circle (Fig. 4-1). A rule-of-thumb method for determining the region in which most of the roots occur is as follows: the radial spread of the roots in feet is equal to the diameter of the tree (1 foot above the soil) in inches. For example, a

Fig. 4-1. Fertilization of shade trees, showing the location of the holes to which fertilizers are added. The holes should be 18 inches deep, about 2 feet apart, and slanted toward the tree, as shown in diagram A.

tree whose diameter 1 foot above the ground is 9 inches, will have most of its roots within a 9-foot radius and its feeding roots in the outer 6-foot-wide band.

Another point to be borne in mind: it is the roots of smaller diameters, $1/16$ inch or less, that function in absorption of nutrients.

The extent of spread of tree roots cannot always be determined by the spread of the branches. Roots can extend at least $1\frac{1}{2}$ to 3 times beyond the spread of the branches. Most of the feeding roots are therefore not found within the 'drip line' area.

Surface Applications. Fertilizers may be broadcast under small trees growing in open soil. Satisfactory results are obtained only when such fertilizers are hoed or watered into the soil thoroughly. As already mentioned, most of the fertilizer elements, especially phosphorus and to a lesser extent potash, remain where they are placed and do not move through the soil readily. When a fertilizer is spread on the surface for a period of years, the tree tends to develop roots near the soil surface. If the tree is growing in a lawn, these roots not only interfere with mowing, but they affect the growth of the grass beneath the trees. Moreover, a tree with a shallow root system is more apt to suffer from dry spells than one with a deeper root system. Elms and maples normally produce roots near the soil surface. Application of fertilizers to the soil surface merely aggravates that condition.

No dry commercial fertilzer should be applied within one foot of the trunk, since injury to the root collar and trunk base might result.

Trenching. The trench method was developed in an effort to place nutrients nearer to the root system. A trench about 2 feet wide is dug in a circle beneath the outer spread of the branches. This area is then filled with rich composted soil to which fertilizers have been added. The disadvantages of this method are obvious. First, the soil is enriched in only a small part of the total area covered by the roots; second, many roots are injured when the trench is dug; and third, large amounts of sod must be lifted and replaced where trees are growing in lawns.

Punch-bar Method. The most practical method for large trees and those growing on lawns is the punch-bar method, because it distributes the fertilizer throughout the root area. Holes spaced about 2 feet apart and about 18 inches deep are made with some implement throughout the area to be fertilized (Fig. 4-2). The correct amount of fertilizer is evenly distributed in the holes, which are then filled completely with loosely packed peat moss, shredded manure, or topsoil and closed by a push with the heel of the shoe.

An ordinary crowbar is the implement most readily available to home owners for making the holes. Obviously the small, closely compacted hole made with such an implement will keep the fertilizer localized. For

Fig. 4-2. The author's son Joseph is shown punching holes with a special apparatus known as Pok-a-hol, prior to inserting fertilizers near the tree's roots.

this reason it is essential that a large number of holes be made, about 10 to 20 for each inch in diameter of the tree. A soil auger, which bores into the soil without compacting the sides of the hole, is a more efficient implement. A post-hole digger is recommended by some authorities, but the holes made by this implement are much too large to be satisfactory for fertilizing trees growing in lawns.

Many commercial arborists and park and cemetery superintendents have discarded punch-bars in favor of more modern equipment, such as electric and compressed-air drills or augers. With these, a great number of holes can be bored to the desired depth in a very short time.

Holes should be made in a slanting direction (Fig. 4-1) rather than vertically, regardless of the implement used. This increases the fertilizable area to a small extent.

If no response becomes evident from fertilizing applications, one should check by probing in a few spots to see whether the plant food was placed near roots. Some investigators have found that some trees have no feeding roots as far out as the branch drip area. In some trees the bulk of the feeding roots are within 6 to 8 feet of the trunk.

Automatic Feeding Machine. The Ferti-Feeder (Fig. 4-3) invented by the well-known arborist Gary H. Maier of Des Moines, Iowa, has recently been introduced for commercial use. This self-contained tree-feeding device carries its own power and fertilizer, and drills and fills holes automatically. Powered by a gasoline engine with reversing transmission, it drills about 4 holes a minute. Up to 100 pounds of fertilizer can be carried in and dispensed by a hopper.

Compressed-air Feeding. A method invented by a well-known commercial arborist in the Middle West, the late Charles F. Irish, and one that represents a great improvement over previous methods, involves the use of compressed air. Holes are made with compressed-air drills or augers as outlined above. A pipe that tapers toward the lower end is inserted in the hole, and compressed air is forced into the soil to drive off accumulations of soil gases and to fracture the soil. (This treatment alone often helps to stimulate tree growth.) Dry fertilizer is then placed in the hole, and compressed air is again forced in.* The fertilizer is thus distributed as well as possible with the least disturbance to the sod. Fertilizing with compressed air is most effective in homogeneous soils. It is not so effective in soils made up of several different layers.

Feeding Needles. Several types of feeding needles or guns are available. With these, fertilizers either in dry form or in water solution are placed in the holes. The addition of fertilizers in water is especially helpful when the soil moisture supply is low and water is a limiting factor. Aside

---

* To prevent the air and fertilizer from blowing back into the operator's face, a metal cover resembling an inverted funnel is attached to the pipe.

Fig. 4-3. The newest machine for applying dry fertilizers is the Ferti-Feeder, developed by Gary H. Maier of Des Moines, Iowa.

from supplying much-needed water, the method ensures almost instant availability of the nutrients, since these must be in solution before the roots can absorb them (Fig. 4-4). The soluble fertilizer elements are dissolved in water in a tank and are then pumped through the needle into the soil. Among the more commonly used soluble fertilizers are Ra-pid-gro—discussed later in this chapter under Foliage Feeding.

Another type of gun includes a hopper, holding about a pound of fertilizer. The water from the spray tank or main is turned off, and a valve is opened to release the charge of fertilizer from the hopper. Another valve then permits water to enter the gun and force the fertilizer down into the soil.

These latest improvements in feeding methods are now used by many of the larger tree-preservation companies and have proved more effective than the simpler methods outlined earlier in this chapter.

Tree owners who want to feed their trees with an apparatus resembling that used by professional tree men can use the Ross Root Feeder (Fig. 4-5), manufactured by Ross Daniels, Inc., 1970 Fuller Road, West Des Moines, Iowa 50265. A plant-food cartridge is placed in the chamber at the top of the apparatus, the garden hose is attached at the proper end, and the pointed rod end inserted into the soil to the proper depth. When the water is turned on, it dissolves the plant food and delivers the solution to the root area** (Fig. 4-6).

Fertilizers in liquid form have the following advantages over the dry fertilizers: they are immediately available to the roots and are more uniformly distributed through the soil; their application requires less labor, provides an additional use for the sprayer, and gives the tree a good watering.

Among the disadvantages are: they do not last very long, and some of the constituents leach out rather quickly; they do not work so well in heavy, poorly drained soil; they offer no opportunity to improve the soil by incorporating organic matter, as is the case with dry fertilizer applications.

When and How Frequently Trees Should Be Fertilized

Trees may be fertilized either in late fall or in early spring. Fall applications should not be made until all possibility of top growth is past. In the New York City area, the first of October is a safe date to start such treatments. Fall applications have an advantage in that some nutrients will enter the roots immediately and some in very early spring. The remainder will be available later. Tree roots always become active long

---

** A multi-feed root feeder has been introduced by Ross Daniels, Inc. It operates in gangs of 3 or more units on one water line for feeding large areas.

Fig. 4-4. Professional arborists apply nutrients with a tree-feeding needle attached to a pressure sprayer.

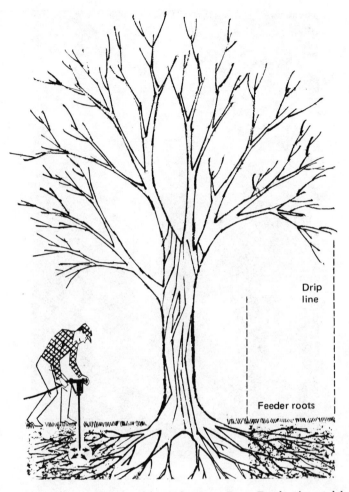

Fig. 4-5. Diagrammatic sketch of how the Ross Root Feeder is used by home owners who want to feed their own trees.

before the buds begin to swell, and fertilizers already in place can be more quickly utilized. Fertilizer applications in the spring may be made from the time the frost is out of the ground until May 1 around New York, but the later the application the less will be the returns as measured in root and top growth.

Dr. Harold B. Tukey, Jr. at Cornell University found that roots of dormant plants continue to grow and absorb nutrients. At soil temperatures of 35°F. (2°C.) there is some absorption of nutrients, while at 45° and 55°F. (7° and 13°C.) the uptake of nutrients is rather large. Applying fertilizers in the fall increases growth the following spring.

Fig. 4-6. Inserting cartridges into a Ross Root Feeder.

Summer applications are not recommended, as such treatments stimulate the production of soft succulent tissues, which do not harden properly and are therefore subject to winter injury. A starving tree, however, should be fed regardless of the season.

The frequency of the fertilization treatments depends on the kind of tree involved, the growth response, and other factors. It may vary from an annual treatment to one made every 3 or 4 years.

Cost of Fertilizers

Price alone should not be the deciding factor in the purchase of fertilizers. Some fertilizers costing $75 or more a ton are worth no more than some costing only $25. Others, manufactured by reliable firms that honestly attempt to include materials known to produce the desired results, may cost more but are well worth the additional price. Some tree fertilizers are more expensive because they contain more nitrogen, some of which may be in the more expensive organic forms such as cottonseed meal, tankage, or dried blood. The synthetic ureaform fertilizers are even more expensive.

Home-mixing of fertilizers as outlined on page 61 is not recommended unless a substantial saving would be realized over the cost of ready-mixed formulas.

Feeding Above-ground Parts of the Tree

Foliage Feeding. Interest in foliage applications of nutrients has increased by leaps and bounds during recent years. If one individual could be selected as the moving force behind this method of feeding plants, it would be the late Thomas Reilly of Dansville, New York, a member of one of America's early tree-growing families. Mr. Reilly was an early advocate of high analysis, completely soluble plant foods which could be applied as foliage sprays. His product, Ra-pid-gro, was the first complete chemical fertilizer to be made commercially available for spraying on trees, shrubs, flowers, and food plants. Ra-pid-gro is a 23-19-17 completely soluble chemical fertilizer with minor elements added. The nitrogen is obtained from crystal urea, monoammonium phosphate, and potassium nitrate; the phosphoric acid from monoammonium phosphate and monopotassium phosphate; and the potassium from potassium nitrate and monopotassium phosphate.

Scientific corroboration of Mr. Reilly's early observations that plants could benefit from foliage applications of nutrients has appeared in recent years. Most notable was the work with radioisotopes at the Michigan Agricultural Experiment Station under professors Tukey, Wittwer, Bukovac, and others. These men were among the first to report that leaves are not completely covered with cutin (except for the stomatal openings), as was believed formerly. It is now known that both the upper and lower surfaces of leaves consist of intermittent parallel layers of pectinlike substances interspersed with the cutinized layers (Fig. 4-7). The pectinaceous substances have a great capacity for absorbing and releasing water and nutrients. Leaf surfaces, therefore, are no longer considered to be relatively impervious to materials in solution.

Formerly it was thought that the lower leaf surface was more efficient in absorbing solutions because of the greater number of stomata on that surface. This apparently is not the case, because the upper surface of some leaves can absorb as much phosphate as the lower surface, even though it has only one seventh as many stomata.

It is not easy to appreciate the potential absorbing surfaces involved. The leaf area of a 12-year-old apple tree, for example, is about 10 times

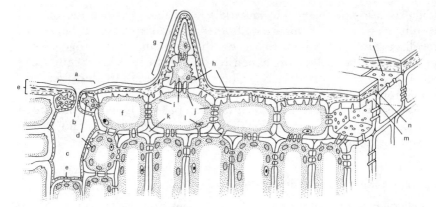

Fig. 4-7. Diagrammatic representation of leaf epidermal cells and cuticle. Modified after Wittwer, 1963. (Drawing not to scale.) (a) stoma, (b) stomatal opening, (c) stomatal cavity, (d) chloroplasts, (e) cuticle interspersed with pectinaceous substances, (f) vacuole, (g) hair, (h) ectodesmata, (i) protoplasm, (j) plasmodesma, (k) intercellular space, (l) nucleus, (m) cellulose cell wall, (n) pectic lamella.

the land area it occupies. And the ratio between leaf area of a shade tree growing along a city street and the constricted land area it occupies is even greater. A 47-foot-tall silver maple growing in the open, for example, was found to have 177,000 leaves with a combined leaf blade area of a sixth of an acre (7,000 square feet).

The absorption of nutrients by leaves is generally greater during daylight hours.

Among other factors which favor absorption and transport of nutrients are high humidity, proper temperature, and incident radiation; a carbohydrate supply; and vigorous growth. Chemical and physical properties of the nutrient spray, such as pH, carrier ions, and surface active agents, also exert a great influence.

Factors inherent in the leaves themselves also influence nutrient intake. Among these are thickness of the cuticle, number of discontinuities (interspersed pectinaceous areas), hairiness or smoothness of leaf surface, and other surface properties that influence adherence.

Young, rapidly expanding leaves absorb more nutrients per unit area than do fully mature ones. Generally speaking, the more vigorous the plant, the more nutrient it can absorb via the leaves.

Not all plants have the same capacity for absorbing nutrients via foliage sprays. Apple leaves, for example, can absorb more than peach leaves can.

Nitrogen applied in the form of urea is the most readily absorbed of the major elements. In fact, the entire nitrogen requirements of some crops can be satisfied by means of foliage sprays. After the urea in solution is absorbed into the leaf, it is split up into ammonia and carbon dioxide by means of the enzyme urease.

Sodium and potassium are two other elements readily absorbed by leaves, and they are among the most highly mobile once inside the leaves. Phosphorus, chlorine, sulfur, zinc, copper, manganese, iron, and molybdenum are less mobile in the order given. Calcium is absorbed but does not move out of the leaves. Despite this fact, calcium and its close relative magnesium can be applied successfully to the leaves of some plants to overcome a deficiency of those elements.

The rate of movement of nutrients such as nitrogen, phosphorus, and potassium absorbed by leaves has been estimated at 1 inch in 5 minutes.

The leaves are not the only tree parts capable of absorbing nutrients. The bark, buds, petioles, and flowers are also capable of some absorption.

Phosphorus and potash applied to the bark of apple and peach trees moved into the branches 18 to 24 inches from the points of application within a 24-hour period. Most absorption via the bark occurs when the nutrient is applied just before the buds begin to swell in early spring. And the nutrient solution applied to the bark can be ten times as strong as that applied to the leaves, without causing damage to the tree.

This method makes it possible to supply important nutrients, before the start of the growing season, to trees that have suffered from some winter injury or that may have a nutrient deficiency.

Foliage sprays are particularly effective in maintaining good growth in dry seasons because the tree can start using the evenly distributed sprays immediately. Dry fertilizers placed in holes around the tree are not available to tree roots in dry spells.

Foliage-nutrient sprays should be applied either with a pressure sprayer or with one of the specially designed fertilizer spray guns available in garden supply stores. The latter have a siphoning device and can be attached to the garden hose. As a rule they cannot reach high enough to leaf-feed tall trees.

The amount of high analysis all-soluble plant food to use will vary with the grade or formula. Generally speaking, no more than the following amounts should be dissolved in each 10 gallons of water used: 5 ounces of a 12-12-12, 13-13-13, or 13-26-13; 4 ounces of a 15-15-15, 15-30-15, or 16-16-16; 3 ounces of an 18-18-18, 20-20-20, or 23-21-17.

The tree should be sprayed until the nutrient solution begins to drip heavily from the leaves.

Tree owners are cautioned that not all fertilizers that are quickly soluble in water are safe to spray on the leaves. The manufacturer will indicate clearly on the label whether his product can be used safely in foliage sprays.

Most of the concentrates that are safe to use as foliage sprays can be combined with such organic pesticides as ferbam and malathion. This enables the tree owner or commercial arborist to feed the tree and control pests and diseases in one operation. Here, too, the manufacturer of the plant food can advise the gardener as to which pesticides are compatible with his product.

Leaves act as a two-way avenue for plant nutrients. Not only are nutrients taken in, but nutrients absorbed either through roots or leaves can be leached out of the leaves during rains.

In the not-too-distant future, large areas such as forests will be fertilized by applying the plant food by airplane. Early experiments revealed this method to be quick and relatively inexpensive, and the forest trees responded by making good growth within 2 years of the applications.

Tree Injection. Direct injection of essential nutrients into the trunk has been moderately successful. But the method cannot yet be recommended as a standard commercial practice. Probably the only exception is the injection of iron salts into chlorotic trees that are known to suffer from iron deficiency.

Though fertilization by injection into the trunk or branches is still in the experimental stage, some recent work indicates that it is feasible, inasmuch as favorable responses have been obtained in some instances. Apple trees have been injected with complete fertilizer solutions containing 0.25 per cent potassium phosphate plus 0.25 per cent urea, at rates varying from $1/30$ to $1/6$ pound per tree. Sufficient quantities of these materials were absorbed in 24 hours to bring about an increase in growth equivalent to that resulting from heavy applications to the soil. Moreover, the injection of urea at the rate of 1 gram of the salt to each inch of the branch diameter produced no injury and increased the nitrogen content of the tissues of some trees.

The greatest danger in tree injections is the possibility of injuring the tree tissues. Another danger is that of introducing wood-rot fungi in the bored holes.

For the present, injections should be attempted only where single salts are needed to overcome a particular deficiency, or where soil treatments are not easily applied because of pavement, walks, and other obstructions over the root area.

Feeding Trees with Micropore Release Packets

A new approach to fertilizing trees and other plants is with so-called micropore release packets sold under the names of Eeesy Grow and Root Contact Paket.

The fertilizer packet is a heat-sealed polyethylene-paper laminated envelope containing specified quantities of water-soluble 16-8-16 fertilizer. The sides of the packets are pierced with a predetermined number of 'pinholes' of precisely measured diameter. When the tree is planted, the packet is placed *unopened* near the feeding roots. Vapor in the soil enters the micropore openings and slowly dissolves the fertilizer, which escapes through the holes in liquid form and is taken up by the plant roots. The combined effect of slow release and the relatively minimal amounts of fertilizer delivered to the plant at any one time assures that fertilizer burn of the feeding roots will not occur.

In practice, the activity of the packets is largely controlled by the seasons. With the arrival of colder weather, the reduction of vapor pressure again develops, and the packet releases the fertilizer to the roots fertilizer is not delivered to the plant roots during the very cold period of the dormant season. When the soil thaws in spring, however, vapor pressure again develops, and the packet releases the fertilizer to the roots in line with the plant's growth needs. Because of these unique features, the perforated packets operate through a timing mechanism which is triggered by vapor pressure in warm soil and halted when the soil is cold.

For established trees, the 4-ounce packets are recommended by the manufacturer, S and D Products, Prairie Du Chien, Wisconsin.* The number to use per tree depends on the size or age of the tree. The 4-ounce packets should be inserted into the soil to a depth of 8 to 10 inches midway between the trunk and outer branch drip. The opening in the soil is made with a spade and is closed after the packet is inserted. According to the manufacturer, the 4-ounce packets supply trees with sufficient nutrients for up to 8 years after insertion into the soil.

Other Methods of Feeding Trees

International Spike of Lexington, Kentucky, has introduced Jobe's Tree Food Spike, which can be driven into the soil with an ordinary carpenter's hammer. The 16-8-8 fertilizer is held together with a patented resin binder. A plastic cup is supplied to facilitate the driving of the spike into the soil. Leaching studies by Purdue University research workers showed that nitrogen and potassium from the spike move into the root zone rapidly and are available for utilization by the tree as soon as the fertilizer is placed in the root zone at a depth of 18 inches. Fertilizing a large tree with the spike is approximately 2½ times faster than drilling.

---

* In the northeastern United States, Eeesy Grow Packets are available from Specialty Fertilizer Company, Box 355, Suffern, New York 10901.

Ross Daniels, Inc., the manufacturer of the Ross Root Feeder, has more recently introduced the Ross Super Tree Stakes, which are driven into the ground at the drip-line of the tree. The stakes have a formulation of 16-10-9 plus iron and zinc.

Selected Bibliography

Attoe, O. J. 1967. 'New long-term plant feeding.' *Horticulture*. p. 45. Oct. 1967.

Attoe, O. J., F. L. Rasson, W. C. Dahnke, and J. R. Boyle. 1970. 'Fertilizer release from packets and its effect on tree growth.' *Proc. Soil Science Soc. of America*. Vol. 34 (No. 1). p. 137–41.

Beilmann, A. P. 1934. 'Experiments on the fertilization of shade trees.' *Proc. Tenth National Shade Tree Conference*. p. 114–25.

———. 1936. 'Feeding the shade tree.' *Missouri Bot. Gard. Bul*. Vol. 24 (No. 4). p. 95–113.

Bettes, R. M. 1972. 'Feeding shade and ornamental trees.' *American Nurseryman*. Oct. 1, 1972. p. 100–102.

Boynton, Damon. 1949. 'Spray fertilization of shade trees.' *Proc. Twenty-fifth National Shade Tree Conference*. p. 6–15.

Broadfoot, W. M. 1966. *Five years of nitrogen fertilization in a sweetgum-oak stand*. U.S. Forest Service Research Note SO-34. Southern Forest Experiment Station, New Orleans, Louisiana.

Bukovac, M. J. and S. H. Witwer. 1957. 'Absorption and mobility of foliar-applied nutrients.' *Plant Physiology*. Vol. 32 (No. 5). p. 428–35.

Cannon, Thomas. 1956. 'Foliar analysis as an index of fertilizer requirements of some ornamental trees.' *Proc. Thirty-second National Shade Tree Conference*. p. 84–93.

Chadwick, L. C. 1934. 'The fertilization of shade trees in the nursery.' *Proc. Am. Soc. Hort. Sci*. Vol. 32. p. 357–60.

———. 1935. 'The fertilization of shade trees in the nursery.' *Proc. Amer. Soc. Hort. Sci*. Vol. 32. p. 357–60.

———. 1936. 'Fertilization of shade trees.' *American Nurseryman*. Vol. 64. p. 9–10.

———. 1937. 'Modern methods of shade tree fertilization.' *Proc. Thirteenth National Shade Tree Conference*. p. 63–76.

———. 1945. 'Fertilizers' action in the soil.' *American Nurseryman*. Vol. 82. p. 7–8, 29–32. Sept. 15, 1945, p. 12–16, Oct. 1, 1945.

———. 1947. 'Some shade tree fertilization problems.' *Arborist's News*. Vol. 12 (No. 2). p. 9–12.

———. 1965. 'Some shade tree fertilization practices.' *Arborist's News*. Vol. 30 (No. 8). p. 57–61.

Chandler, R. F. Jr. 1939. 'The influence of nitrogenous fertilizer applications upon the growth and seed production of beech and sugar maple trees.' *Arborist's News*. Vol. 4. p. 17–19.

Cook, R. L. and C. E. Millar. 1936. 'The residual effect of fertilizer.' *Mich. Agr. Exp. Sta. Quart. Bul*. 18. p. 227–34.

Davies, W. J. et al. 1972. 'Effects of transplanting on physiological responses and growth of shade trees.' *Proc. Forty-eighth International Shade Tree Conference.* p. 22–30.

Heinicke, A. J. 1939. 'The physiology of trees with special reference to their food supply.' *Proc. Fifteenth National Shade Tree Conference.* p. 26–37.

Himelick, E. B., Dan Neely, and W. R. Crowley. 1965. *Experimental field studies on shade tree fertilization.* Illinois Natural History Survey, Biological Notes. 53. 12 p.

Himelick, E. B. and Dan Neely. 1966. 'Recent studies on shade tree fertilization.' *Proc. Forty-second International Shade Tree Conference.* p. 71–79.

Irish, C. F. 1929. 'The process of aeration and fertilization of tree roots by means of compressed air.' *Proc. Fifth National Shade Tree Conference.* p. 35–37.

Jacobs, H. L. 1929. *Fertilization of shade trees.* Part 1. 'Fall vs. spring fertilization.' Davey Tree Expert Co. Res. Bul. 4. 27 p.

———. 1930. *Fertilization of shade trees.* Part 2. 'Chemical fertilization of conifers.' Davey Tree Expert Co. Res. Dept. Bul. 5. 15 p.

———. 1937. 'Fertilizer formulae-tree responses.' *Proc. Thirteenth National Shade Tree Conference.* p. 51–63.

Kenworthy, A. L. 1955. 'Leaf analysis to determine fertilizer needs of trees and shrubs.' *Trees Magazine.* Mar.-Apr. p. 8, 18.

Lunt, H. A. 1938. 'The use of fertilizers in a coniferous nursery.' *Conn. Agr. Exp. Sta. Bul.* 416. p. 723–66.

Lucks, Hartl. 1969. 'Fertilizers: what's new and what can we expect in the future?' *Proc. Forty-fourth International Shade Tree Conference.* p. 20–28.

May, Curtis. 1932. 'A discussion of tree feeding.' *Proc. Eighth National Shade Tree Conference.* p. 31–35.

Mitchell, H. L. and R. F. Chandler. 1939. *The nitrogen nutrition and growth of certain deciduous trees of northeastern United States.* Black Rock Forest Bul. 11. 94 p.

Murphy, R. C. and W. E. Meyer. 1969. *The care and feeding of trees.* Crown Publishers, New York. 164 p.

Neely, Dan, E. B. Himelick, and W. R. Crowley, Jr. 1970. 'Fertilization of established trees.' *Illinois Natural History Survey.* Vol. 30. p. 235–66.

Neely, Dan and E. B. Himelick. 1971. *Fertilizing and watering trees.* Illinois Natural History Survey. Circular 52. 20 p.

Parr, F. L. 1970. *Standard for fertilizing shade and ornamental trees.* National Arborist Assoc., McLean, Virginia. 2 p.

Pirone, P. P. 1951. 'Foliage application of nutrients.' *Proc. Twenty-seventh National Shade Tree Conference.* p. 23–35.

———. 'Advances in general tree maintenance.' *Arborist's News.* Vol. 39 (No. 3). p. 55–60.

Sprague, H. (ed.) 1964. *Hunger signs in crops.* 3rd ed. David McKay Co., New York. 461 p.

Teubner, F. G., S. H. Witwer, W. G. Long, and H. B. Tukey. 1957. 'Some factors affecting absorption and transport of foliar-applied nutrients as revealed by radioactive isotopes.' *Quart. Bul. Mich. Agr. Exp. Sta.* 39 (No. 3). p. 398–415.

Tukey, H. B. 1952. 'The uptake of nutrients by leaves and branches of fruit trees.' *Rept. Thirteenth Int. Hort. Congress,* London. p. 297–306.

Tukey, H. B. and M. M. Meyer, Jr. 1965. 'Nutrient applications to dormant plants.' *American Nurseryman.* June 1, 1965. p. 7–8.

White, D. P. 1965. *Survival, growth, and nutrient uptake by spruce and pine seedlings as affected by slow-release fertilizer materials.* Forest-Soil Relationships in North America, p. 47–63. Oregon State U. Press, Corvallis, Oregon.

White, D. P. and Albert L. Leaf. 1956. *Forest fertilization.* A bibliography, with abstracts on the use of fertilizers and soil admendments in forestry. Syracuse University College of Forestry. Tech. Pub. 81. 305 p.

Wikle, Jack. 1969. 'Fertilization of trees, shrubs and woody ground covers.' *American Hort. Magazine.* Vol. 48 (No. 2). p. 57–61. Spring 1969.

5
Pruning Trees and Treating Wounds

The pruning of trees and the subsequent treatment of wounds are probably the most important of all tree maintenance practices. Proper and systematic pruning helps trees better to withstand adverse environmental conditions. In addition, properly pruned trees require less fertilizing, bracing, and spray materials to keep them healthy. Correct wound treatments reduce losses due to wood-decay fungi. Pruning trees and treating their wounds are so closely related that the two practices must be considered together.

Need for Pruning

Trees are pruned principally to preserve their health and appearance and to prevent damage to human life and to property.

Pruning for Health. Broken, dead, or diseased branches are pruned to prevent decay-producing fungi from penetrating into the part of the tree to which these branches are attached. Live branches are removed to permit penetration of sunlight and circulation of air through the canopy or to compensate for loss of roots. Overlapping branches and those that interfere with utility wires are removed to prevent rubbing and eventual decay. Branch stubs are removed to promote proper healing.

Tops are sometimes cut back to revitalize the remaining parts of the tree. Such pruning, if properly done, increases the general vigor of the tree by supplying additional nourishment to the parts that remain. Drastic pruning involving the removal of much potential leaf surface may, however, seriously affect the food supply and weaken the trees. The removal of a large portion of the top may also favor fungus and insect attack and increase the possibility of scalding of the bark by suddenly exposing tender tissues to the direct rays of the sun. The removal of many small branches rather than a few large ones not only reduces the possibility of sun scald but also makes the pruning less conspicuous and facilitates maintaining the desired shape. In addition, the many small wounds will heal more rapidly and completely than the few large ones.

Since the removal of dead or dying branches constitutes one of the major objectives of pruning, it is well to list some of the principal causes of dieback. These include: lack of adequate or proper plant food; damage to the root system; a deficient or overabundant moisture supply; poisonous elements in the atmosphere or soil; inadequate aeration of the root system owing to grade changes; excessively dense crown; fungus, bacterial, or insect attack; mechanical injury to the trunk and branches; and lightning injury. While it is imperative that all dead wood resulting from any of these causes be removed, it is extremely important that the causal factors be eliminated or corrected whenever feasible.

Pruning for Appearance. Only in formal plantings or to restore the characteristic form to a badly misshapen tree is pruning for appearance warranted. An appreciation of landscape values and some idea of the normal form of the tree being pruned are essential for success in pruning trees in formal plantings. Certain branches on many street trees, particularly Norway maples, tend to develop faster than others. These should be pruned back to preserve the tree's form.

Occasionally it is desirable to keep normally large-growing shade or ornamental trees within restricted bounds of small properties. Judicious pruning of the new growth during summer will produce the desired dwarfing effect, with no harm to the tree.

Pruning for Safety. Dead, split, and broken branches are a constant hazard to human life and to property. Danger from falling limbs is always greatest in trees along city streets and in public parks. Low-hanging live branches must be removed to a height of 10 to 12 feet when they interfere with pedestrian and vehicular traffic. This phase of pruning is probably the most important of all street tree maintenance practices.

Pruning Equipment

Adequate equipment (Fig. 5-1) is an essential of good pruning. Equipment must be maintained in first-class condition both for the safety of the operator and the good of the tree. The chart on page 84 lists the most essential pieces of pruning equipment and their use.

Fig. 5-1. Some of the equipment essential for pruning, bracing, and cavity work.

The knack of using ropes properly in climbing and working in a tree can best be developed through visual instruction and practice; consequently, a discussion of this subject is beyond the scope of this book.* Men most skilled in the use of ropes have been trained principally by the staffs of large tree companies. The use of ropes in tree work contributes safety, comfort, and dexterity to the climber. The amateur would best use saws and pruners that he can operate from the ground for most of the work, and employ experienced tree climbers to remove high limbs in older trees.

Among the well-known manufacturers or distributors of tree pruning tools at present are Ackley Manufacturing Company, Clackamas, Oregon 97015; Bartlett Manufacturing Company, Detroit, Michigan 48202; Fairmont Hydraulics, Chicago, Illinois 60604; Fanno Saw Works, Chico,

---

* *Tree Preservation Bulletin Number 4* of the U.S. Dept. of Interior, National Park Service, presents a complete discussion of the use of ropes in climbing and working in trees. This is available for a small charge from the Superintendent of Documents, U.S. Government Printing Office, Washington, D.C. 20402.

Equipment	Specifications	Use
Hand saw	At least 6 teeth to an inch	Normal pruning cuts
Crosscut saw	3 feet long	Large cuts
Power chain saws	Several sizes (see Fig. 5-2)	Speediest and most efficient to prune large branches
Pole pruner Pole saw	10-12 feet long	Removing small limbs not reached by hand saw
Manila rope	150 feet, ½ inch in diameter	Climbing
Manila rope	100 feet, ¾ inch in diameter	Lowering large limbs
Pruning shears	Hand operated	Cutting back small trees and pruning roots
Ax	Small size	Removing short stubs that cannot readily be removed with a saw
Mallet and chisel	Small size	Point and shape final cuts
Belt snaps (2)		Hold saw and paint cans
Shellac	See page 99	Paint cambial region of cuts
Wound dressing	See page 99	Paint cuts
Safety belt		Fasten operator securely

California 95926; Leonard and Son, Piqua, Ohio 45356; Limb-lopper Company, Santa Fe Springs, California 90670; Muench Co. Inc., Stamford, Connecticut 06902; H. K. Porter, Somerville, Massachusetts 02143; Seymour Smith and Son, Oakville, Connecticut 06779,* and Wachtel Supply Company, Wauwatosa, Wisconsin 53213.

World War II speeded the development of one of the most useful of arborists' tools—the *power* chain saw (Fig. 5-2). This saw is designed for high-speed cutting of trees. One type can fell a hardwood tree 15 inches in diameter in less than a minute and a softwood tree of the same size in a quarter of that time.

The chain saws are simple to operate and light in weight. They reduce limbing, felling, or bucking time to a minimum. Some types can be operated by one man; others require two. The power to run these high-speed saws is usually generated by a light-weight gasoline engine.

Among the manufacturers of chain or power saws are: Fairmont Hydraulics, Chicago, Illinois 60604; Homelite, Textron Div., Charlotte, North Carolina, 28217, makers of the Homelite E-Z chain saw; Envin-

---

* An excellent 32-page booklet *How to Prune and Trim* is available for a small charge from this company.

Fig. 5-2. The power chain saw is an indispensable tool for pruning large branches.

rude and Johnson, Galesburg, Illinois 61401, makers of the Pioneer Holiday 2; and McCulloch Company, Los Angeles, California 90045, makers of the McCulloch Power Mac 6.

A free booklet on chain saw maintenance is available from the Sabre Saw Chain Co., Lewiston, New York 14092.

To facilitate pruning and line-clearing jobs on trees growing along streets and highways, engineers have perfected hydraulically operated aerial lifts to which are attached one or two crows' nests or baskets. From these the operator can reach any point in the ordinary city tree. The apparatus is powered by a conventional power take-off from the truck engine. Among the manufacturers of such equipment are Baker Equipment Engineering Co., Richmond, Virginia 23211; Chance, Pitman Manufacturing Company, Grandview, Missouri 64030, makers of the Pitman Pelican; McCabe-Powers Company, St. Louis, Missouri 63134, makers of Skymaster Aerial Beams; and Mobile Aerial Towers, Fort Wayne, Indiana 46800, makers of the Hi Ranger (Fig. 5-3).

Fig. 5-3. The mobile aerial lift Hi Ranger is helpful in pruning and line clearing jobs in trees along streets and highways.

When To Prune

Though there are advantages and disadvantages in pruning during certain seasons, trees may be pruned at any time of the year, and the selection should be governed generally by practical considerations.

Trees can be best pruned to the desired shape when they are in foliage. It is easier to see weakened or dead branches then.

Since most rapid healing occurs on wounds made in early spring, this season is also a good time for pruning. But some trees, like maples and birches, bleed so profusely when cut in spring that it is better to delay pruning them until summer, when the sap runs less freely. Street and park trees, except maples, are usually pruned during the winter in order to distribute tree maintenance work more evenly over the entire year.

How To Prune

There is no standard method of pruning, but certain procedures and precautions generally are followed by competent arborists to ensure best results. In general, it is best to start pruning operations in the upper parts of the tree and work downward. This facilitates shaping the tree properly and saves time in clearing the tree of pruned branches, which become lodged in the lower branches as they fall. All dead, broken, fungus- and insect-infested, and interfering branches are removed. Small branches that may prove undesirable within a few years should be treated as interfering branches. Clean cuts should be made as nearly flush as possible with the branch that is to remain. Dead branches should be cut back to a healthy crotch, so that healthy tissue surrounds the final cut.

The treatment of bark on the trunk and branches is included in the pruning operation. All dead bark areas should be cut to healthy tissue and old wounds not healing properly should be recut, and then shellac and a wound dressing applied.

Shaping the Final Cuts

All final cuts should be made as close as possible to the remaining part. Stubs or protruding 'lips' should never be left, since they inhibit proper healing, and water pockets that promote wood decay may develop. The branches of some trees, such as the Norway maple, are so shaped that wounds resulting from their removal are flat at the top or bottom. Such wounds do not heal properly because the sap flow fails to reach some of the bark. Wounds of this type should be shaped, as shown in Figure 5-4, by pointing the bark above and below the circular cut, and by removing the protruding wood with a chisel. As will be discussed in Chapter 6, sap movement runs parallel to the length of the branch, and abrupt cuts

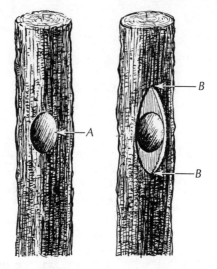

Fig. 5-4. How to shape pruning cuts. **Left:** Branch removed at A. **Right:** The bark is cut away and pointed at B.

across the conducting vessels result in a decrease or stoppage of the sap flow to the bark and in the drying and death of these unfed areas. Wounds made by removing branches at sharp crotches should also be pointed with a chisel to facilitate proper healing.

Theoretically, all wounds, regardless of size, should be painted with a dressing. In actual practice, however, only wounds 2 or more inches in diameter usually are painted. One should bear in mind, however, that decay may readily develop in smaller untreated wounds, especially in trees low in vigor, in which healing progresses slowly.

Removing Large Branches

A good-sized saw with teeth so set as to make a wide cut is best for removing large branches. The procedure is the same as that followed in removing smaller branches, except that additional precautions must be taken to prevent injury to the tree itself.

The tree will suffer considerable damage if only a single pruning cut is made in a large branch, as shown in Figure 5-5. As the cut deepens, the remaining wood will become too weak to support the weight of the limb, and much of the bark below will be ripped off. The proper way to remove a large branch is shown in Figure 5-6. About a foot beyond the proposed final cut, a preliminary undercut is made by sawing until the blade begins to bind. On the upper side of the branch an inch or so beyond the first cut, a second cut is made to sever the branch. The short stub remaining can then be removed by making the final cut as nearly flush with the main branch as possible. The stub should be held in place by the operator's free hand, or by rope, to prevent tearing of the bark. When an entire branch is small enough to be held firmly in place by ropes or by hand, the first and second cuts may be omitted.

Large final cuts cannot always be made as close to the remaining branch as necessary. In such cases, the cut surface must be smoothed over with a chisel.

Removing large limbs from trees along city streets, in parks, and in cemeteries entails an additional precaution. In many instances, such branches must be lowered to the ground in pieces or as a unit, to avoid damage to electric wires, private property, monuments, or shrubs and lawns. This is usually accomplished by means of two or more heavy ropes which lower and guide the branches in their descent.

Removal of V-Crotches

The removal of one or two limbs that have developed adjacent to each other and are connected by a V-shaped crotch is commonly necessary. The actual point of union of the wood of these two limbs may be several feet below the visible joining of the bark. Only careful cutting at the right

Fig. 5-5. Left: The wrong way to prune a large branch. A single cut close to the main stem may result in tearing of the bark.

Fig. 5-6. Right: The correct way to prune a large branch. A preliminary undercut is made at A; a second cut is made at B, to sever the main part of the branch. The remaining stub is removed by cutting at C.

point will ensure proper healing. Preliminary cuts, as described for removing large branches, are made a foot or so above the crotch, to remove the upper part of the branch. A final cut starting from the main trunk and slanting upward to the point of union of the two limbs completes the operation (Fig. 5-7). After this stub is removed it may be necessary to finish the cut with a chisel to form a pointed wound that will heal rapidly.

Dehorning

The practice known as dehorning involves the drastic cutting back of the larger limbs of a tree. The operation may completely disfigure the tree by removing the normal canopy. Moreover, it may eventually lead to serious branch decay beginning at the severed ends, and to the scalding of the bark, which is suddenly exposed to the full rays of the sun. This practice must be employed, however, where there is considerable dying back of the branches due to severe insect or fungus attack, or where a reduced root area cannot sustain a large canopy. It may also be necessary as an invigorating measure, as a means of eliminating interference with overhead wires or other objects, and as a safety measure along city streets.

Certain precautions will help to reduce many of the detrimental

Fig. 5-7. Removal of V-shaped crotch. A preliminary undercut is made at A, and the second cut at B to remove the major part of the branch. The final cut, starting at point C, slants upward to the point of union of two limbs.

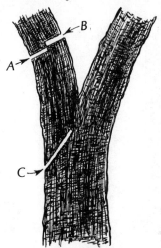

after effects. The branches should be removed with a slanting cut starting just above a vigorous bud or shoot and running back and across the limb at an angle of about 45 degrees. The bud or shoot must always be at the peak of this cut and should point in the direction where new limb development is desired. It is well to remember that a cut made at right angles to the long axis of the branch is not likely to heal, while one made at too sharp an angle will weaken the elbow and eventually result in breaking or splitting of the new limb when it has attained sufficient size. All cut ends should, of course, be properly painted.

As a rule, elm, linden, locust, planetree, and silver maple can be cut back severely without seriously reducing the vigor of the tree, but hickory cannot withstand such drastic treatment. Many Carolina poplars and willows growing along city streets are cut back every few years to prevent their canopies from becoming too large and unsafe. Some attention must be given to pruning suckers or small twigs that usually develop at the severed ends.

Though dehorning is justified under certain conditions, it would be unnecessary in many instances if the tree had received early and judicious pruning.

Pruning Suckers or Watersprouts

Adventitious buds often give rise to thin slender twigs that grow nearly parallel and closely appressed to the branches or trunk. The presence of a large number of such shoots, or suckers, is usually an indication of structural injuries, fungus or insect attack, changes in environmental conditions, or excessive or improper pruning.

The number and size of suckers, the species of tree on which they form, their position on the tree, and the cause of their formation determine what disposition is to be made of them. The presence of sprouts on the upper branches of an elm, for instance, is a natural phenomenon with this species.

Suckers at the base of the trunk of any ornamental or street tree should be removed as they develop, since they not only detract from the appearance of the tree but are also a nuisance.

When the top of a tree has been cut back severely, the suckers that form should be allowed to remain to provide protection from sun scalding of the bark.

Pruning Storm-damaged Trees

Drastic pruning is sometimes necessary after a hurricane or after ice and wind storms. When the damage to large branches or the entire tree is severe enough to endanger human life and property, the pruning should be done as quickly as possible. Except for such emergencies, however, pruning can be delayed until mild weather comes along.

Large damaged branches or uprooted trees are best handled by a professional arborist. The tree owner can undertake repair jobs on smaller trees whose damaged branches are relatively close to the ground. Trees should be examined carefully to determine the extent of injury. If this is not too extensive and the tree is worth saving, a definite plan of rehabilitation should be worked out. Broken branches should be cut back to the next lower crotch if possible. In some instances, especially where a main branch is involved, it may be desirable to leave a considerable part of the stub. Treatment in such cases should follow that outlined earlier in this chapter under Dehorning. Many limbs or crotches that are split can be saved by artificial bracing with bolts. Wounds made by splitting limbs should be cleaned of splinters, the wood smoothed, and the bark traced to the proper shape to ensure rapid healing. Unbroken branches should be left untouched: they should never be headed back to conform with cuts made on broken branches. Though the immediate effect of long and short branches in the canopy may appear odd, additional judicious pruning within a few years will help to fill the wide openings and will eventually result in a well-shaped tree.

Pruning for Disease Control

Very often it is necessary to prune trees that are partially affected by diseases, such as fire blight of apple, pear, and mountain-ash; sycamore anthracnose; Cytospora canker of blue spruce; Diplodia tip blight of conifers; wilt of maples and elms; and twig blight of chestnut oak. In such cases, the infected twigs or branches should be removed at least 3 inches below the point of visible infection.

Extreme caution must be exercised so as not to transmit the causal organism from a diseased to a healthy tree by means of the pruning tools. After use on a tree suspected of being diseased, the cutting edges of all tools should be thoroughly disinfected by dipping them in, or wiping them with a cloth saturated with, 70 per cent denatured ethyl alcohol. Furthermore, pruning when the leaves are wet should be avoided, since parasitic organisms are easily spread under such circumstances.

Pruning Evergreen Trees

Evergreens do not usually require the periodic pruning necessary for deciduous trees. Dead branches in evergreens rarely give rise to such extensive cavities as are found in shade trees, partly because decay is checked by the presence of resins in the wood. If the removal of large branches is necessary, however, the methods previously discussed should be followed.

The main objective in pruning evergreens is to produce a more bushy or compact plant. Pruning the growth at the ends of young shoots forces the plant to make new growth along the branches.

Not all evergreens can be pruned in the same manner or at the same time. The method depends on the species and the type of growth.

Pines and spruces make only one growth during the year. They can be trimmed at any time, but best results are obtained when the new growth is soft. In pruning spruces, especially the blue spruce, the long ends should be removed at the point where side shoots are formed. This will check the terminal growth for a year or two and will enable the branches to fill out. Most pines are best pruned before the new needles start to unfold, that is, when the new growth still gives the appearance of candles. No damage is done to the needles, and the tree will retain its original healthy appearance.

Most of the other evergreens, including arborvitae, junipers, yew, cypress, and chamaecyparis, continue to develop during the entire growing season. These may be trimmed up to the month of August in the New York City area, although June or July pruning is preferable, since new growth will then cover the cuts before the end of the growing season.

Winter pruning is sometimes preferable when an evergreen has become straggly as a result of long neglect. The long branches are cut to encourage new bud development early in the next growing season. When pruning is postponed until summer, new buds will not develop until the following spring, and in the interim the plant will appear unattractive.

Evergreens with a distinctive shape should be so pruned as to retain the desirable effect. Only the long shoots should be removed. Formal evergreen hedges are best pruned with hedge shears. Hemlocks may well be pruned to increase their branching and fullness. In the New York City area late June appears to be the best month, since new growth soon starts and continues throughout the summer. By early fall, the effects of pruning are well hidden by the new growth.

Pruning for Line Clearance

Friction is bound to arise when any two objects attempt to occupy the same area. Such a situation exists when trees grow along highways and city streets where there are light, power, or communication wires. Tree lovers argue that the wires should be set underground or moved out of the way, while the public utility officials often feel that the trees should go. Both trees and wires are essential to the health, prosperity, and happiness of communities, and the only immediate remedy when such an unhappy situation exists is intelligent trimming of trees.

Many utility companies employ a reliable tree-trimming organization for this type of work, as the use of inexperienced help often results in complaints by tree lovers of unnecessary butchering of the trees.

There are four types of pruning usually employed in the vicinity of overhead wires: topping, side pruning, directional pruning, and drop-crotching.

Topping merely involves the removal of the ends of the branches much as a hedge is sheared. It is usually practiced when young trees are growing directly below the wires. This method spoils the natural shape of the tree.

Side pruning is the removal of the side branches of large trees when these interfere with the wires. Usually the opposite side of the tree is pruned to preserve the symmetrical shape.

Directional pruning involves the opening of paths for the wires through the trees by removing smaller branches. Branches are also trained to grow away from the wires before the two meet. An expert pruner can anticipate the direction of future growth and by early and correct pruning reduce the necessity of later pruning. While this method is more expensive than the others, it results in least disfigurement of the tree and gives the most lasting benefits (Fig. 5-8).

Drop-crotching is the cutting back of large branches to laterals, in order to encourage growth to the side and away from the wires. This method provides a longer duration of clearance, but it may have disastrous effects on the tree because of the danger of decay at the cut ends of the branches.

Disposing of Prunings

The disposal of tree prunings in cities has always been a problem. It has been aggravated by the passage of laws, as in New Jersey and New York, that curtail the burning of such material in city dumps because of the resulting increase of air pollutants.

One remedy for municipal arborists, at least insofar as disposing of the branches and twigs is concerned, is the so-called chipper (Fig. 5-9). The pruned branches are fed into the revolving blades of a chipping machine and are broken up into small pieces or chips. Four truckloads of brush (branches, twigs, and leaves) can be reduced to one load of chips. The chipper best known among professional arborists is made by the Asplundh Chipper Company of Willow Grove, Pennsylvania.

The Vermeer Manufacturing Company, Pella, Iowa 50219, has re-

Fig. 5-8. Trees can be pruned so as not to interfere with power lines.

cently introduced the Vermeer 604 Log Chipper. This machine is capable of grinding into chips pieces of tree trunks 6 feet in length and up to 4 feet in diameter. It has a high-speed, 8-inch diameter rotary cylinder, with 45 carbide-tipped cutting teeth, which slice chips away at approximately 1800 RPM, as the wood is hydraulically fed over the cylinder at 20 cycles per minute. Heretofore only relatively small branches could be ground up in chippers.

The wood chips, incidentally, can be used in many ways. They make fine soil conditioners after being composted for a year or two, and they make excellent mulching material. On farms they can be used as poultry-house litter and as animal bedding. Recreational departments are using the chips as a cushion under playground swings and slides.

Pruning with Chemicals

Because of the high cost of pruning trees manually, less expensive ways are being investigated. One is the use of growth-retarding substances such as Slo Gro, developed by a United States Rubber Company scientist. In an untreated tree shoot, a cell expands until at a certain

Fig. 5-9. Disposing tree prunings with a wood chipper. The chopped-up remains are blown onto a truck.

point it divides into two new cells. This process of expansion and division is repeated many times during the growing season. When a tree shoot is treated with Slo Gro, however, the chemical is absorbed into the tree through the leaves, then moves to the rapid-growing terminals. The cells continue to expand, but they do not divide. Growth is inhibited, but the tree remains healthy and vigorous.

Details on how and when to use Slo Gro to reduce the need for pruning of certain trees can be obtained by writing to Uniroyal Chemical, Division of Uniroyal, Bethany, Connecticut 06525.

One way to inhibit growth of sprouts after pruning of certain street trees such as elms, maples, oaks, and sycamores is to apply a plant hormone to the cut surfaces where the branches have been removed. Tre-hold, manufactured by, The Agricultural Products Division, Union Carbide Corp., New York, is an asphalt-base tree paint containing 1 per cent of the ethyl ester of alpha napthalene acetic acid, which, when painted on freshly made pruning cuts, reduces the number of sprouts originating near the cut area and inhibits the growth of sprouts that do start. Tre-hold comes in cans for brush application and in aerosol cans.

The Asplundh Tree Expert Company, Willow Grove, Pennsylvania, also makes a similar product, Inhibitor-Fortified Tree Paint.

Safety Hints to Pruners

Determine the general condition of the tree. Greater precautions are necessary when working in an old or weakened tree than in a sound young one.

Examine pruning equipment often for safety and efficiency.

Know the type of wood in the tree. Greater precautions are necessary in pruning weak-wooded trees, such as poplars, silver maple, willow, and tulip, than in pruning elm, oak, hickory, and plane, which have strong flexible wood.

Danger is greatest when branches are wet and when temperatures are low.

Bark peeling and fungus growths are signs of dead and dying branches. Limbs showing these symptoms should never be depended upon for support.

When electric wires run through a tree, remember that the danger of electric shocks is increased when the tree is wet.

Do not allow tools to come in contact with wires, even though the wires are supposed to be insulated.

Most important of all, *always have a safety rope properly attached.* Any branch, no matter how sound in appearance, may give way under the weight of the climber.*

Treatment of Wounds

A major cause of decay and premature death of trees can be traced directly to neglected wounds made years earlier. The bark of trees, like the epidermis of humans, acts to protect tissues beneath. Once the protective cover is broken, the parts below are subject to infection by fungi, bacteria, and other parasites.

Wounds made by a tree owner's pruning saw in removing a dead, broken, or unwanted branch, by a skidding automobile, or even by a mischievous boy's ax, should be treated as soon as possible after the damage is done. The sooner the treatment, the less chance of invasion by wood-decaying fungi or insect pests.

A tree wound heals by the formation of successive annual layers of callus tissue around the edge of the wound (Fig. 5-10). The callus tissue averages about ½ inch in thickness each year. Consequently, the smaller the wound, the sooner the healing. When a branch is cut very close to the trunk, the the wound is much larger than it should be. On the other hand, if the branch is cut so that a stub remains, callus tissue must

---

* *Tree Preservation Bulletin No. 2* 'Safety for Tree Workers,' revised 1956, is obtainable for a small charge from the Superintendent of Documents, U.S. Government Printing Office, Washington, D.C. 20402.

Fig. 5-10. Callus tissue has completely covered the wound on this tree.

develop up along the sides of the stub before it can cover the cut surface. The proper cut should be in between the two extremes.

All large wounds should first be smoothed over by removing stubs or lips of wood and then shaped into a pointed ellipse to aid rapid callus formation. The cambial region, from which regenerated tissue (callus) will develop later, should then be immediately painted with shellac. When the shellac has dried, a wound dressing should be applied over the entire surface exposed by pruning or by injury to the bark.

Wound dressings on living trees help to protect exposed surfaces and to facilitate healing. These are best applied when the wound is thoroughly dry.

Bark-deep wounds, in which only the bark is damaged and the cambium layer is undisturbed, will heal more rapidly if the damaged area is covered immediately with new burlap or polyethylene film. Shading the damaged bark of elms, maples, and hackberry promotes excellent healing. The shade is provided by a burlap or canvas cover placed on supports of wood or steel frames about six inches from the tree. Just before the damaged area is shaded, the wound is shaped with a sharp knife, as described earlier in this chapter (p. 87), and the cut edge painted with orange shellac. There is no need to paint the exposed cambium area inside the margins of the wound. Four to eight weeks of shading is usually sufficient to ensure the survival and recovery of the injured cells.

Wound Dressing

An ideal wound dressing would disinfect the area treated, prevent entrance of wood-rotting fungi and checking of wood, stimulate callus formation, and be toxic to parasitic organisms with which it comes in contact. It would be easily applied, sufficiently porous to allow excess moisture to evaporate from the wound underneath, and not crack on drying or weathering.

No single dressing has yet been developed to meet all these qualifications, but the following wound dressings are most commonly used:

Orange Shellac. One of the least harmful of all materials available, orange shellac, which is sometimes used as an undercoat for spar varnish or ordinary house paint, is most commonly used to cover traced bark and the adjacent sapwood (Fig. 5-11). While the shellac is not specifically a wound dressing, the alcohol in it is a good sterilizing agent. Shellac applied alone is not very durable.

Asphaltum Paints. Various tree paints that contain asphaltum as the principal ingredient are available. These may be obtained from paint manufacturers and horiticultural supply houses. They may be made up as follows: For each pound of solid asphaltum melted over a slow fire, add about a quart of turpentine, or petroleum oil, or one of its refined fractions, mineral oil. When cooled, the resulting mixture is ready for use. This type of asphaltum paint is more harmful to tree tissues than those made up of water emulsions, but it dries out and weathers more slowly.

Creosote Paints. These are best for painting large surfaces in the interior of a cavity where fungi may have become established. They

Fig. 5-11. Applying orange shellac to freshly made wound.

should be used with extreme caution in the vicinity of fresh wounds when rapid healing is desired.

Ordinary commercial creosote is one of the best materials for destroying and preventing the growth of wood-decay fungi. Most paints will not stick to creosote, but coal tar or hot asphalt will adhere readily. Creosote, like creosote paint, is toxic to live tissues and should be used principally on dead heartwood.

A mixture of equal quantities of creosote and asphaltum is also satisfactory and apparently not so injurious as creosote alone

Grafting Waxes. Prepared with alcohol, these are satisfactory for treating small surfaces.

House Paints. Exterior paints containing oxides of lead and zinc mixed with linseed oil are fairly satisfactory. They are not so durable as asphaltum paints and will injure tender tissues unless the tissues have been previously painted with shellac.

Lanolin Paints. Tree paints containing lanolin as the major ingredient have also found wide acceptance in recent years. By protecting the cambial and bark tissues, this ingredient allows wound callus to develop unchecked.

Workers at the Northeastern Forest Experiment Station at Philadelphia have reported that mixtures of lanolin, rosin, and crude gum promoted wound healing and provided a greater degree of protection to the most crucial zone, the wound edges, than did either shellac or asphaltum.

A suggested mixture of these ingredients is lanolin 10 parts by weight, rosin 2, and crude gum 2. The ingredients are blended simply by melting them and gently stirring together.

The author did considerable research with lanolin mixtures while employed at the New Jersey Agriculture Experiment Station. He found that a mixture of 2 parts of lanolin, thinned with 1 part of raw linseed oil to which .25 per cent of the total mixture of potassium permanganate solution was added, gave better results in wound callus development than any of several commercial tree paints used in the tests. Because the permanganate is not soluble in the lanolin-linseed-oil mixture, it must be dissolved in a small quantity of acetone before being stirred into the mixture.

Bordeaux Paste. This is prepared by slowly stirring raw linseed oil into dry bordeaux powder until a thick paint is produced. It has antiseptic properties but hinders callus development the first year after it is applied. In addition, it weathers rapidly and must be replaced often.

Commercial Tree Paints. Ready-made tree paints are also available. While many of these can be depended upon to give satisfactory results, a few are known to be incapable of killing parasitic organisms that get into them. Diseases may actually be spread through use of infested tree paints.

Tree paints are now available in aerosol cans. The du Pont Company manufactures such a product in which Freon is the propellant for the dressing. Other manufacturers and their products include Amchem Products Company, Tre-hold; Boyle-Midway, Antrol Tree Wound Dressing; Samuel Cabot, Cabot's Tree Healing Paint; and Chevron Chemical Company, Ortho Pruning Paint.

A rubberized tree-wound dressing containing butylnite, Lamot Tree Surgeon Sealant, has recently been introduced to the trade. According to the manufacturer, the product is flexible, unaffected by weather, won't chip, peel or run, and is permanent.

Regardless of the wound dressing used, best results are assured when the dressed surfaces are inspected periodically and recoated once or twice a year. This is especially necessary when the dressing blisters, cracks, or peels (Fig. 5-12). Before old wounds are recoated, it is best to clean the surface with a stiff wire brush to remove all blisters and loose flakes. The new callus growth should not be covered with the dressing.

Wounds callus over more rapidly when no dressings, with the possible exception of shellac and certain asphalt emulsions, are used. There is some evidence that wounded trees form certain gums that aid in healing and help to retard decay. Since the rapidity of healing is of secondary importance to the entrance of wood-rotting fungi, it is best to continue the use of some good dressing.

Fig. 5-12. Tree wounds should be inspected periodically and recoated with tree paint.

Wounded or pruned branches may continue to bleed for a long time. This condition is discussed in detail under Slime Flux on page 207.

Cracks in the wood of large flat wounds constitute important foci for wood-decay fungi. These can be largely prevented, especially when wood is sound at the start, by covering the freshly dressed wound with heavy cloth. The cloth should be cut smaller than the scar, so as to allow room for callus formation. It should then be tacked firmly to the wood, and dressed with the same kind of material previously applied over the wound.

It was formerly believed that trees which produce considerable amounts of resin, such as conifers, are not so subject to heartwood decay as are most deciduous trees. The resins which exude from wounds of some pines and spruces do not have fungicidal properties, and hence wood-decaying fungi can enter through the wounds. Large wounds on conifers should be protected with wound dressings and should be inspected regularly just as with wounds on shade trees.

Recently, in some carefully conducted tests to determine the effectiveness of wound dressings in preventing fungi from entering tree wounds, Doctor A. L. Shigo and C. L. Wilson of the U.S. Department of Agriculture found that these materials had no effect on invasion by microorganisms or on the process of wood discoloration. Most of the organisms isolated from the wood behind the painted surfaces of red maple were common non-decay-producing kinds. They included *Alternaria, Cladosporium, Pestalotia, Epicoccum,* and *Penicillium.* The organisms recovered from elm wood previously treated with a wound dressing also included a number of other non-decay-producing kinds.

Although this investigation throws considerable doubt on the value of applying wound dressings to trees, the author feels that it is still good practice to apply a tree paint over large wounds, if for no other reason than the aesthetic value.

Selected Bibliography

Anonymous. 1972. *American national standard safety requirements for tree pruning, trimming, repairing, or removal.* American National Standard Institute. Z 133. 1-1972. New York. 16 p.

———. 1974. 'Your tree troubles may be you.' *Agriculture Information Bulletin No.* 372. Forest Service, USDA, Washington, D.C. p. 1–21.

———. 1976. 'Rx for wounded trees.' USDA, Forest Service AIB-387. Washington, D.C. 20402. p. 1–37.

Alvarez R. G. 1977. 'Growth regulators.' *Jour. Arboriculture* Vol. 3. (No. 5). p. 94–97.

Armstrong, Norman. 1938. 'Basic principles of shade tree pruning.' *Proc. Fourteenth National Shade Tree Conference.* p. 126–40.

————. 1946. 'Pruning and training the young shade tree.' *Arborist's News*. Vol. 11 (No. 7). p. 49–51. July 1946.

Baumgardt, J. P. 1968. *How to prune most everything*. M. Barrows, New York. 192 p.

Beilmann, A. P. 1930. 'The pruning of ornamental trees and shrubs.' *Missouri Bot. Garden Bul.* 18 (No. 3). p. 45–48.

————. 1933. 'When is the best time to prune a tree (maples)?' *Missouri Bot. Garden Bul.* 21 (No. 4). p. 61–75.

Brown, G. K. 1968. 'An analysis of the effects of the growth inhibitor "Tre-hold".' *Proc. Forty-fourth International Shade Tree Conference.* p. 172–74.

Cathey, H. M. 1970. 'Chemical pruning of plants.' *American Nurseryman*. May 1, 1970. p. 8–11, 51–55.

Ellis, A. H. 1964. 'Use of MH-30 on trees.' *Arborist's News*. Vol. 29 (No. 7). p. 49–53.

Everett, T. H. 1957. 'Tree pruning pointers.' *Garden Jour. New York Bot. Garden.* Jan.-Feb. 1957. p. 16–18.

Evrard, T. O. 1966. 'Chemical tree pruning.' *Weeds, Trees, and Turf.* p. 12–14. Jan. 1966.

Fenska, R. R. 1954. *The new tree experts manual.* A. T. De La Mare, New York. 192 p.

Giles, F. A. and W. B. Siefert. 1971. *Pruning evergreens and deciduous trees and shrubs.* Univ. of Illinois. Cooperative Extension Service. Circular 1033. Urbana-Champaign, Illinois. 57 p.

Harris, R. W. 1975. 'Pruning fundamentals.' *Jour. Arboriculture.* Vol. 1 (No. 12). p. 221–26.

Harris, R. W. *et al.* 1969. *Pruning landscape trees.* Univ. Cal. Agr. Ext. Service AXT-288. Feb. 1969. 30 p.

Harris, R. W. *et al.* 1974. 'Pruning landscape trees.' *Arborist's News*. Vol. 39 (No. 8). p. 133–40.

Kemmerer, H. 1957. *Pruning trees, shrubs, and roses.* Illinois Agr. Extension Service. 15 p.

————. 1977. 'Contract versus in-house managing tree care.' *Grounds Maintenance,* Vol. 12 (No. 1). p. 24, 26, 28. Intertec Publ. Co. Overland Park, Kansas 66212

Kozel, P. C. 1969. 'Chemical pruning shows promise.' *Weeds, Trees, and Turf.* p. 12–13. July 1969.

Kuemmerling, Karl *et al.* 1953. 'Safe practices for arborists.' *Trees.* Nov.-Dec. 1953. p. 10–22.

Leiser, A. T. 1958. 'Polyethylene treatment for tree bark wounds.' *American Nurseryman.* Vol. 107 (No. 9). p. 13, 49.

Le Seur, A. D. C. 1936. 'Care of old trees.' *Jour. Roy. Hort. Soc.* Vol. 61. p. 149–59.

Lesser, M. A. 1946. 'Tree wound dressings.' *Agricultural Chemicals.* Aug. 1946. p. 26–27.

Marshall, R. P. 1931. 'A rubber dressing for tree wounds.' *Phytopathology* Vol. 21. p. 1091.

————. 1931. 'Water blistering of wound dressings.' *Phytopathology* Vol. 21. p. 1173–80.

————. 1931. *The relation of season of wounding and shellacking to callus formation in tree wounds.* USDA Tech. Bul. 246. 28 p.

May, Curtis. 1962. *Pruning shade trees and repairing their injuries.* USDA Home & Garden Bul. 83. 15 p.

————. 1976. *Pruning shade trees and repairing their injuries.* USDA Home and Garden Bul. 83. 15 p.

McQuilkin, W. E. and J. W. Showalter. 1945. 'Lanolin mixtures as dressings for tree wounds.' *Arborist's News.* Vol. 10 (No. 3). p. 3, 17–19.

Neely, D. 1970. 'Healing wounds on trees.' *Am. Jour. Hort. Sci.* Vol. 95. p. 536–40.

Sachs, R. M. 1969. 'Growth control in trees—anatomical and physiological aspects.' *Proc. Forty-fifth International Shade Tree Conference.* p. 60–70.

Shigo, A. L. 1971. 'Wound dressing research on red maples.' *Proc. Forty-seventh International Shade Tree Conference.* p. 97a–98a.

Shigo, A. L. and W. C. Shortle. 1977. ' "New" ideas in tree care.' *Jour. Arboriculture.* Vol. 3. (No. 1). p. 1–4.

Shigo, A. L. and C. L. Wilson. 1977. 'Wound dressings on red maple and American elm: effectiveness after five years.' *Jour. Arboriculture.* Vol. 3. (No. 5). p. 81–87.

Snodsmith, R. L. 1969. 'Proper pruning practices.' *Trees.* Mar.-Apr. 1969. p. 12–13.

Strife, F. W. 1940. 'Safety practices.' *Proc. Fourteenth National Shade Tree Conference.* p. 41–54.

Thompson, A. R. 1955. *Shade tree pruning.* Rev. 1955. Tree Preservation Bul. No. 4. Supt. Documents, Washington, D.C.

Tilford, P. E. 1940. 'Tree wound dressings.' *Proc. Sixteenth National Shade Tree Conference.* p. 41–54.

Truelsen, A. C. 1967. 'Safety practices in tree pruning.' *Trees.* Sept.-Oct. 1967. p. 21–22.

Wyman, Donald. 1963. *Pruning ornamental shrubs and trees.* Arnoldia Vol. 23 (No. 8) p. 107–10.

Young, H. C. and P. E. Tilford. 1937. 'Tree wound dressings.' *Ohio Agr. Exp. Sta. Bimonth. Bul.* 22. p. 83–87.

Zukel, J. W. 1964. 'Slowing tree and shrub growth with retardant MH-30 T.' *Weeds, Trees, and Turf.* Aug. 1, 1965. p. 20.

6

Cavity Treatments

Filling cavities in the trunk and branches is the most spectacular of all tree maintenance practices. The layman has the impression that this is also the major phase of tree care. Although cavity work has a place in any balanced tree program, it does not rank in usefulness with such practices as fertilizing, pruning, and spraying. Its importance in the mind of the layman probably arises from the similarity to the filling of dental cavities. Oddly enough, though only dentists treat cavities in teeth, anyone having access to some cement feels capable of filling a cavity in a tree (Fig. 6-1). The treatment of cavities in trees, however, involves more problems than appear on the surface and should be entrusted only to a reliable arborist.

History of Cavity Work

The impulse to beautify unsightly objects is perhaps as old as man. Conceivably, even in prehistoric times a decaying cavity in an otherwise beautiful tree would have been a good subject for improvement. Attempts to cover cavities with mud and stone are recorded in many ancient writings. In his book *Enquiry in Plants,* written about 300 B.C., the Greek scientist Theophrastus described 'plastering wounds with mud' to prevent trees from decaying. Within the last 200 years many investigators have written on this subject and have advocated the use of wood, brick, clay, mortar, lime, and many odd and 'secret' mixtures. The last 65 years have witnessed greater advance in cavity treatments than in all

105

previously recorded history, primarily because of the impetus furnished by several tree-preservation companies in the United States. Within this period, cement, cork products, wood and rubber blocks, asphalt compounds, and various kinds of sheet metals have attained extensive popularity. In addition, several patented mixtures have been developed that are definitely superior to any of the materials used before the start of the present century. Without doubt, more satisfactory materials will be discovered in the future.

How Cavities Start

All cavities originate from neglected bark injuries (Fig. 6-2). Sound bark forms an effective protective barrier for the more susceptible tissues beneath it. The sapwood dries out shortly after an opening is made, either mechanically or by some natural agent. When the tree is growing vigorously and the injury is not extensive, the open area is covered by a layer of healing tissue (callus) within a year or two, and little damage follows. Where considerable injury occurs (Fig. 6-3) or where a branch

Fig. 6-1. Left: An amateurish job of cavity filling on horsechestnut. Notice how cement is being pushed out of the cavity.

Fig. 6-2. Right: How cavities start. As a result of improper treatment after pruning, the wood has begun to decay. The upper part of the wound is not healing because the bark has not been properly treated.

Fig. 6-3. Extensive bark injuries near the trunk base serve as entrance points for wood decay fungi.

stub remains after faulty pruning (Fig. 6-4) or breakage by wind, healing proceeds slowly or not at all. In such cases, wood-rotting fungi and boring insects have ample time to enter and cause decay. The action of these organisms in turn prevents additional healing, and in time a large cavity is formed. Where the heartwood is exposed by some injury, decay progresses more rapidly, because of the formation of so-called checks or deep fissures in the wood.

A cavity in the heartwood does not seriously impair the vigor of the tree, as is commonly believed. Its presence, however, weakens the tree structurally, making the parts above more susceptible to breakage by wind and ice storms. It also serves as a breeding place for ants, boring insects, and vermin. An extensive opening in the trunk may reduce the vigor of the tree indirectly, because the loss of bark, cambium, and sapwood (which normally would occupy this area) greatly decreases the food transportation and tissue-building facilities.

Decay by most wood-rotting fungi progresses rather slowly, the rate being about equal to that of the annual growth of the tree. For this reason, a vigorous tree may attain great size despite the presence of an extensive cavity. Dr. Ray Hirt, emeritus plant pathologist at the New York State College of Forestry, found that the fungus *Fomes igniarius,* growing in aspen, travels 23 inches in 10 years, or slightly over 2 inches

Fig. 6-4. Stubs such as the one shown not only prevent callus formation, but furnish ideal points of entrance for wood decay fungi.

each year. The same fungus in maples moved about 18 inches in a 10-year period. A few highly virulent fungi, however, may cause extensive decay within a short time.

Some trees, like cherry and willow, decay more rapidly than other trees. The older a tree, the more susceptible it is to decay.

Major cavities occur in trunk, branch, crotch, base, and root. Trunk cavities usually originate from mechanical injuries and broken or improperly pruned large branches; branch cavities, from broken or diseases twigs or from rubbing of interfering branches; crotch cavities, from splitting of the main branches; base cavities, from mechanical injuries, fire, root diseases, and feeding of animals; and root cavities, from mechanical injury and from animal, fungus, and insect attack.

Objectives of Cavity Treatments

The primary objectives of cavity work are to improve the appearance of the tree by removing decayed and insect-riddled wood and to eliminate a breeding place for boring insects, ants, mosquitoes, termites, snails, and rodents.

Many persons have the impression that cavity work includes several other objectives—the principal one being to eradicate and cure heartwood decay. Cavity treatment will not cure decay, and rarely will it check further spread, unless a very small area is involved. As a rule, the fungus threads extend from a few inches to several feet beyond the rotted zone into apparently sound wood. Although the gouging out of such wood is theoretically possible, it is neither economical nor practicable. Extensive laboratory work must be conducted to determine whether all fungus-infected wood has been removed. Moreover, the extensive removal of all wood containing fungus tissue would so weaken the tree that it would be a menace to life and property. Occasionally trees are killed outright when extensive removal of heartwood exposes the sapwood, which then dries out. Such trees might have lived for many years if only badly decayed portions had been removed.

For many years it has been standard practice to remove as much of the fungus-invaded wood as possible prior to filling the cavity. Recent research by Doctors C. L. Wilson and A. L. Shigo indicates that trees are capable of walling off decay that follows wounding. After the tree is wounded, a wall or barrier begins to form. The wall separates tissues present at the time the tree was wounded, which may be invaded by decay-producing fungi, from tissues that form after wounding and remain free of decay. Wilson and Shigo advise leaving some of the decayed wood when filling a tree cavity so as to allow the protective wall to remain. If this wall is broken, decay will spread into the healthy wood that surrounds the decay.

Dr. A. L. Shigo and Mr. A. Shigo recently developed the Shigometer,* an electrical device for detecting discolored and decayed wood in living trees (Fig. 6-5). The Shigometer measures the resistance of wood to a pulsed electric current. According to the inventors, 'As invaded tissues die, discolor, and decay, concentrations of minerals increase; and as mineral concentrations increase, resistance to a pulsed current decreases.'

Plant pathologists of the United States Department of Agriculture Forest Service have developed a mobile X-ray unit which helps to diagnose the extent of decay and defect in a tree.

Method of Treating Cavities

Though greatest emphasis in the past was placed on filling cavities with some solid material, the tendency in more recent years has been to leave the cavity open, once it has been cleaned out, sterilized, and painted. This is especially true in the tree programs of large public enterprises, such as city and county park systems, whose limited budgets do not permit extensive work on individual trees.

* Details on how the Shigometer works and how to use it are given in USDA Forest Service Research Paper NE-294, available from Northeastern Forest Experiment Station, U.S. Dept. of Agriculture, Upper Darby, Penna 19082. The device is manufactured by Northeast Electronics Corp., Concord, New Hampshire.

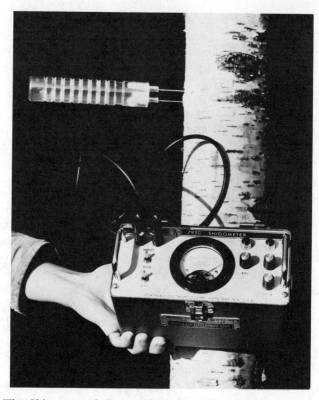

Fig. 6-5. The Shigometer being used to determine the amount of decay in a white birch tree.

The principal steps in treating a cavity according to the standardized methods are cleaning, shaping, bracing, and sterilizing and dressing.

Cleaning Out the Cavity. To remove the decayed and insect-riddled wood, the following tools are needed: a wooden or composition-rubber mallet, a chisel, several gouges with curved edges, and a knife. The knife is used on the bark and cambium and the other tools on the sapwood and heartwood. For large-scale cavity operations, one needs chisels, gouges, and a special cutting tool known as a Rotacutter. The latter operates on the same principal as a wood chipper (Fig. 6-6).

All discolored and water-soaked wood should be removed from small cavities, even though the discolored wood appears relatively sound, for such wood harbors the most active stages of the wood-rotting fungi. Discretion must be used in treating extensive cavities, however, since the removal of much discolored wood may so weaken the tree structurally that it may become dangerously liable to breakage.

As a rule, old neglected cavities have such an extensive callus growth

Fig. 6-6. The A-4 Rotacutter, developed by Danish arborist Niels Hvass, is an excellent tool for cleaning out tree cavities. Attached to a power saw, it rapidly grinds out decayed and fungus-invaded wood.

over their edges that the opening may be nearly completely closed, making it almost impossible to clean out the rotted wood (Figs. 6-7 and 6-8). The removal of this callus from the sides may result in considerable weakening, since it will eliminate important food-conducting tissues of the tree. Judgment must determine whether the cavity is better left alone or whether it should be widened to permit easier access to the decayed wood. If a considerable amount of callus is cut away, the foliage of the tree should be reduced proportionately by pruning to compensate for the loss in water- and nutrient-conducting tissues. The lengthening of the cavity interferes little with the function of the tree.

Shaping the Cavity. The interior of the cavity should be so shaped that no water pockets remain. When the cavity penetrates downward to form a pocket in the trunk or branch, the outer shell should be cut away to eliminate the pocket. If cavities are so shaped that deep water pockets cannot be avoided, some provision must be made to drain off the water. A hole should be bored from the outer bark below the pocket into the lowest point of the depression and a drainpipe placed at the opening. Because of the presence of sap and moisture, which collect near the opening, drainpipes are excellent foci for development of yeast, fungi, bacteria, and insects, and should be avoided wherever possible. A

Fig. 6-7. Left: An old cavity nearly closed by callus growth. Such a tree might be left untouched, because removal of the callus tissue incident to clearing out the decayed wood may weaken the tree considerably.

Fig. 6-8. Right: Cross section of a trunk showing callus development over a cavity.

drainpipe cannot be inserted when a cavity extends below the soil surface. In such cases the lower part, after being properly cleaned and dressed, should be filled with a satisfactory solid material to a few inches above the soil level, and the upper surface of the filling sloped to allow water to drain out of the cavity.

The treatment of the edge of the cavity unquestionably requires more care than any other phase of cavity shaping. Proper and vigorous healing will not take place unless the bark and cambium are healthy and sufficient sapwood is left under these tissues to prevent drying out. The bark should be cut only with a sharp knife to ensure smooth, clean edges, and orange shellac applied to the cut edges immediately to prevent drying of these tender tissues. The bark on the sides of the cavity should be shaped as nearly parallel to the line of sap flow as is practicable, and the upper and lower ends should depart from this line so gradually that they form a long tapering point. When the conducting channels in the bark and sapwood are cut across abruptly, as in round or slightly oval wounds, the sap does not move laterally with sufficient ease to promote healing or prevent death of unfed tissues.

Bracing the Cavity. Many large cavities require some type of support to keep the sides rigid or to hold some solid material more securely if a filling is to be used later. Only an arborist with a good knowledge of the mechanics and physiology of the tree should be allowed to install the supports.

Bolts are placed in the tree by any of the methods shown in Figures 6-9 and 6-10. A strip of healthy bark and cambium, at least 2 inches wide, should be left between the edge of the cavity and the point where the holes are bored into the bark with a sharp bit. Bolts (made by a mechanic or obtained from an arboricultural supply store) of the proper length and diameter are inserted through the holes, oval iron washers placed in position, and the nuts screwed on. The washers and nuts should be countersunk into the wood deep enough to allow callus to form over them. All cut surfaces are then covered with tree paint.

So-called screw rods are commonly substituted for bolts, because they provide more support and eliminate the need for washers and nuts. Briefly, the installation of a screw rod is as follows: A hole is bored through the trunk at the proper point with a bit $^1/_{16}$ inch smaller in

Fig. 6-9. Upper: Cross section of trunk with extensive cavity, showing the installation of a single bolt to keep the sides rigid.

Fig. 6-10. Lower: Cross section of the trunk showing the installation of double bolts to reinforce the thin sides of the tree.

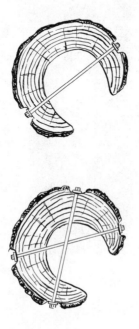

diameter than the screw rod that is to be inserted. The openings in the bark are then reamed down to the wood and the cut surfaces shellacked. The length of the bore is carefully measured and marked on a piece of screw rod. At the marked point the rod is cut about two thirds through with a hacksaw. It is then screwed into the hole with a pipe wrench or some other suitable implement. When the rod is completely in place, the projecting end can easily be snapped off at the point previously weakened.

The importance of bracing long cavities by inserting bolts or screw rods in the sound wood above and below the wound (Fig. 6-11) should not be overlooked. Such a practice minimizes the possibility of the cracking of the wood by frost.

Additional mechanical support is also needed when treating split or crotch cavities. Before the holes are bored and the bolts set in place, the split sides should be drawn together by means of a block and tackle in the main branches arising from the split crotch. At least two bolts must be used above the crotch, and wire cables should be placed higher in the same branches so that all parts will sway as a unit and thus prevent separation of the split sides.

Fig. 6-11. Bracing a long cavity. Aside from bracing at A, it is also essential to brace at B and C to minimize the possibility of cracking of the heartwood by frost action.

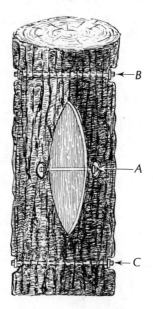

Sterilizing and Dressing. The final essential operations in cavity work include sterilizing and dressing. Sterilization is accomplished by painting all exposed parts of the wood with creosote or copper sulfate solution, 1 pound of copper sulfate crystals dissolved in 4 gallons of water.

The copper sulfate should be dissolved in a wooden container or a crock, never in a metal container. It is poisonous to human beings and animals when taken internally and extreme caution must be exercised in handling it.

After sterilization, a dressing of some ready-made tree paint should be applied over all exposed wood, and also over the bark and sapwood which were previously shellacked.

Open Cavities

The judgment of the arborist and the desires of the tree owner should determine whether a cavity treated in the manner described is to be left open or is to be covered or filled with some suitable material. If the cavity is left open, it should be inspected frequently to determine whether additional dressings are necessary or new rot has developed, in which case prompt attention should be given. The newly developing callus should also be inspected periodically and additional bark traced or cut back wherever healing is not progressing satisfactorily.

Covered Cavities

Occasionally, very old trees are so weakened structurally by decay that no extensive excavating, bolting, and reinforcing can be done, nor can such trees withstand the excessive weights of solid fillings. In other cases, the tree owner may decide that the open cavity is unsightly or otherwise undersirable and may wish to cover the opening. The so-called shell-filling can be used in such circumstances.

After the removal of decayed tissues, the cavity walls are sterilized and dressed as already described. A half-inch strip of bark is cut around the entire opening, leaving a ledge of wood exposed. The cut area is immediately shellacked. A large sheet of paper is then placed over the opening, and a pattern is made to fit the opening and overlap the half-inch ledge of wood. Sheet tin or copper is cut to the exact size of the paper pattern, the back is painted with asphalt or tar, and the metal sheet is nailed to the ledge of wood. Finally the entire surface is waterproofed with some dressing.

Decay continues in many hollow shells despite the most careful cleaning of the cavities. Shell-filling, however, is inexpensive, keeps out vermin and decaying leaves, and is a quick, simple way to cover a cavity.

Filled Cavities

Though the various individuals, firms, and institutions interested in tree preservation are agreed that the practices already discussed—that is, cleaning, shaping, and sterilizing—should be employed in treating any cavity, they disagree about whether such a properly treated cavity should be filled or left open. The author does not intend to take sides in this controversy but will attempt to present both points of view. Here, too, the judgment of the arborist and the desires of the tree owner should determine subsequent treatment.

It is commonly assumed that the principal objectives of filling a cavity are prevention of further decay, addition of mechanical support, provision of a foundation for healing callus, and improvement in appearance of the tree.

The first of these objectives has already been discussed, but some points merit repetition. The evidence at hand today indicates that when decay is well established in the heartwood, it is economically impossible by methods now in use to eradicate all the fungus tissue responsible for decay. Where decay is confined to the outer wood and sapwood or to small cavities in small branch stubs, however, proper treatment is effective.

Advocates of cavity fillings argue that since normal callus growth has been repeatedly observed to seal small wounds perfectly and to check further decay, similar checking should also occur if an opening can be sealed perfectly by artificial means. Perfect closing of a wound, however, can take place only when the materials used as fillers do not become defective under the stresses set up by the swaying of the trees, and when the contraction and expansion of the wood are about equal to those of the filler. Some tree men argue that no filling is completely effective in sealing wounds or in preventing reinfection, since microscopic openings are present along the edge of the filling and beneath the callus and surface of the filling. Such openings appear constantly during the growing season and even during cold winter days. Normal trees shrink in diameter during the day while most fillings expand, and the reverse occurs during the night. Thus perceptible openings may be present several times each day between the filling and the tree. These openings allow tiny fungus spores to enter and cause infection.

Whether or not filling a tree with any material adds structural strength is another disputed point. Solid materials such as cement may actually weaken the tree by their excessive weight or by creating a fulcrum over which the part above the filling may snap off during wind or ice storms. When the cavity is left open, the normal rolling over of successive layers of callus provides extra support to the tree. The principle involved is much the same as that used in making T- or H-shaped structural steel beams. A thick rolling callus over an open cavity imparts considerably more strength to a tree than does a thin flat one growing over a filling.

However, long narrow cavities close much more rapidly when a firm base is provided for the callus.

A large mass of concrete in a cavity will not bend with the swaying of the tree. As a result, either the concrete cracks or crumbles or the wood wears away at the point where friction occurs. Some patented fillers are more flexible than concrete, thus minimizing the latter possibility.

A properly filled cavity improves the appearance of a tree and imparts the feeling to passersby that the tree is receiving proper care. It also provides a considerable amount of personal satisfaction to most owners of trees.

Many trees are well worth the effort and expense required to excavate and fill the decayed portions, but before much money is spent, the following points should be carefully considered.

Factors Determining Whether To Fill a Cavity

Size of Cavity. The more extensive the cavity, the more difficult it is to remove wood-rotting fungi. The greater the size of the wound opening, the more difficult it is to maintain an effective and permanent barrier.

Age of the Tree. As a rule, callus formation proceeds very slowly in old trees, thus leaving a relatively large area exposed to the danger of reinfection for some time. Old trees are also subject to other troubles.

Vitality of the Tree. Trees that have been struck by lightning, injured by manufactured illuminating gas, covered with a grade fill, or otherwise weakened should not be filled until the condition has been remedied and the trees have regained their vigor through pruning and fertilization.

Longevity of the Tree and Susceptibility to Virulent Fungus or Insect Attack. Extensive fillings are not justified on such short-lived or 'weed' trees as the tree-of-heaven. As a general rule, cavities should not be filled in any of the following trees: chestnut, black locust, boxelder, white birch, cultivated cherries, dogwood, yellowwood, Lombardy poplar, redbud, mountain-ash, goldenrain-tree, and most deciduous magnolias. Neither should trees already infected by some wilt fungi, such as *Verticillium*, be filled. Cavities may be filled in the following, but only if the specimen is in otherwise excellent condition: apple, catalpa, black oak, mimosa, paulownia, and willow.

Filling the Cavity

The preliminary procedure for filling a cavity should always include excavating, shaping (Fig. 6-12), sterilizing, and dressing as already described, with one modification. To hold the filling in place more securely, the sides of the cavity should be cut (undercut) as shown in Figure 6-13. This cut must not be made too close to the outer edge, since the wood between the cut area and the edge may be too thin and may dry out the sapwood. As a substitute for undercutting, strips of wood or lath

Fig. 6-12. An extensive cavity ready for filling.

can be nailed along the edge of the cavity, just below the cambial region. These should be waterproofed with tar or asphalt.

Where a cavity is to be filled with a material such as concrete, some provision must be made for draining sap and moisture which may collect behind the filling. Drainage grooves, resembling in form the veins of a leaf, are cut in the back and sides of the cavity; that is, a center groove corresponding to the midrib, with side grooves leading into it, as do the lateral veins. A hole is then bored from the outer bark up into a pocket just below the lower end of the main drainage groove, and a drainpipe inserted. After being sterilized and painted, the entire inner face of the cavity is lined with 3-ply roofing paper held in place with tacks. This paper will prevent clogging of the drainage grooves and will eliminate seepage of the liquids to the surface of the filling. Nails may be driven halfway into the sides and back of the interior of the cavity to provide additional support for the filler (Fig. 6-13).

The surface of a filling should never extend above the level of the cambium. The filling of cavities above the level of the inner bark not only reduces callus development but in many instances inhibits its growth completely. As a guide to determine the proper level of the filling, the

Fig. 6-13. Left: Cross section of the trunk showing insertion of nails to help hold the filling in place. The wood is undercut at A to further help hold the filling.

Fig. 6-14. Right: Filling the cavity with cement.

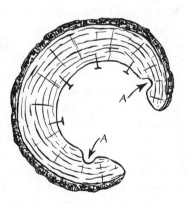

bark should be cut around the edge of the cavity, exposing a ledge of wood ⅛ to ¹⁄₁₆ inch wide. The surface of the filling should be level with that of the exposed wood.

Extreme care must be exercised at all times to prevent bruising of sound bark. An accidental blow from the mallet or the careless use of the chisel or knife may severely injure the cambial layer. In such cases, callus formation must start farther away from the edge of the cavity. This leaves the wood beneath the injured area subject to decay fungi for one to several years longer than normally.

Specification for a Good Filler

Before beginning the filling operations, select a good filling material. The following are the specifications for a good filler:

Durability. The material should not decompose, crack during sharp temperature changes, or melt during the summer heat.

Safety. The filler should not contain harmful chemicals likely to injure the tree.

Flexibility. It must be sufficiently flexible (either by itself or because of the way it is placed in the cavity) to allow for the swaying and twisting to which the part filled is subjected during windy or stormy weather. Without flexibility, the filling breaks or crumbles or grinds away the margin of the wood adjacent to it.

Plasticity. A good filler should be plastic enough to conform to the outline of the cavity.

Waterproofness. The filler must not absorb moisture, since a moist environment adjacent to the wood is conducive to decay.

Filling Materials

Special Fillers. Several patented materials used by some of the larger tree companies meet the specifications for a good filler. They cannot be used, however, without the permission of the patent holders.

Concrete. Probably the cheapest and most readily available filling material is cement mortar or concrete. Two parts of clean sharp sand are mixed dry with one part of cement, and sufficient water is added to produce a stiff mortar. The mixture is then placed in the cavity with a trowel and tamped firmly, especially near the walls of the cavity. Large fillings should be placed in layers or sections not over 6 inches wide to prevent cracking from expansion and contraction and from twisting and bending when the tree is swayed by the wind (Fig. 6-14). Three-ply roofing paper or some other suitable material is used to separate the layers. In wide cavities the sections should have vertical as well as horizontal layers with the roofing paper in between. After the surface is smoothed, the concrete should be painted with a waterproofing material. Cement fills are most satisfactory in small cavities or in large root or trunk-base cavities, where no twisting occurs when the wind sways the tree.

Asphalt Mixtures. Several asphalt mixtures make better fillers than cement, but are more difficult to prepare and put in place. A commonly used mixture is prepared as follows: Melt asphalt in a container over a fire and slowly add dry hardwood sawdust, excelsior, or wood shavings. Continue adding and stirring the solid material as long as it is blackened by the asphalt. The pasty granular mixture formed can then be put in the cavity and tamped into place. When the cavity is very large, or the mixture is too soft, the filling will slump or flow out of the base of the cavity. Canvas, burlap, or thin strips of lath can be fastened over the surface to hold the filling in place. After the filling has hardened, the barriers are removed and the face is smoothed with a hot iron and dressed with tar, asphalt, or paint.

The principal disadvantage of asphalt mixtures is their tendency to soften and slump when exposed to hot summer sunlight. They are much more flexible than concrete, however.

Other Cavity Fillers. Wood blocks, cork products, rubber blocks, and other materials are commonly used for filling cavities. Most of these have some outstanding advantages over the concrete and asphalt fillers.

The newest material for filling cavities is a polyurethane foam. This material is tough, somewhat resilient, and adheres well to both sapwood and heartwood. Moreover, it is light in weight, can be poured into the cavity, is compatible with many fungicides, expands and solidifies rapidly, is somewhat flexible after setting, and permits callus initiation along the edges of the filled cavity.

Details on the use of polyurethane for filling tree cavities are given in University of Massachusetts Publication No. 58, 1970. Amherst, Massachusetts 01002. The polyurethane, available from General Latex and Chemical Company, Cambridge, Massachusetts 02138, is sold under the name Vulta Foam.

Quality Cavity Fills. In the various methods outlined for filling cavities, no attempt has been made to discuss many of the details that might arise during the operation. Actual practice, rather than reading, makes the tree expert. For that reason, the filling of a particularly valuable tree should be entrusted only to a reliable commercial arborist who thoroughly understands not only the mechanics of tree structure but also the materials and their use (Figs. 6-15, 6-16, 6-17). The skilled arborist takes greater pride in filling cavities than in any other phase of his work. Several companies are so confident of their results that they guarantee their cavity work. A reliable tree expert will not promise to cure a tree of heartwood decay by some secret preparation. He will not undertake extensive fillings if the tree is not vigorous enough to stand the treatment. Above all, he realizes that a good tree poorly filled will suffer far more in health and appearance than one left untouched.

Fig. 6-15. A properly filled trunk cavity on the Princeton University campus. Notice the thick roll of callus one year after filling and points where bolts were inserted to reinforce the sides of the tree.

Fig. 6-16. A very large cavity filling on a very old Kentucky coffee tree at Sunnyside, Tarrytown, New York.

Fig. 6-17. A properly filled basal cavity.

Advice to Tree Owners

A written contract covering certain phases of the work is usually advisable when a tree owner employs a commercial arborist to take care of his trees. Any reliable concern will readily agree to the following specifications:

1. The type of cavity work to be done—that his, whether the cavity is to be filled, covered, or left open—should be agreed upon.

2. All badly diseased, punky, or worm-eaten wood should be removed.

3. Orange shellac or some other efficient and harmless covering should be applied to the cut edges of the sapwood, cambium, and bark

immediately after the final tracing cut, or as soon afterward as the cut surface becomes sufficiently dry to ensure a good coverage.

4. All other cut surfaces should be painted with some disinfectant, followed by some effective and more or less permanent tree paint or dressing.

5. Climbing spurs should not be used on any part of the tree, and only soft-soled shoes should be worn by workmen.

6. A guarantee to repair free of charge any defects of workmanship appearing within a reasonable period (a year or so) should be given.

7. Regular inspection of the trees every year should be provided unless the owner prefers to do this himself.

Selected Bibliography

Anonymous. 1967. 'Tree cavity work needs to be based on judgment of the professional.' *Weeds, Trees, and Turf.* July 1967. p. 7, 17, 25.

———. 1973. 'Treating tree cavities.' *Grounds Maintenance.* Vol. 8 (No. 7). p. 27–29. Intertec Publ. Corp., Overland Park, Kansas 66212.

Armstrong, Norman. 1935. 'Importance and place of cavity work in arboriculture.' *Proc. Eleventh National Shade Tree Conference.* p. 61–68.

Blair, M. F. 1936. 'The solid type of cavity repair.' *American Nurseryman.* Vol. 64. p. 7–9.

Eslyn, W. E. and T. L. Highley. 1976. 'Decay resistance and susceptibility of sapwood of fifteen tree species.' *Phytopathology.* Vol. 66 (No. 8). p. 1010–17.

Freeman, G. K. 1936. 'Cavity treatment—shell and open type.' *American Nurseryman.* Vol. 63. p. 5–6.

Jacobs, H. L. 1935. 'A modern view of twenty-five years of cavity treatment.' *Proc. Eleventh National Shade Tree Conference.* p. 55–61.

King, Gordon. 1970. Polyurethane for filling tree cavities. *Proc. Forty-sixth International Shade Tree Conference.* p. 113a.

King, Gordon, Charles Beatty, and Malcolm McKensie. 1970. *Polyurethane for filling tree cavities.* U. of Mass. Publ. No. 58. 6 p.

Le Seur, A. D. C. 1934. *The care and repair of ornamental trees.* Country Life Ltd., London. 257 p.

———. 1934. 'The repair of wounds in trees.' *Gardener's Chronicle* (London). Vol. 95. p. 76.

Marshall, R. P. 1935. 'Scientific aspects of handling tree cavities.' *Proc. Eleventh National Shade Tree Conference.* p. 51–55.

May, Curtis. 1962. 'Possible use of urethane for filling tree cavities.' *Plant Disease Reptr.* Vol. 46 (No. 5). p. 384.

May, C. and J. G. Palmer. 1968. 'Experiments with a combination of two plastics for filling tree cavities.' *Arborist's News.* Vol. 33 (No. 12). p. 1–4.

Palmer, J. G. and C. May. 1970. 'Additives, durability and expansion of a urethane foam useful in tree cavities.' *Plant Disease Reptr.* Vol. 54 (No. 10). p. 858–62.

Rankin, W. H. 1932. 'Wound gums and their relation to fungi.' *Proc. Ninth National Shade Tree Conference.* p. 111–115.

Shigo, A. L. 1975. 'Some new ideas in tree care.' *Jour. Arboriculture.* Vol. 1 (No. 12). p. 234–37.

———. 1975. 'Compartmentalization of decay associated with *Fomes annosus* in trunks of *Pinus resinosa.' Phytopathology.* Vol. 165 (No. 9). p. 1038–39.

———. 1976. 'Decay: a problem in both young and old trees.' *American Nurseryman,* July 1, 1976. p. 24, 25, 226, 228, 232, 234.

———. 1977. ' "New" ideas in tree care.' *Jour. Arboriculture* Vol. 3 (No. 1). p. 1–6.

Shigo, A. L. and E. vH. Larson. 1969. *A photo guide to the patterns of discoloration and decay in living northern hardwood trees.* USDA Forest Service Research Paper. NE 127. 100 p.

Shigo, A. L. and W. E. Ellis. 1973. 'Heartwood, discolored wood and microrganisms in living trees.' *Ann. Rev. Phytopathology.* Vol. 11. p. 197–222.

Welch, D. S. 1949. 'The occurrence of active wood-rotting fungi in apparently sound wood of living trees.' *Arborist's News.* Vol. 14 (No. 2). p. 18–19.

———. 1949. 'The cause and treatment of cavities in trees.' *Proc. Twenty-fifth National Shade Tree Conference.* p. 126–31.

7
Bracing and Cabling

The importance of supplying artificial support to structurally weak or injured trees has been recognized. Some trees, such as oak, beech, and locust, rarely need artificial support because they consist of tough wood fibers and usually have a single major stem from which branches arise at approximately right angles. Despite the absence of tough food fibers, even pine, spruce, and fir seldom need support because of their single stem and type of branching. Other trees, such as elm, maple, and poplar, which have inherent structural weakness resulting from the manner in which their branches arise, often require considerable mechanical support.

The provision of some support by means of iron braces or wire cables is an inexpensive form of tree insurance and is an important phase of any complete tree maintenance program. Artificial supports prevent such injuries as crotch splitting and branch breakage, both of which eventually lead to wood decay. They also prolong the life of many trees after decay or extensive cavities have already developed. It is well to bear in mind that the principal function of the heartwood, or center of the tree, is to provide mechanical support, and that a tree can live for many years despite the presence of a cavity or extensive rotting of this tissue. In such cases, most of the sapwood is free of decay, and together with the cambium and bark above it, can continue to function in the tree's metabolic processes for a long time.

When Is Artificial Support Justified?

In many situations the proper installation of braces and cables proves to be extremely helpful in prolonging the life of a tree. This is especially true of trees having tight V-shaped crotches, split crotches, or inherent susceptibility to breakage.

Tight V-Shaped Crotches. These occur commonly in certain trees in the course of normal development. In others, they result from lack of proper pruning of the young trees. A brief discussion of how V-shaped crotches develop is essential for a better understanding of preventive and subsequent treatments.

In the narrow angle between two sharply forking major branches, the bark and cambium are hindered from developing normally or may even be killed by the pinching action of the branches as they increase in size. This results in a weak union, of the type that readily splits when the branches are subjected to heavy wind or ice storms. In contrast, in trees with a single main trunk, the lateral branches arise more nearly at right angles, forming a U crotch (Fig. 7-1). which does not split off so readily in times of stress.

Split Crotches. The factors favoring ease of splitting are present very early in the tree's life. In many cases, early and judicious pruning by an expert will eliminate the possibility of a split crotch later. As a rule, the arborist finds it difficult to convince the tree owner that preventive practices should be applied when the tree is young, and that because of improper early care, considerable work is necessary in repairing split crotches on older trees.

Split crotches should be supported and treated not only to prevent further splitting and complete loss of one or both branches, but also to check wood decay, which is sure to follow.

Susceptibility to Breakage. Because of such inherent properties as heavy foliage production and brittleness of the wood, some species of trees are more susceptible than others to breakage by wind and ice storms.

Among the trees that are quite susceptible to breakage by winds are: chestnut oak, honey locust, horsechestnut, mimosa (silk-tree), poplars, maples (red, silver, and sugar), sassafras, Siberian elm, tuliptree, and willows.

The following trees are more resistant to wind damage, although they too can lose branches and be toppled by winds of very high velocity: American beech, American elm, ginkgo, hackberry, littleleaf linden, London planetree Norway maple, red oak, sweetgum, and white oak.

Among other conditions that govern the need for supporting a tree are the following: weakening of the tree as a result of removal of some roots during wall or curb construction or grade changes; decay of large areas in the trunk or roots; removal of nearby trees which previously

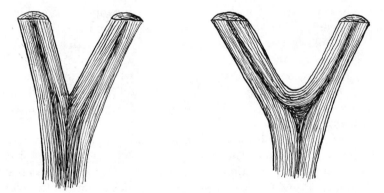

Fig. 7-1. Left. A V-shaped crotch results in a weak union. Branches that form such a crotch are easily broken during storms. **Right:** Branches joined by a U-shaped crotch do not split or break off so easily.

helped to support the tree with their intertwining root systems or to shield it; and exposure to high winds and sleet storms.

Types of Artificial Supports

Despite the fact that bracing and cabling of trees is an old practice, real improvements in materials and methods have been made only in rather recent years. The iron collars, rods, and chains formerly used were expensive, unsightly, inefficient, and often harmful. The iron collar in particular caused considerable damage by preventing normal sap flow in the limb it was supposed to help. Today improved and standardized materials are readily available at tree-surgery supply houses.

Modern tree-supporting technique is divided into two main types: rigid and flexible bracing. Rigid bracing involves the use of bolts and threaded rods for supporting weak or split crotches, long cracks in the trunk or branches, and cavities. The types for cavities are discussed in Chapter 6. Flexible bracing involves the installation of wire cables high in the tree to reduce the load on weak crotches and long arching limbs without hindering the normal branch sway. Both rigid and flexible braces are commonly installed in the same tree.

Rigid Bracing

Prepared lengths of steel or duralumin rods with lag threads at both ends (screw rods) are commonly used in rigid bracing. The holding power of such rods is similar to that of ordinary wood screws used in fastening two boards together. Rods or bolts with machine thread, when used, are held in place by washers and nuts of appropriate size. Though these do not supply so much support as do lag-thread rods, they must be used in the following instances: when more than half the wood in the area where they are to be inserted is decayed; where only a thin shell of sapwood remains around large cavities; and where future decay may develop at the point of insertion. All rods should be covered with a tree wound dressing before they are inserted, and all exposed metal portions painted with a metal preservative paint.

Crotch Bracing. The installation of artificial support is justified on sound trees with weak crotches and when crotch cavities have already developed. To provide additional support, as a rule, wire cables must be installed higher in the tree whenever the branches extend more than 20 feet above the crotch. In small trees or in secondary crotches of large trees, a single rod may be inserted through the center of the two limbs above the crotch (Fig. 7-3). Larger limbs may need the support of two parallel rods (Fig. 7-2). These are usually placed above the crotch at a distance twice the diameter of the limbs at the point of rod insertion, and horizontally separated by a distance equal to about half this diameter.

Split crotches between large limbs should first be closed by pulling the limbs together with properly placed rope and tackle blocks high in the tree. When the crack is closed, a hole is bored through the split parts with a bit $\frac{1}{16}$ inch larger than the bolt to be used. The bolt is then inserted and held in place with washers and nuts. Additional support is provided by inserting a second bolt a few feet above, in the same branches, as shown in Figures 7-4 and 7-5.

Fig. 7-2. Left: For larger limbs, two parallel screw rods provide more support than a single rod.

Fig. 7-3. Center: Installation of a single screw rod to support a V-shaped crotch.

Fig. 7-4. Right: For very large limbs, the installation of a third rod above the parallel rods is suggested.

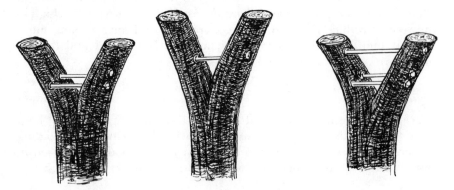

Fig. 7-5. The three rods sketched in Figure 7-4 are shown installed in an American beech.

Split Limbs or Trunks. Screw rods may be used to hold split limbs together or to support the sides of long splits in the trunk. They are usually placed about a foot apart and are staggered so as not to be in the same direct line of sap flow.

Cavity Bracing. Cavity bracing is described in detail in Chapter 6.

Rubbing Limbs. Limbs that rub against each other can be braced together or kept separated by proper bracing. A single rod screwed through the center of each limb at the point of contact will hold the limbs rigidly together and thus eliminate rubbing (Fig. 7-6). If it is desirable to keep such limbs separated, a length of pipe equal to the desired space between the two limbs can be placed over the rod before the branches are fastened together (Fig. 7-7). If the limbs are to be separated and free movement between them is desired, the installation of a U bolt in the upper limb, which rests on a wood block attached to the lower limb, will prove satisfactory (Fig. 7-8). In time the wood block will need replacement because of wear.

Flexible Bracing

Wire cables are used to brace trees together and to strengthen weak crotches. These are usually placed rather high in the tree to provide maximum support from the use of materials of minimum size and cost. Copper-covered steel wire, although more expensive than ordinary galvanized wire, is stronger, size for size, and does not rust.

Fig. 7-6. Upper Left: Method of inserting a screw rod to hold two limbs together and thus prevent rubbing.

Fig. 7-7. Upper Right: Separating two branches by means of a screw rod and a short piece of pipe.

Fig. 7-8. Below: Method of installing a V-bolt to prevent rubbing of two limbs and at the same time allow free movement of the branches.

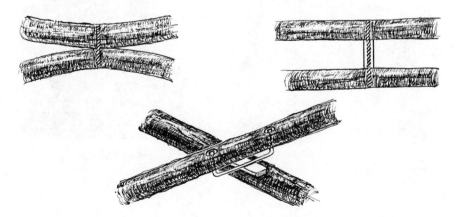

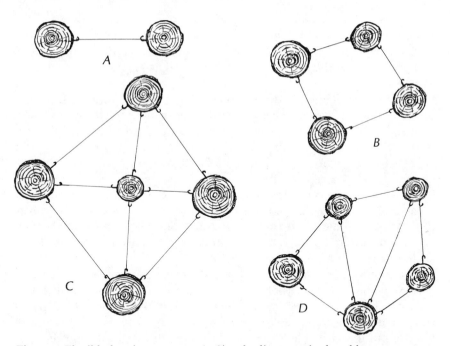

Fig. 7-9. Flexible bracing systems. A, Simple direct: a single cable supports two limbs arising from a single crotch. B, Box: cables attached to all large limbs in a rotary manner. C, Hub and spoke: cables radiate from a limb or metal ring in the center of the main branches. D, Triangular: cables placed in triangular form.

Flexible bracing system commonly employed are of several types. In the simple direct system, a single cable is installed to support two limbs arising from a single crotch (Fig. 7-9A). In the box system, cables are attached to all large limbs of a tree in a rotary manner. This arrangement provides lateral support and maximum crown movement, but little support to weak crotches (Fig. 7-9B). The hub and spoke system, in which cables radiate from a limb or a metal ring in the center of the main branches (Fig. 7-9C), provides little direct or lateral support. In the triangular system cables are placed as shown in Figure 7-9D to provide direct support to weak or split crotches and lateral support to the branches. Triangular bracing is probably the most efficient of the various types described.

Materials and Installation Procedure for Flexible Bracing

The wire cables are usually placed at a point approximately two thirds the distance from the crotch to the top of the tree. They should be so placed as not to rub against each other.

Lag hooks, hook bolts, bent eyebolts, and other materials are most often used to anchor the cables. Such anchors should be well separated when more than one is used on a single branch and should be placed in a straight line with the cable and as nearly at right angles to the branches as possible.

Lag-Hook Installation. Cadmium-plated lag hooks (½ to ⅝ inch diameter and 6-inch thread) are recommended as anchors for most branches. The exact size selected is governed by the amount of stress and the size of the branches. Holes about ⅟₁₆ inch smaller than the hooks are bored at the proper anchorage points, and the hooks are screwed in just far enough to allow a cable to be slipped over the open ends. After the lag hooks are in place, the limbs are pulled together sufficiently so there will be no slack in the cable after it is hooked on. A thimble is inserted over the hook and the cable is then passed through it and spliced to form a permanent union between the two anchors. All spliced areas should be coated with a metal preservative paint.

Eyebolt Installation. Where wood decay is present or considerable stress occurs, eyebolts or hook bolts are generally used as anchor units. The hole for these is drilled completely through the wood, the bark is countersunk to a depth below the cambium, and the bolt, washer, and nut are put in place. The cable ends are then inserted through the eyes and' properly spliced.*

Selected Bibliography

Beilmann, A. P. 1932. 'Weak branching in trees.' *Missouri Bot. Gard. Bul.* 20. (No. 6). p. 92–93.

Felt, E. P. 1940. 'Cabling and the use of wood screws.' *Scientific Tree Topics* 1 (No. 2). Bartlett Tree Expert Co., Stamford, Conn.

Hemming, E. S. 1967. 'Guying trees.' *American Nurseryman.* Dec. 1, 1967. p. 46–47.

Herder, R. R. 1976. 'Problems of safety in tree work.' *Jour. Arboriculture.* Vol. 2 (No. 2). p. 33–35.

Johnson, L. M. 1940. 'Cabling and bracing structurally weak trees.' *Scientific Tree Topics* 1 (No. 3). Bartlett Tree Expert Co., Stamford, Conn.

Luckner, W. Jr. 1951. 'Proper guying practices of transplanted trees.' *Proc. Twenty-ninth National Shade Tree Conference.* p. 47–50.

* The reader desiring more detailed information on the engineering principles involved in the installation of cables and braces is referred to the excellent bulletin *Tree Bracing,* prepared as *Tree Preservation Bulletin No.* 3 of the National Park Service, United States Department of the Interior. The Superintendent of Documents, U.S. Government Printing Office, Washington, D.C. 20402 will send copies at a small charge.

Mayne, L. S. 1975. 'Cabling and bracing. *Jour. Arboriculture.* Vol. 1 (No. 6). p. 101–106.

Parr, F. L. 1970. *Bracing, cabling, and guying standard for shade trees.* National Arborist Assoc., McLean, Va. 4 p.

Thompson, A. R. 1936. 'Tree cabling materials.' *Proc. Twelfth National Shade Tree Conference.* p. 30–43.

Wachtel, C. L. 1951. 'Proper bracing practices.' *Proc. Twenty-ninth National Shade Tree Conference.* p. 60–62.

Wagner, Fred. 1968. 'Cabling and bracing.' *Arborist's News.* Vol. 33 (No. 8). p. 1–5.

———. 1969. 'Cabling and bracing techniques.' *Proc. Forty-fifth International Shade Tree Conference.* p. 202–11.

8

Trees Suitable for Various Locations

Tree species vary greatly in their ability to grow in different environments. Before selecting a tree, therefore, one should know something about the different kinds of trees, the conditions under which they are to grow, and what to expect of them.

When the author wrote his first book on trees about 35 years ago, the consensus among shade-tree commissions, park department officials, arboricultural firms, and other agencies empowered to regulate the selection, planting, and care of trees on public property was that tall-growing trees such as elms, oaks, planes, and maples were best suited for planting along city streets.

Times have changed and so have ideas on the proper kinds of trees to plant. Many officials now realize that it is best to select trees that will give the least trouble and require the lowest maintenance costs in future years. While many of the tall-growing or standard shade and ornamental trees have long been favorites on wide city streets, they are rapidly losing their popularity because of high maintenance costs. Such trees are more expensive to spray and prune, and during severe wind, ice, and snowstorms or hurricanes cause great damage to power and telephone wires. Moreover, tall-growing trees have a greater tendency to crumble curbstones or push them out of line, crack and raise sidewalks, and clog sewer pipes. Tall-growing trees, discussed later in this chapter, should be planted where they have plenty of room to grow and where they will not interfere with public and private utility services.

136

The modern city planner realizes that trees should be fitted into the available space. This idea developed from a street tree program started fifty years ago by the late Barney Slavin in Rochester, New York, and then continued most vigorously by Edward H. Scanlon, now deceased, starting when he was shade-tree commissioner for the City of Cleveland in 1946.

People acquainted with tree raising realize that such tall-growing trees as elms, pin oaks, and planetrees were popular in the past for several reasons. They are easy to reproduce either from seeds or from cuttings, they grow rapidly, transplant readily, and require relatively little after-care.

The low-growing trees, on the other hand, require more skill to grow and maintain. For the first four or five years after being transplanted they must be helped more and perhaps sprayed and pruned more. Although these practices are more expensive, the small type trees are well worth it, for they usually serve their purpose two or three times as long as the tall-growing types, without the many disrupting habits of the latter. And should they have to be removed for any reason, the cost of removal is only one quarter to one sixth that of tall trees.

Not only are most of the small type trees suitable for streetside planting, but they are ideal for modern ranch-type houses.

Proponents of the tall-growing trees claim that low-growing trees have several serious drawbacks: their relative scarcity as compared with tall-growing kinds; their low-hanging branches, which interfere with vehicular and pedestrian traffic; their inability to provide as much shade as tall-growing kinds.

In time, as more nurserymen grow the low-growing forms, the first drawback will be overcome. The second problem can be overcome if low-growing trees are grown properly with a central leader; for example, with Kwanzan flowering cherry, the graft is made 6 to 7 feet above the ground level. The drawback of low-hanging branches can also be overcome if communities would permit the planting of small-type trees inside the property line instead of between the street and sidewalk. The third drawback is not solved so easily, but actually shade is not so important as it was formerly. Street beauty and stabilization of property values are more important today. Where more shade is desired, close planting of low-growing trees is suggested.

The ideal small type tree should grow rapidly; it should reach a useful size soon after being transplanted to its permanent site and should then abruptly slow down. It should be reasonably free from insect pests and diseases and should have pleasing growth habits.

The initial cost of such trees of streetside planting size is much greater than that of the standard tall-growing types, but, as has been said, overall maintenance and, when necessary, removal costs are much lower.

Low-growing Trees for Streetsides and Lawns

Many of the following low-growing trees can be used for streetside planting in situations where their low height will not interfere with traffic or where children are not apt to break branches for their showy flowers. All of them are ideally suited for lawn planting on small properties or near ranch-type houses. A few, like *Magnolia Kobus* and *M. grandiflora*, may grow to considerable size, however.

Ash (*Fraxinus*)

Flowering ash (*Fraxinus ornus*) is a low-growing, round-headed tree with fragrant, whitish flowers.

Modesto ash (*F. velutina glabra*) is a fast-growing, lovely tree which reaches a height of 25 feet. It has a smooth green trunk and bright crisp green, slightly pendulous branches. Male trees are recommended.

'Rose Hill' is a seedless form of white ash (*F. americana* 'Rose Hill') that grows well in different sites and is resistant to insects and diseases.

'Marshall's Seedless' is a form of green ash (*F. pennsylvanica lanceolata* 'Marshall's Seedless') that grows rapidly to 50 feet, is drought resistant, and has dark green glossy foliage.

The 'Hesse European' ash (*F. excelsior hessei*), introduced by Cole Nursery Company,* Circleville, Ohio 43113, has single leaves rather than the compound leaves that most ashes have. It forms a straight sturdy trunk well filled with branches and reaches a height of 60 feet. It can withstand temperatures as low as −40°F. (−40°C.).

'Autumn Purple,' (*F. americana* 'Autumn Purple') a seedless form of white ash whose green leaves turn deep purple to mahogany in the fall, was recently introduced by the same company.

The newest white ash introduced to the trade is 'Champaign County,' which has a tight, dense crown and lustrous leaves throughout the summer. The dense crown results from close placement of the numerous branches.

Sorbus alnifolia is a handsome small mountain-ash from Asia. Bright green leaves turn orange and red in autumn, and deep pink berries persist well into the winter months. It is virtually resistant to boring insects.

Sorbus aria is another pleasant small mountain-ash. Its leaves, bright green above and white tomentose below, contrast with the large orange-red to scarlet fruit. The variety *aurea* has yellow leaves; those of *chrysophylla* are even deeper yellow.

Other desirable ashes are the Manchurian ash and the blue ash.

* The present name of this company is American Garden Cole.

Cherry (*Prunus*)

Varieties of the oriental cherry *Prunus serrulata* produce an unsurpassed display of flowers in early spring. They should be planted in full sun and in well-drained fertile soil. The most popular variety, Kwanzan, is the showiest, hardiest, and best of all flowering cherries for street tree use (Fig. 8-1). When grafted on 6½-foot stems, its upright branches do not interfere with vehicular and pedestrian traffic as do those of other varieties. More than a hundred Kwanzan cherries are planted in the gardens of the United Nations Headquarters in New York. Other good cherries being grown for streetside planting are Akebono, Daikoku, and Shirotae.

Yoshino cherry (*P. yedoensis*), another excellent cherry, grows rapidly when young, then slows down. It is covered with pendant clusters of fragrant pale pink to white flowers in spring. It and Kwanzan are the major components of the famous cherry display at the Tidal Basin in Washington, D.C.

Fig. 8-1. Kwanzan Flowering Cherries grafted on 6½ foot stems make excellent streetside trees. These, growing in Portland, Oregon, are about 30 years old and 24 feet tall.

Other excellent flowering cherries are Sargents (*P. Sargentii*) and double-flowered Mazzard (*P. avium plena*).

Crabapple (*Malus*)

Crabapples can be both ornamental and utilitarian. In addition to the truly magnificent flowers in early spring, some produce bright-colored fruits that make an excellent jelly. Others are grown primarily for their showy flowers.

Among the best known that serve the dual purpose are Arnold crab (*M. Arnoldiana*) and Aldenham crab (*M. purpurea aldenhamensis*). Two recent introductions that fall in the same category are 'Redfield' and 'Redford.' Both are hardy and produce good-sized fruits with flesh that is red throughout. Other good varieties are Dolgo and Young America. The former is a Russian variety introduced into America by the South Dakota Experiment Station, while the latter is an old variety of unknown origin. Fruits of both make excellent jelly.

'White Casade,' a recent introduction of American Garden Cole Nursery Company, is a white-flowered, yellow-fruited weeping crabapple of refined and graceful beauty. It is disease resistant.

'Radiant' and 'Royal Ruby' are two other flowering crabapples. The former has deep red buds which become deep pink blossoms and has small, persistent, bright red fruit. The latter has an abuandance of dark red, double, cup-shaped flowers, often 2 inches or more in diameter.

Among the older varieties of crabapples grown primarily for their flowers are Bechtel's crab, with fragrant double pink blossoms; Carmine crab, with large rose-madder flowers; and 'Dorothea,' with bright tyrian rose flowers. Newer ornamental crabapples are 'Van Eseltine,' which produces double pink blossoms and retains its small fruits during the winter, thus providing food for birds; and the very hardy 'Crimson Brilliant,' with semidouble, vivid crimson flowers. Other excellent crabapples are Shakespeare, with pink flowers; 'Beauty,' with white flowers; and 'Frau Louise Dittman,' with bright pink flowers.

Other recently introduced crabapples are 'Sparkler,' a low-growing spreading from; 'Coralburst,' with small, tightly-spaced leaves, rose-pink double blooms and yellow fruit; 'Red Jewell,' with white flowers in spring, rich dark green summer foliage, and small cherry-red fruit in fall; 'Indian Magic,' with golden-orange fruit that persists all winter; 'White Candle,' with glossy leaves and exceptionally large, double white flowers; and 'Pink Cascade,' with an unusually narrow, weeping form.

Among other beautiful crabapples available at Princeton Nurseries (New Jersey) are 'American Beauty,' with deep pink, double flowers, 'Pink Perfection,' with light pink flowers, and 'Snowcloud,' with snow-white double blooms.

Dogwood (*Cornus*)

The dogwoods are among the most popular of the low-growing trees. Best known and most widely planted is the flowering dogwood (*Cornus florida*) (Fig. 8-2). It does best in the eastern United States from Massachusetts to Florida in well-drained soils. It flowers either in full sun or in partial shade. The large white bracts surrounding the flowers are very conspicuous in spring, and its leaves and fruits are colorful in autumn. It is most successfully transplanted in spring immediately after flowering. There are a number of pink and red strains of the flowering dogwood. The Prosser flowering dogwood has deeper red bracts than the older red-flowering kinds. The 'Rainbow' dogwood (*C. florida* 'Rainbow') has bright yellow and green variegated leaves in summer, these change to a scalet and blue-lavender in the fall.

Fig. 8-2. The flowering dogwood is one of the most beautiful low-growing trees.

A close relative of our native dogwood, the Japanese dogwood (*C. Kousa*), grows about 20 feet tall and blooms about three weeks after the flowering dogwood. Its small yellow flowers, which last about a week, are surrounded by four conspicuous white bracts which are pointed at the tips and not notched and rounded as are those of the flowering dogwood. Because the flowers and fruit are borne on the upper side of horizontal branches, the tree is best planted where it can be seen from above, the Japanese dogwood is more resistant to insect pests and diseases than the flowering dogwood.* The Chinese dogwood (*C. Kousa chinensis*) usually has larger bracts than the Japanese species.

Dogwoods are extremely sensitive to droughts. Hence, water should be supplied to the soil around dogwoods when no rains have fallen for a week or so during the summer months. Otherwise, the leaves will begin to wilt at the tips and turn red, then brown, long before they ordinarily would.

Magnolia (*Magnolia*)

The outstanding magnolia for northern areas, except for the extremely cold regions, is the star magnolia (*M. stellata*). It produces semidouble white flowers more than 3 inches across. The variety *rosea,* with pink buds that open to pinkish flowers, is even more striking. A newer form, *M. stellata rubra,* has dark pink or purplish-red petals. Waterlily is a white hybrid with slightly smaller flowers but more compact growth than the species.

Star magnolia does best in rich, porous soil, although it tolerates clay soils. It withstands city conditions rather well. It definitely dislikes lime and fresh manure. It is most successfully moved with a soil ball in spring after growth starts.

The saucer magnolia (*M. soulangeana*) is best known for its large pink to purple flowers, which are 5 to 10 inches across in early spring. It also does well under city conditions.

The best magnolias for streetside plantings are *M. Kobus* and *M. Loebneri.*

Southern magnolia (*M. grandiflora*) is a magnificent tree with large evergreen foliage and fragrant white flowers up to 8 inches across. It thrives in hot, humid climates and will tolerate some cold but not prolonged freezing. Although a few old specimens are growing as far north as Long Island, this tree does best in the southern part of the United States. It is sometimes used as a street tree but is more effective in lawn plantings.

* A pink-bracted form of Japanese dogwood (*C. Kousa rubra*) is available at a few nurseries.

Maples* (*Acer*)

There are a goodly number of low-growing maples suitable for streetside plantings, for lawns, and for small properties. Many of these are of Asiatic origin; a few are native species.

Amur maple (*Acer ginnala*) does best in the northern United States in rich, well-drained soil. It will thrive either in full sun or in partial shade. It has excellent foliage and will grow in dry spots. It is most effective when planted in groups of two or three.

Hedge maple (*A. campestre*) is an unusual low-growing tree that thrives in the eastern United States in well-drained, deep, fertile soil. Its growth resembles that of the Japanese maple, and its foliage is yellow in fall.

Japanese maple (*A. palmatum*) is a fine-textured, graceful tree with deeply lobed leaves. Some varieties, such as *atropurpureum,* have beautiful red leaves which retain their color throughout the season; others, such as *Oshiu-beni,* have 9-lobed red leaves in spring which turn green when mature.

Mountain maple (*A. spicatum*) grows well in the northern states on rocky hillsides. It is a very hardy tree with light green leaves that turn orange and scarlet in fall, and with fruits that are bright red in summer.

Two outstanding low-growing maples are David's striped-bark maple and the paperbark maple. The former is an upright grower of great value for streetsides. The latter has cinnamon-brown bark which exfoliates in paper-thin strips similar to the bark of certain birches. The peculiar bark, noticeable at some distance, makes the tree outstandingly interesting throughout the year.

Other low-growing maples are the trident maple (*A. buergerianum*); coliseum maple (*A. cappadocicum*) and its varieties *aureum* and *rubrum;* and the Montpeliar maple (*A. monspessulanum*).

Among other excellent low-growing maples, which unfortunately are not yet widely available, are *A. truncatum, A. diabolicum purpurascens, A. mandshuricum,* and *A. mono* var. *tricuspis.*

Miscellaneous Trees

Big-flowered European birdcherry (*Prunus padus* var. *grandiflora*), introduced from England by Edward H. Scanlon, is hardy and handsome. The showy flower spikes are up to 8 inches in length.

Crapemyrtle (*Lagerstroemia indica*), though usually considered a shrub, in the South can become a tree reaching a height of 25 feet (Fig. 8-3). Its showy, lilaclike clusters of flowers, which vary from deep red to purple, pink, lavender, and white, appear from late summer into early fall.

* Tall-growing maples are discussed on page 157.

Fig. 8-3. Crapemyrtle is a low-growing lovely tree in the warmer parts of the country.

Although reliably hardy only as far north as Baltimore, good-sized specimens are to be found in sheltered spots in New York City and along the coast to Cape Cod. Crapemyrtle does best in a hot, dry climate and in a fertile, well-drained loam.

Dove-tree (*Davidia involucrata*) is a small to medium-sized tree valued for its unusual flower, which is a yellowish-tan ball surrounded by white bracts. It is also known as the lady's handkerchief tree because the white bracts resemble a handkerchief.

Franklin-tree (*Franklinia alatamaha*), a native of the southeastern United States, is now known only in cultivation. Its beautiful flowers, up to 3 inches across with yellow stamens in the center, appear in late summer and early fall when most other flowering trees are through for the season. It prefers a moist but well-drained soil and is more difficult to establish than most trees.

Fringe-tree (*Chionanthus virginica*) grows best in the East and in Gulf Coast states in moisure-retentive sandy loam soils. It is fairly tolerant of smoky city conditions. In late May and early June it forms numerous white blossoms. Later, purple fruits resembling grapes appear. These are devoured by birds.

Golden-chain tree, or Waterer laburnum (*Laburnum Watereri*), an upright, rather stiff tree, bears many pendulous clusters of bright yellow pealike flowers. It does best in moist soils with a limestone base but will tolerate a wide variety of soils. It is reliably hardy only in the southern parts of the country. *L. Vossi*, a hybrid between the common laburnum and the Scotch, is said to be even more desirable than the Waterer laburnum.

Goldenrain-tree (*Koelreuteria paniculata*) grows almost anywhere but is most common in the Midwest and does especially well in dry soils. It is drought-resistant and has average resistance to windstorms and ice. It forms showy panicles of yellow flowers in summer, followed by conspicuous bladderlike pods that are handsome in autumn.

A fall-flowering form, 'September GOLDenrain,' is available from Edward H. Scanlon and Associates, Olmsted Falls, Ohio 44138. A similar cultivar* is named 'Autumn Gold.' A fastigiate form of goldenrain-tree is also available.

Hawthorns (*Crataegus* species), like the crabapples, are especially attractive when in flower and fruit. They do best in the northern and eastern states, in well-drained, fertile soils. Nursery-grown trees are transplanted easily. Hawthorns are excellent trees to plant around modern ranch-type houses. Best of the older kinds are Paul's scarlet thorn (*C. oxyacantha pauli*), with clusters of half-inch blossoms of deep rose color, and the Washington thorn (*C. phaenopyrum*), with white blossoms in May followed by scarlet berries and brilliant foliage in autumn. Lavalle hawthorn (*C. lavallei*) is considered the best of the white-flowering kinds. Another thorn that is available from Edward H. Scanlon and Associates, is the Glastonbury thorn or Holy Thorn of Glastonbury (*C. monogyna biflora* or *praecox*), which has had long association with early Christian history.

American hop-hornbeam (*Ostrya virginiana*) is a low-growing tree with very hard wood. A mysterious fungus disease has been killing this tree in recent years.

A low-growing graceful tree, Yeddo hornbeam (*Carpinus tschonoskii*), does well in the eastern United States from New York southward. It makes a compact head and has up-reaching branches which lend it an illusion of tallness. Its leaves are an attractive reddish-bronze color in the fall, and best of all, it has no serious faults. Three other excellent members of this genus are Japanese hornbeam (*C. japonica*), pyramidal

---

* Cultivar, designated by the abbreviation 'cv.,' or indicated by placing a plant name in single quotes or in distinctive boldface type, is internationally used to signify a cultivated or horticultural variety. As opposed to botanical variety, designated by the abbreviation 'var.,' and applying to a population of wild-occurring, similar, but sexually reproduced plants, the cultivar comprises one or more essentially identical individuals, usually vegetatively propagated.

European hornbeam (*C. betulus pyramidalis*), and weeping European hornbeam (*C. betulus pendula*).

Katsura-tree (*Cercidiphyllum japonicum*) forms numerous upward-branching trunks somewhat like the American elm. If the tree is allowed to grow with a single trunk, its habit is columnar, like the Lombardy poplar. It grows best in fertile, moist soil in eastern and northern United States. Its rounded leaves, nearly 4 inches long when mature, are markedly resistant to insect pests and fungus parasites.

Mulberry trees (*Morus*) are unusually resistant to diseases and pests. They make excellent lawn trees. The fruits produced on female trees, however, are highly undesirable. Hence only the male tree, 'Kingan' fruitless mulberry (*Morus alba* 'Kingan'), is recommended where fruits are unwanted.

Eastern redbud (*Cercis canadensis*) may be grown throughout the South and in the eastern United States along the coast as far north as Boston. It prefers a rich soil and a sunny or slightly shaded area. Its pea-shaped purplish-pink flowers are very showy in early spring. It is used as a street tree in the South and as a lawn specimen in the North. A white-flowering form is also available. Recently introduced by American Garden Cole Nursery Company is 'Forest Pansy' (*C. canadensis* 'Forest Pansy') whose leaves on the tip growth are glossy and dark purple. The Chinese redbud (*C. chinensis*), less hardy than the ordinary species, produces dense clusters of flowers that completely hide the twigs which bear them.

Russian-olive (*Elaeagnus angustifolia*), one of the hardest of the low-growing trees, withstands extremely low temperatures far up into Canada. It has beautiful gray-green to near-silver leaves, which are very striking when ruffled by the breeze. Unfortunately it does not transplant easily, and hence large specimens must be moved with a soil ball.

Silk-tree or mimosa (*Albizia julibrissin rosea*) has leaves composed of many small leaflets which give the tree a delicate lacy appearance. The fernlike leaflets curl up at night. Round clusters of dainty pink flowers resembling fluffy balls 1 to 2 inches in diameter cover the tree in midsummer. This tree will grow on almost any soil, including poor, dry rocky ones. It is not reliably hardy north of Washington, D.C., although large specimens are growing along the east coast as far north as Boston. It is a fast-growing tree, and its wood is so brittle that heavy rain and wind storms frequently cause branch breakage. Although it is one of our prettiest flowering trees in midsummer, it is not very handsome in winter when bare of foliage.

Carolina silverbell (*Halesia carolina*) is an interesting small tree whose branches are covered with small, pendant white flowers in spring. It does best in protected, partially shaded spots and prefers a rich moist loam that is reasonably well drained.

Smoke-tree (*Cotinus coggygria*) is a low-growing tree which is hardy from Boston through Ohio, Missouri, Kansas, Oklahoma, and eastern Oregon. Its flowers, which hang in misty panicles about 8 inches long in June and July, give the tree an appearance of being enveloped in purplish smoke. It will grow in dry soils of low fertility.

The Japanese snowbell (*Styrax japonica*) is a small tree of flat-topped form with curved, horizontal branches, dense foliage, and pendulous, bell-shaped flowers appearing after the foliage, but not hidden by it. It does best in light, well-drained soil and in open situations. The fragrant snowbell (*S. obassia*) is a more or less columnar tree with large leaves. When in bloom in early summer it it exceptionally beautiful.

Sorrel-tree or sourwood (*Oxydendrum arboreum*) is an eastern tree that grows well in moist, acid soils and in partial shade. Its late fall flowers are very striking, as is the scarlet color of its leaves at the same season. It is relatively free from pests and diseases and hence needs little if any spraying.

Stewartia (*Stewartia koreana*), though little known, is an excellent, hardy tree with interesting bark resembling that of the sycamore, white flowers in summer and orange-red leaves in autumn.

Hardy rubber tree (*Eucommia ulmoides*) is a round-headed tree with large, glossy, dark green leaves. It is unusually free of insects and diseases.

'Gum Ball' sweetgum (*Liquidambar styraciflua* 'Gum Ball') is a very dwarf form which reaches a height of 8 to 10 feet when mature. It was introduced by Forest Nursery Company, McMinnville, Tennessee.

Less Common Species

Kentucky coffee tree (*Gymnocladus dioicus*) grows best in rich, light soils in the northern United States. It is more useful for lawns than for streetsides. It is unusually resistant to storm damage and has an attractive silhouette in winter. Male trees are recommended, since they do not produce seeds that litter streets.

Japanese pagoda-tree (*Sophora japonica*) grows well in the eastern United States except in the very cold regions. Its pealike white flowers appear in late summer. It tolerates city conditions but is rather subject to branch breakage during ice storms and occasionally to winter injury. This tree should not be planted near automobile parking areas because the falling flowers stain paint. A weeping form (*S. japonica pendula*) is also available.

Turkish filbert (*Corylus colurna*) is a broadly pyramidal, structurally strong tree with excellent foliage. It is drought tolerant and grows well in almost any type of soil.

Trees with Upright Growth Habit

In the last 25 years, the demand has increased for trees with upright (fastigiate) or columnar form for planting along narrow streets and on small city lots. The old familiar Lombardy poplar and the Bolleana poplar were the only kinds available for such planting 45 or so years ago. The high mortality among poplars affected by the Chondroplea canker disease (p. 458), however, makes the planting of these trees a gamble in most parts of the country.

Many nurserymen and most particularly Edward H. Scanlon and Associates are now offering upright forms of shade and ornamental trees. Following are a few of the better kinds to plant along narrow streets or where space is a limiting factor:

Two narrow upright froms of the sugar maple are 'Temple's Upright' and 'Newton Sentry.' The former has many ascending branches, no dominant central leader, and dark green leaves with leathery texture and wavy margins like those of black maple. The latter has few ascending branches; a strong central leader, which produces stubby lateral branches, especially when secondary branches are removed; and yellow-green, nonleathery leaves. Both trees were introduced into the trade in the late nineteenth century.

The 'Scanlon' red maple (*Acer rubrum conica* 'Scanlon') (Fig. 8-4), one of the newest forms of red maple, is an exquisitely handsome pyramidal tree with strong crotches and upsweeping branches. Its green leaves turn vivid red and orange in fall.

Another good selection of upright red maple is Armstrong, which resembles Lombardy poplar in growth habit.

The sentry ginkgo (*G. biloba fastigiata*) maintains its narrow columnar habit and hence is ideal for planting along very narrow city streets.

Other kinds of fastigiate trees available are: improved columnar Norway maple (*Acer platanoides columnare*), upright English oak (*Quercus robur fastigiata*), and upright American linden (*Tilia americana fastigiata*).

A fastigiate form of the black maple (*Acer nigrum*), which is taller-growing and with clearer-yellow fall color and more compact growth than the species, is also available.

Other superior upright trees are *Carpinus betulus fastigiata*, *Crataegus monogyna stricta*, *Acer pseudoplatanus pyramidalis*, *Sophora japonica pyramidalis*, *Fraxinus excelsior pyramidalis*, *Prunus Sargentii columnare*, and *Sorbus aucuparia columnare*.

The Augustine ascending elm is an unusually fine columnar-shaped elm for use along narrow city streets and for landscaping that needs an accent. It is said to be unusually resistant to wind and ice storms and eventually reaches 100 feet in height.

Not only can the upright trees be used on narrow streets or small

Fig. 8-4. The late Edward H. Scanlon of Olmsted Falls, Ohio, in front of a 10-year 'Scanlon' red maple, a conical-shaped, exquisitely handsome tree.

properties, but they have the following advantages over the parent species from which they were derived: first, maintenance costs are lower because they require no heavy pruning; second, their root system is more restricted and compact and they therefore can be planted in crowded conditions such as near driveways, sewers, and underground conduits without causing so much trouble as the standard types; third, fastigiate trees are less susceptible to damage by sleet, snow, and wind because their branches offer less resistance to the elements; finally, they interfere less with street lighting than do the ordinary types.

Standard Trees for Streetside and Lawn Planting

Because some of the more desirable trees mentioned earlier in this chapter will not be widely available for some time, it is necessary to list the species of the tall-growing or standard trees which are still in plentiful supply. It is well to reiterate that while many of these trees have highly desirable characteristics, such as ease of transplanting and wide availability, they eventually grow to great size, making their maintenance costs very high and their removal expensive, if they die from one cause or another. Moreover, they conflict more frequently with power and telephone lines, often causing a complete loss of light, heat, and telephone services when they fall during hurricanes or ice storms.

These trees are better planted in parks, along very wide streets, or in backyards where their height does not interfere with public utilities and where their roots will not clog sewer pipes, lift sidewalks, or push curbstones out of line.

The most widely used groups—oaks, maples, elms, planes, and lindens—are discussed in greatest detail because they presently constitute the great majority of trees planted along eastern and midwestern streets. Lists of trees for these and other parts of the country are presented later in this chapter.

Ash (Fraxinus)

Ashes have several characteristics that make the standard species undesirable as street trees. They are subject to infestations by scale insects, are not particularly attractive at any season, drop their leaves early, produce large numbers of viable seed, and have wood that is inclined to be brittle.

White ash (*F. americana*) is probably the best of the standard ashes as a streetside tree where the soil is particularly favorable.

Red and black ashes thrive only in swampy soils and are, therefore, of little value as streetside trees.

Fig. 8-5. The cork tree, *Phellodendron Lavallei,* makes an excellent tree for streetside or lawn planting.

Cork Trees (*Phellodendron*)

Cork trees (*P. amurense, P. lavallei, P. sachalinense,* and *P. chinense*) are slow-growing species with feathery leaves, which give as much shade as littleleaf linden and more than silk-tree (Fig. 8-5). They grow well in dry soils, are resistant to smoke, and consequently thrive in large cities. They are rather free from insect attack, but some species such as *P. amurense* and *P. lavallei* produce fruit that litters the streets. Hence only males trees are recommended.

Elm (*Ulmus*)

The unfortunate introduction of the Dutch elm disease (p. 391) into the United States and the appearance of the mycoplasma disease phloem necrosis (p. 397) have somewhat dampened enthusiasm for planting elms (Fig. 8-6).

Despite its susceptibility to these highly destructive diseases, the American elm is still one of our most popular trees. It is easily transplanted and becomes quickly established. Because it requires con-

Fig. 8-6. The American elm, one of our most beautiful trees, is rapidly losing its popularity because of its great susceptibility to insects and diseases.

siderable room, it should be planted only on wide streets where the two diseases have not made inroads. The American elm is susceptible also to several insect pests. These, however, can easily be controlled by periodic applications of the proper insecticide.*

Another elm that might be considered for planting in areas where the Dutch elm disease is prevalent is the Hansen Manchurian elm. This species was introduced into America by the late Dr. N. E. Hansen, who collected it in the rugged mountains near the Manchurian-Siberian border, where it withstands temperatures of −76°F (−60°C.). It has strong, sturdy limbs which branch out with firm crotches that do not split easily like those of the American and Chinese elms. The leaf is similar to that of the Chinese elm, discussed below, but is larger and more glossy green. The Manchurian elm grows fast, as much as 8 to 12 feet in one season, and is decidedly resistant to the Dutch elm disease.

---

* Where elms are planted close to a house, the owner must choose between insect control, with the resulting unsightly accumulation of spray residues on the roof, windows, and screens, and the possibility of a serious insect infestation on the foliage.

Golden elm (*U. carpinifolia wredei*) has a pyramidal shape and rich golden leaves that hold their color all season.

Moline elm (*U. americana moline*) is a rapidly growing strain of the American elm, with darker green foliage. It must be carefully pruned to eliminate the formation of weak crotches to which it is subject. It is more upright and less spreading than the common American elm. It does best in the Rocky Mountain area.

Chinese elm (*U. parvifolia*) has small leaves, which turn bright yellow in the autumn. Its flowers are formed in August and September. It is easily transplanted but is very subject to insects and breakage by wind and ice.

Siberian elm (*U. pumila*) is a small tree with sparse growth and brittle wood. It grows well in poor soil and is resistant to the Dutch elm disease. This elm should not be planted with the expectation that it will take the place of the American elm, which it does not resemble in shape or form.

Ginkgo (*Ginkgo biloba*)

Ginkgo, also known as maidenhair tree, a native of Asia, is now used extensively as a street tree in large cities. It does well in all parts of the United States except in the extremely cold areas. Its greatest assets are ability to withstand city conditions, wide tolerance of soil types, ease of transplanting, resistance to ice and wind storms, and remarkable freedom from insect and fungus attack. Its ability to produce shade can be augmented by pruning to increase the branch spread. The leaves are distinctly fan-shaped.

It is best to plant male trees only, because female trees bear brown, olivelike fruits with a disagreeable odor. Fruit formation can be prevented, however, by spraying the tree at blossom time with a dilute solution of maleic hydrazide (sold under the name Slo Gro by Uniroyal Chemical, Division of Uniroyal, Bethany, Connecticut 06525).

Hackberry (*Celtis*)

Hackberry (*C. occidentalis*) is tolerant of city conditions, but in many localities its use is not recommended because of its extreme susceptibilty to witches' broom (p. 406). The Chinese hackberry (*C. sinensis*) and the southern hackberry (*C. mississippiensis*) are less subject to this abnormality. Both species, especially the latter, should be used more extensively along city streets.

Horsechestnut (*Aesculus*)

Horsechestnut (*A. hippocastanum*) is valued for its shape and for its large white flower clusters. The nuts are objectionable because they litter the streets or are sought by boys, who often break branches in collecting them. Nut formation can be prevented, however, by spraying the trees at blooming time with a dilute solution of Amid-thin, manufactured by the Agricultural Products Division, Union Carbide Corp., New York.

The most serious objections to the horsechestnut are the continuous dropping of foliage during the summer and the susceptibilty to leaf-blotch disease.

The double-flowering variety, *A. hippocastanum Baumanii,* does not produce nuts, but it is likely to scorch badly in summer and is also susceptible to leaf blotch.

The pink-flowering horsechestnut (*A. carnea*) is a very beautiful tree when in bloom. It is a cross between the common horsechestnut and the redflowering buckeye.

The ruby-red horsechestnut (*A. carnea briotii*) is similar to the common horsechestnut but is smaller and produces deep red flowers, which are outstanding.

Linden (*Tilia*)

Lindens are commonly used as street and shade trees. They thrive best in fertile, moist soil. Most of the species are favorite hosts for Japanese beetles.

Silver linden (*T. tomentosa*), with leaves that are dark green above and silvery white beneath, produces an interesting effect in the wind. It grows into a compact specimen, especially desirable for lawns or parks. Among the lindens it withstands dry sandy soils best, it loses fewest leaves in summer, and is most resistant to red spider attack. A weeping form of this linden, the silver pendent linden (*T. petiolaris*), has more finely serrated leaves on its pendulous branches.

American linden (*T. americana*) thrives in deep, moist soil and is therefore not very satisfactory as a streetside tree. A valuable forest tree, it is surpassed by other varieties for landscape purposes.

Littleleaf European linden (*T. cordata*) is a small tree that develops a compact, pyramidal head to 30 feet. It is the best of the lindens for streetside plantings in most localities. The 'Rancho' linden *T. cordata* 'Rancho' (Fig. 8-7) has an upsweeping, narrow-branching form that is unique among the lindens. Two other forms of *Tilia cordata* are 'Greenspire' and 'Chancellor.' The former makes a dense, high, narrow, oval top up to 50 feet, and the latter makes a more narrow top up to 35 feet.

Crimean linden (*T. euchlora*), one of the finest of the lindens, with very glossy foliage, grows to about 40 feet. Recently introduced is 'Redmond,' which has striking cerise-red new growth and buds.

Fig. 8-7. 'Rancho' linden, an outstanding form among lindens.

The bigleaf European linden (*T. vulgaris*), with very large leaves, though occasionally planted along city streets, is a less desirable kind.

Locust, Black (*Robinia*)

Black locust (*R. pseudoacacia*) is rapidly disappearing from the eastern landscape because of the ravages of the locust borer (p. 420).

Two excellent locusts are the globe (*Robinia pseudoacacia umbraculifera*) and the Idaho (*Robinia pseudoacacia* × *hispida*). Although these must be sprayed occasionally, they are beautiful and functional. The former has a fine-textured, round head on a base that eventually becomes coarse-textured. It has no spines and rarely sets flowers.

Locust, Honey (*Gleditsia*)

Honey locust (*G. triacanthos*) is more commonly used as a lawn tree than along streets. Its finely divided foliage and its open spreading habit provide partial shade. It is very hardy, grows fairly rapidly, although at first its branches droop considerably and it is difficult to keep erect. Its falling leaflets in autumn curl and dry up, and consequently are not so much of a nuisance as most other deciduous tree leaves. The long fruit pods, which litter the ground in autumn, and the numerous branched thorns, however, are highly undesirable. In playgrounds where children are likely to climb trees, only the thornless variety (*G. triacanthos inermis*), or the 'Moraine' locust mentioned below, should be planted. Some shade-tree men consider thornless honey locust one of the best trees, especially for the larger eastern cities.

Honey locusts are particularly difficult to maintain in good condition in the Washington, D.C.-Philadelphia area because of their great susceptibility to the mimosa web-worm (p. 372).

The best known and most generally available of the new honey locusts is the 'Moraine' locust (*G. triancanthos inermis* 'Moraine') (Fig. 8-8), developed by the Siebenthaler Nursery Company of Dayton, Ohio. It is a thornless variety which is said to be sterile and hence forms no fruit pods.

The locust 'Sunburst' developed by the American Garden Cole Nursery Company of Circleville, Ohio, has bright golden-bronze foliage, is said to be thornless and more resistant to insect pests than the common honey locust. Its brilliant coloring is limited to 8 to 10 inches of branch tips early in the season. By fall the contrast is not sharp because all the foliage turns green. Another recent honey locust introduced by the same company is 'Imperial.' It is said to grow straight and strong without staking and produces a dense, uniform crown with a minimum of trimming.

Fig. 8-8. A seven-year-old 'Moraine' locust.

Princeton Nurseries at Kingston, New Jersey 08528, introduced 'Shademaster' honey locust, a fast, upright grower that frequently retains the leader branch, an unusual property of honey locusts.

'Rubylace' is another honey locust which is thornless, seedless, has ferny foliage with red-maroon color all season. It is a slower grower than other honey locusts.

Maple (Acer)*

The maples constitute a very important group of streetside trees. Some species have many excellent qualities, whereas others are virtually worthless.

Silver maple (*A. saccharinum*) has been planted most extensively in the past, despite the fact that it is the least desirable maple. Because its brittle wood breaks readily even in mild windstorms and its rooting habit lifts

---

* Low-growing maples are discussed on page 143.

pavements and clogs sewers, and because it is extremely susceptible to rapid wood decay and to infestations by many species of insects, this species should never be considered for streetside plantings. Its use is prohibited in many cities and towns.

Norway maple (*A. platanoides*), the most widely planted maple at the present time, is a fairly satisfactory city tree. It is easily transplanted, grows rapidly but not too large.

Because of the dense foliage and shallow rooting habit of Norway maples, lawns cannot be maintained beneath them. Branches must be pruned frequently to allow sufficient penetration of light, and water and fertilizers applied occasionally to compensate for the heavy withdrawal of these materials by the trees' roots. The shallow roots also break or lift pavements, walks, and street curbs. Although relatively free from insect pests, this species is rather susceptible to the Verticillium wilt disease (p. 297). During midsummer the leaves, and certain sucking insects on them, excrete a sticky material that disfigures automobiles and other objects left beneath the trees.

Many municipal tree men are now planting seedling Norway maples less frequently along city streets. The constant pruning required to remove low-hanging branches and to keep them well shaped greatly increases maintenance costs. Specially selected strains of Norway maple do not have the many faults of the ordinary kinds grown from seeds. Hence these will be used more extensively in time. Among the selections in wide use now are: Charles F. Irish, Cleveland, and Almira.

Though the Norway maple is considered hardy by some arborists, it is often injured by extremely low winter temperatures. The climate in Montreal, Canada, is too severe for it. Moreover, it is extremely susceptible to the fungus *Ganoderma* (p. 430), which appears as reddish conks, or fruiting bodies, with coatings like varnish or lacquer, at the base of the trunk or on surface roots.

A. platanoides 'Undulatum' has paler green leaves than *A. platanoides*, with slightly wavy margins. Unlike the ordinary maples, it forms a full-headed crown supported by multiple branches which are rather erect and much lighter than the main species.

The most recently introduced cultivar of *A. platanoides* and one of the very best is 'Cavalier' (Fig. 8-9). It forms a compact, round head, is a fast grower, and is suitable for large, open areas.

Two other forms of Norway maple recently introduced are 'Emerald Queen' and 'Summer Shade.' The former resembles the sugar maple but is more tolerant to adverse conditions. The latter does well in the more southerly parts of the country where the ordinary Norway maple does not do well.

Another cultivar of Norway maple is 'Crimson King,' a seedling of the Schwedler maple. Unlike its parent, it holds its bright red color through-

Fig. 8-9. Norway maple 'Cavalier' has a compact round top and is suitable for large, open areas.

out the growing season. A strain closely resembling 'Crimson King,' 'Faassen's Red-Leaf,' has dark red foliage.

Nikko maple (*A. Maximowiczianum*) is a rare species with three leaflets and forms a broad oval head to a height of 40 feet.

Sycamore maple (*A. pseudoplatanus*) is more attractive than the Norway maple but in some areas it is not so satisfactory as a streetside tree. It grows fairly rapidly with a more spreading and open habit than the Norway. It has not attained widespread use because of its more exacting soil requirements. When planted, it should be given a large growing area.

Two varieties of sycamore maple are particularly outstanding: wine-leaved sycamore maple (*A. pseudoplatanus Spaethii*) and the variegated *A. pseudoplatanus Leopoldii*.

Sugar maple (*A. saccharum*) requires a relatively large area and a moist but well-drained soil for best development. It is subject to sunscorch, is sensitive to the heat reflected from city pavements, and consequently does better along roadsides and highways than in cities. It has fine symmetry, produces moderate shade, and its leaves are brilliantly colored in autumn. 'Green Mountain' is an upright-growing variety that shows more tolerance to heat, drought, and smog than ordinary sugar maples.

Red maple (*A. rubrum*) thrives only in rich, moist soils and does not retain its vitality when planted in dry situations and under city conditions. It does best in suburban areas. Two excellent cultivars of this maple are 'Gerling' and 'Tilford.' 'October Glory' is another form of red maple that colors well in the fall and forms a shapely head up to 50 feet.

Black maple (*A. nigrum*) is sometimes used in highway plantings in the Midwest. It is a close relative of our eastern sugar maple.

Schwedler maple (*A. platanoides schwedleri*) looks much like the Norway maple except for its dark red foliage throughout the early growing period. Although more subject to winter injury than Norway maple, it is being planted rather extensively in many cities.

Boxelder (*A. negundo*), the only common species of maple with compound leaves, is unsatisfactory as a streetside tree because of the extreme brittleness of its wood.

Many other maples, including upright or fastigiate forms, are discussed on page 148, and low-growing forms, some of which are suitable for streetside plantings, are discussed on page 143.

Oak (*Quercus*)

As a group, the oaks are probably one of the best of the older street trees. They are hardy, strong-wooded, long-lived, and relatively free of serious insect and fungus troubles. In addition, they add a great deal of color to the fall landscape.

Oaks have not been planted more extensively because they are thought to be slow growers and difficult to transplant. Although this is true of white and live oaks, most of the other species used as street trees grow fairly rapidly and can be transplanted rather easily. In fact, oak trees that are properly watered and fed will outgrow many other species, the trunk increasing from ½ to 1 inch in diameter a year.

Pin oak (*Q. palustris*) is one of the most commonly planted species in

Fig. 8-10. A row of fine pin oaks along a street in Mount Vernon, New York.

eastern cities (Fig. 8-10). It does not do well in some midwestern areas. It is easily transplanted, becomes established quickly, grows rapidly, thrives in very wet or extremely dry soils, and is resistant to most insect and fungus attacks. Its single, erect trunk with many small drooping branches on the lower part distinguishes it from the other commonly planted species. It is pyramidal when young and assumes a rounded crown at maturity.

The most objectionable characteristics of the pin oak are its drooping branches, which must be pruned to prevent interference with traffic, and its tendency to become chlorotic in limestone soils and in filled-in areas. The latter condition, however, usually can be remedied (p. 236). Other objectionable features are the tendency of the leaves of some trees to hang on during most of the winter, and the dense branch formation that necessitates frequent pruning. 'Sovereign' is a recently introduced pin oak whose branches grow more upright than those of the ordinary pin oak.

Red oak (*Q. borealis maxima*), one of the fastest-growing and best oaks for street planting in most sections of the country, is one of the few species that will thrive along ocean fronts. It requires a relatively large area for proper development. Its growth habit is more open than that of pin oak, thus facilitating the passage of electric wires through it. The red oak becomes established rather slowly, and best results are obtained if it is moved with a soil ball.

Scarlet oak (*Q. coccinea*) grows best in dry, sandy soils, because its roots prefer good air drainage. It withstands droughts better than other oaks and requires less room than red oak. Its fall color is more striking than that of most other oaks. It is very difficult to move.

White oak (*Q. alba*) is probably one of the slowest-growing and longest-lived species in the eastern United States. Because it is difficult to transplant, it is rarely planted along streets. When it is used as a street tree, however, its spreading branch habit allows electric wires to pass through without interference. Although its leaves do not color so brilliantly in fall as do those of the scarlet oak, its broad, round head and spreading branches make it one of the most beautiful oaks at all other seasons.

Live oak (*Q. virginiana*) is planted commonly in the South and on the West Coast as a street tree. Several other species of oaks are also used for street planting in these sections of the country.

Willow oak (*Q. phellos*) is one of the finer-textured oaks. Its light green, shiny, narrow pointed leaves, 2½ to 5 inches long, resemble those of willow. It is easy to transplant, does best in fertile, acid soils but is not hardy in the colder regions of the country.

Shingle oak (*Q. imbricaria*) and Shumard oak (*Q. shumardii*) are also desirable species to plant in the more southerly parts of the country.

Sawtooth oak (*Q. acutissima*) is an excellent tree for parks and streets. It forms a shapely, round head with lustrous green leaves that are narrow and bristle-pointed like American chestnut leaves.

Pear (*Pyrus*)

One of the best medium-tall trees is the 'Bradford' ornamental pear (*Pyrus calleryana* 'Bradford'). This is a nonspiny species from China, introduced about 1918 by the United States Department of Agriculture and named for the late F. C. Bradford, horticulturist of the U.S. Plant Introduction Station, Glenn Dale, Maryland. The tree is unusually handsome, with white flowers in spring, crisp glossy green foliage in summer, and brilliant plum-colored foliage in fall. The original tree, on the grounds of the station in Glenn Dale, is nearly 55 years old and more than 50 feet tall. A superior conic-shaped cultivar of this tree, the 'Chanticleer' pear (*P. calleryana* 'Chanticleer') (Fig. 8–11), is available from Edward H. Scanlon and Associates, Olmstead Falls, Ohio 44138.

Fig. 8-11. A superior conic-shaped form of *Pyrus calleryana* is the cultivar 'Chanticleer.'

These cultivars are said to be resistant to the fire blight disease described on page 287.

Recently introduced by American Garden Cole Nursery Company is *P. calleryana* 'Korean,' which has the same shiny leaves, tiny fruit, and good fall color as *P. calleryana* 'Bradford' but is lower-growing and wider, forming a sturdy, medium-sized tree.

Planetree (*Platanus*)

Planetrees constitute an important group in the tree population of eastern and midwestern cities and towns. For example, of the 158,000 trees planted along Philadelphia streets, 50,000 are planetrees, and all except two are London planetrees (*P. acerifolia*). Their odd method of shedding patches of olive and brown bark, exposing lighter color bark beneath, is known to nearly everyone (Fig. 8–12 and frontispiece).

Some confusion persists regarding the names of several species used. The tree that is generally planted along city streets and that thrives well is the London planetree. This vigorous tree is a hybrid between buttonwood (*P. occidentalis*), also commonly known as sycamore, and the oriental planetree (*P. orientalis*). The true oriental planetree is rare in the United States, despite its general appearance in nursery catalogues. It has deep-lobed leaves and single-fruit balls. The hybrid (London planetree) is intermediate, with lobes starting nearly at the middle of the leaf and with fruit balls usually borne in pairs but at times singly or in threes. The seeds in the fruit balls of the London planetree have sharp points; those of the buttonwood do not. The London planetree, which is unquestionably the best of the planetrees, is better adapted than most other trees for planting in unfavorable city environments. It is occasionally subject to freezing injuries,* is extremely susceptible to the destructive cankerstain disease (p. 452) and Botryosphaeria canker (p. 456), and is difficult to maintain in an erect position for the first two or three years after it is planted along city streets.

An upright form, *P. acerifolia pyramidalis*, makes a fine tree for streetside planting.

Buttonwood is a native tree that grows to great size in the woodlands. It does not withstand city conditions so well as the London planetree and drops much of its foliage during the summer. It is repeatedly attacked by the blight disease, to which it is much more susceptible than the London planetree is.

Poplar (*Populus*)

Poplars are not recommended for streetside plantings. Some of the species, in fact, have such outstanding faults that many communities prohibit their use along public rights-of-way.

Eugene poplar (*P. canadensis eugenei*) has very brittle wood, which breaks easily and is a constant menace to the safety of pedestrians. Though it tolerates city conditions and is a rapid grower, it is short-lived. Its roots clog sewers and break up pavements and walks.

Lombardy poplar (*P. nigra* var. *Italica*) is rapidly disappearing in the eastern United States because of its extreme susceptibility to the Chondroplea canker disease (p. 458). Its rapidity of growth and columnar habit have made it a favorite for windbreaks and crowded situations.

White poplar (*P. alba*) appears to thrive under city conditions but has

* The extremely low temperatures in the winter of 1977 resulted in the death of thousands of London planetrees growing along streets in many cities in the northeastern United States.

Fig. 8-12. The author is examining the trunk of a very old London planetree at The New York Botanical Garden.

many of the undesirable qualities of the Carolina poplar. The variety Bolleana, with an upright form resembling Lombardy poplar, is often used in parks and open areas. This variety is not much better than Lombardy poplar, however.

Sweetgum (*Liquidambar*)

Sweetgum (*L. styraciflua*), with its star-shaped leaves, excellent fall coloration, and deep corky bark, is one of our most beautiful trees. It requires a deep, friable soil and full sunlight. It grows well between the curb and walk in some cities. Drastic pruning of the top at transplanting time greatly increases its chances of survival. It should be used more extensively as a streetside tree when it can be given ample space. Its hard, spiny fruits, which fall on lawns and streets, are objectionable because they damage lawn mowers and even automobile tires that pass over them (Fig. 8-13).

Fig. 8-13. A row of young sweetgum trees growing along a New Jersey street.

Three forms of sweetgums are available: 'Palo Alto,' a West Coast form; 'Festival,' an East Coast form with burgundy and green foliage; and 'Burgundy,' with very dark red fall foliage.

Tuliptree (Liriodendron)

The tulip (*L. tulipifera*) is one of the tallest of our native eastern trees and is considered one of the most beautiful. It requires deep, rich soil and is very difficult to transplant. An excellent tree for private estates and other landscape plantings, it is not recommended as a streetside tree because of its extremely brittle wood and its intolerance to city smoke.

Three columnar cultivars, 'Arnold' and 'Fastigiata' and a form 'Ardis' with small leaves and low in growth, are available.

Wingnut, Caucasian (Pterocarya fraxinifolia)

This very handsome tree, related to walnut, produces very showy racemes 20 inches long. Its foliage is leathery and yellow-green in color. It was the opinion of the late Edward H. Scanlon that the tree should do well in the Midwest and along the East Coast of the United States. The tree is a native of China.

Yellowwood (Cladratis)

Yellowwood (*C. lutea*) is an excellent tree for cities and towns and should be planted more extensively. Some authorities believe it is more suitable than American elm. It has a graceful top, a relatively short trunk with yellow wood and smooth bark, and often reaches a height of 50 feet.

It should be planted in a sunny location. In late spring or early summer it produces hanging clusters of white, fragrant flowers resembling those of white wisteria. Unfortunately, multibranched specimens have a strong tendency to split at the crotches during heavy wind and ice storms.

Zelkova (Zelkova serrata)

This tree, also known as Japanese Keaki, is a member of the *Ulmaceae* and is recommended as a replacement for the American elm. It is resistant to the Dutch elm disease. Its leaves are dark green and resemble those of the American elm. The bark is smooth, like that of American beech, and its growing habit is similar to the elm. The form 'Village Green' is very hardy and fast-growing, with larger leaves than the ordinary Zelkova.

Less Common Species

Cucumber-tree (*Magnolia acuminata*) is more suited for lawns than for streetside planting. It has large, interesting leaves and a cucumberlike fruit, which is inedible. Its winter silhouette is excellent, and it is very resistant to wind and ice storms.

The dawn redwood (*Metasequoia glyptostroboides*) existed in North America about 15 million years ago. It was reintroduced to this hemisphere via seeds collected from living trees in central China in 1945 through the efforts of the late Dr. E. D. Merrill of the Arnold Arboretum.

Dawn redwood somewhat resembles the deciduous bald cypress in foliage character, although its flat needles are nearer the size of a hemlock's. The trees are not particularly handsome.

Hundreds of dawn redwood trees are now growing throughout the United States. Young trees are available from several nurseries, including Kelly Brothers, Dansville, New York 14437. Some seedlings make as much as 4 feet of growth in a single season. Their rapid growth rate suggests they may eventually serve as a good source of lumber. They are not recommended for streetside planting but are well-suited to lawns.

A selected form of the dawn redwood known as 'National' (*Metasequoia glyptostroboides* 'National') can grow to a height of 35 feet in 10 years. When fully grown it will reach a height of 65 to 70 feet.

Trees for Wet Areas

Some properties have an unusually high water table which cannot be corrected by installation of tile drains, breaking up of hardpan, or the incorporation of organic matter.

A number of trees that can tolerate poorly drained locations better than others include: alder (*Alnus*), arborvitae (*Thuja*), bald cypress (*Taxodium distichum*), fringe-tree (*Chionanthus virginicus*), London planetree (*Platanus acerifolia*), quaking-aspen (*Populus tremuloides*), red maple (*Acer rubrum*) river birch (*Betula nigra*), serviceberry (*Amelanchier canadensis*), southern hackberry (*Celtis laevigata*), swamp white oak (*Quercus bicolor*), sweetbog magnolia (*Magnolia virginiana*), sourgum (*Nyssa sylvatica*), sweetgum (*Liquidambar styraciflua*), and tamarack (*Larix laricina*).

Trees for Seashore Planting

Because of the unusually difficult conditions along seashores, relatively few trees do well. Some, however, are markedly tolerant of the salt-laden air, constant winds, and sandy soil.

Japanese black pine (*Pinus thunbergii*) is one of the most satisfactory evergreen trees for seashore planting along the east coast. It withstands salt- and sand-laden air and light sandy soils better than most trees. This tree, however, is not reliably winter hardy in some parts of Canada. For example, the unseasonable frost which hit the Pacific coast of northwestern United States and southwestern Canada on November 11, 1955, killed Japanese black pine that had been growing there for 20 years. Austrian pine (*Pinus nigra austriaca*) suffered no ill effects from the same frost, and it is almost as resistant as Japanese black pine to salt spray on the west coast of Canada.

Red oak (*Quercus borealis maxima*), mentioned earlier, is one of the best oaks to plant along the eastern United States seashore.

Blackjack oak (*Q. marilandica*), sometimes referred to as 'scrub oak,' also makes an excellent tree for seashore plantings.

Russian-olive (*Elaeagnus angustifolia*), also mentioned earlier, is an unusually hardy tree that can withstand seashore conditions.

Other trees that can tolerate trying seashore conditions, provided they are given some slight protection or are planted a bit farther inland than the trees mentioned above, are mugho pine and pitch pine, American holly, post oak, honey locust, weeping willow, laurel willow, red maple, Norway maple, London planetree, gray birch, hawthorns, shadbush, and crabapple.

Trees as Windbreaks

The northern Great Plains area of the United States with its extremely low winter temperatures and very dry summers is one of the more difficult areas in which to grow trees, especially those used as windbreaks. In tests to determine hardiness for farm windbreaks conducted over a 38-year period, workers in the United States Department of Agriculture found that boxelder (*Acer negundo*), green ash (*Fraxinus pennsylvanica*), and the shrubby silver buffaloberry (*Shepherdia argentia*) were most satisfactory.*

Planting Streetside Trees

Since trees are more difficult to grow in the unnatural environment of cities, successful culture of streetside trees involves many problems not usually encountered in forest and country plantings.

Trees in large cities have a particularly difficult time to do their best. City conditions are so unfavorable for most trees that it is a wonder they grow at all. Smoke and other air pollutants, mechanical injuries, a

---

* The most detailed publication on the use of trees as windbreaks, *Tree Against the Wind*, was published as P M W Bulletin No. 5, January 1953, by the State College of Washington Extension Service and the U.S. Department of Agriculture, co-operating, Pullman, Washington 99163.

disrupted water table, highly compacted soil, lack of organic matter, limited root space, reflected heat from buildings, visitations by dogs, lack of water, use of salt on sidewalks to melt ice—these are but a few of the external forces which make the lot of a city tree so difficult. Add to these, invasions by insects and infection of the roots by soil-inhabiting parasitic fungi, and one is almost ready to forego planting trees in cities. Despite these hazards and handicaps, however, millions of trees do grow in large cities, including Brooklyn.

In cities, the runoff of rainfall is nearly 100 per cent. Hence the small open soil area between the street curb and the sidewalk, where most city trees are planted, has little chance to absorb rain water.

Another important point to bear in mind is that a soil which may have had adequate aeration at the time a tree was planted will deteriorate until the aeration is entirely inadequate. Trees growing along city streets are an excellent case in point. When the tree is first planted in the area between the street and the sidewalk, conditions may be satisfactory. As the roots extend into the areas covered by the street and sidewalk, conditions become less favorable. In addition, trampling of the open soil area by pedestrians also compacts the soil and makes it as nearly imprevious to air and water as concrete.

Still another factor which makes the growing of trees along city streets difficult is the lack of adequate plant food. Dr. Curtis May of the United States Department of Agriculture once wrote, 'Street trees are even more likely to decline from lack of soil fertility than lawn trees, because the soil mass in which their roots can develop well is likely to be even more restricted than it is for lawn trees.'

Three factors largely govern success in planting trees along public rights-of-ways—selection of the proper species, good growing conditions, and reasonable aftercare and protection.

Selection of Species for City Streets

Tall-growing trees like the London planetree, the ginkgo, and the honey locust are known to tolerate city conditions better than trees like the sugar maple. The usual explanation is that the foliage of the first three is more tolerant of air pollutants. The author is of the opinion that some deciduous trees are more tolerant because their roots can survive under the extremely poor soil conditions prevalent in most cities; that is, they are better able to tolerate excessively dry soils, poor soil aeration, high concentrations of soluble salts, and other adverse below-ground factors.

A great variety of trees suitable for planting along city streets, especially in the eastern and midwestern parts of the United States, are described earlier in this chapter. Trees suitable for these areas and for other parts of the country are listed at the end of this chapter.

Persons entrusted with the selection and care of streetside trees should adopt programs for proper selection and maintenance. Many of the more desirable low-growing trees need more frequent spraying than the older tall-growing kinds. But in the long run, the former will be better and less expensive. One example will suffice to indicate how expensive the American elm plantings in the eastern and midwestern United States can be. Not only do such trees require frequent sprayings to control scale insects, elm leaf beetles, and European bark beetles, but once they become infected by a fatal disease such as the Dutch elm, or phloem necrosis, then great amounts of money are needed to remove them. The City of New York appropriates many thousands of dollars each year to remove diseased and dead elms. Such costs will continue each year until all susceptible individuals have been removed.

Size of Tree. The best size for street planting varies from ¾ to 1½ inches in caliper at the base. Larger trees are also used but become established more slowly and are more expensive.

Spacing. Most city trees are planted too closely. No trees should be planted closer than 40 feet, and large spreading types should be spaced 60 to 75 feet apart. Narrow streets are best planted in ginkgo, European linden, or some of the pyramidal varieties of maple, oak, elm, and hornbeam described earlier in this chapter.

Location. Street trees are customarily placed between the walk and street curb. Planting one of the tall-growing kinds in this area is bound, in time, to conflict with overhead wires and with the sidewalks and curbs. This area can be properly planted with the kind of tree that will not lead to such difficulties. The decision on where to locate the tree will depend on site factors.

Where tall-growing trees are used, the area between the walk and property line is more satisfactory (Fig. 8-14). This, of course, is feasible only where the house is set back some distance from the property line. The advantages of such an arrangement are many. It removes trees from the area where they are continually subject to injury by street traffic, the trees have more favorable soil conditions, they are less apt to tangle with overhead wires, the crowns do not form over the street area, and the street looks wider. Moreover, less damage to the tree will occur if the street is widened at a later date.*

Trees should be planted alternately along the street rather than opposite one another, to allow more space for development.

Time of Planting. Most street trees are planted in spring, fall, or winter, depending on local conditions. They can also be planted during the summer, provided anti-transpirants are used as suggested in Chapter 3.

---

* A disadvantage of locating trees near or on the property line is that the jurisdiction over such trees is taken away from the Shade-Tree Commissioner or Department of Parks. In Massachusetts, municipally managed trees can be planted as far as 20 feet in on private property.

Fig. 8-14. The ideal location for street trees is not along the curb but back on the property line. Trees are less subject to vehicular injuries and have more favorable growing condition.

Preparation of the Planting Area. The soil along many city streets is so impoverished that some good soil should be substituted. The usual practice is to remove about a cubic yard of soil and replace it with good topsoil to which a liberal amount of manure or peat moss has been added. The holes are approximately 4 feet square by 3 feet deep. If possible they should be dug beforehand to reduce delay at planting time.

Treatment of Top. Most shade-tree men prune all lateral branches back to one or two buds. Young trees thus treated appear rather thin at first, but they soon regain their shape.

Supporting. An angle-iron fence post, 8 feet long, should be inserted about 1½ feet down on the street side; or wooden supports described in Chapter 7 can be used.

Protection. The benefits derived from protecting the trunk with burlap, kraft crepe paper, wax, or other materials, and from supporting the trunk with stakes have been discussed under Transplanting (Chapter 3).

Aftercare. The first and second summers after planting are the most critical periods in the life of the young tree. Artifical watering must be practiced, especially if the rainfall is low. Installation of a Rex-Keyser system, as illustrated on page 51, will make the job easier and more effective. In the absence of such a system, a mulch of wood chips around the base of the newly planted tree is suggested. Such a mulch will not only conserve moisture, but will also help control weeds and prevent soil compaction and deep freezing.

Some of the less desirable trees such as ailanthus, silver maple, poplars, and mulberry are well adapted to air pollutants, drought, low humidity, heat, wind, and other rigors of the inner city and industrial areas. They will thrive with little to no maintenance and might be considered for use in vacant lots, industrial areas, and various bits of 'leftover' land. Professor Russell A. Beatty of the Dept. of Landscape Architecture at the University of California, Berkeley, says their lack of aesthetic appeal is balanced by their ability to 'bring a measure of amenity to otherwise ugly and unhealthy landscapes.'

Trees for Different Areas of the United States*

Shade Trees for the Northeast

Maples —Norway and varieties, Schwedler, Sugar, Red, and varieties	American Yellowwood European Beech
Elms—American, Rock, English	Thornless Honey Locust

* Compiled largely from *Trees, Yearbook of Agriculture* 1949, U.S. Government Printing Office, Washington, D.C. 20402.

Shade Trees for the Northeast (Continued)

Oaks—Pin, Red, Scarlet, White
Ginkgo
Tuliptree
Sweetgum
American Linden
American Sycamore
London Planetree

Cherries—Columnar Sargent Cherry,
Sargents, Double-Flowered Mazzard,
Kwanzan, Akebono, Daikoku, Shi-
rotae
Hackberry
Magnolia Loebneri and *M. Kobus*

Trees of Limited Use for the Northeast

American Mountain-Ash
Black Tupelo
Amur Cork Tree
Goldenrain-Tree
Japanese Pagoda-Tree
Paper Birch
Silver Maple

Green Ash
Kentucky Coffee Tree
Black Walnut
Ohio Buckeye and Common
  Horse-chestnut
Weeping Willow (around lakes or ponds
  —not on city lots)

Evergreen Trees for the Northeast

Eastern Hemlock
Red Pine
Eastern White Pine
White Fir
Nikko Fir

Oriental Spruce
Colorado Blue Spruce
White Spruce
Eastern Arborvitae

Shade Trees for the Southeast

Live Oak
Southern Magnolia
Camphor Tree
Willow Oak
Red Maple
Flowering Dogwood
Sweetgum

American Holly
American Beech
Eastern Redbud
Water Oak
Mimosa or Silk-Tree
Winged Elm
American Elm

Less-Used Trees for the Southeast

Sugarberry
Pecan
Eastern Red Cedar
Goldenrain-Tree
Tuliptree
Canary Date
American Sycamore

Carolina Laurel-Cherry
White Oak
Scarlet Oak
Pin Oak
Laurel Oak
Cabbage Palmetto
Weeping Willow

Southern Florida

Oxhorn Bucida
Australian Pine
Coconut
Royal Poinciana
Benjamin Fig

Mango
Cajeput Tree
Cuban Royal Palm
African Tuliptree
West Indian Mahogany

Shade Trees for the Plains

Green Ash
Cottonwood
American Elm

Siberian Elm
Hackberry
Bur Oak

Trees of Limited Use for the Plains

Ailanthus
Boxelder
Northern Catalpa
Kentucky Coffee Tree
Chinese Elm
Sugarberry
Black Locust

Common Honey Locust
Silver Maple
Russian-Olive
American Sycamore
London Planetree
Eastern Black Walnut
Weeping Willow

Evergreens for the Plains

Eastern Red Cedar
Ponderosa Pine
Douglas-Fir
White Fir
Austrian Pine

Scots Pine
Colorado Blue Spruce
Black Spruce
Western White Spruce

Shade Trees for the Rockies

Ailanthus
Green Ash
White Ash
Boxelder
Northern Catalpa
American Elm
Common Hackberry
Thornless Honey Locust

Linden
Black Locust
Norway Maple
Red Mulberry
Poplars (Lance-Leaf, Narrow-Leaf,
   Lombardy, and Plains)
Russian-Olive
Tamarisk

Evergreens for the Rockies

Arizona Cypress
Eucalyptus
Rocky Mountain Juniper
Aleppo Pine
Austrian Pine

Canary Pine
Colorado Pinyon Pine
Ponderosa Pine
Colorado Spruce
Englemann Spruce

Shade Trees for California

California Live Oak
Camphor Tree
Red Iron-Bark
California Pepper Tree
Cape Chestnut
Ginkgo
California Black Walnut
Chinese Pistache
Panicled Goldenrain-Tree
White Mulberry
Canary Pine

Norway Maple
London Planetree
Sweetgum
Modesto Ash
Pin Oak
Southern Red Oak
Coulter Pine
Lawson Cypress
California Incense Cedar
Deodar Cedar
European White Birch

Shade Trees for the North Pacific Area

Common Hackberry
American Yellowwood
Sweetgum
Tuliptree
Northern Red Oak
Oregon White Oak

Pin Oak
Big-Leaf Maple
Norway Maple
American Elm
Pacific Madrone
California Sycamore

Conifers for the North Pacific Area

Atlas Cedar
Lawson Cypress
California Incense Cedar

Himalayan Pine
Common Douglas-Fir

Following are some less desirable trees and the reasons for so classifying them:

Acer negundo (boxelder)—a weedy tree attractive to insects.

Acer saccharinum (silver maple)—soft and brittle wood very subject to storm damage.

Aesculus octandra (yellow buckeye)—loses foliage early, unsightly.

Ailanthus altissima male (male tree-of-heaven)—flowers have offensive odor.

Catalpa bignonioides (southern catalpa)—objectionable flowers and seed pods, subject to caterpillar attack.

Catalpa speciosa (western catalpa)—objectionable seed pods, short-lived, weak wood.

Diospyros virginiana (persimmon)—objectionable fruits.

Fraxinus americana (white ash)—subjectto diseases difficult to control.

Gleditsia triacanthos (honey locust)—objectionable thorns and seed pods (thornless, seedless clones good).

Juglans nigra (black walnut)—objectionable nuts, roots secrete substance toxic to rhododendrons and other species.

Maclura pomifera (osage-orange)—objectionable fruits.

Morus species (all fruiting mulberries)—objectionable fruits.

Paulownia tomentosa (empress-tree)—unsightly seed pods, coarse leaves.

Populus species (poplar—most species)—weak wood, roots clog sewers.

Prunus serotina (black cherry)—objectionable fruits, subject to tent caterpillars.

Robina pseudoacacia (black locust)—subject to borers.

Selected Bibliography

Anonymous. 1965. *Trees for New Jersey streets.* New Jersey Federation of Shade Tree Commissions. Rutgers University, New Brunswick, N. J. 45 p.

———. 1974. *Trees for New Jersey streets.* Second Revision. New Jersey Federation of Shade Tree Commissions. Rutgers University, New Brunswick, N.J. 44 p.

———. 1966. *Trees for shade and beauty.* USDA Home and Garden Bul. 117. 8 p.

———. 1970. 'Home planner's guide to modern shade trees.' *Flower & Garden.* Feb. 1970. p. 36–39.

Ayres, S. L. *et al.* 1964 *Flowering trees for year-round color in southern California.* Cal. Arboretum Foundation, Arcadia, Cal. 34 p.

Barker, P. A. 1964. 'Tree selection and use.' *Am. Hort. Magazine.* Vol. 43 (No. 3). p. 151–57.

Baumgardt, J. P. 1975. 'Trees for special situations.' *Grounds Maintenance.* p. 12, 14, 20, 22–24, 38. Intertec Publ. Co. Overland, Kansas 66212.

Brarmann, E. F. Jr. 1960. 'Planting street trees in curb excavations in business sections.' *Proc. Thirty-sixth National Shade Tree Conference,* p. 102–12.

Caddick, J. W. 1955. *Care and selection of trees in Rhode Island.* Rhode Island Agr. Exp. Sta. Misc. Publ. 46. 10 p.

Carter, J. C. 1966. Illinois trees: *selection, planting, care.* Illinois Natural History Survey Circ. 51. 123 p.

Collins, W. H. 1972. 'Match tree selection to use area.' *Weeds, Trees, and Turf.* Vol. 11 (No. 1). p. 20–24.

———. 1975. 'New tree selections.' *Jour. Arboriculture.* Vol. 1 (No. 6). p. 113–15.

Crockett, J. U. 1972. *Trees.* Time-Life Books, New York. 160 p.

Curtis, R. W. and Donald Wyman. 1934. *Ornamental trees for New York State.* Cornell Agr. Exp. Sta. Ext. Bul. 287. 32 p.

Daniels, Roland. 1975. *Street trees.* College of Agriculture. Pennsylvania State Univer., University Park, Penna. 47 p.

Davis, W. B. 1963. *Landscape trees for the great central valley of California.* U. of Cal. Agr. Ext. Ser. AXT-93. 9 p.

de Vos, Francis. 1968. 'New trees for landscape and street planting.' *Proc. Forty-fourth International Shade Tree Conference.* p. 220–24.

Eickhorst, W. E. 1976. 'Trees with potential.' *American Nurseryman.* Nov. 1, 1976. p. 14, 110–12, 114, 115.

————. 1976. 'Making the right choice for a street tree planting.' *American Nurseryman.* Nov. 15, 1976. p. 70–79.

Everett, T. H. 1961. 'Guide to trees at the N.Y. Botanical Garden.' *The Garden Journal.* New York Botanical Garden. Vol. 2 (No. 2). p. 53–61.

————. 1969. *Living trees of the world.* Doubleday, New York. 315 p.

Felt, E. P. 1938. *Our shade trees.* O. Judd Publishing Co., New York. 187 p.

Flemer, William, III. 1965. *Shade and ornamental trees in color.* Grosset and Dunlap, New York. 114 p.

————. 1968. 'Weeping trees.' *Horticulture.* Nov. 1968. p. 24, 25, 46.

————. 1970. 'Narrow trees.' *Horticulture.* Apr. 1970. p. 25, 26, 46–48, 51.

————. 1972. 'To plant a tree in the city or suburb.' *Garden Journal.* New York Botanical Garden. Vol. 22 (No. 4). p. 117–18.

————. 1972. 'Trees for urban and suburban planting—part II. New flowering trees.' New York Botanical Garden. Vol. 22 (No. 3). p. 82–86.

————. 1972. 'Recent progress in tree breeding and production.' *Arborist's News.* Vol. 37. p. 38–44.

————. 1973. 'Growing trees in containers.' *Garden Journal,* New York Botanical Garden. Vol. 23 (No. 3). p. 82–88.

Gerling, Jake. 1951. 'Better shade trees and more practical use.' *Proc. Twenty-ninth National Shade Tree Conference.* p. 101–11.

————. 1957. *Progress towards better trees. American Nurseryman.* Vol. 105. p. 97–98.

Harris, R. W. 1969. 'Beautification and conservation potentials of the off-street planting concept.' *Proc. Forty-fifth International Shade Tree Conference.* p. 158–60.

Hill, H. M. 1969. 'Better street trees through research at Ohio State.' *Arborist's News.* Vol. 34 (No. 14). p. 1–6.

Hui-Lin Li. 1957. 'The origin and history of the cultivated planetrees.' *Morris Arboretum Bul.* March 1957. p. 3–9.

Jepson, W. L. 1959. *Trees, shrubs and flowers of the Redwood region.* Save-the-Redwoods League. U. of Cal. 16 p.

Kozel, P. C. and Marti Jansen. 1976. 'A new look at the red maple.' *American Nurseryman.* June 15, 1976. p. 7, 70, 71, 72, 83.

————. 1976. 'The exciting sassafras.' *American Nurseryman.* Oct. 15, 1976. p. 10, 111–13.

Martel, D. J. 1970. 'The use of trees in the unusual landscape design.' *Proc. Forty-fifth International Shade Tree Conference.* p. 235–41.

Mathias, Mildred E. and Elizabeth McClintock. 1963. *A checklist of woody ornamental plants of California.* Cal. Agr. Exp. Sta. Ext. Service Manual 32. 65 p.

Matkin, O. A. 1963. 'Planting street trees in California.' *Am. Hort. Magazine.* Oct. 1963. p. 219–20.

May, Curtis. 1972. *Shade trees for the home.* USDA, Handbook 425. Washington, D.C. 48 p.

————. 1973. *Selecting and growing shade trees.* USDA, Home and Garden Bulletin 205. Washington, D.C. 22 p.

McDaniel, J. C. 1970. 'Ornamental tree and shrub improvement.' *American Nurseryman.* Apr. 1, 1970. p. 107–8.

McKenzie, Malcolm. 1970. 'The role of shade trees in urban arboriculture.' *Trees.* Mar.-Apr. 1970. p. 10–11.

Mower, R. G., R. J. Scannel and A. S. Lieberman. 1965. *Trees for the home grounds.* Cornell Univ. Ext. Bul. 1096. 8 p.

———. 1973. 'Some observations on street tree plantings.' *Jour. Arboriculture.* Vol. 49 (No. 3). p. 49–55.

Mulford, F. L. 1927. *Trees for town and city streets.* USDA Farmer's Bul. 1208. 30 p.

———. 1938. *Planting the roadside.* USDA Farmer's Bul. 1481. 37 p.

———. 1938. *Trees for roadside planting.* USDA Farmer's Bul. 1482. 50 p.

Neil, J. W. 1959. 'Street trees—a systemic approach to their selection.' *Arborist's News.* Vol. 24 (No. 10). p. 73–80.

Nelson, P. K. 1957. 'The hundred finest trees and shrubs for temperate climates.' *Brooklyn Botanic Garden Record.* Plants and Gardens. 13 (No. 3). 80 p.

Norcross, A. C. 1968. 'Trees for late flowers and for fall fruits and leaf color.' *Horticulture.* April 1968. p. 46, 48, 49.

Olson, R. J. and J. P. Nagle. 1965. *Adaptation tests of trees and shrubs for the intermountain area of the Pacific northwest.* Wash. Agr. Exp. Sta. Circ. 450. 43 p.

Peck, K. O. 1969. 'Some ecological bases for selection of trees for suburban planting.' *Arborist's News.* Vol. 34 (No. 13). p. 1–5.

Perkins, H. O. and Carol Woodward. 1963. 'Flowring trees.' *Brooklyn Botanic Garden Record.* Plants and Gardens. Vol. 19 (No. 1). 81 p.

Preston, R. J. 1961. *North American trees.* Iowa State University Press, Ames, Iowa. 395 p.

Santamour, F. S., Jr. 1972. 'Developing and using superior shade trees.' *Arborist's News.* Vol. 37 (No. 4). p. 93a–96a.

———. 1975. 'Better trees and shrubs.' *American Nurseryman.* Sept. 1, 1975. p. 60–63.

———. 1973. 'Genes and plant improvement.' *Arnoldia.* Vol. 33 (No. 2). p. 127–34.

Scanlon, E. H. 1955. 'Selection and use of trees to minimize public area conflicts.' *Proc. Thirty-first National Shade Tree Conference.* p. 183–96.

———. 1965. 'Proper selection of trees for municipal streets.' *Trees.* Nov.-Dec. 1965. p. 6–10.

Scott, H. C. 1965. 'Trees for southern landscapes.' *American Nurseryman.* Oct. 15, 1965. p. 58, 60, 62, 66.

Skinner, H. T. 1964. 'European beech.' *Trees.* Nov.-Dec. p. 14–15.

Stefferud, Alfred. 1969. *Trees: Yearbook of Agriculture* 1949. Supt. of Documents. Washington, D.C. 944 p.

Stone, G. E. 1916. 'Shade trees, characteristics, adaptation, diseases, and care.' *Massachusetts Agr. Exp. Sta. Bul.* 170. p. 123–264.

Tattar, T. A., A. L. Shigo, and T. Chase. 1972. 'Relationship between the degree of resistance to a pulsed current and wood in progressive stages of discoloration and decay in living trees.' *Canadian Jour. Forest Research.* Vol. 2. p. 236–43.

Ticknor, R. L. 1976. 'Results of landscape tree testing.' *American Nurseryman.* Jan. 15, 1976. p. 10, 11, 61–65, 68.

Viehmeyer, Glenn. 1966. 'Deciduous trees for the Plains.' *Horticulture.* Mar. 1966. p. 48–50.

Walter, Richard. 1964. 'Street trees.' *Horticulture.* July 1964. p. 18–20.

Whitehouse, W. E., J. L. Creech, and G. A. Seaton. 1963. 'A new flowering shade tree—the "Bradford" pear.' 1963. *Am. Hort. Magazine.* Vol. 42 (No. 3). p. 151–57.

Woodward, K. W. 1922. *Shade trees in New Hampshire.* New Hampshire Agr. Ext. Service Circ. 53. 16 p.

Wyman, Donald. 1938. *Narrow upright trees in the Arnold Arboretum.* Harvard Univ. Arnold Arboretum Bul. of Popular Information. 6 (No. 11).

———. 1952. 'Forty-five of the best trees for Massachusetts gardens.' *Arnoldia.* Vol. 12 (No. 1). p. 1–20.

———. 1956. 'Eighty trees for the small place.' *Arnoldia.* Vol. 16 (No. 3). p. 9–15.

———. 1956. 'New and rare ornamental and woody plants recently distributed by the Arnold Arboretum.' *Arnoldia.* Vol. 16 (Nos. 7–9). p. 33–51.

———. 1961. 'Majestic beech requires space to display beauty.' *American Nurseryman.* Jan. 1961. p. 16, 17, 112, 113.

———. 1963. 'Trial plot for street trees.' *Arnoldia.* Vol. 23 (No. 1). p. 1–7.

———. 1964. 'Some excellent flowering trees.' *American Nurseryman.* Dec. 1, 1964. p. 12, 13, 37, 42.

———. 1965. *Trees for American gardens.* Rev. and enlarged ed. Macmillan, New York. 502 p.

———. 1968. 'The best fastigiate trees.' *American Nurseryman.* Dec. 1, 1968. p. 10, 11, 90.

II

Specific Abnormalities of Trees

9
Diagnosing Tree Troubles

During the last thirty-five years the author has been asked by commercial arborists, city park departments, landscape architects, public utility companies, and private home owners to diagnose the cause of decline or death of shade and ornamental trees. At the request of a public utility company, during the summer of 1956, for example, he personally examined and then diagnosed the cause of many abnormalities among more than 300 trees in New York City. Since then he has examined a thousand more trees in New York, New Jersey, and Long Island, New York.

As a result of this experience, the author feels he is in a position to help others in diagnosing tree ailments. After all, successful treatment of any abnormality of trees, as of human beings, depends primarily on correct diagnosis. Some troubles occur so frequently on certain trees and have such specific symptoms that they are readily diagnosed by the competent tree man; others are so complex than even the most expert arborist cannot fathom them.

A reliable arborist will not hesitate to admit his inability to diagnose some abnormalities nor will he hesitate to recruit the aid of a specialist to help in the diagnosis, much as medical doctors often consult specialists in difficult cases. He will try corrective treatments of unknown value only as a last resort—after all attempts at a correct diagnosis have failed.

Qualifications of a Tree Diagnostician

The most important qualification of a good diagnostician is plain ordinary common sense; some refer to it as knack, intutition, or good judgment. He must also have a thorough understanding of a so-called normal tree, including the species he is examining. Not only is it necessary that he knew the name of the tree, but he must know its characteristics as to winter-hardiness, tolerance to dry and wet soils, and reactions to other environmental factors.

The good diagnostician will not be afraid to ask questions. Some tree owners and park officials, for some mysterious reason, withhold information essential for a proper diagnosis. The diagnostician must know the history of the tree, such as when and how it was planted. He must also have some information on the past climatic history. This is acquired either from his own records or by asking the owner or person in charge of the tree about it. He must have information regarding drought periods, severity of previous winters, and prevalence of hurricanes or other unusual weather.

The tree diagnostician must also have a thorough understanding of the relation between the soil and the tree. Is the soil properly drained; is it well-aerated; does it hold enough moisture; is it fertile? Soil fertility can be determined only by a complete soil test. The expert must also have a working knowledge of entomology and plant pathology. Many of these phases are treated in some detail in various parts of this book. But additional reading and certainly extensive field experience are necessary before one can really qualify as an expert diagnostician.*

Sometimes it is unwise to become so absorbed in detailed symptoms that important gross symptoms are completely overlooked. It is here that common sense is important.

Correct Diagnosis Important

An incorrect diagnosis at the start will quite naturally lead to improper treatment. For example, a few years ago the author was called to explain the branch dieback in several large oaks growing on an estate in Westchester County, New York. The oaks had been under the care of a professional arborist who had diagnosed the problem as due to lack of food. The trees were fed for several years, but branches continued to die back until the top of one of the trees was nearly bare.

A little digging at the base of the trees and probing into the bark just below the soil line showed that the shoestring root rot fungus (p. 292) had

* Members of the American Society of Consulting Arborists are among the most highly qualified to diagnose tree problems and advise on any phase of tree care. Executive Secretary of the organization is Dr. Spencer Davis, 12 Lakeview Ave., Milltown, New Jersey 08850.

invaded and killed virtually all of the important tissues beneath the bark. In all probability, this fungus had been present in the roots for years and was the prime cause of the dying back of the top. All the plant food in the world applied to trees whose roots were diseased would never have done any good.

Following is another example of how an improper diagnosis can lead to an incorrect conclusion. During the summer of 1957, the author was asked by a public utility company to diagnose the cause of death of several dozen trees growing along streets of a New Jersey community.

One, a 16-inch DBH Norway maple, was said by a plant pathologist who examined the tree earlier to have been killed by escaping natural gas from leaking mains. The only basis for his diagnosis was that a gas leak had been repaired in the general vicinity. The author removed the soil around the base of the tree and found that someone had completely girdled the tree belowground at least a year or so before. The uneven cuts made by an instrument were still plainly visible! Here was a case, then, where a little digging by the first 'expert' might have resulted in an entirely different diagnosis.

In another case, the author was asked to determine the cause of death of a 150-year-old white oak (*Quercus alba*) on a private property in Glencoe, Illinois. The tree's owner planned to sue the local utility for $6000 on the basis of a statement by a professional arborist that the tree had died as a result of a natural gas leak about 45 feet away.

The leaves on the tree were wilted and brown when the author examined them in late October 1960. This indicated that the tree had been at least partially alive earlier that growing season. Many trees, including another white oak of approximately the same age located closer to the leak, appeared to be perfectly healthy.

A study of the terrain and of the past history of the tree and the property elicited the following information:

A very expensive and beautiful house had been built about 7 years earlier, the front of which was within 25 feet of the tree. The grade had been changed. In the area nearest the house at least 2 feet of soil had been placed over the original soil level.

In addition to raising the soil level, a circular driveway of macadam had been constructed around the tree. This paved area covered 67 per cent of the feeding root area of the tree.

One of the lower branches, about 4 inches in diameter, was removed from the tree and cut into one-foot lengths for more detailed study.

Examination of the annual rings in the author's laboratory later revealed that the tree had begun to do poorly about 6 years earlier or about one year after the house and the driveway had been constructed. This is clearly indicated in the enlarged photograph of a cross-section of the branch (Fig. 9-1A and 9-1B). The rate of growth of a tree can be

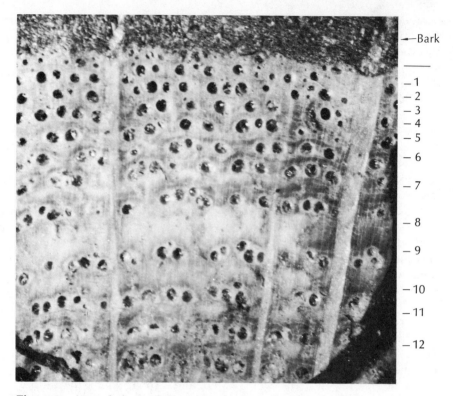

Bark

—1
—2
—3
—4
—5
—6
—7
—8
—9
—10
—11
—12

Fig. 9-1A. Annual rings of white oak. Note rings made in the last 6 years are closer to each other than those made 7 to 12 years earlier.

measured by the spacing between the large-holed cells which forms in the spring and are known as spring wood. The wider the space between each row of spring wood cells, the more vigorous the tree's growth.

The tree's demise was actually caused by several factors, including a change in grade (see p. 199), construction of the driveway around the tree, and the use of poor soil fill.

When faced with the facts and observations gathered by the author, lawyers representing the owner of the tree refrained from damage claims against the utility supplying the natural gas.

One of the more difficult diagnoses involves troubles caused by nutrient deficiencies. One reason is that fewer studies have been made on shade and ornamental trees than on fruit trees and vegetables.

Generally speaking, foliage deficiencies of the various elements become apparent either at the base or at the tip of the current season's growth. A deficiency of nitrogen, phosphorus, potassium, magnesium, and zinc is apparent on the older leaves. A deficiency of iron, man-

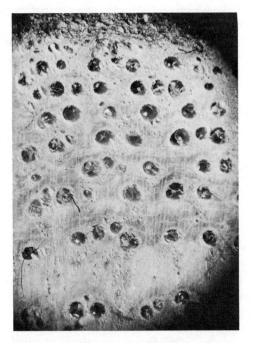

Fig. 9-1B. A larger magnification of Fig. 9-1A showing annual rings of the 8 years prior to the tree's demise.

ganese, sulfur, calcium, boron, and copper is first apparent on the young leaves.*

A machine called the spectrograph enables the scientist to determine quickly whether a plant is suffering from a nutrient deficiency or from an overdose of some nutrient. The procedure is to collect, in July or August, some leaves from a tree suspected of having a nutritional disorder, dry them, and then grind them to a fine powder and reduce them to ashes at a temperature of 500-600°F. The ash is then dissolved and the solution placed on an electrode and burned with a high-voltage electric spark or arc. Each of the elements present will emit its own characteristic light, which is passed through a prism and recorded on a photographic plate as a series of dark lines or bands. These bands indicate the amounts of the various elements present. The spectrograph can determine how much calcium, magnesium, phosphorus, manganese, copper, boron, iron, and zinc are in leaves. Potassium is determined with a so-called flame photometer and nitrogen by chemical methods.

* Space limitations prevent a detailed discussion of nutrient deficiencies. More details can be obtained from the book *Hunger Signs in Crops,* 3rd ed., edited by H. B. Sprague, published by David McKay Co., New York, New York (1964).

Several state colleges of agriculture now provide this type of leaf analysis service for professional nurserymen and arborists. In time, it is hoped that all such colleges will have facilities for making leaf analyses to aid tree men and owners of trees in calculating the fertilizer needs of plants and diagnosing ailments due to nutrient deficiencies.

Procedure in Diagnosing

Following are the standard procedures used by specialists in diagnosing tree troubles. They will vary somewhat with the individual. Some diagnosticians take more stock in symptoms aboveground than belowground. Others, like the author, feel that the most serious tree troubles and those most difficult to diagnose are more frequently associated with belowground symptoms and factors. More about this later.

Before examining any part of an ailing tree, one should study the general surroundings. Are other nearby trees healthy? Have any special treatments been given prior to the appearance of the abnormal condition? Is the tree under diagnosis so situated that a leaf bonfire beneath it may have played a part in its decline? After these and related questions have been answered, one should then proceed with the direct examination of the tree.

Examination of Leaves. The leaves constitute the best starting point because they are most accessible and are first to show outwardly the effects of any abnormal condition. Here, also, a complete understanding of a normal leaf is essential, because the size and the color of normal leaves vary greatly among the different tree species and even among trees of the same species.

Insect injuries to leaves are rather easily diagnosed, either by the presence of the pest or by the effect of its feeding. The leaves may be partly or completely chewed, or they may be yellowed as a result of sucking of the leaf sap, blotched from feeding between the leaf surfaces, or deformed from feeding and irritation.

Leaf injuries produced by parasitic fungi are not diagnosed so readily, however, because the causal organisms are usually not visible to the unaided eye. In some instances, tiny, black pin-point fungus bodies in the dead areas, visible without a hand lens, are indicative of the causal nature. Lesions resulting from fungus attack are more or less regular in outline with varying shades of color along the outer edges. They may range in size from tiny dots to spots more than half an inch in diameter. When several spots coalesce, the leaves may wilt and die.

Atmospheric conditions preceding the appearance of spots on leaves can often be used to advantage in determining the cause of the injury. For example, when leaf spots appear after a week or 10 days of continuous rains and cloudy weather, one can safely assume that some parasitic organism is responsible, because such conditions are favorable for its spread. When leaves are spotted or scorched following a week or more of extremely dry, hot weather, lack of water, as discussed under Leaf Scorch (p. 233), may be responsible. Low temperatures in late spring may also result in much injury to the tender leaves (p. 209).

Changes in leaf structure, appearance, or function may result from such widely different causes as fume injury, deficient or excessive moisture, lack of available food, poor soil aeration, root injuries, or diseases. All but the last two of these can be disregarded if nearby trees of the same species as the one under study are perfectly healthy.

Examination of Trunk and Branches. A careful inspection of the branches and trunk should follow the leaf examination. Sunken areas in the bark indicate injury to tissues beneath. They may have been produced by fungus or bacterial infection or by nonparasitic agents, such as low and high temperatures. The presence of fungus bodies in such areas does not necessarily indicate that the fungus is the primary cause. Only a person with considerable mycological training can distinguish the pathogenic from the nonparasitic species. The diseased wood beneath the bark, if it is the direct result of fungus attack, shows a gradual change in color from diseased to healthy tissue. It is usually dark brown in the earlier, more severely infected portions, then changes to a deep green or a light brown, and finally to a lighter shade of either in the more recently affected parts. On the other hand, injuries resulting from low or high temperatures are usually well defined, an abrupt line of demarcation appearing between affected and unaffected tissues.

The bark of the trunk and branches should also be examined for small holes, sawdust frass, and scars or ridges. These indicate borer infestations in the inner bark, sapwood, or heartwood. As a rule, most borers become established in trees of poor vigor. Because of this, it is necessary to investigate the cause of the weakened condition rather than to assume that the borers are primarily responsible. Branches and smaller twigs should always be examined for infestations of scale insects. Although most scales are readily visible, a few so nearly resemble the color of the bark that they are sometimes overlooked.

Branches or twigs with no leaves or with wilted ones should be examined for discoloration of the sapwood, the usual symptom of wilt-producing fungi. The service of a mycologist is needed for determining the species of fungus involved, because positive identification can be made only by laboratory isolations from the discolored tissue.

The appearance of suckers or watersprouts along the trunk and main branches may indicate a sudden change in environmental conditions, structural injuries, disease, or excessive, incorrect, and ill-timed pruning.

Although galls or overgrowths occasionally present on the main trunk may be caused by parasites and by disturbances in the water relations between the soil and the tree, many are produced by factors not clearly understood by scientists.

The general vigor of a tree usually can be ascertained from the color in the bark fissures and the rapidity of callus formation over wounds. In vigorously growing trees, the fissures are much lighter in color than the bark surface. A rapidly developing callus roll over the wound also indicates good vigor.

Examination of Roots. Because of their inaccessibility, roots are rarely inspected by many arborists. In diagnosing a general disorder in a tree, however, the possibility of root injury or disease must be carefully considered. More than half of the abnormalities in the hundreds of street and shade trees examined by the author during the last 35 years were found to be caused by injuries to or diseases of the root systems.

The sudden death of a tree usually results from the destruction of nearly all the roots or from the death of the tissues at the trunk base near the soil line. The factors most commonly involved in such cases are infection by fungi such as the shoestring fungus (p. 292), the wilt fungus (p. 297), and the *Ganoderma* fungus (p. 430), winter injury, rodent damage, lightning strikes, and toxic chemicals like gasoline, oil, salt, and weed killers. Trees that become progressively weaker over a period of years may be affected by girdling roots, decay following sidewalk and curb installations or road improvement, poor soil type, poor drainage, lack of food, changes in grade, and excessively deep planting from the start.

Nemas, more commonly referred to as nematodes, are responsible for the decline of many shade trees. The root-knot nema *Meloidogyne incognita* produces small swellings or knots on the roots of susceptible trees. But such swellings or knots are not always caused by nemas; those found on the roots of *Alnus, Casuarina,* and *Elaeagnus* are natural outgrowths.

Diagnostic Tools

Certain implements are essential in diagnosing tree troubles (Fig. 9-2). Most important of these is a shovel or small spade for removal of soil around the base of the trunk to facilitate detection of girdling roots, rodent damage, winter injury, and infection by the shoestring fungus or other parasitic fungi. In addition, it is used for digging soil in the vicinity of the smaller roots to be examined for the presence of decay. A soil auger is essential for collecting representative samples of soil for analytical tests and for determining the nature of the subsoil and the drainage. Pruning shears are necessary for cutting twigs and small branches to determine the presence of discoloration in the sapwood caused by wilt fungi and other injuries in the inner bark, cambium, and wood. A small saw is helpful where branches larger than can be handled with pruning shears must be cut. The author finds a sectional pole pruner, consisting of four 4-foot lengths, is excellent for cutting branch

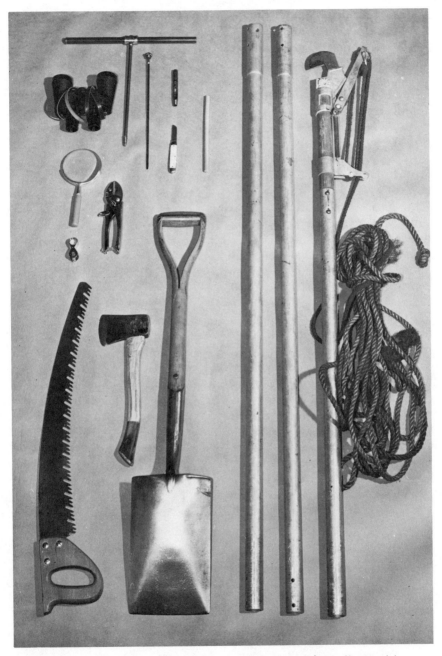

Fig. 9-2. Some of the implements used by a tree disease diagnostician.

samples. This pruner is easily assembled and then disassembled and stored in the automobile luggage compartment.

A most important tool is a chisel or a curved gouge with a heavy handle for tapping the bark to locate dead areas and for making incisions into the bark and sapwood. Bark and sapwood specimens needed for further study are also collected with this instrument with the aid of strokes from a 2- or 3-pound composition mallet. A sharp instrument such as an ice pick is also useful to help determine the extent of soft, decayed wood.

An increment borer facilitates sampling for study of the annual growth rate of the tree, for determining the extent of heartwood decay, and for checking on the presence of vascular infections of fungi like *Verticillium.** One must be reasonably careful with this instrument on living trees, for it is known that discoloration and decay frequently develop around holes made by it. An increment hammer is also available for collecting more shallow samples of the bark and wood.

A hand lens is valuable for detecting the presence of red spider mites and tiny fungus bodies in leaf lesions.

Screw-top vials should be available for collecting insects to be submitted to a professional entomologist for identification. Glassine bags for holding leaf specimens and Kraft paper bags or other containers for holding bark and sapwood specimens, or soil samples, should also constitute part of the diagnostician's working kit.

The Port-A-Lab (Fig. 9-3) is a compact unit containing most of the equipment needed for diagnosing tree problems. In addition to the various materials shown, a sharp digging spade, a pole pruner, and a soil auger would also be useful. Port-A-Lab is available from the Maier Tree Care Service Center, 2419 Easton Blvd., Des Moines, Iowa 50317.

A high-powered microscope for determining the presence of a foreign body in the plant tissues is helpful to persons familiar with its use and capable of recognizing what it reveals.

Following is a questionnaire the author sends to tree owners who desire a tree diagnosis by mail:

Name and Address of Sender

GENERAL QUESTIONS
1. Kind, age, and size of tree?
2. Where is the tree situated? Along street, on lawn, in a park? Near body of water, salt or fresh? On level ground or on a slope?

---

* The Shigometer, mentioned under cavity treatments on page 109, is also helpful in detecting the presence of the Verticillium wilt disease and cold temperature injury and measuring the vigor of a tree.

Fig. 9-3. The Port-A-Lab developed by Gary H. Maier, contains the following materials and instruments: 1. Dissecting microscope (Bausch & Lomb - 15x). This latches in place and folds into the bottom of the instrument case. 2. Microscope light with 6 volt battery and on/off switch. 3. Dissecting block (hardwood). 4. Magnifying glass (Bausch & Lomb - 5 x). 5. Soluble salt testing meter, with test jar, indicator submerging probe, and solution thermometer. 6. Six insect-specimen collection vials. 7. Four soil-sample collection jars. 8. Soil pH indicator. 9. 100' lawn measuring tape. 10. Tree trunk diameter measuring tape. 11. Binoculars (7×35×). 12. Soil moisture tester and tester probe. 13. Soil thermometer. 14. High quality pruning shears. 15. Dissecting knife with two replacement blades. 16. Reference book (*Diseases and Pests of Ornamental Plants* by P. P. Pirone). 17. Soil core extractor. 18. Styrofoam block with probing instruments. 19. Business calling card holder. 10. Drawer (self-locking when instrument case is closed). Contains complete instructions for operation of all instruments, instrument warranties, and suggested diagnostic procedures.

3. How long has the tree exhibited the trouble? If the trouble appeared suddenly, describe the weather conditions occurring just previously. Describe any other unusual conditions.

4. Is the trouble visible all over the tree, on only one side, in the lower or upper branches?

5. Do any other trees of the same species in the near vicinity show the same injury? Do other species show it?

6. How much annual growth have the twigs made during the past 3 years?

7. Has the grade around the tree been raised or lowered during the past 7 years? If so, explain amount of change and describe the prcedure and type of fill used.

8. Has any construction work been done nearby within the past 3 years— house, road, driveway, curbstone, garage, or ditches for laying water or sewer pipes?

9. What work has been done on this tree recently? Has it been pruned within the past 2 years? If so, how much? Fertilizer treatments—when, what, and how much?

10. If a young tree, how long since it was planted in present location? How deeply was it planted? (Use a spade to determine depth of roots.) What treatments were given during the first year after transplanting?

QUESTIONS ABOUT THE SOIL

Answers to these are extremely helpful, particularly if the tree has been dying back slowly over a period of years.

1. What kind of soil surrounds the tree? Sandy, loamy, or clayey? What soil cover—asphalt, cement, crushed rock, cinders, sand, grass, mulch, weeds, or no cover? How much open area is there?

2. What is the depth to subsoil, to rock or shale, to hardpan?

3. What is the pH reaction of the soil?

4. Does water stand on the soil after a heavy rain?

QUESTIONS ABOUT THE ROOTS

These are the most difficult to answer, since considerable digging may be required. The answers are most important, however, especially when a general disorder is involved.

1. Is a girdling root present? Sometimes such roots are well below ground and you may have to dig a foot or so before you can be sure.

2. Are the larger roots normal in color? Do they have rotted bark or discolored wood? If so, submit specimens.

3. What is the appearance of the finer roots? Are root hairs abundant and white? (Dig down a foot or so beneath the outer spread of the branches.)

QUESTIONS ABOUT THE TRUNK

1. Are there any long, narrow open cracks present? If so, in which direction do they face?

2. Are cavities present? If so, describe size of opening, condition of interior if unfilled. If filled, give details.

3. Is there any bark bleeding? If so, how extensive? (Submit specimens including bark and sapwood.)
4. Are there any swollen areas? Describe.
5. Is there a swollen area completely around the trunk? If so, cut into the swelling with a chisel to determine the possible presence of some foreign object such as a wire.
6. Are there any fungi (mushrooms or bracket-type) growing out of the bark? (If so, include a few specimens.)
7. Are there cankers (dead sunken areas in the bark)? Submit specimens.
8. Are there any borer holes or other evidences of insect work?
9. Is the bark at or just below the soil line healthy? (Use a curved chisel to determine this.)
10. If wood beneath this bark is discolored, describe color and extent. Submit several pieces of bark and wood.

QUESTIONS ABOUT THE BRANCHES
1. Is the bark cracked for some distance? On what side of the branches?
2. Are there any cankers in the branch?
3. Is there any discoloration in the branches or twigs which have wilted leaves or which are leafless?

SPECIFIC POSSIBILITIES
1. Did the trouble appear
    a. Immediately after a thunderstorm?
    b. After chemicals were injected into the trunk?
    c. After sprays were applied? (Name the ingredients used and when applied.)
    d. After weed killers were applied in the vicinity?
    e. After treating a nearby cellar for termite control?
    f. After any other chemical treatment?

SHIPPING THE SPECIMENS
By the time you've answered the questions that pertain specifically to your particular case, you are ready to collect and ship us specimens.
Woody specimens without leaves should be wrapped in newspaper and packed in a pasteboard box. Twigs and small branches should be cut to approximately one foot in length.
Include with diseased branches or twigs a portion of the adjacent healthy parts. (When submitting branches without leaves be sure to tell us the name of the tree.)
Leaves should be wrapped dry, preferably individually, in ordinary wax paper, then in wrapping paper or in a pasteboard box. Never wrap leaves in wet paper towelling, wet cotton or plastic sheets because many of the specimens will be decayed or covered with all kinds of organisms by the time they reach us.
Trunk specimens should include a portion of the dead bark and sapwood. If possible, adjacent healthy tissue also should be included on the same specimens. Bark and sapwood specimens should be about 2 inches long and 1 inch wide and separately packed in wax paper.

Label all specimens and have this label correspond with the description in your letter.

Return questionnaire and specimens to P. P. Pirone, New York Botanical Garden, Bronx, New York 10458.

The following chapters treat problems that are rather readily diagnosed by the use of most of the diagnostic tools described above.

Selected Bibliography

Anonymous. 1973. *A tree hurts, too.* U.S. Dept. Agr. Forest Service. NE-INF. 16-73. Supt. Documents, Washington, D.C. 28 p.

————. 1973. 'Recognizing, treating tree and shrub cankers.' *Grounds Maintenance.* Vol. 8, (No. 11). p. 32–33. Intertec Publ. Corp., Overland Park, Kansas 66212.

————. 1974. *Your tree's trouble may be you.* U.S. Dept. Agr. Forest Service. Agr. Information Bulletin No. 372. Supt. Documents, Washington, D.C. 21 p.

Beilmann, A. P. 1935. 'The use of instruments in tree diagnosis.' *Proc. Eleventh National Shade Tree Conference.* p. 18–27.

————. 'Possible use of instruments in tree diagnosis.' *Trees.* May-June 1941. p. 14, 16.

Carter, J. C. 1959. 'Tools useful in diagnosing tree troubles.' *Arborist's News.* Vol. 24 (No. 12). p. 89–92.

Chadwick, L. C. 1943. 'Diagnosis of nutritional requirements of ornamental plants.' *Proc. Nineteenth National Shade Tree Conference.* p. 5–19.

Davis, S. H. 1974. 'How accurate are you in diagnosing your tree problems?' *Arborist's News.* Vol. 39 (No. 5). p. 53–60.

Dodge, A. W. 1938. 'Diagnosing shade tree troubles.' *Proc. Fourteenth National Shade Tree Conference.* p. 118–26.

Flemer III, W. 1972. 'Recent Progress in Tree Breeding and Production.' *Arborist's News.* Vol. 37 (No. 1). Urbana, Ill. 38a–44a.

Hacskaylo, John, R. F. Finn and J. P. Vimmerstedt. 1969. *Deficiency symptoms of some forest trees.* Ohio Agr. Res. and Development Center, Research Bull. 1015. 68 p.

Hamilton, C. C. 1946. 'Diagnosis of insect injury.' *Trees Magazine.* May-June 1946. p. 18.

Hanson, J. B. and William Lautz. 1971. 'Photography as an aid in estimating *Annosus* root rot-caused tree mortality.' *Plant Disease Reptr.* Vol. 55 (No. 9). p. 761–63.

Hepting, G. H., E. E. Roth and Bailey Sleeth. 1949. 'Discolorations and decay from increment borings.' *Jour. Forestry.* Vol. 47 (No. 5). p. 366–70.

Hough, A. F. 1935. 'A method of preparing wood sections for accurate age counts.' *Jour. Forestry.* Vol. 33 (No. 7). p. 698–99.

Houston, D. R. 1972. *The use of large-scale aerial color photography for assessing forest tree diseases.* U.S. Dept. Agr. Forest Service Research Paper. NE-230. 7 p.

————. 1974. 'Diebacks and declines: Diseases initiated by stress, including defoliation.' *Arborist's News.* Vol. 39 (No. 5). p. 73–78.

Howe, Hollis. 1945. 'Relation of complete facts to diagnosis.' *Trees.* Aug. 1945. p. 15, 18.

Hubert, E. E. 1924. 'The diagnosis of decay in wood.' *Jour. Agr. Res.* Vol. 29 (No. 11). Dec. 1924. p. 523–67.

Long, W. H. 1931. 'Data to be noted in studying heart rots of living trees.' *Phytopathology.* Vol. 31 (No. 12). p. 1199–1200.

Mitchell, J. H. 1954. 'Practical shade tree maintenance.' *Proc. Thirtieth National Shade Tree Conference.* p. 319–23.

Mower, R. G. 1973. 'Some observations on street tree plantings.' *Proc. Forty-ninth International Shade Tree Conference.* Vol. 49: 49–55.

Neely, Dan. 1972. 'Hints on diagnosis of tree problems.' *Proc. Forty-eighth International Shade Tree Conference.* p. 33–37.

Neely, Dan, ed. 1972. 'X-ray diagnosis of trees.' *Arborist's News.* Vol. 37 (No. 5). p. 56–57.

Pirone, P. P. 1947. 'How to get help in diagnosing tree troubles.' *The Shade Tree.* New Jersey Federation of Shade Tree Commissions. Jan. 1947.

Pirone, P. P. and R. S. Halliwell. 1966. 'How to diagnose tree diseases.' *Weeds, Trees, and Turf.* Vol 5 (No. 5). p. 14–17, 28.

Rusden, P. L. 1965. 'How to diagnose shade tree root diseases.' *Weeds, Trees, and Turf.* Feb. 1965. p. 12–14, 32.

Schoeneweiss, D. F. 1971. 'Diagnosis of physiological disorders in woody ornamentals.' *Proc. Forty-seventh International Shade Tree Conference.* p. 33a–38a.

————. 1972. 'Diagnosis of physiological disorders in woody ornamentals.' *Arborist's News.* Vol. 37 (No. 1). p. 1–5.

Shaw, C. G. and M. R. Harris. 1960. 'Key to the fruiting bodies of fungi commonly associated with decay.' *Washington State Agr. Ext. Ser. Bul.* 540. p. 33–35.

Shigo, A. L. 1969. 'The death and decay of trees.' *Natural History Magazine.* Vol. 78 (63). p. 42–47.

Shigo, A. L. and E. vH. Larson. 1969. *A photo guide to the patterns of discoloration and decay in living northern hardwood trees.* U.S. Dept. Agr. Forest Research Paper NE-127. 100 p.

Shigo, A. L. and Paul Berry. 1975. 'A new tool for detecting decay associated with *Fomes annosus* in *Pinus resinosa.*' *Plant Disease Reptr.* Vol. 59. (No. 9). 739–42.

Staples. M. W. 1973. 'Diagnosing tree ailments.' *Flower and Garden.* July 1973. p. 40–41.

Streets, R. B. Sr. 1969. *The diagnosis of plant diseases.* Univ. of Arizona Agr. Exp. Sta. Extension Service. Tucson, Arizona. Aug. 1969. 230 p.

Tattar, T. A. 1976. 'Use of electrical resistance to detect *Verticillium* wilt in Norway and sugar maple.' *Proc. American Phytopathological Soc.* Vol. 3. p. 266–67.

Tattar, T. A. and R. O. Blanchard. 1977. 'Electrical techniques for disease diagnosis.' *Jour. Arboriculture.* Vol. 3 (No. 2). p. 21–24.

Tilford, P. E. 1945. 'Diagnosing shade tree troubles.' *Proc. Twenty-first National Shade Tree Conference.* p. 17–25.

Vaughn-Eames, H. 1932. 'The increment borer in diagnosis.' *Proc. Eighth National Shade Tree Conference.* p. 48–50.

Welch, D. S. 1941. 'The diagnosis of shade tree troubles.' *Proc. Seventeenth National Shade Tree Conference.* p. 45–50.

White, R. P. 1931. 'Four unusual symptomatic pictures and their diagnosis.' *Proc. Seventh National Shade Tree Conference.* p. 82–86.

Worley, C. L., H. R. Lesselbaum, and T. M. Mathews. 1941. 'Deficiency symptoms for the major elements in seedlings of three broad-leaved trees.' *Jour. Tenn. Acad. Science.* Vol. 6. p. 239–47.

10

Nonparasitic Injuries

Many of the causes of poor growth and even death of trees are non-parasitic agents. Following are some of the most common ones.

Damage Caused by Grade Changes around Trees

The addition or removal of soil may seriously disturb the delicate relationship between roots and soil and thus result in considerable damage or death of the tree. Yet such procedures may be necessary when new homes and highways are built, lawns or terraces graded, or street improvements made.

The author is often asked to diagnose the cause of the gradual weakening and even the death of beautiful oaks, maples, or beeches on properties in newly developed residential sections. He first examines the trunk base to see whether it flares out. Where no fill has been applied, the trunk is wider at the soil line than it is a foot or so above. If the trunk has no flare at its base and it enters the ground in a straight line, then a fill has probably been applied. Of course some digging with a good spade will then reveal the depth of the fill.

Other visible symptoms are small yellow leaves, the presence of numerous suckers along the main trunk and branches, many dead twigs, and, in some instances, large dead branches. When the owner is questioned as to what precautions were taken to minimize the shock of placing the roots in a new environment, the usual answer is that none was thought necessary. The building contractor dug the subsoil from the cellar location and spread it promiscuously around the trees. He placed a foot of good topsoil over this, and his job was done!

Persons who plan to build a new house, or who have just moved into a new house surrounded by trees, or who plan construction changes near large trees, would be well advised to pay particular attention to the discussion that follows.*

Why Trees Suffer from Soil Fills. Before methods of reinvigorating trees suffering from existing grade changes and ways of preventing injury from fills and removals of soil are considered, it is well to stress again some of the basic principles involved. Air (primarily oxygen) and water are essential for normal functioning of roots. Soil microorganisms, necessary to break down organic matter that serves as food for the roots, also need air. In addition, when air is lacking, certain gases and chemicals increase and become toxic to roots. Toxins produced by anaerobic bacteria may be more harmful than the damage resulting from asphyxiation due to lack of oxygen. The tree roots have become established within a certain area in the soil where the essential materials are present. The moment a blanket of soil is placed over the existing soil level, a marked disturbance occurs in the balance between the roots and these essential materials. As a result, the roots die, and the symptoms soon become visible in the aboveground parts. These symptoms may appear within a month, or they may not appear for several years.

The piling around trees of large heaps of sand or soil to be used for road and building construction may also have a detrimental effect (Fig. 10-1).

Factors Governing Extent of Injury from Fills. The extent of injury from fills varies with the species, age, and condition of the tree; the depth and type of fill; drainage; and several other minor factors. Sugar maple, beech, dogwood, oak, tuliptree, pines, and spruces are most severely injured; birch, hickory, and hemlock suffer less; and elm, poplar, willow, planetree, pin oak, and locust are least affected. Trees in weak vegetative condition at the time the fill is made are more severely injured than trees in good vigor.

Obviously the deeper the fill, the more marked is the disturbance to the roots, and consequently the more serious are the effects. Clay soil fills cause most injury, because the fineness of the soil shuts out air and water most completely. The application of only an inch or two of clay soil may cause severe injury. Gravelly fills cause least trouble, because both air and water permeate them more readily. As a rule, the application of a layer several inches deep of gravelly soil, or even of the same kind of soil

* Additional information is presented in Home and Garden Bulletin 104, *Protecting Shade Trees During Home Construction,* and Agriculture Information Bulletin 285, *Protecting Trees Against Damage From Construction Work,* both available for a small fee from Superintendent of Documents, U.S. Government Printing Office, Washington, D.C. 20402.

Fig. 10-1. Piling soil over the root zone of trees can be very harmful.

in which the tree has been growing, will do no harm. In such cases, trees eventually become accustomed to the new situation by producing additional roots near the surface.

Some trees, such as pin oaks, are able to survive despite the addition of a considerable amount of soil over the original level. These produce a layer of roots above the original ones and about a foot or so below the new level.

Methods of Saving Trees in Existing Fills. Unfortunately, little can be done to save trees that have been suffering from grade fills over a long period. Much can be done, however, to restore trees surrounded by recent fills or trees that do not yet appear to have suffered seriously from older fills. Corrective treatments, which should be undertaken as quickly as possible, must have as their objective the duplication, in so far as possible, of conditions existing before the fill was made. The following are the best methods:

Where a relatively shallow layer of soil has been added, the soil is periodically broken up or cultivated, compressed air is forced into the soil, and fertilizers and water are added.

Where the fill is moderately deep, the soil directly around the trunk is removed to the original level and a dry well is constructed. Holes are dug to the original level every few feet over the entire root area, and 6-inch bell tiles are placed in them. Fertilizers are then placed in the soil as near to the root zone as possible.

Where the fill is deep or where a particularly valuable tree is involved, more work and expense are required. The following procedure will help to overcome some of the harmful effects: Remove the soil to the original level around the trunk. Dig trenches radiating from this area to points below the outer spread of the branches. The level of the radial trench should slope downward from the trunk to the outside in order to drain water away from the trunk. Connect the ends of the radial trenches by digging a circular trench to the same level. Add ground limestone and fertilizer in the exposed area in the radial and circular trenches, but *not* around the trunk. Build a well of loosely joined stones around the trunk. Place lines of 6- or 8-inch split sewer pipe, 4-inch horseshoe drain tile, or 4-inch agricultural tile in the radial and circular trenches. The first two types are laid downward. Join the tile tightly enough to hold out soil, but loosely enough to allow air and water to enter. Cover the joints with cardboard, old tin, or some other material to prevent clogging by the soil. Place 6-inch bell tile upright over the junction of the tile in the circle and the radii, and pile stones around to hold them in position. Then place rocks followed by crushed stone and gravel over the ground tile, and fill the remaining space (about 12 inches) with good topsoil.

Preventing Injury from Soil Fills. Although the initial cost of proper precautionary measures is high, prevention of injury is much more effective than the curative measures just described. Before undertaking such a program, however, one should carefully consider the following points:

First, the age of the tree: An old or weak tree may not be worth the expense involved unless it has historical or unusual aesthetic value. A young tree can be replaced at less cost than that necessary for precautionary measures. Second, vigor: If the tree is in low vigor or has an extensive cavity, its possible life span may be too short to justify the expense. Third, species: If the tree belongs to a short-lived species (Norway maple or tree-of-heaven), the added expense may not be justified, though it might be with long-lived trees, such as oaks or beeches. Fourth, the number of other trees in the immediate vicinity: obviously, if only one or two large trees are on the property, any attempt to save them will be worth while, since they greatly enhance the beauty of the home. Lastly, the susceptibilty to some deadly disease: there might be some question, for instance, of the justification of precautionary measures around an elm if the tree is in an area infested by the Dutch elm disease (p. 391).

Preparation for Raising Grades. When all the aforementioned factors have been considered and the decision to undertake the necessary measures has been made, the procedure illustrated in Figure 10-2 should be followed.

The ground around the base and underneath the branch spread is

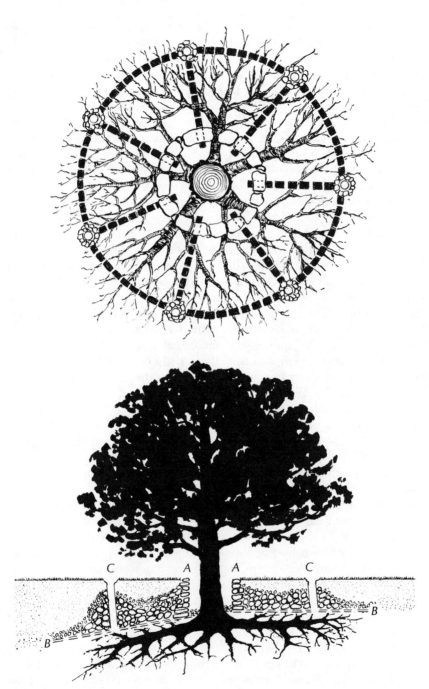

Fig. 10-2. Preventing injury by soil fills. **Upper:** Bird's-eye view. **Lower:** Side view showing A, the dry well; B, ground tile; and C, upright bell tile.

cleared of all plants and sod, and the soil is then broken up without disturbing the roots. Commercial fertilizers are applied according to the method outlined on page 61. Four- or six-inch agricultural tile or split sewer pipes are laid in a wheel-and-spoke design with the tree as the hub. The radial lines of tile near the tree should be at least 1 foot higher than the ends joining the circle of tile. A few radial tiles should extend beyond the circle and should slope sharply downward to ensure good drainage. An open-jointed stone or brick well is then constructed around the trunk up to the level of the new fill. The inner circumference of the stone well should be about 2 feet from the circumference of the trunk. Six-inch bell tiles are placed above the junction of the two tile systems, the bell end reaching the planned grade level, and stones are placed around the bell tiles to hold them erect. All ground tiles are then covered with small rocks and cobblestones to a depth of 18 inches. Next, the large rocks are covered with a layer of crushed stone, and these in turn with gravel, to a level of about 12 inches from the final grade. Cinders should never be used as a part of the fill. A thin layer of straw or hay should be placed over the gravel to prevent soil from sealing the air spaces. Then good topsoil should be spread over the entire area except in the tree well and the bell tile. To prevent clogging, crushed stone should be placed inside the dry well over the openings of the radial tile.

The procedure outline can be followed where a grade is to be raised around several trees in a group. In such cases the tile can run from one tree to another, increasing the air circulation.

To prevent children from falling into the hole, the area between the trunk and the stone well should be either covered by an iron grate or filled with a 50-50 mixture of crushed charcoal and sand. The latter practice will prevent not only filling with leaves and consequent impairment of the efficiency of air and water drainage, but also rodent infestation and mosquito breeding.

Children are often tempted to fill bell tiles with soil. To prevent this, the tiles should be filled with crushed rock and covered with a screen.

Other Methods. The method outlined constitutes an ideal one to ensure the least disturbance by fills, but a number of other methods can be substituted. Where water drainage is not a serious problem, coarse gravel in the fill can be substituted for the tile. This material has sufficient porosity to ensure air drainage. Instead of bell tile in the system, stones, crushed rock, and gravel can be added so that the upper level of these porous materials slants toward the surface in the vicinity below the outer branch spread.

Lowering Grades. Although removing soil around trees is not so disastrous as increasing the soil level, four changes take place: valuable topsoil is removed, feeding roots are exposed to drying out and low temperature injury, roots below the removed soil may be damaged, and the water table is changed. Most trees, however, will not suffer appreciably when only a few inches of topsoil are removed, since the roots soon become adjusted to the new conditions.

Injury to the tree as a result of lowering the grade can be reduced to a minimum by avoiding damage to roots. Exposed roots, if cut or broken, should be treated and covered with peat moss to prevent drying. Leaf mold, peat moss, or rotted manure should be incorporated in the remaining soil to increase the water-holding capacity. If large roots are cut or damaged, a few branches should be pruned to maintain the proper balance between these parts. Fertilizers should be applied, especially on the upper or undisturbed area.

Under some conditions injury can be reduced by terracing the new slope around the tree, rather than cutting the soil away in a uniform gradient (Fig. 10-3).

Protecting Trees from Excavations. Insofar as possible, trees should be protected when excavations are made for water and sewage lines. The trenches should be located away from the trees. If these cannot be routed around the trees, the best alternate is to tunnel under them.

Fig. 10-3. Construct a retaining wall when the grade is lowered.

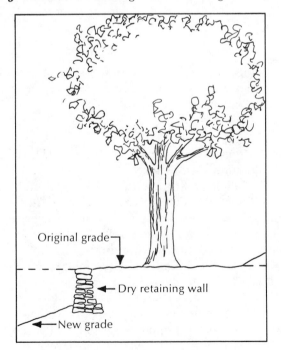

Original grade⌐

←- Dry retaining wall

←—New grade

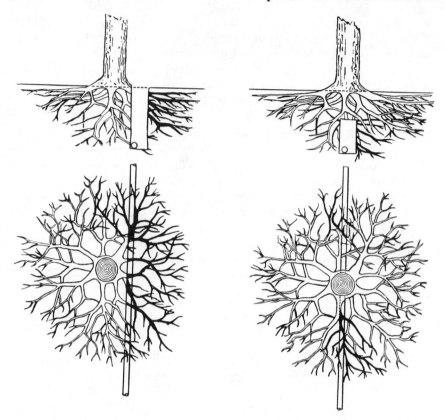

Fig. 10-4. Tunnel beneath root systems. Drawings at left show trenching that would probably kill the tree. Drawings at right show how tunneling under the tree will preserve many of the important feeder roots.

Power-driven soil augers are available for this job. Figure 10-4 illustrates what to do in situations of this sort.

Mr. Charles Schmalz of Rochester, New York, found a surer way of getting trees to form new root systems where earth fills are to be made over the original level. Wounding the bark on the lower trunk or major roots just before the soil level is raised is his method. Where the soil level is to be raised a foot or more, the wounds are made in the trunk. Where the fills are to be shallow, wounds made in the larger roots will result in the growth of roots up into the filled area.

The wound in the trunk or larger roots should be deep enough to penetrate into the sapwood, and a pebble or some other object should be placed in the wound to keep it open to prevent healing at that point. The principle is much the same as that used in air-layering of woody plants indoors.

Mr. Schmalz reported that a gully 2 to 14 feet deep in a residential area was to be filled. Trees included Norway spruce, black oak, and native varieties of maple and poplar. Those in the area to be filled were notched in several parts of the trunk about a foot below the level of intended fill.

Although the roots of the trees in the gully were covered to a depth varying from 14 feet at the center to 2 feet at the edges, Mr. Schmalz reported that not a single tree died. All were doing well 32 years after the fill was applied.

The author feels this may be one solution for treating areas where the methods described earlier are not feasible because of the great expense involved. The one unfavorable factor, of course, is the possibility of decay setting in at the point where the incisions are made.

Slime Flux

The foul-smelling and unsightly seepage from wounds in the bark or wood of various shade trees is known as slime flux (Fig. 10-5). It occurs most commonly on profusely bleeding trees, such as birch, elm, and maple, especially on those in declining vigor.

There are two types of slime flux, brown and alcoholic, distinguished on the basis of origin, color, and mode of development. Brown slime flux originates from heartwood sap. Before reaching the wounded surface, the sap is a clear watery fluid containing several nutrients. On the surface it soon changes to a brown, slimy ooze, as a result of the feeding by fungi, bacteria, and insects. Alcoholic slime flux, on the other hand, develops from the sap of bark and sapwood. It is white and frothy and usually forms near the base of the trunk. The sap is rich in starches, sugars, and proteins and thus makes an excellent growing medium for various bacteria and yeasts. These organisms produce fermentation, and the resulting odor is attractive to many species of insects.

Slime flux contains acids and aldehydes that are toxic to tree tissues. When the exudations persist for some time, much of the bark and cambium over which they flow is killed.

Treatment of Slime Flux. Thus far no effective preventive or curative measure is known. Alcoholic flux is usually of short duration and results in less damage than the more persistent brown flux. Bark tracing of the wounded area, shellacking, and dressing with a good paint to stimulate rapid healing are suggested for the former. Brown flux is more difficult to check, since the sap from which it originates is forced out of the heartwood by positive pressure. The sap may continue to flow despite cauterization of the wound with a blow torch followed by a covering of thick tar, the treatment most commonly recommended. Some arborists find that considerable reduction in the flow can be obtained by boring holes into the heartwood below the wound and inserting pipes to drain

Fig. 10-5. Slime flux oozing from a pruned branch stub of an American elm.

off the sap. Semirigid plastic drainage tubes have been found to be more satisfactory than those made of metal. They are less injurious to trees, people, or saws. These tubes relieve the positive pressure and allow the wound to heal. After the wound heals, the drain pipes are removed and the holes are plugged with a filler. Trees with slime flux should be fertilized to promote vegetative growth, which in turn hastens callus development over the wound.

Occasionally a report appears in professional aborists' and nurserymen's magazines on the use of sulfa drugs and antibiotics for preventing slime flux. Such reports, however, have not been substantiated by scientific tree workers. It is to be hoped that an effective chemical will be devised in the near future to control slime flux.

Injuries Caused by Low Temperatures

Low temperatures may injure trees in either vegetative or dormant condition. Injury is most common in regions where seasonal variations are greatest. For purposes of discussion, low-temperature injuries may be divided according to the season of the year in which they occur, that is, spring, fall, and winter.

Spring Frosts. Sudden drops to freezing temperature or below result in wilting, blackening, and death of tender twigs and leaves of deciduous trees, or reddening of the needles and defoliation of coniferous trees. Injury is most severe when the low temperatures occur in very late spring, when new growth is well advanced. Because of frost pockets, trees growing in hollows and valleys are damaged more often than those on higher ground.

Warm days in early spring stimulate premature growth, which is readily injured by the cold days and nights that follow. Among plants susceptible to this type of injury are: boxwood, Japanese dogwood, pyracantha, red and white oaks, hackberry, and white ash.

Autumn Frosts. A cool summer followed by a warm autumn prolongs the growing season. Under such conditions twigs, buds, and branches fail to mature properly and therefore are more subject to injury by early autumn frosts. Unseasonable cold waves in the fall may also result in much damage. The disastrous frost which hit the Pacific Northwest on November 11, 1955, severely injured and killed thousands of trees and shrubs.

Winter Injury. Despite their dormant condition, trees frequently suffer severely during the winter. Their winter-hardiness is influenced by drainage, location, natural protection, species of tree, and character of the root system, as well as by a combination of unfavorable weather conditions.

The roots of trees are more likely to freeze in poorly drained than in

well-drained soils—maple, ash, elm, and pine roots being most susceptible. The effects of frozen roots are seldom noted until the following
summer, when the aboveground parts wilt and die. Injury to roots
occurs most commonly during winters of little snowfall or in soils bare of
small plants and other vegetation.

The ability of the tree to withstand low temperatures is also governed
by the maturity of the wood. Trees fed with excessive amounts of high
nitrogenous fertilizers, or those making considerable growth in late fall,
are most commonly injured.

Aside from extensive damage to branches and roots, unfavorable
temperatures during the winter produce more or less localized injuries
on the trunks and branches. These are known as frost cracks, cup-
shakes, and frost cankers.

FROST CRACKS: Longitudinal separations of the bark and wood are
known as frost cracks. These openings may be large enough to permit
the insertion of a hand, and may extend in a radial direction to the
center of the tree or beyond.

Frost cracks are most likely to form in periods of wide temperature
fluctuations. The water in the wood cells near the outer surface of the
trunk moves out of the cells and freezes during sudden drops in
temperature. The loss of water from these cells results in the drying of
the wood in much the same way as green lumber drys and cracks when
exposed to the sun. At the same time, the temperature of the cells in the
center of the trunk remains much higher and little drying of these cells
or shrinkage of the wood takes place. The unequal shrinkage between
the outer and the inner layers of wood sets up great strain, which is
released only by the separation of the layers. The break occurs suddenly
along the grain of the wood and is usually accompanied by a loud report
(Fig. 10-6).

Cracks formed in this manner appear principally on the south and
west sides of the trunk, since these are heated by the sun's rays and a
greater gradient prevails when the temperatures drop suddenly during
the night. If all exposures of the trunk were heated evenly, tension and
frost cracks would not develop, as all tissues would shrink at the same
rate.

Dr. E. B. Himelick of Illinois reported some interesting observations
as to why frost cracks on London planetrees reopen during the winter.
He found that frost cracks on such trees pop open when the air
temperature gets as low as 8°F. (−13°C.) and not because of a sudden
drop in temperature, as had been believed previously. The cracks
opened wider with the lowering of the temperature at night and closed
during the day as the air temperature increased. Installation of half-inch
rods screwed into a $7/16$-inch hole drilled through the crack every 12
inches prevented reopening of the cracks the following winter.

Fig. 10-6. Frost crack on trunk of a young horsechestnut tree.

Deciduous trees appear to be more subject to cracking then do evergreens. Among the former apple and crabapple, ashes, beech, goldenrain-tree horsechestnut, linden, London planetree, certain maples, tuliptree, walnut, and willow suffer most. Isolated trees are more susceptible than those growing in woodland areas, and trees at their most vigorous age (6 to 18 inches in diameter) are more subject than very young or old ones. Probably because of the higher moisture content of their tissues, trees growing in poorly drained sites are more subject to cracking than are those growing in drier, better drained soils.

When warmer temperatures arrive, the frozen tissues thaw, absorb more water, and the crack closes. The cracked zone in the heartwood never closes completely even though the surface may be sealed by callus formation. Because of insufficient support, however, the same area again splits open the following winter. The repeated splitting and callusing eventually results in the formation of a considerable mass of tissue over the affected area.

The most serious aspect of frost cracks is that they provide conditions favorable for the entrance of wood-decay fungi. The open surfaces should be treated and dressed in the same way as open cavities are. The installation of bolts as described under Bracing the Cavity (p. 113) may prevent the repeated annual splitting and thus enable adequate bark and sapwood to develop without disturbance.

Young trees susceptible to frost cracks can be protected by attaching sisal-kraft paper or strips of burlap to the trunk in late fall, or applying a coat of whitewash. Tying a wide board upright on the south side of the trunk will also help.

CUP-SHAKES: Wide temperature fluctuations within a relatively short period produce another type of injury known as cup-shakes. This results from conditions that are the reverse of those responsible for frost cracks. A sudden heating by sunshine of the outer tissues of the trunk, following low temperatures, will cause these tissues to expand more rapidly than the inner tissues, resulting in a cleavage or separation along an annual ring.

FROST CANKERS: Low-temperature injuries may be confined to small localized areas on the trunk, branches, or in crotches. The lesions or cankers resulting from this limited injury are common on maple and London planetree and are confined principally to the southern and western exposures of the trunk. Scalding by the sun's rays on these exposures may penetrate as deeply as the cambium, resulting in a well-defined lesion.

The inner bark and cambium at or near the soil line can also be damaged by unseasonably low temperatures. The live tissues in these areas mature later than the twigs and branches. When low temperatures occur before the tissues are sufficiently hardened, these tissues are apt to be damaged. The area affected may be confined to one side, or it may extend completely around the trunk and cause girdling. Old Baldwin apple trees appear to be especially susceptible to this type of damage. The practice known as bridge grafting can be adopted to save trees so injured.

Winter Drying of Evergreens. Winter injury to such plants as rhododendron, laurel, holly, pines, spruces, and firs is rarely caused by excessive cold during the winter. The damage is caused, rather, by excessive and rapid fluctuations in temperature or by late spring freezes after the plants have resumed activity.

Evergreen plants lose water continuously. Although water loss is less during the winter months, it may be considerably increased when the plants are subjected to drying winds or are growing in warm sunny spots. Unless the water lost during this period is replaced by absorption through the roots, the leaves wilt, turn brown, and many die.

In the earlier stages, winter injury on broad-leaved evergreens is evident as a scorching of the leaves at the tips and along the outer margins (Fig. 10-7). The color of the affected parts tends to be brown

Fig. 10-7. Winter injury to rhododendrons and other broad-leaved evergreens appears as a browning along the edges of the leaves.

rather than yellow. On narrowed-leaved evergreens, the needles are browned entirely or from the tips downward along part of their length. The terminal buds and twigs are brittle and snap readily when bent.

Prevention of Winter Injury. From the foregoing discussion it is obvious that the ability of a plant to withstand low temperatures depends on many factors beyond man's control. In some instances, however, several precautions can be taken to reduce the possibility of winter damage.

The selection of well-drained soils as sites for trees cannot be overemphasized. Trees considered susceptible always withstand low temperatures better when planted in soil with good aeration and water drainage.

Fertilization and soil aeration not only increase root growth but also tend to encourage deeper rooting, both of which help to reduce the possibility of winter injury. Better aeration can be obtained by spading the open soil area around the tree and by improving the water drainage. Digging should be shallow, so as not to disturb the feeding roots growing near the surface.

To protect broad-leaved evergreens, such as rhododendron and laurel, windbreaks of coniferous evergreens, which as a rule suffer less severely, are to be encouraged. Heavy mulches of oak-leaf mold or acid peat moss to prevent deep freezing and thus to facilitate water absorption by the roots are of great assistance in avoiding winter injury. To ensure an ample water supply during the winter months, soils around evergreens should be thoroughly soaked before freezing weather sets in.

Winter-browning can be prevented, or at least greatly reduced, by spraying the leaves with the liquid plastic Wilt-Pruf NFC (p. 52). This material should be applied with a pressure sprayer on a mild day in late November or early December in the latitude of New York City. The author has seen many kinds of evergreens, including rhododendrons, boxwood, and mountain laurel, which came through the winter undamaged following an application of Wilt-Pruf NCF in late fall or early winter.

Care of Winter-Injured Plants. In any attempt to aid a winter-injured plant to regain its vigor, several precautions should be noted.

Drastic pruning of such plants is not advisable, since additional harm is apt to occur. Moreover, pruning should be deferred until the buds open in the spring, when dead wood can easily be distinguished from the live. A moderately pruned tree will recover more quickly than one severely pruned or one not pruned. It is impractical to prune winter-injured needles or leaves of evergreens, but all dead wood should, of course, be removed.

Some disagreement exists among tree men as to the specific fertilizer practices to be followed on severely winter-injured trees. Those who favor omission of fertilizer for the entire season following injury claim that heavy spring applications may either further injure already damaged roots, or result in the production of much foliage. A reduction in the root mass would lower the water intake, whereas an overabundance of foliage would require more water than could be transported by the winter-injured conducting tissues. These advocates say that a moderate application of fertilizer might be justified about the first of July, since some new water-conducting tissue will have been formed by that time.

Advocates of medium to heavy applications of fertilizers in the spring following winter injury claim that such treatments encourage the formation of new tissue, thus making it possible for the tree better to withstand summer conditions.

Lightning Injury

Every year hundreds of shade and ornamental trees are struck by lightning throughout the country. The amount and the type of injury are extremely variable and appear to be governed by the voltage of the charge, the moisture content of the part struck, and the species of tree involved.

The woody parts of the tree may be completely shattered (Fig. 10-8) and may then burn, a thin strip of bark parallel to the wood fibers down the entire length of the trunk may be burned or stripped off, the internal tissues may be severely burned without external evidence, or part or all of the roots may be killed. The upper trunk and branches of evergreens, especially spruces, may be killed outright, while the lower portions remain unaffected. In crowded groves, trees close to the one directly hit will also die. In many cases, grass and other vegetation growing near the stricken trunk will be killed.

So-called 'hot bolts' with temperatures over 25,000°F. will make an entire tree burst into flames, while cold lightning can make it literally explode as it strikes at 20,000 miles per second. On occasion, both types fail to cause apparent damage, but months later the tree dies from burned roots and internal tissues.

Tall trees or those growing alone in open areas and trees with roots in moist soils or those growing along bodies of water are most likely to be struck. Though no species of tree is totally immune, some are definitely more resistant to lightning bolts than others. Beech, birch, and horsechestnut, for example, are rarely struck, whereas elm, maple, oak, pine, poplar, spruce, and tuliptree are commonly hit. The reason for the wide variation in susceptibility is not clear. Some authorities attribute it to the difference in composition of the trees: for example, trees high in oils (beech and birch) are poor conductors of electricity, whereas trees high in starch content (ash, maple, oak, etc.) are good conductors. In addition, deep-rooted or decaying trees appear to be more subject to attack than are shallow-rooted or healthy trees.

It is commonly believed that lightning never strikes twice in the same

Fig. 10-8. Shattering of the trunk on a lightning-struck tuliptree.

place. This is not true, for some trees have been struck by lightning as many as seven times, judging from the scars on their trunks.

Repairing Lightning-Injured Trees. The injured tree should be inspected carefully before any attempt is made to repair the damage. Many trees are severely injured internally or below ground, despite the absence of external symptoms, and will soon die regardless of treatment. Consequently, expensive treatments should not be undertaken until the tree appears to have a good chance of recovery.

Where external damage is not great or where the tree is particularly valuable, several immediate measures are justifiable. Some benefit is derived by tacking on and covering with burlap any long thin pieces of bark that have been split or lifted from the sapwood. Shattered limbs and torn bark should be removed carefully and all open surfaces dressed. In addition, some rapidly available fertilizer should be placed around the root area to stimulate vigorous growth.

Lightning Protection. Trees growing in locations favorable for strikes, and large, rare, or otherwise valuable ones can be adequately protected at comparatively small cost by the installation of proper equipment.*

The principles governing the protection of buildings and other structures from lightning bolts are employed also in safeguarding trees. The major difference is in the type of materials used and their method of installation. Tree protection systems must have flexible cables to allow for the swaying of the trunk and branches, and adjustable units to allow for the tree's growth.

A vertical conductor is fastened along the trunk with copper nails, from the highest point in the tree to the ground. The ground end is fastened to several radial conductors, which are buried underground and extend beyond the root area. These, in turn, are attached to ground rods 8 feet in length, which are driven vertically into the ground.

The system should be inspected every few years, the air terminals extended to the new growth, and other adjustments necessitated by expansion of the tree should be made. Ground terminals should also be checked periodically.

A well-known company that handles lightning protection equipment is The Independent Protection Co., Inc., Goshen, Indiana 46526. An excellent brochure entitled 'Lightning The Destroyer' is available from the company.

Wires carrying electric current may also cause some injury to trees. Suitable nonconductors should be placed over wires passing in the

---

* The theories and details of installing lightning-protection equipment are too involved to permit discussion in this book. This information is available in *Tree Preservation Bulletin No. 5*, which may be obtained from the Superintendent of Documents, U.S. Government Printing Office, Washington, D.C. 20402, for a small fee. Installation must be entrusted to a specialist in tree care and should never be attempted by the layman.

vicinity of the trunk and branches. Much of the injury by wires can be avoided by judicious pruning, as discussed under Line Clearance (p. 93), so that branches and wires do not interfere with each other. Outdoor evergreens bedecked with lights at Christmas time can be damaged if there are too many poorly placed bulbs or if worn equipment is used. The bulbs should be placed so that they do not come into direct contact with the needles or twig tips.

Gas Injury

In the third and fourth editions of this book, the author stated that natural gas leaking from gas mains was not toxic to trees. This conclusion was based on experiments conducted by him during 1956 and 1957 in which the roots of young Norway maples, pin oaks, and London planetrees were subjected to natural gas for periods up to 7 weeks. No toxic effects were noted, whereas trees of the same kind and age subjected to manufactured gas died within 2 weeks.

The author was also influenced in arriving at the conclusion that natural gas was not toxic because this substance did not contain any unsaturated hydrocarbons (ethylene, acetylene, benzene, butylene, propylene), carbon monoxide, cyanogen compounds, or hydrocyanic acid—all known to be toxic to trees and other plants.

To further support this conclusion, the author found that the great majority of a thousand streetside trees examined by him died from root and trunk infections caused by fungi, such as *Ganoderma lucidum, Verticillium albo-atrum, Armillaria,* and *Phytophthora* species, from insect attacks, girdling roots, mechanical injuries, or certain chemicals. In 13 per cent of the cases investigated, death was not attributable to any of the aforementioned factors.

It was not possible, for example, to pinpoint the cause of death of 12 large Norway maples on a Brooklyn, New York, street in 1961 and of 10 Norway maples in Passaic, New Jersey, in the same year, as well as a number of trees in the coastal towns of New Jersey. Natural gas leaks had occurred in these areas. In most instances the trees that had died from unknown causes were growing in areas where the roots were almost completely covered with pavement imprevious to air. The author assumed, therefore, that the escaping natural gas had replaced the soil oxygen and the trees had died of asphyxiation.

A more specific reason for the death of trees near natural gas leaks was presented in a research paper by Dr. J. Hoeks of the Netherlands in 1972. He found that after an extended period, certain species of bacteria consumed the methane in the natural gas by their own metabolic processes, depleted the available oxygen, and increased the amount of carbon dioxide in the soil. Their metabolic processes would explain how long exposures to natural gas would result in the death of some trees.

More recently, Dr. J. H. B. Garner of the Environmental Protection Agency at the National Environmental Research Center in North Carolina observed similar harmul effects to vegetation by natural gas. After extensive tests along streets in Wilmington, North Carolina, he concluded that natural gas, in addition to displacing the soil air to some extent, provides food for certain species of bacteria, particularly *Desulfovibrio desulfuricans*. Anaerobic conditions result when there is a rapid uptake of natural gas. Under such conditions the bacteria transform sulfates to hydrogen sulfide. This substance inhibits root respiration and nutrient uptake and results in the death of the tree or shrub. Dr. Garner also stated that nitrous oxides which are formed under anaerobic conditions by microbial action may also be involved in the death of plants.

On the basis of the research of Doctors Hoeks and Garner, it appears that natural gas can under certain conditions be harmful to trees. One should not overlook the possibility, however, that even in the presence of leaking gas, other agents or factors may also be involved in the death of a tree. Streetside trees will continue to die from fungi, insects, girdling roots, mechancial injuries, chemicals, and so forth, whether they are near gas leaks or miles away from them. Each case of injury or death of trees allegedly related to leaking gas mains must be based on individual examination and laboratory tests by a qualified person.

Injury by Girdling Roots

Many trees are weakened and some are killed by the growth habits of certain of their roots. Such roots grow closely appressed to the main trunk or large laterals in such a way as to choke the members they surround, much as does a wire left around a branch for a number of years. This choking action restricts the movement of nutrients in the trunk or in the strangled area of the large roots. When a large lateral root is severely girdled, the branches that depend upon it for nutrients commonly show weak vegetative growth and may eventually die of starvation. If the taproot of a tree is severely girdled, the main branch leader may die back. As a rule, trees affected by girdling roots do not die suddenly, but become progressivly weaker over a 5- or 10-year period despite good pruning and feeding practices.

Girdling roots which develop below ground level can often be detected by examining the trunk base. If the trunk ascends straight up from the ground, as it does when a soil fill has been made (p. 199), or is slightly concave on one side, instead of showing a normal flare (swelling) or buttress at the soil line, then one can suspect a girdling root. Of course digging the soil alongside the trunk should reveal whether the strangling member is present.

Trees growing along paved streets always suffer more from girdling roots than do those in open areas, and middle-aged or old trees more than younger ones. Norway and soft maples, oaks, elms, and pines are affected most frequently.

How Girdling Roots Develop. Roots are deflected from their normal spreading course by unfavorable environmental conditions. They grow most rapidly in areas where air, moisture, and food supply are best. A good case in point is that of a tree growing along a city street. The roots of such a tree, when newly planted, are usually spread out in all directions by the planter. For a number of years, the roots spread in the general direction in which they were originally placed. Because of unfavorable conditions under the pavement, the larger roots and especially the younger ones will eventually grow away from the street toward the open areas between the curb and sidewalk and toward lawns. In the course of bending, the younger roots cross over older roots and become closely appressed to the base of the main trunk. Such roots grow and expand rapidly because of the more favorable conditions and eventually press against or strangle the roots they cross or the trunk base they touch (Fig. 10-9).

Root girdling frequently occurs where a street tree is planted in a hole filled with good soil and surrounded by hard, impervious subsoil. Inability to penetrate the more unfavorable soil forces the roots to develop within the filled area, thus favoring girdling.

Careless placement or overcrowding of the roots at transplanting time may also lead to root girdling and the rotting of the crowns. This has been observed not only with shade trees along city streets, but also with red, white, and Scots pines planted in reforestation projects. In the latter case, a direct correlation exists between careless placement of roots and the amount of subsequent infection in the root crown by fungi and bacteria. As twisted roots develop, air and water pockets are formed. These make ideal breeding places for organisms that produce root and crown decay.

In a few instances, fertilization of the soil in the immediate vicinity of young street trees has stimulated new root production, produced overcrowding, and eventually resulted in the formation of girdling roots.

Girdling roots are always more numerous in compacted than in loose soils, and on soft-wooded than on hard-wooded trees.

Container-grown trees are more apt to be subject to girdling roots than are uncontained trees. Trees left too long in containers develop roots that spiral the walls. Unless such roots are straightened out at the time of final transplant, they may cause girdling of the stem later on.

How To Diagnose Girdling Roots. The best time to determine the presence of girdling roots is in late fall just before frost. At that time, the side of the tree over the girdled area will show lighter green leaves, which

Fig. 10-9. Treatment of girdling roots. **Top:** A girdling root. **Center:** Removing the root with a chisel and mallet. **Bottom:** The girdling root has been removed. The cut should be covered with tree paint.

tend to absciss earlier than normally. One must always bear in mind, however, that other factors may produce similar symptoms and that the most positive sign is the discovery of girdling roots. Such roots can be uncovered by carefully removing the soil around the trunk on the side showing weak top growth, poor bark devlopment, or a pronounced swelling at the base of the trunk. Usually the girdling root is to be found at or a few feet below the soil surface. Occasionally it may be deeper if the taproot is being strangled.

Treatment for Girdling Roots. If the girdling root has not yet seriously impaired the tree's chance of recovery, it should be severed with a chisel and mallet (Fig. 10-9) at its point of attachment to the trunk or to the large lateral root. A few inches should be cut from the severed end to prevent its reuniting with the member from which it was severed. Then the cut surfaces, on the trunk or main root and on the severed root itself, should be painted to hinder insect and fungus invasion. Finally the soil is replaced in its original position. If the tree has been considerably weakened, judicious pruning should be practiced and some good fertilizer applied.

Smoke and Soot Injury

It is estimated that each year more than 150 million tons of pollutants are released into the air over the United States.

Smoke emanating from chimneys of manufacturing plants, apartment house incinerators, and other instruments of combustion, including automobiles, contain ingredients which are harmful to the leaves of trees and other plants.

Smoke from factories frequently contains one to several chemicals which do the actual damage. The three major pollutants are sulfur dioxide, fluorine compounds, and the so-called smog typical of the Los Angeles area. The first two are so-called acid-forming gases, whereas smog is a peculiar combination of many different chemicals.

Sulfur Dioxide and Fluorine Pollutants. Sulfur dioxide, perhaps the most common ingredient in the smoke from factories, can injure vegetation in concentrations as low as one or two parts in a million parts of air. Although highly toxic to plants, it is relatively nontoxic to humans at these low concentrations. At concentrations high enough to injure plants, it may irritate the mucous membranes of individuals who are exposed to it for long periods.

Both sulfur dioxide and fluorine produce leaf markings that are quite distinctive. When the gas concentration is high, the leaf cells become water-soaked and then collapse and dry out rapidly, leaving blanched or scorched areas. Mild attacks will merely cause the leaves to turn yellow.

Maple and other broad-leaved trees exposed to sufficiently high concentrations of sulfur dioxide show ivory-white markings, mostly between the main veins. Sometimes the markings occur along the margins, with branches extending into the interveinal areas. With some broad-leaved trees the markings are darker brown in color.

Sulfur dioxide causes a reddish discoloration of the needles on Douglas-fir and Ponderosa pine, followed by shriveling of the affected tissues. The discoloration may occur at the tips only or as a band over the entire length of the needles.

When the concentration is too low or the time of exposure to sulfur dioxide is too short to cause any visible lesions or yellowing of the leaves, the growth of the plant will not be affected. In other words, sulfur dioxide is not a systemic poison and its action is not cumulative. As a matter of fact, at low concentrations of about three tenths of a part per million parts of air, it is absorbed by the leaves and changed to the sulfate form.

When relatively high concentrations of one or more parts per million are absorbed for an hour or more, sulfurous acid or sulfite forms in the interior cells. These compounds cause visible damage to the leaf cells and prevent them from functioning normally.

Middle-aged leaves are most susceptible to sulfur dioxide, while the young or growing leaves are markedly resistant. Brownish-red or yellow areas between the leaf veins are a rather characteristic symptom. The margins or tips of some leaves may also be discolored or blanched. On coniferous trees, the tips, bases, or centers of the needles turn red and then, especially when the gas concentration is high or the gas has been present for a long period, turn completely brown and drop off.

Sulfur dioxide and fluorine damage often cannot be told apart in the field. Only a chemical analysis of the leaves will reveal which gas is responsible.

Flourine compounds are much more toxic to vegetation than is sulfur dioxide. Industries which produce aluminum, steel, ceramics, and phosphates are the principal contributors of fluorine compounds to the atmosphere.

Smog—Unusual Pollutant. Smog is a term used to designate a mixture of smoke and fog. In the Los Angeles area, however, this term refers to a complex of liquids, solids, and gases, comprising more than 50 chemical elements and compounds. Smog damage also occurs on the eastern seaboard.

The harmful ingredients are believed to be products resulting from a combination of unsaturated hydrocarbons and the ozone in the atmosphere. The hydrocarbons come from oil refineries and related industries as well as from automobile exhausts.

Silvering, glazing, streaking, and speckling of the leaves are among the more common symptoms of the Los Angeles type of smog. The symptoms vary according to the type of vegetation and the structure of the leaf. Leafy vegetables are more susceptible than trees. They will show a metallic sheen or glazed appearance on their lower leaf surfaces from 1 to 3 days after exposure to smog.

A great deal of research is now being conducted in California to determine ways of eliminating smog or of reducing its damage. One investigator has already observed that smog damage to certain crops can be prevented by applying dusts or sprays containing dithiocarbamates, a widely used group of fungicides. Others have reported that a light spraying with ascorbic acid (vitamin C) on the leaves of some plants prevented the burning and bronzing symptoms of smog.

Many factories, particularly in the Los Angeles area, which formerly released large quantities of sulfur dioxide into the atmosphere, have installed special equipment to trap the harmful gases. Others have built extremely tall chimneys so that the smoke is well diluted before it reaches susceptible crops.

Chlorine and Hydrogen Sulfide Pollutants. Two other gases may also cause damage to vegetation—chlorine and hydrogen sulfide. The former produces most unusual markings. Dead areas develop between the veins and generally toward the center of the leaf, resulting in a netted appearance. Hydrogen sulfide (which has the odor of spoiled eggs) differs from most other pollutants in its effects. The youngest leaves are most sensitive and hence are marked first. The markings are usually light tan to white.

Smoke. Though not so toxic as sulfur dioxide or fluorine, soot, the solid residue of smoke, may also damage plants. This material slowly settles on the leaves and eventually may coat them completely. Here the damage does not result from clogging of the breathing pores (stomata), as some believe, but from the screening out of sunlight. The sharp reduction in light reduces the capacity of the leaf to manufacture food, and consequently results in a serious impairment of the general vigor of the plant. Because the leaves of evergreens remain attached throughout the year, and in some species for several years, a considerable deposit may accumulate and thus greatly reduce the chances of survival of these trees. Soot is one factor that makes it difficult to grow evergreens in large cities.

Trees vary considerably in their tolerance to smoky atmospheres. Tree-of-heaven, ginkgo, and Carolina poplar seem to withstand such conditions best, and London planetree, pin oak, Norway maple, elm, linden, and tulip show decreasing tolerance in the order mentioned. As has been pointed out, other factors, including tolerance of roots to harmful chemicals, also enable some trees to tolerate adverse city conditions better.

Toxic gases in the atmosphere may harm vegetation indirectly as well as directly. The acidity of a soil may increase as a result of the interaction between acid gases and the lime particles in the soil. Such a change not only reduces the population of certain beneficial soil bacteria, but also decreases the activity of others. Excessive soil acidity, whether speeded up by air pollutants or from natural leaching by rainfall or irrigation, can be counteracted by the application of lime.

Obviously one way to reduce injury from smoke is to eliminate the production of the most harmful constituents at their source. Where this is not feasible, trees most tolerant to city conditions should be planted. Injury to small evergreens by soot deposits can be minimized by spraying with a soapy solution followed by syringing with clear water. A material known at Calgon (sodium hexametaphosphate) can also be used to remove soot from broad- and narrow-leaved evergreens.

Trees at intersections are particularly vulnerable to exhaust fumes from autos and buses. Interestingly, the damage occurs where vehicles must linger for traffic lights, congestion, and bus stops. The author's studies showed that as one works back along the block, the trees get progressively healthier toward the middle of the block, then begin to fail as one works toward the next intersection. Bus exhaust fumes deposit an oily film that can be felt by rubbing the leaves. This film is extremely damaging to vegetation. Formaldehyde, another ingredient in bus exhausts, is also toxic to tree leaves.

Arborists and others interested in the care of trees should not be too hasty in concluding that leaf abnormalities are necessarily caused by air pollutants. They should bear in mind that unfavorable weather, insects, fungi, bacteria, spray materials, growth regulators, and viruses also produce symptoms that might be confused with symptoms of air pollution.

Over the last 35 years the author has examined literally hundreds of cases of alleged air-pollution injury to vegetation and has found that only a small percentage of the damage was actually caused by smoke or gases. And this experience was gained in areas that were highly industrialized! Before blaming poor growth of vegetation on air pollutants, therefore, one would do well to call in a competent diagnostician. Plant pathologists at some of the state agricultural colleges are available to render this service.

Lichen Injury

Lichens often appear as a green coating on the trunks (Fig. 10-10) and branches of trees. They are actually two plants in one, being composed of a fungus body and an algal body, which live together in complete harmony. The alga supplies elaborated food to the fungus and, in turn, receives protection and some food from the fungus.

Fig. 10-10. Lichens growing over a tree trunk.

Lichens do not parasitize trees, but merely use the bark as a medium on which to grow. They are more unsightly than injurious, although when extensive they may interfere with the gaseous exchange of the parts they cover. They are common on trees throughout the southern states and appear less frequently in the northern states. Because of their extreme sensitivity to sulfur dioxide released from facory chimneys, lichens seldom appear on trees in the larger cities. They rarely develop on rapidly growing trees, because the bark is shed before the lichens have an opportunity to grow over much of the surface.

As a rule, lichens can be eradicated by spraying the infested parts with bordeaux mixture 2-2-50 or any ready-made copper spray.

Chemical Injuries

Weed Killers. The various chemicals used as weed killers severely damage or even kill trees in the immediate vicinity. The author has noted many cases of toxicity to trees caused by such materials.

When carelessly used, the selective weed killers containing 2,4-D (2,4-dichlorophenoxyacetic acid), among others, have caused widespread damage to trees (Fig. 10-11).

Persons treating lawns for weed control or using weed killers for controlling poison ivy and other undesirable plants along highways and

Fig. 10-11. 2,4-D injury to mulberry leaves.

rights-of-way should exercise extreme caution to avoid drifting of the 2,4-D and similar materials to nearby trees.

Symptoms of injury from weed killers vary according to the concentration of material which reaches the tree, the kind of tree, temperature, and other factors. The most general symptom is a distortion of leaves and twigs. Leaves roll upward or downward, at the midrib or along the edges, so as to be cupped. Leaf stems may curl downward, in some cases forming loops resembling a curled pigtail. From a distance, severely affected trees appear wilted because of this leaf and stem distortion.

The author has noted 2,4-D injury on many trees, including elm, dogwood, boxelder, hawthorn, Norway maple, tuliptree, pin, red, white, and black oaks, and sassafras. Unless the trees received an unusually heavy dose or repeated lighter doses, they usually recovered.

To avoid possible damage to trees, it is suggested that one of the less volatile forms of 2,4-D be used, and that it be applied on windless days and in a coarse spray (at low pressure), rather than as a fine mist such as that used for spraying trees with fungicides and insecticides.

The author was among the first to draw attention to the possibility that trees such as pin oaks growing in lawns treated in the fall with 2,4-D can absorb enough of the hormone in their dormant buds to produce distorted leaves the following spring. Arborists should bear in mind that wooden spray tanks cannot be made free of 2,4-D once this hormone has been used in them. Such a sprayer cannot safely be used later for normal pest control operations.

Where a sprayer with a metal tank has been used, the 2,4-D can be removed as follows: Fill the tank with warm water and household ammonia at the rate of one gallon of the ammonia or 5 pounds of Sal soda for each 100 gallons of water. Then pump out a few gallons to wash pump parts, hose, and nozzles, and allow the remainder to stay in the tank for 2 hours or so. Finally, drain the tank and rinse several times with clear water.

Activated charcoal or a 1 percent mixture of Norit A will also rid spray tanks of 2,4-D residues.

It is well to stress the fact that even minute traces of 2,4-D in such sprayers will cause severe distortion of leaves and twigs. Injury to susceptible plants has been observed with dilutions as low as ½ part 2,4-D in a million parts of water.

In the 1960's combinations of lawn fertilizer and chemicals which kill broad-leaved weeds were used in great quantities. Very often severe damage was done to trees growing in the lawn areas as a result of the chemical weed killers, which either entered the trees via the tree roots or volatilized and entered the leaves. The author has seen dozens of cases where the leaves of magnolia, dogwood, and flowering cherry were severely distorted as a result. In some cases, the trees actually died.

Soil sterilants used to destroy vegetation along walks, fences, or driveways can harm roots of trees growing nearby. Such materials can be moved by surface and underground water for considerable distances to the vicinity of tree roots and cause serious damage. Simazine and dichlobenil are among the more toxic pre-emergence herbicides.

Calcium Chloride. Trees growing along country roadsides may be damaged by the calcium chloride used to keep down dust on dirt roads. Heavy rains wash the chemical off the roads and carry it down to the roots, which absorb it and then transport it to the leaves, where it causes injury. Correct grading of the roadside so as to facilitate removal of flood waters and prevent their being soaked into the soil around the roots will greatly reduce the chances of damage.

Tree species vary in their tolerance to calcium chloride. Red oak, white oak, and American elm are most tolerant, whereas balsam fir, white spruce, beech, sugar maple, cottonwood, and aspen are least tolerant.

Damage to the leaves appears as a leaf scorch which is difficult to distinguish from physiological leaf scorch caused by lack of water in the soil.

Salt. Sand treated with salt and piled along roadsides for use on icy roads may also damage trees. The salt is leached down into the roots and causes burning. Sand piles thus treated should, obviously, be placed at some distance from the root areas of the trees.

Salt is frequently scattered over sidewalks in winter to melt ice or prevent water from freezing. When the salty solution finds its way to open soil near roots it can be very toxic. As a matter of fact, sodium chloride (ordinary table salt) is five to ten times more toxic to some trees than calcium chloride. Sand or sawdust should be used to prevent slipping in areas near a tree and other plant roots.

In 1976 more than 9 million tons of salt (sodium chloride) were applied along streets and highways in the United States for de-icing.

At the University of New Hampshire, Dr. Avery E. Rich and his students have been investigating the association of salt applications and tree mortality. They observed that trees within 30 feet of the highways were affected, while the trees beyond that distance were nearly always healthy. Salt injury appears as a marginal leaf scorch, early fall coloration and defoliation, dieback of twigs and branches, and in severe cases death of the entire tree.

Dr. Rich and his co-workers observed that some trees were more tolerant to salt than others and classified them as follows:

Very tolerant: Black cherry, red cedar, red oak, and white oak.

Tolerant: Black birch, black locust, gray birch, largetooth aspen, paper birch, white ash, and yellow birch.

Moderately tolerant: American elm, basswood (American linden), ironwood, Norway maple, red maple, shagbark hickory.

Intolerant: Beech, birch, hemlock, red pine, speckled alder, sugar maple, white pine.

Very often decline of trees along roadsides may not be entirely due to salt deposits but to a lack of moisture as well. Dr. Walter Banfield of the University of Massachusetts observed that only those sugar maples fully exposed to the sun and wind and growing on dry soils, unprotected by a ground cover, showed progressive dieback. On the other hand, sugar maples growing close to the road on low lying, protected sites where the soil remained moist showed no decline—this despite the fact that they were subjected to maximum salting and car exhausts.

One substitute for the highly toxic calcium and sodium chlorides is Ferti-Thaw. According to the manufacturer, the National Chemsearch Corporation, Irving, Texas 75060, Ferti-Thaw will melt snow and ice and is noninjurious to vegetation. In fact, it is reported actually to aid in promoting plant growth the following spring.

Another product, Tred-Spread, is also said to melt snow and ice without injuring vegetation.

Cinders. Hard and soft coal cinders, especially those that have been unexposed to weathering, should not be placed over the soil beneath trees. Toxic materials in such cinders will be washed down in rainwater and harm the roots.

Salt Spray. Trees growing along the Atlantic coast are often injured by salt spray blown from the ocean. During hurricanes the spray actually damaged leaves 50 miles from salt water. Most of the damage, however, is usually confined to within a few miles of the coast.

Among the broad-leaved trees, elm, magnolia, Norway maple, sugar maple, tuliptree, and sourgum appear most susceptible to salt-water spray, whereas red oak and horsechestnut are very resistant. Among the evergreens, white pine, hemlock, junipers, and Scots pine are most harmed, whereas Japanese black pine, Colorado blue spruce, Austrian pine, holly, spruce, and yew suffer least.

Removal of badly damaged trees and pruning of mildly affected ones are all that can be suggested.

Fungicides and Insecticides. The various sprays recommended in the latter part of this book for disease and insect control may occasionally injure trees. In general, damage from fungicides and insecticides is more severe on undernourished trees and on those growing in poorly drained soils than on vigorous specimens. Insect injury and frost damage also predispose leaves to spray injuries. Cool, damp weather favors the chances of injury from bordeaux mixture and other copper fungicides. High temperatures and humidities increase the chances of injury from lime sulfur and other sulfur sprays.

Copper in Rainwater. The author is of the opinion that rainwater that passes through copper leaders and drainpipes of homes may injure trees. He has noted the gradual weakening and death of a number of trees whose roots were continuously wetted with such water.

To prevent damage, the water passing through copper leaders should be drained directly into the sewer or the street gutter.

Copper Sulfate. This chemical is frequently mentioned as a control for algae (green scum) in ponds and lakes. The usual concentration is 1 part of the copper sulfate in a million parts of water, by weight. When the concentration is in excess of this figure, there is danger of harming trees growing around the edge of the pond or lake.

Tree Bands. Banding trees with a sticky substance to trap insects such as cankerworm moths, can be dangerous unless means are taken to prevent the inner bark and cambium from absorbing the material. If the banding material is applied directly to the bark, or if the thicker outer bark is shaved or cut away and the material then applied, severe damage may follow.

Sugar maples appear to be more susceptible than other trees to banding substances applied directly to the bark.

Hail Injury

At times, hailstorms cause considerable damage. They may completely defoliate the trees or shred the leaves sufficiently to check growth sharply. They are most injurious to young trees or to those with undeveloped foliage in early spring. Areas in the bark and cambium may be severely bruised or even killed from the impact of the hailstones. When the bark injuries do not callus over rapidly, they often serve as entrance points for wood decay fungi.

Mechanical Injuries

Damage to trees, especially the trunks, by motor vehicles, by children, and even by thoughtless adults occurs too commonly to warrant much discussion. Injury by automobiles and trucks is often unavoidable.

Most mechanical injuries are confined to the outer portions of the trunk. These should receive immediate treatment. Cut the bark along the edge of the wound in the form of a pointed ellipse (Fig. 10-12), shellac the cut edges, and then dress the wound with a tree paint.

Where constant danger of mechanical injury exists, young trees should be protected by a tree guard.

Wire, unless covered with a piece of garden hose or some other suitable material, should never be used to aid in the support of trees. As

Fig. 10-12. Two examples of correct treatment of bark injuries. Note the pointed cuts and excellent callus development.

the trunk expands, the bare wire will tend to girdle the trunk and cause severe weakening or even death of the tree (Fig. 10-13).

Accumulations of snow, especially on evergreens such as yews, hemlocks, and junipers, can cause severe branch breakage. Such accumulations should be gently shaken off as soon as possible with a broom or bamboo rake. Ice-covered trees should be handled even more carefully. If the temperature is on the rise, rinsing the ice-coated trees with water from a hose will thaw the ice.

Some deciduous trees are prone to cracking and splitting of branches in ice and wind storms. Among those most subject are the ashes, catalpas, hickories, horsechestnuts, red maple, empress-tree, Siberian elm, silk-tree, tuliptree, and yellowwood.

The lawnmower is a more destructive instrument for debarking trees than are automobiles and malicious children. Careless use of this instrument results in severe damage to the inner bark and cambium near the soil line. Parasitic fungi like Ceratocystis, which infects planetrees (p. 452), and wood-destroying fungi can get started in wounds made by lawnmowers.

If no grass is planted close to the base of a tree, there is less chance of causing damage. Installation of a so-called No-Trim Tree Guard eliminates the need for edging and trimming grass around lawn trees.

Fig. 10-13. Wire used to help support this tree caused complete girdling of the trunk.

Leaf Scorch

Although the trouble known as leaf scorch is most prevalent on Japanese red, sugar, silver, Norway, and sycamore maples, it also occurs on horsechestnut, ash, elm, and beeches and to a lesser extent on oaks and other deciduous trees.

The Katsura-tree (p. 146) is particularly subject to leaf scorch when planted near hard-surfaced pavements. The tree apparently cannot tolerate a paved surface over its roots.

Symptoms. Scattered areas in the leaf first between the veins or along the margin, turn light or dark brown. The edges of the discolored areas are very irregular. All the leaves on a given branch appear to be affected more or less uniformly. When a considerable area of the leaf surface is discolored, the canopy of the tree assumes a dry, scorched appearance (Fig. 10-14). In severe cases, the leaves dry up completely, then fall prematurely. When such defoliation occurs before midsummer, new leaves are formed before fall. In mild cases, the leaves remain on the tree, and little damage results.

The position of the most severely affected leaves can be used, in many instances, as a means of distinguishing leaf scorch from leaf spot and

Fig. 10-14. The tree in the center shows severe leaf scorch.

blight damage caused by fungi. Leaves affected by scorch are usually most abundant on the side of the tree exposed to the prevailing winds or to the most intense rays of the sun, whereas spotted and blighted leaves resulting from fungus attack are usually scattered throughout the treetop, the greatest numbers being on the lower, more densely shaded parts.

Cause. Leaves are scorched when the roots fail to supply sufficient water to compensate for that lost at critical periods. They are most severely affected during periods of high temperatures and drying winds. The inability to supply the necessary water is influenced by the moisture content of the soil and by the location and condition of the root system. Obviously, even the most extensive root system cannot supply enough water to compensate for the tremendous amounts lost through the leaves if the soil moisture content is low because of a prolonged drought.

Though of less common occurrence, scorch may appear in trees growing in excessively wet soils. Under such conditions the water-absorbing capabilities of the roots may be greatly reduced because of lack of air.

Trees with diseased roots, those whose root systems have been reduced as a result of curb installation or building operations, and those whose roots are restricted or covered with impervious materials are most subject to leaf scorch. For example, sugar maples adjacent to concrete-paved driveways and near street intersections are commonly observed to have more scorch than those more favorably situated along the same street or those growing on lawns or along country roads.

Where injury to a part of the root system is severe and permanent, or where soil conditions are continuously unfavorable, leaf scorch may occur regularly.. In fact, some trees show leaf scorch every year regardless of whether the season is cool and moist or hot and dry.

Heavy infestations of aphids and other sucking insects usually contribute to the severity of leaf scorch. Some investigators feel that the trouble is associated with a deficiency of potash in the leaves. They believe that potash-deficient leaves tend to lose water more rapidly and consequently become scorched more readily.

Control. Any practice that increases root development and improves the tree generally will help to reduce leaf scorch. The application of chemical fertilizers, especially those containing large quantities of potash, is suggested. In addition, insects and fungus diseases should be kept under control.

The tops of trees with restricted or injured root systems should be reduced by judicious pruning to increase the supply of water to the remaining leaves.

Where soils are likely to become dry, water should be applied, especially during seasons of low rainfall. Where the soil is heavy and compacted, some improvement will result from breaking up the surface layers or from inserting upright tile to facilitate penetration of water. In the rarer cases where scorch results from the inability of the roots to absorb water because of excessively wet soils, the installation of drain tiles in the manner suggested under Injuries Caused by Grade Changes (p. 199) will help.

Leaf scorching in particularly valuable trees can be prevented, or at least reduced, by spraying the leaves with Wilt-Pruf NCF before the regular 'scorching' period.

Chlorosis

The uniform yellowing of leaves resulting from a reduction in the normal amount of chlorophyll is termed chlorosis. Loss of the green coloring matter reduces the efficiency of the leaf in manufacturing food.

Chlorotic leaves may result from fungus, virus, or insect attack; low temperatures; toxic materials in the air or soil; excessive soil moisture; surpluses of soil minerals; lack of nonavailability of nutrients.

Chlorosis of many shade trees, especially of pin oak, appears to be associated with nonavailability of iron rather than with a lack of this element. This is especially true in soils containing limestone, ashes, or other alkaline materials, where the pH of the soil varies from 6.7 to 8.5. Iron may be present in such soils, but in a form that cannot be absorbed by the plant. Whether the chlorosis of boxelder, catalpa, cottonwood, bur and white oaks, sweetgum, and red, silver, and sugar maples, like that of pin oak, is caused primarily by nonavailability of iron is not known definitely. Chlorosis in many other trees, especially fruit, may result also from deficiencies or nonavailability of zinc, magnesium, boron, or nitrogen, elements apparently rarely involved in chlorosis of shade trees growing along city streets.

Symptoms. The leaves of affected trees first turn uniformly yellowish-green, or they may remain green along the veins but turn yellow in the intravenal areas (Fig. 10–15). The terminal growth of twigs is small, and the tree is generally stunted. The tissue between the leaf veins or along the leaf edge may die on trees affected for several years with chlorosis. Eventually whole branches or the entire tree may die prematurely unless the condition responsible is corrected.

Control. Chlorosis due to a deficiency or nonavailability of iron can often be corrected by special treatments. The newest treatment involves the use of so-called iron chelates. These are generally more effective than such chemicals as iron sulfate and iron ammonium citrate used formerly.

The iron chelate is strongly held in soluble form against the action of phosphates and other chemicals in the soil. Because it remains in solution rather than in dissociated form, the iron is readily absorbed by

Fig. 10-15. Gardenia leaves showing iron deficiency symptoms.

the plants. Moreover, the iron in chelated form is needed in much smaller amounts than the chemicals formerly used. For example, a gram of chelated iron applied to the soil around an iron-deficient tree is as effective as a pound of iron sulfate.

Iron chelates are applied in either of two ways: in powdered form directly to the soil, or dissolved in water and sprayed on the leaves.

For best results with soil applications the iron chelate should be distributed uniformly over the soil surface beneath the tree and thoroughly watered to a depth of 6 inches. To assure an even distribution, the proper amount of chelated iron powder should be mixed with fertilizer or with some inert material such as sand, or the required amount should be dissolved in water and sprayed or sprinkled over the soil. Pin oaks from 3 to 6 inches DBH will require about one pound of iron chelate; those over 6 inches DBH about 2 pounds.

Leaf sprays should be applied as thorough cover sprays, that is, sufficient liquid should be applied to wet thoroughly all leaf surfaces. The sprays are best applied when the leaves are fully expanded and should not be applied to shade trees in blossom or to fruit trees in blossom or in fruit. Pin oaks can be sprayed with a solution containing 8 ounces of iron chelate in 25 gallons of water.

Sequestrene of iron, made by the Geigy Company, Ardsley, New York 10502, was the first of several iron chelates to appear on the market. Presently this company markets its products as Sequestrene 330 Fe Iron Chelate for use on alkaline or slightly acid soils and as Sequestrene NaFe Iron Chelate for more acid soils.

Iron chelates are also sold under such trade names as Perma Green Iron 135 by Refined Onyx Division, Lyndhurst, New Jersey 07071, and Iron Tetrine by Glyco Chemicals, Inc., Greenwich, Connecticut 06830.

Perhaps it might be well to restress what has been said earlier. One should not conclude that all yellowing of leaves is caused by a deficiency of iron. Chlorotic leaves may also result from fungus, virus, insect, or mite attack; low temperatures; lack of nitrogen; toxic materials such as 2,4-D in the air, or other chemicals in the soil; excessive soil moisture; surpluses of such metals as copper, manganese, or zinc. Correct diagnosis (see Chapter 9) is therefore important to obtain preventive or curative results with iron chelates.

Other metallic chelates are available for curing deficiencies of elements other than iron.

Other Methods for Curing Iron Deficiency. Until the development of iron chelates, iron deficiency was cured by spraying leaves with a solution containing 5 pounds of ferrous sulfate and 2 pounds of soybean flour in 100 gallons of water. A few ounces of a wetting agent added to the water, before the ferrous sulfate and flour were mixed in, helped to stick the spray on the leaves and make it more effective.

Iron salts such as iron ammonium phosphate injected into holes bored into the trunk also were used to cure trees affected with chlorosis. This method has several drawbacks, including the danger of initiating infections by wood-decay fungi in the vicinity of the bore holes.

Finally a 50-50 mixture of ferrous sulfate and powdered sulfur was applied to the soil. One pound of this mixture for each inch of trunk diameter can be distributed evenly early in spring throughout the root area in the manner outlined for inserting dry chemical fertilizers (p. 65).

Rodent Damage

Young trees with thin, succulent bark are subject to damage by rodents such as field mice, pocket gophers, and rabbits during winters of heavy snowfall, or where the trees have been mulched with some strawy material. Placing a collar of a quarter-inch wire mesh or even ordinary window screening around the base of such trees will prevent much damage. Use of strawy mulches in which mice are apt to nest should be avoided. The trunk bases of susceptible trees can also be painted with a specially developed repellent. Ringwood Repellent, made by Panogen, Inc., Woodstock, Illinois 60098, is effective against rabbits.

Sapsucker Damage

Yellow-bellied sapsuckers, *Sphyrapicus varius varius*, have been observed feeding on 26 kinds of trees in the northeastern United States. The birds under observation fed particularly on hemlock, red maple, yellow, paper, and gray birches, and mountain-ash. Both conifers and hardwoods were damaged by the pecking of the birds. The injury, though rarely fatal, is commonly seen in apple orchards. No effective preventive measures have been developed.

Selected Bibliography

Anonymous. 1964. *Protecting trees against damage from construction work.* USDA Inform. Bul. 285. 26 p.

——. 1965. *Protecting shade trees during home construction.* 1965. USDA Home and Garden Bul. 104. 8 p.

——. 1973. 'Air pollution damages trees.' U.S. Forest Service. Northeastern Area State and Private Forestry, Upper Darby, Pa. 32 p.

Beilmann, A. P. 1940. 'Lightning and trees.' *Missouri Bot. Gard. Bul.* Vol. 28 p. 209–16.

Benedict, H. M. and J. P. Nielsen. 1956. 'The markings produced by various air pollutants on leaves.' *Proc. Thirty-second National Shade Tree Conference.* p. 205–15.

Bieberdoff, F. W., C. I. Shrewsbury, H. C. McKee, and L. H. Krough. 1958. *Vegetation as a measure indicator of air pollution.* Part I. Bul. Torrey Bot. Club 85 (No. 3). p. 197–200.

Blaser, R. E. 1976. 'Plants and de-icing salts.' *American Nurseryman.* Dec. 15, 1976. p. 8, 9, 48, 50, 52, 53.

Bray, D. F. 1958. 'Gas injury to shade trees.' *Scientific Tree Topics* 2 (No. 5). p. 19–22.

Brennen, Eileen, Ida Leone, and Charles Holmes. 1969. 'Accidental chlorine gas damage to vegetation.' *Plant Disease Reptr.* Vol. 53. p. 873–75.

Campana, Richard. 1964. 'Non-infectious diseases; Part I: Effect of cold injury and freezing.' *Weeds, Trees, and Turf.* Aug. 1964. p. 10–11, 22–23.

——. 1965. 'Non-infectious diseases; Part II. Influence of heat and imbalance of water.' *Weeds, Trees, and Turf.* May 1965. p. 12–15.

——. 1976. 'Air pollution effects on urban trees.' *Trees.* Vol. 35 (No. 2). p. 35–38.

Carpenter, E. D. 1970. 'Salt tolerance of ornamental plants.' *American Nurseryman.* Jan. 1, 1970. p. 12, 54, 56, 58, 60, 62, 64, 68, 70–71.

Carter, J. C. 1957. 'Non-parasitic tree troubles.' *American Nurseryman.* Oct. 15, 1957. p. 110–14.

Covert, E. N. 1926. *Protection of buildings and farm property against lightning.* USDA Farmer's Bul. 1512. 32 p.

Crocker, William. 1931. 'The effect of illuminating gas on trees.' *Proc. Seventh National Shade Tree Conference.* p. 24–34.

Daines, R. H., Eileen Brennan, and Ida Leone. 1967. 'Air pollutants and plant response.' *Jour. Forestry.* Vol. 65 (No. 6). 381–84.

Davis, S. H. Jr. 1970. 'Pollution damage to ornamental trees and shrubs.' *Proc. Forty-fifth International Shade Tree Conference.* p. 28–33.

Davis, D. D. and J. B. Coppolino. 1974. 'Relative ozone susceptibility of selected woody ornamentals.' *Hort. Science,* Vol. 9. p. 537–39.

———. 1974. 'The relative susceptibility of eighteen coniferous species to ozone.' *Phytopathology.* Vol. 62 (No. 1). p. 14–19.

———. 1976. 'Ozone susceptibility of selected woody shrubs and vines.' *Plant Disease Reptr.* Vol. 60 (No. 10). p. 876–78.

Davison, A. W. 1971. 'Effects of de-icing salt on roadside verges; soil and plant analysis.' *Jour. Applied Ecology.* Vol. 8. p. 555–61.

Day, W. R. and T. R. Peace. 1937. 'The influence of certain accessory factors on frost injury to forest trees.' IV. Air and soil conditions. *Forestry* (Gr. Brit.). Vol. 11. p. 92–103.

De Wolf, Gordon Jr., 1970. 'What can we do about pollution.' *Arnoldia.* Vol. 30 (No. 2). p. 33–55.

Dirr, M. A. 1976. 'Selection of trees for tolerance to salt injury.' *Jour. Arboriculture.* Vol. 2 (No. 11). p. 209–16.

Dodge, A. W. 1936. 'Lightning damage to trees.' *Proc. Twelfth National Shade Tree Conference.* p. 43–55.

———. 1968. 'Lightning protection and treatment.' *Proc. Forty-fourth International Shade Tree Conference.* p. 64–69.

Duling, J. Z. 1968. 'Lightning protection for trees.' *Proc. Forty-fourth International Shade Tree Conference.* p. 69–71.

———. 1969. 'Recommendations for treatment of soil fills around trees.' *Arborist's News.* Vol. 34 (No. 6). p. 1–4.

Foss, E. W. 1965. *Lightning protection.* Cornell Ext. Bul. 1150. 16 p.

Fowler, M. E. and G. F. Gravatt. 1945. *Reducing damage to trees from construction work* USDA Farmer's Bul. 1967. 22 p.

Freier, G. D. 1977. 'Lightning and trees.' *Journ. Arboriculture.* Vol. 3 (No. 7), p. 131–137.

Garner, J. H. B. 1974. 'The death of woody ornamental plants associated with leaking natural gas.' *Arborist's News.* Vol. 39 (No. 12). p. 13–17.

Giles, F. A. and J. B. Gartner. 1972. *Tree damage around construction sites.* Univ. Illinois Cooperative Extension Service. Circular 1061. 6 p.

Guba, E. F. 1934. 'Slime flux.' *Proc. Tenth National Shade Tree Conference.* p. 56–61.

———. 1942. 'Slime flux of shade trees.' *Trees.* March-April 1942. p. 2, 9.

Hacskaylo, John, R. F. Finn, and J. P. Vimmerstedt. 1969. *Deficiency symptoms of some forest trees.* Ohio Agr. Res. and Development Center, Research Bul. 1015. Wooster, Ohio.

Hartley C. and T. C. Merril. 1915. 'Storm and drought injury to foliage trees.' *Phytopathology.* Vol. 5. p. 20–29.

Hepting, G. H. 1963. 'Climate and forest diseases.' *Am. Rev. of Phytopathology.* Vol. 1. p. 31–50.

———. 1968. 'Diseases of forest and tree crops caused by air pollutants.' *Phytopathology.* Vol. 58. p. 1098–1101.

Hibben, C. R. 1969. 'Ozone toxicity to sugar maple.' *Phytopathology.* Vol. 59 (No. 10). p. 1423–28.

Himelick, E. B. 1970. 'Frost cracks on London plane an important outdoor winter thermometer.' *Arborist's News.* Vol. 35. (No. 1). p. 5, 6.

Hitchcock, A. E., William Crocker, and P. W. Zimmerman. 1932. 'Toxicity of illuminating gas in soil.' *Proc. Ninth National Shade Tree Conference.* p. 34–36.

Hoeks, J. 1972. *Effect of leaking natural gas on soil and vegetation in urban areas.* Agr. Research Report 778. Centre for Agricultural Publishing and Documentation. Wageningen, Holland. 120 p.

———. 1972. 'Changes in composition of soil air near leaks in natural gas mains'. *Soil Science.* Vol. 13 (No. 1). p. 46–54.

Holmes, F. W. 1964. 'Effect of use of snow control chemicals on street trees.' New Jersey Federation of Shade Tree Commissions, Thirty-ninth Annual Meeting. p. 38–45.

Jacobs, Homer. 1950. '2,4-D, friend or foe.' *Proc. Twenty-sixth National Shade Tree Conference.* p. 23–37.

Jacobson, J. S. and A. C. Hill (eds.). 1970. *Recognition of air pollution of vegetation.* Informative Dept. No. 1. TR-7. 100 p. Agr. Committee Air Pollution Control Assoc., Pittsburgh, Penna.

Jennings, O. E. 1934. 'Smoke injury to shade trees.' *Proc. Tenth National Shade Tree Conference.* p. 44–49.

Jensen, K. F. 1973. 'Response of nine forest tree species to chronic ozone fumigation.' *Plant Disease Reptr.* Vol. 47 (No. 11). p. 914–16.

Knight, L. J. and William Crocker. 1913. 'Toxicity of smoke.' *Bot. Gaz.* Vol. 55. p. 337–71.

Kreag, K. K. 1939. 'Nature and control of shade tree chlorosis.' *Proc. Sixteenth National Shade Tree Conference.* p. 32–40.

Kuhns, L. J. and T. D. Snydor. 1976. 'Copper toxicity in woody ornamentals.' *Jour. Arboriculture.* Vol. 2 (No. 4). p. 68–71.

Linzon, S. N., W. D. McIllveen, and R. G. Pearson. 1972. 'Late-spring leaf scorch of maple and beech trees.' *Plant Disease Reptr.* Vol. 56 (No. 6). 526–30.

Lumis, G. P., G. Hofstra, and R. Hall. 1975. 'Salt damage to roadside plants.' *Jour. Arboriculture.* Vol. 1 (No. 1). p. 14–16.

MacDougal, D. T. 1902. 'Effect of lightning on trees.' *Journ. New York Bot. Gard.* Vol. 3. p. 131–35.

Marsden, D. H. 1951. 'Gas injury to trees.' *Brooklyn Botanic Garden Record.* Plants and Gardens. Vol. 7. p. 156–58.

———. 1952. 'Some common noninfectious diseases of shade and ornamental trees in New England.' *Proc. Twenty-eighth National Shade Tree Conference.* p. 73–79.

Marshall, R. P. 1942. *Care of damaged shade trees.* USDA Farmer's Bul. 1896. 34 p.

Meserve, A. W. 1937. 'Effect of changing grades around trees and suggested treatment.' *Proc. Thirteenth National Shade Tree Conference.* p. 36–51.

Middleton, J. T. 1956. 'Response of plants to air pollution.' *Jour. Air Poll. Control Assoc.* May 1956. p. 7–11.

Mielke, J. L. and J. W. Kimmery. 1942. 'Heat injury to the leaves of California black oak and some other broadleaves.' *Plant Disease Reptr.* Vol. 26. p. 116–19.

Neely, Dan. 1973. 'Pin oak chlorosis—trunk implantations correct iron deficiency.' *Jour Forestry.* Vol. 71 (No. 6). p. 340–42.

———. 1976. 'Iron deficiency chlorosis of shade trees.' *Jour. Arboriculture.* Vol. 2 (No. 7). p. 128–30.

Parr, F. L. 1970. *Lightning protection installation standard.* National Arborist Assoc., McLean, Va. 3 p.

Pirone, P. P. 1940. 'Chlorosis of pin oak and its control.' *The Shade Tree.* Vol. 13 (No. 12). p. 1–6. New Jersey Federation of Shade Tree Commissions.

———. 1946. '2,4-D injury to shade trees.' *Proc. Twenty-second National Shade Tree Conference.* p. 107–14.

———. 1946. 'Before you build, safeguard your trees.' *Amer. Home.* June 1946. p. 32–33.

———. 1954. 'Chelates will cure iron deficiency.' *Flower Grower.* Nov. 1954. p. 20–21.

———. 1956. 'Air pollution—an ever increasing problem.' *Flower Grower.* Sept. 1956. p. 28–29.

———. 1966. 'Nonparasitic ailments of trees and shrubs in urban areas.' *Plants and Gardens (n.s.).* Brooklyn Botanic Garden 22 (No. 1). p. 92–97, 104.

Raup, H. M. 1937. 'Recent changes of climate and vegetation in southern New England and adjacent New York.' *J. Arnold Arboretum.* Vol. 18. p. 79–117.

Rich, A. E. 1971. 'Salt injury to roadside trees.' *Proc. Forty-seventh International Shade Tree Conference.* p. 77a–79a.

Rhoads, A. F. 1976. 'Effects of air pollution stress on urban plantings in New Jersey.' *American Nurseryman,* Dec. 1, 1976. p. 11, 48, 50, 51, 54, 55.

Rhoads, A. F. and Eileen Brennen. 1975. 'Fluoride damage to woody vegetation in New Jersey in 1974.' *Plant Disease Reptr.* Vol. 59. p. 427–29.

———. 1976. 'Response of ornamental plants to chlorine contamination in the atmosphere.' *Plant Disease Reptr.* Vol. 60 (No. 5). p. 409–11.

Roberts, B. R. 1977. 'The response of urban trees to abiotic stress.' *Jour. Arboriculture.* Vol. 3 (No. 4). p. 75–78.

Rusden, P. L. 1955. 'Trees and the changing weather.' *Scientific Tree Topics* Vol. 2. p. 13–14. Bartlett Tree Expert Co.

———. 1961. 'Six major noninfectious diseases of shade trees.' *Scientific Tree Topics.* Vol. 2 (No. 8). p. 20–21. Bartlett Tree Expert Co.

Rushmore, F. M. 1969. *Sapsucker damage varies with tree species and seasons.* USDA Forest Service Research Paper NE-136. 19 p.

Scheffer, T. C. and G. C. and G. G. Hedgcock. 1955. *Injury to northwestern forest trees by sulfur dioxide from smelters.* USDA Tech. Bul. 1117. 49 p.

Shurtleff, M. C. 1970. 'Plants vs. pollution.' *Flower and Garden.* Oct. 1970. p. 12–16.

Siegel, S. M. 1961. 'Effects of reduced oxygen tension on vascular plants.' *Physiologia Plantarum.* Vol. 14. p. 554–57.

Sinclair, W. A. 1969. 'Polluted air: Potent new selective force in forests.' *Journal of Forestry.* Vol. 67 (No. 5). p. 305–9.

Skelly, J. M., L. D. Moore, and L. L. Stone. 1972. 'Symptom expression of eastern white pine located near a source of oxides of nitrogen and sulfur dioxide.' *Plant Disease Reptr.* Vol. 5 (No. 1). p. 3–5.

Slankis, V. 1974. 'Soil factors influencing formation of mycorrhizae.' *Ann. Rev. Phytopathology.* Vol. 12. p. 437–57.

Smith, E. M. 1976. 'Pin oak chlorosis.' *American Nurseryman.* Feb. 1, 1976. p. 15, 55.

Stone, G. E. 1914. *Electrical injuries to trees.* Mass. Agr. Exp. Sta. Bul. 156. 19 p.

———. 1916. 'Frost cracks, winter killing of cork cambium, and sunscald.' *Mass. Agr. Exp. Sta. Bul.* 170. p. 204–8.

Thomas, H. E. and L. H. MacDaniels. 1933. *Freezing injury to the roots and crowns of apple trees.* Cornell Agr. Exp. Sta. Bul. 556. 23 p.

Van Camp, John. 1970. 'Protecting trees from physical damage on construction sites.' *Arborist's News.* Vol. 35 (No. 12). p. 129–32.

Van Wormer, H. M. 1937. 'Effect and treatment of girdling roots.' *Proc. Thirteenth National Shade Tree Conference.* p. 30–36.

———. 1940. 'Effects of girdling roots on trees.' *Arborist's News.* Vol. 5. p. 81–84.

———. 1968. 'Lightning protection for trees.' *Proc. Forty-fourth International Shade Tree Conference.* p. 70–71.

Wagener, W. W. 1961. 'Past fire incidence in Sierra Nevada forests.' *Jour. Forestry.* Vol. 59 (No. 10). p. 739–47.

Warne, L. C. 1934. 'The distribution of potassium in normal and scorched foliage.' *Ann. Bot.* Vol. 48. p. 57–67.

Weaver, L. O. 1965. 'Diebacks and declines of hardwoods attributed to climatic changes—a review.' *Arborist's News.* Vol. 30 (No. 5). p. 33–36.

Went, F. W. 1958. 'Plant damage due to air pollution and the use of plants as indicators of air pollution.' *Air Poll. Control Assoc. News* Jan. 1958. p. 3–5.

Westing, A. H. 1969. 'Plants and salt in the roadside environment.' *Phytopathology.* Vol. 59. p. 1174–81.

White, P. M. 1973. 'Plant tolerance for standing water: an assessment.' *Arborist's News.* Vol. 38 (No. 4). p. 41–42.

Whitehead, J. B. 1933. 'Lightning protection for trees.' *Science.* Vol. 78. p. 507–8.

Wilson, C. L. 1970. 'Soil pollution and trees.' *Trees.* May-June 1970. p. 6, 7.

Wilson, J. D. and H. A. Runnels. 1931. 'Bordeaux mixture as a factor increasing drought-injury.' *Phytopathology.* Vol. 21. p. 729–38.

Witte, C. P. 1936. 'Frost cracks.' *Proc. Twelfth National Shade Tree Conference.* p. 181–88.

Wood, F. A. and J. B. Coppolino. 1972. *The influence of ozone on deciduous forest tree species. Effects of air pollutants on forest trees.* VII International Symposium of Forest Fume Damage Experts. Vienna, Sept. 1970. p. 233–53.

Yelenosky, George. 1964. 'Tolerance of trees of deficiencies of soil aeration.' *Proc. Fortieth International Shade Tree Conference.* p. 127–46.

Young, H. C. 1930. 'Spray injuries.' *Proc. Sixth National Shade Tree Conference.* p. 83–86.

11

Insect Control

A working knowledge of insect pests, of how they injure plants, and of methods of combating them is essential to any tree preservationist. The author does not intend to present a detailed discussion on methods of identifying insects. This is best left to texts written specifically for that purpose. Moveover, accurate identification of any insect can be obtained by submitting the specimen to the Division of Insect Identification, United States Department of Agriculture, Beltsville, Maryland 20705, or to the state entomologist, usually located in the state capital or in the state agricultural experiment station.

A brief discussion of the life history and structure of insects, however, will help to clarify many of the terms used in the latter part of this book.

Life History of Insects

One of the most interesting and unfathomable mysteries of nature is found in a study of the life cycle of the insect as it passes through various stages from egg to adult. The process that embodies all these changes in form is known as metamorphosis.

The life cycle of butterflies, beetles, sawflies, true flies, and moths comprises four separate stages: egg, larva, pupa, and adult. Insects with this life cycle are said to have complete metamorphosis.

After mating, the female deposits her eggs in a safe place that will prove a favorable environment for the wormlike animals, larvae, when they emerge; or she produces the eggs in such large numbers that there is a sufficient survival to keep the insects abundant. The names of the larval forms vary according to the groups to which they belong. The larvae of butterflies and moths are called caterpillars; those of beetles, grubs (Fig. 11-1A); those of sawflies, false caterpillars; and the legless larvae of flies, maggots.

As a larva grows it sheds its skin, or molts, several times, each successive skin being larger and better able to accommodate the animal's ever-increasing body. Finally the larva becomes full grown and is ready to enter the third stage of development, the pupa. Larvae of many insects prepare a protective covering for this stage. The cocoon of the moth and of the sawfly, the pupal case of true flies, and the pupal cell of the beetle represent this phase of the transformation.

Although the pupal stage is considered a resting period, it is marked by considerable metabolic activity and many important changes, which culminate in the emergence of the adult insect.

A different form of development characterizes some insects. Grasshoppers, plant lice, plant bugs, lace bugs, and leafhoppers belong to a group having incomplete metamorphosis. The egg develops into a small wingless creature, called a nymph. Resembling the adult except for its ungainly head and small body, the nymph passes through several periods of molting. Wings develop and become more prominent with each successive molt; gradually the entire body assumes the appearance of the adult insect. Thus, the last stage is attained directly, no pupa being formed in the life cycle.

Fig. 11-1A. Left: Flat-headed borers.

Fig. 11-1B. Right: Adult beetle of one of the flat-headed borers. The wing covers are hard and horny.

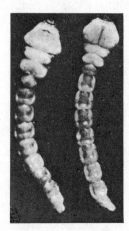 

Structure of Insects

The body of an adult insect is composed of three principal parts: head, thorax, and abdomen. The head consists of one section to which are attached the feelers or antennae; the mouth parts; and the eyes. The thorax, just behind the head, has three segments from which emanate six true legs and usually four wings. Segmentation of the abdomen, the posterior body part, varies with different insects. The spiracles, small breathing pores, are located in the segments of the abdomen and thorax. In the female a small, sharp-pointed organ for depositing eggs, the ovipositor, is found at the posterior end of the abdomen. Small appendages, called 'prolegs,' are attached to the abdomen of the larvae of many moths, butterflies, and sawflies.

Sawflies, moths, beetles, and countless other insects have 2 pairs of wings. Often the front pair is extremely hard and serves as a protective covering for both the hind wings and the greater part of the abdomen. Such hardened wings, called 'elytra,' may be observed in the beetle (Fig. 11-1B).

Another important group of insects, known as scales, have sucking mouth.parts and are wingless (except for the males). There are three kinds of scales: mealybugs, soft scales, and armored scales.

Mealybugs are white and are motile in all stages.

Soft scales vary widely in appearance, ranging from the woolly maple-leaf scale to the shell-like kermes and lecanium scales. Soft scales such as the lecaniums have two periods of motility: the crawler stage, which moves to the leaves; and the second instar stage, which migrates from the leaves back down to the twigs in the fall.

Armored scales have a waxy secretion formed into a flattened, hard, shell-like covering, which includes old shed skins. Armored scales move only in the first instar, which is also called the crawler. Once the crawler settles and begins feeding, it remains in that place until it dies.

Control Methods

Many of the insecticides used in previous years are now banned completely or their use is limited to special pests. The State of Michigan was among the first to ban the use of DDT. On January 1, 1971, New York State banned a goodly number of materials formerly widely used. Among these are benzene hexachloride, DDD, DDT, endrin, mercury compounds, selenites and selenates, strobane, and Toxaphene. Some of these are highly poisonous. Others persist in soil and water for a long, long time; in other words, they are not easily biodegradable.

Other states have followed New York's example, and more materials will be banned when there is evidence of toxicity to people and animals or where the materials persist for too long a period after application.

The use of some of the materials, such as chlordane and lindane (gamma isomer of benzene hexachloride), are permitted for special pests and in special situations by qualified persons.

In New York State some of the materials may be distributed, sold, purchased, possessed, and used only upon issuance of a *commercial or purchase permit* for any uses listed on the approved lable as registered with the New York State Department of Environmental Conservation. Amateur gardeners do not qualify for permits.

Experimentation with fungicides and insecticides continues and may be expected to develop new and valuable poisons. In recent years many new preparations have come on the market. Until they have been used for some time and under various conditions, it is impossible to say whether they are superior to some of the well-known older products. In using any commercial preparations, old or new, it is important to follow with great care the printed directions on the label.

Where specific commercial products are mentioned by their trade names in subsequent pages, it is not to be understood that we recommend them to the exclusion of other similar materials. They are simply representative and, in most places, readily available products.

Following are some of the materials whose use is permitted provided the regulations are complied with.[1] Also given are chemical names and their relative toxicity values.[2]

Insecticides

*Agritol.** See under *Bacillus thuringiensis.*

Aminocarb, sold under the trade name Matacil,* will control the spruce budworm, jack pine budworm, and other pests. 4-(Dimethylamino)-m-tolyl methylcarbamate. Ld.$_{50}$: 600.

*Amiphos** controls aphids, mites, and scales on many ornamental plants. *O, O*-Dimethyl-*S*-2 (acetylamino ethyl phosphorodithiophosphate). LD$_{50}$: 500.

Bacillus thuringiensis is a microbe which as an insecticide is effective in

1. An asterisk denotes that the product mentioned is a trade name.
2. Relatively toxicity—LD$_{50}$. The term 'LD$_{50}$' stands for 'lethal dose required to kill half (50 per cent) of a group of test animals.' The dosage is expressed as a ratio: the amount of pesticide, in milligrams, per 1000 grams of body weight of the test animal concerned (usually rats). For example, an Ld$_{50}$ of 5 is a dosage of 5 milligrams per 1000 grams of body weight. Since for all pesticides the lethal dose is expressed in standard form, comparison among dosages states, in effect, their relative toxicity. Note, however, that an LD$_{50}$ of 4 is not lower, but higher than an LD$_{50}$ of 5: the lower the dosage (that is the LD$_{50}$ value), the more toxic is the pesticide.

An LD$_{50}$ of 5 or less will kill most animals. For man, pesticides with an LD$_{50}$ value of 500 and above are relatively safe; a probable lethal dose of these would range from one ounce to one pint or one pound.

the control of many kinds of caterpillars. It is harmless to humans and animal pets. The insecticide is sold under the trade names Agritol,* Bakthane L 69,* Biogard,* Biotrol,* Dipel,* Larvatrol,* and Thuricide.*

Bakthane L 69.* See under *Bacillus thuringiensis.*

*Baygon** is a carbamate insecticide used to control the birch leaf miner, and chinch bugs and sod webworms in lawns. 2-Iso-propopoxyphenyl N-methylcarbamate.

*Biogard.** See under *Bacillus thuringiensis.*

*Biotrol.** See under *Bacillus thuringiensis.*

Carbaryl. See under Sevin.*

Carbofuran. See under Furadan.*

Chlorophos. See under Dipterex.*

*Cygon,** also known as dimethoate and Rogor,* is effective in controlling hemlock fiorinia scale, honey locust mite, pine needle scale, and mealybug on yew. Some plants are injured by it, and it should therefore be used only on those recommended by the manufacturer. O,O-Dimethyl $S/(N$-methylcarbamoylmethyl) phosphorodithioate. LD_{50}: 215.

*Cythion.** See under Malathion.

*Diazinon,** also sold as Spectracide,* controls soil insects such as wireworms and root worms as well as turf pests such as chinch bugs and many insects infesting ornamental plants. O, O-Diethyl O-(2-isopropyl-6-methyl-4-pyrimidinyl) phosphorothioate. LD_{50}: 300–400.

*Dibrom,** also known as naled, is effective against many pests including bagworms. 1,2-Dibromo-2,2-dichloroethyl dimethyl phosphate. LD_{50}: 430.

Dimethoate. See under Cygon.*

*Dipel.** See under *Bacillus thuringiensis.*

*Dipterex,** also known under the common names trichlorfon and chlorophos and the trade name Dylox,* is a phosphate insecticide. It is very effective in the control of the omnivorous leafroller, *Platynotus stultana,* and many other caterpillars. Dimethyl (2,2,2-trichloro-1-hydroxyethyl) phosphonate. LD_{50}: 560.

Dormant oil sprays. Petroleum oils, properly prepared, are used to control many pests that live through the winter on the buds, twigs, and trunks of trees and other woody plants. They are applied in spring just before new growth begins and when the air temperature is 45°F. (7°C.) or above. Only one application per season is recommended.

Some oil sprays, those having a viscosity of 90 or more, may be harmful to atlas cedar, beech, birch, black walnut, Japanese maple, hickory, sugar maple, and walnut. In certain seasons they may also damage evergreens such as cryptomeria, Douglas-fir, the true firs (*Abies*), junipers, retinospora, Japanese umbrella pine, and yews. Lime sulfur solution is much safer for these plants.

In tests conducted in 1968, Dr. Spencer Davis and J. L. Peterson of

Rutgers University reported that a 60-second 'superior' oil[3] (Scalecide) sprayed on so-called 'oil-susceptible' trees on the campus and in the arboretum of Rutgers University caused no damage. The concentration used was at the rate of 3 gallons in 100 gallons of water. The spray was applied in early March when the air temperature was about 55°F. (13°C.).

Trees sprayed with Scalecide and which showed no damage included American beech (*Fagus grandifolia*), European beech (*F. sylvatica*), cryptomeria (*Cryptomeria japonica*), Chinese cedar (*Juniperus chinensis*), Pfitzer cedar (*J. c. Pfitzeriana*), Sargent cedar (*J. c. Sargenti*), Savin cedar (*J. sabina*), western red cedar (*J. scopulorum*), pignut hickory (*Carya glabra*), shagbark hickory (*C. ovata*), Japanese maple (*Acer palmatum*), sugar maple (*A. saccharum*), Japanese pagoda-tree (*Sophora japonica*), redbud (*Cercis canadensis*), black spruce (*Picea pungens*), and black walnut (*Juglans nigra*).

On the basis of these tests it appears that some reevaluation of the effect of dormant oils should be made.

*Dylox.** See under Dipterex.*

*Furadan,** also known by the common name carbofuran, is effective in controlling strawberry and black vine weevils on Taxus. 2,3-Dihydro-2,2-dimethyl-7-benzofuranyl methylcarbamate. LD$_{50}$: 10,500.

*Gardona** is very effective in controlling caterpillars such as the juniper webworm. 2-Chloro-1-(2,4,5-trichlorophenyl) vinyl dimethyl phosphate.

*Guthion** is used by some professional arborists, nurserymen, and foresters to control a wide variety of insects on shade trees and ornamentals. It is not recommended for home gardeners' use. O,O-Dimethyl S-(4-oxo-1,2,3-benzotriazino-3-methyl) phosphorodithioate. LD$_{50}$: 11 to 13.

*Imidan,** also known as Prolate,* controls many chewing insects, including gypsy moth caterpillars and elm spanworms, and a wide variety of sucking insects. N-(Mercaptomethyl)phthalimide S(O,O-dimethylphosphorodithioate. LD$_{50}$: greater than 500.

*Larvatrol.** See under *Bacillus thuringiensis.*

Malathion, one of the most widely used organic phosphate insecticides, controls a wide variety of pests including aphids, scale crawlers, mealybugs, and many chewing insects. A premium grade of malathion, sold under the name Cythion,* has less odor than the regular product O,O-Dimethyl phosphorodithioate of diethyl mercaptosuccinate. LD$_{50}$: 1000–1375.

*Matacil.** See under Aminocarb.

3. 'Superior' type oils are highly refined, more paraffinic petroleum oils having a high unsulfonated residue of 94 minimum, a narrow distillation range, and a viscosity index of 85 minimum. Currently recommended oils have 3 weights or viscosities. They are 100-second, 70-second, and 60-second oils. The latter two are more widely used on trees and are less phytotoxic.

*Meta-Systox R** renders plants toxic to aphids, leafhoppers, leafminers, mites, white flies, and many other pests. S-2-(Ethylsulfinyl) ethyl O, O-dimethyl phosphorothioate. LD_{50}: 56–65.

Methoxychlor is an insecticide with long residual action used to control elm bark beetles, which spread the Dutch elm disease fungus, and many kinds of borers. 1, 1, 7 Trichloro-2, 2-bis (p-methoxyphenyl) ethanol. LD_{50}: 6000.

Naled. See under Dibrom.*

*Orthene** is effective in controlling aphids, bagworms, cankerworms, gypsy moths, and many other insect pests. O,S-Dimethyl acetylphos-phoramidothioate. LD_{50}: 950.

Prolate. See under Imidan.*

Pyrethrum is obtained from flowers of a species of chrysanthemum grown in central Africa and Ecuador. Pyrethrin 1, pyrethrin 2, cinerin 1, and cinerin 2. LD_{50}: 1000.

*Rogor.** See under Cygon.*

Rotenone is an insecticide extracted from derris and cubé roots grown in Peru. It is moderately toxic to animals and highly toxic to fish. LD_{50}: 300–1500.

*Sevimol** is a formulation of Sevin* in molasses, which adheres to sprayed foliage better than Sevin used alone.

*Sevin,** known under the common name carbaryl, is used to control many insects infesting trees. Repeated use will result in an increase in spider mites. It is toxic to bees and will defoliate Boston ivy and Virginia creeper vines. 1-Naphthyl N-methylcarbamate. LD_{50}: 500–850.

*Sevin 4 Oil,** a combination of Sevin* and oil, is used to control the spruce budworm and western spruce budworm. It can be applied to large forest areas by airplane. Ground applications can be made to high-value trees with a mistblower.

*Spectracide.** See under Diazinon.*

Supracide 2E* is a recently introduced insecticide-miticide that is effective against certain pests infesting nursery grown trees.

*Thuricide.** See under *Bacillus thuringiensis.*

Trichlorfon. See under Dipterex.*

*Zectran,** also known as mexacarbate, is effective against loopers, tent caterpillars, pine-shoot moth, birch leaf miner, thrips, and leafhoppers. 4-Dimethyl amino-3,5-xylyl N-methylcarbamate. LD_{50}: 15–63.

Miticides

Because spider mites are rarely controlled with the ordinary insecticides, special materials known as miticides or acaricides are used to combat them. Following are those most widely used:

*Acaraben.** See under Chlorobenzilate.

*Aracide.** See under Aramite.*

Aramite,* also sold under the names Aracide* and Niagaramite,* is an excellent mite killer for use on ornamental and nonfood plants. It is compatible with sulfur and with the most commonly used insecticides and fungicides. It should not be used with lime and other highly alkaline materials or with bordeaux mixture. 2-(p-tert-butylphenoxy)-1-methyl ethyl-2-chloroethyl sulfite. LD_{50}: 3900.

Chlorfenson. See under Ovotran.*

Chlorobenzilate is very effective against many species of mites infesting certain trees. Ethyl 4,4-dichlorobenzilate. LD_{50}: 960.

Dicofol. See under Kelthane.*

Kelthane,* known under the common name dicofol, is an extremely effective miticide. 1-1- Bis (p-chlorophenyl)-2,2,2-trichloroethanol. LD_{50}: 809.

Niagaramite.* See under Aramite.*

Omite* is a miticide that is very effective in controlling several species of mites which infest fruit trees. It does not harm beneficial insects like bees. 2-(p-tert-Butylphenoxy) cyclohexyl-2-propynyl sulfite.

Ovex. See under Ovotran.*

Ovotran,* also known by the common names ovex, sulfonate, and chlorfenson, kills all stages of mites including the eggs. It is toxic to the leaves of some ornamentals early in the growing season. Read directions carefully prior to using it. p-Chlorophenyl *p*-chlorobenzenesulfonate. LD_{50}: 2050.

Sulfonate. See under Ovotran.*

Tedion,* also known as tetradifon, is an excellent miticide for certain trees. It does not kill beneficial insects and is harmless to foliage. 2,4,5,4-Tetrachlorodiphenylsulfone. LD_{50}: 14,700.

Tetradifon. See under Tedion.*

Spreading and Sticking Agents

Any material that helps spread spray in an even, unbroken film over the surface of leaves, bark, or insects' bodies is known as a spreader; this action is usually accomplished by lowering the interfacial tension of the spray. Materials that help the spray to adhere firmly to the leaves are known as stickers.

Formerly soaps, household detergents, and some oils were recommended as spreaders. We now know that some, particularly soaps, are alkaline and may completely detoxify the insecticide. Others, such as oils, may not be compatible with fungicides containing sulfur.

Where a spreader-sticker is required it is best to depend on specially prepared products.

Commercial spreaders and stickers widely available include du Pont

Spreader-Sticker (SS₃), Triton B1956, Filmfast, Nu-Film, Ortho Dry Spreader, and Spray Stay. The last named is manufactured by Nursery Specialty Products, the manufacturer of the anti-desiccant Wilt-Pruf NCF.

Borers

Any insect that feeds inside the roots, trunks, branches, or twigs of a tree is known as a borer. The borer is usually in the larval or worm stage, although some beetles, which are the adult stage of certain insects, also may bore into the tree.

Eggs are deposited in bark crevices and scar tissue or, in a few instances, below the bark surface, by the adult during spring, summer, or fall, depending on the species. Tiny larvae hatch from the eggs and penetrate the bark. Once they are below the surface, they cannot be controlled by the ordinary poisons used for leaf-chewing insects.

Factors Favoring Borer Infestations. Although a few borers can attack vigorously growing trees, most species become established in trees low in vigor. Consequently any factor that tends to lower the vitality of a tree predisposes it to borer attack. Among the more important of these factors are prolonged dry spells, changes in the environment unfavorable to the growth of the tree, loss of roots in transplanting, repeated defoliation by insect or fungus parasites, and bark injuries caused by frost, heat, or mechanical agents.

Drought periods weaken trees by checking normal growth and by causing premature defoliation. Rapid environmental changes, including changes in the height of the water table caused by digging drainage ditches, damming, or altering the grade, result in general weakening of the trees. Thinning out a grove makes the remaining trees more subject to sun scald and root injury, because the direct sunshine not only heats the bark but also greatly increases the soil temperatures. The effects of moving a tree to a new location have already been discussed in the chapter on Transplanting. Repeated defoliation by insects and fungi undermines the general health of the tree. Bark injuries, aside from weakening trees, result in the production of scar tissue, a preferred site for oviposition.

Prevention of Borer Attack. Many borer infestations can be prevented by improving, when feasible, any unfavorable situation around the trees. Proper fertilization, adequate watering during dry spells, periodic spraying for leaf-chewing insects and blighting fungi, and pruning of infested or weakened branches are recommended. All bark wounds should receive immediate treatment to facilitate rapid healing and thus reduce the amount of scar tissue.

Borer infestations, common in recently transplanted trees, can be materially lessened by placing a barrier over the trunk and larger limbs immediately after the trees are set in their permanent location. Newspaper, wrapping paper, burlap, or specially prepared Kraft crepe paper is used. The last, also known as Tree Wrap, is now employed most extensively because it provides greater protection, is applied more easily, and is neater in appearance than the other materials. The crepe paper consists of two layers cemented together by asphaltum and is sold in 4- and 6-inch widths, wound in bolts of 25 or more yards. It is wrapped around the tree in much the same way as surgical bandage is applied, at an angle that permits sufficient overlap to make a double thickness. Binder twine is wound in the opposite direction to hold the paper in place. Both the twine and the paper remain in place for about two years before disintegrating. This is long enough to provide protection during the most susceptible period.

Asphaltum-impregnated Kraft paper should not be treated with an oil base insecticide because the oil will dissolve the asphaltum.

Polyethylene wrap has not proved satisfactory because it holds too much moisture, which causes the tree to sweat and thus favors the development of fungus cankers.

Aluminum foil has been tried with considerable success. Not only is it attractive and easily applied but it does not need to be tied down with binder twine as do some of the other wrapping materials.

Control. The method used to control borers already established depends on the part of the tree infested and the species of borer involved. Twig and root borers are controlled by pruning and discarding infested parts or by spraying or injecting certain chemicals into the unpruned infested parts.

Application of insecticides to the bark during the adult's egg-laying period or before the eggs hatch and the borers enter the bark is standard procedure for controlling trunk and branch borers. The most generally used material at this time is methoxychlor. A sticking and wetting agent (p. 251) added to the spray will increase the efficiency of the material.

The bark on the main trunk and larger branches can be sprayed or painted with the solution. Unless one is also trying to control leaf-infesting insects, it is not necessary to spray the leaves with borer-controlling materials.

Three or four applications at weekly to 10-day intervals may be necessary with some borers to provide protection over the entire egg-laying period. Details on these applications are given later under the different trees susceptible to borers.

Borers that make galleries which lead to the bark surface (sawdustlike frass is a telltale sign) can be controlled by injecting a toxic paste into the holes and then sealing them with a small wad of chewing gum, grafting wax, or putty. The pastes are sold under such trade names as Bor-Tex, Borer-Kil, and Borer-Sol.

Some borers inside the tree can be killed by crushing them with a flexible wire inserted into the opening or, after probing for them, with a sharp knife.

Insect Control by Trunk Injections

Techniques and materials have been developed for controlling specific insects in certain trees by injecting insecticides into the sapstream of the trunk. The insecticides then move throughout the tree to provide protection and control.

Outstanding in the field of trunk injections is the J.J. Mauget Company of Burbank, California, which manufactures injector units Inject-a-Cide and Inject-a-Cide B. The former contains Meta-Systox R and the latter Bidrin as the active ingredient.

These are used by arborists, nurserymen, and horticulturists who have participated in a special training course.

Apparatus is also available for injecting liquid insecticides and fungicides into the tree under high pressure. Small holes are first bored into the tree trunk to the depth of the outer layers of sapwood. A special injector screw is then inserted into the hole. A high-pressure hose is connected at one end to the screw and at the other end to a hydraulic sprayer capable of building pressures up to 400 psi. The insecticide and/or fungicide is then pumped into the tree at high pressure.

The use of such apparatus is limited to experienced professional arborists.

Termites and Ants in Trees

Termites are usually associated with damage to wood in buildings. But they are occasionally found in decaying wood of live trees. Once they became established in a tree, their feeding is not confined to the decaying wood; they also feed on sound heartwood and sapwood. Several different kinds of termites can infest trees. The so-called dry-wood kinds can cause damage, but the so-called subterranean species are more destructive. The latter nest underground and may enter the tree through injured or dead roots, or they may build so-called shelter tubes of mud along the outer bark which connect the underground galleries with the breeding and feeding place up on the trunk.

Ants of several kinds also are capable of damaging live trees. Some feed on the bark at the base of trees; others eat out the heartwood. (Fig.

Fig 11-2. Larval and adult stages of carpenter ants infesting wood of black birch (*Betula lenta*).

11-2). Ants are built differently from termites. The principal difference is that ants have a noticeable constriction of the body between the thorax (where the legs and wings are attached) and the abdomen, whereas termites have a broad connection between these two sections. The wings of termites have finer venation and protrude farther beyond the abdomen than do those of ants.

Ants can be controlled with Diazinon. A hand duster can be used to blow Diazinon dust into the colony, or a small hand sprayer can be used to wet the infested areas with a Diazinon or Baygon solution.

Termites can be controlled with chlordane. In some states, such materials can be applied only by professional exterminators.

Certain carriers or solvents for some termite-proofing materials are extremely toxic to trees and shrubs. Hence any extensive use of such materials for termite-proofing homes should be used with due regard to their toxic properties, especially where tree and other plant roots are growing nearby.

Biological Control of Insects

Biological control of insects includes the use of parasites, predators, and bacterial and viral organisms. More broadly, it also includes the use of microbial insecticides, sterilizing agents, and attractants or lures.

One of the outstanding examples of biological control was the introduction of the Vedalia ladybird beetle from Australia in 1887 into citrus orchards in California to control the cottony-cushion scale. Within two years of its release into the orchards, the larval and adult stages of this predator had annihilated the scale, a pest that threatened to wipe out California's citrus industry.

The bacterium *Bacillus thuringiensis* produces a toxin which kills leaf-chewing larvae of butterflies and moths. When a caterpillar eats 40,000 to 80,000 live spores of the *B. thuringiensis*-sprayed leaf, it is poisoned by the toxic crystals produced by the bacteria during spore production. The *B. thuringiensis* dust is sold under such trade names as Agritol, Bakthane L 69, Biogard, Biotrol, Dipel, Larvatrol, and Thuricide.

Insect viruses are also being tested as a means of controlling certain caterpillars on trees and other plants. A virus has been used to wipe out an infestation of the great basin tent caterpillar (*Malacosoma fragilis*). The virus, taken from dead caterpillars which had succumbed naturally from the virus infection, was sprayed on healthy caterpillars in the laboratory. After these contracted the disease and died, their bodies were ground to make a suspension of the virus. A pint of ground, virus-killed caterpillars was sufficient to spray 30 to 50 acres of trees infested with tent caterpillars. Tests are now under way to determine whether the virus spreads from the areas where it is applied by man. If the artificially applied virus spreads a considerable distance, the treatment would be economically feasible.

Dr. C. G. Thompson of the United States Department of Agriculture Forest Service in Oregon recently isolated a naturally occurring virus capable of controlling the tussock moth that is the scourge of Douglas-fir forests in the Pacific Northwest.

Another example of biological control on a large scale was reported some years ago. Pines infested with European pine sawfly larvae were sprayed by airplane in May with an infectious virus suspension. Twenty-three days later, 89 per cent of the worms were dead. There was a 100 per cent kill on 60 per cent of the trees and only a slight defoliation. Trees not sprayed with the virus suspension were nearly 100 per cent defoliated.

Sterilization of the males of certain harmful pests is another form of biological control. The insects are exposed to gamma radiation, rendering them sterile. Females mating with gamma ray-treated males produce no offspring; thus the insect population is greatly reduced.

A number of chemosterilants are also being tested. These affect the genetic material in the insects' reproductive organs, resulting in abortion of the fertilized egg.

Another important phase of biological control involves the use of sex attractants or sex lures. These chemicals are placed in poisonous baits to attract males, which then die of poisoning.

Scientists in the United States Department of Agriculture have extracted several sex lures from natural organisms. One, from virgin elm bark beetles, attracts adult elm bark beetles of both sexes. When the lure is synthesized in sufficient amounts, it will be subjected to large-scale tests to control the bark beetles which disseminate the highly fatal Dutch elm disease fungus.

A synthetic sex attractant for the gypsy moth, a serious pest of fruit, forest, and shade trees in the northeastern United States, known as Disparlure, has also been developed. Also available are sex lures for monitoring the population of codling moth (Pherocon CM), obliquebanded leafroller (Pherocon OBLR), Oriental fruit moth (Pherocon OFM), and red-banded leafroller (Pherocon RBLR) in orchards.

Scientists in the United States Department of Agriculture have recently developed the insecticide Dimilin, which interrupts the growth process of the gypsy moth caterpillars, resulting in premature death. Under normal conditions, before each molt (shedding the skin) the body begins to produce chitin, which forms the new outer layer or shell. The Dimilin ingested by the caterpillar interferes with chitin production and results in death. Dimilin has been registered by the Environmental Protection Agency for use against the gypsy moth.

The degree of insect control by some predators such as the ladybird beetle (lady bug) and the praying mantis is often overemphasized.

Most ladybird beetles feed primarily on aphids rather than on insects in general. Although an adult ladybird beetle can consume as many as 50 aphids a day, and the larval stage can devour 25, these numbers are not sufficient to keep aphids under control.

Some kinds of ladybird beetles also feed on mealybugs and scales when the alphids are all consumed.

Ladybird beetles can be purchased by the quart or the gallon from several firms in the western United States. Unfortunately, however, these beetles do not necessarily stay in the vicinity of their release.

Another predator frequently mentioned as a control for other insects is the praying (or preying) mantis. This insect feeds on harmless and beneficial insects as well as harmful ones. It cannot be depended on to do a thorough job of pest control.

While it is true that, in a few instances, parasites and predators have controlled destructive insects successfully, it is unrealistic to expect biological controls alone to control pests completely. During the past 80 or so years the United States Department of Agriculture has imported 520 natural enemies of pests. Only 115 of these have survived and become established, and only approximately 20 have substantially controlled the pests they were imported to combat.

Selected Bibliography

Anonymous. 1967. *Suggested guide for the use of insecticides to control insects affecting groups, livestock, households, stored products, forests and forest products.* Agriculture Handbook No. 331, USDA Agricultural Research Service, Washington, D.C.

——. 1968. *Dictionary of pesticides.* Farm Chemicals. Meister Publ. Co., Willoughby, Ohio. p. 317–99.

——. 1970. *Cornell recommendations for commercial production and maintenance of trees and shrubs.* Cornell Miscellaneous Bulletin. 44 p.

——. 1971. *Farm chemicals handbook.* Meister Publ. Co., Willoughby, Ohio. 500 p.

——. 1974. *Insect and mite control on ornamentals.* Ohio State Univ. Cooperative Ext. Ser. Bull. 504. 33 p.

——. 1974. *Pesticide directory.* Meister Publ. Co., Willoughby, Ohio. 212 p.

——. 1975. *A guide to safe pest control around the home.* N.Y. State College of Agriculture and Life Sciences, Ithaca, N.Y. 56 p.

Anderson, R. F. 1960. *Forest and shade tree entomology.* Wiley, New York. 428 p.

Appleby, J. D. 1976. 'Current control of insect pests.' *Jour. Arboriculture.* Vol. 2 (No. 3). p. 41–50.

Baker, W. L. 1972. *Eastern forest insects.* USDA, Forest Service Misc. Publ. 1175. 642 p.

Billings, S. C. 1975. *Pesticide handbook-entoma.* 26th ed. Entomological Soc. of America. College Park, Md. 290p.

Blickenstaff, C. C. 1965. 'Common names of insects.' *Bul. Ent. Soc. of America.* Vol. 11 (No. 4). p. 278–320.

——. 1970. 'Common names of insects.' *Bul. Ent. Soc. of America.* Vol 16 (No. 3). p. 169–71.

Borror, D. J., D. M. De Long, and C. A. Triplehorn. 1976. *An introduction to the study of insects.* 3rd ed. Holt, Rinehart and Winston, New York. 852 p.

Craighead, F. C. 1950. *Insect enemies of eastern forests.* USDA Miscellaneous Publication 657. 679 p.

Creighton, J. T. 1947. 'New developments in insecticides and application equipment.' *Proc. Twenty-third National Shade Tree Conference.* p. 106–21.

Davis, Spencer Jr. 1969. 'Newer dormant oils on oil-susceptible trees.' *Arborist's News.* Vol. 34 (No. 15). p. 1-4.

——. 1972. 'The effect of natural gas on trees and other vegetation.' *Arborist's News.* Vol. 37 (No. 12). p. 139–41.

Doane, C. C. and P. W. Schaefer. 1971. *Aerial application of insecticides for control of the gypsy moth.* Conn. Agr. Exp. Sta. Bull, 724. 23 p.

Dunbar, D. M. 1973. 'Effective chemicals for nursery pest control.' *American Nurseryman.* Oct. 1. p. 8, 51–53, 56–57.

Eads, C. O. 1970 'The three "Rs" of effective insect control.' *Proc. Forty-fifth International Shade Tree Conference.* p. 251–54.

——. 1976. 'Visual aids of insect damage to trees and shrubs.' *Jour. Arboriculture.* Vol. 2 (No. 11). p. 201–5.

Essig. E. O. 1958. *Insects and mites of western North America.* Rev. ed. Macmillan, New York. 1050 p.

Estores, R. A., 1972. 'Systemic insecticides.' *Arborist's News.* Vol. 37 (No. 7). p. 73–75.

Felt, E. P. 1934. 'Fundamentals in the control of insect pests.' *Proc. Tenth National Shade Tree Conference.* p. 37–44.

———. 1965. *Plant galls and gall makers.* Reprint. Hafner Publ. Co., New York. 364 p.

Flint, W. P. and M. D. Farrar. 1940. 'Dormant spraying materials for shade trees.' *Arborist's News.* Vol. 5 (No. 1). p. 1–2.

Frear, D. E. H. 1970. *Pesticide handbook-entoma.* 22nd ed. College Science Publishers, State College, Penna. 284 p.

Graham, S. A. 1929. *Principles of forest entomology.* McGraw-Hill Book Co., New York. 339 p.

Hamilton, C. C. 1934. 'Experiments in the control of boring insects.' *Proc. Tenth National Shade Tree Conference.* p. 31–37.

———. 1957. 'Systemic insecticides: their nature and use in agriculture.' *Proc. Thirty-third National Shade Tree Conference.* p. 128–45.

———. 1958. 'Insect pest control for ornamental stock.' *American Nurseryman.* Mar. 15, 1958. p. 76–87.

Harding, W. C. Jr. and W. T. Johnson. 1960. *Insects of ornamental tress and shrubs.* Maryland Ext. Serv. Bul. 169.

Harrigan, W. R. and J. L. Saunders. 1976. *Cornell recommendations for pest control for commercial production and maintenance of trees and shrubs.* N.Y. State College of Agriculture and Life Sciences, Ithaca, N.Y. 60 p.

Hartzell, A. and W. J. Youden. 1935. 'Efficiency of banding for the control of cankerworms.' Boyce Thompson Inst. 7. p. 365–77.

Hayes, W. L. Jr. 1963. *Clinical handbook on economic poisons.* U.S. Dept. H. E. & W., Pub. Health Ser. Pub. 476. 144 p.

Herrick, G. W. 1935. *Insect enemies of shade trees.* Comstock Publishing Co., Ithaca, N.Y. 417 p.

Himelick, E. B. 1972. 'High pressure injections into trees.' *Arborist's News.* Vol. 37 (No. 9). p. 97–103.

Houser, J. S. 1937. 'Borer control experiments.' *Proc. Thirteenth National Shade Tree Conference.* p. 159–69.

Howard, L. O. 1901. *The insect book.* Doubleday, New York. 429 p.

Johnson, W. T. and H. H. Lyon. 1976. *Insects that feed on trees and shrubs.* Comstock Publishing Associates. Cornell University, Ithaca, N.Y. 463 p.

Mac Aloney, H. J. and H. G. Ewan. 1964. *Identification of hardwood insects by type of tree injury, north-central region.* USDA Forest Service Res. Paper LS-11. 71 p.

Mallis, E. 1964. *Handbook of pest control.* 4th ed. MacNair-Dorland Co., New York. 1148 p.

Marx, J. L. 1973. 'Insect control (II): hormones and viruses.' *Science.* Vol. 181. p. 833–35.

Metcalf, C. L. 1962. *Destructive and useful insects.* 4th ed. McGraw-Hill Book Co., New York. 1087 p.

Middleton, Wm. 1932. 'Some conditions leading to the attack of shade and ornamental trees by borers.' *Proc. Eighth National Shade Tree Conference.* p. 23–31.

Neiswander, R. B. 1956. 'Insect pests of ornamentals: borers and gall makers.' *Arborist's News.* Vol. 21 (No. 5). p. 33–37.

Nielsen, D. G. 1976. 'Insect-tree- relationships in an urban environment.' *Weeds, Trees, and Turf.* May 1976. p. 22, 27.

O'Brien, R. D. 1967. *Insecticides, action, and metabolism.* Academic Press, New York. 332 p.

Olkowski, W. and H. Olkowski. 1975. 'Establishing an integrated pest control program.' *Jour. Arboriculture.* Vol. 1 (No. 9). p. 167–72.

Pirone, P. P. 1954. 'Plan your dormant spray operations now.' *Flower Grower.* Feb. 1954. p. 10–13.

———. 1976. 'A matter of responsibility: a pesticide revolution.' *Garden Journal.* N.Y. Botanical Garden. Vol. 26 (No. 2). p. 48–51.

Sanderson, E. D. and L. M. Peairs. 1931. *Insect pests of farm, garden, and orchard.* Wiley, New York. 568 p.

Saunders, J. L. and W. T. Johnson. 1974. *Cornell recommendations for pest control for commercial production and maintenance of trees and shrubs.* N.Y. State College of Agriculture and Life Sciences, Ithaca. N.Y. 52 p.

Schread, J. C. 1970. *Control of scale insects and mealybugs on ornamentals.* Conn. Agr. Exp. Sta. Bull. 710.27 p.

———. 1971. *Control of borers in trees and woody ornamentals.* Conn. Agr. Exp. Sta. Circ. 11 p.

Snyder, T. E. 1935. *Our enemy the termite.* Comstock Publishing Co., Ithaca, N.Y. 196 p.

Spence, E. Y. 1968. *Guide to chemicals used in crop protection.* Canada Dept. Agr. Publ. 1093. 5th ed. 483 p.

Thomson, W. T. 1969. *The ornamental pesticide application guide.* Thomson Publications, Davis, Cal. 471 p.

Turner, Neely. 1963. *The gypsy moth problem.* Conn. Agr. Exp. Sta. Bull. 655. 36 p.

Vasvary, L. M. and S. H. Davis, Jr. n.d. *Tree, shrub, and flower pest control for the homeowner.* Co-op. Ext. Service, Rutgers University, Leaflet 328B. 12 p.

Vertrees, J. D. 1970. 'The small world—private lives of insects.' *Proc. Forty-fifth International Shade Tree Conference.* p. 229–34.

Wallner, W. E. 1964. 'Fiorinia hemlock scale, pest of ornamental hemlocks.' *Farm Research.* N.Y. St. Agr. Exp. Sta. and Cornell Agr. Exp. Sta. 30 (No. 1). p. 1–3.

Weidhaas, J. A. 1968. 'The effects of chemicals on insect systems.' *Proc. Forty-fourth International Shade Tree Conference.* p. 73–85.

———. 1968. 'Importance and control of scale insects.' *Proc. Forty-fourth International Shade Tree Conference.* p. 246–56.

Westcott, Cynthia. 1973. *The gardener's bug book.* 4th ed. Doubleday, New York. 689 p.

Westcott, Cynthia and P. K. Nelson. 1960. 'Biological control of plant pests.' *Brooklyn Botanic Garden.* Plants and Gardens. Vol. 16 (No. 3). 97 p.

Westcott, Cynthia and J. Walker (Eds.). 1966. *Handbook on garden pests.* Special printing of Plants and Gardens, XXII. No. 1. Brooklyn, N.Y. Brooklyn Botanic Garden.

Wilson, J. D. 1931. *Insects and their control.* Interstate Printing Corp., Plainfield, N.J. 383 p.

Wilson, L. F. 1962. *Forest insects and diseases in the northern great plains—a survey.* Lake States Forest Exp. Sta. Paper 101.

Wysong, Noel. 1953. "Termites as tree pests.' *American Nurseryman.* July 15, 1933. p. 84–88.

12

Spraying Equipment and Practices

Successful control of insect pests is ensured not only by proper selection and preparation of the insecticide but also by correct placement of the material on the infested or susceptible parts of the tree. The latter is best accomplished with good spraying equipment.

Equipment

Small trees and shrubs can be sprayed with barrel or bucket types sprayers or a small sprayer carried on the operator's back, or with small power sprayers (Fig. 12-1). Large trees can be properly sprayed only with large spraying machines (Figs. 12-2 and 12-3). Such machines are expensive and are owned principally by commercial arborists and park and shade-tree departments that do considerable shade-tree work.

Hydraulic Sprayers. The modern spray machine consists of a large wooden or steel tank, ranging in capacity from 100 to 1,000 gallons, for holding the spray material; an agitator inside the tank, which revolves to keep the spray material uniformly dispersed; and a gasoline-driven pump, which forces the material from the pump through the spray hose. These parts are usually mounted as a unit on skids to facilitate moving onto a truck or some other carrier, or they may be permanently mounted on a chassis and drawn by a truck, tractor, or other vehicle. Certain accessories, such as adequate hose and spray guns with special nozzles, complete the equipment.

Spray machines are available with pumping capacities ranging from

Fig. 12-1. A small power sprayer is excellent for spraying low-growing trees.

5^1/$_2$ gallons a minute at 300 pounds pressure, to 55 gallons at 800 pounds. Specially made hose of ^{3}/$_4$- or 1-inch size must be used to withstand some of the higher pressures.

The following are among the companies that manufacture large spraying machines: John Bean Division, FMC Corp., Lansing, Michigan 48909; Buffalo Turbine Agricultural Equipment Co., Gowanda, New York 14070; Friend Mfg. Corp., Gasport, New York 14067; H. D. Hudson Mfg. Co., Chicago, Illinois 60611; Lockwood Corp., Gering, Nebraska 69341; and F. E. Myers and Bros. Co., Ashland, Ohio 44805.

The stream of spray material and the height to which it will reach are governed by the size and construction of the nozzle, the amount of material discharged, and the pressure behind it. There are five principal types of spray nozzles. These are the disk nozzle, which throws a hollow cone-shaped spray; the Vermorel nozzle, which throws a misty, more or less cone-shaped spray; the bordeaux nozzle, which throws a flat, fan-shaped driving spray; the spray gun, which throws a cone-type to

Fig. 12-2. A hydraulic sprayer applying a dormant spray.

Fig. 12-3. A 400-gallon capacity hydraulic sprayer in action on a tall tree.

solid-stream spray; and the park nozzle, which throws a solid-stream spray. Each type has its own particular advantages and uses.

The pressure of the spray material at the nozzle opening, as well as the type of nozzle, governs the success of a spraying operation. Other factors remaining the same— for example, the size of the nozzle opening—any increase in pressure breaks up the spray material into finer particles, forces them to a greater distance from the nozzle, and results in the application of a greater volume of the insecticide or fungicide.

To spray a tree approximately 20 feet high, it is necessary to have a nozzle with a ⅛-inch opening in the disk, which will deliver 6 gallons of spray a minute at 180 pounds pressure. A tree 90 feet high can be adequately sprayed with a nozzle having a ⁵/₁₆-inch opening, releasing 44 gallons a minute at a pressure of 300 to 400 pounds. Because of friction as the spray moves through the hose, the pressure at the nozzle is much lower than that developed by the pump at the spray tank. For each 100-foot increase in length of 1-inch hose from the tank to the nozzle in the example cited above, the pressure in the tank must be increased by 33 pounds in order to provide sufficient pressure at the nozzle to enable coverage of the 90-foot tree.

Sprays are applied to tall trees in a so-called solid stream, that is, the material leaves the nozzle much as water issues from a fire hose. This stream, forced out under great pressure, soon reaches a height, however, at which it breaks into a mist, which drifts onto the leaves and stems.

In contrast to solid-stream spraying, so-called mist spraying is used on trees less than 20 feet high. In the latter case the spray breaks into a fine mist as soon as it leaves the nozzle, giving rapid and complete coverage.

Hydraulic sprayers must be handled properly to keep them at peak efficiency. To achieve this objective: lubricate daily, particularly all moving parts; always pour chemical mixtures through a good strainer before they enter the tank; rinse out the tank, hose, and nozzles with clean water at the end of the day; carry, rather than drag, the spray hose over rough terrain.

For low-growing trees, the 'Trombone' sprayer is very efficient and easy to operate (Fig. 12-4).

Mist Blowers. The discovery of insecticides such as DDT (now banned in many parts of the United States) speeded the development of new types of pest-control applicators. Water serves as the vehicle for the insecticides used in the conventional hydraulic sprayers, whereas the so-called mist blowers, or air sprayers, use blasts of air to propel the insecticide in liquid form (Fig. 12-5). With such machines it is possible to cover more trees in shorter time and at far less cost. The use of highly concentrated materials not only speeds up the refilling time but sharply

Fig. 12-4. The Trombone is available for spraying shrubs and low-growing trees.

reduces runoff or drip waste, which causes heavy loss of more dilute materials applied with the hydraulic sprayer.

Some of the mist sprayers can disperse spray particles for relatively long distances, often up to 100 feet, against a mild wind. One should bear in mind, however, that if the liquid phase disappears before the insecticide reaches its target, the dry insecticide will not adhere to the leaf surface. In other words, to deposit a coating of insecticide properly, the liquid-insecticide mixture must reach the leaves before the liquid phase evaporates.

There are several sizes and types of mist blowers on the market. Some are more suitable for use on large shade trees, and others are better adapted for watershed, park, and forest plantings.*

Among the manufacturers of mist blowers are: John Bean Division, FMC Corporation, Lansing, Michigan 48909; Besler Corp., Oakland, California 94604; Buffalo Turbine Agricultural Equipment Co., Gow-

---

* *Concentrated Spray Equipment* by S. F. Potts, published by Dorland Books, Caldwell, New Jersey 07006, gives details on mist blowers and concentrated sprays.

Fig. 12-5. A Rotomist mist blower in action.

anda, New York 14070; Friend Manufacturing Co., Gasport, New York 14067; Homelite, Textron Div., Charlotte, North Carolina; Lockwood Corp., Gering, Nebraska 69341; F. E. Myers and Bros. Co., Ashland, Ohio 44805; and Todd-CEA, Inc., Grandview, Missouri 64030.

Smaller one-man-operated mist blowers are made by Solo Motors, Inc., Newport News, Virginia 23605, and Stihl American, Inc., Oakland, New Jersey 07432 (Fig. 12-6).

Helicopters are now being used to apply insecticides and fungicides to large uninhabited areas such as woodlands and golf courses. The insecticide carbaryl (Sevin) has been applied by helicopters to control gypsy moth caterpillars in woodland areas.

Spraying Practices

Although correct spraying technique can be perfected only by actual practice, a number of suggestions to help in its acquisition are in order.

The intensity and direction of the wind must be considered before spraying operations begin. Unless the operator has had considerable experience, poor coverage and considerable waste of material are bound to occur on windy days. Maximum coverage on such days is obtained when the spray is directed toward the leeward sides of the leaves and twigs. As the spray is caught by the wind, it is blown back in the opposite

Fig. 12-6. A Stihl SG 17 mist sprayer in action.

direction, thus ensuring complete coverage. The wind factor is of even greater importance when using mist blowers; that is to say, there should be little to no wind.

Another factor to be considered is the proximity of the trees to buildings and other structures. The operator should determine beforehand how best to cover the tree with the least disfigurement to these objects. Where mist blowers are used near parked automobiles, the operator must take into account the possibility of coating the automobiles with the spray. The problem can be solved by enforcing regulations which prevent parking of automobiles under trees that are to be sprayed.

The spray gun should be adjustable to meet the situation in hand. It must be opened to the solid-stream discharge rate when the tops of tall trees are being sprayed, and cut down to a mist spray where lower branches are involved. There is no ironclad rule as to the amount of spray that should be applied to any particular tree. The object of spraying is to cover every leaf, twig, and branch that is infested or that might later become infested by some insect. Once complete coverage is obtained, the operator should move on to another part of the tree or to another tree. Usually it is not necessary to spray until the material drips from the leaves.

Safety Precautions

Following are some additional safety precautions:

Always read the label before using spray materials. Respect warnings and precautions listed.

Keep sprays out of reach of children, pets, and irresponsible adults. Do not store them near the pantry.

Store spray materials in their original containers.

Do not smoke while spraying.

Avoid inhaling sprays.

Do not spill spray materials on skin or clothing. Should some be accidentally spilled, remove contaminated clothing as quickly as possible and wash the skin thoroughly.

Wash hands and face thoroughly with soap and water and change to clean clothing after spraying.

Dispose of empty containers so they pose no hazard to humans, pets, or plants.

If symptoms of illness occur, call a physician or call the poison control center in your community.

Spray formulations, including insecticides, fungicides, miticides, and combination sprays, are presented toward the end of the next chapter.

Selected Bibliography

Carr, J. P. and J. M. Patterson. 1954. 'Application of chemicals with air sprayers.' *Jour. Agr. and Food Chem.* Vol. 2 (No. 22). p. 1102–4.

Cleveland, C. R. 1938. 'Spray materials and practices.' *Proc. Fourteenth National Shade Tree Conference.* p. 64–91.

Hamilton, C. C. (Ed.). 1939. *Entoma.* Eastern Branch of American Assoc. of Economic Entomologists. New Brunswick, N.J. 172 p.

Harding, G. W. 1947. 'Operator experience with mist blower.' *Proc. Twenty-third National Shade Tree Conference.* p. 194–99.

Langford, G. S. 1941. 'Tolerance of shade trees to spray materials.' *Proc. Seventeenth National Shade Tree Conference.* p. 19–30.

Mason, A. F. 1936. *Spraying, dusting, and fumigating of plants.* Macmillan, New York. 539 p.

Potts, S. F. 1947. 'Concentrated spray applications.' *Proc. Twenty-third National Shade Tree Conference.* p. 183–94.

————. 1958. *Concentrated spray equipment.* Dorland Books, Caldwell, N.J. 598 p.

Rankin, W. H. 1932. 'Spraying for leaf disease of shade trees.' *Proc. Eighth National Shade Tree Conference.* p. 64–70.

Wester, H. V. 1953. *General spraying and other practices.* Tree Preservation Bulletin No. 6. Rev. 1953. Supt. Documents, Washington, D.C.

13
Tree Diseases and Their Control

Although disease control unquestionably constitutes one of the major phases of successful tree maintenance, it is the least clearly understood by the tree worker. This lack of understanding is due partly to the difficulty of recognizing disease symptoms and partly to the rather complex nature of the parasitic agents. Insufficient knowledge of the various chemicals used to combat diseases and of their proper applications is also a contributing factor.

Broadly speaking, a tree is considered diseased when its structure or functions deviate from the normal as discussed in the first chapter. Such a definition includes abnormalities caused by drought, excessive moisture, lack of nutrients, and chemical and electrical injuries. The present discussion, however, is limited to those diseases caused by infective agents such as fungi, bacteria, and viruses. The symptoms they produce, their nature, and the chemicals and arboricultural practices used to combat them are also included in the discussion.

Symptoms

A diseased tree exhibits one or several characteristic symptoms, depending on the species of tree, its environment, and the causal agent. Three general groups of symptoms occur: dying of the tissues, or necrosis; dwarfing or underdevelopment, hypoplasia; and overgrowth, or hyperplasia.

Necrotic symptoms include dead twigs or leaves—blights; sunken

271

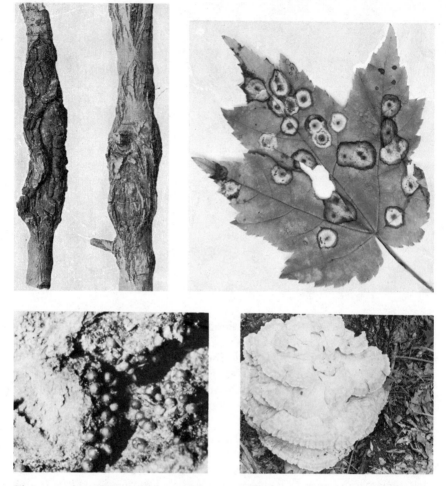

Fig. 13-1. Symptoms of Fungus Diseases. **Upper Left:** Cankers on ash stems. **Upper Right:** Circular spots on maple leaf caused by the fungus *Phyllosticta*. **Lower Left:** Pin-point fruiting bodies of the *Nectria* canker fungus. **Lower Right:** Fruiting bodies of the fungus *Polyporus sulphureus*.

decayed areas on the trunk, branches, or roots—cankers (Fig. 13-1); small, well-defined dead areas on the leaves—leaf spots (Fig. 13-1); and dead or wilted tops owing to the killing or obstructing of the conducting tissue—wilts.

Chlorosis, or yellowing of the leaves resulting from underdevelopment of chlorophyll, is a hypoplastic symptom often associated with virus diseases. Stunting of twig growth and the production of undersized leaves are other hypoplastic symptoms.

The various types of galls produced by both fungi and bacteria are hyperplastic symptoms. Probably the most striking example is the overgrowth produced on trees and shrubs affected by the crown gall disease discussed in Chapter 14. Leaves affected by the so-called curl diseases, wherein small areas or the entire leaf grows to twice the normal size, exhibit another type of hyperplastic symptom.

In addition to symptoms produced on the plant attacked, certain signs, such as fruiting and vegetative structures of the causal organisms, help in diagnosing the disease. For example, many fungi produce on the affected areas fruiting bodies that are easily recognized and facilitate diagnosis. Such bodies vary in size from pin-point dots (Fig. 13-1), which are barely visible to the unaided eye, to bodies a foot or more in diameter (Fig. 13-1). The latter commonly occur in wood-decay diseases and appear as shelves or brackets adhering to the dead bark.

Additional signs may also occur that aid in determining the cause of a disease. For example, droplets of colorless or milky ooze appear on the bark of trees affected by the fire blight disease, and spruces affected by the Cytospora canker disease nearly always have grayish-white resins exuding along the affected branches.

Nature of Parasitic Agents

Most diseases of shade and ornamental trees are caused by one of four agents: bacteria, fungi, viruses, or mycoplasma-like organisms.

Bacteria and fungi are plants that differ from those most familiar to everyone in that they do not contain the green coloring matter, chlorophyll, which is necessary for the manufacture of food. As a result, they are dependent on the higher plants for their sustenance. Bacteria and fungi that depend entirely upon decaying organic matter for their food source are known as saprophytes. These forms are frequently beneficial, in that they hasten decay and the liberation of minerals for use in future plant growth. Forms that are able to obtain their nourishment by direct attack upon living plant cells are known as parasites or pathogens. It is this group that is concerned in disease production.

Bacteria are microscopic, single-celled plants which multiply by simple fission, a single individual dividing to form two. Some types of bacteria possess flagella or hairlike appendages which effect a limited amount of locomotion in liquids. Bacteria have several forms, but those that parasitize plants are usually rod-shaped.

Fungi, as a rule, are much more complex than bacteria. They may possess two distinct stages—vegetative and reproductive. The vegetative stage consists of a weft or mass of microscopic, threadlike strands called 'hyphae.' Unlike the bacteria, a single fungus plant may be composed of innumerable cells, joined together. Certain tissues in this complex are capable of performing highly specific functions. The reproductive stage may be simple or very complex, either microscopic or visible to the

Fig. 13-2. Spore tendrils of the fungus *Cytospora* (*Valsa*) *Kunzei* oozing from infected pine bark.

naked eye, often reaching 12 or more inches in diameter. In all cases, however, the reproductive bodies produce microscopic spores of various shapes and colors, which function much as do the seeds of higher plants. The spores may be ejected, drop out, or ooze (Fig. 13-2) from the reproductive bodies and are carried by some means to susceptible plant parts. In a moist environment, these spores germinate by pushing forth a tiny strand known as a germ tube. Once inside the host plant, the tube branches into numerous strands, which constitute a new fungus plant. Eventually this plant produces a new crop of spores directly, or fruit bodies capable of producing spores.

Viruses are ultramicroscopic principles generally carried from diseased to healthy plants by insects. The infective principle usually occurs in all parts of the plant and survives the winter in plant tissues.

Mycoplasma-like organisms, intermediate between bacteria and viruses both in size and other properties, have recently been implicated as plant pathogens. Lethal yellowing of palms and phloem necrosis of elms, previously thought to be caused by viruses, are now known to be caused by these organisms. Among the reasons for this conclusion are the facts that the symptoms are suppressed by antibiotics and the organisms have long resisted isolation and visualization.

Dissemination of Bacteria and Fungi

Bacterial plant pathogens and many fungus pathogens gain entrance into the plant tissue through the natural openings, such as the stomata, or breathing pores, and the hydathodes in the leaf tissues, or the lenticels in the stem. Wounds caused by insects or by mechanical means also afford convenient openings. Many fungi, however, are also able to penetrate directly the unbroken epidermis of the leaves. By growth or multiplication within the host tissue, fungi and bacteria absorb the cell contents and cause death, or by their presence cause overgrowth or dwarfing of the invaded tissues.

Fungus parasites are disseminated primarily in the spore stage. They may be splashed by rain or carried by air currents, by insects, by animals, on the hands of the tree worker, or on tools, from tree to tree or from place to place.

Wind-blown rain is probably the most important agent in the local dissemination of spores, particularly of those fungi that cause leaf spots, leaf blights, and twig cankers. Spores produced on the surface of infected leaves or in cankers are splashed or washed to nearby healthy leaves and twigs, on which new infections occur.

Air currents are also important agents of dissemination. For example, the spores of the chestnut blight fungus are blown by the wind many miles from the tissues on which they are formed.

Insects are well-known agents of dissemination. Bees and flies are known to spread the bacteria that cause the fire blight disease. Several species of bark beetle are believed to be chiefly responsible for the spread of spores of the fungus causing the Dutch elm disease.

The chestnut blight fungus is known to be spread by birds and squirrels lighting on or traveling over extensive bark cankers, on the surface of which spores are produced in large numbers. These spores adhere to the talons or feet and may be deposited again on some distant tree.

Spores may be spread on tree workers' hands and clothing, as is the case with the Cytospora canker disease of spruce, especially when diseased branches are pruned during wet weather. The fungus responsible for planetree cankerstain may be disseminated on infested pruning saws, and even in many types of wound dressings (p. 455).

Pruning saws, shears, and other metal tools can be disinfested by dipping them in or wiping them with 70 per cent denatured alcohol. Tree-climbing ropes contaminated with fungi can be disinfested by confining the rope for 3 hours in a 10-gallon closed receptacle containing 4 ounces of liquid formaldehyde.

Soil-inhabiting organisms capable of producing diseases such as wilts and root and collar rots are carried largely by the transfer of infested soil on tools, on shoes, or by washing during heavy rains. Winds, by lifting soil particles and carrying them from place to place, may also be a means of dissemination of this group of plant parasites.

Many soil-inhabiting organisms live as saprophytes in the soil until they come in contact with susceptible tree roots. They enter such roots, even unwounded ones, and become parasites. Wilt fungi grow directly into the conducting tissues, where they cause a partial clogging or secrete poisons that are carried in the water stream to the leaves. There they accumulate and cause a collapse of the leaf tissues.

Many fungi that normally are weak parasites, which do little damage to trees growing under proper conditions, can readily destroy trees growing under adverse conditions.

To avoid damage by so-called weak parasites, one should provide the best possible growing conditions for trees. The trees should be well fed, the soil provided with organic matter, drainage improved if necessary, and the trees watered during extended periods of drought.

Overwintering of Bacteria and Fungi

Leaf-spotting and leaf-blighting bacteria and fungi overwinter in fallen infected leaves, on dormant buds, and in small twig cankers; canker-producing bacteria and fungi overwinter in the margins of the cankers; and wilt fungi pass the winter in the vascular tissues of infected trees and in the soil.

Principles of Tree Disease Control

The control of shade and ornamental tree diseases is based largely on the principles of eradication and protection, and to a lesser degree on exclusion and immunization.

Eradication. The removal and destruction of the fungus or bacterial parasites either at their source or at the point where infection occurs constitutes one phase of eradication. For example, the collection and destruction of fallen diseased leaves eliminates an important source of inoculum. In the same manner, the pruning of branches infected by pathogenic fungi or bacteria also removes an important source of inoculum for subsequent infections.

Another commonly employed eradicatory practice is the application of dormant or delayed dormant sprays at the point where infection occurs. For example, lime sulfur solution is often recommended for the control of dieases such as leaf blisters and anthracnoses, in which spores pass the winter in the bud scales and on the twigs. Such a spray actually disinfests the buds and twigs before the spores have an opportunity to germinate or to penetrate the tree's tissues in the early spring.

The removal of decayed wood in trunks and branches may also be considered an eradicatory measure. As has already been pointed out in the chapter on Cavity Treatments, however, such a practice rarely, if ever, accomplishes its objective, inasmuch as the causal fungi extend well beyond the zone of visible decay.

Protection. Protection of trees from attacks by pathogenic organisms includes those measures involving the use of sprays and manipulation of the environment in order to make conditions unfavorable for the pathogen, favorable for the tree, or both.

Exclusion and Immunization. The principles of exclusion and immunization are less commonly used to control tree diseases. Exclusion involves the prevention of importation of trees known to be susceptible to certain highly contagious diseases into an area that is still uninfested, such as the movement of elms from the Dutch elm disease quarantine area to uninfested zones. Immunization involves the use of strains of trees that are resistant to some particular disease. This field is not so highly developed in regard to trees as it is with smaller plants, though some work is now being conducted in various parts of the country on breeding trees for disease resistance.

Manipulation of the Environment

Certain arboricultural practices can be executed to change the environment and effect disease control. For example, judicious pruning of many deciduous trees reduces the density of the crown and results in a reduction of the severity of anthracnose disease. Most fungus spores must be exposed to high humidity or free water for at least several hours in order to germinate and infect. Thinning out of the tree's crown enables more rapid drying after rains or heavy dews, thus materially reducing the number of infections.

Improving soil drainage by the installation of drain tiles increases the ability of the tree to withstand attacks by many soil-borne organisms. The addition of fertilizers high in nitrogenous materials will aid many trees to outgrow certain diseases. Probably the best example is in the treatment of maples mildly infected with the Verticillium fungus. The increased growth resulting from the fertilization enables the formation of a thick layer of sapwood, which seals the invading fungus in the heartwood, where it is harmless.

It is well to remember, however, that certain practices may change the environment so as to make conditions more favorable for the pathogen. Excessive applications of nitrogenous fertilizers, for example, will increase the susceptibility of such trees as apple, hawthorn, and mountain-ash to the fire blight disease. Consequently, the application of fertilizers low in nitrogen and relatively high in phosphorus and potash is recommended in such cases.

It is now well recognized that trees growing in good, well-drained, and well-aerated soils usually show less disease than those in poor soils. Supplying such conditions, whenever feasible, will naturally result in healthier trees.

Spraying for Disease Control

Three points must be kept foremost in mind to ensure success with sprays: they must be applied at the proper time; they must be applied thoroughly; and they must contain the proper ingredients.

All protective sprays must be applied before rainy periods, because fungi and bacteria penetrate plant tissues when the plants are wet. Most of the failures to control leaf diseases that are reported by tree men are due to lack of appreciation of the importance of timely application.

Complete coverage with the spray is also essential, for the most efficient material will do little good unless it is applied as a fine mist, which will deposit an even protective film. The lower surfaces of the leaves are the most common entrance points for leaf-infecting fungi. Consequently, these should be thoroughly coated. The various types of spray machines discussed in Chapter 12 are satisfactory for the application of disease-preventing sprays.

Bactericides

A number of serious diseases caused by bacteria are best controlled with bactericides. Bordeaux mixture and fixed copper fungicides are fairly effective in controlling these diseases, but some of the antibiotics are even more effective.

Fire blight, a bacterial disease of hawthorn, mountain-ash, and other members of the rose family, can be controlled with streptomycin or mixtures of this antibiotic and another known as Terramycin.* Antibiotics for bacterial plant disease control are sold under such names as Bacticin,* Agrimycin,* Agri-Strep,* and Phytomycin.*

Fungicides

Many fungicides are available for controlling tree diseases. Following are some of the materials approved in most parts of the United States:

Acme Bordeaux Mixture.* See under Bordeaux Mixture.

Acti-dione,* also known as cycloheximide, is an antibiotic which con-

* Trade name.

trols cedar-apple rusts. 3-2-(3,5-dimethyl-2-oxocyclohexyl)2-hydroxy-ethyl)-glutarimide.

*Agrimycin.** See under Streptomycin.

*Agri-Strep.** See under Streptomycin.

*Arasan.** See under Thiram.

*Basi-Cop.** See under Bordeaux Mixture.

*Basic Copper Sulfate.** See under Bordeaux Mixture.

Benlate,[1] sold under the names of Benlate Benomyl Fungicide,* Bonide Benomyl (DuPont New Systemic Fungicide),* Science Systemic Fungicide,* Miller's Systemic Fungicide,* Lignasan BLP,* controls many fungus leaf spots and blotches, blights, rots, scabs, and powdery mildews. It appears promising as a control of Verticillium wilt of some plants and of the Dutch elm disease. Methyl 1(butylcarbamoy 1)-2-benzimidazole-carbamate. LD_{50}: 10,000.

*Benlate Benomyl Fungicide.** See under Benlate.

*Black Leaf Bordeaux Powder.** See under Bordeaux Mixture.

*Bonide Benomyl (DuPont New Systemic Fungicide).** See under Benlate.

Bordeaux Mixture is one of the oldest and still one of the most useful fungicides. The killing principle in the spray, after it is made up and ready for use, is a mixture of certain salts of copper. It is prepared by mixing copper sulfate (blue vitriol) and hydrated lime in various proportions. The formula 4-4-50, for instance, means that 4 pounds of copper sulfate and 4 pounds of hydrated lime are used with 50 gallons of water. The above proportions are so generally useful that this may be considered a standard mixture. It has been found, however, that the amount of lime may be considerably reduced. For example, 2-1-50 or even 3-1-50 has been found satisfactory for certain plants, and the residue does not spot the foliage so badly. Certain plants are rather susceptible to burning by lime.

To prepare small quantities of bordeaux, the following procedure is suggested: Dissolve 4 ounces of copper sulfate crystals in 1 gallon of water. Then dissolve 2 ounces of hydrated lime in 2 gallons of water. Finally, add the copper sulfate solution to the lime water. This makes 3 gallons of approximately a 4-2-50 bordeaux.

Mixing the two solutions together forms an insoluble or 'fixed' gelatinlike copper precipitate. When it dries on the leaves, it forms a membranous coating which clings. Since the adhesiveness is lost if the mixture stands too long, bordeaux mixture should always be fresh when used.

Ready-made bordeaux mixture is sold under the names Acme Bordeaux Mixture,* Copper Hydro Bordow,* Bor-dox,* Pratt Bordeaux Mix,* Black Leaf Bordeaux Powder.*

1. Benlate is used throughout this book for the sake of brevity. Actually, the full name is Benlate Benomyl Fungicide.*

Wherever bordeaux mixture is mentioned in this book as a disease-preventing materials, one may safely substitute one of the so-called fixed coppers.

Among the fixed coppers on the market are Basic Copper Sulfate,* Tribasic Copper Sulfate,* Basi-Cop,* Microcop,* Copper 53 Fungicide,* and T-B-C-S 53.* Other copper fungicides are sold as Bordo,* Bordo-Mix,* C-O-C-S,* Kocide 101,* Miller 658,* Ortho Copper Fungicide,* and Coprantol.*

One objectionable feature of bordeaux mixture and other copper compounds is that they may cause some injury to plants when used during cool, wet weather.

*Bordow.** See under Bordeaux Mixture.

*Bordo-Mix.** See under Bordeaux Mixture.

*Bor-dox.** See under Bordeaux Mixture.

*Captan,** also sold under the name Orthocide,* is effective in preventing scab on crabapple leaves and fruits and many other leaf spot diseases of trees.

*Carbamate.** See under Ferbam.

*Chem-Bam.** See under Nabam.

*Chem-Neb.** See under Maneb.

*Chem-Zineb.** See under Zineb.

*C-O-C-S.** See under Bordeaux Mixture.

*Copper 53 Fungicide.** See under Bordeaux Mixture.

*Copper Hydro Bordo.** See under Bordeaux Mixture.

*Coprantol.** See under Bordeaux Mixture.

*Coromate.** See under Ferbam.

Cycloheximide. See under Acti-dione.*

*Cyprex,** commonly known as dodine, is effective against the leaf blight of sycamores and black walnuts. n-Dodecyguanidine acetate. LD_{50}: 1000.

*Dexon** is effective in controlling root rot diseases caused by *Pythium* and *Phytophthora* fungi. Sodium [4-(dimethylamino)phenyl] diazene sulfate. LD_{50}: 100.

*Difolatan.** See under Folcid.

Dinocap. See under Karathane.*

Dithane D-14.* See under Nabam.

Dithane M-22.* See under Maneb.

Dithane M-45* is effective in preventing many fungus diseases of ornamental trees. Eighty per cent coordination product of zinc ion and manganese ethylene bisdithiocarbamate. LD_{50}: 8000.

Dithane Z-78.* See under Zineb.

Dithiocarbamate. See under Dithane D-14,* Dithane M-22,* Dithane M-45,* Dithane Z-78,* Ferbam, Fermate,* Fore,* Maneb, Manzate,* Parzate,* and Zineb.

Dodine. See under Cyprex.*

Ferbam, also sold under the names Coromate,* Fermate,* Fermate Ferbam Fungicide,* Carbamate,* Karbam Black,* and Ferbam Fungicide,* is one of the first so-called carbamates to be marketed. It controls the cedar rust disease of crabapples, many leaf spots, blights, and scab. Ferric dimethyl dithiocarbamate. LD_{50}: 17,000.

*Ferbam Fungicide.** See under Ferbam.

*Fermate.** See under Ferbam.

*Fermate Ferbam Fungicide.** See under Ferbam.

Folcid, sold under the trade name Difolatan,* is effective against anthracnose of sycamores and London planetrees. *cis*-N8(1, 1, 2, 2-Tetrachloroethyl) thio-4-cyclohexene-1,2-dicarboximide. LD_{50}: 6200.

Folpet. See under Phaltan.*

*Fore** is a special formulation of Dithane M-45* for use in controlling many leaf diseases of such trees as holly and horsechestnut. LD_{50}: 8000.

*Karathane,** also known as dinocap and Mildex,* is used to control powdery mildew on many trees. It also controls several species of mites. 2-4-Dinitro-6-octyl-phenylcrotonate, 2,6-dinitro-4-octylphenylcrotonate, and nitrooctylphenols (principally dinitro). LD_{50}: 980.

*Karbam Black.** See under Ferbam.

Kocide 101.* See under Bordeaux Mixture.

Lignasan. Used as an aid in the control of Dutch elm disease. Injected into the trunk of elms in late spring. Methyl 2-benzimidazole carbamate phosphate.

*Lignasan BLP.** See under Benlate.

Lime sulfur is effective in controlling powdery mildews on many trees. It also help to combat infestations of spider mites. In concentrated form it is used during the plants' dormant period to destroy overwintering stages of aphids, mites, and scale insects. As a dormant spray it is diluted 1 part of the concentrated lime sulfur in 8 or 10 parts of water. Lime sulfur should not be used near buildings, walls, or trellises because it will stain such objects. It can be diluted 1 part in 50 parts of water and used as a spray during the growing season. Lime sulfur is also available as a dust. Neither the dust nor the spray should be used when the air temperature is above 85°F. (29°C.). Calcium polysulfide.

Maneb, also sold as Dithane M-22,* Manzate,* and Chem Neb,* is effective in combating leaf spot diseases of trees. Manganese ethylene bisdithiocarbamate. LD_{50}: 7500.

*Manzate.** See under Maneb.

Mertect 160 has recently been found to be effective against the Botrytis blight of dogwood. LD_{50}: 3100.

*Microcop.** See under Bordeaux Mixture.

*Mildex.** See under Karathane.*

Miller 658.* See under Bordeaux Mixture.

*Miller's Systemic Fungicide.** See under Benlate.

Nabam, also sold as Dithane D-14,* and Chem-Bam,* is occasionally used to control certain fungus diseases of ornamental trees. Disodium ethylene-1,2-bisdithiocarbamate. LD_{50}: 395.

*Orthocide.** See under Captan.*

*Ortho Copper Fungicide.** See under Bordeaux Mixture.

Oxycarboxin. See under Plantvax.*

*Parzate.** See under Zineb.

PCNB. See under Terraclor.*

*Phaltan,** also sold under the common name folpet, is used to control many fungus diseases of trees. It is one of the carbamate fungicides presently available that will control powdery mildew. N-(trichloro-methylthio)phthalimide. LD_{50}: greater than 10,000.

*Phytomycin.** See under Streptomycin.

Piperalin. See under Pipron.*

*Pipron,** also known by the common name piperalin, is effective in combating powdery mildew of catalpa and many ornamental plants. 3-(2-Methylpiperidino)propyl 3,4-dichorobenzoate.

*Plantvax,** also known by the common name oxycarboxin, is effective in controlling rust diseases, especially of cedar-apple and hawthorn rusts.   5,6-Dihydro-2-methyl-1,4-oxathin-3-carboxanilide-4,4-dioxide. LD_{50}: 2000.

*Polyram** controls fungus diseases of many ornamental plants. A mixture of ethylene bis(dithiocarbamate) zinc and (dithiobis(thio-carbonyl)-iminoethylene)bis (dithiocarbamate) zinc. LD_{50}: over 10,000.

*Pratt Bordeaux Mix.** See under Bordeaux Mixture.

*Science Systemic Fungicide.** See under Benlate.

Streptomycin, also known as Agrimycin,* Agri-Strep,* and Phytomy-cin,* is effective in controlling diseases such as fire blight of apple, crabapple, pear, and walnut.

Sulfur has long been used to control many plant diseases such as powdery mildew. It also controls spider mites. See under Lime sulfur for details.

T-B-C-S 53.* See under Bordeaux Mixture.

*Terraclor** is an excellent soil fungicide. Pentachloronitrobenzene. LD_{50}:12,000.

*Terrazole,** also sold as Truban,* is effective against soil-borne fungi such as *Pythium.* 5-Ethoxy-3-trichloromethyl-1,2,4-thiadiazole. LD_{50}: 2,000.

Thiram, also sold as Arasan* and Thylate,* is used to control rust and scab of crabapples and other diseases. Tetramethylthiuram disulfide. LD_{50}: 780.

*Thylate.** See under Thiram.

*Tribasic Copper Sulfate.** See under Bordeaux Mixture.

*Truban.** See Terrazole.*

Zineb, also sold as Parzate* and Dithane Z-78,* is used as a preventive fungicide for anthracnose of planetrees and other fungus diseases. Zinc ethylene bisdithiocarbamate.

Combination Sprays and Compatibility. Some materials may be safely combined with others to control fungus or bacterial diseases and insects in a single operation. Because improper mixing of these materials may cause injury to the sprayed plants or reduce the efficiency of one or several of the materials in the mixture, one should seek advice from state entomologists and plant pathologists as to the best and safest combinations. A spray compatibility chart is also available from the Meister Publishing Company, Willoughby, Ohio 44094, for a small charge.

Spray Formulas[2]

Actidione—100 parts per million—one level teaspoon of 0.5 per cent Actidione, plus 5 level tablespoons of spreader-corrective, in 3 gallons water.

Aramite 15 per cent wettable powder, 2 pounds in 100 gallons water, or 2 tablespoons in 1 gallon.

Aramite 25 per cent emulsion, 1 pint in 100 gallons, or 1 teaspoon in 1 gallon.

Bordeaux mixture 4-4-50, copper sulfate 4 pounds, hydrated lime 4 pounds in 50 gallons water. To make 3 gallons, dissolve 4 ounces copper sulfate in 1 gallon water and 4 ounces hydrated lime in 2 gallons water. Then pour copper sulfate solution into limewater and use immediately.

Captan 50 per cent wettable powder, 2 pounds in 100 gallons water, or 1½ tablespoons in 1 gallon.

Chlorobenzilate 25 per cent emulsifiable solution, 1 pint, in 100 gallons, or 1 teaspoon per gallon.

Chlorobenzilate 25 per cent wettable powder, 1 pound in 100 gallons, or 1 level tablespoon per gallon.

Copper fungicides (fixed), as directed by manufacturer.

Copper sulfate (snow), 8 pounds plus hydrated lime, 12 pounds plus linseed oil, 1 pint in 100 gallons water.

Dinitro powder (DN Dry Mix), 4 pounds in 100 gallons water, or ½ cup in 3 gallons.

Dinitro Slurry (Elgetol or Krenite), 1 gallon in 100 gallons water.

Dormant sprays (Dendrol, Scalecide, Sunoco, etc.), as directed by the manufacturer.

Elgetol, 1 gallon in 100 gallons water, or 2½ tablespoons in 1 gallon.

Ferbam 76 per cent, 2 pounds in 100 gallons water, or 2½ tablespoons in 1 gallon.

2. These are some of the more commonly used insecticides, miticides, fungicides, bactericides, and combination sprays presently in common use.

Ferbam 76 per cent, 1½ pounds, plus summer spray oil emulsion, 1 quart in 100 gallons water.

Ferbam 76 per cent, ½ pound plus wettable sulfur 3 pounds in 100 gallons.

Fermate—see ferbam.

Ferradow—see ferbam.

Karathane, as directed by the manufacturer.

Kelthane 18.5 per cent emulsifiable solution, 1 pint in 100 gallons or 1 teaspoon per gallon.

Kelthane 25 per cent wettable powder, 1 to 1½ pounds in 100 gallons or 1 tablespoon per gallon.

Malathion 25 per cent wettable powder, 3 pounds in 100 gallons water, or 3 tablespoons in 1 gallon.

Malathion 50 per cent emulsifiable liquid, 1½ pints in 100 gallons water, or 1 tablespoon per gallon.

Maneb 80 per cent wettable powder, 1 pound in 100 gallons water, or ½ teaspoon per gallon.

Methoxychlor 25 per cent emulsion, 3 quarts in 100 gallons water, or 2 tablespoons per gallon.

Methoxychlor 50 per cent wettable powder, 3 pounds in 100 gallons water, or 3 tablespoons per gallon.

Nabam, 1⅓ quarts plus zinc sulfate, 1 pound plus hydrated lime ½ pound plus Triton X-100 one ounce in 100 gallons water.

Rotenone 1 per cent emulsifiable solution, 1 quart in 100 gallons, or 1 tablespoon per gallon.

Streptomycin, as directed by the manufacturer.

Sulfur (wettable), 2 pounds in 100 gallons, or 1 tablespoon per gallon.

Sulfur sprays, as directed by the manufacturer.

Superior dormant miscible oil (Orthol D, Neutrona, Superior), as directed by the manufacturer.

Zineb 70 per cent wettable powder, 1½ pounds in 100 gallons water, or 1 tablespoon per gallon.

Ziram 70 per cent wettable powder, 2 pounds in 100 gallons, or 2 tablespoons per gallon.

Selected Bibliography

Anonymous. 1970. 'Plant disease control guide.' *Grounds Maintenance*. March 1970. p. 43–46.
———. 1977. 'G M Guide to 1977 horticultural chemicals.' *Grounds Maintenance*. Vol. 12 (No. 3). p. 76–83.
Beattie, R. K. 1939. 'Virus diseases of forest and shade trees.' *Proc. Fifteenth National Shade Tree Conference*. p. 12–22
Bega, R. V., T. W. Childs, G. H. Hepting, C. S. Hodges, Jr., and L. F. Roth. 1963. 'Symposium on root diseases of forest trees.' *Phytopathology*. Vol. 53 (No. 10). p. 1120–36.

Bier, J. E. 1964. 'The relation of some bark factors to canker susceptibility.' *Phytopathology*. Vol. 54 (No. 3) p. 250–53.

Boyce, J. S. 1961. *Forest pathology*. 3rd ed. McGraw-Hill Book Co., New York. 572 p.

Campana, Richard. 1970. 'Systemic fungicides for the control of tree diseases.' *Trees*. July-Aug. 1970. p. 6–11.

Carter, J. C. 1953. 'Fungicides for use on shade and ornamental trees.' *Proc. Twenty-ninth National Shade Tree Conference*. p. 118–22.

———. 1961. *Illinois trees: their diseases*. Illinois Natural History Survey Circ. 46. 99 p.

———. 1963. 'New controls for shade tree diseases.' *American Nurseryman*. Nov. 15, 1963. p. 13, 89–102.

Davidson, A. C. and R. M. Prentice. 1967. *Important forest insects and diseases of mutual concern to Canada, the United States, and Mexico*. Minister of Forestry and Rural Dev. Ottawa, Canada. 248 p.

Felt, E. P. and S. W. Bromley. 1931. 'Insecticides and fungicides for ornamentals.' *Proc. Seventh National Shade Tree Conference*. p. 115–21.

Gregory, S. F. and T. W. Jones. 1975. *An improved apparatus for pressure-injecting fluid into trees*. Northeastern Forest Experiment Station. USDA Forest Service Res. Note NE-214. 6 p.

Hartig, Robert. 1894. *Diseases of trees*. Macmillan, London, 331 p.

Heald, F. D. 1926. *Manual of plant diseases*. McGraw-Hill Book Co., New York. 891 p.

Helburg, L. B., M. E. Shomaker, and R. A. Morrow. 1973. 'A new trunk injection technique for systemic chemicals.' *Plant Disease Reptr*. Vol. 57 (No. 6). p. 513–14.

Hepting, G. H. 1960. 'Climate change and forest disease.' *Proc. Fifth World Forestry Congress*. Vol. 2. p. 842–47.

———. 1963. 'Climate and forest diseases.' *Ann. Rev. Phytopathology* 1. p. 31–50.

Hepting, G. H. and M. E. Fowler. 1962. *Tree diseases of eastern forests and farm woodlands*. Agr. Inf. Bul. 254 p.

Hock, W. K. 1970. 'Present status of research on systemic fungicides.' *Arborist's News*. Vol. 35 (No. 6). p. 57–61.

Hubert, E. E. *An outline of forest pathology*. Wiley, New York. 543 p.

James, R. L., F. C. Strong, W. F. Morofsky, and A. E. Mitchell. 1959. *Control of insects and diseases on ornamental trees*. Mich. Sta. Univ. Ext. Bul. 269 p.

Kienholz, Raymond and C. B. Bidwell. 1938. *A survey of diseases and defects in Connecticut forests*. Conn. Agr. Exp. Sta. Bul. 412. 66 p.

Kimmey, J. W. 1957. *Dwarf misletoes of California and their control*. Tech. Paper 19. Cal. Forest and Range Exp. Sta. 12 p.

King, C. L. 1963. *Shade tree diseases*. Kansas State Univ. Ext. Circ. 310.

Kurtz, A. R. 1965. *Pests and diseases of trees and shrubs*. Wisconsin State Dept. Agr. Bul. 351.

Lortie, M. E. W. Ross, A. L. Shigo, F. A. Wood, J. M. Skelly, and R. A. Zabel. 1964. 'Symposium on tree cankers.' *Phytopathology*. Vol. 54 (No. 3). p. 261–78.

Massee, George. 1915. *Diseases of cultivated plants and trees*. Duckworth and Co., London. 605 p.

McWain, P. and G. F. Gregory. 1971. *Solubilization of benomyl for xylem injection in vascular wilt disease control.* Northeastern Forest Exp. Sta., USDA Forest Service Res. Paper NE-234.

Neely, Dan. 1970. 'Fungicides and their use.' *Arborist's News.* Vol. 35 (No. 11). p. 117–20.

———. 1975. 'Treatment of foliar diseases of woody ornamentals with soil injections with benomyl.' *Plant Disease Reptr.* Vol. 59 (No. 4). p. 300–303.

Nichols, L. P. n.d. *Tree diseases: description and control.* Penn. State Univ. Special Circ. 85. 29 p.

———. 1974. *Tree diseases—description and control.* Penn. State Univ., Northeast Extension Publ. 28 p.

Peace, T. R. 1962. *Pathology of trees and shrubs.* Oxford Univ. Press, London. 753 p.

Peterson, G. W. and R. S. Smith, Jr., 1975. *Forest nursery diseases in the United States.* USDA Forest Service, Agr. Handbook No. 470. 125 p.

Peterson, J. L. and S. H. Davis, Jr. 1977. 'Update on tree disease and fungicide research.' *American Nurseryman* Jan. 15. p. 14, 15, 104, 105.

Pirone, P. P. 1959. 'Why shade trees die along city streets.' *Garden Journal* N.Y. Bot. Garden. Nov.-Dec. 1959. p. 207–10.

———. 1972. 'Plant ailments.' *Arnoldia.* Vol. 33 (No. 1). p. 37–45.

Raabe, R. D. 1970. 'Soil-borne diseases of shade trees.' *Proc. Forty-fifth International Shade Tree Conference.* p. 259–61.

Rankin, W. H. 1918. *Manual of tree diseases.* Macmillan, New York. 398 p.

Shurtleff, M. C. 1966. *How to control plant diseases in the home garden.* 2d ed. Iowa State Univ. Press. 649 p.

———. 1970. 'New developments in systemic fungicides.' *Flower and Garden.* July 1970. p. 34–37.

———. 1975. 'GM guide to horticultural chemicals.' *Grounds Maintenance.* March 1975. p. 62, 64, 66, 70.

Shurtleff, M. C. and G. W. Simone. 1977. 'Fungicide and disease control. Spray programs for woody ornamentals.' *Jour. Arboriculture.* Vol. 3 (No. 3). p. 41–54.

Silverborg, S. B. and R. L. Gilbertson. 1962. *Tree diseases in New York State plantations.* N.Y. State College Forestry. Syracuse. Bull. 44. 61 p.

Smith, E. F. 1920. *An introduction to bacterial diseases of plants.* Saunders, Philadelphia. 688 p.

Stevens, F. L. 1925. *Plant disease fungi.* Macmillan, New York. 469 p.

Stevens, F. L. and J. G. Hall. 1933. *Diseases of economic plants.* Macmillan, New York. 507 p.

Wilson, C. L. 1977. 'Emerging tree diseases in urban ecosystems. *Jour. Arboriculture.* Vol. 3 (No. 4). p. 69–71.

Young, H. C. 1940. 'Fungicides and their use on ornamental shade trees.' *Arborist's News.* Vol. 5 (No. 5). p. 33–36.

Zabel, R. A., S. B. Silverborg, and M. E. Fowler. 1958. *A survey of forest tree diseases in the Northeast.* 1957. USDA Forest Service. Station paper No. 110. 30 p.

14
General Parasitic Diseases

This chapter discusses some of the more prevalent diseases caused by bacteria and fungi, which occur on a wide variety of shade and ornamental trees.

Fire Blight

Although fire blight is known primarily as a disease of apple and pear trees, and consequently is of most concern to orchardists, it also occurs on many ornamental trees and shrubs in the rose family. Commercial arborists, and estate superintendents, and even the owner of a single susceptible tree must often cope with this very destructive disease. Besides attacking apple and pear trees, fire blight appears commonly on several species of cotoneaster (*Cotoneaster* spp.), cockspur thorn (*Crataegus crusgalli*), English hawthorn (*C. oxyacantha*), and mountain-ashes) (*Sorbus* spp.). It occurs less commonly on fire thorn (*Pyracantha coccinea*), serviceberry (*Amelanchier canadensis*), flowering quince (*Chaenomeles japonica*), cultivated quince (*Cydonia vulgaris*), Christmas berry (*Photinia villosa*), flowering plum (*Prunus triloba* var. *plena*), spirea (*Spirea vanhouttei*), rose (*Rosa* spp.), and *Stransvaesia davidiana*. It also has been recorded on such widely different trees as walnut (*Juglans* spp.) and persimmon (*Diospyros* sp.).

Symptoms. The leaves near the growing tips and the flowers suddenly wilt, turn brown and black, and look as though they have been scorched by fire. Twigs also are blighted on most of the ornamental hosts. In some, the mountain-ashes, for example, the infection spreads down to involve large branches. Extensive cankers on the trunk and main branches develop on the larger ornamental trees, as well as on apple and pear (Fig. 14-1). The flowering quince is susceptible principally to blossom blight, the disease being rare on the woody parts. The presence of bloom infection and the absence of typical twig blight in such cases give the infected tree the appearance of having been injured by frost.

Cause. Fire blight is caused by a germ known as *Erwinia amylovora.* The bacteria are carried from oozing cankers on nearby pear, apple, or other infected hosts to the open blossoms by bees, flies, and other insects and by splashing rains. They multiply rapidly in the blossoms and are spread to other blossoms by bees in quest of nectar and pollen. In this manner hundreds of blossoms are contaminated in a relatively short period. The bacteria penetrate and infect the blossom tissues, then continue downward into the fruit spurs, twigs, and even branches, killing the various tissues infected.

The application of excessive amounts of nitrogenous fertilizers increases the tree's susceptibility to fire blight bacteria.

Fig. 14-1. Fire blight canker and blight on pear.

Control. Blighted twigs should be pruned well below the infected areas and destroyed. This practice eliminates an important potential source of inoculum for subsequent epidemics. The pruning must be done carefully, all large wounds properly dressed, and the pruning tools carefully sterilized with denatured alcohol or a 10 percent solution of sodium hypochlorite (Clorox) to prevent spreading this highly contagious disease.

The antibiotic streptomycin or a mixture of streptomycin and Terramycin is very effective.

The antibiotic should be sprayed when the trees are in the early-bloom and full-bloom stages. Poor control results when the sprays are delayed until the petal-fall stage. In the eastern United States three applications are needed for good control; in California as many as five may be necessary. The antibiotic is not capable of killing fire blight germs that have become deeply established inside the tree. It does prevent infections from becoming firmly established, provided the sprays are timed properly.

Less streptomycin is absorbed into a plant if rain falls within a few hours of application. A rain one or more days after application has little effect on the amount absorbed.

There are three formulations of antibiotics now widely available to large-scale users (orchardists, nurserymen, arborists, etc.) for fire blight control. Their active ingredient is streptomycin in either the sulfate or the nitrate form. Of these, Merck's Agri-Strep and Squibb's Phytomycin contain only strepomycin. Pfizer's Agrimycin 100 contains Terramycin in addition to streptomycin.

The preventive measures mentioned above usually suffice for most ornamental trees and shrubs. Where large ornamental trees and apple or pear develop cankers on the trunks and larger branches, additional treatments may be necessary. To eliminate an important source of contagion, the cankers should be removed by surgical methods or the bacteria in them destroyed by means of chemical paints.

The surgical removal of the canker involves cutting back into the healthy bark about 4 inches around the margin of the canker during the dormant season and removing all tissues inside the cut zone. The resulting wound is then disinfected with bichloride of mercury solution followed by the application of any good wound dressing. Such a treatment is effective for small cankers but is not recommended for large cankers extending around more than half of the affected branch. The best procedure in the latter case is to remove the branch completely, inasmuch as its chances of survival are small.

A more rapid method for destroying the bacteria in large cankers without surgical treatment involves the application of chemical paints to the cankered area. These paints penetrate the bark and destroy the harmful bacteria without severely injuring the tree. One of the best paints for such purposes, developed by Dr. H. E. Thomas of California, contains the following ingredients:

cobalt nitrate	3½ ounces
commercial glycerine	1.7 fluid ounces
oil of wintergreen	3.4 fluid ounces
acetic acid	1.7 fluid ounces
ethyl (or denatured) alcohol	27.2 fluid ounces

The last four ingredients are mixed together by stirring, and the cobalt nitrate powder is added slowly until it is completely dissolved. This cobalt nitrate canker paint should be applied over large cankers with a brush, so that it covers not only the infected portions but several inches of the surrounding bark as well. It will not penetrate and kill the bacteria if the canker is covered with rough, corky bark. Consequently, best results are obtained if the rough layer of outer bark is scraped away before the paint is applied.

The mixture should be kept in a tightly stoppered bottle when not in use.

Crown Gall

Crown gall (Fig. 14-2) is a common disease of trees in the rose family, such as apple, cherry, pear, plum, quince, and flowering almond. The disease also occurs on such widely different trees as chestnut, Arizona cypress, European juniper, incense cedar, sycamore maple, oleander, poplar, English walnut, willow, English yew, and in Hawaii on the macadamia tree (*Macadamia ternifolia*).

Symptoms. Roughened swellings or tumorlike galls of varying sizes appear at the base of the tree or on the roots. On poplar and willow, these galls may also appear on the aerial parts. Growth of the tree may be retarded, the leaves may turn yellow, or the branches or roots may die as a result of the presence of these galls. Although old, established trees are rarely damaged appreciably, young trees may be killed.

Cause. Crown gall is caused by the bacterium *Agrobacterium tumefaciens*. The organism does not kill the parts attacked, but stimulates cell growth in them. It enters the susceptible plants through wounds and is primarily a parasite of young nursery stock.

Control. Nurserymen should discard all young fruit and ornamental trees showing galls on the stem or main roots. They should avoid wounding the stems and roots of young trees in the nursery. They should also be aware that irrigation water is capable of carrying the crown gall bacteria.

Fig. 14-2. Crown gall on walnut stem.

Where the disease is known to be present in the nursery, dipping the roots in a solution containing 200 parts per million of Agrimycin 100 (4 tablespoons in 5 gallons of water) for half an hour is suggested as a possible preventive practice.

The newest material to be introduced as a control for crown gall is 'Bacticin' manufactured by the Tuco Products Co., a Division of Upjohn Co., Kalamazoo, Michigan 49001. The active ingredients are 2, 4-Xylenol and meta-cresol. The material is applied directly to the galled area. The manufacturer's directions as to use and necessary precautions should be followed to the letter.

Powdery Mildews

The leaves and the twigs of many deciduous trees and shrubs are occasionally covered with a grayish-white dusty material known as powdery mildew. The mildew is made up of delicate, hyaline, cobweblike strands of fungus tissue covered with microscopic colorless spores. Many minute, spherical, black bodies, fruiting structures of the sexual stage of the fungus, may be visible to the unaided eye on the grayish-white areas. The spores of the fungus overwinter in these bodies.

Although mildew fungi grow mainly over the surface, they also penetrate the leaf surface with fine sucking organs in many places and extract the juices of the host plant. Heavily mildewed leaves may turn yellow and fall prematurely. Mildews appear most commonly toward the end of summer and in late fall and are most prevalent on trees growing in shaded and damp locations.

Cause. There are a number of distinct species of powdery mildew fungi that can be distinguished only by microscopical examination. The following list includes most of the species, together with the trees or shrubs they parasitize:

Microsphaera alni on alder, birch, lilac, planetree, and walnut; *Phyllactinia corylea* on ash, beech, catalpa, chestnut, dogwood, elm, hawthorn, hornbeam, oak, and tulip; *Podosphaera oxyacanthae* on apple, hawthorn, pear, persimmon, plum, serviceberry, and spirea; *Sphaerotheca pannosa* on peach; *Uncinula salicis* on poplar and willow; *U. circinata* on maple; *U. flexuosa* on buckeye; *U. macrospora* on elm; *U. clintonii* on linden; and *Erysiphe aggregata* on alder.

Control. Lime sulfur 1-50 or wettable sulfurs were formerly recommended for powdery mildew control. These have been largerly supplanted in recent years by Karathane. As a rule, however, only particularly valuable larger specimens or small nursery trees are sprayed to control mildew. Certain precautions listed on the package must be followed.

Shoestring Root Rot

Some of our most valuable shade and ornamental trees are susceptible to the so-called shoestring root rot disease. The name is derived from the long, round, black strands of tissue, closely resembling shoestrings, produced by the fungus underneath infected bark, over infected roots, or in the soil. Other names often given to the same disease are Armillaria root rot, crown rot, and mushroom rot. Among shade and ornamental trees, oaks and maples appear to be most commonly infected, although the disease is occasionally destructive on apple, birch, black locust, chestnut, empress-tree, eucalyptus, goldenrain-tree, Katsura-tree, larch, mountain-ash, pine, planetree, poplar, redbud, rhododendron, and spruce. In all probability the disease may occur on almost any tree or shrub grown, if the necessary conditions for infection are present.

Symptoms. The above ground symptoms cannot be differentiated from those produced by many other diseases or agents that cause root or trunk injuries. Probably the most striking external symptom is a decline in vigor of a part or the entire top of the tree (Fig. 14-3). Where the progress of the disease is slow, branches die back from time to time over a period of several years.

The most positive signs of this disease, however, are found at the base

Fig. 14-3. Branch dieback and general decline in this oak are symptoms of shoestring root rot.

of the trunk at or just below the soil line, or in the main roots in the vicinity of the root collar. Here, fan-shaped, white wefts of fungus tissue closely appressed to the sapwood are visible when the bark is cut away or lifted. Scraping or lifting the white wefts of mycelia, which have a strong mushroom odor, will reveal water-soaked sapwood. Where the entire top has wilted, the fungus tissue will be found completely around the trunk. Where a large branch has died back, or one side of the tree shows poor vigor, the fungus will be found only on one or two main roots or on one side of the trunk base. Where the tree has been dead for some time, the dark brown to black 'shoestrings' may occur beneath the bark or in the soil near the infected parts. Clusters of light brown mushrooms, so-called honey mushrooms, may appear in the vicinity of the rotted wood in late autumn (Fig. 14-4). These rarely occur near infected street and shade trees, however, inasmuch as conditions are usually unfavorable for their development, or the infected trees are removed before the mushrooms have a chance to form.

Cause. Shoestring rot is caused by the fungus *Armillaria mellea.* The fruiting stage, the honey mushroom, somewhat resembles the mushroom sold in stores but is slightly larger, is yellowish brown, and the top of the cap is dotted with dark brown scales. The mushrooms usually grow in close clusters with their stem bases pressed together. Spores released from the underside of the cap are blown by the wind to bark injuries at the base of living trees or to dead tree stumps. Under

Fig. 14-4. The mushroom state of the shoestring root rot fungus.

favorable conditions, the spores germinate and produce mycelium, which penetrates and infects the tree tissues. Later, fungus strands (shoestrings) grow out from the tissues and through the soil. These strands may then contact healthy roots of nearby trees and penetrate and infect them. In fact, infection of living trees is thought to occur almost exclusively by means of these fungus strands. The author has seen infected trees in cities, however, that were isolated by whole blocks from other possible sources of infection, indicating that infection must have occurred by means other than fungus strands growing through the soil.

Some doubt exists as to the virulence of *Armillaria mellea*. Because the disease is almost constantly associated with trees that were previously in poor vigor, several investigators believe that the fungus is only weakly parasitic and cannot attack vigorously growing trees. Others, including the author, believe the causal fungus is capable of attacking living roots and can penetrate sound, healthy bark. It can also enter the tree through dead roots and through bark injuries. But no matter how it enters, the fact remains that once the fungus gains a hold in trees, it usually kills them in a relatively short while.

Control. Because much of the evidence at hand indicates that shoe-string root rot is associated with weak trees, probably the best precautionary measures are fertilization, water, and soil improvement.

An infected tree whose entire root system or trunk is diseased cannot be saved. The larger roots in the vicinity of the trunk as well as the trunk itself should be removed and destroyed. Soil in the immediate vicinity should also be removed.

Attempts to save partly infected valuable trees are occasionally successful, especially where only one or two main roots or one side of the trunk is involved. In such cases, the soil within a radius of about 2 feet around the trunk should be removed in the spring or summer to expose the root collar and the larger roots. Roots whose bark is completely rotted should be removed and the affected bark on partly diseased roots and on the trunk carefully cut away. All visible fungus tissue and water-soaked wood should be removed. The bark edges should be shellacked and the entire wounded surface covered with a good tree paint. Branches should be thinned out and small plants growing nearby removed to allow as much sunlight and air as possible in the vicinity of the treated parts. In addition, the trees should be fed with some quickly available plant food to stimulate additional growth. The exposed roots and root collar should be covered with fresh soil in late fall to prevent freezing.

Where the disease has killed one tree in a group, spread to nearby trees can occasionally be delayed or even completely checked by removing the tree and the main roots and by digging a circular isolation trench.

The trench should be about 1 foot wide, 2 feet deep, and about 5 or 6 feet from the former location of the trunk. All soil from the trench as well as that within the circle should be carted away. All roots within the trenched area should be removed, even if they belong to nearby healthy trees. Although this complete treatment is expensive, it is warranted where particularly valuable trees are growing near a tree that has succumbed to shoestrong root rot. The remaining trees should, of course, be fertilized, watered, and given all possible care to ensure continued vigorous growth.

The problem of planting another tree in the site on which one has previously died from this disease occasionally confronts the shade-tree commissioner, arborist, or property owner. The author has known of cases where three successively planted trees have died from shoestring root rot under such conditions.

Where a tree must be planted in the same place, several precautions are necessary to ensure the safety of the new tree. The old soil, including the larger roots and as many as possible of the smaller roots of the dead tree, should be carted away. New soil should be used in its place but it should not be placed around the trunk. The immediate vicinity of the trunk should be filled with a layer a foot wide and 6 inches or so deep of ¾-inch crushed stone. This will help aerate the trunk base and provide a barrier between the soil and the trunk through which the fungus would have difficulty in spreading and becoming established.

Where such a procedure involves considerable expense or where it cannot be practiced because of obstructions, such as pavements and walks, an attempt may be made to destroy all traces of fungus tissue by disinfecting the soil and roots with some chemical. The best material for such purposes is formaldehyde solution, prepared by dissolving 1 gallon of 37 per cent formaldehyde in 50 gallons of water. Enough of this mixture should be poured over the root zone to penetrate to the subsoil. The treated area should be covered for a few days with canvas to enclose the fumes, after which the soil is uncovered and aerated for several weeks. All traces of formaldehyde fumes must be gone before a tree can be safely replanted. This treatment cannot be used where trees or other forms of vegetation are growing near by.

Carbon disulfide has been successfully used on the West Coast to control the shoestring fungus in citrus groves while infected trees are still standing. Doses of 1½ ounces of the chemical are inserted 8 inches below the surface and 18 inches apart. The top of the soil is kept moist, or wet soil is applied to enclose the fumes. From 30 to 60 days are required for the chemical to kill the fungus in the soil and in diseased roots. The dead trees are removed and new trees are then set in their places.

British scientists have recently developed a refined creosote, sold under the trade name Armillatox, which appears to be effective against active infections of *Armillaria mellea* in living trees.

Verticillium Wilt

Verticillium wilt, one of the most common fungus diseases, is found on more than 300 kinds of plants, including shade and ornamental trees, food and fiber crops, annual and perennial ornamentals. Among its more immportant suscepts are the many species of maples planted along city streets. In fact, this disease has caused the death of more maples during the last 35 years than any other disease. A survey in New Jersey by the author revealed that the silver maple (*Acer saccharinum*) is the most susceptible of the streetside maples, with the Norway maple (*A. platanoides*), red maple (*A. rubrum*), and sugar maple (*A. saccharum*) decreasingly susceptible in that order.

The following additional trees known to be susceptible to Verticillium wilt are listed in alphabetical order of their botanical names: hedge maple (*Acer campestre*); broad-leaved maple (*A. macrophyllum*); painted maple (*A. mono*); boxelder (*A. negundo*); California boxelder (*A. negundo* var. *Californicum*); black maple (*A. nigrum*); Japanese maple (*A. palmatum*); Japanese red maple (*A. palmatum* var. *rubrum*); Schwedler's maple (*A. platanoides* var. *Schwedleri*); sycamore maple (*A. pseudo platanus*); Drummond maple (*A. rubrum* var. *Drummondi*); trident maple (*A. rubrum* var. *trilobum*); tatarian maple (*A. tataricum*); horsechestnut (*Aesculus hippocastanum*); tree-of-heaven (*Ailanthus altissima*); Spanish chestnut (*Castanea sativa*); southern catalpa (*Catalpa bignonioides*); western catalpa (*C. speciosa*); carob (*Ceratonia siliqua*); redbud (*Cercis canadensis*); Judas tree (*C. Siliquastrum*); camphor-tree (*Cinnamomum camphora*); yellowwood (*Cladrastis lutea*); flowering dogwood (*Cornus florida*); smoketree (*Cotinus coggygria*); quince (*Cydonia oblonga*); Japanese persimmon (*Diospyros Kaki*); Texas persimmon (*D. texana*); persimmon (*D. virginiana*); Russian-olive (*Elaeagnus angustifolia*); beech (*Fagus* spp); white ash (*Fraxinus americana*); green ash (*F. pennsylvanica* var. *lanceolata*); black ash (*F. nigra*); European ash (*F. pennsylvanica* var. *subintegerrima*); Kentucky coffee tree (*Gymnocladus dioica*); China tree (*Koelreuteria japonica*); goldenrain-tree (*K. paniculata*); tuliptree (*Liriodendron tulipifera*); osage-orange (*Maclura pomifera*); bull bay (*Magnolia grandiflora*); saucer magnolia (*M. soulangeana*); star magnolia (*M. stellata*); apple (*Malus* spp); banana (*Musa paradisiaca* var. *sapientum*); sourgum (*Nyssa sylvatica*); olive (*Olea europea*); tea olive (*Osmanthus ilicifolius*); avocado (*Persea americana*); cork tree (*Phellodendron amurense*); pistachio (*Pistacia vera*); aspen (*Populus tremula*); almond (*Prunus amygdalus*); apricot (*P. Armeniaca*); sweet cherry (*P. avium*); cherry plum (*P. cerasifera*); sour cherry (*P. cerasus*); Morello cherry (*P. cerasus* var. *austera*); garden plum (*P. domes-*

tica); Mahaleb cherry (*P. mahaleb*); Japanese apricot (*P. mume*); prune
(*Prunus* spp.); pear (*Pyrus* spp.); pin oak (*Quercus palustris*); black locust
(*Robinia pseudo-acacia*); sassafras (*Sassafras variifolium*); Brazil pepper-tree
(*Schinus terebinthifolius*); Japanese pagoda-tree (*Sophora japonica*); cacao
(*Theobroma cacao*); American linden (*Tilia americana*); littleleaf linden (*T.
cordata*); Crimean linden (*T. euchlora*); American elm (*Ulmus americana*);
English elm (*U. campestris*); slippery elm (*U. fulva*); Scotch elm (*U. glabra*);
and Siberian elm (*U. pumila*).

Symptoms. Wilt symptoms vary somewhat with the kind of tree, its age,
location, and other factors, but there are some symptoms common to all
situations. A sudden wilting of the leaves on one limb, on several limbs,
or even on the entire tree is a general symptom (Fig. 14-5). The severity
of this symptom depends less on species of tree than on the amount of
infection in the belowground parts. Long before wilting becomes visible,
the fungus has been at work belowground. If most of the roots are
infected, the tree will die quickly. On the other hand, if infections in the
roots are confined to one side of the tree, only the parts above that side
will show wilt symptoms. Periods of drought frequently accentuate the
wilting symptoms and speed the death of the infected tree.

The wilted leaves may fall after they have dried completely, or they
may hang on for the remainder of the season. Sometimes a few branches
or even the entire top of the tree will die during the winter and hence fail
to leaf out the following spring. Cases of this sort are usually attributed
to winter injury.

Because many other agents can cause similar symptoms, positive
diagnosis of Verticillium wilt can be made only by culturing sapwood
tissue in the laboratory. The cultures are taken from discolored sapwood, which occasionally appears in the branches but more commonly
and more reliably near the base of the main trunk or in the main roots.
There is some evidence that in the case of tomatoes and eggplant, the
spores of *Verticillium* can infect the plants via the leaves. This has not
been shown to be the case with infection of trees. It is a soil-inhabiting
fungus primarily, and hence its most common avenue of entrance is via
the roots. One would expect, therefore, that the discoloration of the
sapwood would be more marked and more common closer to the point
of entrance. This is actually the case, as the author discovered in his
studies on the cause of dying of streetside trees over the last twenty
years.

When the *Verticillium* fungus is present, the outer sapwood rings
(those nearest the bark) will show a discoloration. The color varies with
the species of tree and the duration of the infection. In Norway maple it
is a bright olive-green; in American linden, dark gray; in tree-of-heaven,
yellowish-brown; in black locust, brown to black; in northern catalpa,
purple to bluish-brown; in American elm, brown (like the Dutch elm

Fig. 14-5. This maple is heavily infected by the fungus *Verticillium albo-atrum*.

disease fungus); and in Japanese pagoda-tree, greenish-black. But the presence of discolored sapwood tissue cannot be used as an exact diagnostic symptom. It merely indicates that a fungus may be involved. For example, the author has isolated at least six different kinds of fungi from sapwood of Norway, silver, and red maples which showed the bright green discoloration! Moreover, he reproduced the same discoloration in young healthy maples by inoculating them with these fungi.

Recently Terry A. Tattar of the Department of Plant Pathology, Shade Tree Laboratories, University of Massachusetts, was able to determine the presence of the *Verticillium* fungus with a Shigometer, mentioned on page 109.

It is well to reiterate, therefore, that a positive diagnosis for Verticillium wilt, as for the Dutch elm disease, can be made only by laboratory isolation tests.

Cause. Wilt is caused by the fungus *Verticillium albo-atrum.** Many strains or segregates of this fungus are known to exist. The fungus can live in soil for some time without actually parasitizing roots. Although it is thought to enter roots and stems only through injuries, infection may occur via young, uninjured roots. Some research workers believe air currents may spread spores over long distances. When such spores lodge in tree wounds, aboveground infection may occur. Sapwood wounds are usually necessary for the start of an infection in the aerial portions of the tree. Contaminated pruning tools may serve to promote aerial infections.

Once inside the water-conducting tissues, the *Verticillium* fungus grows upward longitudinally; that is to say, the infection spreads upward from the point of inoculation. The actual discoloration which results may be due to the presence of the fungus itself or to a chemical change resulting from the action of the fungus.

Control. Trees showing general and severe infection by the *Verticillium* fungus cannot be saved. Such trees should be cut down at once and destroyed quickly and completely. As many of the roots as possible should also be removed. A species of tree satisfactory for the particular location but not susceptible to wilt should be planted. A few commercial arborists, faced with the request to replant the same kind of tree in infested soil, have reported good results from drenching the soil with formaldehyde solution, 1 part in 50 parts of water, several weeks to a month before replanting the new tree. Not only must formaldehyde be handled with care, however, but its reliability for doing the job under large-scale conditions is questionable.

---

* Some investigators claim that the fungus *Verticillium dahliae* causes wilt, on the basis that it forms small black fruiting bodies (sclerotia) in laboratory culture whereas *V. albo-atrum* does not. This difference is not enough, however, to designate it as the causal fungus.

Some trees appear to be highly or completely resistant to Verticillium wilt. Narrow- and broad-leaved evergreens appear to be safe as replacements where a tree has died from the wilt disease. Following is a list of deciduous trees not now known to be susceptible to wilt and which might be used as replacements: beech, birch, ginkgo, hackberry, hawthorn, honey locust, hop-hornbeam, hornbeam, Katsura-tree, mountain-ash (European), mulberry, oak (white and bur), pawpaw, pecan, serviceberry, sweetgum, sycamore, willow, and Zelkova.

Several investigators, including the author, have noted recovery of trees from mild cases of Verticillium wilt after liberal applications of a high nitrogenous soluble fertilizer such as Ra-pid-gro. The material must be used early in the growing season on trees which show only one or two wilted branches. The heavy fertilization apparently stimulates leaf growth, which in turn enables the rapid formation of a thick layer of sapwood that seals in the infected parts beneath (Fig. 14-6).

Other investigators have found that heavy nitrogenous fertilizer treatment increased the spread of the fungus in the tree. A number of investigators have also tried injecting chemicals into infected trees or applying them to the soil around the roots as a curative measure. Such treatments are not reliably effective and hence must be kept in an experimental category for the present.

Vapam is another material reported to be effective in treating

Fig. 14-6. Greenish discoloration of sapwood may be caused by the *Verticillium* fungus. Several layers of healthy sapwood now cover the infected area in this branch.

infested soil prior to replanting a tree in the same area. Two pints of Vapam in 300 gallons of water are poured into a basin formed by making a ring or depression 12 feet in diameter around the former tree's location. The solution should be allowed to soak into the soil and the soil should be left undisturbed for at least 2 weeks before replanting.

Other General Diseases

Many other general parasitic diseases affect a wide variety of trees. Among these are canker and dieback caused by the fungus *Botryosphaeria dothidea* (p. 456), canker caused by several species of *Cytospora* (p. 546), and trunk and root rot caused by species of *Ganoderma* (p. 430).

Selected Bibliography

Agrios, G. N. 1975. 'Virus and mycoplasm diseases of shade and ornamental trees.' *Jour. Arboriculture*. Vol. 1 (No. 3). p. 41–47.

Ark, P. A. and J. P. Thompson. 1960. 'Experimental greenhouse control of crown gall and olive knot with antibiotic drenches.' *Plant Dis. Reptr*. Vol. 44 (No. 3). p. 197–203.

Beer, S. V. 1976. 'Fire blight control with streptomycin sprays and adjuvants at different application volumes.' *Plant Disease Reptr*. Vol. 60 (No. 6). p. 541–44.

Beer, S. V. and D. C. Opgenorth. 1976. '*Erwinia amylovora* on fire blight canker surfaces and blossoms in relation to disease occurrence.' *Phytopathology*. Vol. 66 (No. 3). p. 317–22.

Boyd, R. J., A. C. Hildebrandt, and O. N. Allen. 1971. 'Retardation of crown gall enlargement after bacteriophage treatment.' *Plant Disease Reptr*. Vol. 55 (No. 2). p. 145–48.

Caroselli, N. E. 1957. *Verticillium wilt of maples*. Rhode Island Exp. Sta. Bul. 335.

Carter, J. C. 1961. *Illinois trees: their diseases*. Illinois Nat. Hist. Survey Circ. 46. Second printing with alterations). 99 p.

———. 1961. 'Verticillium wilt of ornamental plants.' *Arborist's News*. Vol. 26 (No. 12). p. 89–94.

Day, W. R. 1927. 'Parasitism of *Armillaria mellea* in relation to conifers.' *Quart. Jour. Forestry*. Vol. 21. p. 9–21.

Deep, I. W. and H. Hussin. 1965. 'Influence of temperature on initiation of crown gall in woody hosts.' *Plants Dis. Reptr*. Vol. 49 (No. 9). p. 734–35.

Dochinger, L. S. 1957. 'Verticillium wilt: its nature and control.' *Proc. Thirty-third National Shade Tree Conference*. p. 202–12.

Dowson, W. J. 1957. *Plant diseases due to bacteria*. 2nd ed. Cambridge University Press, Cambridge, England. 232 p.

Drain, B. D. 1938. *Fire blight canker treatments*. Tennessee Agr. Sta. Circ. 62. 4 p.

Dunegan, J. C. 1957. 'Antibiotics for tree disease control.' *Proc. Thirty-third National Shade Tree Conference*. p. 116–26.

Hepting, G. H. 1971. *Diseases of forest and shade trees of the United States.* U.S. Dept. Agr., Forest Service, Agriculture Handbook 386. 658 p.

Hildebrand, E. M. 1969. *Fire blight and its control.* Cornell Agr. Exp. Sta. Ext. Bul. 405. 32 p.

Himelick, E. B. 1969. *Trees and shrub hosts of Verticillium albo-atrum.* Illinois Nat. Hist. Survey. Biological Notes No. 66. 8 p.

———. 1969. 'Verticillium wilt.' *Proc. Forty-fourth International Shade Tree Conference.* p. 256–62.

Hock, W. C. 1971. 'Crown gall of woody plants.' *Weeds, Trees, and Turf.* Vol. 10 (No. 6). p. 20–21.

Keil, H. L. and T. van der Zwet. 1967. 'Sodium hypochlorite as a disinfectant of pruning tools for fire blight control.' *Plant Dis. Reptr.* Vol. 51 (No. 9). p. 753–55.

Leaphart, C. D. 1963. *Armillaria root rot.* U.S. Dept. Agr. Forest Pest Leaflet 78 p. 8.

Luepschen, N. S. 1960. *Fire blight control with streptomycin, as influenced by temperature and other environmental factors and by adjuvants added to sprays.* Cornell Univ. Memoir 375. Dec. 1960. 39 p. Ithaca, N.Y.

McCown, M. and J. A. McClintock. 1935. *Controlling fire blight by canker treatment and spraying.* Indiana Agr. Exp. Sta. Bul. 208. 8 p.

McIntyre, J. L., J. Kuc, and E. B. Williams. 1975. 'Protection of Bartlett pear against fireblight with deoxyribonucleic acid from virulent and avirulent Erwinia amylovora.' *Physiological Plant Pathology.* Vol. 7. p. 153–170.

Moore, L. W. 1976. 'Research findings of crown gall and its control.' *American Nurseryman.* Nov. 15, 1976. p. 8, 9, 68, 69, 122, 128.

———. 1977. 'Prevention of crown-gall on *Prunus* roots by bacterial antagonists.' *Phytopathology* Vol. 67 (No. 1). p. 139–44.

Munnecke, D. E., W. Wilbur, and E. F. Darley. 1976. 'Effect of heating or drying on *Armillaria mellea* or *Trichoderma viride* and the relation to survival of *A. mellea* in soil.' *Phytopathology.* Vol. 66 (No. 11). p. 1363–68.

Parker, K. G. 1959. 'Verticillium hadromycosis of deciduous tree fruits.' *Plant Dis. Reptr. U. S. D. A. Supplement* 255. p. 39–61. May 15, 1959. Beltsville, Md.

———. 1961. *Verticillium wilt and its prevention.* Cornell Univ. Extension Bul. 1072. 8 p.

Parker, K. G., E. G. Fisher, and W. D. Mills. 1957. *Fire blight on pome fruits and its control.* Cornell Univ. Ext. Bul. 966. 23 p. July 1957. Ithaca, N.Y.

Pawsey, R. G. and M. A. Rahman. 1976. 'Chemical control of infection by honey dew fungus, *Armillaria mellea:* a review.' *Jour. Arboriculture.* Vol. 2 (No. 9). p. 161–69.

Pirone, P. P. 1957. '*Ganoderma lucidum,* a parasite of shade trees.' *Bull. Torrey Bot. Club.* Vol. 84 (No. 6). p. 424–28.

———. 1959. 'Why shade trees die along city streets.' *Proc. Thirty-fifth National Shade Tree Conference.* p. 6–15.

———. 1967. 'Learn to know fire blight on pears, apples.' *Flower and Garden.* Feb. 1967. p. 20, 58–59.

Raabe, R. D. 1962. 'Host list of the root rot fungus *Armillaria mellea.*' *Hilgardia.* Vol. 33 (No. 2). p. 25–88.

——. 1965. 'Some previously unreported hosts of *Armillaria mellea* in California.' *Plant Disease Reptr.* Vol. 49 (No. 10). p. 812.

——. 1966. 'Variation of *Armillaria mellea* in culture.' *Phytopathology.* Vol. 56 (No. 11). p. 1241–44.

——. 1967. 'Variation in pathogenicity and virulence in *Armillaria mellea.*' *Phytopathology.* Vol. 57 (No. 1). p. 73–75.

——. 1970. '*Armillaria mellea*, the oak root fungus.' *Arborist's News.* Vol. 35 (No. 12). p. 132–34.

Reed, G. M. 1913. 'The powdery mildews—*Erysiphaceae.*' *Amer. Micros. Soc. Trans.* Vol. 32. p. 219–25.

Rudolph, B. A. 1931. 'Verticillium hadromycosis.' *Hilgardia.* Vol. 5 (No. 9). p. 197–361.

Shaffer, W. H. and R. N. Goodman. 1970. 'Control of twig blight with a combination spray of streptomycin, sulfur, and glyodin.' *Plant Disease Reptr.* Vol. 54 (No. 3). p. 203–5.

Sinclair, W. A. and W. T. Johnson. 1969. *Verticillium wilt.* Cornell Tree Pest Leaflet A-3. N.Y. State College of Agr. 7 p.

——. 1972. *Crown gall.* State Univ. N.Y. College of Agr. Cooperative Extension. Tree Pest Leaflet A-5. 12 p.

Strong, F. C. 1941. 'Root and root crown troubles.' *Trees Magazine.* Sept.-Oct. 1941. p. 10–14.

Thomas, H. E. 1934. 'Studies on *Armillaria mellea*, infection, parasitism, and host resistance.' *Jour. Agr. Res.* Vol. 48. p. 187–218.

Thomas, H. E. and P. A. Ark. 1934. *Fire blight of pears and related plants.* Cal. Agr. Exp. Sta. Bul. 586.

Wilson, C. L. and C. E. Seliskar. 1976. 'Mycoplasma-associated diseases of trees.' *Jour. Arboriculture.* Vol. 2 (No. 1). p. 6–12.

Zabel, R. A., S. B. Silverborg and M. E. Fowler. 1958. *A survey of forest tree diseases in the Northeast*—1957. Station Paper 110. Northeastern Forest Exp. Sta. Station Paper. 110.

15

Diseases and Insect Pests
of Low-growing Trees

This chapter deals primarily with the diseases and insect pests* of the low-growing deciduous trees discussed in the early part of Chapter 8. Where both low-growing and tall-growing kinds occur in the same genus, as with ashes and magnolias, the disease and insect problems of both are discussed in this chapter.

For each tree, the individual diseases are first presented in the logical order: symptoms, cause, and control. Next comes a description of the damage caused by each insect pest, followed by very brief descriptions of the various stages of the insect, and by the control measures.

The cultural requirements of some of the trees are discussed briefly before describing the more common diseases and pests. Where this information is omitted, it may be found in Chapter 8.

ACACIA (Acacia)

Acacias are beautiful flowering trees grown outdoors in the warmer parts of the United States and in greenhouses in the colder parts.

Diseases

The fungus diseases of acacia are not important. A twig canker caused by *Nectria ditissima* and *Fusarium lateritium* (*Gibberella baccata*) has been reported from California. Leaf spotting by the fungus *Physalospora*

* Although mites are not true insects, they are treated under this group for the remainder of the book.

fusca, a species of *Cercospora,* and the alga *Cephaleuros virescens* occasionally develops in the South. In California powdery mildew caused by the fungus *Erysiphe polygoni* is common. Root and trunk rots caused by the fungi *Phymatotrichum omnivorum, Armillaria mellea, Clitocybe tabescens,* and *Fomes applanatus* have been reported from the south and the west.

Insects

COTTONY-CUSHION SCALE. *Icerya purchasi.** This 'ribbed scale barklouse,' which has been a serious pest of acacia, citrus, and other plants in California, has been troublesome in greenhouses in the eastern states for a number of years. The mature insect has a ribbed, cottony covering through which may be seen its soft body, sometimes ¼ inch long. The white, fluted mass that extends from the scale is composed largely of eggs covered by a protecting waxy mass. The scale itself is much smaller and is usually inconspicuous. At its earliest stage the scale is greenish and not contained in a woolly excretion.

Several other species of scale occasionally infest acacia. These are: California red, which is round and reddish in color; greedy, a small gray species; oleander, a pale yellow kind; and San Jose, which is small and gray with a nipple in its center.

Control. Malathion sprays or aerosols are effective against the crawler stage of scale insects.

CATERPILLARS. *Argyrotaenia citrana* and *Sabulodes caberata.* The former, known as the orange-tortrix, a dirty-white, brown-headed caterpillar, webs and rolls the leaves of many trees and shrubs on the West Coast. The latter, known as the omnivorous looper, a yellow to pale pink or green caterpillar, with yellow, brown, or green stripes on the sides and back, also feeds on a wide variety of plants in the same region.

Control. Spray with carbaryl (Sevin) when the caterpillars are young.

ALDER *(Alnus)*

Most species of alder grow best in moist soils. Those grown in ornamental plantings are less subject to diseases than to insect pests. The few diseases that occasionally appear produce little permanent damage.

Diseases

CANKER. A number of fungi cause cankers and dieback of the branches. Among the most common are *Nectria coccinea, Solenia anomala,* and *Physalospora obtusa.* Trunk cankers may also be caused by *Diatrypella oregonensis, Hymenochaete agglutinans,* and *Didymosphaeria oregonensis.*

---

* The scientific name of the insect is given after the common name.

Control. No simple control measures are known. Cankered branches should be pruned to sound wood and the trees fed and watered to increase their vigor.

LEAF CURL. *Taphrina macrophylla.* The leaves of red alders grow to several times their normal size, are curled and distorted, and turn a decided purple when affected by this disease. Infection is apparent on the leaves as soon as they appear in the spring.

Three other species, *T. amentorium, T. occidentalis,* and *T. robinsoniana,* are known to cause enlargement and distortion of the scales of female catkins. These project as curled, reddish tongues, which are soon covered with a white glistening layer of fungus tissue.

Control. Spray the trees with either ferbam or ziram in late fall or while they are still dormant in the spring. This will destroy most of the spores, which overwinter in the bud scales and on the twigs and which are largely responsible for early infections. Sprays are suggested only for valuable specimens.

POWDERY MILDEW. Several species of powdery mildew fungi attack the female catkins of alder. The most common, *Erysiphe aggregata,* develops as a white powdery coating over the catkin. Two other species, *Microsphaera alni* and *Phyllactinia corylea,* occur less frequently.

Control. These fungi rarely cause enough damage to warrant control measures. Where justified, Benlate or Karathane sprays will give control.

LEAF RUST. *Melampsoridium hiratsukanum.* Some damage is done to alder leaves by this rust, which breaks out in small yellowish pustules on the leaves during the summer. The leaves later turn dark brown. It is suspected that the alternate host of this rust is a conifer.

Control. The disease is never severe enough to justify control measures.

Insects

WOOLLY ALDER APHID. *Prociphilus tessellatus.* The downward folding of leaves, in which are found large woolly masses covering bluish-black aphids, is typical of this pest. Eggs are deposited in bark crevices and pass the winter in these locations. Maples are also infested by this species.

Control. Malathion sprays when the young begin to develop in spring give excellent control.

ALDER FLEA BEETLE. *Altica ambiens.* The leaves are chewed during July and August by dark brown larvae with black heads. The adult, a greenish-blue beetle $1/5$ inch long, deposits orange eggs on the leaves in spring.

Control. Carbaryl (Sevin) sprays when the larvae begin to feed will control this heavy feeder.

ALDER LACE BUG. *Corythucha pergandei.* This species infests not only alder but occasionally birch, elm, and crabapple.

Control. Spray with malathion or carbaryl (Sevin) in late spring.

ALDER PSYLLID. *Psylla floccosa.* This sucking insect is common on alders in the northeastern United States. The nymphal stage produces large amounts of wax. When massed on the stems, the psyllids resemble piles of cotton.

Control. Spray with malathion when the nymphs or adults are seen.

ALMOND, FLOWERING (*Prunus triloba*)

Diseases

BLOSSOM BLIGHT and DIEBACK. *Monilinia fructicola.* This disease causes serious damage to flowering almond. Leaves turn brown and entire branches wilt.

Control. Prune and destroy infected twigs and branches. During wet springs, particularly if the disease was prevalent the previous year, spray with captan or wettable sulfur just before the blossoms open and again 10 days later.

LEAF DROP. Bordeaux mixture and some of the fixed copper fungicides will cause defoliation of flowering almond, peach, and some other members of the genus *Prunus.* Hence they are not recommended for these hosts.

OTHER DISEASES. Flowering almond is susceptible to bacterial fire blight caused by *Erwinia amylovora,* bacterial leaf spot by *Xanthomonas pruni,* powdery mildew by the fungus *Podosphaera oxyacanthae,* root rot by the fungus *Armillaria mellea,* and mosaic by a virus.

Control. Controls are given under more favored hosts.

ASH (*Fraxinus*)*

White, green, and black ash are unusually free from attacks by fungus parasites but are frequently attacked by several insect pests.

Diseases

DIEBACK. Ringspot like virus. In the northeastern United States, white ash has been affected by a branch dieback, and since 1940 occasional death of the tree has been reported. The primary cause of the disease has not been clearly established, although a ringspot-like virus has been associated with it by Dr. Craig Hibben of the Brooklyn Botanic Garden. The virus was transmitted both by grafting and nemas.

Control. Control measures have not been developed.

---

* Some species of ash are tall-growing trees. Many, however, are low-growing kinds.

WITCHES' BROOM. Mycoplasma-like organism. More recently Dr. Hibben was successful in transmitting the mycoplasma-like organism from declining white ash trees by means of the parasitic flowering plant known as dodder.

Control. No controls are known.

ANTHRACNOSE. *Gloeosporium aridum.* Brown spots occur over large areas of the leaves, especially along the veins (Fig. 15-1). In wet seasons, infected leaves drop prematurely.

Control. Valuable specimens should be sprayed with a copper fungicide 3 times at 2-week intervals, starting when the buds break open.

LEAF SPOTS. Several leaf spotting fungi occur on ash, including *Cercospora fraxinites, C. lumbricoides, C. Texensis, Cylindrosporium fraxini, Mycosphaerella effigurata, Phyllosticta fraxinicola, Septoria besseyi, S. leucostoma,* and *S. submaculata.*

Fig. 15-1. Anthracnose of white ash caused by the fungus *Gloeosporium aridum.*

Control. Gather and destroy fallen leaves. This practice is usually sufficient to keep leaf spot diseases at a minimum. In cases where the disease was severe the previous year and spring conditions remain wet, spray with captan or zineb 2 or 3 times at 10-day intervals, beginning when the buds begin to open.

CANKERS. *Cytospora annularis, Diplodia infuscans, Dothiorella fraxinicola, Nectria cinnabarina, N. coccinea,* and *Sphaeropsis* sp. At least six fungi cause branch and trunk cankers on ash. The author found that a species of *Dothiorella* was associated with the death of many white ash trees in the metropolitan New York area in 1977.

Control. Prune out infected branches. Maintain trees in good condition by proper feeding, watering, and spraying.

RUST. *Puccinia sparganioides.* The leaves of green and red ash are conspicuously distorted and the twigs are swollen by this fungus. The spores of the fungus, yellow powder in minute cups, appear over the swollen areas. The spores produced on ash are incapable of reinfecting ash, but infect the so-called 'marsh and cord' grasses.

Control. The disease is rarely destructive enough to warrant special control measures. Sulfur sprays can be used where the disease is serious on valuable specimens.

Insects and Related Pests

ASH BORER. *Podesesia syringae fraxini.* This borer attacks ash and mountain-ash in the Prairie States. It burrows into the tree trunk at or just below the soil line.

Control. Cut out and destroy severely infested trees. Methoxychlor or Dursban sprays applied around the trunk when the adult moths are depositing eggs may be helpful.

BROWN-HEADED ASH SAWFLY. *Tomostethus multicinctus.* Trees may be completely defoliated in May or early June by yellow sawfly larvae. The adult is a beelike insect that lays eggs in the outer leaf margins. Winter is passed in the pupal stage in the ground.

Control. Spray with carbaryl (Sevin) about the middle of May.*

CARPENTER WORM. *Prionoxystus robiniae.* Large scars along the trunk, especially in crotches, and irregularly circular galleries about ½ inch in diameter, principally in the heartwood, are produced by a 3-inch, pinkish-white caterpillar, the carpenter worm. The adult moth, with a wingspread of nearly 3 inches, deposits eggs in crevices or rough spots on the bark during June and early July. A period of 3 years is necessary to complete the life cycle.

---

* Unless specifically noted otherwise, the dates mentioned for appearance of symptoms and time of control apply to the latitude of New York City.

Control. Spray or paint bark of trunk and main branches with methoxychlor in late June and repeat twice at 2-week intervals. Inject commercial borer paste such as Bortox into burrows and seal openings.

OTHER BORERS. Many other borers infest ash. Among the more common are brown wood, California prionus, flatheaded apple tree, and the Pacific flatheaded borer.

Control. State entomologists will supply spraying dates and other information necessary to control these pests.

LILAC LEAF MINER. *Gracillaria syringella.* Light yellow, ¼-inch larvae first mine the leaves of ash, deutzia, privet, and lilac and then roll and skeletonize the leaves. Small moths emerge from overwintering cocoons in the soil in May to deposit eggs in the undersides of the leaves. A second brood emerges in July.

Control. Spray with Diazinon or malathion before larvae curl the leaves. Repeat in mid-July.

LILAC BORER. *Podosesia syringae syringae.* Rough, knotlike swellings on the trunk and limbs and the breaking of small branches at the point of injury are indications of the presence of the lilac borer, a brown-headed, whitebodied larva ¾ inch long. The adult female appearing in early fall is a moth with clear wings having a spread of 1½ inches, the front pair of which is deep brown. The larvae pass the winter underneath the bark.

Control. Spray the trunk and main branches with methoxychlor in early May and repeat twice at 3-week intervals.

FALL WEBWORM. *Hyphantria cunea.* In fall webworm infestations, the leaves are chewed in August and September, and the branches are covered with webs or nests, which enclose skeletonized leaves and pale-yellow or green caterpillars 1 inch long. The adult moth has white-to brown-spotted wings with a spread of 1½ inches.

Control. Cut out or remove nests, or spray thoroughly with *Bacillus thuringiensis,* Diazinon, Dylox, or carbaryl (Sevin) when the webs are first visible.

ASH FLOWER GALL. *Aceria fraxinivorus.* This disease is caused by small mites which attack the staminate flowers of white ash. The flowers develop abnormally and form very irregular galls up to ½ inch in diameter (Fig. 15-2). These galls dry out, forming clusters which are conspicuous on the trees during winter.

Control. Kelthane spray applied after the buds swell and before the new growth emerges in spring will provide control.

OYSTERSHELL SCALE. *Lepidosaphes ulmi.* Masses of brown bodies shaped like an oystershell and about ¹/₁₀ inch long, covering twigs and branches, are characteristic of this insect. The pests overwinter in the egg stage under the scales. The young crawling stage appears in late May.

Control. Spray in late spring, before the buds open, with 1 part concentrated lime sulfur in 10 parts of water, or with dormant oil plus

Fig. 15-2. Ash flower gall caused by mites.

ethion according to the directions of the manufacturer. Malathion or carbaryl (Sevin) sprays applied when the young are crawling about in May and June also give control.

SCURFY SCALE. *Chionaspis furfura.* A grayish scurfy covering on the bark indicates the presence of this pest. The scale covering the adult female is pear-shaped, gray, and about $^1/_{10}$ inch long. The pest overwinters as purple eggs under the female scale.

Control. Spray in late spring, before the leaf buds open, with dormant oil plus ethion, or in mid-May and again in early June with malathion or carbaryl (Sevin).

ASPEN—See Poplar (Chapter 16).

AVOCADO (*Persea*)

Diseases

ANTHRACNOSE. *Colletotrichum gloeosporioides.* Greenhouse plants in the northern states and garden plants in the southern are subject to attack by this fungus. It causes a general wilting of the ends of branches and the development of cankers on the stem and spots on the leaves and flowers.

Control. If necessary, spray with bordeaux mixture or some other copper fungicide.

ROOT ROT. *Phytophthora cinnamomi.* Root rot, also known as 'decline,' is the most destructive disease of avocado in California. The causal fungus is soil-borne and seed-borne.

Control. Treat seed in hot water at 120° to 125°F. (49° to 50°C.) for 30 minutes to eliminate seed-borne infections. The avocado variety Duke is said to be rather resistant to attack by the causal fungus.

SCAB. *Sphaceloma perseae.* This is a serious disease of avocado in Florida and Texas.

Control. Copper sprays will control this disease.

OTHER DISEASES. Other important diseases of avocado are canker, caused by *Botryosphaeria dothidea,* root rot by *Armillaria mellea,* and wilt by *Verticillium albo-atrum.*

Control. Measures for the control of these diseases are discussed in Chapter 14.

BANANA (*Musa*)

Plants of the cultivated banana, *Musa paradisiaca* var. *sapientum*, are subject to a number of serious bacterial and fungus diseases, as well as many insects. Such plants grown in northern greenhouses for display and educational purposes are subject to mealybugs, whiteflies, and scales. These can be controlled with malathion sprays.

In Florida the dwarf banana, *M. nana*, is subject to anthracnose caused by the fungus *Gloeosporium musarum,* leaf blight by the bacterium *Pseudomonas solanacearum,* and the southern root-knot nema, *Meloidogyne incognita.* The burrowing nema, *Radopholus similis,* occurs in Louisiana on the roots of ornamental banana trees.

Control. Plant pathologists at southern agricultural experiment stations will provide control measures.

BIRCH (*Betula*)

The birches are graceful as well as beautiful (Fig. 15-3). Extremely particular about soil conditions, they are unable to adapt themselves as street trees and are used principally on lawns.

The canoe birch (*B. papyrifera*) has attractive bark and a single trunk. Gray birch (*B. populifolia*) is gray-barked, and many specimens have several trunks.

Ornamental birches are susceptible to several fungus parasites and insect pests. Of these, the bronze birch borer is mainly responsible for the death of trees used in ornamental plantings.

The Monarch birch (*B. maximowicziana*), introduced into the United

Fig. 15-3. The bark and growth habit of the gray birch (*Betula populifolia*) are very interesting.

States from Japan in 1893 by Professor Sargent of the Arnold Arboretum, is highly resistant to the bronze birch borer. Its leaves are larger than those of native species and more distinctly heart-shaped. Monarch birch does better in urban environments than the other birches. It should be more widely planted as a lawn or park tree.

Diseases

LEAF BLISTER. Three fungi cause leaf blister on many species of birch. *Taphrina bacteriosperma* and *T. carnea* produce red blisters and curling of the leaves on many of the birch species, and *T. flava* forms yellow blisters on gray and canoe birches.

Control. Gather and destroy all fallen leaves. Spray with ferbam or ziram just before buds open in spring.

LEAF RUST. *Melampsoridium betulinum.* Leaves of seedlings and of mature trees are sometimes attacked by a rust which causes spotting and defoliation. The rust pustules are bright reddish-yellow. The spores from these pustules carry the infection from leaf to leaf. The alternate or sexual stage causes a blister rust on larch. In mixed forest plantings both hosts may be seriously injured.

Control. In ornamental plantings the disease rarely becomes destructive enough to warrant special control measures.

LEAF SPOT. Several leaf spot fungi attack birch. The fungus *Gloeosporium betularum* produces brown spots with a dark brown to black margin. The fungus *Cylindrosporium betulae* forms smaller spots with no definite margin. Both fungi may become sufficiently prevalent to cause some premature defoliation.

Control. Gathering and destroying fallen leaves usually suffices for practical control. Bordeaux mixture or any other copper spray may be used in late spring as a preventive.

CANKER. Black, paper, sweet, and yellow birches are particularly susceptible.

Symptoms. Young cankers are usually not readily visible. Upon close examination, however, they are seen to be darker in color than the adjacent healthy tissue and appear water-soaked. Later the edge of the diseased area cracks, thus exposing the canker (Fig. 15-4). Callus tissue forms over the cracked area, but becomes infected and dies. The process is repeated annually, forming concentric rings of dead callus. The bark

Fig. 15-4. Canker on black birch.

within the cankered zone falls away, leaving the wood exposed. When the canker completely girdles the stem or trunk, the distal portion dies.

Cause. Canker is caused by the fungus *Nectria galligena.* Small, globose, dark red fruit bodies of the fungus are barely visible to the unaided eye on the dead bark.

Control. In thick stands it is advisable to remove trees with trunk infections. Trees having cankers or galls on the branches may be saved by pruning out and destroying the cankers. Since the cankers originate on young growth, inspection of the plantings and early destruction of the cankered young trees are advisable. Trees in ornamental plantings should be fed and watered to keep them in good vigor.

DIEBACK. *Melanconium betulinum.* Trees weakened by drought may be attacked by this fungus, which causes a progressive dieback of the upper branches. Infestations of the bronze birch borer mentioned below may cause similar symptoms, however.

Control. Prune affected branches to sound wood, and fertilize and water heavily to help revitalize the tree.

WOOD DECAY. A number of wood-decay fungi attack birches. One, *Polyporus betulinus,* attacks dying or dead birches and produces shelf- or hoof-shaped, gray, smooth, fungus bodies along the trunk. Others, such as *Torula ligniperda, Fomes fomentarius, F. igniarius, F. applanatus, Poria laevigata,* and *P. obliqua,* are associated with decay of living trees.

Control. Wood decays cannot be checked once they have become extensive. Avoidance of wounds and maintenance of the trees in good vigor by fertilization are the best preventive practices.

OTHER FUNGUS DISEASES. Birches are subject to several other fungus diseases: powdery mildews caused by *Microsphaera alni* and *Phyllactinia corylea,* leaf spots by *Gloeosporium betulae-luteae* and *Septoria betulicola,* and stem cankers by *Physalospora obtusa* and *Diaporthe alleghaniensis.*

Control. Control measures are rarely necessary for these diseases.

VIRUS DISEASE. Line pattern mosaic. Apple mosaic virus. Decline, dieback, and death of both white and yellow birches in forest plantings may be virus-induced. White birch in ornamental plantings may also be affected but to a lesser extent. Yellow to golden line and ringspot patterns on the leaves are the most striking symptoms.

Control. Control measures have not been developed for this virus disease.

Insects and Related Pests

APHIDS. *Euceraphis betulae* and *Calaphis betulaecolens.* The former, known as the European birch aphid, is yellow and infests cut-leaved and other birch varieties. The latter, the common birch aphid, is a large green species which produces copious quantities of honeydew followed by sooty mold.

Control. Spray thoroughly with Diazinon, dimethoate, or malathion as soon as these aphids appear.

WITCH-HAZEL LEAF GALL APHID. *Hormaphis hamamelidis.* This insect, which causes the formation of cone galls on witch-hazel, migrates from this host to birches in summer. It feeds on the undersides of the leaves and resembles nymphs of whiteflies.

Control. Spray with malathion when aphids are present.

CASE BEARER. *Coleophora salmani.* Leaves are mined and shriveled and small cases are formed under the leaves by the case bearer, a light yellow to green caterpillar, $^1/_5$ inch long with a black head. The adult is a brown moth with a wingspread of $^2/_5$ inch. The pest overwinters as a larva in a case attached to the bark.

Control. Spray in late spring, before growth begins, with 1 part concentrated lime sulfur in 8 parts of water, or with standard malathion solution in late July or early August.

BIRCH LEAF MINER. *Fenusa pusilla.* Gray, canoe, and cut-leaf birches are especially susceptible to attacks by the leaf miner, a small white worm which causes leaves to turn brown in late spring or early summer (Fig. 15-5). The adult is a small black sawfly which overwinters in the soil as a pupa. The first brood begins to feed anytime from very early to late May, depending on the season and the location of the trees. The first brood causes most damage because it attacks the tender spring foliage. Other broods hatch during the summer, but these cause less damage because they do not attack mature foliage but confine their feeding to leaves on sucker growths and to newly developing leaves in the crowns of the trees.

Control. Diazinon, Meta-Systox R, or carbaryl (Sevin) sprays will control the birch leaf miner. The first spray should be applied about May 1. If the spring is a cold one, the first application can be delayed a week or so. For best control, two additional applications should be made at 10-day intervals. To control the second brood of leaf miners, spray again about July 1 and July 10.

In Connecticut Dr. John Schread found that Cygon used as a soil drench or surface applications of either Baygon or Cygon in granular form also controlled the birch leaf miner.

BIRCH SKELETONIZER. *Bucculatrix canadensisella.* The lower leaf surface is chewed and the leaf is skeletonized and may turn brown as a result of feeding by this skeletonizer, a yellowish-green larva ¼ inch long. The adult moth has white-lined, brown wings with a spread of ⅜ inch.

Control. Spray the upper and lower sides of the leaves with carbaryl (Sevin) about mid-July.

BRONZE BIRCH BORER. *Agrilus anxius.* Varieties of birch grown in parks as ornamental shade trees, especially where the soil is poor, and trees grown elsewhere under adverse conditions, become prey to this borer. The grub is from ½ to 1 inch long, flat-headed and light-colored. The adult stage is a beetle ½ inch long. The beetles, which feed on foliage for

Fig. 15-5. The leaf miner causes brown blotches on birch leaves. The tiny adult flies and the larvae are also shown.

a time, deposit their eggs in slits in the bark. The borers make flat, irregular, winding galleries just beneath the bark of the main trunk. Heavy infestations usually kill the trees (Fig. 15-6).

Control. Spray the trunk and branches thoroughly and the leaves lightly in early June and twice more at 2-week intervals with methoxychlor as directed by the manufacturer. Dimethoate (Cygon 2E) at the rate of 1 quart of the emulsifiable liquid per 100 gallons of water applied in mid-June and again in late June for 2 consecutive years, will also provide control. Keep the trees in good vigor by feeding and watering when needed.

SEED MITE GALL. *Eriophyes betulae.* Another conspiculous gall on paper birch and other species is caused by the seed mite. The galls are about 1 inch in diameter, made up of many adventitious branches and deformed buds. They may resemble witches' brooms.

Control. This pest is never serious enough to require control measures.

Fig. 15-6. These birches are dying back because of infestations of the bronze birch borer.

CALLIANDRA (*Calliandra*)

Diseases and Insects

The roots of the Surinam calliandra in Florida may be rotted by the fungus *Clitocybe tabescens*. In Arizona the rust fungus *Ravenelia reticulatae* occurs on this host. Control measures have not been developed.

The green peach aphid, *Myzus persicae*, attacks the powder-puff tree (*Calliandra inaequilatera*) when this beautiful tree is grown in northern greenhouses. The aphids are frequently held in check by the parasitic braconid wasps. The wasps thrust their eggs into the abdomens of the aphids. There, after the eggs hatch, the little grubs feed on the body content. The parasite punctures a hole in the under side of the aphid and fastens it to the leaf; the aphid then swells up and turns brown and the skin becomes tough and leathery. When the wasp is about to emerge it cuts a round hole in the body of the abdomen, sometimes leaving a hingelike portion which holds the lidlike cover in place. The aphids are also controlled by syrphid flies, the sluglike larvae of which feed on the aphids. Ladybugs also are natural enemies of these insects. Aphid infestations that are too heavy to be controlled by natural parasites can be handled with malathion sprays.

CAMELLIA (*Camellia japonica* and *C. sasanqua*)

Camellias are grown outdoors in the warmer parts of the country and indoors in the colder parts. The *sasanqua* varieties are said to be more winter hardy than the *japonica* varieties in the northeastern part of the country along the Atlantic coast.

Fungus and Algal Diseases

BLACK MOLD. *Meliola camelliae*. The abundant black fungus growth of the *Fumago* stage covers the leaves and twigs of this host. The ascospores are brown, each provided with several crosswalls.

Control. Spray with malathion to control insects such as aphids and scales which secrete the substance on which this fungus grows. Promptly pick off and destroy infected leaves and get rid of all debris from infected plants.

CANKER. *Glomerella cingulata*. A canker and dieback of camellias is widespread and frequently destructive in the southern states. It also occurs on greenhouse-grown plants in the North. The fungus enters only through wounds. In nature, the usual entrance points are scars left by the abscission of leaves in spring.

In Florida a species of *Phomopsis* causes somewhat similar symptoms.

Control. Prune and destroy cankered twigs. Where the cankers occur on the main stem of large plants, surgical removal of the diseased portions should be attempted, followed by use of a tree paint containing a fungicide. Copper fungicides applied periodically to the leaves and stems may help to prevent new infections.

FLOWER BLIGHT. *Sclerotinia camelliae.* This blight is confined to the flowers, which turn brown and drop. It occurs in the Pacific Coast states and in Gulf and other southern states from Texas to Virginia. All species and varieties of camellias appear equally susceptible to the blight.

Another flower-blighting fungus, *Sclerotinia sclerotiorum,* has been reported from North Carolina. A bud and flower blight is occasionally caused by *Botrytis cinerea,* particularly after the plants have been subjected to frost.

Control. To control the *Sclerotinia camelliae* blight, pick off and discard all old camellia blossoms before they fall. Benlate, ferbam, sulfur, or Fore sprays help to prevent infection. Infections can also be prevented by placing a 3-inch mulch of wood chips or other suitable material around the base of each plant. Such a barrier will prevent the fungus bodies in the soil beneath from ejecting their spores into the atmosphere and onto the leaves. Soils heavily infested with sclerotia (which later produce ascocarps) may be treated with ferbam or Captan. PCNB (Terraclor) provides even more effective control but must be used in soils free of plants.

No special controls have been developed for the *Botrytis* bud and flower blight or for *Sclerotinia sclerotiorum.*

LEAF BLIGHT. *Cephaleuros virescens.* The epidermal cells are attacked by this alga, which spreads rapidly over the leaf and causes it to blacken and die.

Control. Remove diseased leaves. Badly infested specimens may be sprayed with a copper fungicide.

LEAF GALL. *Exobasidium camelliae.* The leaves and stems of new shoots are thickened and distorted by this fungus.

Control. Spray once before the leaves unfurl with either ferbam or zineb.

LEAF SPOT. *Cercospora theae.* This leaf spot, first reported from Louisiana, develops under conditions of overcrowding, partial shade, and high humidity of a lath house.

Control. No controls have been developed.

ROOT ROT. *Phytophthora cinnamomi.* This disease is common not only on camellia but also on avocado, maple, pine, and rhododendron, as well as many other woody plants. Excessive moisture and poor soil drainage favor its development.

Control. Improve drainage. Drenching soil around living plants with either nabam or zineb may help.

SPOT DISEASE. *Pestalotia guepini.* More or less irregular round blotches run together, causing a silvery appearance of the upper surface of the leaves. The diseased area is sharply marked off from the healthy portion. The pycnidia or fruiting bodies of the fungus are visible as black dots. Leaf fall sometimes results. Several other fungi produce leaf spotting: *Phyllosticta camelliae, P. camelliaecola,* and *Sporonema camelliae.* A species of *Sphaceloma* causes scabby spots on the leaves.

Control. Collect and destroy all diseased leaves. Spray larger plantings with some fungicide, such as bordeaux mixture, if spotting of the foliage is not objectionable; otherwise spray the plants with wettable sulfur.

Physiological Diseases

BUD DROP. Camellias grown in homes, in greenhouses, and even outdoors frequently lose their buds before opening, or the tips of the young buds and edges of young petals turn brown and decay. (Fig. 15-7). Bud drop from indoor-grown plants usually is due to overwatering of the soil or to some other faulty environmental condition such as insufficient light, excessively high temperatures, or a potbound condition of the roots. Bud drop in the Pacific Northwest may result from a

Fig. 15-7. Lower: Bud drop of camellia. **Upper:** Yellow mottle virus symptoms.

severe frost in September or October, severe freezing during the winter, or an irregular water supply. In California it may result from lack of adequate moisture.

CHLOROSIS may be caused by deficiency of some elements in the soil.

EDEMA. Frequently brown, corky, roughened swellings develop on camellia leaves grown in greenhouses. The condition is associated with overwatering of the soil during extended periods of cloudy weather.

SUNBURN. This condition appears on leaves as faded green to brown areas with indefinite margins. It occurs on the upper exposed sides of bushes, particularly those transplanted from shaded to very sunny areas.

SALT INJURY. Camellias cannot tolerate high soil salinity even though they grow best in the acid soils and temperate climate of our eastern and Gulf Coast areas. Salt levels above 1800 parts per million in the soil solution were fatal to camellias in greenhouse tests conducted at the Virginia Truck Experiment Station in Norfolk. Azaleas were found to be equally susceptible to high salt concentrations.

Virus Diseases

The virus diseases of camellia are not well understood. Leaf and flower variegation is presumed to be caused by a virus, inasmuch as the condition was transmitted by graftage from variegated *Camellia japonica* to uniformly green varieties of *C. japonica* and *C. sasanqua*. Some yellow variegation, however, may be due to genetic changes rather than virus infection. Such variegations usually follow a uniform and rather typical pattern which is more or less similar on all leaves. The author has observed many greenhouse-grown camellias in the North with typical ringspot patterns in the leaves. The symptoms caused by camellia yellow mottle virus are illustrated in Figure 15-7.

Control. Plants suspected of harboring a virus should be discarded, or at least isolated from healthy plants.

Insects and Other Animal Pests

FLORIDA RED SCALE. *Chrysomphalus aonidum.* This scale insect, common on citrus and other plants in the greenhouse, has been found to live on camellia leaves. The scales are dark brown and more or less circular. It is easy to remove the scale with a needle; this exposes the very light yellow body of the insect, firmly attached to the leaf by its sucking organ. The leaf shown in Figure 15-8 was photographed after several of the scales had been thus removed; the insects appear as white spots.

Many other species of scales infest camellias. They include black, California red, camellia, chaff, cottony taxus, degenerate, Florida wax, glover, greedy, hemispherical, latania, Mexican wax, oleander, oyster-

Fig. 15-8. Florida red scale on camellia.

shell, peony, and soft scale. Two other scales known as the camellia parlatoria and the olive parlatoria also attack this host.

Control. Spray with malathion or carbaryl (Sevin) to control the young crawling insects. Repeat the treatment at 2-week intervals for heavily infested plants. In the South, Florida Volck and similar oil emulsions are quite effective on outdoor plants. Oil sprays should not be applied when the temperature is above 85°F. (29°C.), but malathion and carbaryl (Sevin) may be applied at any time.

FULLER ROSE BEETLE. *Pantomorus godmani.* This snout-beetle occasionally infests camellias, roses, palms, and many other plants.

A number of other beetles also infest this host. The most common are rhabdopterus, flea beetle, and the grape colaspis.

Control. Carbaryl (Sevin) sprays will control the various kinds of beetles.

MEALYBUGS. *Planococcus citri* and *Pseudococcus adonidum.* These two white insects are usually found in the leaf axils and shoot buds.

Control. Spray with malathion.

SPOTTED CUTWORM. *Amathes c-nigrum.* This cutworn has been found feeding on the blasted buds of camellias in greenhouses. Apparently it is able to climb up among the branches, leaves, and flower buds.

Control. Spray with carbaryl (Sevin).

TEA SCALE. *Fiorinia theae.* The most serious pest of outdoor camellias in the South, this scale also infests greenhouse-grown camellias in the North as well as ferns, palms, orchids, figs, and several other plants. It can be distinguished superficially by its oblong shape and the ridge down the center parallel to the sides.

Control. The same as for Florida red scale.

THRIPS. the browning of the tips of buds, followed by decay and dropping, has frequently been found to be due to the attacks of a species of thrips. This should be clearly distinguished from the bud drop caused by overwatering (see above).

Control. Spray with malathion.

WEEVILS *Otiorhynchus sulcatus* and *O. ovatus.* The black vine weevil and the strawberry root weevil feed on the leaves; the larval stages feed on the roots and the base of the stem.

Control. Spray the lower parts of the plants and the soil surface with Diazinon.

OTHER INSECTS. A great number of other insects infest camellias in greenhouses, homes, and outdoors. These include the following aphids: black citrus, melon, green peach, and ornate. The following caterpillars chew the leaves: omnivorus looper, orange tortrix, and western parsley. The fruit tree leafroller and the greenhouse leaf tier also chew the leaves and roll or tie them together. The greenhouse whitefly is common on greenhouse-grown plants.

Control. Most of these pests can be easily controlled with malathion. The caterpillars can also be controlled with carbaryl (Sevin).

ROOT NEMA. *Meloidogyne incognita.* Camellias are unusually resistant to root-knot nemas, although the pests have been recorded on these plants in Texas. Another species of nema, *Hemicriconemoides gaddi,* has been reported on the roots of camellia in Louisiana.

Control. Drenching the soil around infested trees with Nemagon may provide control.

CHASTE-TREE *(Vitex)*

This low-growing tree or shrub produces showy purple clusters of blooms in late summer in the North and earlier in the South.

Diseases

LEAF SPOT *Cercospora viticis.* This disease occurs on chaste-tree along the Gulf Coast.

Control. The disease is rarely severe enough to warrant control measures.

ROOT ROT. *Phymatotrichum omnivorum.* The root rot is present on chaste-tree in Texas.

Control. Control measures are not practicable.

CHERRY, JAPANESE FLOWERING
(Prunus serrulata, P. yedoensis, and related species)

Flowering cherries are used rather extensively as ornamentals. In latitudes north of southern New Jersey they are occasionally damaged by low winter temperatures, as is evidenced by longitudinal cracks (Fig. 15-9) on the south or west side of the trunk or in the branch crotches. Flowering cherries are best planted in fall.

Fig. 15-9. Winter injury to flowering cherry. This species is particularly susceptible in eastern areas north of Philadelphia.

Flowering cherries are susceptible to some of the fungi and insect pests that attack the common cherry. These parasites, however, have not been studied in detail on flowering cherries, and any treatment must be based on the control measures suggested for ordinary cherry. Information on the diseases and insects of ordinary cherry is readily available from the state agricultural experiment stations.

Bacterial and Fungus Diseases

SHOT-HOLE. *Xanthomonas pruni*. The bacterium that attacks peaches and cherries in orchards is known to attack Japanese cherries also, causing a familiar 'shot-hole' appearance. The infected tissue dries up and falls out, leaving a hole about ⅛ inch in diameter. Shot-holes in cherry leaves may also be due to the fungus *Coccomyces hiemalis*, discussed below, and to virus infection.

Control. Where the *Xanthomonas* bacterium causes serious damage to flowering cherries, spray with Cyprex, mentioned below under leaf spot.

LEAF SPOT. *Coccomyces hiemalis*. During rainy springs this disease is rather prevalent. The reddish spots on the leaves drop out, leaving circular holes. Complete defoliation may follow.

Control. Benlate, Cyprex, or Dodine sprays will control this rather prevalent disease. The first application should be made when the flower petals fall, followed by 2 more applications at 2-week intervals.

BLACK KNOT. *Apiosporina morbosa*. Black, rough cylindrical-shaped galls (Fig. 15-10) develop on the twigs or apricots, cherries, and plums. Neglected trees appear to be especially subject to this disease.

Control. Prune knotted twigs and excise knots on large branches during the winter. Then spray with Dodine or Benlate when the trees are dormant, at pink bud stage, at full-bloom stage, and 3 weeks later.

POWDERY MILDEW. *Podosphaera oxyacanthae*. The Japanese cherry is subject to the same powdery mildew that attacks edible cherries. The leaves and twigs become coated with a mat of fungus growth, which causes dwarfing and death of these branches. The disease is uncommon.

Control. Karathane or Benlate sprays will control this disease.

WITCHES' BROOM. *Taphrina cerasi*. *Prunus yedoensis* seems to be rather susceptible to this disease. Large branches will sometimes become deformed by development of many irregular dwarfed branches to form a witches' broom. Blossoms develop and leaves come out on the brooms earlier than on the normal branches. Sometimes large numbers of very small brooms develop all over the tree, killing the end-branches and eventually the whole tree.

Control. Cut off and destroy the brooms. Spray with ziram or ferbam in fall or in early spring.

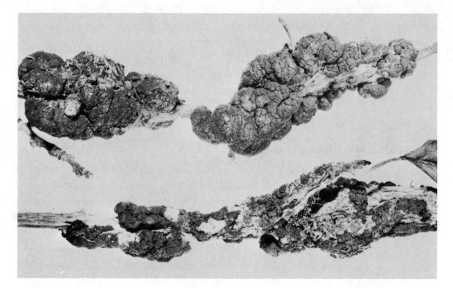

Fig. 15-10. Black knot of cherry caused by the fungus *Apiosporina morbosa.*

Virus Disease

Normal-appearing Japanese cherries of the varieties Kwanzan and Shirofugen have been found to carry a virus of the Little Cherry type. This fact is important only to cherry virus research workers who use flowering cherries for test plants.

Physiological Disease

YELLOWING. Very often yellowing and premature defoliation of flowering cherry occur without previous spotting of the leaves. These symptoms are associated with excessively wet or dry soils or with low-temperature injuries to the crown and roots. As a rule, a second set of leaves is formed after the premature defoliation in spring or early summer. The new leaves are normal to all appearances.

Insects and Other Animal Pests

ASIATIC GARDEN BEETLE. *Maladera castanea.* The leaves are chewed during the night by a brown beetle ¼ inch long. During the day the insect hides just below the soil surface.

Control. Carbaryl (Sevin) sprays will keep this pest in check.

PEACH BORER. *Sanninoidea exitiosa.* Masses of gum exuding from the base of the tree are the work of the peach borer within the trunk. The adult is a clear-winged moth, which appears and deposits eggs in July and August.

The lesser peach borer, *Synanthedon pictipes,* may also attack flowering cherry. The adult, a metallic, blue-black, yellow-marked moth, emerges in June in the vicinity of New York City and in May in the South to deposit eggs on the bark higher up in the tree than the peach borer.

Control. Four applications of methoxychlor to the trunk and branches will control both types of borers. The first application should be made about June 15 in latitudes of New York City, a few weeks earlier in the South. The other applications should follow at about 2-week intervals.

ORIENTAL FRUIT WORM. *Graphiolitha molesta.* Wilting of the tips of twigs may be due to boring by the oriental fruit worm, a small pinkish-white larva, about ½ inch long. The adult female is about ½ inch long and is gray with chocolate-brown markings on the wings. Larvae overwinter in the soil.

Control. Where only a few trees are involved, removal and destruction of wilted tips as they appear is usually sufficient. Large numbers of trees can be protected by periodic applications of methoxychlor sprays to which a compatible mite killer such as Kelthane has been added. Applications should be started as soon as the leaves begin to emerge and should be repeated twice at 10- to 12-day intervals.

PEAR SLUG. *Caliroa cerasi.* These so-called slugs, olive-green, semitransparent, and slimy, are the larvae of a sawfly. They are about ½ inch long, swollen at the front, and shaped somewhat like a tadpole (Fig. 15-11). They occasionally infest *Prunus* and may completely skeletonize the

Fig. 15-11. Pear-slug sawfly larvae skeltonizing cherry leaf.

leaves. There are two generations a year in the northern states and three in the southern.

Control. Spray with malathion when the slugs begin to feed.

PLANTHOPPERS. *Metcalfa pruinosa* and *Ormensis septentrionalis.* These planthoppers injure shrubs and trees by sucking the juices of the more tender branches, which they cover with a woolly substance. One species is illustrated in Figure 15-12.

Control. Apply sprays containing pyrethrum or rotenone, or a combination of the two, forcefully enough to wet the insects thoroughly.

EASTERN TENT CATERPILLAR. *Malacosoma americanum.* Wild cherries are the natural hosts of the tent caterpillar (Fig. 15-13). Unless these plants are valued as ornamentals, they should be destroyed.

Control. When the caterpillar occurs on Japanese cherry, it can be controlled by spraying the tree with carbaryl (Sevin) as soon as the caterpillars appear in the spring.

SAN JOSE SCALE. *Aspidiotus perniciosus.* Gray, closely appressed masses of circular scales, $1/10$ inch in diameter, with a raised nipple in the center, are characteristic of the San Jose scale. The winter is passed in the immature stage on the bark.

Control. Dormant oil sprays or lime sulfur 1-10 on the trunk, branches, and twigs before the buds open in spring is effective. A more complete

Fig. 15-12. Planthopper (*Ormensis septentrionalis*) on cherry branch.

Fig. 15-13. Eastern tent caterpillars on wild cherry. **Inset:** Egg masses on twigs.

control can be obtained by following with carbaryl (Sevin) or malathion sprays in May and June.

WATERLILY APHID. *Rhopalosiphum nymphaeae*. Ornamental species of *Prunus* grown near waterlily ponds are seriously attacked by the waterlily aphid. The insects migrate to the trees in May and June and in autumn.

Control. Spray with malathion when the insects appear on the leaves.

WHITE PEACH SCALE. *Pseudaulacaspis pentagona*. The presence of this scale is indicated by white incrustrations on the bark, masses of circular white scales ¹/₁₀ inch in diameter, which suck juices from below the bark.

Control. While the tree is dormant, spray with 1 part concentrated lime sulfur in 10 parts of water, or with dormant strength oils. Diazinon, methoxychlor, or carbaryl (Sevin) sprays applied when the young are crawling about in spring will also control these pests.

ROOT NEMA. *Pratylenchus penetrans*. Research at the New York State Experiment Station revealed that this nema attacks the roots of edible cherry trees. It is possible that the roots of Japanese flowering cherries are also susceptible to the same nema.

JAPANESE BEETLE. See under Linden (Chapter 16).

CORK TREE *(Phellodendron)*

Cork trees are unusually free of pests. The only insects recorded on this host are the lesser snow scale, *Pinnaspis strachani,* and the pustule scale, *Asterolecanium pustulans.*

Malathion or carbaryl (Sevin) sprays applied in late spring or early summer will control the crawler stages of these pests.

CRABAPPLE, FLOWERING *(Malus)*

Flowering crabapple trees used for ornamental purposes are subject to attack by many of the fungi and insects that occur on the common apple.

Some species and cultivars that are unusually resistant to the four most common diseases—fire blight, cedar-apple rust, powdery mildew, and scab—include 'Adams,' *baccata jackii,* 'Beauty,' 'Beverly,' 'Centennial,' 'Goldfinch,' *halliana parkmani,* 'Pink Spires,' 'Royalty,' 'Snow Drift,' 'White Angel,' and 'Winter Gold.'

Bacterial and Fungus Diseases

FIRE BLIGHT. *Erwinia amylovora*. This disease will not be serious on the flowering crab if commercial orchards of pears and apples are not nearby. Several varieties of hawthorns are far more susceptible to this bacterial disease, which causes blighting of the ends of branches.

Control. See under fire blight (Chapter 14).

CANKER. *Physalospora obtusa* and *Phoma mali.* Two species of fungi cause cankers on the trunks of crabapples. They often gain entrance through wounds made by lawn mowers and other maintenance equipment.

Control. Avoid wounding trees. Increase the tree's vigor by feeding and watering.

RUST. *Gymnosporangium juniperi-virginianae.* When common red cedar with cedar-apple galls is transplanted from the wild to a garden, a number of brown or orange spots, bearing the pycnidial stage of the rust, may later be very conspicuous on the leaves of flowering crabapples nearby. Much defoliation may follow heavy infection.

Control. If practicable, eliminate any red cedars (*Juniperus*) within a mile radius, or spray with Fore as directed by the manufacturer or with ½ pound of ferbam and 3 pounds of elemental sulfur per 100 gallons of water. Four to five applications at 7- to 10-day intervals are needed, starting when the orange fungus masses appear on junipers. For most effective results, the sprays should be applied before rainy periods. Plantvax sprays are also effective in combating rusts. In the New England states, Thylate sprays will control rusts, scab, and several other crabapple diseases.

SCAB. *Venturia inaequalis.* Olive-drab spots ¼ inch in diameter appear on the leaves, which drop prematurely, and the fruits are disfigured. The imperfect stage of the fungus, *Fusicladium dendriticum,* overwinters on the twigs.

Control. Spray with captan, dodine or Fore 4 or 5 times at 10-day intervals, starting when leaves are half-grown.

Insects and Related Pests

Most insects that infest the leaves and twigs, such as aphids, alder lace bug, leafhoppers, and several kinds of caterpillars, are easily controlled with malathion if applied when the young are feeding. Oystershell, San Jose, and Putnam scales can be controlled with a dormant oil spray, or with malathion or carbaryl (Sevin) when the young scales are crawling about in late spring. Malathion can be safely combined in the ferbam-sulfur spray recommended for rust control.

PERIODICAL CICADA. *Magicicada septendecim.* This pest (Fig. 15-14), also known as the 17-year locust, damages branches of crabapple, apple, and many other fruit trees by making deep slits in the bark during the egg-laying period. Such branches are easily broken during windy weather.

Control. A spray containing 1 ounce of carbaryl (Sevin) in 5 gallons of water gives excellent control if applied in July at the time the cicadas are in the trees.

EUROPEAN RED MITE. *Panonychus ulmi.* This species also infests the

Fig. 15-14. Female periodical cicadas lay their eggs in young twigs and branches.

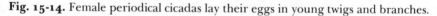

leaves of black locust, elm, mountain-ash, and rose, in addition to many kinds of fruit and nut trees.

Control. A 'superior'* type dormant oil applied in early spring just before new growth begins will provide control. When infestations are particularly heavy, applications of chlorobenzilate, Keltane, or Tedion in late May, and again two weeks later, may be necessary.

CRAPEMYRTLE (*Lagerstroemia*)

This beautiful shrubby tree is reliably hardy only in the South, although fine specimens are growing in protected places in the latitude of New York City.

* See footnote p. 249.

Diseases

POWDERY MILDEW. *Erysiphe lagerstroemiae*. This mildew is most serious in the spring and fall months. The leaves and shoots are distorted and stunted. Inflorescences are also attacked, the flower buds failing to open. The shoots and leaves may be coated with white growth, the leaves tending to assume a reddish color beneath the mildew. The whole plant may sometimes be affected.

Two other species, *Phyllactinia corylea* and *Uncinula australiana*, occasionally infect this host.

Control. Actidione PM spray is very effective in controlling the powdery mildew on this host. Wettable sulfur and Karathane sprays also control it. A dormant lime sulfur spray just before buds open in spring is recommended, in addition to the other sprays, where mildew is unusually prevalent.

OTHER FUNGUS DISEASES. Black spot caused by a species of *Cercospora*, tip blight by *Phyllosticta lagerstroemia*, leaf spot by *Cercospora lythracearum* and *Pestalotia guepini*, and root rot by *Clitocybe tabescens* are other diseases of this host.

Control. Leaf spots and tip blight can be controlled with several applications of a copper fungicide at 3-week intervals, starting when the new growth appears in spring. Root rot cannot be controlled.

Insects

CRAPEMYRTLE APHID. *Myzocallis kahawaluokalani*. This species attacks only crapemyrtle. It exudes a great amount of honeydew, on which the sooty mold fungus, *Capnodium* sp., thrives.

Control. Spray with Meta-Systox R, malathion, or carbaryl (Sevin) early in the growing season.

FLORIDA WAX SCALE. *Ceroplastes floridensis*. This reddish- or purplish-brown scale covered with a thick, white, waxy coating tinted with pink attacks a wide variety of shrubs in the South.

Control. Spray with malathion or carbaryl (Sevin) when the crawling stage is about.

DOGWOOD (*Cornus*)

The dogwoods, among our best ornamental low-growing trees, are subject to several important fungus diseases and insect pests.

Diseases

CROWN CANKER. The most serious disease of flowering dogwood (*C. florida*), crown canker, is prevalent in several northeastern states.

Symptoms. An unthrifty appearance is the first general symptom. The leaves are smaller and lighter green than normal and turn prematurely red in late summer. At times, especially during dry spells, they may curl and shrivel. Later, twigs and even large branches die. At first the diseased parts occur principally on one side of the tree, but within a year or two they may appear over the entire tree.

The most significant symptoms and the cause for the weak top growth is the slowly developing canker on the lower trunk or roots, at or near the soil level. Although the canker is not readily discernible in the early stages, it can be located by careful examination. Cutting into it will reveal that the inner bark, cambium, and sapwood are discolored. Later, the cankered area becomes sunken, and the bark dries and falls away, leaving the wood exposed. When the canker extends completely around the trunk base or the root collar, the tree dies.

Cause. Crown canker is caused by the fungus *Phytophthora cactorum.* The same parasite apparently causes the so-called bleeding canker disease of maples (p.428) and canker of American beech (p. 381). It also parasitizes a large number of other plants. *P. cactorum* can live over in the soil in partly decayed organic matter, and its spores may be washed to nearby uninfested areas. It appears to gain entrance primarily through wounds, and then invades the tissues in all directions. Thus far the disease of maples (p. 428) and canker of American beech (p. 381). It also on transplanted trees in ornamental plantings.

Control. Crown canker cannot be controlled after the fungus has invaded most of the trunk base or root collar. Control is possible if the infection is confined to a relatively small area at the trunk base. After the cankered area is outlined, a strip of healthy bark approximately one inch wide should be removed all around the edge of the canker. The bark removal should be deep enough to uncover the cambium. Within the area thus left bare, all discolored bark and sapwood should be carefully cut out with a gouge. The edge of the wound should be painted with orange shellac and the area between with any good tree paint. Success with this procedure will depend on early detection of the infection and thorough and complete surgical treatment.

Because the disease has been found only on transplanted trees, and because the fungus appears to enter the host plants more readily through wounds, some observers have suggested that infection occurs primarily through unavoidable injuries inflicted during transplanting. Another avenue of entrance suggested, especially on long-established trees, is wounds made by lawn machinery and cultivating tools. Consequently, all wounds should be painted immediately with shellac and then with a good tree paint, after they have been properly shaped. The possibility of injury to valuable lawn specimens can be decreased by providing some protection around the trunk base, such as a No-Trim Tree Guard.

Areas where dogwoods have died from *Phytophthora* infections should not be replanted with dogwoods for several years unless the soil is fumigated. Where losses have occurred in nurseries, drench the soil with Dexon or Terrazole to kill any of the fungus still present in the soil. The chemical treatments will not cure already infected trees.

DIEBACK. *Botryosphaeria dothidea.* Dieback of dogwood branches, particularly the pink-flowering kinds, is frequently caused by this species of *Botryosphaeria.* The dieback is often erroneously attributed to dogwood borers by some arborists.

Control. No effective control measures have been developed.

FLOWER AND TWIG BLIGHT. *Botrytis cinerea.* In rainy seasons in the eastern United States, the white flower bracts fade and rot and infect leaves on which they fall (Fig. 15-15). In some cases twigs are also blighted.

Control. Spray the entire tree lightly with Benlate, captan, Mertect 160, or zineb early in the flowering period.

Fig. 15-15. Blight on flowering dogwood leaves caused by the fungus *Botrytis cinerea.*

LEAF SPOTS. *Ascochyta cornicola, Cercospora cornicola, Colletotrichum gloeosporioides, Elsinoë corni* (Fig. 15-16), *E. floridae, Phyllosticta globifera, Ramularia gracilipes, Septoria cornicola,* and *S. floridae.* Many species of fungi cause leaf spots on this host.

Control. A number of fungicides are effective in combating leaf spots. Among these are Fore, maneb, and Captan. Applications should be made once a month, starting in April when the flower buds are in the cup stage and continuing until the flower buds for the following year are formed in late summer.

POWDERY MILDEWS. *Microsphaera alni* and *Phyllactinia corylea.* Powdery mildews may attack dogwood, entirely covering the leaves with a thin white coating of the fungus.

Control. Spray with Benlate or Karathane.

TWIG BLIGHTS. *Myxosporium everhartii, Cryptostictis* sp., and *Sphaeropsis* sp. Cankering and blighting of dogwood twigs may be caused by three species of fungi.

Control. Prune and destroy infected twigs. Fertilize and water to increase vigor of the tree.

OTHER DISEASES. Other diseases of dogwood include root rots caused by *Armillaria mellea* in the North, its counterpart *Clitocybe tabescens* in the South, and *Phymatotrichum omnivorum.* The Pacific dogwood (*Cornus Nuttallii*) is subject to canker caused by *Nectria galligena,* and collar rot by *Phytophthora cactorum.*

Control. Control measures are not available.

The native dogwood, *Cornus florida,* is especially sensitive to dry soils. In prolonged dry spells its leaves wilt at the margins and turn brown and appear as though scorched by fire. Applying water to specimens growing in lawns during dry spells will help to prevent this condition.

Insects

BORERS. At least seven kinds of borers attack dogwoods. The most serious are the flatheaded borer, *Chrysobothris femorata* (Fig. 15-17), and the dogwood borer, *Thamnosphecia scitula* (Fig. 15-18).

Control. In the latitude of New York, paint or spray the trunks and branches with methoxychlor 3 times at 20-day intervals starting in mid-May. Endosulfan (Thiodan) spray in early June and again 2 weeks later also gives control. In some states this material can be used only by arborists and nurserymen under permit.

DOGWOOD CLUB GALL. *Mycodiplosis alternata.* Club-shaped galls or swellings, ½ to 1 inch long, on twigs of flowering dogwood are caused by a reddish-brown midge which attacks the twigs in late May. Small orange larvae develop in the galls, which drop to the ground in early fall (Fig. 15-19).

Fig. 15-16. Upper: Small slightly raised reddish-gray spots on dogwood leaves are caused by the fungus *Elsinoë corni*. **Lower:** Spots on the white bracts are also caused by *Elsinoë corni*.

Fig. 15-17. Flatheaded apple tree borer and galleries in dogwood branch.

Control. Pruning and destroying twigs with the club galls during summer will provide control. Spraying weekly 6 to 7 times with carbaryl (Sevin) starting in late May will also control this pest.

LEAF MINER. *Xenochalepus dorsalis.* The flat yellowish-white larvae, up to ¼ inch long, occasionally attack dogwood leaves, making blisterlike mines on the under side. The adult beetles skeletonize the leaves by feeding on the under side.

Control. Spray with malathion when the adult beetles are feeding on the leaves, or before the larvae enter the leaves.

SCALES. Five species of scales may infest dogwood: dogwood, cottony maple (Fig. 15-20), obscure, oystershell, and San Jose.

Control. Spray with a line sulfur or miscible oil, dormant strength, in

Fig. 15-18. Adult stage of the dogwood borer *Thamnosphecia scitula.*

late fall or early spring. Follow with malathion or carbaryl (Sevin) in mid-May and again in June.

WHITEFLY. *Tetraleurodes mori.* Leaves of dogwood, mulberry, holly, maple, and planetree infested by whitefly are usually sticky from honeydew secreted by black, oval, scalelike young, $1/35$ inch long, with a prominent white border. The adults are tiny whiteflies, which dart away when the leaves are disturbed.

Control. Spray with malathion in midsummer and again in late summer.

OTHER INSECTS. Among other insects which occasionally infest dogwood are melon aphid, pitted ambrosia bettle, red-humped caterpillar, giant hornet, leafhoppers, locust leaf miner, leafroller, and the dogwood sawfly. The control for most of these is achieved with carbaryl (Sevin) sprays.

EMPRESS-TREE (*Paulownia*)

The empress-tree is prized most for its showy clusters of violet flowers in early spring. It is relatively free of pests, but it is quite sensitive to extremes in the weather. No important insects are known to attack the empress-tree.

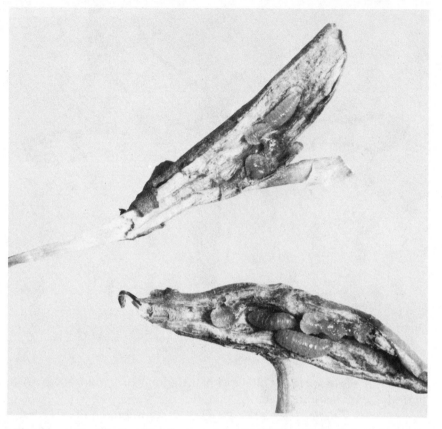

Fig. 15-19. Dogwood club gall opened to show larvae. (*Mycodiplosis alternata*).

Diseases

LEAF SPOTS. *Ascochyta paulowniae* and *Phyllosticta paulowniae*. Two species of fungi cause leaf spots on this host in very rainy seasons.

Control. Gather and destroy fallen leaves. Preventive sprays containing copper or dithiocarbamate fungicides can be used on extremely valuable specimens in rainy seasons.

MILDEW. *Phyllactinia guttata* and *Uncinula clintonii*. Two species of powdery mildew fungi occasionally infect *Paulownia* leaves.

Control. Benlate, wettable sulfur, or Karathane sprays will control these fungi.

WOOD DECAY. *Polyporus spraguei* and *P. versicolor*. These fungi are constantly associated with a wood decay of this host.

Control. As with other wood-decaying fungi, control is difficult. Avoiding wounds near the trunk base and keeping the tree in good vigor by feeding and watering when necessary are suggested.

Fig. 15-20. Cottony maple scale on dogwood leaves.

TWIG CANKER. *Phomopsis imperialis.* Occasionally twigs and small branches are affected by this disease.

Control. Prune and destroy infected branches.

FRANKLIN-TREE (*Franklinia alatamaha*)*

Diseases

LEAF SPOT. *Phyllosticta gordoniae.* Spots on the leaves of this host occasionally occur in rainy seasons.

Control. Valuable specimens can be sprayed with copper or dithiocarbamate fungicides.

BLACK MILDEW. *Meliola cryptocarpa.* In the deep South, leaves of the Franklin-tree may be covered by this black fungus.

ROOT ROT. *Phymatotrichum omnivorum.*

Control. Measures are rarely adopted to control black mildew or root rot.

* The Franklin-tree was formerly called *Gordonia alatamaha.*

WILT. *Phytophthora* sp. Rutgers University plant pathologists recently reported a highly destructive wilt disease in container-grown Franklin-trees. Affected trees wilt suddenly during hot weather and then drop their leaves. Infected roots are brownish-black in color and black cankers occur along the stems.

Control. Early tests indicate that soil drenched with the experimental chemical M-4109 provides control.

Insects

SCALES. Three species of scale insects are known to attack the Franklin-tree: red bay, *Chrysomphalus perseae;* walnut, *Aspidiotus juglans-regiae;* and *Lecanium* sp. The last-named was found by the author on specimens submitted from New York State.

Control. Spray with malathion or carbaryl (Sevin) when the young are crawling in late spring.

GIANT HORNET WASP. *Vespa crabro germana.* This wasp tears the bark not only from the Franklin-tree but also from birch, boxwood, poplar, willow, and other trees and shrubs. The wasp is dark reddish-brown with orange markings on the abdomen. It is the largest wasp in the United States—1 inch long.

Control. Apply a carbaryl (Sevin) spray to the trunk when the pest begins to tear the bark in July.

FRINGE-TREE (*Chionanthus*)

Diseases

LEAF SPOTS. Four species of fungi, *Cercospora chionanthi, Phyllosticta chionanthi, Septoria chionanthi,* and *S. eleospora,* are known to cause leaf spotting on this host.

Control. Spray with a copper fungicide or with one of the dithiocarbamates.

POWDERY MILDEW. *Phyllactinia corylea.* The leaves of fringe-tree are occasionally affected by this disease.

Control. Where mildew is severe, spray with Benlate, Karathane, or wettable sulfur.

OTHER DISEASES. Fringe-tree is occasionally subject to several canker diseases caused by *Botryosphaeria pyriospora, Phomopsis diatrypea,* and *Valsa chionanthi.*

Control. Prune diseased branches.

Insects

SCALES. The rose scale *Aulacaspis rosea* and the white peach scale *Pseudaulacaspis pentagona* infest *Chionanthus.*

Control. A dormant oil spray applied in early spring will control these pests. Malathion or carbaryl (Sevin) applied in mid-May and again in mid-June will control the crawler stage.

GOLDEN-CHAIN (Laburnum)

Diseases

LEAF SPOT. *Phyllosticta cytisii.* Leaves are subject to spotting when infected by this fungus. The spot, at first light-gray, later turning brown, has no definite margin. The black fruiting bodies (pycnidia) of this fungus dot the central part of the spot. Another fungus, *Cercospora laburni,* also causes leaf spots.

Control. In areas where these leaf spots are troublesome, apply a copper fungicide several times at 2-week intervals during rainy springs.

TWIG BLIGHT.*Fusarium lateritium.* Brown lesions on the twigs followed by blighting of the leaves above the affected area in very wet springs is characteristic of this disease. The sexual stage of this fungus is *Gibberella baccata.*

Control. Prune and destroy infected twigs and spray as for leaf spot.

LABURNUM VEIN MOSAIC (virus). Conspicuous vein-banding of *Laburnum alpinum* in Maryland is said to be due to a virus. Although tobacco ringspot virus was isolated from infected plants, there was no evidence that it caused the disease.

Control. Remove and destroy infected plants.

Insects and Related Pests

APHIDS. *Aphis craccivora.* The cowpea aphid, black with white legs, clusters at the tips of the branches. The bean aphid, *A. fabae,* also infests golden-chain.

Control. Spray with malathion or carbaryl (Sevin) when the aphids appear in late spring.

GRAPE MEALYBUG. *Pseudococcus maritimus.* The grape mealybug occasionally infests golden-chain both aboveground and belowground.

Control. Mealybugs infesting the branches and twigs can be controlled with malathion sprays. Those infesting the roots can be curbed by wetting the soil with Diazinon.

NEMA. *Meloidogyne hapla.*

Control. Control measures are rarely practiced for this pest.

GOLDENRAIN-TREE (Koelreuteria)

Diseases

CORAL SPOT CANKER. *Nectria cinnabarina.* Small, depressed, dead areas in the bark near wounds or branch stubs are caused by this fungus. Tiny, coral-pink bodies are formed on the dead bark.

Control. Prune infected branches back to sound wood. Fertilize and water to maintain vigor.

OTHER FUNGUS DISEASES. The only other fungus diseases reported as affecting *Koelreuteria* are a leaf spot caused by a species of *Cerocospora,* wilt by *Verticillium albo-atrum,* and root rot by *Phymatotrichum omnivorum.*

Control. For wilt, see Chapter 14. The other diseases are never destructive enough to warrant control measures.

Insects

SCALES. Three species of scales infest *Koelreuteria:* the lesser snow, *Pinnaspis strachani;* mining, *Howardia biclavis;* and white peach, *Pseudaulacaspis pentagona.*

Control. Dormant oil sprays applied in early spring will control these scales. Malathion or carbaryl (Sevin) sprays applied in late May and in mid-June will control the crawler stage of the pests.

GUAVA (*Psidium guajava*)

Diseases

In Florida this host is subject to a leaf and fruit spot caused by the fungus *Glomerella cingulata,* a thread blight by *Pellicularia koleroga,* a leaf spot by *Cercospora psidii,* and a root rot by *Clitocybe tabescens.*

Control. Effective control measures are unavailable.

Insects and Other Animal Pests

SCALES. Nine species of scale insects infest guavas: barnacle, black, chaff, Florida red, Florida wax, greedy, green shield, hemispherical, and soft.

Control. Spray with malathion or carbaryl (Sevin) to control the crawling stage of these pests.

OTHER INSECTS. Occasionally guava is attacked by the Mexican fruit fly, *Anastrepha ludens;* the long-tailed mealybug, *Pseudococcus adonidum;* and the eastern subterranean termite, *Reticulitermes flaviceps.*

Control. Control measures have not been developed.

SOUTHERN ROOT-KNOT NEMA. *Meloidogyne incognita.* This nema infests guava roots in Florida.

Control. This pest is difficult to control on plants growing outdoors.

GUMBO-LIMBO (*Bursera*)

Diseases

SOOTY MOLD. *Fumago vagans.* A heavy growth of this sooty mold develops on the plant as a result of infestation with the brown soft scale (see below). The results are sometimes very serious.

Control. Spray with malathion or carbaryl (Sevin) to control the scale insect which secretes the substance on which the sooty mold fungus lives.

OTHER DISEASE. In the deep South, branches of this host may be killed by the fungus *Physalospora fusca.*

Control. Prune infected branches.

Insects

BROWN SOFT SCALE. *Coccus hesperidum.* This scale insect, which often remains inconspicuous because of its tendency to assume the color of the twigs or leaves upon which it is feeding, does great damage to greenhouse plants. The lower sides of the leaves are sometimes heavily infested with light green scales, which often choose the petioles or twigs and the upper parts of the trunk on which to develop their mature stages. The scales are arranged longitudinally along the smaller branches and main stem. They are very flat and thin, more or less transparent. Though the young are usually sluggish, not migrating far from the mother scale, they do travel to the upper leaves. This scale is said to be a general feeder, attacking many plants in the greenhouse and also tropical fruit outdoors. Eight other species of scales may infest gumbo-limbo.

Control. Spray the plants with malathion or carbaryl (Sevin) every 2 weeks until all the young scales are destroyed.

HAWTHORNS (*Crataegus*)

Hawthorns, sometimes called thorns, are members of the rose family, to which the apple and pear belong. As such, they are frequently attacked by the same fungi, bacteria, and insects that attack those trees.

Diseases

LEAF BLIGHT. In late summer English hawthorn (*Crataegus oxyacantha*) and Paul's scarlet thorn (*C. oxyacantha pauli*) may be completely defoliated by the leaf blight disease. Cockspur thorn and Washington thorn appear to be much more resistant to the trouble.

Symptoms. Early in spring small, angular, reddish-brown spots appear on the upper leaf surface (Fig. 15-21). As the season advances, the spots enlarge, then coalesce, and the leaves finally drop.

Cause. The fungus *Diplocarpon maculatum* causes leaf blight. It is primarily a parasite of hawthorns, although some investigators believe it is also responsible for a similar disease of pear and quince.

Numerous black, flattened, orbicular bodies are visible, with the aid of a hand lens, in the discolored spots on both leaf surfaces. These bodies contain spores that initiate numerous infections during rainy springs.

Fig. 15-21. Leaf blight of hawthorn caused by the fungus *Diplocarpon maculatum*.

Control. Gather and destroy all the leaves in the fall to reduce infections the following spring, inasmuch as the fungus survives from one season to the next primarily in diseased leaves.

There is some evidence that the fungus also overwinters as mycelium in small cankers on the bark. Because such sources of inoculum cannot be completely eliminated, sprays containing Actidione, Benlate, Dithane M-45, or zineb are needed. These fungicides should be applied 3 times at 10-day intervals. The first application should be made immediately after the leaves have unfolded.

Trees that have been subjected to several consecutive years of severe leaf blight infections may be considerably weakened. A good tree fertilizer, applied in fall or spring, will help such trees to regain their vigor.

FIRE BLIGHT. Hawthorns, especially the English hawthorn, are subject to the bacterial disease fire blight, discussed on page 287.

RUSTS. At least nine rust fungi attack hawthorns. Of these the orange rust *Gymnosporangium clavipes* and *G. globosum* are the most common on ornamental species. The former, shown in Figure 15–22, attacks both

Fig. 15-22. Rust on hawthorn caused by the fungus *Gymnosporangium clavipes*.

the leaves and the fruits of hawthorn, causing severe defoliation and deformation of fruit. The twigs are also attacked and deformed, developing abnormal, antlerlike branches. The fungus breaks out in little cuplike structures called cluster-cups, from which quantities of bright orange spores are shed. These spores are borne by the wind to nearby red cedars and infect their leaves and young twigs. The fungus is perennial in the cedars but annual in the hawthorns (see under Juniper, Chapter 17). *G. globosum* produces on the leaves spots which vary from light gray to brown. The cluster-cups are long, slender, tubelike. This fungus also attacks apple trees; it seldom does much damage to hawthorn. Another stage of the fungus lives for two or three years on the red cedar before killing the small branches which it attacks (see under Juniper, Chapter 17).

Another rust, *G. confusum*, was reported as attacking *Crataegus oxyacantha* in California in 1967. This was the first case in the United States. The alternate host is *Juniperus sabina*.

The Washington thorn (*Crataegus phaenopyrum*) and the cockspur thorn (*C. crus-galli*) are resistant to rusts.

Control. If practicable, eliminate susceptible junipers within one mile of hawthorns. If not practicable, spray the hawthorns with Daconil 2787, Dithane M-45, ferbam, or a mixture of ferbam and wettable sulfur 4 to 5 times at 7- to 10-day intervals when orange masses appear on junipers.

Rusts can also be controlled by spraying the alternate hosts, junipers, with cycloheximide (Actidione).

LEAF SPOTS. A large number of fungi are known to cause leaf spots on hawthorns. Among the more common ones are: *Cercospora confluens, C. apiifoliae, Cercosporella mirabilis, Cylindrosporium brevispina, C. crataegi, Gloeosporium crataegi, Hendersonia crataegicola, Septoria crataegi,* and *Monilinia johnsonii.* The last also causes spots on the fruits, as does the scab fungus *Venturia inaequalis.*

Control. Zineb sprays will control most of the fungi listed.

POWDERY MILDEW. Two species of powdery mildew fungi, *Phyllactinia corylea* and *Podosphaeria oxyacanthae,* attack hawthorns.

Control. The dithiocarbamates, which control leaf blight and rust, are ineffective against powdery mildew. For these fungi use either Benlate, sulfur, or Karathane.

SCAB. *Venturia inaequalis.* Olive-drab spots ¼ inch in diameter appear on the leaves, and smaller ones on the fruits. Leaves drop prematurely, and the fruits are disfigured. The fungus may also overwinter on the twigs.

Control. Spray with captan, dodine, or Fore, 4 or 5 times at 10-day intervals when the leaves are half-grown.

Insects and Other Pests

APHIDS. Many species of aphids infest hawthorns: apple, apple grain, hawthorn, rosy apple, woolly apple, and woolly hawthorn.

Control. Spray with malthion or Diazinon before the pests become numerous.

APPLE LEAF BLOTCH MINER. *Phyllonorycter crataegella.* This leaf miner can be very destructive in hawthorn nurseries and ornamental plantings near New York City. The principal damage is done during May or June. The first symptom is a small channel in the leaf, which widens to a blisterlike area light brown in color. The miner begins work at one edge of the leaf near the stalk and continues on that side toward the point of the leaf. The inner parts of the leaf are usually completely consumed, only the epidermis and veins remaining. Only the leaves that are unfolding are attacked. Much defoliation follows the work of these insects. The same species attacks many fruit trees, including apple, cherry, plum, quince, and sweet-scented crabapple.

Control. Spray in early May and repeat twice at 2-week intervals with malathion or carbaryl (Sevin).

APPLE AND THORN SKELETONIZER. *Anthophila pariana.* This pest feeds on leaves of apple, pear, and hawthorn in the northeastern United States. The adult moth is dark gray to reddish-brown with a ½-inch wing expanse. The full grown larva is ½ inch long, with a yellowish-green body and a pale brown head.

Control. Spray with carbaryl (Sevin) when the larvae begin to feed.

BORERS. Four borers infest hawthorns: flatheaded apple tree, round-headed apple tree, pear, and the shot-hole.

Control. Maintain trees in good vigor by feeding when necessary and watering during dry spells. Paint or spray the trunk and branches with methoxychlor at periodic intervals during the growing season. State entomologists will supply the proper dates for each locality.

LACE BUGS. *Corythucha cydoniae, C. arcuata.* Lace bugs are not common on hawthorn but occasionally appear to be rather serious. They feed on the undersides of the leaves, depositing small, brown, sticky spots of excreta. Once the infestation is started, the insects breed during summer and become rather numerous.

Control. Spray with Diazinon, malathion, or carbaryl (Sevin).

PLANTHOPPER. *Ormenis septentrionalis.* These sucking insects often attack wild grape vines and feed on the tender shoots. They are also found on *Crataegus* at times. The insects are a beautiful pale bluish-green, covered with white powder. The powder and other whitish excretions also cover the young on the limbs and branches. The insects are nearly ½ inch long, very thin vertically.

Control. Spray the trees forcefully with pyrethrum or rotenone sprays, or a combination of both. The insects must be thoroughly wetted by the sprays.

SCALES. The following kinds of scales infest hawthorn: barnacle, cottony maple, European fruit lecanium, Florida wax, lecanium, Putnam, scurfy, soft, and San Jose.

Control. Spray with lime sulfur or miscible oil, dormant strength, just before plant growth begins in spring. Follow in mid-May and in June with malathion or carbaryl (Sevin) sprays to control the crawling stages.

WESTERN TENT CATERPILLAR. *Malacosoma pluviale.* Tawny or brown caterpillars with a dorsal row of blue spots feed primarily on hawthorns as well as wild cherry and alder, making tents at the same time as the fall webworm. The moths are smaller and somewhat lighter than the eastern tent caterpillar adults.

Other caterpillars that may feed on hawthorns include the eastern tent, the forest tent, the red-humped, the variable oak leaf, and the walnut caterpillar. The caterpillar stages of the gypsy moth and the western tussock moth also occur on this host.

Control. Spray with *Bacillus thuringiensis*, Dylox, methoxychlor, or carbaryl (Sevin) when the caterpillars begin to chew leaves.

TWO-SPOTTED MITE. *Tetranychus urticae.* During the summer months, especially in dry weather, these mites often become sufficiently numerous to injure foliage. The symptoms are the same as those on other plants attacked by the mites.

Control. If the hawthorn is given a dormant clean-up spray in spring with commercial lime sulfur, the eggs of the mites are killed. If not, spray with chlorobenzilate, Kelthane, Meta-Systox R, or Tedion in early June and repeat in a few weeks, if necessary.

HOP-HORNBEAM (Ostrya)

Hop-hornbeam, also known as ironwood, is a slow-growing tree with a rounded crown and slender, pendulous, often contorted branches.

Diseases

Hop-hornbeam is susceptible to cankers caused by *Aleurodiscus* spp., *Nectria* sp., and *Strumella coryneoidea*; to leaf spots by *Cylindrosporium dearnessi*, *Gloeosporium robergei*, and *Septoria ostryae*; to powdery mildews by *Microsphaera alni*, *Phyllactinia corylea*, and *Uncinula macrospora*; to root rots by *Armillaria mellea* and *Clitocybe tabescens*; to a leaf blister by *Taphrina virginica*; and to a rust caused by *Melampsoridium carpini*.

Control. The controls for these diseases are discussed under more seriously affected hosts.

Insects

Among the insects that attack hop-hornbeam are the birch lace bug, the melon aphid, pitted ambrosia beetle, two-lined chestnut borer, and two species of scales, cottony-cushion and latania.

Control. These insects are rarely serious enough to require control measures.

HOP-TREE (Ptelea)

Diseases

LEAF SPOTS. *Cercospora afflata*, *C. pteleae*, *Phleospora pteleae*, *Phyllosticta pteleicola*, and *Septoria pteleae*. These five species of fungi cause leaf spots on hop-tree.

Control. Pick off and destroy spotted leaves. Other control measures are rarely necessary.

RUST. *Puccinia windsoriae*. This fungus occasionaly occurs on hop-tree. The alternate stage of the fungus is found on grasses.

Control. No controls are required.

ROOT ROT. *Phymatotrichum omnivorum*.

Control. Control measures have not been developed.

Insects

TWO-MARKED TREEHOPPER. *Enchenopa binotata*. These little sucking insects, ⅛ inch or slightly more in length, with a long, proboscislike head portion, resemble miniature quail or partridges; they are dark brown in color with two white spots. When disturbed, the insects jump very rapidly from place to place. They secrete honeydew. The egg masses are covered by a snow-white frothy substance (shown in Fig. 15–23) like that secreted by spittle insects but much firmer in consistency. From a distance, infested branches resemble those infested with woolly aphids or cottony-cushion scale.

Control. Spray with malathion or with a pyrethrum-rotenone compound.

SCALE. *Pseudaulacaspis pentagona.* This pest, also known as West Indian peach scale, infests a wide variety of trees in the warmer parts of the country.

Control. Malathion or carbaryl (Sevin) sprays when the crawling stage is moving about in the early spring will provide control.

HORNBEAM (*Carpinus*)

Diseases

LEAF SPOTS. *Clasterosporium cornigerum, Gloeosporium robergei, Gnomoniella fimbriella, Phyllosticta* sp., and *Septoria carpinea.* These five fungi cause leaf spotting of hornbeam.

Fig. 15-23. Treehopper (*Enchenopa binotata*) egg masses on hop-tree.

Control. Leaf spots are rarely serious enough to warrant control measures. Copper or ferbam sprays are effective in preventing heavy outbreaks.

CANKERS. *Pezicula carpinea, Solenia ochraceae,* and *Nectria galligena.* These three species of fungi frequently cause bark cankers, sometimes leading to severe dieback of branches.

Control. Badly cankered trees cannot be saved. Prune out twigs and branches of mildly infected ones. The use of copper sprays may also be justified in some situations.

TWIG BLIGHT. *Fusarium lateritium.* In the South this fungus causes a twig blight on hornbeam. The sexual stage of this fungus is *Gibberella baccata.*

Control. Prune and destroy infected twigs on valuable ornamental specimens.

OTHER DISEASE. The felt fungus, *Septobasidium curtisii,* occurs on a number of trees in the South. The felt is purplish-black and covers the insect it parasitizes.

Control. Control measures are not needed.

Insects

MAPLE PHENACOCCUS. *Phenacoccus acericola.* Although this scale is more common on sugar maple, it occasionally infests hornbeam, where it forms large white cottony masses on the lower leaf surface.

Control. Malathion or carbaryl (Sevin) sprays directed to the lower leaf surfaces in late spring are effective.

SOURGUM SCALE. *Phenacaspis nyssae.* This scale is nearly triangular, flat, and snow-white.

Control. The same as above.

JUNEBERRY—See Serviceberry.

KENTUCKY COFFEE TREE (*Gymnocladus*)

This species is remarkably free of fungus parasites and insect pests.

Diseases

LEAF SPOT. Three fungi, *Cerospora gymnocladi, Phyllosticta gymnocladi,* and a species of *Marssonia,* have been reported on this host.

Control. Special control measures are rarely required, but periodic applications of copper or dithiocarbamate fungicides will protect valuable specimens.

OTHER DISEASES. A root rot caused by the fungus *Phymatotrichum omnivorum* and a wood rot by *Polyporus pulchellus* are the only other fungus diseases known on *Gymnocladus*.

Control. Control measures have not been developed.

Insects

OLIVE SCALE. *Parlatoria oleae*. This insect is purplish-brown, and its female shell is ovate, circular, dirty gray, and very small. The female begins laying eggs in spring.

Control. Spray in late spring with either malathion or carbaryl (Sevin) to control the crawler stage.

MAGNOLIA (Magnolia)*

Magnolias are subject to a number of fungus diseases and insect pests. Only the more important are treated here.

Fungus Diseases

BLACK MILDEWS. *Irene araliae, Meliola amphitrichia, M. magnoliae*, and *Trichodothis comata*. A black, mildewy growth covers the leaves of magnolias in the deep South.

Control. Deciduous magnolias may be sprayed with Actidione PM; others with wettable sulfur.

LEAF BLIGHT. *Pellicularia koleroga*. The leaves of *Magnolia grandiflora* may be blighted by this fungus, which also affects apple, citrus, dogwood, Japanese persimmon, pecan, quince, and many shrubs in the South.

Control. Valuable specimens can be protected with two or three applications of copper fungicides or Difolatan.

LEAF SPOTS. *Alternaria tenuis, Cladosporium fasciculatum, Mycosphaerella milleri, Colletotrichum* sp., *Coniothyrium olivaceum, Epicoccum nigrum, Exophoma magnoliae, Glomerella cingulata, Hendersonia magnoliae, Micropeltis alabamensis, Phyllosticta cookei, P. glauca, P. magnoliae, Septoria magnoliae*, and *S. niphostoma*. These 15 species of fungi cause leaf spots on magnolias.

Control. Fungus leaf spots on valuable specimens can be controlled by periodic applications, early in the growing season, of copper or dithiocarbamate fungicides.

DIEBACK. *Phomopsis* sp. Cankers with longitudinal cracks in the bark are formed on the larger limbs and trunks. The wood is discolored a blue-gray. The bark is dark brown over the affected areas. Apparently healthy branches also may be discolored.

Control. No suggestion for control has been made.

* Some species of magnolia are tall-growing trees. Many, however, are low growing kinds.

NECTRIA CANKER. *Nectria magnoliae*. This fungus produces symptoms similar to those of *N. galligena* (see under Walnut, Chapter 16), but infects only magnolias and tuliptrees.

Control. Prune and destroy cankered branches. Keep trees in good vigor by watering, spraying, and feeding when necessary.

LEAF SCAB. *Elsinoë magnoliae*. In the deep South *Magnolia grandiflora* leaves may be spotted by this fungus.

Control. The disease is not serious enough to warrant control measures.

WOOD DECAY. A heart-rot, associated with the fungi *Fomes geotropus* and *F. fasciatus*, has been reported on magnolia. Affected trees show sparse foliage and dieback of the branches. In early stages the rot is grayish-black, with conspicuous black zone lines near the advancing edge of the decayed area. The mature rot is brown. The causal fungi gain entrance through wounds.

Control. No control measures are effective once the rot has become extensive. Avoid trunk wounds and maintain good vigor by fertilization and watering.

Other Diseases

ALGAL SPOT. *Cephaleuros virescens*. Leaves and twigs infested by this alga have velvety, reddish-brown patches.

Control. Control measures are usually unnecessary.

Wilt caused by *Verticillium albo-atrum*, angular leaf spot by *Mycosphaerella milleri*, and leaf scab by *Sphaceloma magnoliae* are among other diseases of magnolia.

Control. Same as above.

Insects

MAGNOLIA SCALE. *Neolecanium cornuparvum*. Undeveloped leaves and generally weak trees may result from heavy infestations of the magnolia scale, a brown, varnishlike hemispherical scale, ½ inch in diameter, with a white, waxy covering (Fig. 15–24). The young scales appear in August and overwinter in that stage.

Control. A dormant oil-ethion spray in early spring just before new growth emerges will control the adult, overwintering scales. The crawler stage of both this and tuliptree scale, unlike most scales, appears in late summer. Hence, the use of carbaryl (Sevin) or a mixture of malathion and Sevin for the crawler stage should be delayed until late August or early September.

TULIPTREE SCALE. *Toumeyella liriodendri* also infests magnolias and lindens at times.

Fig. 15-24. Magnolia scale (*Neolecanium cornuparvum*).

Control. The same as for magnolia scale.

OTHER PESTS. The following scales also occur on magnolias: black, chaff, cottony-cushion, European fruit lecanium, Florida wax, glover, greedy, oleander, purple, and soft. Spray the young, crawling stages of these scales in May and June with malathion or carbaryl (Sevin).

The Comstock mealy bug, the omnivorous looper caterpillar, and the citrus whitefly also infest magnolias. Malathion sprays, applied when the pests appear, give good control.

A species of Eriophyid mite infests *Magnolia grandiflora* in the South. Kelthane or Tedion sprays will control this pest.

The sassafras weevil *Odontopus calceatus* occasionally infests magnolias. Carbaryl (Sevin) sprays applied when the weevils begin to feed, or after the eggs hatch, should provide control.

MANGO (*Mangifera indica*)

Diseases

ANTHRACNOSE. *Glomerella cingulata*. This is perhaps the most prevalent disease of mango in the South. Leaves are spotted, flowers and twigs blighted, and fruits rotted by this fungus.

Control. Spray valuable specimens periodically with a copper or dithiocarbamate fungicide.

POWDERY MILDEW. *Oidium mangiferae*. Flower panicles and foliage may be injured when infected by this powdery mildew fungus.

Control. Spray with Benlate, Karathane, or wettable sulfur when mildew appears.

OTHER FUNGUS DISEASES. In Florida mango is subject to twig blight caused by a species of *Phomopsis*; leaf spots by *Pestalotia mangiferae*, *Phyllosticta mortoni*, and *Septoria* sp.; scab by *Elsinoë mangiferae*; and sooty mold by species of *Capnodium*.

Control. Control measures are rarely necessary.

Insects

SCALES. Twenty-six species of scale insects infest mango.

Control. Spray with malathion or carbaryl (Sevin).

OTHER INSECTS. The long-tailed mealybug and greenhouse thrips also infest mango.

Control. Same as for scales.

MIMOSA—See Silk-Tree.

MOUNTAIN-ASH (*Sorbus*)

Because mountain-ashes belong to the rose family, they are subject to most of the same diseases and insects common in this family.

Bacterial and Fungus Diseases

CANKER. Four fungi, *Cytospora chrysosperma*, *C. massariana*, *C. microspora*, and *Fusicoccum* sp., occur occasionally on mountain-ash, especially on weakened trees.

Control. Prune severely affected branches and fertilize. The latter practice may increase the tree's susceptibility to fire blight, however, if high nitrogenous fertilizers are used.

LEAF RUSTS. The alternate stages of the rust fungi *Gymnosporangium aurantiacum*, *G. cornutum*, *G. globosum*, *G. tremelloides*, *G. nelsoni*, *G. nootkatense*, and *G. libocedri* occur on *Juniperus* or *Libocedrus* species. On mountain-ash leaves, circular, light yellow, thickened spots first appear during summer. Later, orange cups develop on the lower surfaces of these spots.

Control. Where mountain-ashes are highly prized, and where practicable, remove the alternate hosts. If such removal is impracticable, valuable trees can be protected by sprays recommended for rust control of flowering crabapples (Malus).

CROWN GALL. See Chapter 14.

FIRE BLIGHT. See Chapter 14.

SCAB. See under Crabapple.

OTHER DISEASES. Mountain-ash is subject to many other diseases. These are discussed under rosaceous hosts in other parts of this book.

Insects

APHIDS. The rosy apple and woolly apple aphids frequently infest this host.

Control. Spray with malathion or carbaryl (Sevin).

JAPANESE LEAFHOPPER. *Orientus ishidae.* This insect causes a characteristic brown blotching bordered by a bright yellow margin, the yellow zone merging into the color of the leaf.

Control Spray with dimethoate, carbaryl (Sevin), or malathion in late May or early June.

MOUNTAIN-ASH SAWFLY. *Pristiphora geniculata.* Green larvae with black dots feed on mountain-ash leaves from early June to mid-July, leaving only the larger veins and midribs. The adults, yellow with black spots, deposit eggs on the leaves in late May.

Control. Spray with carbaryl (Sevin) when the leaves are fully expanded.

PEAR LEAF BLISTER MITE. *Eriophyes pyri.* Tiny brownish blisters on the lower leaf surface and premature defoliation result from infestations of the pear leaf blister mite, a tiny, elongated, eight-legged pest, $^1/_{125}$ inch long. The pests overwinter beneath the outer bud scales. Eggs are deposited in spring in leaf galls, which develop as a result of feeding and irritation by the adult.

Control. Spray the trees with lime sulfur in late fall or early spring or with Kelthane early in the growing season.

ROUNDHEADED BORER. *Saperda candida.* Trees are weakened and may be killed by the roundheaded borer, a light yellow, black-headed, legless larva 1 inch long. Galleries in the trunk near the soil level, frass at the base of the tree, and round holes of the diameter of a lead pencil in the bark are typical signs of this pest. The adult is a beetle ¾ inch long, brown with two white longitudinal stripes on the back. It emerges in April and deposits eggs on the bark.

Control. Spray trunk and branches thoroughly with methoxychlor starting in mid-May and repeating 3 times at 2-week intervals.

SCALES. Five species of scale insects infest mountain-ash: black, cottony maple, oystershell, San Jose, and scurfy.

Control. Dormant oil or lime sulfur sprays, followed by malathion or carbaryl (Sevin) sprays during the growing season, will control these insects.

ORCHID-TREE (*Bauhinia*)

Several species of orchid-trees are grown as lawn specimens and as framing for small houses in Florida and other warm parts of the country.

Diseases

LEAF SPOT. *Colletotrichum* sp. and *Phyllosticta* sp. The former has been reported from Texas and the latter from Florida.

Control. Controls are usually unnecessary.

Insects

The Cuban may beetle *Phyllophaga bruneri*, two species of mealybugs—citrus and long-tailed—and 19 species of scales attack orchid-trees.

Control. Methoxychlor sprays should be effective against the adult stage of the Cuban may beetle. Malathion or carbaryl (Sevin) sprays will control mealybugs and the crawler stage of the scales. A summer oil emulsion is also effective against mealybug and scales.

PAGODA-TREE, JAPANESE (*Sophora japonica*)

This member of the legume family produces clusters of white, showy flowers in summer. It should be more widely planted as a specimen tree. Japanese pagoda-trees do well in cities. The single-stemmed form 'Regent,' should be used along city streets. The falling flowers in summer will stain automobiles, and hence this tree should not be planted in parking lots or similar areas.

Diseases

CANKER. *Fusarium lateritium.* Oval, 1- to 2-inch cankers, with definite, slightly raised, dark red-brown margins and light tan centers, occasionally appear on this host. When the cankers completely girdle the stem, the distal portion dies. The sexual stage of this fungus is *Gibberella baccata.* Another fungus, *Cytospora sophorae,* is also found on dead branches. Both fungi are usually associated with frost damage in late fall or early spring.

Control. Prune diseased or dead branch tips to sound wood and apply a copper fungicide several times during the growing season.

DAMPING-OFF. *Pellicularia filamentosa.* In Connecticut and the southern states this fungus causes a damping-off of seedlings.

Control. Use steam-pasteurized soil, or soil treated with PCNB (Terraclor).

TWIG BLIGHT. *Nectria cinnabarina* and *Diplodia sophorae.* Two fungi cause cankers and dieback of twigs of this host.

Control. The same as for canker.

OTHER FUNGUS DISEASES. Japanese pagoda-tree is also subject to powdery mildew caused by *Microsphaera alni,* root rot by *Phymatotrichum omnivorum,* leaf spot by *Phyllosticta sophorae,* and rust by *Uromyces hyalinus.*

Control. Controls are unnecessary.

Insects

SCALES. Cottony-cushion *Icerya purchasi* and long soft *Coccus elongatus* have been reported on Japanese pagoda-tree.

Control. Malathion or carbaryl (Sevin) sprays will control the crawler stage in late spring and early summer.

OTHER PESTS. A nema, *Meloidogyne* sp., and mistletoe, *Phoradendron flavescens,* also attack Japanese pagoda-tree.

Control. Control measures are not available.

PAPER-MULBERRY (*Broussonetia*)

Diseases

CANKER. *Fusarium solani.* Branch dieback results from cankers produced by this fungus. The disease was first found in Ohio in 1965. The same fungus also infects cottonwood, red oak, and sweetgum.

Control. Prune infected branches. Keep trees in good vigor by feeding and by watering during dry spells.

ROOT ROT. *Phymatotrichum omnivorum.* This root rot, common on many plants in the southern states, has been reported from Texas on the paper-mulberry tree.

Control. Control measures have not been developed.

OTHER DISEASES. Among the other diseases reported from the southern states are a dieback and canker caused by the fungus *Nectria cinnabarina,* a leaf spot by *Cercosporella mori,* a mistletoe disease by *Phoradendron flavescens,* and root knot by the nema *Meloidogyne incognita.*

Control. These diseases are usually not serious enough to warrant control measures.

Insects

WHITE PEACH SCALE. *Pseudaulacaspis pentagona.*
Control. Carbaryl (Sevin) or malathion sprays will control the crawler stage.

PEACH, FLOWERING (*Prunus*)

Varieties of peach grown for ornament are subject to all the diseases and insect pests that affect those grown for their fruits. The following are among the more common problems.

Diseases

LEAF CURL. *Taphrina deformans.* When this fungus is involved, leaves appear much thickened, and individual leaves are puffed and folded with the edges curled inward. The affected leaves acquire red or purplish tints.
Control. Spray either with ziram or ferbam in late fall after the leaves drop or in spring before buds open.

Insects

GREEN PEACH APHID. *Myzus persicae.* This insect has been found to be very injurious during the summer to a number of varieties of flowering peach and related ornamentals.
Control. Spray with malathion, Meta-Systox R, or carbaryl (Sevin) when insects first appear, and repeat a week later if necessary.
BLACK PEACH APHID. *Brachycaudus persicae.* This aphid is common on commercial plantings of peaches.
Control. The same as for green peach aphid.
PEACH TREE BORER. *Sanninoidae exitiosa.* The grubs of the peach borer cause a great amount of damage to flowering peach as well as to related forms, frequently causing death of the trees. The damage is marked by profuse gummosis at the crown and on the main roots just below the surface of the soil. The trees fail to grow properly and the leaves turn yellowish. The frass or borings of the grubs becomes mixed with the gum. If one follows down the burrows with a chisel or a penknife, white flat grubs from ½ to 1 inch long, with brown heads, may be found.
Control. The grubs must be removed from young trees by hand-grubbing; that is, the ground should be pulled back from the base of the tree and the grubs dug out with the aid of a grubbing chisel or other implement with a curved blade. The burrows should be followed down until the grubs are found. Young trees up to 3 years old should be examined twice a year. In trees over 3 years old, the grubs can be

controlled by the use of paradichlorobenzene (PDB). The soil should be dug away from the base of the tree to a depth of 3 or 4 inches and the cavity leveled off. For trees 3 years old, apply ½ to ¾ of an ounce of the fumigant in a circle around the base. For older trees, use 1 to 1½ ounces. The soil is then replaced in the hole and mounded around the base of the tree. While paradichlorobenzene may be applied during the summer, it is safer to use it in late September or October. If it is applied earlier in the summer, the soil should be removed about 1 month or 6 weeks later. If it is allowed to remain too long in the soil during hot weather, injury is likely, especially to young trees.

Spraying or painting the trunk with methoxychlor in early July and repeating 3 times at 2-week intervals is a good preventive treatment. Dursban applications also provide control.

LESSER PEACH TREE BORER. *Synanthedon pictipes.* This borer attacks growing tissue anywhere in the trunk from the ground to the main branches. The eggs are laid mainly in cracks of the trunk. Other species of *Prunus* also are attacked.

Control. The adult female of this borer begins to deposit eggs earlier than does the peach tree borer. Hence the methoxychlor applications should be started by mid-June. The insecticide should be applied to the main branches as well as to the main trunk.

WHITE PEACH SCALE. *Pseudaulacaspis pentagona.* Where flowering peaches and close relatives are planted in parks near the Japanese cherry, the trees may be infested with the same scale insect.

Control. Spray in mid-June with malathion or carbaryl (Sevin) to control the crawling stage.

PEAR, ORNAMENTAL (*Pyrus*)

The 'Bradford' pear (*Pyrus calleryana 'Bradford'*), described on page 162, is said to be quite free of fungus diseases. However, in 1967 W. L. Klarman, plant pathologist at the University of Maryland, found a number of trees with cankers on their trunks produced by a species of *Coniothyrium.* All infected trees were growing in highly unfavorable situations. Those growing in better areas appeared to be free of cankers.

Control. Providing good growing conditions should help to avoid the disease.

PERSIMMON (*Diospyros*)

Persimmons in the wild and those grown for their fruits are subject to a great number of diseases and pests. Ornamentals, however, are relatively free of problems.

Diseases

WILT. Caused by the fungus *Cephalosporium diospyri*, it is perhaps the most destructive disease of this host. Originally discovered in Tennessee in 1933, it now occurs from the Carolinas to Florida and west to Texas. Oriental persimmons appear to be resistant to this disease.

Control. Controls have not been developed.

Other diseases of lesser importance on this host include dieback, caused by *Botryosphaeria dothidea,* twig blight by *Physalospora* spp., and root rot by *Phymatotrichum omnivorum.*

Control. Control measures are usually not required.

Insects

Among the many insects that attack persimmons are the Fuller rose beetle; three species of borers—flatheaded apple-tree, persimmon, and redheaded ash; three kinds of caterpillars—hickory horned devil, red-humped, and variable oak leaf; twenty-five species of scales, and the greenhouse thrips, citrus whitefly, and several kinds of beetles.

Control. Entomologists at the Agricultural Experiment Stations in the southern state will provide control measures for these insects.

QUINCE, FLOWERING (*Chaenomeles*)

Bacterial and Fungus Diseases

CROWN GALL. *Agrobacterium tumefaciens.* This disease occasionally affects this host.

Control. See Chapter 14.

FIRE BLIGHT. *Erwinia amylovora.* Flowering quince, like other rosaceous hosts, is subject to this disease.

Control. Destroy nearby neglected and unwanted pear and apple trees. Spray with an antibiotic at mid-bloom stage.

BROWN ROT. *Monilinia fructicola* and *M. laxa.* These fungi are usually more destructive on fruit trees than on the ornamental varieties. They cause a leaf blight and a blossom and twig blight of flowering quince.

Control. Periodic applications of captan or wettable sulfur sprays during the early growing season are effective.

RUST. *Gymnosporangium clavipes.* This bright, orange-colored rust is more commonly found on fruiting trees than on the flowering varieties. It attacks the fruit as well as the leaves and young twigs. It also attacks apples and hawthorns. The alternate host is the common red cedar, *Juniperus virginiana.* Though very destructive to the common quince, it does little damage to the cedar. (See under Juniper, Chapter 17, and also under Hawthorn in this chapter.)

Another rust, *G. libocedri*, also attacks flowering quince leaves.

Control. Spray periodically with ferbam or wettable sulfur during the growing season.

LEAF SPOTS. *Diplocarpon maculatum* and *Cercospora cydoniae*. These leaf spots can become quite troublesome and cause premature defoliation in rainy seasons.

Control. Spray with Benlate or zineb early in the growing season.

OTHER DISEASES. Among other diseases occasionally found on flowering quince are: twig blight caused by *Botryosphaeria dothidea*, cankers by *Nectria cinnabarina*, *Phoma* sp. and *Physalospora obtusa*, and root-knot nema *Meloidogyne* sp.

Control. These diseases are rarely serious enough on flowering quince to warrant control measures.

Insects

COTTON APHID. *Aphis gossypii*. Young leaves and upper ends of tender branches may be heavily infested with these aphids.

Control. Spray with malathion when the insects appear.

REDBUD (*Cercis*)

Diseases

CANKER. *Botryosphaeria dothidea*. This, the most destructive disease of redbud, also affects many other trees and shrubs. (See p. 456.) On redbud the cankers begin as small sunken areas and increase slowly in size. The bark in the center of the canker blackens and cracks along the edges. The wood beneath the cankered area becomes discolored. When the canker girdles the stem, the leaves above wilt and die. The causal fungus is easily recovered from discolored wood by standard tissue culture techniques in the laboratory. The causal fungus was formerly known as *Botryosphaeria ribis*.

Control. Prune and destroy branches showing cankers. Surgical excision of cankered tissue on the main stem is occasionally successful if all infected bark and wood is removed. Paint all wounds promptly with a wound dressing containing 200 ppm Benlate fungicide. Periodic applications of a copper fungicide during the growing season may help to prevent new infections.

LEAF SPOTS. A conspicuous leaf spot disease occurs on redbud throughout the range of this tree in the eastern half of the United States. Scattered circular to angular brown spots, about ¼ inch in diameter, appear on the leaves early in summer. The spots increase in size until they attain a diameter of nearly ½ inch by fall.

The fungus *Mycosphaerella cercidicola* produces circular to angular spots with dark brown borders on the leaves. Spores from overwintered fallen leaves initiate spring infections. The fungi *Cercosporella chionea* and *Phyllosticta cercidicola* also cause leaf spots on redbud.

Control. Valuable specimens can be protected by periodic applications of copper or dithiocarbamate fungicides in late spring and early summer.

OTHER DISEASES. Among other fungus diseases of redbud are wilt caused by *Verticillium albo-atrum* and root rots by *Clitocybe tabescens, Ganoderma curtisii,* and *Phymatotrichum omnivorum.*

In Mississippi, branch dieback attributed to automobile exhaust fumes has been noted.

Insects

CATERPILLARS. The larval stage of the California tent caterpillar, *Malacosoma californicum,* and the grape leaf folder, *Desmia funeralis,* occasionally infest redbuds.

Control. Spray with *Bacillus thuringiensis* or carbaryl (Sevin) when the young caterpillars begin to chew the leaves.

COTTON APHID. *Aphis gossypii.* The young leaves and upper ends of tender branches may be heavily infested with these aphids.

Control. Spray with malathion, Meta-Systox R, or carbaryl (Sevin) as soon as the aphids appear on the leaves, and repeat in 2 weeks if necessary.

TWO-MARKED TREEHOPPER. *Enchenopa binotata.* The leaves and stems of redbud are occasionally punctured by a dusky-brown insect $^3/_{10}$ inch long. A hornlike projection from the upper part of its body makes the insect resemble, in outline, a bird at rest. Locust, sycamore, hickory, and willow are also infested by this treehopper.

Control. Spray the leaves and stems with Diazinon, Meta-Systox R, or carbaryl (Sevin) when the insects are young.

SCALES. Eleven species of scales infest the twigs and branches of redbud.

Control. Dormant lime sulfur or oil sprays usually are sufficient to control scales. Severely infested trees should also be sprayed in May and June with malathion or carbaryl (Sevin).

OTHER INSECTS. The Rhabdopterus beetle *Rhabdopterus deceptor,* the redbud leafroller *Fascista cercerisella,* and the greenhouse whitefly *Trialeurodes vaporariorum* all attack redbud.

Control. Carbaryl (Sevin) sprays will control these pests.

RUSSIAN-OLIVE *(Elaeagnus)*

Russian-olive, an excellent tree for very difficult situations, is relatively free of fungus parasites and insect pests.

Diseases

CANKERS. *Botryodiplodia theobromae, Nectria cinnabarina, Fusicoccum elaeagni, Fusarium* sp., *Phomopsis elaeagni,* and *Phytophthora cactorum.* Cankers on the branches and trunk of Russian-olive may be caused by any of these fungi. The first-named fungus has killed large numbers of Russian-olives in shelterbelts in Nebraska and other Great Plains states. Bark, cambium, and phloem tissues are killed in strips along the trunk and major branches. Infection is rapid up and down stems but slow around them. Hence, complete girdling and death may take several years.

Control. No control measures have been developed.

LEAF SPOTS. Several fungi including *Cercospora carii, C. elaeagni, Phyllosticta argyrea, Septoria argyrea,* and *S. elaeagni* cause spots on leaves of this host.

Control. These fungi are rarely severe enough to warrant the use of protective fungicides.

RUST. *Puccinia caricis-shepherdiae* with the alternate host *Carex,* and *P. coronata* f. *elaeagni* with the alternate host *Calamagrostis* occur on Russian-olive in the midwestern United States.

Control. These diseases are not important enough to warrant control measures.

WILT. *Verticillium albo-atrum.* This disease was first found on Russian-olive in a nursery planting in New Mexico in 1958.

Control. See Chapter 14.

OTHER DISEASES. Russian-olive is occasionally affected by crown gall caused by *Agrobacterium tumefaciens* and hairy root by *A. rhizogenes.*

Control. Control measures are rarely necessary.

Insects

OLEASTER-THISTLE APHID. *Capitophorus braggii.* This pale yellow and green aphid, which lives on thistles during the summer, overwinters on Russian-olive.

Control. Control measures are unnecessary.

SCALES. *Parlatoria oleae* and *Lepidosaphes beckii.* The olive and the purple scale occasionally infest this host. Seventeen other species of scales have also been recorded on Russian-olive.

Control. Spray with malathion or carbaryl (Sevin) in late May and again in late June to control the crawler stage of scales.

SASSAFRAS (*Sassafras*)

Sassafras, an excellent tree for landscape plantings, is extremely susceptible to Japanese beetle infestations. Like American holly, it is dioecious, that is, the pistillate and staminate flowers grow on different trees. The slate-blue fruits are ornamental and provide food for birds.

Diseases

CANKER. Two fungi, *Nectria galligena* and *Physalospora obtusa*, are frequently associated with branch cankers (Fig. 15-25).

Control. Pruning affected branches to sound wood is suggested.

LEAF SPOTS. *Actinopelte dryina, Diplopeltis sassafrasicola, Glomerella cingulata, Metasphaeria sassafrasicola, Phyllosticta illinoisensis,* and *Stigmatophragmia sassafrasicola.* These six species of fungi cause leaf spots on sassafras. They are rarely serious enough to warrant control measures.

OTHER DISEASES. Powdery mildew caused by the fungus *Phyllactinia corylea*, wilt by a species of *Verticillium,* shoestring root rot by *Armillaria mellea,* and a disease of the yellows type have also been recorded on sassafras. The last causes bunching and fasciation of the branch tips, leaf rolling, and leaf dwarfing.

This host is also subject to curly top caused by the beet curly top virus and to aster yellows caused by a mycoplasma-like organism.

Insects

JAPANESE BEETLE. *Popillia japonica.* The topmost leaves, exposed to the bright sun are the first to be attacked by this beetle (Fig. 15-26).

Control. Sassafras trees used in ornamental plantings can be protected by spraying with Diazinon, methoxychlor, or carbaryl (Sevin), first when the beetles begin feeding on the leaves and then with two repetitions at weekly intervals.

PROMETHEA MOTH. *Callosamia promethea.* The leaves are chewed by the promethea moth larva, a bluish-green caterpillar that grows to 2 inches

Fig. 15-25. Cankers on sassafras stem caused by the fungus *Nectria galligena.*

Fig. 15-26. Japanese beetles feeding on a sassafras leaf.

in length. The adult female has reddish-brown wings, near the tips of which eyelike spots are visible; the wingspread is nearly 3 inches. The cocoons of this pest are suspended in the trees.

The caterpillars of the hickory horned devil *Citheronia regalis*, the io *Automeris io*, and the polyphemus moth *Antheraea polyphemus* also chew sassafras leaves.

Control. Spray with *Bacillus thuringiensis*, Imidan, or carbaryl (Sevin) when the caterpillars are small.

SASSAFRAS WEEVIL. *Odontopus calceatus*. This small snout weevil begins to feed as soon as the buds break and before the leaves have expanded, making numerous holes in the leaves. The female adults then deposit eggs on the midribs of the leaves, and the larvae which hatch from these mine into the leaves to cause blotches. Tuliptree and magnolia are also susceptible.

Control. Carbaryl (Sevin) sprays applied when the adults begin to feed in June, or after the eggs hatch, should provide control.

SCALES. The oystershell and San Jose scales occasionally infest sassafras. Valuable specimens can be protected from these pests with two applications of malathion or carbaryl (Sevin) sprays, one in May and the other in June.

OTHER SCALES. In addition to the two scales mentioned above, sassafras is occasionally infested by the European fruit lecanium (*Lecanium corni*), Florida wax (*Ceroplastis floridensis*), and pyriform (*Protopulvinaria pyriformis*).

Control. The crawler stage of scales can be controlled by spraying with carbaryl (Sevin) or malathion.

SERVICEBERRY (*Amelanchier*)

Serviceberry, also known as Juneberry, shadblow, and shadbush, is an excellent low-growing tree of the rose family. As such, it is subject to many of the diseases and insects common to members of that family.

Diseases

FIRE BLIGHT. *Erwinia amylovora.* This bacterial disease, which is serious on certain hawthorns and other pomaceous trees, occasionally occurs on serviceberry.

Control. See Chapter 14.

FRUIT ROTS. *Monilinia amelanchieris* and *M. fructicola.* The fruits of serviceberry are rotted in rainy seasons by these fungi.

Control. Infections on particularly valuable specimens can be prevented by periodic applications of captan or wettable sulfur sprays.

LEAF BLIGHT. *Diplocarpon maculatum.* Only occasionally is serviceberry attacked by this fungus. It is more serious on hawthorn and apple.

Control. See under Hawthorns, p. 347.

MILDEWS. *Erysiphe polygoni, Phyllactinia corylea*, and *Podosphaera oxyacanthae.*

Control. These three species of powdery mildew fungi can be controlled with Benlate, sulfur, or Karathane sprays.

RUST. More than 10 species of rust occur on serviceberry, with alternate hosts on juniper, chamaecyparis, and incense cedar.

Control. Same as for hawthorn rusts (p. 348).

WITCHES' BROOM. Several species of serviceberry are subject to the witches' broom disease, which rarely causes much damage.

Symptoms. The production of many lateral branches from a common center results in a bunching or broomlike effect. The lower surfaces of leaves attached to such twigs are covered with sooty fungus growth.

Cause. The fungus *Apiosporina collinsii* causes witches' broom. It penetrates the twigs in spring and stimulates the production of the many lateral branches. The black growth of the fungus on the leaves contains small, round fruiting bodies in late summer. These produce spores for the following season's infections.

Control. Prune and destroy affected leaves and twigs.

Insects and Related Pests

BORERS. A number of borers, including the lesser peach tree (*Synanthedon pictipes*), apple bark (*Thamnosphecia pyri*), roundheaded apple tree (*Saperda candida*), and the shot-hole (*Scolytus regulosus*), occasionally attack serviceberry.

Control. Keep trees in good vigor by feeding and watering. Spraying the trunk and branches with methoxychlor at 2- to 3-week intervals during late spring and early summer will control these borers.

LEAF MINER. *Nepticula amelanchierella.* Broad irregular mines, especially in the lower half of the leaf, result from infestation by the larvae.

Control. See under birch leaf miner, page 317.

PEAR LEAF BLISTER MITE. See under Mountain-Ash.

PEAR SLUG SAWFLY. See under Cherry, Japanese Flowering.

WILLOW SCURFY SCALE. See under Willow (Chapter 16).

SHADBLOW—See Serviceberry.

SHADBUSH—See Serviceberry.

SILK-TREE (*Albizia*)

Silk-tree (*Albizia julibrissin*), also known as mimosa, is used as a street and lawn tree in the South and as an ornamental in protected places along the Atlantic Coast as far north as Boston. Its most destructive disease is wilt, and its most destructive insect the webworm.

Diseases

WILT. This highly destructive disease is extremely prevalent from Maryland to Florida and along the Gulf Coast into Louisiana. The author found the first cases in New Jersey many years ago and more recently found diseased trees at the New York Botanical Garden in New York City. This is the northernmost known location of the disease at this time.

Symptoms. Wilting of the leaves, which soon die, is the most striking symptom. A brown ring of discolored sapwood, usually in the current annual ring of the stem and branches, is another positive symptom. Bleeding along the stems occurs occasionally. Large numbers of spores are formed in the lenticels on the trunk and branches of affected trees, at times even before actual wilting of the leaves occurs. Such spores may account for widespread outbreaks of the disease. Trees usually die within a year or so of infection.

Cause. The fungus *Fusarium oxysporium* f. *perniciosum* is known to cause wilt. The fungus lives in soil and spreads in this medium. It also can be carried over in seed collected from diseased trees. According to Dr. Richard Toole of the United States Department of Agriculture, there are two races of this fungus. One will infect silk-tree and not *Albizia procera*. The other, from Puerto Rico, will infect *A. procera* and not the silk-tree.

Control. Dead and dying trees should be cut down and destroyed to avoid the spread of the disease. Until recently the only control known was to use wilt-resistant trees. These were sold by southern nurserymen under the names 'Tryon' and 'Charlotte.' However, in 1964 Dr. D. L. Gill of the United States Department of Agriculture reported finding infected 'Tryon' and 'Charlotte' trees in Georgia. In 1967 Dr. Gill recovered *Fusarium oxysporum* f. *perniciosum* from roots of one apparently healthy resistant 'Charlotte' tree. This may explain the poor rooting of cuttings and death of inoculated trees after several years.

OTHER FUNGI. Several other fungi are reported on silk-tree. *Nectria cinnabarina* causes dieback and canker; *Coniothyrium insitivum* and a species of *Phomopsis* damage the twigs; and *Thyronectria austro-americana* is weakly pathogenic to twigs. The last is much more destructive to honey locust. *Ganoderma curtisii* is associated with a root rot. The rust fungus *Sphaerophragmium* sp. has been reported on *Albizia lebbeck* in Florida.

Insects

WEBWORM. *Homadaula anisocentra*. The larvae of this pest appear on the foliage in early spring. They are also highly destructive to honey locust (p. 424). The larvae are $^3/_5$ inch long when full grown and are gray-brown, sometimes pinkish, with 5 narrow, white, lengthwise stripes. At first they feed together in a web, but later spread throughout the tree, tying the leaves in conspicuous masses and skeletonizing them. When mature, they drop to the ground on silken threads and spin cocoons in various kinds of cracks and crevices. The moths, gray with a wingspread of about ½ inch, appear in June to lay eggs on the silk-tree flowers and leaves.

Control. When the young caterpillars are just beginning to feed, spray with carbaryl (Sevin) or Diazinon. The spraying must be repeated several times, because there are as many as 4 generations of this pest each year in some areas.

LESSER SNOW SCALE. *Pinnaspis strachani*. This white, semitransparent scale occasionally infests silk-trees, in addition to avocado, citrus, hackberry, palms, and other trees and shrubs in the deep South.

Six other species of scales also infect silk-tree.

Control. Spray with malathion, carbaryl (Sevin), or Meta-Systox R when the young are crawling about.

OTHER INSECTS. Blister beetle and citrus mealybug also infest this host.

NEMAS. *Meloidogyne arenaria* and *Trichodorus primitivus*. The former, known as the peanut root-knot nema, causes small knots or galls on silk-trees in the South. The latter, known as the stubby root nema, infests *Albizia julibrissin* roots in Maryland and azaleas in California.

Control. See under Boxwood (Chapter 17).

SILVERBELL (*Halesia*)

Silverbell is subject to few diseases, and no insects of importance are reported.

Diseases

LEAF SPOT. In rainy seasons, brown circular spots are caused by the fungus *Cercospora halesiae*.

Control. This leaf spot rarely becomes serious enough to warrant periodic applications of a copper fungicide.

WOOD DECAY. A decay of the wood, caused by *Polyporus halesiae*, has been reported from Georgia.

Control. Wood-decay fungi are difficult to control. Avoid bark wounds and keep the tree in good vigor.

SMOKE-TREE (*Cotinus*)

The smoke tree, a close relative of ordinary sumac, is occasionally used in ornamental plantings. When it is grown in soils where nitrates tend to become deficient, its leaves show red spots or blotches. The application of a commercial fertilizer high in nitrogen usually helps to overcome this trouble.

Diseases

WILT caused by the fungus *Verticillium albo-atrum* is the only serious disease of smoke-tree.

Control. See Chapter 14.

RUST. Two rusts have been reported on this tree: *Puccinia andropogonis* f. *onobrychidis* and *Pileolaria cotini-coggyriae*. The latter, found in Georgia several years ago, produces conspicuous spots with hypertrophied centers surrounded by dead tissue.

Control. These diseases are not serious enough to warrant control measures.

LEAF SPOTS. Four species of fungi are known to cause leaf spots on smoke-tree: *Cercospora rhoina, Pezizella oenotherae, Septoria rhoina,* and *Gloeosporium* sp.

Control. Valuable specimens can be protected with copper fungicides.

Insects

OBLIQUE-BANDED LEAF ROLLER. *Choristoneura rosaceana.* The leaves may be mined and rolled in June by pale yellow larvae. The adult moth is reddish-brown and has a wingspread of 1 inch, with the front wings crossed by 3 distinct bands of dark brown.

Other trees subject to this pest are apple, apricot, ash, birch, cherry, dogwood, hawthorn, horsechestnut, linden, maple, oak, peach, pear, plum, and poplar.

Control. Spray early in June with carbaryl (Sevin).

SAN JOSE SCALE. *Aspidiotus perniciosus.* This scale occasionally infests smoke-tree.

Control. Malathion or carbaryl (Sevin) sprays will control the crawler stage.

SORREL-TREE (Oxydendrum)

Diseases

TWIG BLIGHT. *Sphaerulina polyspora.* This fungus occasionally causes blighting of leaves at the tips of the branches. Trees injured by fire or in poor vigor appear to be most subject to this disease.

Control. Pruning infected twigs is usually sufficient to keep this disease under control. Feed and water when necessary to keep trees in good vigor.

LEAF SPOTS. Two fungi, *Cercospora oxydendri* and *Mycosphaerella caroliniana,* occasionally spot the leaves of sorrel-tree. The latter produces reddish or purple blotches with dry brown centers in midsummer.

Control. Spray with a copper fungicide, starting when the leaves are fully expanded and repeating in 2 weeks.

Insects

No insects of any consequence attack this tree.

SOURGUM—See Tupelo (Chapter 16).

STRAWBERRY-TREE (*Arbutus*)

Diseases

LEAF SPOTS. *Septoria unedonis* and *Elsinoë mattirolianum*. The former fungus produces small brown spots on leaves of *Arbutus unedo* in the Pacific Northwest, and the latter a spot anthracnose in California.

Control. If only a few plants are involved, pick off the infected leaves; if necessary, spray with wettable sulfur.

CROWN GALL. *Agrobacterium tumefaciens*. This bacterial disease occurs occasionally on strawberry-tree in California and Connecticut.

Control. Remove and destroy infected parts.

Insects

CALIFORNIA TENT CATERPILLAR. *Malacosoma californicum*. This species occasionally feeds on the leaves of strawberry-tree in California. It makes large tents in the trees like those of the eastern tent caterpillar.

Control. Spray with *Bacillus thuringiensis,* Dylox, methoxychlor, or carbaryl (Sevin) when the caterpillars are small.

SCALES. *Saissetia oleae, Aspidiotus camelliae,* and *Coccus hesperidum*. These three species of scales—black, greedy, and the brown soft, respectively—are known to attack strawberry-tree in the West.

Control. Spray with malathion or carbaryl (Sevin) from time to time to control the young crawling stages of these pests.

TREE-OF-HEAVEN (*Ailanthus*)

Tree-of-heaven, also called ailanthus, is never used as a streetside tree but thrives in the larger cities where no other tree will grow. It frequently sprouts in parks and yards of large cities. Only the seed-bearing kinds should be planted, as the male or pollen-bearing form has an offensive odor when it blooms.

Diseases

WILT. *Verticillium albo-atrum* is the most destructive fungus parasite of this host. Many trees have been killed by it in the Philadelphia-New York environs in the last 30 years.

Control. See Chapter 14.

SHOESTRING ROOT ROT. *Armillaria mellea* is another fungus that has been destroying this tree in the northeastern United States in recent years.

Control. See Chapter 14.

LEAF SPOT. Three leaf-spotting fungi, *Cercospora glandulosa*, *Phyllosticta ailanthi*, and *Gloeosporium ailanthi*, occasionally attack this tree.

Control. Control measures are never applied for leaf spots.

TWIG BLIGHT. *Fusarium lateritium*. This fungus also causes branch and twig cankers on Japanese pagoda-tree. The sexual stage of this fungus is *Gibberella baccata*.

Control. Control measures are rarely necessary.

OTHER DISEASES. Other fungus diseases causing dieback or cankers of ailanthus include *Botryosphaeria dothidea*, *Cytospora ailanthi*, *Coniothyrium insitivum*, *Nectria coccinea*, *Physalospora obtusa*, and *P. rhodina*.

Control. Control measures are rarely needed.

Insects

CYNTHIA MOTH. *Samia cynthia*. The larvae of this moth can completely defoliate a tree-of-heaven in a few days. Mature larvae are 3½ inches long, light green, and covered with a glaucous bloom. The adult moth is beautifully colored and has a wingspread of 6 to 8 inches (Fig. 15-27). A crescent-shaped, white marking is present in the center of each of the grayish-brown wings.

Control. Spray with carbaryl (Sevin) in June when the caterpillars begin to chew the leaves.

AILANTHUS WEBWORM. *Atteva punctella*. Olive-brown caterpillars with

Fig. 15-27. Cynthia moth (*Samia cynthia*). The larval stage of this insect feeds voraciously on *Ailanthus* (tree-of-heaven) foliage.

five white lines feed in webs on the leaves in August and September. Adult moths have bright orange forewings, with four cross-bands of yellow spots on a dark blue ground.

Control. Spray with carbaryl (Sevin) in August.

OTHER INSECTS. Among other caterpillars which attack this host, particularly in cities, are the fall webworm, *Hyphantria cunea,* and the white-marked trussock moth, *Hemerocampa leucostigma.* Another species, the pale tussock moth, *Halisidota tessellaris,* attacks a wide variety of deciduous trees.

Control. Methoxychlor or carbaryl (Sevin) sprays will control these pests.

Oystershell scale and citrus whitefly occasionally infest *Ailanthus.*

Control. Carbaryl (Sevin) or matathion sprays will control these pests.

Selected Bibliography

Anonymous. 1976. 'Detecting, controlling tree diseases and pests: ornamental crabapple.' *Grounds Maintenance.* June 1976. p. 42, 45–47, 50, 51.

Arthur, J. C. 1934. *Manual of the rusts in the United States and Canada.* Purdue Research Foundation. Lafayette, Ind. 438 p.

Beattie, R. K. 1933. 'Diseases threatening ornamental and forest trees.' *Jour. Econ. Ent.* Vol. 26. p. 621–24.

Chambers, E. L. and N. F. Thompson. 1931. *Some of the more important insects and plant diseases of Wisconsin trees and shrubs.* Wis. Dept. Agr. and Mkts. Bul. 123. 58 p.

Chambers, E. L. 1933. *Pests and diseases of trees and shrubs.* Wis. Dept. Agr. and Mkts. Bul. 145. 87 p.

Cook, M. T. 1918. *Common diseases of shade and ornamental trees.* N. J. Agr. Exp. Sta. Circ. 98. 28 p.

Felt, E. P. and W. H. Rankin. 1932. *Insects and diseases of ornamental trees and shrubs.* Macmillan, New York. 507 p.

Flemer, William III. 1973. 'Disease-resistant crab apples.' *American Nurseryman.* Apr. 1, 1973. p. 9, 67–71.

Gambrell, F. L. and R. M. Gilmer. 1956. 'Insects and diseases of fruit nursery stocks and their control.' N. Y. Agr. Exp. Sta. Bul. 776. p. 5–50.

Gill, D. L. 1964. 'Wilt of mimosa wilt-resistant cultivars.' *Plant Disease Reptr.* Vol. 48 (No. 8). p. 648.

Gottlieb, A. R. and J. B. Berbee. 1973. 'Line pattern of birch caused by apple mosaic virus.' *Phytopathology.* Vol. 63 (No. 12). p. 1470–77.

Graves, A. N. 1919. 'Some diseases of trees in greater New York.' *Mycologia.* Vol. 11. p. 111–24.

Hansen, L. C. and E. Hasselkus. 1974. 'Recommended varieties of scab resistant crab apples.' *American Nurseryman.* Jan. 1, 1974. p. 13, 61.

Hepting, G. H. 1939. *A vascular disease of the mimosa tree.* USDA Circ. 535. 10 p.

———. 1960. 'Spot anthracnose and other diseases of dogwood.' *Arborist's News.* Vol. 25(No. 4). p. 25–28.

Hibben, C. R. 1966. 'Transmission of a ringspot-like virus from leaves of white ash.' *Phytopathology.* Vol. 56 (No. 3). p. 323–25.

———. 1971. 'Research on ash dieback.' *Plants and Gardens (n.s.),* Brooklyn Botanic Garden. Vol. 26 (No. 4). p. 28–29.

Hibben, C. R. and B. Wolanski. 1971. 'Dodder transmission of a mycoplasma from ash witches' broom.' *Phytopathology.* Vol. 61 (No. 2). p. 151–56.

Herrick, G. W. 1935. *Insect enemies of shade trees.* Comstock Publishing Co., Ithaca, N.Y. 417 p.

Inman, R. E. 1962. 'Cycloheximide and the control of hawthorn leaf blight under nursery conditions.' *Plant Disease Reptr.* Vol. 46 (No. 12). p. 827–30.

Jones, S. G. 1925. 'Life-history and cytology of *Rhytisma acerinum.*' *Ann. Bot.* Vol. 39. p. 41–75.

Klarman, W. L. 1968. 'Coniothyrium canker on ornamental pear.' *Plant Disease Reptr.* Vol. 52(No. 10). p. 972.

Langford, G. S. and E. N. Cory. 1939. *Common insects of lawns, ornamental shrubs, and shade trees.* Md. Agr. Exp. Sta. Ext. Bul. 81. 54 p.

May, Curtis. 1965. 'Rust of juniper, flowering crab apple, and hawthorn.' *Am. Hort. Magazine.* Vol. 44 (No. 1). p. 29–32.

Nichols, L. P. 1969. 'Occurrence of the apple scab fungus on twigs of flowering crab apples and one cultivar of commercial apple.' *Plant Disease Reptr.* Vol. 53(No. 12). p. 974–75.

———. 1970. 'Crab apples that are still valuable though vulnerable.' *American Nurseryman.* May 15, 1970. p. 10, 51–53.

———. 1975. 'Disease-resistant crab apples.' *American Nurseryman.* June 1, 1975. p. 13, 93–98.

———. 1976. 'Disease-resistant crab apples for 1976.' *American Nurseryman.* p. 14, 75–80.

Peterson, G. W. 1976. 'Disease of Russian-olive caused by *Botryodiplodia theobromae.*' *Plant Disease Reptr.* Vol. 60 (No. 6). p. 490–94.

Peterson, J. L. and S. H. Davis, Jr. 1965. 'A Fusarium canker of *Sophora japonica.*' *Plant Disease Reptr.* Vol. 49 (No. 10). p. 835–36.

Pirone, P. P. 1939. *Diseases of ornamental plants.* N. J. Agr. Exp. Sta. Cir. 385.

———. 1940. 'Diseases of shrubs and small trees.' *Proc. Sixteenth National Shade Tree Conference.* p. 91–112.

Schuder, D. L. 1961. 'The mimosa webworm and its control.' *Trees.* Apr. 1961. p. 18–19, 29.

Silverborg, S. B. and R. W. Brandt. 1957. 'Association of *Cytophoma pruinosa* with dying ash.' *Forest Science.* Vol. 3 (No. 1). 75–78.

Strong, F. C. 1938. 'Some important shade tree diseases of the midwest.' *Proc. Fourteenth National Shade Tree Conference.* p. 106–16.

16

Diseases and Insect Pests
of Tall-growing Trees

The diseases and insect pests of tall-growing deciduous trees are treated here. As discussed in Chapter 8, most of these are best planted along wide streets, in parks, and on larger properties.

ASH—See Chapter 15.

ASPEN—See Poplar.

BASSWOOD—See Linden.

BEECH (Fagus)

Beeches are among our most beautiful trees, their dormant shapes and winter bark contribute much to any landscape.

The American beech (*F. grandifolia*) is a handsome, low-branched, slow-growing tree. Its dense foliage and shallow rooting habit, however, make difficult the maintenance of a lawn under it. It grows best in cool, moist soils and cannot withstand constant trampling over the soil nor does it withstand city conditions very well. Under ordinary conditions it is extremely difficult to transplant.

The European beech (*F. sylvatica*) is similar to the American species except that its bark is darker gray and its foliage more glossy. Its many horticultural varieties include purple beech, variety *atropunicea,* with deep purple leaves; weeping beech, variety *pendula,* one of the world's most beautiful weeping trees; weeping purple beech, variety *purpureo-pendula;* and cut-leaf, variety *laciniata,* with very beautiful, narrow, almost fernlike leaves. Other new or interesting kinds are Darwyck beech, *F. sylvatica fastigiata;* golden-leaved beech, variety *aurea;* a red fern-leaved beech, variety *Rohanni;* and the tricolor beech with pink, white, and green leaves that turn a coppery bronze.

Diseases

The dying of a large number of American beeches is believed by some investigators to be related to drought and subsequent death of the roots. Associated with the progressive weakening of some of the trees, however, is a trouble known as leaf mottle or scorch.

LEAF MOTTLE. This disease was first reported by Dr. W. H. Rankin in 1928 as being prevalent on American beech in the vicinity of Philadelphia. Since that time it has appeared somewhat sporadically, although it has been unusually abundant in the eastern United States during the last 30 years.

Symptoms. In spring, small translucent spots surrounded by yellowish-green to white areas appear on the young unfurling leaves. These spots turn brown and dry, and by the first of June the mottling is very prominent, especially between the veins near the midrib and along the outer edge of the leaf. Within a few weeks the brown areas increase in number until the entire leaf presents a scorched appearance. A considerable part or, in some instances, all of the leaves then drop prematurely. Where complete defoliation occurs, new leaves begin to develop in July. The second set of leaves in such cases appears quite normal and drops from the trees at the normal time in the fall.

The extensive loss of foliage early in the season exposes the branches to the direct rays of the sun. Because beeches are rather sensitive to such rays, considerable scalding of the bark occurs. Such injury predisposes the tree to attacks by the two-lined chestnut borer and possibly by other insects. Heavy infestations of borers will kill large branches or even the entire tree.

Cause. The cause of leaf mottle is not known. Investigations by the author many years ago failed to reveal definite clues. Site, age of tree, water supply, or atmospheric conditions do not appear to be correlated with the incidence or severity of the trouble. For example, trees growing in open lawns appear to be as subject as trees in the woods; young trees seem to contract the trouble as readily as old ones; trees growing in light, well-drained soils apparently are as susceptible as those in heavy moist soils; and the disease appears to be as prevalent in wet seasons as in dry ones. The symptoms are not typical of any known nutrient deficiency, and injections of magnesium nitrate and ferrous sulfate into the trunks have failed to produce any improvement.

Dr. Spencer Davis of Rutgers University has reported that leaf mottle is actually a form of leaf scorch. Trees that exhibit mottling have a different protoplasm or genetical background than those that are not mottled, according to Dr. Davis. Hence one tree responds differently from the other to the same soil conditions.

Control. Until more is known about the causal nature, the only recommendation that can be made is to provide adequate fertilization. The bark of particularly valuable specimens that are completely defoliated might well be protected from the midsummer sun with burlap or some other material until the second set of leaves has developed sufficiently to provide the necessary shade.

BLEEDING CANKER. *Phytophthora cactorum.* This disease, first reported on maples in Rhode Island about 1939, is now known to occur on almond, apricot, beech, cherry, dogwood, elm, maple, peach, and plum. The name suggests the most common symptom visible on beech, maple, and elm, an oozing of a watery light brown or thick reddish-brown liquid from the bark.

The fungus also causes crown canker on dogwood; and trunk cankers on fruit trees.

Control. No effective preventive measures are yet known. Infected specimens should be cut down and destroyed to prevent spread to nearby trees. Mildly affected trees have been known to recover. Avoid bark wounds near the base of the tree.

BEECH BARK DISEASE. The natural stands of beech in eastern Canada and northeastern United States have been severely damaged by this disease in the last 45 years. Although it is primarily a disease of forest beech, it is potentially dangerous to ornamental beech.

The combined attack of the woolly beech scale, *Cryptococcus fagi,* and the fungus *Nectria coccinea* f. *faginata* cause this disease.

Infestations of the scale on the bark always precede those of the fungus. During August and September, countless numbers of minute, yellow, crawling larvae appear over the bark. By late autumn they settle down and secrete a white fluffy material over their bodies. This substance is very conspicuous, and the trunks and branches appear as though coated with snow. Through the feeding punctures of the insect, the *Nectria* fungus then penetrates the bark and kills it. The insects soon die because of the disappearance of their source of food.

Death of the infected bark is followed by drying; infected areas on the trunk thus are depressed and cracked. Eventually, deeply sunken cankers are formed, which assume a more or less circular or oval shape. The destruction of the bark and other tissues of the tree leads to a progressive dying of the top. Late in the season the leaves usually curl and turn brown, the twigs die, and new buds fail to form. The dead leaves remain attached throughout the winter. In spring, affected branches fail to produce foliage, and other branches, lacking reserve food materials, produce small yellow leaves that usually die during summer. Eventually, the entire tree dies.

Control. Because of infestations of the woolly beech scale must precede fungus penetration, the eradication of the insect pest will prevent the start of the disease. Malathion sprays applied to the trunks and branches of valuable ornamental trees growing in the infested areas in early August and in September should control the young scales. A dormant lime sulfur spray applied to trunks and branches will control overwintering adult scales. Oil sprays are also effective but are not reliably safe on beech trees.

CANKERS. *Asterosporium hoffmanni, Cytospora* sp., *Strumella coryneoidea, Nectria galligena,* and *N. cinnabarina.* Canker and branch dieback of beech may be caused by any one of the five fungi listed.

Control. Prune and destroy infected branches.

LEAF SPOTS. *Gloeosporum fagi* and *Phyllosticta faginea.* Leaf spots develop late in the growing season.

Control. Control can be achieved by spraying with copper or dithiocarbamate fungicides.

POWDERY MILDEW. *Microsphaera alni* and *Phyllactinia corylea.* Two species of powdery mildew fungi occasionally develop on beech leaves in late summer.

Control. Benlate, Karathane, or wettable sulfur sprays will control powdery mildews.

Insects

BEECH BLIGHT APHID. *Prociphilus imbricator.* The bark is punctured and juices are extracted by the beech blight aphid, a blue insect covered with a white cottony substance. The pests also feed on the leaves.

Control. Spray with carbaryl (Sevin) or malathion when the pests first appear in spring. Repeat 2 weeks later if necessary.

WOOLLY BEACH APHID. *Phyllaphis fagi.* Leaves are curled and blighted by the woolly beech aphid, a cottony-covered insect, the cast skins of which adhere to the lower leaf surface. The purple beech is more commonly infested than the American beech.

Control. Before the leaves are curled, spray with the same formula as that recommended for the beech blight aphid.

BEECH SCALE. *Cryptococcus fagi.* White masses of tiny circular scales, each $1/40$ inch in diameter, on the bark of the trunk and lower branches are the common signs of beech scale infestation. The eggs are deposited on the bark in late June and early July, and the young crawling stage appears in August and September. The pest overwinters as a partly grown adult scale. Beech scale is primarily a pest of forest trees and is mentioned here only because of its association with the beech bark disease. It is present in at least twelve New York State counties.

Control. See under beech bark disease.

CATERPILLARS. Many caterpillars chew the leaves of beech, including the eastern tent, hemlock looper, saddled prominent, walnut, and the yellow-necked. The larval stage of the following moths also infest the leaves of this host: gypsy, imperial, io, leopard, luna, and the rusty tussock.

Control. Valuable ornamental specimens can be protected from any of these pests with methoxychlor or carbaryl (Sevin) sprays. These are most effective if applied when the caterpillars are small.

BROWN WOOD BORER. *Parandra brunnea.* Winding galleries in the wood, made by the white-bodied, black-headed borers, 1¼ inches long, and tiny holes in the bark, made by emerging shiny, brown bettles ¾ inch long, are typical signs of brown wood borer infestation. The eggs are deposited in bark crevices or in decayed wood.

Control. Infestations can be prevented to a large extent by avoiding mechanical injuries to bark and wood and by treating open wounds.

TWO-LINED CHESTNUT BORER. *Agrilus bilineatus.* Trunks and branches of trees defoliated by the leaf mottle disease or of those weakened by other causes are subject to attacks by the two-lined chestnut borer. Cankers of varying sizes appear on the sides of the branches exposed to the sun's rays. A dark red liquid exudes from a small puncture in the center of the canker. The formation of several cankers along a branch reduces the sap flow and weakens the distal portions of the infested branch. A description of the pest is presented under Oak on page 448.

SCALES. In addition to the *Cryptococcus* scale mentioned above, beech trees are subject to the following scales: black, cottony-cushion, European fruit lecanium, oystershell, Putnam, and San Jose.

Control. Spray with malathion when the young scales are crawling about and with dormant lime sulfur in early spring.

EASTERN TENT CATERPILLAR. See under Willow.

DATANA CATERPILLAR. See yellow-necked caterpillar under Oak.

GYPSY MOTH. See under Elm.

CATALPA *(Catalpa)*

Two species of catalpa, common and western, are used in ornamental plantings. Common catalpa (*C. bignonioides*) should be planted only where its flowers and fruits are not objectionable. Western catalpa (*C.*

speciosa) is hardy and grows rapidly. Several leaf spots and powdery mildews, in addition to the Verticillium wilt disease (p. 297), occur on these hosts. Insects are usually more of a problem than the diseases.

Diseases

LEAF SPOT. A common disease of catalpa, leaf spot is most prevalent during rainy seasons.

Symptoms. Tiny water-soaked spots, scattered over the leaf, appear in May. The spots turn brown and increase in size until they attain a diameter of about ¼ inch. Holes in the leaves are common as a result of dropping out of the infected tissue. Where the spotting is unusually heavy, the leaves may drop prematurely.

Cause. Three fungi, *Phyllosticta catalpae*, *Alternaria catalpae*, and *Cercospora catalpae*, are frequently associated with these spots (Fig. 16–1). Injury by the catalpa midge, discussed below, and infection by bacteria are believed to increase the susceptibility to leaf spots.

Control. Gather and destroy the leaves in fall. Spray valuable susceptible trees three times with bordeaux mixture or any other copper fungicide, first, as the leaves unfurl, then when the leaves are half-grown, and again when full grown.

POWDERY MILDEW. Two species of mildew fungi, *Microsphaera alni* f. *vaccinii* and *Phyllactinia corylea*, attack catalpas.

Control. Spray valuable trees with either Benlate, wettable sulfur, or Karathane.

WOOD DECAY. The western catalpa is extremely susceptible to heartwood decay caused by the fungus *Polyporus versicolor*. The heartwood becomes straw-yellow, light, and spongy. Another fungus, *Polyporus catalpae*, causes decay of the trunk near the soil line. The wood becomes brown, tough, brittle, and full of cracks.

Control. Avoid wounds, inasmuch as the spores of both fungi enter through bark injuries. Keep the trees in good vigor by fertilizing and watering.

OTHER DISEASES. Among other diseases of Catalpa are twig dieback, caused by *Botryosphaeria dothidea,* root rot by *Armillaria mellea* and *Phymatotrichum omnivorum,* and canker by *Physalospora obtusa.*

Control. Control measures have not been developed.

Insects

COMSTOCK MEALYBUG. *Pseudococcus comstocki.* Distorted growth of twigs, limbs, and trunk may be produced by the sucking of this small, elliptical, waxy-covered insect. The leaves may be covered with black sooty mold, which develops on so-called honeydew secreted by this pest. Winter is passed as eggs in masses of white waxy secretions on the bark.

Fig. 16-1. Leaf spot caused by the fungus *Phyllosticta catalpae*.

Control. Before the buds open, spray with 1 part concentrated lime sulfur in 10 parts of water, or with winter-strength dormant oil.* A malathion or carbaryl (Sevin) spray applied to the trunk and branches in late spring and again in early summer will provide additional control.

CATALPA MIDGE. *Cecidomyia catalpae.* Leaves are distorted, and circular areas inside the leaves are chewed, leaving a papery epidermis, as a result of infestation by tiny yellow maggots. The adult, a tiny fly with a wingspread of 1/16 inch, appears in late May or early June to lay eggs on the leaves. Winter is passed in the pupal stage in the soil.

* See footnote page 249.

Control. Cultivate the soil beneath the trees to destroy the pupae, and spray in late May with malathion.

CATALPA SPHINX. *Ceratomia catalpae.* Leaves may be completely stripped from a tree by a large yellow and black caterpillar, the sphinx, which attains a length of 3 inches. The adult female is a grayish-brown moth with a 3-inch wingspread. The winter is passed as the pupal stage in the ground.

Control. Spray the foliage with carbaryl (Sevin) early in May and again in mid-August.

CHESTNUT *(Castanea)*

Diseases

BLIGHT. The rapid disappearance of one of our best forest, ornamental, and nut trees, the American chestnut, as a result of infection by one of the most virulent tree parasites, is too well known to warrant much discussion in this book. Despite tireless effort and tremendous monetary expenditures, dead and diseased chestnut trees are all that remain of the losing battle man has waged to check this invader. Despite the lack of many optimistic signs, a few individuals maintain that it is yet too early to predict the ultimate fate of this valuable tree. They point out that cankers on diseased trees appear to develop less rapidly than in former years and that more and more partly healed cankers are visible. Other hopeful signs, they assert, are the fact that sprouts continue to develop at the base of dead stumps and from the roots, some attaining a height of more than 30 feet and a trunk diameter of 8 or more inches, and the fact that thousands of other sprouts, though not attaining so large a size, are able to produce nuts before they succumb.

No one will dispute the statement that the chestnut blight disease has done more than any other single factor in American history to make the public tree-conscious. Within the span of 70 years many persons have witnessed the passing of this irreplaceable tree. Believed to be of minor importance when first reported by the late Hermann Merkel, who found a few infected trees in Bronx Park, New York City, in 1904, the disease proceeded to wipe out the chestnut stands in New England forests and along the eastern slopes of the Allegheny and Blue Ridge mountains, the principal range of this host. Today some chestnuts still stand in the extreme southern and western parts of this tree's natural range: in Tennessee, Georgia, and South Carolina. It is safe to say, however, that they too will soon suffer the same fate as their northern kin, for blight has been reported in these states, as well as in many midwestern and several far-western states.

Though blight is essentially a disease of the American chestnut, it commonly occurs on the chinquapin *(Castanea pumila)* as well. The causal fungus has been found growing on red maple, shagbark hickory, live oak, and staghorn sumac (*Rhus typhina*), and on dead and dying white, black, chestnut, and post oaks.

Symptoms. The only evidences of the once magnificent chestnut trees are the tremendous barkless trunks that still stand among living trees of other species, or the rotting stumps around whose edges vigorous living sprouts and small trees continue to appear. Many of the young trees seem to escape the disease for the first dozen years of their lives. Whether this is owing to their smooth bark, which is relatively free from injury during this period, or whether they have some degree of resistance in infancy, is not definitely known. Once the destructive fungus gains a strong foothold, however, the leaves on one branch, or several branches, or even on the entire young tree suddenly wilt, turn brown, and hang dry on the branches (Fig. 16-2). The death of the leaves and of the stems to which they are attached results from the death and girdling of some portion below. When the infection occurs rather high in the tree, only the distal parts are affected. When it develops at the base near the soil line, the entire top of the tree dies.

Close inspection of the lower parts of dying twigs, branches, or trunks reveals the presence of cankers. These are discolored, slightly sunken areas in the bark. Layers of flat, fan-shaped, buff-yellow wefts of fungus tissue are usually revealed between the bark and the sapwood when the bark in the cankered area is lifted or peeled carefully.

Cause. Blight is caused by the fungus *Endothia parasitica*. When a considerable bark area has been invaded, tiny, pin-point fruiting bodies, the tips of which barely protrude from the bark, are developed. In damp weather, sticky, yellowish-orange masses of spores ooze from the openings in these bodies. The spores are splashed by rain or are carried by birds and by crawling and flying insects to wounds in the bark below or to nearby trees, where they cause new infections. A second type of fruiting structure is also developed. This is a small, black, flask-shaped body embedded in the bark with a relatively long beak protruding above the surface. The spores from this type are shot into the air and are blown for many miles by the wind. In fact, spore traps placed on high buildings in New York City, when the epidemic was at its peak years ago, caught many spores of this type. The windblown spores lodge in open wounds on chestnut trees and produce new infections when conditions are favorable. The mycelium, the vegetative stage of the fungus, penetrates the bark, cambium, and sapwood with considerable rapidity and soon completely girdles the infected twig, branch, or trunk. Chestnut blight has been unchecked by man because of his inability to prevent the dissemination of spores by wind, birds, and insects.

Control. Although many suggestions and recommendations have been published, none has proved effective in controlling chestnut blight. Per-

Fig. 16-2. Chestnut blight on young sprouts. The leaves hang dry and brown on girdled stems. Notice the stump of the original tree.

sistent efforts have been made to find some chemical that when injected into the tree would check the development of cankers. Numerous claims for such chemicals have been advanced, but the author is unaware of the existence of any really effective material at the present time.

Some recent research at the Connecticut Agricultural Experiment Station, New Haven, indicates that cankers can be restricted and caused to heal by the introduction of a hypovirulent (weak) parasitic strain of *Endothia parasitica* into the canker.

After 60 years of research in this country, no American chestnut has been found with sufficient resistance to be of practical value.

When research scientists finally realized that the chestnut blight fungus was uncontrollable, substitutes were sought. The answer seemed to be the introduction of Asiatic chestnuts which were known to be resistant to blight. Although a few of these chestnuts were introduced as long ago as 65 years, the greatest numbers were introduced in the late 1920's. But their introduction has resulted in the appearance of other diseases, such as the blossom-end rot of the nuts caused by the fungus *Glomerella cingulata* and twig canker, discussed below.

Asiatic chestnuts (*C. japonica* and *C. mollissima*) are now widely available from many nurseries. Most of them are best suited for ornamental plantings and nut production rather than as forest trees. Many have a shrublike growth habit, with multiple trunks arising near the ground level. They do not grow so tall and straight as the American chestnut and cannot compete on wooded areas when interplanted with other trees. The varieties of *C. mollissima* that are best for orchard cultivation are Abundance, Kuling, Meiling, and Nanking.*

TWIG CANKER OF ASIATIC CHESTNUTS. The increased use of Asiatic species of chestnuts, because of their resistance to blight, has revealed that these species are susceptible to a less destructive disease, twig canker.

Symptoms. Cankers on trunks, limbs, or twigs result from fungus invasion of the bark, cambium, and sapwood. Cankers on the branches may cause complete girdling, followed by death within a single season. When complete girdling does not take place in one season, the canker may callus over temporarily, and the infection then may continue the following season, to cause death of the parts above the canker.

Cause. Several fungi have been associated with this disease, the most common and virulent one being *Cryptodiaporthe castanea*. It has been found to kill young trees in nurseries and older trees in permanent plantings, but more commonly it kills individual branches, thus decreasing growth and deforming the trees.

Control. Twig canker is most prevalent on trees in poor vigor. Maintaining good vigor will do much to ward off attacks. Planting sites should be carefully selected, and fertilization and watering practiced to ensure vigorous growth. All unnecessary injuries to the trees should be avoided, since the causal organisms penetrate and infect most readily through bark wounds. Trees should be carefully inspected in early summer, when symptoms are most apparent, and affected twigs should be pruned to sound wood and destroyed. Large cankers on the trunk or larger branches should be removed by surgical methods.

* For a small charge, the Superintendent of Documents, U.S. Government Printing Office, Washington, D.C. 20402, will send on request Farmer's Bulletin 2068, *Chestnut Blight and Resistant Chestnuts*. The Connecticut Agricultural Experiment Station, New Haven, Connecticut, also has an excellent publication on the same subject, Bulletin 657.

OTHER DISEASE. The fungus *Monochaetia kansensis* causes a leaf spot of *Castanea mollissima* in Kansas and Mississippi.

Insects

WEEVILS. *Curculio auriger* and *C. proboscideus.* Two species of weevils native to the United States may seriously damage the nuts of the Asiatic species of chestnuts.

Control. Spray the trees with methoxychlor before the weevils lay eggs in August. Treat the soil beneath Asiatic chestnut trees with ethylene dibromide in spring to kill the larval stage. Nuts harvested from infested trees which have not been treated as described above should be enclosed with methyl bromide in a tight container for 3 hours.

The insect pests which attack American chestnut are of no importance because of the destruction of the trees by blight. Following, however, are some insects that can attack living American chestnuts:

BROWN WOOD BORER. See under Beech.

DATANA CATERPILLAR. See yellow-necked caterpillar under Oak.

JAPANESE BEETLE. See under Linden.

LECANIUM SCALE. See under Oak.

TWIG PRUNER. See under Maple.

SPRING CANKERWORM. See under Elm.

WHITE-MARKED TUSSOCK MOTH. See under Elm.

TWO-LINED CHESTNUT BORER. See under Oak.

COTTONWOOD—See Poplar.

ELM (*Ulmus*)

Bacterial and Fungus Diseases

WETWOOD. A term applied to certain forms of wilt, branch dieback, and internal and external fluxing of elms. It occurs in American, Moline, Littleford, English, Siberian, and slippery elms.

Symptoms. Elms affected by wetwood have dark, water-soaked malodorous wood. The condition is usually confined to the inner sapwood and heartwood in trunks and large branches. Little or no streaking occurs in the outer sapwood, and no discoloration is seen in the cambial region or phloem.

Cause. Wetwood is caused by the bacterium *Erwinia nimipressuralis.* In the course of their development the bacteria produce gas, which often creates pressures ranging from 5 to 20 pounds in the tree.

Control. Injections of such chemical substances as mercuric chloride, copper sulfate, silver nitrate, and 8-hydroxyquinoline benzoate into in-fected trees have failed to control the disease. Although no effective control has been found, some relief to fluxing trees is possible through installing drainpipes in the trunk. Drainpipes do not reduce the infec-tion but provide a way for the sap and toxic gas to escape. Semi-rigid plastic pipes are more satisfactory than metal ones. (See under slime flux, p. 207.

DUTCH ELM DISEASE. Much has been written in the last 40 years both in the United States and in Europe on the Dutch elm disease, the most destructive fungus disease attacking elms. The misleading name given the disease merely refers to the place where it was first identified in 1919, the Netherlands. The disease is believed to have entered the United States in the late 1920's on burled elm logs from Europe. After killing literally thousands of elms in the eastern United States, it now is known to be present in at least 36 states, including California.

Symptoms. Wilting leaves on one or more branches followed by yellow-ing, curling, and dropping of all but a few of the leaves at the branch tips about midsummer are the first outward symptoms. The disease is often recognizable in winter by the tuft of dead brown leaves adhering to the tips of curled twigs. When diseased twigs or branches are cut, spots or flecks are visible in the sapwood near the bark (Fig. 16-3). A longitudinal section of the diseased twig shows long brown streaks following the grain of the wood.

Discoloration in the wood also occurs in several other less destructive elm diseases. Consequently, a positive diagnosis can be made only after the fungus responsible for the discoloration has been isolated. Plant pathologists at the state agricultural experiment stations are equipped to make a diagnosis, provided adequate twig specimens showing internal discolorations are submitted to them.

Cause. The Dutch elm disease is caused by the fungus *Pesotum ulmi* (Fig. 16-4), the sexual stage of which is *Ceratocystis ulmi.*

Several species of insects are largely responsible for the spread of the fungus from diseased to healthy trees. Among the most common vectors in this country are the smaller European elm bark beetle, *Scolytus multi-striatus*, and the native elm bark beetle, *Hylurgopinus rufipes*. A number of other boring insects are also known to transmit the causal fungus, or are suspected of transmitting it. The fungus may occasionally be spread by rainwater and through grafting of roots of a diseased with a healthy elm. Other suspected means of spread are wind-blown spores, birds, and pruning tools, although no clear-cut evidence is available.

The fungus penetrates the tree only through wounds. Once inside the wood, it can spread rapidly either by spores developed in the wood vessels and carried in the sap stream, or by growth of the fungus hyphae (Fig. 16-5). Death of affected branches is believed to be due to toxins

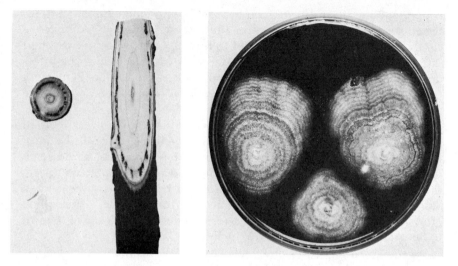

Fig. 16-3. Left: Discoloration in twig resulting from infection by the Dutch elm disease fungus, *Ceratocystis ulmi*.

Fig. 16-4. Right: The Dutch elm disease fungus as it appears in pure culture when isolated from infected elm twigs.

produced by the fungus or to lack of water as a result of the plugging of the vessels by materials formed in the process of fungus invasion.

Control. After almost 40 years of research, no positive control has been developed. Control is indirect, that is, against the insects (bark beetles) which are the principal disseminators of the fungus.

One way to control the insect carriers is to search out and destroy their breeding places. These include all dead, dying, or devitalized elm material such as sick trees, hurricane-damaged ones, broken limbs, elmwood piles, and elm fence posts. To do a good job, such material must be removed from a relatively large area because the smaller European elm bark beetle, the principal disseminator in this country, can fly more than 3 miles and frequently does. The long flights are usually made in search of suitable breeding places, but these same bettles may also feed on living trees. Such beetles have been found to carry viable spores of the Dutch elm disease fungus for more than 2 miles. The elm bark beetles breed and feed in all species of elms that grow in this country.

Bark beetle development in standing diseased trees can be prevented by injecting oxydemetonmethyl or cacodylic acid under pressure. Broods already established in such trees are also destroyed.

The best way to prevent the movement of these beetles is to use a residual type contact insecticide on elm trees in March or April.

Fig. 16-5. Spore-bearing coremia of the asexual stage of the Dutch elm disease fungus *Pesotum ulmi.*

For hydraulic sprayers use 2 per cent methoxychlor. This is made up by mixing 8 gallons of 25 per cent methoxychlor emulsifiable concentrate in 92 gallons of water to make 100 gallons of spray.

For mist blowers use methoxychlor with xylene or xylene-type formulations. This is made by mixing 50 gallons of 25 per cent emulsifiable concentrate to 50 gallons of water to make 100 gallons of spray.

It has been observed that healthy trees that are pruned in late July, August, and September are more apt to contract the disease than those pruned at other times of the year.

Pruning diseased branches has often been suggested as a means of checking this disease. However, J. H. Hart of the Michigan Agricultural Experiment Station found that this practice was effective in only 23 per cent of the cases. Because of the low percentage of success and the high cost of trimming large trees, he concluded that this method of control is neither effective nor practical.

More recently, however, Dr. Richard Campana found that elimination of the disease was inversely related to depth of infection. The infected tree had a better chance of survival if the infection in the excised branch had not penetrated too far down in the branch. He found that 87 per cent of the trees survived where the removed branch had 10 linear feet of apparent disease-free wood; 42 per cent with 5 to 10 feet; and 12 per cent with less than 5 feet.

Some spread of the disease may occur via root grafts between a diseased and a healthy tree. Vapam soil treatments will kill roots of diseased trees and thus prevent transmission via root grafts.

Oil used to lubricate chain saws that are used to prune trees may be another way of disseminating the Dutch elm disease fungus. Scientists at the University of Maine and at Yale University found that spores (conidia) of the fungus survived immersion in S.A.E. 30 oil for as long as 7 days.

Frequent reports appear in the press and in scientific literature about a chemical which will prevent the Dutch elm disease or cure mildly infected ones. One, recently introduced is Lignasan BLP, a water-soluble form of Benlate, which was tested on 7000 mature trees by 1500 cooperators in 15 states. Trunk injections are made under pressure with special apparatus any time during the growing season but preferably in spring when the trees reach full leaf.

Details on dosage and procedures are available from Lignasan BLP manufacturer, the E. I. duPont Co., Wilmington, Delaware.

Some recent research by Dr. Richard Campana at the University of Maine suggests that some strains of the Dutch elm disease fungus develop a tolerance to Benlate.

Plant pathologists of the United States Department of Agriculture, Plant Science Research Dvision, Delaware, Ohio, found that 6 isolates of the Duth elm disease fungus from 6 states were able to tolerate tremendous concentrations of a soluble form of Benlate (MBC-HCl) in laboratory tests. The six isolates grew on agar containing 1,000 micrograms of the chemical per gram of nutrient, whereas the growth of 23 other isolates was inhibited by one microgram per gram.

'Arbotect' 20-S, manufactured by Merck and Company, Rahway, New Jersey, is the most recently developed systemic fungicide for use as a Dutch elm disease preventive and as a therapeutic treatment for mildly infected trees. The active ingredient is thiabendazole.

The Dutch elm disease fungus is highly variable. Some strains of the fungus are apparently highly resistant to the Benlate.

At the moment and for all practical purposes, as thorough a sanitation program as possible is perhaps the most important control practice.

The greatest hope for eventual control lies in the discovery of American elms that have natural immunity to the disease. A number of such individuals are being watched carefully by scientists of the United States Department of Agriculture. Scientists at the Shade Tree and Ornamental Plants Laboratory, Delaware, Ohio, have developed a hybrid elm, 'Urban Elm,' which is resistant to the Dutch elm disease. This elm is a cross between an elm from the Netherlands (*Ulmus hollandica* var. *vegeta* X. *U. carpinifolia*) and a Siberian elm. The new tree will grow to moderate size, making it more suitable for urban planting than the American elm. It has an upright branching form as compared with the very familiar umbrella shape of the American elm.

Several commercial nurseries are now propagating 'Urban Elm,' and planting-size specimens should be available within a year or so.

Another disease-resistant hybrid clone, 'Sapporo Autumn Gold,' was developed by tree breeders at the University of Wisconsin. Several commercial nurseries are now propagating it, and like 'Urban Elm,' it should be available in 1979 or 1980.

The 'Christine Buisman' elm, formerly thought to be highly resistant to the disease, has been found to be susceptible to both Dutch elm disease and the mycoplasma disease phloem necrosis. The Hanson Manchurian elm, like most Asiatic elms, is decidedly resistant to the disease. A close relative of the American elm, Japanese keaki (*Zelkova serrata*) is much more resistant to the disease than is the American elm. It is vase-shaped and has bark resembling beech and elmlike foliage that turns red in the fall.

The tiny wasp *Dentrosoter protuberans* from France was introduced into the United States by the Forest Service in the late 1960's in the hope that it would help to control the insect that spreads this disease. The wasp is a parasite on the fungus-carrying European bark beetle. The female wasp locates hidden beetle larvae and deposits eggs beside them. When the eggs hatch, the wasp larvae attack and kill the bark beetle larvae by sucking their body juices. If and when the wasps become established in large enough quantities, they may be an important factor in reducing the bark beetle population and thus reducing the spread of the causal fungus.

Scientists in the United States Department of Agriculture have extracted several sex lures from natural organisms. One, from virgin elm bark beetles, attracts adult elm bark beetles of both sexes. When the lure is synthesized in sufficient amounts, it will be subjected to large-scale tests to control the beetles which disseminate the Dutch elm disease fungus.

Occasionally one reads that well-fed elms are less apt to contract Dutch elm disease. Actually, the reverse is true. Fertilizers increase the vessel group size, which makes the trees more susceptible to the disease. Unless the trees show a severe nutrient deficiency, they should not be fertilized more often than once every 3 or 4 years.

CANKERS. At least eight species of fungi, *Apioporthe apiospora*, *Botryosphaeria dothidea*, *Coniothyrium* spp., *Cytospora ludibunda*, *Nectria coccinea*, *N. cinnabarina*, *Phomopsis* sp., and *Sphaeropsis ulmicola*, cause cankers and dieback of twigs and branches of elms.

Control. Many small cankers can be eradicated by surgical means. The cuts should extend well beyond the visibly infected area to ensure complete removal of fungus-infected tissue. The edge of the wound should be painted with shellac and the entire exposed area finally dressed with a good tree paint. If the canker has completely girdled the stem, prune well below the affected area, and destroy the prunings.

BLEEDING CANKER. *Phytophthora cactorum.* This disease also affects maple.

Control. See under Maple.

LEAF CURL. *Taphrina ulmi.* Small blisters which lead to abnormal leaf development follow an attack by this fungus. Infection usually takes place soon after the leaves unfold.

Control. Valuable specimens subject to this disease should be sprayed with concentrated lime sulfur in spring just before growth starts.

LEAF SPOTS. *Cercospora sphaeriaeformis, Cylindrosporium tenuisporium, Coryneum tumoricola, Gloeosporium inconspicuum, G. ulmicolum, Gnomonia ulmea, Monochaetia monochaeta, Phyllosticta confertissima, P. melaleuca, Mycosphaerella ulmi, Septogloeum profusum,* and *Coniothyrium ulmi.* There are so many fungi that cause leaf spots of elms that only an expert can distinguish one from another. Probably the most prevalent leaf spot, however, is that caused by *Gnomonia ulmea,* the first symptom of which appears early in spring as small white or yellow flecks on the upper leaf surface. The flecks then increase in size, and their centers turn black (Fig. 16-6). If infections occur early and are heavy, the leaves may drop prematurely. Usually, however, the disease becomes prevalent in late fall about the time the leaves drop normally, and consequently little damage to the tree occurs.

Control. Gather the fallen leaves in autumn and place them in trash cans to be carted away. Ferbam or zineb sprays applied 3 times at 10- to 12-day intervals, starting when the leaves are half-grown, will give good control of leaf spots.

POWDERY MILDEWS. Three species of powdery mildew fungi, *Microsphaera alni, Phyllactinia corylea,* and *Uncinula macrospora,* develop their mycelia on both sides of the leaves and cause a yellowish spotting.

Control. Damage is so slight that spraying is usually unnecessary.

CEPHALOSPORIUM WILT. *Deuterophoma ulmi.* The disease was once called Dothiorella wilt. Early symptoms are the drooping and yellowing of the

Fig. 16-6. Leaf spot of elm caused by the fungus *Gnomonia ulmi.*

leaves, which are more or less mottled and which later become brownish
and rolled. The foliage on trees whose trunk is infected is very dwarfed.
Much dieback of twigs and branches occurs. This fungus is spread by
wind, rain, insects, and birds. The parasite enters through wounds and
develops in the water-conducting system, and also invades the medullary
rays, pith, cambium, and other living tissues.

Control. Severely infected trees should be removed and destroyed.
Mildly infected ones should be pruned heavily to remove as much of the
diseased wood as possible. Because the fungus may develop internally
well beyond the area of the external symptoms, pruning does not always
produce the desired results. Heavy fertilization may help mildly diseased
trees to recover. The number of leaf infections can be reduced by
applying combination sprays containing a fungicide and an insecticide.
Fertilization is suggested as a general precautionary measure, despite the
fact that there seems to be no correlation between the vigor of the tree
and its susceptibility to the disease.

VERTICILLIUM WILT. *Verticillium albo-atrum.* The symptoms of this
disease are so much like those of the Dutch elm disease and Cephalosporium wilt that culturing of the fungus is necessary to distinguish
them. This wilt may in time cause the death of large elms but usually
does not become epidemic. The fungus usually spreads upward from
the roots, but some recent research by scientists in the United States
Department of Agriculture has revealed that air-borne spores can cause
infection of aboveground parts.

Control. When infected trees wilt extensively, they should be cut down
and destroyed, along with as many of the roots as possible. Fertilizing
mildly infected trees may aid recovery.

WOOD DECAY. A number of fungi are associated with decay of elm
wood. They cannot be checked once they have invaded large areas of the
trunk. Many can be prevented from gaining access to the interior of the
tree, however, by avoiding bark injuries, by properly treating injuries
that do occur, and by keeping the tree in good vigor by fertilizing and
watering.

Virus and Related Diseases

PHILOEM NECROSIS. Mycoplasma-like organism. This disease is even
more deadly than Dutch elm disease. Thousands of elms in the Middle
West have died from its effects during the last 35 years. At present the
disease has spread as far east as western New York State.

Symptoms. The earliest symptoms appear in the extreme top of the tree
at the outer tips of the branches. Here the foliage becomes sparse, and
the leaves droop because of downward curvature of the leaf stalks.
Individual leaves curl upward at the margin, producing a troughlike

effect that makes them appear narrow and grayish-green. They are often stiff and brittle. The leaves then turn yellow and fall prematurely. These symptoms appear throughout the tree and are not confined to one or several branches, as are wilt disease infections.

In advanced stages of the disease, first the small fibrous roots and eventually the larger ones die. One of the most typical signs is the discoloration of the phloem tissue that precedes the death of the larger roots. The discoloration frequently extends into the trunk and branches. The cambial region becomes light to deep yellow, and the adjacent phloem tissue turns yellow, then brown, with small black flecks scattered throughout. After this, the phloem tissues are browned and killed. Moderately discolored phloem has an odor resembling wintergreen. In chronic cases of phloem necrosis, there is a gradual decline over a 12- to 18-month period before the tree dies. In acute cases, an apparently healthy and vigorous tree may wilt and die within 3 to 4 weeks.

Cause. The phloem necrosis organism can be transmitted experimentally be grafting patches of diseased bark, scions, or roots on healthy trees. In nature the infectious principle is transmitted by the elm leafhopper, *Scaphoideus luteolus.* Actually there are two strains of this insect in the central states where the disease is most concentrated, but only one is capable of transmitting the infectious agent.

Control. Spray June 1 and again August 1 with 2 pounds of 50 percent wettable methoxychlor (50WP) powder per 100 gallons of water to control the insect vector, the elm leaf beetle, and some other foliar pests.

Because of the nature of the causal organism, it may be possible to control phloem necrosis with sprays or injections of the antibiotic tetracycline. Plant pathologists at Cornell University recently reported that tetracycline injected into 42 elms retarded symptom development and death.

MOSAIC. This virus disease, which causes yellow mottling of leaves, is rather rare and relatively harmless. It can be transmitted from diseased to healthy trees through both pollen and pistils.

SCORCH, another virus disease, occurs in the vicinity of Washington, D.C. Foliar necrosis and a gradual crown deterioration and eventual death are the principal symptoms. The causal virus has been transmitted by grafting.

Control. No control is known for mosaic or scorch.

Insects and Other Animal Pests

WOOLLY APPLE APHID. *Eriosoma lanigerum.* Stunting and curling of the terminal leaves result from infestations of bluish-white aphids. The growing tip may be killed back for several inches. The pest overwinters in the egg stage in bark crevices.

Control. In spring just after the buds burst, spray with Diazinon, malathion, or Meta-Systox R. Repeat in 10 days to 2 weeks.

ELM LEAF CURL APHID. *Eriosoma americanum.* This insect may become injurious to elms at times. Another species of leaf-infesting aphid is *Myzocallis ulmifolii.*

Control. The same as for the woolly apple aphid.

ELM CASE BEARER. *Coleophora limosipennella.* When elms are infested by the case bearer, small holes are chewed in the leaves and angular spots mined between the leaf veins by a tiny larva. The adult is a small moth with a ½-inch wingspread. The pest overwinters in the larval stage in small cigar-shaped cases made from leaf tissue.

Control. Carbaryl (Sevin) sprays in May, or a dormant spray before growth starts in spring, will control this pest.

ELM LACE BUG. *Corythucha ulmi.* In eastern states this insect may do considerable damage to elms. It first infests the tender foliage in spring, later causing a characteristic spotting of the leaves, which turn brown and die. Black specks of the excreta on the under side of the leaves are also characteristic.

Control. Spray with malathion or carbaryl (Sevin) when the young bugs appear in spring.

ELM LEAF BEETLE. *Pyrrhalta luteola.* Two distinct types of injury are produced by this pest. Soon after the leaves unfurl in spring, rectangular areas are chewed in them by the adult beetles, brownish-yellow insects ¼ inch long (Fig. 16-7). Later in the season the leaves are skeletonized and curl and dry up as a result of the feeding on the lower surface by the larvae, black grubs with yellow markings. The eggs (Fig. 16-8) are deposited on the lower leaf surface by the beetles.

Control. Spray with carbaryl (Sevin) after the leaves are partly out, and again about 3 weeks later. Mites may increase on leaves sprayed too often with this material. The masses of grubs or pupae around the base of the tree can be destroyed by wetting the soil with a dilute solution of malathion prepared from the emulsifiable concentrate.

ELM LEAF MINER. *Fenusa ulmi.* Leaves of American, English, Scotch, and Camperdown elms are mined and blotched in May and June by white, legless larvae, sometimes as many as 20 in a single leaf. Adult females are shining black sawflies which deposit eggs in slits in the upper leaf surfaces.

Control. Spray the leaves about May 1 and 15 with Diazinon, malathion, or carbaryl (Sevin). Repeat once in June to control the second generation.

SMALLER EUROPEAN ELM BARK BEETLE. *Scolytus multistriatus.* Trees in weakened condition are most subject to infestation by the smaller European elm bark beetle. The adult female, a reddish-black beetle $^1/_{10}$ inch long, deposits eggs along a gallery in the sapwood. The small white

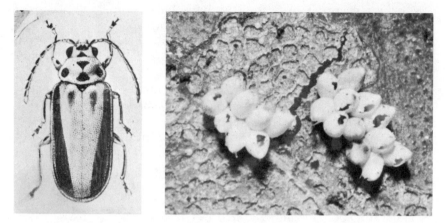

Fig. 16-7. Left: Adult elm leaf beetle, which occasionally becomes a household pest.

Fig. 16-8. Right: Eggs of elm leaf beetle are deposited on the lower leaf surface of elms. Note some have already hatched.

larvae that hatch from the eggs tunnel out at right angles to the main gallery. Tiny holes are visible in the bark when the adult beetles finally emerge. The beetle is of interest because it is one of the principal vectors of the Dutch elm disease fungus. Adult beetles will feed to a slight extent on buds and bark of twigs during summer. (Fig. 16-9).

Control. Remove and destroy severely infested branches or trees, and fertilize and water weakened trees. High concentrations of methoxychlor should be applied in late April or early May to control this pest and thus prevent it from spreading the Dutch elm disease fungus.

ELM COCKSCOMB GALL. *Colopha ulmicola*. Elongated galls which resemble the comb of a rooster are formed on the leaves as a result of feeding and irritation by wingless, yellow-green aphids. Eggs are deposited in bark crevices in fall. Two other species, *Tetraneura graminis* and *T. ulmisaccula*, behave similarly.

Control. A malathion spray applied as the buds open in spring will destroy the so-called 'stem-mother' stage.

DOGWOOD TWIG BORER. *Oberea tripunctata*. This girdler causes the dropping of many small twigs of the elm in May and June. The female partially girdles branches up to ½ inch in diameter. When the eggs hatch, the grubs bore 4 to 5 inches down the center of the twig, which may have broken off at the girdled point. The grubs are dull yellow, ¾ inch long; they winter in the twigs. The adult beetles appear in the spring.

Control. To destroy the larvae, gather and discard all fallen twigs as

Fig. 16-9. Engraving of the wood made by the larvae of the smaller European bark beetle.

soon as they are noticed; to destroy the adults, spray the trees with carbaryl (Sevin) or methoxychlor in June.

SPRING CANKERWORM. *Paleacrita vernata.* Spring cankerworm, also called inch worms or measuring worms, are looping worms, of various colors and about 1 inch in length, that chew the leaves. The adult female moth, which is ½ inch long and is wingless, climbs up the trunk to deposit eggs in early spring.

Control. Spray the leaves with *Bacillus thuringiensis* (Dipel, Thuricide), Imidan, or carbaryl (Sevin) while the worms are small. In spring the trunk may be banded with a sticky material such as Tree Tanglefoot to trap the adult females as they crawl up the tree to deposit their eggs.

FALL CANKERWORM. *Alsophila pometaria*. The leaves are chewed by the fall cankerworm, a black worm about 1 inch in length. The adult female is a wingless moth that deposits eggs in late fall on the twigs and branches.

Control. The spray recommended for spring cankerworm will control this pest. Bands of sticky material should be applied by late September to trap the adult females as they climb the trees.

ELM BORER. *Saperda tridentata*. Weakened trees are also subject to attack by the elm borer, a white grub 1 inch long which burrows into the bark and sapwood and pushes sawdust out through the bark crevices. The adult is a grayish-brown beetle ½ inch long, with brick-red bands and black spots. Eggs are deposited on the bark in June. The larvae overwinter in tunnels beneath the bark.

Control. Spray the bark of the trunk and branches in late June and mid-July with methoxychlor.

ELM SPANWORM. *Ennomos subsigniarius*. This pest, whose adult stage is known as the snow-white linden moth, caused heavy defoliation of deciduous trees in some parts of the northeastern United States in the summer of 1970. It feeds mostly on beech, elm, horsechestnut, linden, maple, and yellow birch. The larvae are about 1½ inches long, brownish-black with bright red head and anal segments. Eggs are laid in midsummer in groups on branches and hatch the following spring. The moths appear in late July in such great numbers that they resemble a snow shower.

Control. Carbaryl (Sevin) or Imidan sprays applied when the trees come in full leaf will control the spanworm.

LEOPARD MOTH BORER. *Zeuzera pyrina*. The young caterpillars enter the twigs at the bases of the buds and wilting results. The borers work downward, making large burrows in the larger limbs and trunks. Borers are whitish or light pink, marked with a number of dark spots. They are 2 to 3 inches long.

Control. Cut out and destroy infested twigs of small trees. Destroy the borers in larger branches by inserting a flexible wire into their tunnels to crush them, or inject a nicotine paste such as Bortox and then seal the openings with putty or chewing gum. The females, which are unable to fly, may be collected and destroyed before they have laid their eggs.

GYPSY MOTH. *Porthetria dispar*. The leaves of a large number of forest, shade, and ornamental trees are chewed by the gypsy moth larva, a hairy, dark gray caterpillar with pairs of blue and red dots down its back, and ranging up to 3 inches in length. Among the most susceptible trees are apple, speckled alder, gray, paper, and red birches, hawthorn, linden, oaks, poplars, and willows. Trees that are also favored as food include ash, balsam fir, butternut, black walnut, catalpa, red cedar, flowering dogwood, sycamore, and tuliptree. The average annual damage caused by feeding of this insect amounts to nearly 3 million dollars. More that a million acres of woodlands have been 25 to 100 per cent defoliated in a single year.

Control. Bacillus thuringiensis, Imidan, methoxychlor, carbaryl (Sevin), and Sevimol sprays all control this pest. They are most effective on young caterpillars.

Destroying the egg masses during winter or early spring also helps to protect valuable ornamental trees.

A synthetic sex lure, Diparlure, has recently been developed by United States Department of Agriculture scientists. Male gypsy moths are lured into special traps by this material, which enables Federal and state officials to determine the presence and density of gypsy moths in any particular area.

MOURNING-CLOAK BUTTERFLY. *Nymphalis antiopa*. The leaves are chewed by the caterpillar stage of this butterfly, which is 2 inches long, spiny, with a row of red spots on its back. The adult has yellow-bordered, purplish-brown wings. It overwinters in bark cavities and other protected places and deposits masses of eggs around small twigs in May.

Control. Spray with *Bacillus thuringiensis* or carbaryl (Sevin) when the caterpillars are small. Prune and destroy infested twigs and small branches.

WHITE-MARKED TUSSOCK MOTH. *Hemerocampa leucostigma*. The leaves are chewed by the tussock moth larva, a hairy caterpillar 1½ inches long, with a red head, longitudinal black and yellow stripes along the body, and a tussock of hair on the head in the form of a Y. The adult female is a wingless, gray, hairy moth which deposits white egg masses on the trunk and branches.

On the West Coast, the larvae of the western tussock moth, *H. vetusta*, feed on almond, apricot, cherry, hawthorn, oaks, pear, plum, prune, walnut, and willows in addition to elms.

Control. Spray the foliage with carbaryl (Sevin) when the young caterpillars begin to feed in spring.

SCALES. Eleven species of scales infest elms: brown elm, calico, camphor, citricola, cottony maple, elm scurfy, European elm, European fruit lecanium, oystershell, Putnam, and scurfy. The European elm scale, *Gossyparia spuria* (Fig. 16-10), is a soft scale not protected by a waxy covering.

Control. Spray all surfaces with a 'superior'* type miscible oil before the buds open in spring, or with malathion or carbaryl (Sevin) in late May and again in mid-June.

* See footnote, p. 249.

Fig. 16-10. European elm scale, *Gossyparia spuria*.

MITES. *Eotetranychus carpini* and *Metatetranychus ulmi*. These pests infest elms, causing the leaves to turn yellow prematurely.

Control. The inclusion of a miticide such as Kelthane in the regular insecticide spray will curb these pests.

CARPENTER WORM. See under Ash (Chapter 15).

ELM CALLIGRAPHA. See under Linden.

ELM SAWFLY. See under Linden.

FALL WEBWORM. See under Ash (Chapter 15).

FOREST TENT CATERPILLAR. See under Maple.

JAPANESE BEETLE. See under Linden.

LINDEN LOOPER. See under Linden.

GINKGO (*Ginkgo*)

Ginkgo, also known as maidenhair-tree, is unusually resistant to fungus and insect attack. A fungitoxic substance, α-hexenal, is believed to be responsible for its resistance to fungus diseases. Leaf spots have been attributed to three fungi: *Glomerella cingulata*, *Phyllosticta ginkgo*, and *Epicoccum purpurascens*. The damage by these fungi is negligible. In 1966 the author isolated a bacterium from another leaf spot (Fig. 16-11) but was unable to prove definitely that it was responsible for the spotting. In Czechoslovakia a similar disease is attributed to a virus.

Several wood-decaying fungi, including *Polyporus hirsutus, P. lacteus, P. tulipiferus, P. versicolor*, and *Fomes meliae*, have also been reported, but these are of rare occurrence.

Control. No effective control is known.

Fig. 16-11. Leaf spot of *Ginkgo biloba*, the cause of which is unknown.

Insects and other Pests

Few insects attack this tree. Among those occasionally found are the omnivorous looper, *Sabulodes caberata*; the grape mealybug, *Pseudococcus maritimus*; the white-marked tussock moth, *Hemerocampa leucostigma*; and the fruit tree leafroller, *Archips argyrospilus*.

The southern root-knot nema *Meloidogyne incognita* has been reported on ginkgo in Mississippi.

Control. Control measures are rarely applied.

HACKBERRY (*Celtis*)

Diseases

GANODERMA ROT. *Ganoderma lucidum.* This fungus is capable of attacking living trees, causing extensive decay of the roots and trunk bases. See under Maple.

LEAF SPOTS. *Cercosporella celtidis, Cylindrosporium defoliatum, Phleospora celtidis, Phyllosticta celtidis,* and *Septogloeum celtidis.* Many fungi cause leaf spots on hackberry in rainy seasons.

Control. Leaf spots are rarely serious enough to warrant control, but a copper or dithiocarbamate fungicide would probably be effective.

POWDERY MILDEW. *Uncinula parvula* and *U. polychaeta.* Both sides of the leaves are attacked, the mildew being visible either as a thin layer over the entire surface or in irregular patches. The small black fruiting bodies, ascocarps, develop mostly on the side opposite the mildew.

Control. Spray valuable specimens with Karathane or Benlate when mildew begins to become prevalent.

WITCHES' BROOM. In the eastern and central states the American hackberry is extremely susceptible to the witches' broom disease.

Symptoms. The early symptoms are visible on the buds during the winter. Affected buds are larger, more open, and hairier than normal ones. Branches that develop from such buds are bunched together, producing a broomlike effect, which is most evident in late fall or winter. The witches' brooms are more unsightly than harmful. Their presence, however, causes branches to break off more readily during wind storms, and the exposed wood is then subject to decay.

Cause. The exact cause of the witches' broom disease is not definitely known. An *Eriophyes* mite and the powdery mildew fungus *Sphaerotheca phytoptophylla* are almost constantly associated with the trouble and are believed to be responsible for the deformation of the buds that results in the bunching of the twigs.

Control. No effective control measures are known. Pruning back all infected twigs to sound wood and possibly spraying it with 1 part of lime sulfur in 10 parts of water in early spring might help. This should be followed with 2 applications of Kelthane at 2-week intervals starting in mid-May. The Chinese hackberry is less susceptible than the common hackberry and should be substituted in areas where the disease is prevalent. The southern hackberry (*Celtis mississippiensis*) is also less subject to witches' broom.

Insects and Related Pests

HACKBERRY NIPPLE-GALL MAKER. *Pachypsylla celtidis-mamma.* Small round galls opening on the lower leaf surfaces and resembling nipples are caused by a small jumping louse or psyllid. Another species of psyllid, *Pachypsylla celtidisvesicula,* produces blister galls.

Control. Spray with Cygon, Diazinon, or carbaryl (Sevin) when the leaves are one-quarter grown.

SCALES. Several species of scales including camphor, cottony maple, oystershell, Putnam, and San Jose occasionally infest this host.

Control. Malathion or carbaryl (Sevin) sprays when the young are crawling about in spring will provide control. Where infestations are heavy, a dormant oil or lime sulfur spray before leaves emerge in spring should also be applied.

MOURNING-CLOAK BUTTERFLY. See under Elm.

PAINTED HICKORY BORER. See under Hickory.

HICKORY (Carya)

Diseases

CANKER. Several canker diseases occasionally occur on hickory. These are associated with the fungi *Strumella coryneoidea, Nectria galligena,* and *Rosellinia caryae.*

Control. Prune dead or weak branches and paint the wounds with a good dressing. Avoid bark injuries and keep the trees in good vigor by fertilizing and by watering during dry spells. Keep borer and other insect infestations under control.

CROWN GALL. *Agrobacterium tumefaciens.* This bacterial disease occurs occasionally on hickory.

Control. Prune and destroy infected twigs or branches.

LEAF SPOTS. Several leaf-spotting fungi occur on hickory. Of these, *Gnomonia caryae* is the most destructive. It produces large, irregularly circular spots, which are reddish-brown on the upper leaf surface and brown on the lower. The margins of the spots are not sharply defined, as are those of many other leaf spots. The minute brown pustules on the lower surface are the summer spore-producing bodies. Another spore stage develops on dead leaves and releases spores the following spring to initiate new infections. The fungus *Monochaetia monochaeta* occasionally produces a leaf spot on hickory but is more prevalent on oaks. The fungus *Marssonina juglandis* also attacks hickory but is more destructive to black walnut. Two species of *Septoria, S. caryae* and *S. hicoriae,* also cause spots on hickory.

Control. Gather and destroy leaves in fall to kill fungi they harbor. To protect valuable specimens, spray the leaves with maneb or zeneb when the leaves unfurl, when half-grown, and again when full-grown.

POWDERY MILDEWS. Two fungi *Phyllactinia corylea* and *Microsphaera alni* cause mildewing of leaves.

Control. Control measures are rarely adopted.

WITCHES' BROOM. *Microstroma juglandis.* This fungus, which causes a leaf spot of butternut and black walnut, is capable of causing a witches' broom disease on shagbark hickory. The brooms, best seen when the trees are dormant, are composed of a compact cluster of branches. Early in the growing season the leaves on these branches are undersized and curled, later they turn black and fall.

Control. No effective control measures have been developed, but a dormant lime sulfur spray, followed by ferbam or ziram sprays during the growing season, is suggested.

Insects and Related Pests

HICKORY LEAF STEM GALL APHID. *Phylloxera caryaecaulis.* Hollow, green galls in June, which turn black in July, on leaves, stems, and small twigs of hickory are caused by the sucking of this small louse. In June the insides of the galls are lined with minute shiny lice of varying sizes. Galls range in size from a small pea to more than ½ inch in diameter.

Control. A dormant spray in late spring just as growth begins should destroy many overwintering lice. Carbaryl (Sevin), Meta-Systax R, or malathion sprays early in the growing season and repeated several times at 2-week intervals also give control. Sprays are not effective once the galls begin to develop.

HICKORY BARK BEETLE. *Scolytus quadrispinosus.* Young twigs wilt as a result of boring by the bark beetle, a dark brown insect ¹/₅ inch in length. The bark and sapwood are mined, and the tree may be girdled by the fleshy, legless larva ¼ inch long. The larvae overwinter under the bark.

Control Spray the foliage with carbaryl (Sevin) when the beetles appear in July. Remove and destroy severely infested trees, and peel the bark from the stump. Increase the vigor of weak trees by fertilization and watering.

CATERPILLARS. The leaves of park trees may be chewed by one of the following caterpillars: hickory-horned devil, red-humped, walnut, yellow-necked, and white-marked tussock moth.

Control. All caterpillars are readily controlled with *Bacillus thuringiensis* or carbaryl (Sevin) sprays.

JUNE BUGS. *Phyllophaga* spp. The leaves may be chewed during the night by light to dark brown beetles, which vary from ½ to ⅞ inch in length. The beetles rest in nearby fields during the day. The larva is ¾ to 1 inch long, white, and soft-bodied with a brown head. Three or more years are required for completion of the life cycle of most of the species.

Control. Spray the leaves with carbaryl (Sevin) during late May or early June, depending on the locality. The larval stage, which feeds on grasses in lawns and golf courses, can be controlled by treating the lawns with Diazinon or Dursban.

PECAN CIGAR CASEBEARER. *Coleophora caryaefoliella.* The leaves are mined, turn brown, and fall when infested by the pecan cigar casebearer, a larva ¹/₅ inch long, with a black head. The adult female is a moth with brown wings that have fringed hairs along the edge and a spread of ²/₅ inch. The larvae overwinter on twigs and branches in cigar-shaped cases ⅛ inch long.

Control. Spray with malathion as soon as the leaves are fully developed.

PAINTED HICKORY BORER. *Megacyllene caryae.* The sapwood of recently killed trees is soon riddled by painted hickory borers, creamy white larvae that attain a length of ¾ inch. The adult beetle is dark brown, has zigzag lines on the back, and is ¾ inch long. Eggs are deposited in late May or early June.

Control. Remove and destroy dead trees immediately. Inject a nicotine paste such as Bortox into the tunnels of live trees and then seal the openings with chewing gum, grafting wax, or putty. Spraying the bark with methoxychlor in early June might also help. Thiodan will also control this borer but its use is restricted to professional arborists and nurserymen in some states.

TWIG GIRDLER. *Oncideres cingulata.* Twigs girdled by this pest, a larva ½ inch long, are then broken off by the wind and fall to the ground. The adult is a reddish-brown beetle ¾ inch long. The larvae overwinter inside the twigs on the ground.

Control. Gather and destroy severed branches and twigs in autumn or early spring.

SCALES. Three species of scales—grape, obscure, and Putnam— occasionally infest hickories.

Control. Spray with malathion or carbaryl (Sevin) during late spring and early summer, or with lime sulfur just before growth starts in spring.

MITE. *Eotetranychus hicoriae.* This pest occasionally infests hickory leaves, causing them to turn yellow and drop prematurely.

Control. Spray with malathion or a miticide such as Aramite, Dimite, or Kelthane.

HORSECHESTNUT (*Aesculus*)

Diseases

ANTHRACNOSE. *Glomerella cingulata.* Terminal shoots become blighted down to several inches below the buds. Diseased tissue is shrunken, and the epidermis and young bark are ruptured; pustules are formed containing the pink spores of the anthracnose fungus.

Control. Spray as described below for leaf blotch.

CANKER. *Nectria cinnabarina.* This disease is said to attack the branches and to cause much defoliaton of old trees.

Control. Remove and destroy diseased branches. Spray 2 or 3 times at 10-day intervals with ziram, starting when the new growth emerges.

LEAF BLOTCH. *Guignardia aesculi.* This fungus disease is very serious in nurseries, where it often causes complete defoliation of the stock. The spots may be small or so large they include nearly all the leaf. At first they are merely discolored and water-soaked in appearance; later they turn a light reddish-brown with a very bright yellow marginal zone (Figs 16-12 and 16-13). When the whole leaf is infected it becomes dry and brittle and usually falls. The small black specks seen in the center of the spot are the fruiting bodies of the imperfect stage of the fungus. The

Fig. 16-12. Left: Early stage of the horsechestnut leaf blotch disease.

Fig. 16-13. Right: Advanced stage of the disease.

leaf stalks are also attacked. This leaf blotch is very similar to scorch, often seen on shade trees along streets and in city parks. The two diseases can be distinguished by the small, black, pimplelike fruiting bodies on the leaf blotch caused by the fungus. The fungus lives over winter on the old leaves where it has produced its perfect stage. The ascospores are the means by which the disease is spread in the spring. The first signs of infection may not appear until some time in July.

Control. Old leaves under diseased trees should be raked up and carted away. Spray with Dithane M-45, dodine, Fore, or zineb, 2 to 4 times at 10-day intervals, starting after the buds open. The total number of applications is governed by the weather. The disease is always more severe during the very wet springs.

LEAF SPOT. *Septoria hippocastani.* Small brown circular spots occasionally develop on the leaves of this host. The slender spores may be seen when the fruiting structures are observed under the microscope.

Control. The sprays recommended for leaf blotch will also control this fungus.

POWDERY MILDEW. *Uncinula flexuosa.* This disease is prevalent in the Middle West, where the undersides of leaves frequently are covered with white mold. The fruiting bodies of the winter stage of the fungus appear as small black dots over the mold.

Control. Spray trees with Benlate, wettable sulfur, or Karathane a few times at weekly intervals, starting when the mildew appears.

WOUND ROT. *Collybia velutipes.* The fungus enters through wounds and destroys the wood, later forming clusters of mushroomlike fruiting bodies. It is one of the fungi which may be found during the winter months still attached to the trees. The fruiting bodies have dark brown, velvety stalks.

Control. Remove limbs that have been killed by this rot and cover the cut surface to prevent the entrance of fungus spores into the wound.

OTHER DISEASES. Horsechestnut is susceptible to two stem diseases: wilt caused by *Verticillium albo-atrum* and bleeding canker by *Phytophthora cactorum.* The former is discussed in Chapter 14 and the latter under crown canker in dogwood, Chapter 15.

Some horsechestnut trees are susceptible to nonparasitic leaf scorch. The scorching usually becomes evident in July or August. First the margins of the leaves become brown and curled. Within 2 or 3 weeks the scorch may extend over the entire leaf. Some observers report that scorch is more prevalent in dry seasons, but serious injury also has been noted in wet seasons. Trees that are prone to scorch will show symptoms every year regardless of the kind of weather.

Control. Prune susceptible trees and provide them with good growing conditions. Feed and water when necessary. The application of an anti-desiccant such as Wilt-Pruf NCF after the leaves are fully expanded may be helpful.

Insect Pests

COMSTOCK MEALYBUG. *Pseudococcus comstocki.* This small, elliptical, waxy-covered insect attacks umbrella catalpa primarily, but it is also found on apple, boxwood, holly, horsechestnut, magnolia, maples, osage-orange, poplar, and Monterey pine. After hatching in late May, the young crawl up the trunk to the leaves, where they suck out the juices and devitalize the tree. Twigs, leaves, and trunks may be distorted as a result of heavy infestations. The eggs winter in bark crevices or in large masses hanging to the twigs.

Control. Malathion sprays in May and June are effective in controlling this pest.

JAPANESE BEETLE. *Popillia japonica.* During the bright hot days of July and August the leaves of the horsechestnut are the preferred food of the Japanese beetle, especially the leaves at the top and on the south side of the tree. The attacks are more or less sudden, and the top of the tree may quickly appear scorched. The large veins of the leaves are about all that is left after the beetles have done their work.

Control. Early in July when the beetles become numerous, spray with Diazinon, methoxychlor, or carbaryl (Sevin), as recommended by the manufacturer.

WALNUT SCALE. *Aspidiotus juglansregiae.* This is a round, saucer-shaped scale with a raised point in the center; it is about $^{1}/_{16}$ inch in diameter. Certain trees are more susceptible than others to infestation by this scale. The main trunks are most seriously attacked. Several layers of the scales collect in cracks and under the bark. They winter in a half-grown stage.

Many other scales also attack horsechestnuts. Among these are the cottony maple, maple phenacoccus, oystershell, Putnam, and scurfy scales.

Control. In spring when the temperature is well above freezing and while the tree is still dormant, spray with miscible oil. Malathion and carbaryl (Sevin) are also effective in late spring and early summer when the young scales are crawling about.

WHITE-MARKED TUSSOCK MOTH. *Hemerocampa leucostigma.* Among the caterpillars that infest park and streetside trees will be found the tussock moth caterpillar, recognizable by its red head and its yellow body with black marks and four tufts of hairs. The mature caterpillars are from ½ to 2 inches long. Late in summer, after the caterpillars have stopped feeding, they may be found crawling rapidly over the limbs and trunks toward the places where they pupate. The egg masses, which live through winter, are ½ inch long and are covered with a white frothy substance. The young hatch in May and can do considerable damage before they are discovered. There are usually two generations a year.

Control. During the days when they are feeding, the caterpillars can be controlled by spraying the trees with *Bacillus thuringiensis,* Dylox, methoxychlor, or carbaryl (Sevin). The egg masses are plainly visible and can be collected and destroyed in fall and winter.

BAGWORM. See under Arborvitae (Chapter 17).

FLATHEADED BORER. See under Maple.

KATSURA-TREE (*Cercidiphyllum*)

The only diseases recorded on this host are cankers caused by a species of *Phomopsis* and a species of *Dothiorella,* and shoestring root rot by *Armillaria.* Pruning cankered branches below the infected area should keep the canker disease under control. See Chapter 14 for the control of shoestring root rot.

LARCH (*Larix*)

Larches grow in almost any type of soil, including clay and limestone. They do best, however, in moist, loamy soils and in full sunshine. They do not tolerate dry soils or sandy hillsides in climates where the summers are hot.

The varieties most commonly used in ornamental plantings are the American larch or tamarack, the European larch, the Japanese larch, and the Western larch.

Diseases

EUROPEAN LARCH CANKER. This disease has been particularly destructive on larches in Europe for a long time. It is discussed here to acquaint tree men with its symptoms so that suspicious cases can be reported to the proper authorities immediately.

A few localized outbreaks arising from the importation of diseased plants from Europe occurred in the New England states from 1927 to 1935. Fortunately, these were stamped out as soon as discovered. Because of the similarity of symptoms to several other less destructive canker diseases, larch canker has been erroneously reported as existing on various trees.

European and American larches are known to be very susceptible to canker, whereas the Japanese larch is relatively resistant.

Symptoms. Stems of young trees and branches of small diameter die suddenly as the result of girdling by cankers. On trunks and branches of large diameter, cankers that increase in size each year are formed. A heavy flow of resin is evident from the cankers. The slowly developing cankers on the trunk or large branches result in considerable distortion and swelling of the affected members. White, hairy, cup-shaped fruiting bodies, about ¼ inch in diameter, develop in the cankered tissues.

Cause. The fungus *Trichoscyphella willkommii* causes larch canker. It enters through wounds and destroys the inner bark and cambium.

Control. European investigators have found that selection of favorable planting sites and maintenance of trees in good vigor discourage severe outbreaks of the disease. It is hoped that any future outbreaks in the United States will be discovered in time and eradicated so as to prevent extensive spread of the disease.

OTHER CANKERS. Four other species of fungi cause cankers: *Trichoscyphella ellisiana, Aleurodiscus amorphus, Leucostoma kunzei,* and *Phomopsis* sp.

Control. Canker diseases are difficult to control. Keeping trees in good vigor by feeding and watering when needed will help to reduce the severity of infection.

LEAF CAST. *Hypodermella laricis.* The needles of the American and Western larches and the spur shoots that bear them may be killed by this disease. Early symptoms are yellowing, followed by browning of the needles. Very small, elliptical, black fruiting bodies of the fungus appear on the dead leaves during the winter.

Several other fungi, including *Cladosporium* sp., *Lophodermium laricis, L. laricinum,* and *Meria laricis,* also cause leaf cast or leaf blights of larch. The leaf cast diseases are most common on ornamental larches in the western United States.

Control. Gather and destroy the needles in late fall or winter to eliminate the most important source of inoculum. This usually ensures satisfactory control. Spraying trees of ornamental value with dilute lime sulfur solution or with bordeaux mixture or any other copper fungicide may be advisable.

NEEDLE RUSTS. Three rust fungi attack larch needles. They develop principally on the needles nearest the branch tips. Affected needles turn yellow and have pale yellow fungus pustules on the lower surfaces.

The fungus *Melampsora paradoxa* occurs on American, European, Western, and Alpine larches. Its alternate hosts are several species of willows. Larches can be infected only by spores developing on willows, but the spores on willows can reinfect the willow.

The fungus *Melampsora medusae* attacks American larch and its alternate host, poplar. As with *M. paradoxa,* spores on larch cannot reinfect larch but must come from poplars.

Melampsoridium betulinum affects American larch and several species of birches. The spore stage on birch can infect birch as well as larch.

Control. Where larches are the more valuable specimens in an ornamental planting, the removal of the alternate host will prevent infection. Infected needles should be submitted to a rust specialist for determination of the exact species involved before attempts to eradicate the alternate hosts are made. Spraying trees of ornamental value with a dilute lime sulfur solution or with a copper fungicide may be advisable.

WOOD DECAY. Several species of fungi are constantly associated with the various types of wood decay of larch. Those most common in the eastern United States are *Fomes annosus, F. roseus, F. pini,* and *Polyporus schweinitzii.* They are found mainly on older, neglected trees.

Control. Little can be done to check wood decays by the time they are discovered. Maintaining valuable specimens in good vigor by periodic fertilization and by watering during dry spells will do much to prevent initial infections. Wounds on the trunks of such trees should be treated promptly.

Insects

LARCH CASEBEARER. *Coleophora laricella.* In May and June larches infested with this caterpillar suffer from an extensive browning of the leaves. The leaves are mined by a small caterpillar which used pieces of the needles to form a cigar-shaped case ¼ inch long. The black-headed caterpillar eats a hole in the leaf either at the end or in the middle and feeds as a miner in both directions as far as it can without leaving the case. The miners winter in the cases, which are attached to the twigs. The moths emerge in late June or July.

Control. To kill the casebearers that have survived the winter, spray in early spring with lime sulfur, dormant strength, or with a miscible oil. If this is not done, spray with carbaryl (Sevin) as soon as the insects begin to feed in late spring.

LARCH SAWFLY. *Pristiphora erichsonii.* In sawfly infestations, the needles are chewed by ¾- to 1-inch-long, olive-green larvae covered with small brown spines. The adult is a wasplike fly with a wingspread of ⁴/₅ inch. Eggs are deposited in incisions on twigs in late May and June. The larvae overwinter in brown cocoons on the ground.

Control. Gather and destroy fallen needles beneath the tree. If necessary, spray with methoxychlor or carbaryl (Sevin) in June or early July as soon as the insect begins to feed.

WOOLLY LARCH APHID. *Chermes strobilobius.* White woolly patches adhering to the needles are typical signs of this pest. The adult aphids are hidden beneath the woolly masses. The winged adults migrate to pines, and another generation returns to the larch the following season. Eggs are deposited at the bases of the needles in the spring. Young aphids overwinter in bark crevices.

Control. Spray with 1 part concentrated lime sulfur in 10 parts of water before growth starts, or with carbaryl (Sevin), Meta-Systox R, or malathion when the young are hatching in May.

OTHER INSECTS. The larvae of the gypsy moth, *Porthetria dispar,* and the white-marked tussock moth, *Hemerocampa leucostigma,* and the adult stage of the Japanese beetle also chew larch leaves.

Control. Spray with *Bacillus thuringiensis* or carbaryl (Sevin) when the pests begin to feed.

LINDEN (*Tilia*)

Diseases

CANKER. *Nectria cinnabarina.* Twigs and larger branches bear cinnabar-colored fruiting bodies of the fungus, each body about the size of a pinhead. These ascocarps break through the bark and are readily seen without a hand lens. The same or similar fungi attack apples, oaks, and other trees.

Other cankers on linden are caused by *Aleurodiscus griseo-canus* and *Strumella coryneoidea.*

Control. Cut out and destroy all cankered branches and remove and destroy twigs and branches that have fallen to the gound. Cover wounds with a good tree paint.

LEAF BLIGHT. *Cercospora microsora.* Circular brown spots with dark borders characterize this disease. The spots are very numerous, sometimes causing the entire leaf to turn brown and fall off. Young trees are most seriously affected. The sexual stage of the causal fungus is *Mycosphaerella microsora.*

Control. The same as for leaf blotch, below.

LEAF BLOTCH. European lindens are occasionally affected by the leaf blotch disease.

Symptoms. Elongated, light brown spots occur along the veins in the various parts of the leaf but chiefly near the tip. A conspicuous, narrow black band appears between the dead and the healthy tissue. In severe infections, the tree may be completely defoliated.

Cause. Leaf blotch is caused by the fungus *Gnomonia tiliae,* which is thought to overwinter on diseased fallen leaves.

Control. Gather and destroy fallen leaves. Spray with bordeaux mixture 4-4-50 or other copper fungicides, first when the leaves begin to grow, then when they are half-grown, and again after they are fully expanded. Ziram, which is effective against leaf blotch diseases of other shade trees, may also be effective on linden.

LEAF SPOTS. *Phlyctaena tiliae* and *Phyllosticta praetervisa.* These leaf spots are relatively rare and hence control measures are unnecessary.

POWDERY MILDEWS. *Microsphaera alni, Phyllactinia corylea,* and *Uncinula clintonii.* Lindens are quite susceptible to powdery mildew fungi. They rarely cause enough damage to require control measures.

Control. Valuable specimens may be sprayed with Benlate, wettable sulfur, or Karathane when the mildew appears.

OTHER DISEASES. Other diseases reported on lindens include canker caused by *Botryosphaeria dothidea,* and wilt by *Verticillium albo-atrum.*

Control. See under London planetree p. 456 and under Verticillium wilt p. 297.

Insects and Related Pests

LINDEN APHID. *Myzocallus tiliae.* Sap is sucked from the leaves and a sticky substance is exuded by a yellow-and-black aphid with clouded wings.

Control. Spray with carbaryl (Sevin) or malathion when the young aphids appear on the leaves in spring.

JAPANESE BEETLE. *Popillia japonica.* This beetle is attracted to certain trees in a planting, feeding high up on a sunny side (Figs. 16-14, 16-15, 16-16).

Control. Trees should be sprayed with a mixture of carbaryl (Sevin) and Kelthane in early July and again 10 days later.

ELM CALLIGRAPHA. *Calligrapha scalaris.* Ragged holes remain in leaves chewed by creamy-white larvae with yellow heads. The adult beetle is ⅜ inch long, oval, yellow, with green spots on the wing-covers and a broad, irregular, coppery-green stripe down the back. Lemon-yellow eggs are deposited on the lower leaf surface in late June or early July. The beetles hibernate in the ground.

Control. Spray the foliage with carbaryl (Sevin) as the larvae appear.

CATERPILLARS. Among the many caterpillars that chew the leaves of this host are cankerworms, the variable oak leaf caterpillar, and the larvae of the gypsy, cynthia, cecropia, and white-marked tussock moths.

Fig. 16-14. Japanese beetles on linden (normal size) and the characteristic appearance of the chewed leaves.

Fig. 16-15. Upper Inset: Japanese beetle enlarged.

Fig. 16-16. Lower Inset: Larval stage of Japanese beetle enlarged.

Control. Spray with carbaryl (Sevin) when the caterpillars are young.

BASSWOOD LEAF MINER. *Baliosus ruber.* The beetles feed on the under side of the leaves, eating out all tissues except the veins. The larvae also work on the under side, making large blisterlike mines. The foliage turns brown, withers, and falls off.

Control. See locust leaf miner under Black Locust.

ELM SAWFLY. *Cimbex americana.* These smooth caterpillars, pale green with a black stripe down the middle of the back, are about 1 inch long. They curl up tightly when at rest. Elm, willow, maple, and poplar are other hosts frequented.

Control. The standard methoxychlor sprays used to control this pest on elms will also work on linden. Straight methoxychlor sprays may bring on an outbreak of mites, and it is therefore wise to include a mite-killer in the mixture.

LINDEN LOOPER. *Erannis tiliaria.* This pest, also known as the basswood looper, infests apple, brasswood, birch, elm, hickory, and maple. The caterpillars are 1½ inch long at maturity, bright yellow, with 10 longitudinal wavy black lines down the back. The moth, buff colored with a 1¾-inch wingspread, deposits its eggs from October to November.

Control. Carbaryl (Sevin) or methoxychlor sprays applied when the young caterpillars begin to feed will provide control.

LINDEN MITE. *Eriophyes tiliae.* In midsummer, especially in dry weather, the leaves become infested with this mite, which causes them to turn brown and dry up.

Light brown woolly patches along the veins on the lower leaf surface are produced by the mite *Eriophyes liosoma.*

Control. Lindens are especially susceptible to mite damage when straight methoxychlor sprays are used. Hence valuable trees should be sprayed with a good miticide such as Kelthane. A good preventive is to use this material with the methoxyclor from the start.

EUROPEAN LINDEN BARK BORER. *Chrysoclista linneela.* This whitish larva with a light brown head bores into the bark of lindens. It does not affect the cambial area but honeycombs the bark to such an extent that decay-producing organisms have easy access.

Control. No control measures have been developed.

LINDEN BORER. *Saperda vestita.* Broad tunnels beneath the bark near the trunk base or in roots are made by the linden borer, a slender white larva 1 inch long. The adult, a yellowish-brown beetle ¾ inch long, with three dark spots on each wingcover, feeds on green bark. Eggs are deposited in small bark crevices made by the beetle.

Other borers that attack lindens are the flatheaded apple tree and the brown wood.

Control. Dig out the borers with a flexible wire, or inject a nicotine paste such as Bortox into the tunnels and seal the openings. Spraying the

trunk base with methoxychlor may control many of the young larvae
after they hatch out of their eggs.

SCALES. Nine species of scale insects infest this host: cottony maple,
European fruit lecanium, oystershell, Putnam, San Jose, terrapin, tuliptree, walnut, and willow.

Control. Valuable specimens should be sprayed from time to time with
malathion or carbaryl (Sevin).

WALNUT LACE BUG. *Corythucha juglandis.* This pest also infests ash,
hickory, and mulberry.

Control. Spray valuable specimens with malathion or carbaryl (Sevin).

LOCUST, BLACK *(Robinia)*

Diseases

CANKER. *Aglaospora anomala, Nectria galligena,* and *Diaporthe oncostoma.*
Cankers on twigs and death of the distal portions may be due to any one
of these three fungi.

Control. Prune and destroy infected twigs.

DAMPING-OFF. *Phytophthora parasitica.* In nurseries, serious damage to
seedings from 1 to 3 weeks old may be caused by this fungus. The young
plants droop and their cotyledons curl. This is followed by wilting and
the collapse of the entire seedling, which decays within a few days.

Control. Use clean soil or steam-pasteurize old soil for setting out
seedlings.

LEAF SPOTS. *Cladosporium epiphyllum, Cylindrosporium solitarium, Gloeosporium revolutum, Phleospora robiniae,* and *Phyllosticta robiniae.* Many fungi
cause leaf spots of black locust.

Control. Control measures are seldom practiced.

POWDERY MILDEWS. *Erysiphe polygoni, Microsphaera diffusa,* and *Phyllactinia corylea.* White coating of the leaves occurs only occasionally on black
locust.

Control. These mildews are never serious enough to warrant control
measures.

WOOD DECAY. Nearly all the older black locusts growing along roadsides and in groves in the eastern United States harbor one of several
wood-decay fungi. Nearly all these decays have followed infestation of
the locust borer, *Megacyllene robiniae.*

The fungus *Fomes rimosus* causes a spongy, yellow rot of the
heartwood. It infects the trunk through tunnels made by the locust
borer or through dead older branches. After extensive decay of the
woody tissues, the fungus grows toward the bark surface where it
produces hard, woody, bracket- or hoof-shaped fruiting structures
nearly 1 foot wide. The upper surface of the structure is brown or black
and is cracked; the lower surface is reddish-brown.

The fungus *Polyporus robiniophilus* produces a soft, white rot of the heartwood. Like the *Fomes,* it infects the tree through locust borer tunnels and dead branches. The fruiting structures, which develop on dead bark, are at first white and firm, later brown and corky.

Control. Because wood decays of black locust become established mainly through locust borer tunnels, their prevention rests primarily on freedom from the insect pests. Effective control of the latter, however, cannot easily be attained, and for this reason heartwood decays will continue to be prevalent. Cavity treatments should never be attempted on black locusts.

WITCHES' BROOM. Black locust and honey locust are subject to this condition. The disease, though common on the sprouts, rarely occurs on the large trees. It is characterized by production in late summer of dense clusters or bunches of twigs from an enlarged axis. The bunched portions ordinarily die during the following winter. The disease was long considered to be virus-induced, but recent evidence educed by Japanese and American scientists indicates that a mycoplasma-like organism is the cause of many witches' broom diseases.

Control. Infected trees appear to recover naturally. No definite control measures are known.

Insects

LOCUST BORER. *Megacyllene robiniae.* Galleries formed by this borer may extend in all directions into the wood, which is discolored or blackened. The trees become badly disfigured. Young plantings may be entirely destroyed. (Fig. 16-17). The adult is a black beetle about ¾ inch long, spotted with bright yellow, transverse, zigzag lines (Fig. 16-18). The young grubs first bore into the inner bark and sapwood.

Control. Cut and destroy badly infested trees. Kill young borers in trunk and branches by inserting Bortox into the burrows and sealing the openings with chewing gum or putty. Spraying with methoxychlor in late August or early September gives effective control. Maintain trees in good vigor by proper watering, pruning, and feeding.

LOCUST LEAF MINER. *Xenochalepus dorsalis.* The beetles live through the winter and attack the young leaves in early May. They skeletonize the upper surface and lay their eggs on the under surface. The larvae enter the leaf and make irregular mines in the green tissue. A second generation of beetles emerges in September.

Control. Spray with Diazinon or carbaryl (Sevin) early in July to kill the young larvae as they begin to mine the leaves.

LOCUST TWIG BORER. *Ecdytolopha insiticiana.* Elongated, gall-like swellings 1 to 3 inches long on the twigs are caused by the feeding and irritation of the pale yellow larvae of the locust twig borer. The adult

Fig. 16-17. Branch dieback of black locust caused by locust borer infestations.

Fig. 16-18. Adult stage of the locust borer, *Megacyllene robiniae*.

female is a grayish-brown moth with a wing expanse of ¾ inch. The pest overwinters in the pupal stage among fallen leaves.

Control. Prune and destroy infested twigs in August, and gather and destroy fallen leaves in autumn.

SCALES. Eight species of scale insects infest black locust: black, cottony cushion, cottony maple, oystershell, Putnam, San Jose, soft, and walnut.

Control. Spray with malathion or carbaryl (Sevin) when the young scales are crawling about in spring. Repeat the application in about 2 weeks.

Other Pests

DODDER. *Cuscuta* sp. This well-known flowering plant, which grows as a parasite on various plants, causes considerable damage to seedlings. It may also be a factor in transmission of certain virus diseases in border plantings.

Control. Dacthal spray applied to the soil in early spring will prevent germination of dodder seed.

LOCUST, HONEY (Gleditsia)

Diseases

LEAF SPOT. *Linospora gleditsiae*. This is rather a serious blight in the southern states. Numerous black fruiting bodies (acervuli) of the fungus develop on the lower side of the leaves. The ascocarpic stage develops throughout the summer and lives through the winter. In the Middle West other leaf spots are caused by *Cercospora condensata* and *C. olivacea*.

Control. Gathering and destroying of all fallen leaves should provide practical control.

CANKERS. Five fungi, *Thyronectria austroamericana*, *T. denigrata*, *Cytospora gleditschiae*, *Dothiorella* sp., and *Kaskaskia gleditsiae*, are known to cause stem cankers on honey locust. The author found that the first-named fungus killed a number of honey locusts at the United Nations gardens in New York several years ago. (Fig. 16-19) The last-named fungus causes extensive areas of necrosis, cracking, and peeling of the trunk bark along with a brown discoloration.

Control. Effective control measures have not been developed.

POWDERY MILDEW. *Microsphaera alni.* This mildew fungus is widespread on honey locusts.

Control. Control measures are never used for this disease on this host.

RUST. *Ravenelia opaca.* One rust disease is known to occur on honey locust.

Control. No control measures are necessary.

Fig. 16-19. The honey locust (*Gleditsia triacanthos*) at left in the United Nations Gardens died as a result of infection by the fungus *Thyronectria austroamericana.*

WOOD DECAY. Like most trees, honey locusts are subject to wood-decaying fungi. Among the more prevalent ones are a species of *Fomes, Daedalea ambigua, D. elegans, Ganoderma curtisii, G. lucidum,* and *Xylaria mali. G. lucidum* occurs on living trees, which suggests that it is a vigorous parasite, as it is on species of maple.

Control. No effective controls are known. Avoid mechanical injuries around the base of the tree, provide good growing conditions, and feed and water the tree to maintain good vigor.

Insects and Related Pests

HONEY LOCUST BORER. *Agrilus difficilis.* A flat-headed borer burrows beneath the bark of honey locust and eventually may girdle the tree. Large quantities of gum exude from the bark near the infested nodes. The adult beetles, which emerge in June, are elongate, ½ inch long, black with a metallic luster.

Control. No really effective controls are known, although it is likely that methoxychlor sprays applied to the trunks during the egg-laying period in mid-June and early July may prove effective.

POD GALL MIDGE. *Dasineura gleditschiae.* This midge causes globular galls ⅛ inch in diameter at the growing tips (Fig. 16-20). The pest seems to prefer some of the newer thornless varieties such as 'Moraine' and 'Shademaster' to the ordinary honey locust. The adult midge appears in April when the leaves begin to emerge. It deposits eggs singly or in clusters among the young leaflets. The larvae hatch within a few days and begin to feed on the inner surface of the leaflets.

Control. No effective control is available at present.

HONEY LOCUST PLANT BUG. *Diaphnocoris chlorionis.* Discoloration of leaves and stunting of new growth is caused by this widely distributed pest (Figs. 16-21, 16-22). Complete defoliation may occur during heavy infestations. Adults are ³/₁₆ inch long and pale green. Both adults and nymphs are difficult to detect because their color blends with foliage and growing tips on which they feed. Yellow-leaved strains of honey locust, such as 'Sunburst,' are more susceptible to this bug than are green-leaved ones like 'Shademaster.'

Control. Spray susceptible varieties with carbaryl (Sevin) a week or 10 days after buds burst.

WEBWORM. *Homadaula albiziae.* This pest is more common on the silk-tree (*Albizia julibrissin*), but in some parts of the country it is a serious pest of honey locust.

Control. Spraying with carbaryl (Sevin) or Diazinon will control this pest, but 3 to 5 applications are necessary to provide season-long protection. A single soil application of either phorate (Thimet) or Di-Syston or injection of Bidrin into the trunk base will also provide control. These

Fig. 16-20. Pod gall of honey locust caused by the insect *Dasineura gleditschiae*. Uninfested leaves are seen on the lower right side.

materials, however, are extremely toxic and should be handled only by a professional arborist or nurseryman who has been issued a use permit.

SPIDER MITE. *Eotetranychus multidigituli.* This mite causes yellow stippling of the leaves, which drop prematurely. Defoliated trees usually leaf out again in late summer but are considerably weakened.

Control. Spray with Kelthane or Tedion early in July and repeat every 2 weeks as needed.

BAGWORM. See under Arborvitae (Chapter 17).

COTTONY MAPLE SCALE. See under Maple.

SAN JOSE SCALE. See under Cherry, Japanese Flowering (Chapter 15).

SPRING AND FALL CANKERWORMS. See under Elm.

MAGNOLIA–See Chapter 15.

Fig. 16-21. Left: Honey locust plant bug injury and discoloration of foliage.
Fig. 16-22. Right: Adult of honey locust plant bug.

MAIDENHAIR–See Ginkgo.

MAPLE (*Acer*)

Fungus and Bacterial Diseases

ANTHRACNOSE. *Gloeosporium apocryptum.* In rainy seasons this disease may be serious on sugar and silver maples and on boxelder and to a lesser extent on other maples. The spots are light brown and irregular in shape. They may enlarge and run together, causing the death of the entire leaves. Leaves partially killed appear as if scorched. Another anthracnose, *Gnomonia veneta,* more frequently found on sycamores, attacks maples also.

Control. Spraying 3 times at 2-week intervals with bordeaux mixture or some other copper fungicide or with zineb, starting when the leaves begin to unfurl in spring, will provide control.

LEAF SPOT (PURPLE EYE). *Phyllosticta minima.* The spots are ¼ inch or more in diameter, more or less irregular, with brownish centers and purple-brown margins. The black pycnidia of the fungus develop in the center of the spots. This disease is most severe on red, sugar, and silver maples but also occurs on Japanese, Norway, and sycamore maples.

Control. Spray with zineb 3 times at 2-week intervals, starting when the leaves are unfolding from the buds.

BASAL CANKER. The author was the first to discover this disease on Norway maples in New Jersey about 35 years ago.

Symptoms. An early symptom is a thin crown resulting from a decrease in the number and size of the leaves. Trees die within a year or two following this period of weak vegetative growth. Another, more striking symptom is the presence of cankers at the base of the trunk near the soil line. The inner bark, the cambium, and in many instances the sapwood are reddish-brown in the cankered area (Fig. 16-23). Death occurs when the entire root system decays or when the cankers completely girdle the trunk.

Cause. Basal canker is caused by the fungus *Phytophthora cinnamomi*. This fungus was known as *P. cambivora* when the author first isolated it from diseased Norway maples. The fungus appears to be most destructive on trees growing in poorly drained or shallow soils.

Control. No effective control measures are known. Diseased trees should be removed and destroyed. New plantings of Norway maples should be made in well-drained soils, high in organic matter. Frost cracks and mechanical injuries near the base of the trunk should be

Fig. 16-23. Bark cut away to show the reddish-brown discoloration of the sapwood produced by the fungus *Phytophthora cinnamomi*.

properly treated and dressed and trees fertilized and watered to maintain good vigor.

BLEEDING CANKER. This highly destructive disease was first reported
from the New England states centering around Rhode Island. The
author found the first case of this disease in New Jersey in October 1940.
Norway, red, sycamore, and sugar maples as well as oaks, elms, and
American beech are susceptible to this disease. The severity of the
disease is associated in some way with hurricane damage.

Symptoms. The disease is named for its most characteristic primary
symptom, the oozing of sap from fissures overlying cankers in the bark.
Infected inner bark, cambium, and sapwood develop a reddish-brown
necrotic lesion, which commonly exhibits an olive-green margin. These
symptoms differ markedly from those produced in trees affected with
basal canker. A secondary symptom, the wilting of the leaves and dying
back of the branches, is said by one investigator to be due to a toxic
material secreted by the causal fungus.

Cause. Bleeding canker is caused by the fungus *Phytophthora cactorum*,
which is closely related to the fungus that causes basal canker. *P. cactorum*
is also responsible for the crown canker disease of dogwoods (p. 336).
The author has produced infection in dogwood with the fungus isolated
from Rhode Island maples. The same organism kills the growing tips of
rhododendrons during rainy seasons and is known to attack a large
number of other trees, including apple, apricot, cherry, peach, and
plum.

Control. As with basal canker, no effective control measures are known.

BACTERIAL LEAF SPOT. *Pseudomonas aceris.* In California the leaves of
Oregon maple (*A. macrophyllum*) may be spotted by a bacterium. Spots
vary from pin-point dots to areas ¼ inch in diameter. They first appear
as though water-soaked and are surrounded by a yellow zone; later they
turn brown and black.

Control. Preventive sprays containing a copper fungicide applied in
early spring should control this organism.

LEAF BLISTER. *Taphrina sacchari.* The lesions produced by this fungus
are circular or irregular in shape, pinkish or buff on the underside, and
ochre or buff above. Sugar and black maple are most susceptible.
Blistering, curling, and blighting of other maples are produced by
different species: *Taphrina lethifer* affects mountain maple; *T. aceris*,
Rocky Mountain hard maple, *T. dearnessii*, red maple; and *T. carveri*,
silver maple.

Control. Leaf blisters on valuable specimens can be prevented by
applying dormant lime sulfur, ferbam, or ziram spray just before growth
starts in spring.

BULL'S-EYE SPOT is a name coined by the author to describe a spot that
occurs on red, silver, sugar, and sycamore maples in particularly shaded

spots in the eastern United States. The spots show a distinct target pattern with layers of concentric rings (Fig. 16-24). The causal organism is *Cristulariella pyramidalis*.

Control. Control measures have not been developed.

TAR SPOT. *Rhytisma acerinum.* Street maples are seldom infected with this fungus, but red maples in forests may be prematurely defoliated. The spots are irregular, shining black tarlike discolorations up to ½ inch in diameter, developed on the upper sides of the leaves. The dark color is due to the masses of brown or black mycelium.

Control. Rake up and discard the leaves in fall. If necessary spray with a copper fungicide or ferbam when buds are opening, and when severe, repeat several times at 2-week intervals.

OTHER FUNGUS LEAF SPOTS. *Rhytisma punctatum* causes a minute black spotting on many species of maples. It is rare in the East but rather prevalent on the Pacific Coast. A number of other leaf spots that occur occasionally are caused by fungi belonging to the genera *Cercospora, Septoria, Cylindrosporium,* and *Monochaetia.*

Control. Spray as for tar spot.

NECTRIA CANKER. *Nectria cinnabarina.* Cankers appear on twigs and branches and occasionally develop on the trunks to such an extent as to cause the death of the trees. Reddish fungus fruiting bodies develop in large numbers. Although the fungus is most common on maples and lindens, it attacks a wide variety of other hardwood trees. Another fungus, *Nectria ditissima*, causes the development of irregular cankers, accompanied by the formation of thick calluses, which later become diseased and leave an open wound. Cankers should be cut out well beyond the diseased areas and the wounds protected by a good tree paint. The vigor of the trees should be increased by fertilization.

Boxelder and red and sugar maples occasionally show another type of

Fig. 16-24. Bull's-eye spot of sycamore maple.

canker, which differs strikingly from that produced by either of the Nectria fungi. The cankers are irregularly circular and contain broad, slightly raised concentric rings of callus tissue. The cankered tissue is firmly attached to the wood with heavy, white-to-buff, fan-shaped wefts of fungus tissue under the bark near the margins. Tiny black fungus bodies are present in the centers of the old cankers. The fungus responsible for this type of canker is known as *Eutypella parasitica*. Other cankers may be caused by the following fungi: *Botryosphaeria dothidea*, *Cytospora* sp., *Fusarium solani*, *Nectria galligena*, *Physalospora obtusa*, *Septobasidium fumigatum*, and *Valsa sordida*.

Control. Cankers on trunks can rarely be eradicated by surgical methods once they have become very extensive. Those on branches can be destroyed by removing and discarding the affected members. Removal of dead branches, avoidance of unnecessary injuries, and maintenance of trees in vigorous condition by fertilization and watering are probably the best means known of preventing canker formation.

GANODERMA ROT. *Ganoderma lucidum.* Rapid decline and death of many trees growing along city streets were found by the author to be due to this fungus. It forms large, reddish fruit bodies with varnishlike coating at the base of the infected tree or on its surface roots (Fig. 16-25 and 16-26). Red and Norway maples appear to be most susceptible.

Control. No control is known for diseases of this type. Planting trees in deep, fertile soil, avoiding bark and root injuries, and fertilizing and watering properly will reduce chances of infection.

PHOMOPSIS BLIGHT. *Phomopsis acerina.* Dying of Norway maples along city streets has been attributed by the author and by Dr. J. C. Carter of Illinois to infection by this fungus.

Control. No controls have been developed.

POWDERY MILDEWS. *Uncinula circinata* and *Phyllactinia corylea.* These mildews, which are rarely serious, can be controlled by spraying with Benlate, wettable sulfur, or with Karathane.

SAPSTREAK. *Ceratocystis coerulescens.* This killing disease of sugar maples was first described by Dr. George Hepting of the United States Forest Service from North Carolina in 1944. It has since been reported from New England and the lake region of the Midwest. Typical symptoms include thinning crowns with undersized chlorotic foliage, followed by death of the tree. Sapstreak also affects tuliptree in woodlands.

Control. No effective control has been developed.

TRUNK DECAY. In New England sugar maples tapped for their sap are subject to a serious trunk decay caused by the fungus *Valsa leucostomoides*. In longitudinal section the affected areas appear as truncated cones with pale yellow centers bordered by deep olive or greenish-black streaks.

Control. Tap holes should be sprayed or painted with a fungicide at the time the spiles are pulled. The trees should be tapped on the diagonal or up and down the butts.

Fig. 16-25. The author is examining a dying Norway maple infected with the fungus *Ganoderma lucidum*. He is holding a live branch cut from the healthy side of this tree. the fungus bodies at the base of the tree. **Inset:** A culture of the *Ganoderma* fungus growing on a synthetic medium in the laboratory.

Fig. 16-26. Close-up of the *Ganoderma* fungus at the base of a dying maple tree.

WILTS. Already discussed in detail in Chapter 14, wilt is perhaps the most important vascular disease of maples. Positive diagnosis of this disease is possible only by collecting adequate specimens of discolored sapwood beneath the bark of the trunk near the soil line and culturing the material in the laboratory. The *Verticillium* fungus, however, is not the only fungus capable of discoloring the sapwood of maples. Several others have been found to do so. Some of these, however, have not killed trees that were artificially inoculated with them, while others have. The parasitic kinds have not yet been identified.

Physiological Disease

MAPLE DECLINE. Weakening and death of sugar maples along heavily traveled highways in the northeastern United States has been attributed to excessive use of salts (sodium and calcium chlorides) during the winter months. (See Chapter 10.)

Insects and Mites That Attack Leaves

Besides the leaf-eating insects described below, there are others that attack maple leaves. These include the elm sawfly, *Cimbex americana*; brown-tail moth, *Nygmia phaeorrhoea*; gypsy moth, *Porthetria dispar*, in certain eastern states; white-marked tussock moth, *Hemerocampa leuco-stigma*; American dagger moth, *Acronicta americana*; saddled prominent caterpillar, *Heterocampa guttivitta*; and the oriental moth, *Cnidocampa flavescens*. These are readily controlled by spraying with carbaryl (Sevin) or methoxychlor. The canker worms, *Paleacrita vernata* and *Alsophila pometaria* (also known as inch worms and measuring-worms), and bag-worms, *Thyridopteryx ephemeraeformis*, also are controlled in this way.

BOXELDER BUG. *Leptocoris trivittatus.* The leaves of boxelder are injured by the sucking of young bright-red bugs. The adult stage is a stout, ½ inch long, grayish-black bug with three red lines on the back (Fig. 16-27). All stages of this pest are clustered on the bark and branches in early fall.

Control. Spray bark with carbaryl (Sevin) when clusters of bugs appear in late May or early June. Because this bug feeds on seeds of pistillate (female) trees, one should plant only staminate (male) trees.

FOREST TENT CATERPILLAR. *Malacosoma disstria.* These caterpillars, bluish with a row of diamond-shaped white spots along the back, feed individually on leaves of maple, birch, oak, and poplar, but do not form a tent in the forks of smaller branches as do the eastern tent caterpillars (*Malacosoma americanum*), which have a white stripe down the back. The egg masses look the same, about ½ inch long, completely surrounding the twig, and having a brown, varnished appearance.

Control. They can be quite easily controlled by spraying with carbaryl (Sevin).

GREENSTRIPED MAPLEWORM. *Anisota rubicunda.* These caterpillars are pale yellowish-green, 1½ inches long, with large black heads; the stripes along the back are alternately pale yellowish-green and dark green. The insects prefer red and silver maples.

Control. They can be quite easily controlled by spraying with carbaryl (Sevin).

Fig. 16-27. Boxelder bug enlarged.

JAPANESE LEAFHOPPER. *Orientus ishidae*. These insects cause a characteristic brown blotching with a bright yellow margin, which merges into the green part of the leaf.

Control. Spray with carbaryl (Sevin) in late May or early June.

LEAFHOPPER. *Alebra albostriella*. The Norway maple may become seriously infested with these yellowish leafhoppers; they also cause swellings on the twigs by depositing eggs under the young bark.

Control. Spray in early spring with carbaryl (Sevin).

LEAF STALK BORER. *Nepticula sericopeza*. Though these small borers more commonly infest the fruit of Norway maples, they may attack the leaf stalks in June. The borers tunnel in the stalks, causing a black discoloration about ½ inch from the base. The lower end of the stalk is somewhat enlarged. These borers occasionally cause severe defoliation. The adult is a minute moth with spinelike hairs on the surface of its wings.

Control. Spray with a dominant miscible oil in early spring to destroy the cocoons. If this is not done, spray with methoxychlor in the latter part of May.

PETIOLE BORER. *Caulocampus acericaulis*. This yellowish, smooth sawfly larva causes leaf fall of sugar maple. It tunnels in the upper end of the leaf stalk about ½ inch from the blade. The leaf blades fall off in May and June and sometimes the leaf stalk itself falls. Only the leaves of the lower branches are usually seriously infested.

Control. Malathion or methoxychlor sprays as the leaves open in May should provide control. This pest is rarely serious enough, however, to warrant control measures.

MAPLE LEAF CUTTER. *Paraclemensia acerifoliella*. Much defoliation of sugar maple and beech trees results from the work of this small caterpillar, which is about ¼ inch long. It cuts out small sections of the leaves and forms a case in which it hides while it feeds. It skeletonizes a ringlike portion, the center of which may fall out.

Control. Rake up and discard all leaf litter in fall to kill the hibernating pupa, or apply carbaryl (Sevin) to the foliage.

MAPLE TRUMPET SKELETONIZER. *Epinotia aceriella*. Red and sugar maple leaves are folded loosely by small green larvae which develop inside a long trumpetlike tube.

Control. Methoxychlor, carbaryl (Sevin), or Diazinon sprays applied in mid-July will control this pest.

NORWAY MAPLE APHID. *Periphyllus lyropictus*. The leaves of Norway maple are subject to heavy infestation by these hairy aphids, which are greenish with brown markings. Like other aphids, they secrete large amounts of honeydew. The leaves attacked become badly wrinkled, discolored, and reduced in size. Defoliation may follow. Several other species, including *Drepanaphis acerifoli*, *Periphyllus aceris*, and *P. negundinis*, also occur on maples.

Control. Spray in early summer with malathion or carbaryl (Sevin), being careful to cover the undersides of the leaves.

OCELLATE LEAF GALL. *Cecidomyia ocellaris.* These galls are less than ½ inch in diameter, with cherry-red margins; they are easily confused with purple eye leaf spot. They occur on red maple but are usually not injurious. The little maggots, which may be seen at the center of the spot, soon drop off.

BLADDER-GALL MITE. *Vasates quadripes.* The upper surfaces of maple leaves are often covered with small, green, wartlike galls, which later turn blood-red. These are caused by the feeding of this mite. If the galls are very numerous, the leaves become deformed.

Control. Spray with dormant oil plus ethion in late April. Kelthane spray in spring when the buds show green color and again 2 weeks later should also protect the foliage.

OTHER MITES. Other maple galls are caused by the mites *Phyllocoptes aceris-crumena* and *Eriophyes acericola.* The galls are about ¹/₅ inch long, tapering at both ends (fusiform). They develop on the upper side of the leaf and, when numerous, render the foliage unsightly. Spray with lime sulfur at blossom time or with Kalthane in early June.

Several other species of *Eriophyes* and *Phyllocoptes* produce large blotches along the veins or between them. Brilliant purple, red, or pink minute blisterlike or pilelike growths are due to the mites. A dormant strength lime sulfur spray just before leaf buds open, or a Kelthane spray when the buds show green color, is recommended for control of these mites.

The mite *Paratetranychus aceris* occasionally infests maple leaves, causing mottling and premature yellowing. A spray containing Aramite, Chlorobenzilate, or Kelthane when these mites are noticed in early June will give good control.

Scale Insects

MAPLE PHENACOCCUS. *Phenacoccus acericola.* The leaves of sugar maple may be covered on the underside by cottony masses that envelop the females in July, as is well shown in Figure 16-28. The males collect in the crevices of the bark and give it a white, chalky appearance. There are several generations a year. Predacious insects feed on the eggs of this scale.

Control. Spray with malathion or carbaryl (Sevin) in spring just as the buds burst. Repeat the spray in early August.

COTTONY MAPLE SCALE. *Pulvinaria innumerabilis.* Silver maples are especially susceptible to infestation by this scale. Smaller branches are often covered with large white cushionlike masses. The scale itself is brown, from ⅛ to ¼ inch in diameter; the whole mass is about ½ inch in diameter. The cottony mass may contain as many as 500 eggs in June.

The young move out and infest the leaves; later they migrate to the branches, being found especially on their undersides.

Control. Spray with lime sulfur in early spring when trees are dormant. Malathion or carbaryl (Sevin) may be applied during midsummer when the young are crawling.

OTHER SCALES. Several other scales attack maples. Among them are the terrapin scale, *Lecanium nigrofasciatum*, gloomy scale, *Chrysomphalus tenebricosus*, and Japanese scale, *Leucaspis japonica*.

Control. These may be controlled by spraying with dormant miscible oil or lime sulfur. The latter is safer. Malathion or carbaryl (Sevin) sprays are most effective when the young scales are crawling.

Fig. 16-28. Maple phenacoccus (*Phenacoccus acericola*) on sugar maple leaf.

Wood Borers

Limbs infested with borers are the first to break after a heavy snowstorm or after they have been coated with ice. Five or six species of wood-boring insects infest maples.

FLATHEADED BORER. *Chrysobothris femorata*. Trees in poor vigor are attacked by this light yellow larva, 1 inch long, which builds flattened galleries below the bark, often girdling the tree. The adult is a dark coppery-brown beetle, ½ inch in length, which deposits eggs in bark crevices in June and July. The pest overwinters underneath the bark in the larval stage.

Control. Increase the tree's vigor by feeding and watering, or protect recently transplanted trees with crepe wrapping paper. Spray the trunk and branches with methoxychlor in mid-May and repeat twice more at 2-week intervals. Borers active in the trees can be killed by inserting a flexible wire in the borer holes.

LEOPARD MOTH BORER. *Zeuzera pyrina.* This brown-headed borer is white or slightly pinkish and marked by blackish spots on the body. Full-grown borers may be 3 inches long and nearly ½ inch in diameter. They winter in the tunnels they make. Besides their cylindrical burrows they make wide cavities which so weaken the limbs that they break off very readily. Soft maples are especially susceptible.

Control. Preventive treatments include spraying the trunk and main branches with methoxychlor in late May and repeating 4 times at 2-week intervals. On valuable young trees that are already infested, the boring caterpillars can be killed by inserting into their tunnels a flexible wire or pastes containing nicotine or a few drops of carbon disulfide, and then sealing the openings with putty or chewing gum.

METALLIC BORER. *Dicerca divaricata.* The larvae of these brass- or copper-colored beetles frequently invade the limbs of peach, cherry, beech, maple, and other deciduous trees. The beetles live 2 or 3 years as borers in the trees and lay their eggs in August and September. The adults have been known to cause much defoliation.

Control. Infested limbs should be cut and destroyed to get rid of the grubs before the adult beetles emerge to lay their eggs.

PIGEON TREMEX. *Tremex columba* bores round exit holes in the bark about ¼ inch in diameter. The larvae usually attack trees which are dying because of the attacks of fungi or other species of borers.

Control. Insert Bortox into the burrows and seal the openings.

SUGAR MAPLE BORER. *Glycobius speciosus* becomes evident through the occurrence of dead limbs among leafy branches or of dead areas on the branches and trunks.

Control. Methoxychlor spray applied to the trunk and branches in mid-August will control this pest.

TWIG PRUNER. *Elaphidionoides villosus.* This pest attacks many shade and fruit trees in addition to maples, cutting off twigs, which fall to the ground. The larvae are found inside the fallen twigs.

Control. Gather and destroy the fallen twigs in July, August, and early September; otherwise the larvae will overwinter in them. A methoxychlor spray applied in mid-August will also control this pest.

CARPENTER WORM. See under Ash (Chapter 15).

JAPANESE BEETLE. See under Linden.

LINDEN LOOPER. See under Linden.

WHITEFLY. See under Dogwood (Chapter 15).

WOOLLY ALDER APHID. See under Alder (Chapter 15).

Other Pests

SQUIRRELS. The red squirrel *Tamiasciurus hudsonicus* bites the bark of young red and sugar maples to drink the sap that flows from the wounds. Cankers develop as a result of fungi which enter the wounds.

NEMAS. Dieback of sugar maples in woodland areas of Wisconsin has been associated with heavy infestations of several species of root nemas. In Massachusetts the dagger nema *Xiphinema americanum* is associated with a decline of sugar maples.

Control. Controls have not been developed.

MULBERRY (*Morus*)

The white mulberry (*Morus alba*) of the Orient is now naturalized in many parts of the United States. The cultivar 'Kingan' is recommended as a shade tree because it does not produce fruits.

Diseases

BACTERIAL BLIGHT. *Pseudomonas mori*. Water-soaked spots appear on leaves and shoots; they later become sunken and black. The leaves are distorted, and the shoots have black stripes. The leaves at the twig tips wilt and dry up.

Control. Some control is obtainable on young trees by pruning dead shoots in autumn and spraying with bordeaux mixture the following spring. Streptomycin sprays may also be effective.

LEAF SPOTS. *Cercospora moricola, C. missouriensis,* and *Cercosporella mori.* The leaves of mulberry are spotted by these fungi in very rainy seasons.

Control. The *Cercosporella* fungus can cause defoliation of older trees. Valuable specimens should be sprayed with a copper fungicide if leaf spots are serious.

POPCORN DISEASE. *Ciboria carunculoides*. This disease, known only in the southern states, is largely confined to the carpels of the fruit. It causes them to swell and remain greenish, and interferes with ripening.

Control. The disease is of little importance. It does not lessen the value of the tree as an ornamental.

FALSE MILDEW. *Mycosphaerella mori.* The foliage of mulberries grown in the southern states may suffer severely from attacks of this mildew. It appears in July as whitish, indefinite patches on the undersides of the leaves. Yellowish areas then develop on the upper sides. The fungus threads that will produce spores emerge from the stomata on the underside and spread out so as to form a white, cobweblike coating; the general appearance is that of a powdery mildew. The asexual spores are colorless, each composed of several cells. The infected leaves fall to the ground, and the overwintering or ascocarpic stage matures in spring on these leaves.

Control. Gather and destroy all fallen leaves in autumn. Spray with bordeaux mixture as soon as the mold appears in July.

CANKERS. At least six species of fungi may cause cankers on twigs and branches and dieback of twigs: *Cytospora* sp., *Dothiorella* sp., *D. mori*, *Gibberella baccata*, f. *moricola*, *Nectria* sp., and *Stemphyllium* sp. These can be distinguished only by microscopic examination or laboratory tests.

Control. Prune and destroy dead branches. Keep trees in good vigor by watering and fertilizing.

POWDERY MILDEWS. *Phyllactinia corylea* and *Uncinula geniculata*. The lower leaf surface is covered by a white, powdery coating of these fungi.

Control. Valuable specimens can be protected by occasionally spraying with Benlate, Karathane, or wettable sulfur.

Insects and Related Pests

CITRUS FLATID PLANTHOPPER. *Metcalfa pruinosa*. This very active insect, also called mealyflata, is ¼ inch long with purple-brown wings and is covered with white woolly matter.

Control. Spray with pyrethrum or rotenone or a combination of the two.

CERAMBYCID BORER. *Dorcaschema wildii*. In the South this borer mines large areas of cambium and tunnels into the wood of mulberry trees. Branches or even entire trees are girdled and killed.

Control. Spray trunks and branches of valuable trees with methoxychlor twice at monthly intervals, starting in mid-May.

SCALES. The following scales infest mulberry: California red, cottony maple, Florida wax, greedy, olive parlatoria, peach, San Jose, and soft.

Control. Spray with malathion or carbaryl (Sevin) to control the crawling stage of these pests.

OTHER PESTS. The Comstock mealybug and the mulberry whitefly also infest this host.

In dry seasons the two-spotted mite *Tetranychus urticae* may be abundant and injurious. Leaves are mottled and yellow.

Control. Malathion or carbaryl (Sevin) sprays are effective, in controlling the mealybug and whitefly. To control the mite, valuable specimens should be sprayed with Chlorobenzilate, Kelthane, Meta-Systox R, or Tedion after the fruits are gone.

OAK (*Quercus*)

Diseases

ANTHRACNOSE. *Gnomonia quercina*. This fungus, whose asexual stage is *Gloeosporium quercinum*, is rather common in the northern states on white and red oaks, American elm, and black walnut. Rainy weather favors the disease, which may cause defoliation. Weak trees, if defoliated, may die. The spots on the leaves run together, causing the appearance of a leaf blotch or blight. The dead areas follow the veins or are bounded by larger veins. These blotches are light brown. Infection may occur in midsummer.

Control. Three applications of zineb will control this disease: the first when leaves unfurl, the second when leaves reach full size, and the third 2 weeks later. Difolatan sprays also provide control.

BASAL CANKER. *Phaeobulgaria inquinans.* This fungus frequently develops in crevices of the sunken bark that overlies basal cankers. It enters through open wounds but then invades the surrounding bark and sapwood and eventually girdles and kills the tree. The mature fruit bodies are cup- or saucer-shaped and grow from short stems that extend into the bark. When moist, the fruiting bodies look and feel like rubber.

Control. The same as for the canker disease described below.

CANKER. *Strumella coryneoidea.* Although primarily a disease of forest oaks, canker occasionally affects red and scarlet oaks in ornamental plantings. American beech, chestnut, red maple, tupelo, and pignut and shagbark hickories are also susceptible. Several types of cankers, depending on the age of the tree and the rate of growth of the causal fungus, are produced on the trunks. Smooth-surfaced, diffuse, slightly sunken cankers are common on young trees with a diameter of 3 to 4 inches. Cankers on older trees have a rough surface ridged with callus tissue. Open wounds may be present in the center of large cankers as a result of secondary decay and shedding of the bark.

Cankers on red oak (*Quercus borealis maxima*) were found to be caused by the fungus *Fusarium solani*, those on basket oak (*Q. Prinus*) by a species of *Botryodiplodia*, those on live oak (*Q. virginiana*) by *Endothia parasitica*, and those on pin oak (*Q. palustris*) by *E. gyrosa*.

Control. Prune dying and dead branches to eliminate an important possible source of inoculum. Remove small cankers on the trunk by surgical means, and fertilize and water the trees to improve their vigor.

LEAF BLISTER. During cool, wet springs almost all species of oak are subject to the leaf blister disease. Circular, raised areas ranging up to ½ inch in diameter are scattered over the upper leaf surface, causing a depression of the same size on the lower surface (Fig. 16-29). The upper surface of the bulge is yellowish-white, and the lower yellowish-brown. The leaves remain attached to the tree, and there is rarely any noticeable impairment in their functions.

Cause. Leaf blister of oaks is caused by the fungus *Taphrina coerulescens*. New infections in spring are caused by spores from overwintered leaves and possibly by spores lodged in bud scales and on twigs.

Control. A single application at bud-swelling time in spring of any of the following fungicides, applied with a power sprayer so as to coat buds

Fig. 16-29. Leaf blister of oak.

and twigs thoroughly, will give control: captan, Fore, maneb, or zineb. Dilute as directed by the manufacturer.

LEAF SPOTS. Like all other trees, oaks are subject to a number of leaf spot diseases. These rarely cause much damage to the trees, inasmuch as they become numerous rather late in the growing season. The following fungi are known to cause leaf spots: *Cylindrosporium microspilum, Dothiorella phomiformis, Gloeosporium septorioides, G. quercinum, G. umbrinellum, Leptothyrium dryinum, L. californicum, Marssonina martini, M. quercus, Microstroma album, Monochaetia monochaeta, Phyllosticta tumericola, P. livida, Septogloeum querceum, Septoria quercus,* and *S. quercicola.*

Control. Gathering and destroying all fallen leaves is usually sufficient to keep down most outbreaks in seasons of normal rainfall. Valuable oaks may be protected by several applications of copper or zineb sprays at 2-week intervals, starting in early spring when the leaves unfold.

POWDERY MILDEW. In the southern and western states *Sphaerotheca lanestris* is the most troublesome mildew-producer. It forms a white mealy growth on the undersides of the leaves; this later turns brown. The entire surface of the leaf, as well as the tip ends of the twigs, may be covered with the brown feltlike mycelium.

Other powdery mildew fungi affecting oaks include *Erysiphe trina, Microsphaera alni,* and *Phyllactinia corylea.*

Control. Leaf-infecting powdery mildew fungi can be controlled with Acti-dione PM, Benlate, or Karathane.

RUST. *Cronartium quercuum.* The alternate hosts of this fungus are species of pine, such as *P. rigida* and *P. banksiana*, to which some damage is done by the development of gall-like growths. On oak leaves small yellowish spots first appear on the undersides; later brown, bristlelike horns of spores develop.

Control. Little damage is done to the oak; hence no control has been found necessary.

TWIG BLIGHTS. Chestnut oak and, at times, red and white oaks in ornamental plantings are affected by twig blights.

Symptoms. A sudden blighting of the leaves on twigs and branches scattered over the tree is the most striking symptom. The dead twigs and small branches, with their light brown, dead leaves still attached, are readily visible at some distance from the tree because of the sharp contrast with unaffected leaves near them.

Diseased bark becomes sunken and wrinkled, and the sapwood beneath is discolored.

Cause. Eight species of fungi are capable of causing twig blight: *Coryneum kunzei, Diplodia longispora, Physalospora glandicola, P. obtusa, P. rhodina, Pseudovalsa longipes, Sphaeropsis quercina,* and *S. malorum.* Most of the fungi winter over in dead twigs and in cankers on larger branches. During rainy weather of the following spring, spores in large numbers ooze from the dead areas and are splashed onto young shoots and into bark injuries, where they germinate and cause new infections.

Control. During summer, prune infected twigs and branches to sound wood. As a rule, cutting to about 6 inches below the visibly infected area will ensure removal of all fungus-infected tissue in the wood. In severely weakened trees, considerably more tissue must be removed, inasmuch as the fungus may penetrate down the branch for a distance of 2 or more feet.

Valuable trees should be fertilized and watered and their foliage covered with a combination spray containing methoxychlor and a copper fungicide to destroy leaf-chewing insects and prevent infections by leaf-spotting fungi.

SHOESTRING ROOT ROT. *Armillaria mellea.* Oaks are a favored host of this disease, which is discussed in Chapter 14.

WILT. This most highly publicized disease of oaks in recent years is causing some concern to arborists, nurserymen, tree owners, and lumber interests in the Middle West. At this writing, the disease has been found in 20 states, from Kansas and Nebraska eastward to western New York state, and from Minnesota southward to Texas.

Cause. The fungus *Ceratocystis fagacearum* is known to cause wilt. When first described in the literature in 1943, it was known as *Chalara quercina.* The fungus causes infections primarily through wounds made by man or other agents. It has been transmitted rather easily by tools used by arborists and foresters. The most susceptible period appears to be during spring-wood development in the tree.

The causal fungus is spread by root grafts and by several insects and related pests, including fruit flies, Nitidulid beetles, the flatheaded borer *Chrysobothris femorata*, and the mite *Garmania bulbicola*. This fungus has also been recovered from a species of bark beetle and from the two-lined chestnut borer. Recently two species of oak bark beetles, *Pseudopityophthorus minutissimus* and *P. pruinosus*, were found capable of carrying the oak wilt fungus. Tools and climbing spurs used by lumberjacks, foresters, or arborists are other ways by which the fungus is spread. Squirrels are also believed to be vectors. Tree species belonging to the red oak group appear to be the most susceptible, whereas the white oak is markedly resistant. In nature the fungus has been found on Chinese chestnuts and related genera, and it has been transmitted experimentally to a wide variety of trees, including apple.

Control. No effective control is known. For the present, eradication and destruction of infected specimens is being advocated. Where diseased trees are not removed and destroyed, infection centers develop. Ammate applied to such trees results in the reduction of fungus inoculum available for spread via roots or root-inhabiting insects. Because the oak wilt fungus appears to be most infectious early in the growing season when the new spring wood vessels are developing, it is suggested that pruning operations in oaks be delayed until July or later.

WOOD DECAY. Oaks are subject to attacks by a number of fungi that cause decays beneath the bark, usually near the soil line. Two types of decay, known as white heart-rot and brown heart-rot, generally result. Fungi belonging to the genera *Stereum, Polyporus, Fomes*, and *Fistulina* are most commonly associated with these rots. The same tree may show infection by more than one of these fungi, although in most cases only one is involved. The fungus *Stereum gausapatum* has been isolated from most basal decays of oaks. In the early stages of decay, it forms white lines through the sound wood, producing a mottled effect when viewed longitudinally. These white lines or channels usually follow the spring wood vertically, but they branch frequently and at times penetrate the annual growth rings. Later much of the summer wood decays, and in the final stages all the wood becomes light-colored and brittle.

Control. Once wood decays have become extensive, little can be done to check their advance. Trees live for a long time, however, despite the presence of these decays. Except to eliminate a breeding place for vermin, cavity work is rarely done where extensive decay occurs.

RINGSPOT. Virus. Plant pathologists at the University of Arkansas have found viruslike particles in black and blackjack oak leaves exhibiting ringspot symptoms.

The symptoms were found in trees with dead crowns as well as in vigorous saplings.

Control. Control measures have not been developed.

Fig. 16-30. Wool sower gall caused by the gall wasp *Callirytis seminator*.

Insects

GALLS.* There are hundreds of kinds of galls on oaks, and a special manual is needed to identify them. Galls are caused by many species of mites and insects which feed and grow completely protected inside the galls. The life cycles of gall insects and mites vary according to the species involved. The pests overwinter either on the trees or on the ground. The adults emerge in spring and travel to the leaves and twigs, in which they deposit eggs. The young which hatch from the eggs then mature in the galls which form around them. Most kinds of galls on oaks rarely affect the health of the trees. One of the most beautiful galls is the wool sower (Fig. 16-30), produced by the gall wasp *Callirytis seminator*. It is found on white, chestnut, and basket oaks. Some, as the gouty gall (Fig. 16-31), the horned gall, and the oak-potato gall (Fig. 16-32), may

---

* An excellent book on galls is *Plant Galls and Gall Makers* by E. P. Felt, Hafner Publ. Co. New York (1965).

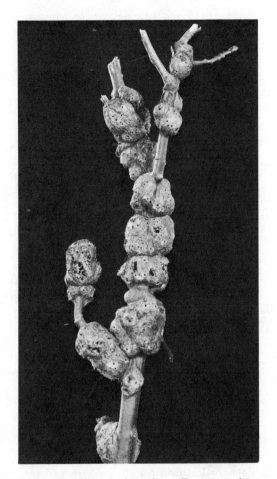

Fig. 16-31. Gouty oak gall caused by the gall wasp *Andricus punctatus*.

affect the health as well as the appearance of the tree by killing branches. Another common gall is the oak apple gall (Fig. 16-33).

Control. Before growth starts in spring, spray the trees either with dormant lime sulfur or with a dormant miscible oil to destroy some of the pests overwintering on the branches. Valuable trees should also be given a carbaryl (Sevin) or a methoxychlor-Kelthane spray in mid-May and again in mid-June. Heavily infested branches should be pruned and destroyed before the adults emerge.

GOLDEN OAK SCALE. *Asterolecanium variolosum*. Shallow pits are formed in the bark by these circular, greenish-gold scales, which attain a diameter of only $1/16$ inch. Infested trees have a ragged, untidy appearance. Young trees may be killed outright, the lower branches dying first.

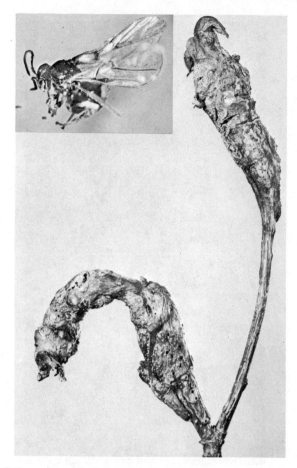

Fig. 16-32. Oak potato gall. **Inset:** Adult of *Neuroterus batatus*, the cause of oak potato gall.

Control. A 'superior' type miscible oil spray applied in early spring will destroy most of the pests. Malathion plus methoxychlor, Diazinon, or carbaryl (Sevin) sprays in July will control the crawler stage. A Cygon spray in August will control the adult stage.

LECANIUM SCALES. *Lecanium corni* and *L. quercifex.* Branches and twigs infested with these pests are covered with brown, down-enveloped, hemispherical scales. The adults are $1/6$ inch in diameter. The winter is passed in the partly grown stage. *L. quercitronis* infests several species of oaks in the eastern states and live oak in California.

Control. Spray with 'superior' type miscible oil or lime sulfur before the buds open in spring, or with malathion or carbaryl (Sevin) in early summer when the young scales are moving about.

Fig. 16-33. Oak apple gall caused by a species of gall wasps.

OAK GALL SCALE. *Kermes pubescens*. Large, globular scale insects, about ⅛ inch in diameter, infest the twigs, leaf stalks, and midribs and tend to gather on the young buds. They are illustrated in Figure 16-34. A red and brown mottling characterizes the pest. The leaves become distorted and many of the twigs are killed, but the tree as a whole is not usually seriously injured.

Control. A dormant oil spray applied in March or early April is very effective. Malathion or carbaryl (Sevin) sprays in late spring are effective against the crawler stage.

OBSCURE SCALE. *Chrysomphalus obscurus*. Tiny, circular, dark gray scales, $1/10$ inch in diameter, may occasionally cover the bark of twigs and branches. The pest overwinters in the partly grown adult stage.

Control. Spray with dormant oil or winter-strength lime sulfur before growth starts in spring or with malathion or carbaryl (Sevin) in late spring.

PURPLE SCALE. *Lepidosaphes beckii*. The female of this species has an elongated, oyster-shaped, slightly curved, brown or purplish body. This species infests citrus trees primarily, but occurs also on many other species in California.

Control. Spray with malathion or carbaryl (Sevin) when the young crawling stage is present.

OAK LACE BUG. *Corythucha arcuata*. The leaves of many oaks, particularly the white oak species, may turn whitish-gray when heavily infested with this lace bug.

Fig. 16-34. Scale (*Kermes pubescens*) on bur oak. The scale insects closely resemble the oak buds in the axils of the leaves and at the tips of twigs.

Control. Spray with Diazinon, malathion, or carbaryl (Sevin) when the young begin to feed in June.

Borers

TWO-LINED CHESTNUT BORER. *Agrilus bilineatus*. Large branches are killed on some trees as a result of the formation of tortuous galleries underneath the bark by the two-lined chestnut borer, a white, flat-headed larva ½ inch long. The adult, a slender greenish-black beetle ⅜ inch long, appears in late June. The larvae pass the winter beneath the bark. Beech and American chestnut are also attacked by this pest.

Control. Cut down and destroy all badly infested trees. Increase the vigor of the remaining trees by fertilizing and watering. Methoxychlor sprays applied to the bark of trunk and branches early in July will also help.

FLATHEADED BORER. *Chrysobothris femorata*. Trees that are not growing vigorously are sometimes attacked by the apple tree borer. The eggs are deposited in crevices in the bark. The young grubs feed on the sapwood and make flat galleries in the wood.

Control. Cut out and destroy dying trees.

OTHER BORERS. Oaks may be invaded by other borers, including the carpenter worm, *Prionoxystus robiniae*, discussed under ash; the leopard moth borer, *Zeuzera pyrina*, and the twig pruner, *Elaphidionoides villosus*, discussed under maple.

OAK BLOTCH LEAF MINERS. *Cameraria hamadryadella* and *C. cincinnatiella*. The former makes pale blotches on many kinds of oak leaves. One leaf miner larva is found in each blotch. The latter makes similar blotches on leaves of white oak, each blotch contaiining 10 or more larvae.

Control. Rake up and destroy fallen leaves because the insect overwinters in the mines of such leaves. Spray with carbaryl (Sevin), malathion, or Trithion in spring when the young miners hatch out of the eggs.

Leaf-Eating Insects

There are so many species of insect larvae that feed on oak leaves that it is impossible to list them all. The following are some of the more important kinds:

YELLOW-NECKED CATERPILLAR. *Datana ministra*. The leaves are chewed by this caterpillar, a black-and-yellowish-white-striped larva 2 inches long. The adult female moth is cinnamon-brown with dark lines across the wings, which have a spread of 1½ inches. Eggs are deposited in batches of 25 to 100 on the lower leaf surface. The insect hibernates in the pupal stage in the soil.

Control. Spray the leaves with methoxychlor or carbaryl (Sevin) when the caterpillars are young.

PIN OAK SAWFLY. *Caliroa lineata*. The lower surfaces of pin oak leaves are chewed by ⅜- to ½-inch-long greenish larvae or slugs, which leave only the upper epidermal layer of cells and a fine network of veins. Injured leaves turn a golden-brown, and when the feeding by the larvae is extensive, the injury can be readily distinguished at a considerable distance. The adult stage is a small, shining-black, four-winged insect ¼ inch long.

Control. Spray the leaves with carbaryl (Sevin) when the larvae begin to feed in early summer. Direct the spray primarily to the lower surfaces of the leaves. This pest appears to prefer the upper parts of the tree.

SADDLEBACK CATERPILLAR. *Sibine stimulea*. This broad, spine-bearing, red caterpillar with a large green patch in the middle of its back attains an inch in length and occasionally chews the leaves of ornamental and streetside oaks. The adult is a small moth with a wingspread of 1½ inches. The upper wings are dark reddish-brown; the lower, a light grayish-brown.

Control. The same as for the yellow-necked caterpillar.

OAK SKELETONIZER. *Bucculatrix ainsliella*. The leaves of red, black, and white oaks may be skeletinized by a yellowish-green larva, ¼ inch long when fully grown. The adult, a moth with a wing expanse of $5/16$ inch, is creamy white, more or less obscured by dark brown scales.

Control. Spray with Diazinon, methoxychlor, or carbaryl (Sevin) when the larvae begin to feed in early June and when the larvae of the second brood begin to feed in August.

ASIATIC OAK WEEVIL. *Cyrtepistomus castaneus.* Severe damage to the leaves of oaks and chestnuts can be caused by a deep red or blackish weevil, ¼ inch long, with scattered green scales which have a metallic lustre. Its long antennae are characteristic of only one other species in this country, the longhorned weevil, *Calomycteris setarius.* Like the elm leaf beetle and the boxelder bug, they move into homes in fall to hibernate.

Control. Methoxychlor sprays on foliage at the time the weevils begin to feed provide good control.

OAK LEAF TIER. *Croesia purpurana.* Buds and leaves are chewed by the larval stage of this pest.

Control. Spray with carbaryl (Sevin) no later than April 15 in the latitude of New York or before the buds begin to break.

OTHER PESTS. Among other insects that chew oak leaves are the caterpillars of the io moth, *Automeris io*; the cecropia moth, *Platysamia cecropia*; the luna moth, *Actias luna*; the gypsy moth, *Porthetria dispar*; the American dagger moth, *Acronicta americana*; the oak leafroller *Argyrotoxa semipurpurana*; Japanese weevil, *Pseudocneorhinus bifasciatus*; and the satin moth, *Stilpnotia salicis.*

Several species of cankerworms and leafrollers also chew the leaves of oaks.

Control. All these can be controlled by spraying with carbaryl (Sevin) or Diazinon when the larvae begin to feed.

Other Pests

OAK MITE. *Oligonychus bicolor.* Mottled yellow foliage results from the sucking of the leaf juices by the oak mite, a yellow, brown, or red, eight-legged pest. The mite usually overwinters in the egg stage.

Control. Spray with dormant oil or lime sulfur during early spring, or with Kelthane, Meta-Systox R, or Tedion in mid-June and again 2 to 3 weeks later.

OSAGE-ORANGE (*Maclura*)

Diseases

LEAF SPOTS. Leaves are occasionally spotted by three species of fungi: *Cercospora maclurae, Ovularia maclurae,* and *Phyllosticta maclurae.*

Control. Leaf spots are rarely serious enough to warrant control measures.

OTHER DISEASES. Osage-orange is susceptible to a leaf blight caused by *Sporodesmium maclurae* and rust by *Physopella fici*.

Research workers at Rutgers University found that the wood of osage-orange contained about 1 per cent of the chemical 2,3,4,5-tetrahydroxystilbene, which was toxic to a number of fungi. This may explain why this host is remarkably resistant to decay-producing fungi.

Insects

SCALES. Five species of scale insects infest osage-orange: cottony-cushion, cottony maple, European fruit lecanium, Putnam, and San Jose.

The citrus mealybug and the citrus whitefly also attack this tree.

Control. Malathion, Meta-Systox R, or carbaryl (Sevin) sprays will control the scales. The synthetic pyrethroid, Resmethrin (SBP 1382), will control whitefly.

PECAN (*Carya illinoensis*)

Diseases

BROWN LEAF SPOT. *Cercospora fusca*. This leaf spot is common throughout the pecan-growing areas in the South. Downy spot, caused by the fungus *Mycosphaerella caryigena*, also occurs in the same localities.

Control. Spray with a low-lime bordeaux mixture as recommended by the plant pathologist in the state where trees are affected.

CROWN GALL. *Agrobacterium tumefaciens*. The roots of young pecan trees may be infected by this bacterial disease. Occasionally older trees in orchards are also infected.

Control. Remove galls from roots of young infected trees. Then try dipping the roots for an hour in a solution containing 400 parts of Terramycin in 1 million parts of water, or treat with Bacticin as recommended by the manufacturer.

SCAB. *Cladosporium effusum*. This is one of the most destructive diseases of pecans in the Southeast. The fungus attacks leaves, shoots, and nuts.

Control. Dyrene or Dodine sprays will control this disease. The local state plant pathologist at the state college of agriculture can provide details on dilution and timing.

OTHER DISEASES. Pecans are subject to a number of diseases that infect other species of *Carya*. They are not treated in detail here because the pecan is not an important ornamental tree.

Insects

BORERS. A large number of borers infest pecans. Following are the most important: dogwood, flatheaded apple tree, pecan, pecan carpenterworm, shot-hole, twig girdler, and twig pruner.

Control. As with borers on other trees, keep ornamental trees in vigorous condition by feeding and watering. Particularly valuable ornamental specimens can be protected from most borers by spraying the trunks and branches with methoxychlor at the time the insects are most vulnerable. State entomologists will provide information on concentrations and application dates.

PEPPERIDGE-TREE—See Tupelo.

PLANETREE, LONDON (*Platanus acerifolia*)*

The London planetree is one of the most commonly planted trees in cities in the northeastern United States because it is more tolerant to air pollutants and other unfavorable growing conditions than most trees. However, it does not do well where extremely low winter temperatures occur. Many trees, 3 to 5 inches in trunk diameter, were killed or severely injured in New York City as a result of the severe 1977 winter.

Fungus Diseases

CANKERSTAIN. Thousands of London planetrees have died from this disease in the eastern United States in the past 45 years. The disease has also occurred in some of the southern and midwestern states (Fig. 16-35).

Symptoms. Conspicuous reduction in both amount and size of foliage is the most obvious symptom. This is followed within a year or two by complete death of the tree.

Shrunken cankers appear on trunks, large limbs, and occasionally on small limbs (Fig. 16-36). The cankers frequently have longitudinal cracks and roughened bark. Bluish-black or brown discolorations appear on freshly exposed bark over the cankers. The callus tissue formed at the margin of a canker usually dies early. Dark-colored streaks extend from the cankers inward through the wood to the central pith, and frequently radiating web-shaped brown streaks extend from the pith outward through the sound wood in other regions (Fig. 16-37). The rays are mostly dark-colored. As the disease progresses, there is a gradual thinning of the leaves, which are smaller than usual. The disease seems to be limited to shade trees. The sycamore, *P. occidentalis,* is said by some to be resistant to this disease; others say it is mildly susceptible.

Cause. Cankerstain is caused by the fungus *Ceratocystis fimbriata* f. *platani.* Several closely related species cause blue stain in lumber, and

---

* Diseases and pests of the American planetree or buttonwood (*Platanus occidentalis*) are discussed under Sycamore.

Fig. 16-35. London planetree affected by the cankerstain disease.

Fig. 16-36. Trunk of London planetree showing infection by the cankerstain fungus *Ceratocystis fimbriata* f. *platani*.

one, *C. ulmi*, is a stage of the organism causing the Dutch elm disease. There is some evidence that as many as 5 species of Nitidulid beetles are capable of disseminating the causal fungus.

The fungus enters the trunk or branches through bark injuries and grows toward the center. From this point it grows outward radially along various lines, forming cankers wherever it reaches the bark. Large numbers of spores are formed beneath recently killed bark or on freshly exposed wood surfaces.

Many cankers center around injuries made by saw cuts, pole pruner cuts, rope burns, accidental saw scratches, and injuries by climbers' boots. Observations indicate that cankers may also start from pruning cuts that have been painted with a wound dressing containing fungus-infested sawdust. The fungus can apparently survive in some of the commonly used asphaltum wound dressings. The disease has been experimentally transmitted from infected to healthy trees by means of contaminated pruning saws. It is highly probable that the use of contaminated tools and tree paints constitutes the chief means of spread on streetside and shade trees. Injuries to the roots and trunk during curb and sidewalk installation and those made by boys with sharp instruments are also important foci for fungus invasion. Natural bark fissures and frost cracks may also constitute entrance points.

Control. Diseased trees should be removed and destroyed as soon as the diagnosis is confirmed. All injuries to sound trees should be avoided. Saws and other implements used in pruning planetrees should be thoroughly disinfested by washing in denatured alcohol or some other strong disinfestant after use on each tree in the more heavily infested zones. Because of the possibility of spreading the fungus by means of infested wound dressings, the addition to the dressing of some mild disinfestant such as Benlate or thiabendazole that are toxic to the fungus but harmless to the tree tissues is suggested. Where such a disinfestant is not used in localities where the disease is prevalent, it is best not to apply a dressing on fresh wounds.

Plant pathologists once believed that the disease could not be spread by way of contaminated saws if pruning was done in winter, from December 1 to February 15. It is now known that this is not the case.

Fig. 16-37. Cross section of planetree trunk infected by *Ceratocystis fimbriata* f. *platani*. The discoloration shows the spread of the fungus through the wood.

Hence all pruning tools should be sterilized with 70 per cent denatured alcohol after use on each tree regardless of the season.

BOTRYOSPHAERIA CANKER. *Botryosphaeria dothidea.* This fungus, like *Verticillium albo-atrum* and *Armillaria mellea*, is far more widespread than most professional arborists and nurserymen realize. It has long been known to cause cankers and dieback of redbud, but the author was among the first to show that its asexual stage, *Dothiorella*, caused a highly destructive disease of London planetrees in New York City. By cross-inoculation tests, he proved that the same fungus can infect other important shade trees, including sweetgum. The fungus also has been isolated from naturally infected sweetgums showing branch dieback and discolored wood. Among other trees known to be susceptible to this fungus are apple, avocado, beech, flowering cherry, flowering dogwood, Japanese persimmon, hickory, horsechestnut, pecan, poplar, quince, sourgum, sycamore maple, and willow.

Many years ago, the author, working with Mr. E. C. Rundlett, then arboriculturist for the New York City Department of Parks, was the first to record that leaf fires beneath streetside trees made the trees more susceptible to infection by the conidial stage *Dothiorella gregaria*. He also pointed out that this is true of infections by the cankerstain fungus discussed earlier.

Control. No control is possible once the fungus has invaded the main trunk. When infections are limited to the branches, pruning well below the cankered area may remove all the infected material. Wounds and damage to the bark by fires should be avoided. Burning of leaves and other materials are now prohibited in most municipalities. The trees should be kept in good vigor by feeding, watering during dry spells, and spraying to control leaf-chewing and leaf-sucking insects.

POWDERY MILDEW. *Microsphaera alni.* London planetrees are especially susceptible to attacks of powdery mildew. Leaves and young twigs are covered with a whitish mold to such an extent that much of the foliage is destroyed. The weather seems to determine the seriousness of the attack; during some seasons no mildew appears, while in others the disease is serious, especially on young trees of a size for transplanting.

Control. In nursery plantings it is practical to spray trees with Benlate, Karathane, or wettable sulfur for this disease. Individual specimens are rarely sprayed to control mildew.

BLIGHT, ANTHRACNOSE. See under Sycamore.

Nonparasitic Diseases

DOG CANKER. Injury to trees planted along streets where it is customary to walk dogs is confined to the lower 2 feet of the trunk. Many trees up to 6 inches in trunk diameter may be killed in this way.

Control. Placing a metal collar around trees visited by male dogs will help to eliminate cankers, but the dogs' urine will still seep into the soil and root area to cause severe damage to the roots and premature death of the tree.

Insects

AMERICAN PLUM BORER. *Euzophera semifuneralis*. London planetrees, particularly streetside specimens whose bark has been damaged are particularly susceptible to this pest. Damage to the inner bark and cambial regions by the larval stage, a dusky-white, pinkish, or dull brownish-green caterpillar, may be so extensive that the tree dies prematurely. Wild cherry, mountain-ash, and all kinds of fruit trees are also susceptible.

Control. Avoid damaging trees and keep them in good vigor by feeding and watering. Spray the main trunk with methoxychlor 3 times at 3-week intervals, starting in mid-May.

LACE BUG. *Corythucha ciliata*. The leaves turn pale yellow and many drop prematurely as a result of the sucking by the lace bug. The adult, ⅛ inch long, white and with lacelike wings, deposits eggs on the lower leaf surface. There are several generations a year. The adult passes the winter in bark crevices and other sheltered places in the vicinity of the trees. London planetree is much more susceptible to this pest than is sycamore.

Control. As soon as the eggs hatch on the leaves (about June 1 in the latitude of New York), spray with carbaryl (Sevin). Some control is possible with a dormant spray applied just before growth begins in spring.

OTHER INSECTS. London planetrees may be attacked by other insects.

POINCIANA (*Poinciana*)

These are discussed under Sycamore.

Diseases

CANKER. This tropical tree is subject to relatively few diseases. Perhaps the most destructive is canker, caused by the fungus *Botryosphaeria dothidea*.

Control. Branches that show cankers should be pruned and destroyed.

Other diseases reported on this host are crown gall caused by the bacterium *Agrobacterium tumefaciens*, anthracnose by a fungus belonging to the genus *Gloeosporium*, a rust by the fungus *Ravenelia humphreyana*, and root rots by two fungi, *Clitocybe tabescens* and *Phymatotrichum omnivorum*.

Control. Control measures are rarely necessary.

Insects

LESSER SNOW SCALE. *Pinnaspis strachani.* The lesser snow scale frequently infests this host. The female is pear-shaped, white, semitransparent, sometimes speckled with brown. The male is narrow and white.

Control. Spray with malathion or carbaryl (Sevin) to control the crawler stage.

POPLAR (*Populus*)

Diseases

Several destructive diseases affect the trunks and limbs of poplars. The generic name of the causal fungus is used to differentiate the various types of cankers produced. A dieback, which is not clearly understood, and a number of leaf diseases, which rarely cause much damage, also occur on poplars.

CHONDROPLEA CANKER. The dying and dead Lombardy poplars (*Populus nigra italica*) in the eastern United States are ample evidence of this destructive disease. Black and eastern cottonwoods and balsam, black, and Norway poplars also may be affected, although these species are much less susceptible than Lombardy poplar (Fig. 16-38).

Symptoms. Elongated, dark, sunken cankers occur on the trunk, limbs, and twigs (Fig. 16-39). The bark and cambium in the cankers are destroyed, and the sapwood is invaded and discolored. When the cankers completely girdle the trunks or branches, the distal portions die. Trees less than 4 years old are usually killed outright in a relatively short time. Older trees do not succumb so rapidly, but are readily disfigured and become virtually worthless as ornamentals or windbreaks.

Cause. The fungus *Chondroplea populea* causes this disease. The sexual stage of this fungus is *Cryptodiaporthe populea*. It forms small raised pustules on diseased bark, from which cream-colored masses of spores ooze out in April and May. The spores are splashed onto leaves and into bark injuries, where they germinate and infect these parts. Invasion often advances down the leaf petiole into the twig, causing death of the latter.

Control. No effective control measures are known. Wounds of all sorts should be avoided. Pruning of diseased parts, as suggested for most canker diseases, does not appear to help control this disease; in fact, it often spreads it.

Fig. 16-38. The Lombardy poplars on the left died as a result of infection by the fungus *Chondroplea populea*.

Inasmuch as the leaves are attacked and the fungus enters the twigs through infected leaves, some investigators have recommended repeated applications of copper sprays to reduce leaf infections. As a rule, individual trees are not sufficiently valuable to justify four or more applications of a fungicide each year. Such a practice may be warranted, however, in nurseries where the disease threatens young stock.

The only hope lies in the development of resistant varieties. The Japan poplar (*P. maximowiczii*) appears to show some resistance. Conflict-

Fig. 16-39. Trunk of Lombardy poplar showing elongated sunken cankers caused by the fungus *Chondroplea populea*.

ing reports exist concerning the susceptibility of the Simon poplar (*P. simonii*); some persons assert that it is very resistant, others, that it is very susceptible.

CYTOSPORA CANKER. Another destructive canker disease of poplar, Cytospora canker, primarily affects trees poor in vigor. Among the factors that most commonly contribute to the weakened condition are drastic pruning and the unfavorable environment of city soils. Carolina and silver-leaf appear to be the most susceptible of the poplars. Maples, mountain-ash, and willows are also susceptible. The Rio Grande cottonwood in the West is resistant to this disease.

Symptoms. Brown, sunken areas covered with numerous red pustules first appear on young twigs. The fungus moves down the stem and invades larger branches or even the trunk. Here, circular cankers are formed, which continue to expand until the entire member is girdled and the parts above die.

Cause. The fungus *Cytospora chrysosperma*, a stage of the fungus *Valsa sordida*, is the causal agent. It lives on dead branches but can attack live branches and trunks when the tree is weakened. Spores are developed in the black pin-point fruiting structures on dead wood. They ooze from these bodies and are splashed by rains or carried by birds and insects to bark wounds or weakened and dead branches, where they germinate and infect.

Control. Because Cytospora canker is primarily a disease of weak trees, the most effective preventive is the maintenance of the trees in high vigor by fertilization, watering, and the control of insect and fungus parasites of the leaves. In addition, dead and dying branches should be removed and all unnecessary injuries avoided.

HYPOXYLON CANKER. A highly destructive disease, Hypoxylon canker occurs less commonly than Chondroplea and Cytospora cankers. In the northeastern states it affects quaking and large-toothed aspens and balsam poplar. It is most harmful to young trees and is more common on forest trees than on ornamentals.

Symptoms. Gray cankers of varying sizes appear along the trunk but never on the branches. The color changes to black as the outer bark falls away from the surface of the canker. When the bark is peeled off, blackened sapwood is visible around the edge of the canker. Wefts of fungus tissue, resembling the chestnut blight fungus but different in color, are also visible beneath the peeled bark. Many cankers attain a length of several feet and cause considerable distortion of the trunk before complete girdling of the trunk and death occur.

Cause. This disease is caused by the fungus *Hypoxylon pruinatum*. Spores are believed to initiate infections through bark injuries.

Control. This disease is so highly contagious and destructive that infected trees should be cut down and destroyed as soon as the diagnosis is confirmed. Injuries should be avoided as much as possible.

SEPTORIA CANKER. A serious stem canker disease of hybrid poplars, Septoria canker may also infect leaves of all species of native poplars.

Symptoms. Leaves on young shoots or lowermost branches of native poplars are spotted early in the season. Cankers appear later on the stems of hybrid poplars with black, balsam, and cottonwood parentage. When cankers girdle the stem, the distal portion dies.

Cause. *Mycosphaerella populorum* causes leaf spot and stem canker. The asexual stage of this fungus is *Septoria musiva*, hence the common name for the disease. Fruit bodies of the Septoria stage are frequently found in the cankered areas.

Control. The most effective way of combating the canker stage of this disease is to use hybrid poplar clones that have proved to be naturally resistant. The leaf spot stage on ornamental poplars can be prevented by periodic applications of a copper fungicide.

FUSARIUM CANKER. *Fusarium solani.* This disease occurs on *Populus deltoides* in the South, Middle West, and Canada.

Control. Control measures have not been developed.

BRANCH GALL. Small globose galls up to 1½ inches in diameter occasionally occur at the bases of poplar twigs. Primarily, the bark is hypertrophied, although some swelling of the woody tissues also occurs. Twigs and some branches may be killed, but the disease rarely becomes serious.

Cause. Small black pin-point fruiting bodies of the fungus *Macrophoma tumefaciens* are embedded in the bark of the gall, especially along the fissures. Fungus penetration is initiated in the developing buds in early spring, and the swelling of the tissue probably results from some stimulant secreted by the fungus.

Control. Pruning the galled branches and dead twigs to sound wood and destroying the removed wood are usually sufficient to hold the fungus in check.

LEAF RUSTS. Several species of rust fungi attack poplars in the eastern United States. These produce yellowish-orange pustules, usually on the lower leaf surface. The two species most common in the East are *Melampsora medusae* and *M. abietis-canadensis*, which require alternate hosts to complete their life cycles. The alternate host of the former is larch, and that of the latter, hemlock. Two other leaf rusts are caused by *Melampsora albertensis* and *M. occidentalis.*

Control. Except for the rust fungus *Melampsora medusae*, which causes heavy losses of young cottonwoods (*Populus deltoides*) in nurseries in the Midwest and South, leaf rusts rarely cause enough damage to necessitate special control measures. *M. medusae* can be controlled in plant nurseries with a summer application of Benlate. Several rust-resistant cottonwood clones are also available.

LEAF BLISTER. Brilliant yellow to brown blisters of varying sizes occasionally appear on poplar leaves following extended periods of cool, wet weather. The blisters, which may be more than an inch in diameter, result from stimulation of the leaf cells by the fungus *Taphrina aurea.* Another species, *T. johansoni*, causes a deformity of the catkins.

Control. Spraying the trees in early spring with ferbam or ziram will control leaf blister. Such a practice is suggested only where particularly valuable specimens are involved.

LEAF SPOTS. *Ciborinia bifrons, C. confundens, Marssonina populi, M. brunnea, Mycosphaerella populicola, Plagiostoma populi,* and *Phyllosticta alcides.* Many species of fungi, including *Mycosphaerella populorum* mentioned under the Septoria canker disease, cause leaf spots of poplars. Of these, *Marssonina populi*, which produces brown spots with a darker brown margin and premature defoliation, is by far the most common. It also invades and kills the twigs.

Control. The first requisite in the control of leaf spot diseases is the gathering and destruction of all fallen leaves to remove an important source of inoculum. Poplars are rarely sprayed with fungicides, but bordeaux or any ready-made copper fungicide may be used early in spring on valuable trees. Difolatan will also control leaf spots.

DIEBACK. A dieback of the top and complete death of Lombardy poplar, cottonwood (*P. balsamifera*), and the goat willow (*Salix caprea*) have been reported on trees in the vicinity of Washington, D. C., and in western Tennessee. On Lombardy poplar, the wood appears first water-soaked, then red, and finally brown. The tree dies when the entire cross section of the trunk is stained brown.

Cause. The cause of this trouble in not known. Bacteria have been isolated from the margins of the discolored area. There is a strong possibility that the water-soaked appearance and the subsequent staining actually result from extremely low winter temperatures and that the bacteria enter after the injury occurs.

Control. No control measures are known.

POPLAR INKSPOT. *Sclerotinia bifrons.* Thick, round or elongated black spots form on leaves and then drop out, leaving holes. Aspen, Lombardy, and Carolina poplars are most subject to inkspot, whereas the large-toothed aspen (*P. grandidentata*) appears to be immune.

Control. Where the fungus attacks valuable specimen poplars, or nursery stock, the use of bordeaux mixture or some fixed copper is suggested.

POWDERY MILDEW. *Uncinula salicis.* This is a common superficial disease, appearing as a white mildew on both sides of the leaves; usually the damage is not serious.

Control. Spray with Benlate, Karathane, or wettable sulfur if the specimens are valuable and the disease is serious.

Insects

APHIDS. *Pemphigus populitransverus* and *Mordwilkoja vagabunda.* The former produces galls on the leaf petioles of certain poplars; the latter is responsible for convoluted galls at the tips of twigs.

Several other species of leaf-infesting aphids occur on this host.

Control. Valuable ornamental specimens can be sprayed with lime sulfur when the trees are dormant or with malathion just as the leaves unfurl in early spring.

BRONZE BIRCH BORER. *Agrilus anxius.* Weakened trees are always more susceptible than vigorous trees to attack by the bronze birch borer. Branches are girdled and the upper parts of the tree die back as a result of feeding by the borer, a white, legless larva, ¾ inch long. The adult beetle, which appears in June and feeds on the leaves for a short time, is ½ inch long and bronze in color. The female deposits eggs in bark crevices in June.

Control. Spray the leaves, trunk, and branches with methoxychlor in early June, and repeat in 3 weeks. Remove and destroy severely infested parts. Water important trees during drought periods.

POPLAR BORER. *Saperda calcarata.* Blackened and swollen scars on the limbs and on the trunk and sawdust at the base of the tree usually result from attack by the poplar borer, a white larva, 1¼ to 1½ inches long when full grown. The upper and lower parts of the larva's body have horny points. The adult female is a bluish-gray beetle, with black spots and yellow patches, and is slightly over an inch in length.

Control. Remove and destroy badly infested trees. Spraying the trees with methoxychlor at 2-week intervals, starting in late July, may be justified on valuable trees.

IMPORTED WILLOW LEAF BEETLE. *Plagiodera versicolora.* Holes are chewed in the leaves by the willow leaf beetle, the metallic-blue adult form ⅛ inch long; and the leaves are skeletonized by the black larvae, which are ¼ inch long. The adult lives through the winter and deposits eggs on the lower leaf surface in spring.

Control. Spray with carbaryl (Sevin) after the eggs hatch in late May or early June.

RED-HUMPED CATERPILLAR. *Schizura concinna.* The leaves are chewed by clusters of red-humped caterpillars, yellow and black striped forms with red heads and red humps. The adult, a grayish-brown moth with a wingspread of 1¼ inches, deposits masses of eggs on the lower leaf surface in July. Winter is passed in a cocoon on the ground.

Control. Spray with *Bacillus thuringiensis* or carbaryl (Sevin) when the caterpillars are small.

SATIN MOTH. *Stilpnotia salicis.* The larval stage, black with conspicuous irregular white blotches, feeds on the leaves of poplar, willow, and sometimes on oaks in late April or May. The adult, satin-white and with a wing expanse up to 2 inches, emerges in July.

Control. Spray with carbaryl (Sevin) in early June and again in early August.

TENTMAKER. *Ichthyura inclusa.* The leaves are chewed and silken nests appear on twigs as a result of infestations of the tentmaker, a black larva with pale yellow stripes, which attains a length of 1¼ inches at maturity. The adult female is a moth with white-striped gray wings. The pupae overwinter in fallen leaves.

Control. Remove and destroy nests or spray with carbaryl (Sevin) when the larvae are small.

SCALES. Many species of scale insects infest populars. Among these are black, cottony maple, European fruit lecanium, greedy, lecanium, oystershell, San Jose, soft, terrapin, walnut, and willow.

Control. Valuable specimens infested with scales should be sprayed with lime sulfur or miscible oil in early spring just before growth starts, or with malathion or carbaryl (Sevin) in mid-May and again in mid-June to control the crawling stages.

FALL WEBWORM. See under Ash (Chapter 15).

REDWOOD, DAWN (*Metasequoia glyptostroboides*)

Diseases

CANKER. *Botryosphaeria dothidea*. This is the only disease known to occur on dawn redwood, described on page 456. Early symptoms include the wilting of leaves on individual lateral branches. Cankers develop on the trunk at the base of the infected branches. Resin exudes from the infected area.

The canker disease also occurs on *Sequoiadendron giganteum* and on *Sequoia sempervirens* planted outside the native range.

Control. Control measures have not been developed.

SOURGUM—See Tupelo.

SWEETGUM (*Liquidambar*)

Because of the increased use of sweetgums in recent years, their diseases and insect pests have received more than the usual amount of attention.

Diseases

BLEEDING NECROSIS. The author was the first to discover the bleeding necrosis disease of sweetgum in New Jersey and on Staten Island, New York, as far back as 1941.

Symptoms. The most striking symptom, readily visible at some distance, is the profuse bleeding of the bark, usually at the soil line or a few feet above, but occasionally observed as high as 20 feet up on the main trunk and lower branches. The exudation looks like heavy motor oil poured over the bark.

The condition of the inner bark and sapwood beneath the oozing area, however, presents a more positive symptom of the disease. Such bark is dark reddish-brown with an occasional pocket containing a white crystalline solid. The outer layer of sapwood may be brown or olive-green in color.

Infected trees may exhibit undernourished foliage and more or less extensive dying-back of terminal branches by the time profuse bleeding is visible on the trunk.

Cause. The fungus *Botryosphaeria dothidea* cuases bleeding necrosis, but when first reported by the author the fungus was listed under the asexual stage *Dothiorella.* There is some evidence that raising the grade around the tree makes it more subject to this fungus.

Control. No control measures are known. Removal and destruction of diseased trees is suggested.

LEAF SPOTS. Six fungi *Actinopelte dryina, Cercospora liquidambaris, C. tuberculans, Exosporium liquidambaris, Leptothyriella liquidambaris,* and *Septoria liquidambaris* may occasionally spot the leaves of this host.

Control. Leaf spots are rarely serious enough to warrant control measures.

OTHER DISEASES. Several other important diseases of sweetgum have been reported in recent years. For most, the causal agent is still unknown. One, leader dieback, is caused by the fungus *Diplodia theobromae.* It was found capable of causing dieback of the leader branch under certain predisposing environmental conditions.

The disease known as sweetgum blight has caused death of many trees in Maryland and adjacent states. At this writing no causal organism has been associated constantly with the disease.

Control. Control measures are unavailable.

Insects

SWEETGUM WEBWORM. *Salebria afflictella.* The leaves are tied and matted together by small larvae.

Control. Spray with carbaryl (Sevin) before the leaves are matted together.

CATERPILLARS. The leaves of sweetgum are occasionally chewed by the caterpillars listed below, as well as by those of several species of moths including the luna, *Actias luna,* polyphemus, *Antheraea polyphemus,* and promethea, *Callosamia promethea.*

Control. Spray with *Bacillus thuringiensis,* Imidan, or carbaryl (Sevin) when caterpillars begin to feed.

COTTONY-CUSHION SCALE. *Icerya purchasi.* This insect, which is more destructive to silver maples, has been known to infest sweetgum branches and leaves.

SWEETGUM SCALE. *Aspidiotus liquidambaris.* This scale is occasionally found on sweetgums in the eastern United States.

Control. Spray with a 'superior' * type miscible oil in spring before growth begins and with malathion or carbaryl (Sevin) in early June.

* See footnote page 249.

WALNUT SCALE. *Aspidiotus juglansregiae*. The insect winters in the adult state, the eggs being laid in spring. Feeding of the young begins early in June. In severe infestations twigs, limbs, and trunks may become encrusted.

Control. See under Horsechestnut.

BAGWORM. See under Arborvitae (Chapter 17).

FALL WEBWORM. See under Ash (Chapter 15).

FOREST TENT CATERPILLAR. See under Maple.

SYCAMORE (*Platanus occidentalis*)

This tree, also known as buttonwood and American planetree, is found from Maine to Minnesota, Florida to Texas. It is occasionally planted as a street tree but is not so desirable as the London planetree (*Platanus acerifolia*) (p. 163).

Diseases

BLIGHT, also known as anthracnose and scorch, is the most serious disease of sycamore. Two western species, *Platanus racemosa* and *P. wrighti*, are also susceptible. The disease is locally severe in some sections of the United States every year. (Figs. 16-40 and 16-41). The London

Fig. 16-40. Left: A sycamore tree lost nearly all its leaves in June as a result of the blight (anthracnose) disease.

Fig. 16-41. Right: The same tree with a new set of leaves by early October.

planetree (*P. acerifolia*), though much more resistant, shows some injury during epidemic years. The destructiveness of this disease is often underestimated. While a single attack seldom results in serious harm, repeated annual outbreaks will eventually so weaken the tree that it becomes susceptible to borer attack and winter injury.

Symptoms. The first symptom, often confused with late frost injury, is the sudden browning and death of single leaves or of clusters of leaves as they are expanding in spring. Later, brown, dead areas along and between the veins appear in other leaves. The dead tissues assume a triangular form as a result of the death of the veinal tissues. The leaf falls prematurely when several lesions develop or when the leaf stem is infected. Many trees are completely defoliated and remain bare until late summer, when a new crop of leaves is formed. Small twigs are also attacked and killed. Cankers appear on the leaf spurs and on twigs as sunken areas with slightly raised margins (Fig. 16-42). When these completely girdle the infected parts, the distal portions, including the leaves, are killed. This is known as the shoot blight stage. Moderately infected trees show clusters of dead leaves scattered over the entire tree; these contrast sharply with the unaffected foliage.

Fig. 16-42. Twig canker of sycamore blight (anthracnose). Note fruiting bodies protruding from the bark.

Cause. Blight is caused by the fungus *Gnomonia platani*. The fungus has several distinctly different types of spores (Fig. 16-43). It may overwinter in the vegetative stage (mycelium) in fallen infected leaves and in twig cankers. In the South it passes the winter in the spore stage on dormant buds. Initial infections of the young leaves in spring may originate from spores formed in overwintered leaves on the ground, from spores developed on infected twigs, and from spores on the dormant buds. Additional crops of spores for late infections are formed on the lower surfaces of the newly infected leaves in early spring (Fig. 16-44).

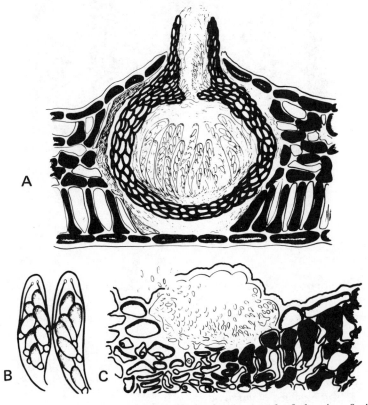

Fig. 16-43. A. Diagrammatic cross section of sycamore leaf showing fruiting body of the fungus *Gnomonia platani*. B. Close-up of so-called ascospores. C. The summer spore (*Gloeosporium*) stage of the fungus.

The prevalence and severity of attack are governed by weather conditions, frequent rains, and cool temperatures favoring rapid spread.

The severity of the shoot blight stage is largely governed by the average temperature during the 2-week period following the emergence of the first leaves. If the average temperature during this period is below 55°F. (13° C.), the injury will be severe. If it is between 55° and 60° F. (16° C.), it will be less severe, and if it is over 60° F., little to no injury will occur.

Control. Control measures are rarely attempted on sycamores growing in open fields or in woodlands. They are justified, however, on particularly valuable specimens and on those used for shade and ornament.

All fallen leaves and twigs should be gathered and discarded in autumn to destroy the overwintering mycelium, which produces spores for the following spring's infections. Infected spurs and dead twigs

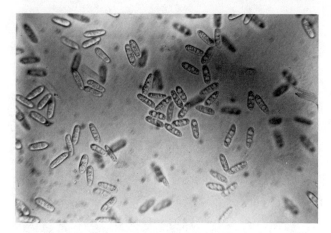

Fig. 16-44. The spores of the summer (*Gloeosporium*) stage of the blight (anthracnose) fungus as they appear through a microscope.

should be pruned, whenever feasible, and destroyed. To protect valuable specimens, spray the leaves with difolatan, maneb, or zineb when they unfurl, when they reach full size, and a third time 2 weeks later.

Trees suffering from repeated attacks should be heavily fertilized in the fall or the following spring to increase their vigor.

OTHER DISEASES. Several diseases of minor importance include brown leaf spots caused by the fungi *Mycosphaerella platanifolia, Phyllosticta platani,* and *Septoria platanifolia.*

Control. These can be controlled by adopting the spray schedule suggested for the control of anthracnose (p. 467).

In the South a bark canker is caused by the fungus *Botryodiplodia theobromae.*

Control. Control measures are rarely adopted.

Insects

APHIDS. *Longistigma caryae.* The giant bark aphid, up to ¼ inch in length, frequently attacks the twigs of sycamore and may gather in clusters on the undersides of the limbs. These insects are also called planetree aphids. They are the largest species of aphids known and exude great quantities of honeydew.

Another species, *Drepanosiphum platanoides,* infests maples in addition to sycamores throughout the country.

Control. Spray with Meta-Systox R, malathion, or carbaryl (Sevin).

SYCAMORE PLANT BUG. *Plagiognathus albatus.* This bug in its adult stage is ⅛ inch long, tan or brown in color, with dark eyes and brown spots on the wings. The young bugs are yellow-green, with conspicuous reddish-brown eyes. These pests suck out the plant juices on the upper sides of sycamore and London planetree leaves, presumably leaving a poisonous material which results in yellowish or reddish spots. As the leaves grow, the injured areas drop out, leaving holes.

Control. Malathion sprays applied in early May and again 2 weeks later will control this insect.

LACE BUG. *Corythucha ciliata.* See under Planetree, London.

SYCAMORE TUSSOCK MOTH. *Halisodota harrisii.* The caterpillar stage of this moth is yellow and has white to yellow hairs on its body. It occasionally becomes abundant on sycamores in the northeastern United States.

Control. Carbaryl (Sevin) sprays will provide control.

SCALES. Several species of scale insects, including black, cottony maple, grape, oystershell, sycamore, and terrapin, occasionally infest the sycamore and other species of *Platanus.*

Control. Malathion or carbaryl (Sevin) sprays in late spring when the young scales are crawling about are effective. A dormant spray containing a 'superior' * type miscible oil should be applied in early spring where the infestations are unusually heavy.

OTHER PESTS. *Platanus* species are infested by other pests, including bagworms, borers, mites, whiteflies, root knot nema (*Meloidogyne* sp.), and several other species of parasitic nemas.

Control. Control measures are rarely needed.

TULIPTREE (Liriodendron)

Fungus Diseases

CANKERS. At least six species of fungi, *Botryosphaeria dothidea, Cephalosporium sp., Fusarium solani, Myxosporium* spp., *Nectria magnoliae,* and *Nectria* sp., cause cankers in tuliptree. The first mentioned is perhaps the most destructive.

Control. Prune and cart away infected branches. Valuable trees should be sprayed with a copper fungicide, and fed and watered to increase their vigor.

LEAF SPOTS. At least six species of fungi, *Cylindrosporium cercosporioides, Gloeosporium liriodendri* (Fig. 16-45), *Mycosphaerella liriodendri, M. tulipiferae, Phyllosticta liriodendrica,* and *Ramularia liriodendri* cause leaf spots of tuliptree.

Control. Leaf spots rarely become sufficiently destructive to warrant control measures other than the gathering and destroying of infected leaves. The use of copper sprays may be justified on valuable trees.

* See footnote page 249.

Fig. 16-45. Anthracnose of tuliptree leaves caused by the fungus *Gloeosporium liriodendri.*

POWDERY MILDEWS. Two species of fungi, *Phyllactinia corylea* and *Erysiphe polygoni*, produce a white coating over the leaves of this host.

Control. Where particularly valuable small trees are affected, spray with Benlate, Karathane, or wettable sulfur.

ROOT AND STEM ROT. *Cylindrocladium scoparium.* This disease has been associated with decline of large tuliptrees in Georgia and North Carolina.

Control. Control measures have not been developed.

SAPSTREAK. *Ceratocystis coerulescens.* Sapstreak occasionally occurs on tuliptree.

Control. No effective control has been developed.

WILT. *Verticillium albo-atrum.* This disease has been found in Connecticut and Illinois.

Control. See Chapter 14.

Physiological Disease

LEAF YELLOWING. Starting in midsummer, during dry, hot periods, many tuliptree leaves turn yellow and drop prematurely. The yellowing is due to climatic conditions and not to any destructive organism. The leaves of recently transplanted trees exhibit yellowing more frequently than those of well-established trees. Very often, small, angular, brownish specks appear on the leaves between the leaf veins as a preliminary stage of yellowing and defoliation.

Insects

TULIPTREE APHID. *Macrosiphum liriodendri.* This small green aphid secretes copius quantities of honeydew. Hence leaves of other plants growing beneath the tree are coated with honeydew, which is then overrun by the sooty mold fungus.

Control. Late spring and early summer applications of Meta-Systox R, malathion, or carbaryl (Sevin) will control this aphid.

TULIPTREE SCALE. *Toumeyella liriodendri.* Trees may be killed by heavy infestations of oval, turtle-shaped, often wrinkled, brown scales, ⅓ inch in diameter (Figs. 16-46 and 16-47). The lower branches, which are usually the first to die, may be completely covered with scales. Like the tuliptree aphid, this scale insect secretes much honeydew. The secretion drops on leaves and is soon covered by sooty, black mold. Tuliptree scales overwinter as partly grown young. They grow rapidly until they mature in August. Young scales are produced in late August, at which time the old females dry up and fall from the tree.

Control. Spray the trees with a dormant miscible oil on a relatively warm day in late March or early April before the buds open. Or spray with malathion, Meta-Systox R, or carbaryl (Sevin) in late August or

Fig 16-46. Left: Adult stage of tuliptree scale.

Fig. 16-47. Right: Crawling stage of tuliptree scales which appears in late summer.

early September when the young are crawling about, and repeat the spray 2 weeks later.

OTHER SCALE INSECTS. In addition to the very common and destructive tuliptree scale, this host is also subject to oystershell and willow scale.

Control. Spray with miscible oil in early spring followed by malathion in late May.

TULIPTREE SPOT GALL. *Thecodiplosis liriodendri.* A gallfly produces purplish spots about ⅛ inch in diameter on the leaves (Fig. 16-48). These are frequently mistaken for fungus leaf spots.

Control. The damage is more unsightly than detrimental to the tree. Hence sprays are rarely used to control this pest.

SASSAFRAS WEEVIL. See under Sassafras (Chapter 15).

TUPELO (*Nyssa*)

Tupelo, also known as sourgum and pepperidge tree, makes a fine lawn or park tree but because it is difficult to transplant, it is not commonly used. Its fall coloration is outstanding.

Fig. 16-48. Tuliptree spot gall caused by the gallfly *Thecodiplosis liriodendri.*

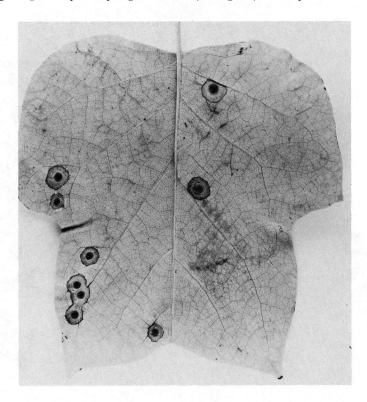

Diseases

CANKER. Five species of fungi, *Botryosphaeria dothidea*, *Fusarium solani*, *Nectria galligena*, *Strumella coryneoidea*, and *Septobasidium curtisii*, produce stem cankers on tupelo.

Control. Prune and destroy infected branches. Keep trees in good vigor by watering and fertilizing when necessary.

LEAF SPOTS. *Mycosphaerella nyssaecola*. Irregular purplish blotches, which later enlarge to an inch or more in width, are commonly scattered over the upper surfaces of the leaves of young tupelo trees in the southeastern states. Minute black fruiting bodies of the fungus are visible in the infected areas.

Two other fungi, *Cercospora nyssae* and *Pirostoma nyssae*, also cause leaf spots.

Control. Copper fungicides are suggested as preventive sprays. Raking and destroying infected leaves in fall should also help to reduce infections.

RUST. *Aplospora nyssae*. This rust fungus occasionally infects tupelos from Maine to Texas.

Control. Control practices are not warranted.

Insects

TUPELO LEAF MINER. *Antispila nyssaefoliella*. Leaves are first mined by the larval stage. When mature, the larvae cut oval sections out of the leaves and fall to the ground with the severed pieces.

Control. Spray with malathion in May when the adult moths emerge. Repeat within 10 days.

TUPELO SCALE. *Phenacaspis nyssae*. This scale is nearly triangular in shape, flat, and snow-white.

Control. A dormant oil spray in early spring will provide control.

OTHER PESTS. Two other pests have been reported on tupelo: the azalea sphinx moth and San Jose scale.

Control. Malathion or carbaryl (Sevin) sprays will control the larval stage of the former and the crawling stage of the latter.

WALNUT (*Juglans*)

Black walnut and butternut are rarely used as street trees. They require exacting soil conditions, are subject to wind and ice damage, are untidy, and their nuts tempt children to cause damage to the trees.

In ornamental plantings, the black walnut may produce detrimental effects on other types of plants growing nearby. The author has observed extensive damage to native and hybrid rhododendrons and to mountain laurel when these plants were grown in close proximity to black walnut roots. Other observers have reported similar damage to apple trees, alfalfa, tomato, potato, and a number of perennial ornamental plants growing near black walnut, and butternut as well.* In most instances, the removal of the nut trees resulted in the disappearance of the harmful effects.

A number of important diseases and insect pests occur on the different species of walnut.

Diseases

CANKER. This disease is also common on apple; aspen; beech; birch; mountain, red, and sugar maples; dogwood; butternut; pignut hickory; and red, white, and black oaks.

Symptoms. Scattered, often numerous, rough, sunken, or flattened cankers with a number of prominent ridges of callus wood arranged more or less concentrically on the trunks or branches are characteristic symptoms. The size of the cankers varies according to age; on larger branches and on the trunk some attain a length of 4 feet and a width of 2½ feet and have as many as 24 concentric ridges. Complete girdling and death of the distal portions may occur within a few years on smaller branches, and in 20 or more years on large trunks. The concentric pattern of the canker is less evident on twigs and smaller branches.

On the dead bark and wood in late fall and winter, small, globose, red masses, the fruiting structures of the causal fungus, are barely visible to the unaided eye.

Cause. Canker is caused by the fungus *Nectria galligena*. In late winter and in spring, the red fruiting bodies produce spores, which are forcibly ejected into the air. These are then carried by wind and rain to bark injuries made by insects, fungi, ice, low temperatures, wind, rubbing plant parts, or dead branch stubs. The spores germinate and produce mycelium, which penetrates the bark and wood. Penetration progresses rather slowly, usually about ½ inch of tissue being killed annually around the developing canker.

In California a bark canker on *Juglans regia* is caused by the fungus *Phomopsis juglandina*.

Control. All badly diseased trees should be felled, and the cankered tissues cut out and destroyed.

Valuable trees only mildly infected can be saved by removing the cankers by surgical methods, followed by shellacking the edges of the wound and thoroughly coating the open area with a good wound dressing. In addition, the trees should be fertilized, watered, and sprayed to control leaf pests and ensure rapid callusing.

Sites exposed to full sunshine should be used for new walnut plant-

* A most exhaustive study of this problem is presented in West Virginia Agricultural Experimental Station Circular 347, by M. G. Brooks.

ings, inasmuch as the fungus does not appear to thrive under such conditions.

BACTERIAL BLIGHT. English and Persian walnuts grown for ornament and for nut production in the eastern United States are susceptible to this destructive blight.

Symptoms. Small, water-soaked spots, which turn reddish-brown, appear on the young, unfolding leaves in spring. Ths spots are usually isolated, but they may coalesce, causing considerable distortion of the leaves. Black, sunken lesions also appear on the twigs, which may be completely girdled, causing death of the parts above. Infection of the husks usually results in premature dropping of the fruit, or in browning and decay of any fruit that remains attached.

Cause. The bacterium *Xanthomonas juglandis* causes blight. It is believed to overwinter mainly in diseased buds and is splashed by rain to various parts of the tree in spring.

Control. Cut out and destroy badly infected shoots. Spray with streptomycin, 50 ppm, plus a spreader-sticker, as flower buds open, at full bloom, and at petal fall.

BARK CANKER. *Erwinia nigrifluens.* This bacterial disease, first found in California in 1955 on Persian walnut, appears as irregular, large, shallow, dark-brown necrotic areas in the trunk and scaffold branches. The cankers enlarge in summer and are inactive in winter.

A phloem canker of *Juglans regia* in California is attributed to the bacterium *Erwinia rubrifaciens.*

Control. Control measures have not been developed for these diseases.

BROWN LEAF SPOT. *Gnomonia leptostyla.* Both butternut and walnut may be badly spotted by this fungus. The leaflets are attacked early in summer and are marked by irregular dark brown or blackish spots, somewhat similar to those caused on elm leaves by a closely related fungus. Much defoliation may result.

Marssonina juglandis forms irregularly circular brown spots in early summer. *Ascochyta juglandis, Cercospora juglandis, Phleospora multimaculans, Marssonina californica,* and *Cylindrosporium juglandis* also occasionally spot leaves. *Cristulariella pyramidalis* forms brown spots with white concentric rings (sometimes referred to as bull's-eye or zonate leaf spot). Complete defoliation of black walnut from this fungus has been reported from Illinois.

Control. Because the leaves harbor the causal fungi, all fallen leaves should be gathered and destroyed to eliminate this important source of inoculum. Black walnuts and butternuts of ornamental value should be sprayed periodically with Benlate, Cyprex, dodine, maneb, or zineb. The first application should be made when the buds start to open, the second about 10 days later, and the third when the leaves are full grown.

YELLOW LEAF BLOTCH. *Microstroma juglandis.* This fungus causes a yellow blotching on the upper sides of the leaves. The snow-white coating of fungus growth on the underside is composed of enormous numbers of spores, which spread the disease. It also causes the witches' broom disease of shagbark hickory.

Control. Same as for brown leaf spot.

DIEBACK. Though black walnut occasionally dies back, this disease is most prevalent and destructive on butternut and the Japanese walnut (*Juglans ailantifolia*).

Symptoms. On butternut the smaller branches first die back; the dying back progressing slowly until the main branches are involved. The bark on the affected branches changes from the normal greenish-brown to reddish-brown, and finally to gray. Small, black pimplelike pustules soon cover the dead bark. These disappear within a year or two, leaving small, irregular holes in the loose outer bark.

Cause. The fungus *Melanconium juglandis* causes the slow dying back and eventual death of the tree. Olive-gray elliptical or kidney-shaped spores are exuded in a black inky mass from the black pustules on the bark to initiate new infections.

Control. Severely affected trees should be removed and destroyed. Where the disease is still confined to the upper ends of the branches, pruning to sound wood will help to check further spread. In addition, fertilization, watering, sanitation, and insect and leaf-disease control measures should be adopted to help the tree regain its vigor.

TRUNK DECAY. The trunks of black walnut and butternut often show a white or a brown decay of the heartwood. The former is caused by the so-called 'false tinder' fungus, *Fomes igniarius,* which forms hard, gray, hoof-shaped fruiting bodies, up to 8 inches in width, along the trunk in the vicinity of the decay. The latter is caused by the fungus *Polyporus sulphureus,* which forms soft, fleshy, shelflike fruiting structures which are orange-red above and brilliant yellow below. The fruiting bodies become hard, brittle, and dirty-white as they age. These fungi usually enter the trunk through bark injuries and dead branch stubs.

Control. Once these decays become extensive, little can be done to eradicate them. Cleaning out the badly decayed portions and applying a wound dressing are suggested. Initial infections can be kept at a minimum by maintaining the vigor of the trees and by protecting the wounds as soon as they are formed.

WALNUT BUNCH DISEASE. Mycoplasma-like organism. This disease, formerly called witches' broom, was once thought to be caused by a virus. It is characterized primarily by the appearance of brooms or sucker growths on main stems and branches, tufting of terminals, profuse development of branchlets from axillary buds, leaf dwarfing, and, at times, death of the entire tree (Fig. 16–49). These symptoms vary from mild to severe and are particularly pronounced on Japanese walnut.

Fig. 16-49. Walnut bunch in Japanese walnut tree caused by a mycoplasma-like organism.

Butternut, Persian walnut, and eastern black walnut are also susceptible but to a lesser degree. The causal organism has been experimentally transmitted by grafting.

Control. Walnut bunch can be transmitted by grafting. An insect vector has not yet been associated with the disease, and hence no control measures have been developed.

OTHER DISEASES. A leaf spot and blasting of the nutlets of *Juglans mandchurica* in California is attributed to the bacterium *Pseudomonas syringae*, which also attacks lilacs. Blackline, a disorder characterized by formation at the graft union of a narrow, dark-brown, corky layer of nonconducting tissue that results in girdling, is suspected of being caused by a virus.

Control. Control measures are rarely needed.

Insects and Related Pests

WALNUT APHID. *Chromaphis juglandicola.* This pale yellow species is common on the undersides of English walnut leaves on the West Coast. It secretes large quantities of honeydew or aphid honey.

The giant bark aphid, *Longistigma caryae,* occasionally infests butternut and walnut.

Control. Spray with malathion.

WALNUT CATERPILLAR. *Datana integerrima.* Trees are defoliated by this caterpillar, which is covered with long white hairs and which grows to 2 inches in length. The adult female moth has a wingspread of 1½ inches. Its dark buff wings are crossed by four brown lines. Eggs are deposited in masses on the lower sides of the leaves in July. Winter is passed in the pupal stage in the soil.

OTHER CATERPILLARS. The following caterpillars also attack walnut: hickory horned devil, orange tortrix, omnivorous looper, red-humped, and yellow-necked.

Control. Spray with *Bacillus thuringiensis* or carbaryl (Sevin) when the larvae are small.

WALNUT LACE BUG. *Corythucha juglandis.* This pest is occasionally abundant on park trees, causing a bad spotting of the foliage.

Control. Spray early infestations with malathion or carbaryl (Sevin).

WALNUT SCALE. *Aspidiotus juglansregiae.* Part or all of a tree may be severely weakened by masses of round brown scales, ⅛ inch in diameter. The adult female is frequently encircled by young scales. The pest overwinters on the bark.

OTHER SCALES. Nut trees are also susceptible to many other scales, including black, California red, calico, cottony-cushion, greedy, oyster-shell, Putnam, scurfy, and white peach.

Control. To control walnut and other scales, spray with lime sulfur when the trees are dormant, or with malathion or carbaryl (Sevin) in late spring and again in early summer.

MITES. The following species of mites infest *Juglans:* European red, platani, southern red, and walnut blister. The last-mentioned, known scientifically as *Aceria erinea,* causes yellow or brown feltlike galls on the undersides of leaves.

Control. Spray twigs and bark with Diazinon, chlorobenzilate (Acaraben), or Kelthane before new growth begins in spring. A second application should be made to the newly formed leaves in late spring.

WILLOW *(Salix)*

Willow are rarely used as street trees or in locations where the breaking off of their weak-wooded branches is likely to cause injury. Some species, however, are used extensively in landscape plantings, especially around ponds and streams.

Diseases

LEAF BLIGHT. Blight, or scab, is the most destructive disease of willows in the United States. It has already killed hundreds of trees in the

northeastern states and appears to be spreading westward and southward.

Symptoms. Soon after growth starts in spring, a few small leaves turn
black and die. Later, all the remaining leaves on the tree suddenly wilt
and blacken, as if they had been burned by fire. Cankers on twigs may
result from the leaf infections. Following rainy periods, dense olive-
brown fruiting structures of the causal fungus appear on the undersides
of blighted leaves, principally along the veins and midribs.

Cause. Leaf blight is caused by the fungus *Venturia saliciperda*. It passes
the winter in infected twigs, on which it produces spores during early
spring. The spores are washed by rain onto the newly developing leaves
and initiate early infections. Such leaves produce large numbers of
spores of the asexual stage, *Pollaccia saliciperda,* which are responsible for
the severe blighting of the remaining leaves later in the season.

Control. Pruning of dead twigs and branches will eliminate the most
important source of inoculum for early-season infections. Spraying
with Fore, maneb, or zineb 3 or 4 times at 10-day intervals, starting when
the leaves begin to emerge in spring, will usually give control. These
practices are recommended only for valuable specimens. A number of
species, including weeping, bay-leaved, osier, purple, and pussy willows,
appear resistant to blight. These should be planted in place of the more
susceptible species, such as the crack and the heart-leaved willow.
Golden willow has been reported by some investigators to be susceptible,
by others to be resistant.

BACTERIAL TWIG BLIGHT. *Pseudomonas saliciperda.* The leaves turn
brown and wilt, and blighted branches die back for some distance.
Brown streaks can be seen in sections of the wood. The parasite winters
in the cankers, so that the young leaves are infected as soon as they
unfold. The disease has so far been serious only in New England. There
it has caused the death of a large number of trees by serious defoliation.
The damage has been confused with frost injury.

Control. Pruning as many infested twigs as possible and spraying as
suggested above for leaf blight are the recommended control measures.

CROWN GALL. *Agrobacterium tumefaciens.* See Chapter 14.

BLACK CANKER. Closely associated with leaf blight is the disease known
as black canker.

Symptoms. The symptoms of black canker resemble those of leaf blight
but usually appear later in summer. Dark brown spots, many of which
show concentric markings, appear on the upper leaf surface. Whitish-
gray or gray elliptical lesions, with black borders, appear subsequently
on the twigs and stems. Clusters of minute black fruiting bodies develop
in the stem lesions. Successive attacks over a 2- or 3-year period usually
result in death of the entire tree.

Cause. Black canker is caused by the fungus *Physalospora miyabeana.*

Two types of spores are produced on the stem lesions: one exuding from fruiting bodies as small pink masses in early summer; and the other released from tiny, black spherical bodies in early spring. The fungus lives over the winter on diseased twigs in the latter type of fruiting bodies.

Control. Pruning and spraying as suggested for leaf blight are recommended. The use of resistant varieties also offers a means of avoiding this destructive disease. The bay-leaved, the osier, and the weeping willow appear to be resistant, whereas the crack, the heart-leaved, the white, the purple, and the almond willow appear to be susuceptible. As in the case of leaf blight, golden willow has been reported by some observers to be extremely suceptible, and by others to be resistant.

CYTOSPORA CANKER. Willows are subject to this canker disease, caused by the fungus *Cytospora chrysosperma,* the perfect stage of which is *Valsa sordida,* already discussed under Poplar. The control measures listed under that host hold true also for willows. In addition, the use of resistant varieties offers a means of avoiding serious trouble. One investigator has observed that the disease occurs rarely on black willow or on peach-leaf willow, whereas crack and golden willows appear to be extremely susceptible.

OTHER CANKERS. Willows are susceptible to other canker diseases caused by *Botryosphaeria dothidea, Cryptodiaporthe salicina, Cryptomyces maximus, Discella carbonacea, Diplodina* sp., and *Macrophoma* sp.

Control. Control measures are rarely needed.

GRAY SCAB. *Sphaceloma murrayae.* This disease affects many species of willow, including *Salix fragilis, S. lasiandra,* and *S. lasiolepis.* Round, irregular, somewhat raised, grayish-white spots with narrow, dark brown margins appear on the leaves. Affected portions of the leaves frequently drop away.

Control. The same as for leaf spots, described below.

LEAF SPOTS. At least ten species of fungi—*Ascochyta salicis, Asteroma capreae, Cercospora salicina, Cylindrosporium salicinum, Marssonina kriegeriana, Myriconium comitatum, Phyllosticta apicalis, Ramularia rosea, Septogloeum salicinum,* and *Septoria didyma*—cause leaf spots on willow. Some may also cause premature defoliation.

Control. Because most leaf spot fungi overwinter on diseased fallen leaves, gathering and destroying the leaves is a recommended practice. Valuable specimens should be sprayed with ferbam, zineb, or copper fungicides when leaf spots cause considerable defoliation annually.

POWDERY MILDEW. *Uncinula salicis.* Leaves infected with this mildew are covered with a whitish feltlike mold. This develops chains of white spores which are shed in clouds. The little black fruiting bodies formed later in the season are characterized by microscopic appendages curled at the end like a shepherd's crook. This is not a serious disease of willows, but may cause some loss of leaves.

Control. Valuable willows infected with this fungus can be protected by an occasional application of Benlate or Karathane spray. Sprays containing wettable sulfur also can be used to control this mildew. Bordeaux mixture, recommended for several other diseases of willow, is also helpful.

RUST. *Melampsora* spp. Three or four species of rust attack willow leaves, causing lemon-yellow spots on the lower surfaces. Later in the season the spore-bearing pustules are dark-colored. The disease may be severe enough to cause dropping of the leaves. Of the rust-causing fungi, one species, *M. paradoxa,* has the larch as the alternate host; *M. abieti-capraearum* has the balsam fir; and *M.arctica* lives a part of the year on a saxifrage.

Control. Although rust infections are not considered serious, they may result in heavy defoliation of young trees. Gathering and destroying fallen leaves will help to prevent serious outbreaks. The use of copper or sulfur fungicides as preventives is suggested only in rare instances.

TAR SPOT. *Rhytisma salicinum.* These spots are usually jet black, very definitely bounded, about ¼ inch in diameter, somewhat raised about the surface of the leaf. They are more common on maple.

Control. Since this fungus winters on the old leaves, care should be taken, where the disease is serious, to rake up and destroy dead leaves. Spray the shrubs or trees early in May with bordeaux mixture or wettable sulfur.

WITCHES' BROOM. Mycoplasma-like organism. Early breaking of axillary buds and subsequent growth of numerous spindly, erect branches with stunted leaves on *Salix rigida* are characteristic symptoms of this disease. The witches' brooms die the winter after they are formed.

Control. Ways of preventing this disease have yet to be developed.

Insects

APHIDS. Several species of aphids infest willows, the most common being the giant bark, *Longistigma caryae.*

Control. Spray valuable specimens with malathion or carbaryl (Sevin).

EASTERN TENT CATERPILLAR. *Malacosoma americanum.* The leaves are chewed and small silken nests are formed in branch crotches by the tent caterpillar, a yellow-haired, black form with white lines down the back (Fig. 15-13). It attains a length of nearly 2 inches, prefers to feed on wild cherry but will feed on apple, peach, and plum in addition to willow. When these trees are scarce, the insects will also defoliate ash, beech, birch, elm, maple, oak, poplar, and many shrubs. The adult female, a fawn-colored moth, has a wing expanse of 2 inches. Eggs are laid in cylindrical clusters on twigs in July.

Control. Remove and destroy egg clusters and nests when they appear, and spray with carbaryl (Sevin) when new twig growth is 2 to 4 inches long in spring.

BASKET WILLOW GALL. *Rhabdophaga salicis.* Swollen, distorted twigs may be produced by yellowish, jumping maggots of the basket willow gall midge. The adults appear in early spring.

Control. Prune and destroy infested twigs.

MOTTLED WILLOW BORER. *Cryptorhynchus lapathi.* Swollen and knotty limbs may be produced by mottled willow borers, white legless larvae ½ inch long, which eat through the cambium, sapwood, and heartwood. The adult beetle, ⅓ inch long, has a long snout and grayish-black, mottled wing covers. Eggs are laid in fall, and the larvae overwinter in tunnels beneath the bark.

Control. Spray the trunk thoroughly during the latter part of August with methoxychlor.

IMPORTED WILLOW LEAF BEETLE. *Plagiodera versicolora.* These beautiful metallic-blue beetles, about ⅛ inch long, live through the winter under the bark scales and in the dead leaves about the tree. They emerge and lay their lemon-yellow eggs sometime in early June. The ugly larvae or grubs feed on the undersides of the foliage, leaving only a network of veins. The adult beetle develops during July and produces a second brood in August. This beetle is so much smaller than the Japanese beetle (*Popillia japonica*) that it can scarcely be mistaken for it. In the vicinity of New York both beetles cause rather serious damage.

Control. Spraying with carbaryl (Sevin) in late May will control this pest. A second spraying in late June may be necessary for the second brood.

PINE CONE GALL. *Rhabdophaga strobiliodes.* Cone-shaped galls at the branch tips that hinder bud development are produced by small maggots. The adult, a small fly, deposits eggs in the opening buds. The larvae hibernate in cocoons inside the galls.

Control. Remove and destroy galls in the fall, or spray thoroughly with malathion when the buds are swelling in spring.

POPLAR BORER. *Saperda calcarata.* This borer penetrates deeply into the wood and may be distinguished from the willow borer by the excelsior-like frass. (See also under Poplar.)

Control. If their tunnels are visible, the borers can be killed by inserting a flexible wire, or by using a preparation containing nicotine sulfate in jelly form, then sealing the hole with wax or chewing gum. Badly infested willows should be cut down and destroyed.

WILLOW FLEA WEEVIL. *Rhynchaenus rufipes.* The overwintering adult beetle emerges in the middle of April. During the latter part of May it excavates a circular mine on the underside of the leaf and it deposits its eggs. The adults feed on the foliage, causing it to become brown and dry. The larvae begin to mine the leaves about the middle of June. By the end of July, where infestation is heavy, the trees appear as if scorched by fires.

Control. To control the adult weevil, spray in mid-May with carbaryl (Sevin).

WILLOW LACE BUG. *Corythucha mollicula.* Willow leaves may be severely mottled and yellowed by this sucking insect.

Control. Malathion or carbaryl (Sevin) sprays in late spring provide excellent control.

WILLOW SHOOT SAWFLY. *Janus abbreviatus.* The female lays its eggs in the shoots in early spring. It then girdles the stem, preventing further growth of the twig, which wilts and dies. The young borers feed in the pith of the shoots, which die eventually.

Control. Prune and destroy infested twigs. Spray with carbaryl (Sevin) when the larvae are small.

WILLOW SCURFY SCALE. *Chionaspis salicis-nigrae.* Branches and even small trees may be killed by heavy infestation of this pest, a pear-shaped white scale ⅛ inch long. The insect passes the winter in the egg stage underneath the scale of the female.

Other scale insects that attack willows are black, California red, cottony-cushion, cottony maple, European fruit, greedy, lecanium, obscure, oystershell, Putnam, soft, and terrapin.

Control. Spray with lime sulfur or a dormant oil in spring when trees are still dormant, then with malathion or carbaryl (Sevin) in May and again in June to control the crawling stage.

BAGWORM. See under Arborvitae (Chapter 17).

CALIFORNIA TENT CATERPILLAR. See under Strawberry-Tree (Chapter 15).

CARPENTER WORM. See under Ash (Chapter 15).

HEMLOCK LOOPER. See under Hemlock (Chapter 17).

GIANT HORNET. See under Boxwood (Chapter 17).

OMNIVOROUS LOOPER. See under Acacia (Chapter 15).

WALNUT CATERPILLAR. See under Walnut.

YELLOWWOOD *(Cladrastis)*

Few diseases and only one insect pest have been recorded on this host. A powdery mildew caused by *Phyllactinia corylea,* canker by *Botryosphaeria dothidea,* wilt by *Verticillium albo-atrum,* and a decay of the butt and roots of living trees by *Polyporus spraguei* occur occasionally. An unidentified species of scale may occasionally infest yellowwood. Control measures are rarely necessary.

Yellowwood is also susceptible to the bean yellow mosaic virus. Affected trees have irregularly shaped leaflets with prominent vein chlorosis, mottle, and some downward rolling along the mid-veins. The importance of this disease has not been assessed. Control measures are not known.

Selected Bibliography

Anonymous. 1954. *Chestnut blight and resistant chestnuts.* USDA Farmer's Bul. 2068. 21 p.

————. 1970. *Cornell recommendations for commercial production and maintenance of trees and shrubs.* N.Y. State College of Agr., Ithaca, N.Y. Rev. of Feb. 1970.

————. 1973. *Pressure injection of methyl 2-benzimidazole carbamate hydrochloride solution as a control for Dutch elm disease.* USDA Forest Service Res. Note NE-176. 9 p.

————. 1976. *Maple diseases and their control.* USDA Home and Garden Bul. 81. 6 p.

————. 1977. Detecting, controlling tree diseases and pests: maple. *Grounds Maintenance.* Vol. 12 (no. 1). p. 47, 50, 53. Intertec Publ. Corp., Overland Park, Kansas 66212.

Anderson, H. W. and David Gottlieb. 1952. 'Plant disease control with antibiotics.' *Economic Botany.* Vol. 6 (No. 3). p. 294–308.

Anderson, P. J. and W. H. Rankin. 1914. 'Endothia canker of chestnut.' *Cornell Univ. Agr. Exp. Sta. Bul.* 347. p. 530–618.

Ashcroft, J. M. 1934. 'European canker of black walnut and other trees.' *W. Va. Agr. Exp. Sta. Bul.* 261. p. 1–52.

Atkinson, G. F. 1901. 'Studies on some shade tree and timber destroying fungi.' *Cornell Agr. Exp. Sta. Bul.* 193. p. 199–235.

Avery, G. S. 1957. 'The dying oaks.' *Scientific American.* May 1957. p. 112–22.

Beattie, R. K. and J. D. Diller. 1954. 'Fifty years of chestnut blight in America.' *Jour. Forestry.* Vol. 52. p. 323–29.

Born, G. L. and J. L. Crane. 1972. '*Kaskaskia gleditsiae* gen. et sp. nov. Parasitic on thornless honey locust in Illinois.' *Phytopathology* Vol. 62. (No. 8). p. 926–30.

Britton, W. E. and R. B. Friend. 1935. 'Insect pests of elms in Connecticut.' *Conn. Agr. Exp. Sta. Bul.* 369. p. 265–307.

Burgess, A. F. 1929. 'Insect pests of trees.' *Proc. Fifth National Shade Tree Conference.* p. 63–64.

Cannon, W. N., Jr. and D. P. Worley. 1976. 'Dutch elm disease control: performance and costs.' USDA Forest Service Res. Paper NE-345. 7 p.

Carter, J. C. 1940. 'Diseases of oaks and Verticillium wilt of woody plants.' *Proc. Sixteenth National Shade Tree Conference.* p. 83–91.

————. 1975. 'Major tree diseases of the century.' *Jour. Arboriculture.* Vol. 1 (No. 8). p. 141–47.

Clapper, R. B. and G. F. Gravatt. 1943. "The American chestnut: Its past, present, and future.' *Southern Lumberman.* Vol. 167 (No. 2105). p. 227–29.

Clapper, R. B. and R. K. Beattie. 1944. 'American and blight-resistant chestnuts.' *Flower Grower.* Vol. 31 (No. 10). p. 488–89, 500.

Clinton, G. P. and F. A. McCormick. 1929. 'The willow scab fungus.' *Conn. Agr. Exp. Sta. Bul.* 302. p. 443–69.

Comstock, J. H. and A. B. Comstock. 1906. *A manual for the study of insects* Comstock Publishing Co., Ithaca, N. Y. 701 p.

Davis, S. H. and J. L. Peterson. 1973. 'A wound dressing to prevent spread of the *Ceratocystis* causing cankerstain of the planetree.' *Plant Disease Reptr.* Vol. 57 (No. 1). p. 28–30.

Day, W. R. 1924. 'The watermark disease of the cricket bat willow.' *Oxford Forestry Mem.* Vol. 3. p. 1–30.

Dietrich, Joseph. 1957. 'A look at Dutch elm disease control.' *Trees.* Nov.-Dec. 1957. p. 16–18.

Doane, R. W., E. C. Van Dyke, W. J. Chamberlain, and H. E. Burke. 1936. *Forest insects.* McGraw-Hill Book Co., New York. 463 p.

Ehrlich, John. 1934. 'The beech bark disease.' *Canad. Jour. Res.* Vol. 10 (Special number). p. 593–692.

Ford, R. E. et al. 1972. 'Discovery and characterization of elm mosaic virus in Iowa.' *Phytopathology.* Vol. 62 (No. 9). p. 987–91.

French, W. J. and S. B. Silverborg. 1967. '*Scleroderris* canker of red pine in New York State plantations.' *Plant Disease Reptr.* Vol. 51 (No. 2). p. 108–9.

Galloway, B. T. 1926. 'The search in foreign countries for blight resistant chestnuts and related tree crops.' *U. S. Dept. Agr. Circ.* 383. p. 1–16.

Garren, K. H. 1949. 'Leader dieback— a "new" disease of sweet gum.' *Plant Disease Reptr.* Vol. 33(No. 9).p. 351–53.

Grant, T. J. and Perley Spaulding. 1939. 'Avenue of entrance for canker forming nectrias of New England hardwoods.' *Phytopathology.* Vol. 29. p. 351–59.

Gravatt, G. F. and L. S. Gill. 1930. *Chestnut blight.* USDA Farmer's Bul. 1641. 18 p.

Hahn, G. G. and T. T. Ayers. 1934. '*Dasyscyphae* on conifers in North America.' *Mycologia.* Vol. 26.p. 73–101, 167–80, 479–501.

———. 1936. 'The European larch canker and its relation to certain other cankers of conifers in the United States.' *Jour. Forestry.* Vol. 34. p. 898–908.

Hart, J. H. 1970. 'Attempts to control the Dutch elm disease by pruning.' *Plant Disease Reptr.* Vol. 54 (No. 11). p. 985–86.

Headland, J. K. et al. 1976. 'Severity of natural *Endothia parasitica* infection of Chinese chestnut.' *Plant Disease Reptr.* Vol. 60 (No. 5). p. 426–29.

Hedgcock, G. G. 1929. 'The large leafspot of chestnut and oak associated with *Monochaetia dezmazierii.*' *Mycologia.* Vol. 21. p. 324–25.

Henry, B. W. 1944. '*Chalara quercina*, n. sp., the cause of oak wilt.' *Phytopathology*, Vol. 34. p. 631–35.

Hepting, G. H. 1939. *A vascular wilt of the mimosa tree.* USDA Circ. 535. 10 p.

———. 1955. 'The current status of oak wilt in the United States.' *Forest Sci.* Vol. 1 (No. 2). p. 95–103.

Hiley, W. E. 1919. *The fungal diseases of the common larch.* Oxford Univ. Press, New York, 204 p.

Hutchins, L. M. *et al.* 1951. 'Diseases of shade and forest trees.' *Brooklyn Botanic Garden Record.* Plants and Gardens. Vol. 7 (No. 2). p. 121–58.

Jaynes, R. A. and N. K. Van Alfen. 1974. 'Control of American chestnut blight by trunk injection with methyl-2-benzimidazole carbamate (MBC).' *Phytopathology*. Vol. 64 (No. 11). p. 1479–80.

Kegg, J. D. 1973. 'Oak mortality caused by repeated gypsy moth defoliations in New Jersey.' *Jour. Econ. Ent.* Vol. 66 (No. 3). p. 639–41.

Kim, K. S. and J. P. Fulton. 1973. 'Association of viruslike particles with a ringspot disease of oak.' *Plant Disease Reptr.* Vol. 57 (No. 12). p. 1029–31.

Marshall, R. P. and Alma Waterman. 1948. *Common diseases of important shade trees.* USDA Farmer's Bul. 1987. 55 p.

McKenzie, M. A. 1936. 'Shade tree diseases of New England.' *Proc. Twelfth National Shade Tree Conference*, p. 100–103.

Miles, L. E. 1921. 'Leaf spots of elm.' *Bot. Gaz.* Vol. 71. p. 100–103.

Munro, G. 1976. 'Recent work with water soluble Benlate in Canada.' *Jour. Arboriculture.* Vol. 2. (No. 4). p. 73–76.

Neely, Dan. 1972. 'Control of the twig blight state of sycamore anthracnose.' *Plant Disease Reptr.* 54 (No. 4). p. 354–55.

———. 1976. 'Sycamore anthracnose.' *Jour. Arboriculture.* Vol. 2 (No. 8). p. 153–57.

Neely, Dan, R. Phares, and B. Weber. 1976. '*Cristulariella* leaf spot associated with defoliation of black walnut plantations in Illinois.' *Plant Disease Reptr.* Vol. 60 (No. 7). p. 587–90.

Neiswander, R. B. 1957. 'The control of some gall makers on shade trees.' *Trees.* May-June 1957. p. 20–22.

Pirone, P. P. 1938. 'The detrimental effect of walnut to rhododendron and other ornamentals.' *N. J. Exp. Sta. Nursery Disease Notes.* Vol. 11 (No. 4). p. 450–52.

———. 1940. 'New diseases of Norway maples.' *Trees.* Mar.-Apr. 1940. p. 7, 15, 16, 18.

———. 1942. 'A new disease of sweet gum.' *American Forests.* Vol. 48. p. 130–31.

———. 1948. 'A new threat to London plane trees.' *Proc. Twenty-fourth National Shade Tree Conference.* p. 97–101.

———. 1953. 'Fire as predisposing (contributing) factor in canker diseases of street trees.' *Trees Magazine.* Vol. 13. Sept.-Oct. 1953. p. 9–10, 20.

Rex, E. G. and J. M. Walter. 1946. *The cankerstain disease of plane trees.* New Jersey Dept. of Agr. Circ. 360. 23 p.

Rexrode, C. O. 1976. 'Insect transmission of oak wilt.' *Jour. Arboriculture.* Vol. 2 (No. 4). p. 66–65.

Rexrode, C. O. and T. W. Jones. 1971. 'Oak bark beetles carry the oak wilt fungus.' *Plant Disease Reptr.* Vol. 55 (No. 2) Feb. 1971. p. 108–11.

Santamour, F. S. 1973. 'Resistance to Dutch elm disease in Chinese elm hybrids.' *Plant Disease Reptr.* Vol. 57 (No. 12). p. 997–99.

Schrenk, H. von and Perley Spaulding. 1929. *Diseases of deciduous forest trees.* U.S. Dept. Agr. Bur. Pl. Ind. Bul. 149, 85 p.

Shigo, A. L. 1976. 'The beech bark disease.' *Jour. Arboriculture.* Vol. 2 (No. 2). p. 21–25.

Sinclair, W. A. and T. H. Filer. 1974. 'Diagnostic features of elm phloem necrosis.' *American Arboriculturist.* Vol. 39 (No. 1). p. 145–49.

Sinclair, W. A., J. L. Saunders, and E. J. Braun. 1975. *Dutch elm disease and phloem necrosis.* N. Y. S. College of Agriculture. Cornell Tree Pest Leaflet. A-9. 20 p.

Sinclair, W. A., E. J. Braun, and A. O. Larsen. 1976. 'Update on phloem necrosis of elms.' *Jour. Arboriculture*. Vol. 2 (No. 6). p. 106–13.

Steward, V. B. 1916. 'The leaf blotch disease of horsechestnut.' *Cornell Agr. Exp. Sta. Bul.* 371. p. 411–19.

Strong, F. C. 1957. 'Nature and control of anthracnose of shade trees.' *Arborist's News*. Vol. 22 (No. 5). p. 33–39.

TeBeest, D. O., R. D. Durbin, and J. E. Kuntz. 1976. 'Stomatal resistance of red oak seedlings infected by *Ceratocystis fagacearum*.' *Phytopathology*. Vol. 66 (No. 11). p. 1295–97.

Townsend, A. M. 1971. 'Relative resistance of diploid *Ulmus* species to *Ceratocystis ulmi*.' *Plant Disease Reptr*. Vol. 55 (No. 1). p. 980–82.

Townsend, A. M. and L. R. Schreiber. 1976. 'Resistance of hybrid elm progenies to *Ceratocystis ulmi*.' *Phytopathology*. Vol. 66 (No. 9). p. 1107–10.

True, R. P., H. L. Barnett, C. K. Dorsey, and J. G. Leach. 1960. *Oak wilt in West Virginia*. West Virginia Univ. Agr. Exp. Sta. Bul. 448T. 119 p.

Turner, Neely. 1969. *The gypsy moth in Connecticut*. Conn. Agr. Exp. Sta. Circular 231. 8 p.

Walter, J. M. 1946. *Canker stain of plane trees*. USDA Circ. 742.

Welch, D. S. 1934. 'The range and importance of Nectria canker of hardwoods in the northeast.' *Jour. Forestry*. Vol. 32. p. 997–1002.

Welch, D. S. and J. G. Matthysse. 1955. *Control of Dutch elm disease in New York State*. Cornell Ext. Bul. 932. 15 p.

Wheeler, A. G., Jr. and T. H. Henry. 1976. 'Biology of the honey locust plant bug, *Diaphnocoris*, and other Mirids associated with ornamental honey locust.' *Ann. Ent. Soc. America*. Vol. 69 (No. 6). p. 1095–1104.

Wicks, T. 1976. 'Persistence of benomyl tolerance in *Venturia inaequalis*.' *Plant Disease Reptr*. Vol. 6 (No. 10). p. 818–19.

Wilson, C. L. 1976. 'Recent advances and setbacks in Dutch elm disease research.' *Jour. Arboriculture*. Vol. 2 (No. 7). p. 136–39.

Wilson, C. L., C. E. Seliskar, and C. R. Krause. 1972. 'Mycoplasmalike bodies associated with elm phloem necrosis.' *Phytopathology* 62 (No. 1). p. 140–43.

Zentmeyer, G. A., J. G. Horsfall and P. P. Wallace. 1946. *Dutch elm disease and its chemotherapy*. Connecticut Agr. Exp. Sta. Bul. 498. 70 p.

17

Diseases and Insect Pests of Evergreen Trees

The treatment of evergreens in this chapter parallels closely that in the preceding chapters. Evergreen trees are used primarily for ornamental purposes. In a few areas in the country some of them are occasionally used as street trees.

ARBORVITAE (*Thuja*)

In the wild, the American arborvitae, also called white cedar, inhabits moist, sometimes swampy areas along banks of streams. When under cultivation, it prefers a moist but well-drained soil. The unthrifty condition of many trees in ornamental plantings is often associated with waterlogged soils.

Many horticultural varieties of American arborvitae are now available from nurserymen. Most of these are subject to the same troubles that affect the parent tree.

Diseases

LEAF BLIGHT. Although most destructive on the giant arborvitae of the Northwest, leaf blight occasionally appears on the American arborvitae. The disease is most prevalent on trees under 4 years old, but may attack trees of all ages.

Symptoms. From 1 to 4 irregularly circular, brown to black cushions appear on the tiny leaves in late spring. The leaves then turn brown, and the affected areas appear as though scorched by fire. Toward fall the leaves drop, leaving the branches bare.

490

Cause. The fungus *Fabrella thujina* causes leaf blight. The brown to black cushions on the leaves are the fruiting bodies of this fungus. Spores are discharged into the air from these bodies during rainy periods in summer, to initiate new infections.

Control. Small trees or nursery stock can be protected by several applications of bordeaux mixture or other copper sprays in midsummer and early autumn.

TIP BLIGHT. This disease resembles leaf blight but occurs primarily on varieties of *Thuja orientalis*, the golden biota or golden arborvitae being most susceptible. The leaves near the branch tips turn brown in late spring or early summer. Tiny black bodies, which are visible through a magnifying lens, occur on infected leaves.

Cause. The fungus *Coryneum berckmanii* causes tip blight. Several other fungi, including *Cercospora thujina, Pestalotia funerea,* and *Phacidium infestans,* are also associated with tip and twig blights.

Control. Spray with a copper fungicide 2 or 3 times at weekly intervals starting in late May.

JUNIPER BLIGHT. The fungus *Phomopsis juniperovora*, which is the cause of the blight of red cedar and other species of *Juniperus*, also attacks arborivitae.

Control. See twig blight, under Juniper.

Physiological Diseases

BROWNING AND SHEDDING OF LEAVES. The older, inner leaves of arborvitae turn brown and drop in fall. When this condition develops within a few days or a week, as it does in some seasons, many persons feel that a destructive disease is involved. Actually it is a natural phenomenon similar to the dropping of leaves of deciduous trees. When the previous growing season has been favorable for growth, or when pests, such as red spider, have not been abundant, the shedding occurs over a relatively long period through fall and consequently is not so noticeable.

WINTER BROWNING. Rapid changes in temperature, rather than drying, in late winter and early spring are responsible for browning of arborvitae leaves.

Insects and Related Pests

ARBORVITAE APHID. *Cinara tujafilina.* This reddish-brown aphid with a white bloom infests roots, stems, and leaves of arborvitae, Italian cypress, and retinospora.

Control. Treat soil with Cygon to control the root-infesting stage, and spray with malathion or Diazinon to control pests above ground.

BAGWORM. *Thyridopterix ephemeraeformis.* This caterpillar builds around itself an elongated sac, 2 or 3 inches in length, out of pieces of leaves of its host plant. If the host is a narrow-leaved evergreen, the bag looks as though it were shingled loosely with little sticks. The larva increases in size, enlarging the bag. The adult stage is a moth. The pest overwinters in the egg stage in the old female bags (Fig. 17-3).

Control. Hand-pick and destroy bags in winter. Spray with Diazinon, Dipterex, or carbaryl (Sevin) when the young worms first appear. The time of this appearance varies from May 1 to June 1, depending on the locality. Spray 7 to 10 days later if live bagworms are still present.

CEDAR TREE BORER. *Semanotus ligneus.* This pest attacks the bark and wood of cedars, redwood, Douglas-fir, and Monterey pine. The adult beetle is ½ inch long, black with orange or red markings on the wing cover. The larval stage bores into the inner bark and wood, frequently girdling the trees.

Control. Spray with malathion, carbaryl (Sevin) plus malathion, or Diazinon when the beetles emerge from the tree.

LEAF MINER. *Argyresthia thuiella.* The leaf tips turn brown as a result of the feeding within the leaves of the small leaf miner maggot. The adult stage is a tiny gray moth with a wingspread of ⅓ inch. The maggots overwinter in the leaves.

Control. Trim and destroy infested leaves. Spray with malathion in mid-June and early July, when eggs are hatching. Soil drenches with Cygon will also give some control.

ARBOVITAE WEEVIL. *Phyllobius intrusus.* White to pink larvae with brown heads feed on the roots of arborvitae and junipers. The adult, covered with greenish scales, feeds on the upper parts of the plants from May to July.

Control. Spray with carbaryl (Sevin) in late May and repeat in mid-June to control the adult stage.

MEALYBUG. *Pseudococcus ryani.* This pest also attacks incense-cedar, Norfolk Island pine, and redwood.

Control. Spray with malathion or Cygon.

SCALE. *Lecanium fletcheri.* This dark brown, flat, more or less hemispherical scale belongs to the so-called naked or unarmored scales. Newly hatched young have an amber color, which changes to pale orange-yellow. The insect overwinters as a partly grown scale on the stems, branches, and leaves. The pest is relatively unimportant on this host but is rather serious on yews.

Three other species of scales also attack arborvitae: European fruit lecanium, juniper, and San Jose.

Control. Malathion or Diazinon sprays are very effective if applied during midsummer when the young are crawling about.

SPIDER MITE. See spruce spider mite, under Juniper.

AUSTRALIAN-PINE (*Casuarina*)

This tree has been widely planted as an ornamental and as windbreaks in southern Florida.

Diseases

In Florida the Australian-pine is subject to a root rot caused by *Clitocybe tabescens* and to a species of root-knot nema. In California it is subject to the shoestring root-rot fungus *Armillaria mellea*.

Control. Effective control measures are not available.

Insects

AUSTRALIAN-PINE BORER. *Chrysobothris tranquebarica*. This flat-headed borer also attacks red mangrove trees. The adult females are greenish-bronze beetles, ½ to ¾ inch long, which deposit eggs on the bark in April.

Control. Cut out beetle-infested branches or trees in fall or winter. Valuable ornamental specimens can be protected by methoxychlor sprays applied in April.

OTHER INSECTS. Two species of mealybugs—citrus and long-tailed—and seven species of scales—barnacle, brown soft, cottony-cushion, Dictyospermum, Latania, long soft, and mining—also may infest Australian-pine.

Control. Control measures are rarely used.

BALD CYPRESS (*Taxodium*)

This genus has both evergreen and deciduous members. It is relatively free of fungus parasites and insect pests.

Diseases

TWIG BLIGHT. This disease, also present on a number of other conifers, including arborvitae, junipers, cypress, and yews, is rarely serious. It causes a spotting of leaves, cones, and bark and, in very wet seasons, a twig blight.

Cause. The fungus *Pestalotia funerea* is frequently associated with twig blight. It is not considered a vigorous parasite but becomes mildly pathogenic on trees weakened by mites, dry weather, sun scald, or low temperatures.

Control. Control measures are rarely applied, although a copper fungicide would probably be effective.

WOOD DECAY. A number of fungi belonging to the genera *Fomes, Lenzites, Poria,* and *Polyporus* are associated with wood decay of bald cypress. The last is sometimes found on living trees.

Control. Avoid wounding the trunk base of valuable trees. Keep trees in good vigor by watering and, if needed, by feeding.

OTHER FUNGUS DISEASES. Canker caused by species of *Septobasidium* and heart rot caused by *Fomes geotropus, F. extensus,* and *Ganoderma applanatum* have been reported from the Gulf Coast.

Control. No control measures are known for these diseases.

Insects

CYPRESS MOTH. *Recurvaria apicitripunctella.* The larval stage of this moth mines the leaves of bald cypress and hemlock, then webs them together in late summer. The female adult is a small yellow moth with black markings and fringed wings.

Control. Spray with carbaryl (Sevin) when the larvae begin to mine the leaves in late spring and before they web the leaves together.

BANYAN (*Ficus benghalensis*)

The only pests reported on this tree are insects: the long-tailed mealybug and four species of scales—black, Chinese obscure, green shield, and mining.

Control. Malathion sprays are suggested for these insects attacking valuable ornamental specimens. Summer oil emulsions are also effective.

BOXWOOD (*Buxus*)

Boxwood requires a well-drained, neutral soil with an occasional light application of ground limestone. In poorly drained soil, it is more susceptible to winter injury and fungus diseases. A few kinds, particularly the tree box, grow into small trees and hence are discussed here.

Diseases

CANKER. One of the most destructive diseases of boxwood is canker.

Symptoms. The first noticeable symptom is that certain branches or certain plants in a group do not start new growth so early in spring as do others, nor is the new growth so vigorous as that on healthy specimens. The leaves turn from normal to light green and then to various shades of tan. Infected leaves turn upward and lie close to the stem instead of spreading out like the leaves on healthy stems. The diseased leaves and branches show small, rose-colored, waxy pustules, the fruiting bodies of the fungus. The bark at the base of an infected branch is loose and peels off readily from the gray to black discolored wood beneath. Infection is frequently found to take place at the bases of small dead shoots or in crotches where leaves have been allowed to accumulate.

Cause. Canker is caused by the fungus *Pseudonectria rousselliana,* which is found on the stem cankers. Another stage of the same fungus, known as *Volutella buxi,* attacks the leaves and twigs, producing pale rose-colored spore masses on yellowed leaves. A species of *Verticillium* is occasionally associated with the dieback of twigs. The fungus *Nectria desmazierii,* whose imperfect stage is known as *Fusarium buxicola,* is also capable of causing canker and dieback of boxwood.

Control. Dead branches should be removed as soon as they are noticeable, and cankers on the larger limbs should be treated by surgical methods. The annual removal and destruction of all leaves that have lodged in crotches is recommended. Four applications of bordeaux mixture 3-3-50 or lime sulfur 1-50 have been shown to be very effective in preventing canker. The first should be made after the dead leaves and dying branches have been removed and before growth starts in the spring; the second, when the new growth is half completed; the third, after spring growth has been completed; and the fourth, after the fall growth has been completed. The boxwood should be fed with occasional applications to the soil of well-rotted cow manure, or commercial fertilizers, and ground limestone.

BLIGHT. Several fungi are associated with the blighting of boxwood leaves. The most common are *Phoma conidiogena* and *Hyponectria buxi.* The exact role of these fungi in this disease complex is not clear.

Control. The fungicides recommended for canker control will also control blight.

LEAF SPOTS. *Macrophoma candollei, Phyllosticta auerswaldii, Fusarium buxicola,* and *Collectotrichum* sp. Leaves turn straw-yellow and are thickly dotted with small black bodies, the fruiting structures of the first fungus listed above. The others also cause leaf spotting. All are apparently limited in their attacks to foliage weakened by various causes.

Control. Leaf spots may be controlled by shaking out all fallen and diseased leaves from the center of the bush and destroying them. All dead branches in the center of specimen plants or hedges should be removed to allow better aeration. An application of bordeaux mixture or any ready-made copper fungicide before growth starts in spring is beneficial. This spray will discolor the foliage, but the unsightly effect is soon hidden by new growth.

ROOT ROT. *Phytophthora cinnamomi.* 'Off-color' foliage followed by sudden wilting and death of the entire plant is characteristic of this disease. Yews and a large number of other woody ornamental plants are also subject to this disease. Another species, *P. parasitica,* also causes a root rot and blight of boxwood. *Paecilomyces buxi* was found to be associated with boxwood decline in Virginia.

Control. Infected plants cannot be saved. Pasteurize infested soil and replant with healthy specimens.

Nonparasitic Diseases

WINTER INJURY and SUN SCALD. Most boxwood troubles in the northeastern United States are due to freezing and sunscalding, which primarily injure the cambium of unripened wood. Several distinct types of symptoms are exhibited by winter injury. Young leaves and twigs may be injured when growth extends far into fall or begins too early in spring. Leaves may turn rusty brown to red as a result of exposure to cold, dry winds during winter. A dieback of leaves, twigs, and even the entire plant may occur on warm winter days when the aboveground tissues thaw rapidly and lose more water then can be replaced through the frozen soil and roots. Another type of winter injury is evinced by the splitting and peeling of the bark. The bark becomes loosened and the stems are entirely girdled, resulting in death of the distal portions.

Control. Fertilizers should be applied in late fall, preferably, or very early in spring. Adequate windbreaks should be provided during winter, especially in the more northern latitudes. In the latitude of New York City spraying with Wilt-Pruf NCF on a mild day in December, and again on a mild day the following February, will provide as much protection from winter winds as do burlap windbreaks. A heavy mulch consisting of equal parts of leaf mold and cow manure should be applied to prevent deep freezing and to aid in supplying water continously.

Insects and Related Pests

BOXWOOD LEAF MINER. *Monarthropalpus buxi*. Oval, water-soaked swellings on the lower leaf surface result from the feeding inside the leaves by the leaf miner, a yellowish-white maggot, ⅛ inch long. The adult is a tiny midge, $1/10$ inch long, which appears in May.

Control. When the adult midges are seen in late May (about the time the weigelas are in full bloom), spray the boxwood leaves with Diazinon, Cygon, malathion, or carbaryl (Sevin).

BOXWOOD PSYLLID. *Psylla buxi*. Terminal leaves are cupped and young twig growth is checked by the boxwood psyllid, a small, gray, sucking insect covered with a cottony or white waxy material (Fig. 17-1). The adult is a small green fly with transparent wings having a spread of ⅛ inch.

Control. Spray in mid-May and again 2 weeks later with Diazinon, malathion, or carbaryl (Sevin).

Fig. 17-1. Cupping of boxwood leaves (left and right) caused by the boxwood psyllid (*Psylla buxi*). Leaves in the center are normal.

BOXWOOD WEBWORM. *Galasa nigrinodis.* This pest chews leaves and forms webs on boxwood.

Control. Spray with malathion or carbaryl (Sevin) when the young larvae begin to feed.

GIANT HORNET. *Vespa crabro germana.* The bark is occasionally stripped from the branches by the giant hornet, which has a 1-inch wing expanse and dark orange markings. The pests nest in trees, in buildings, or underground.

Control. Locate the nests and blow Diazinon powder into the openings. Apply a Diazinon or carbaryl (Sevin) spray in mid-July to the trunks and branches of trees subject to bark-tearing by this pest. Repeat the application in early August.

MEALYBUGS. *Pseudococcus comstocki* and *Rhizoecus falcifer.* The former, known as the Comstock mealybug, attacks many hosts, including catalpa, holly, horsechestnut, maple, pine, and poplar. It is one of the few species capable of wintering outdoors. The latter, the ground mealybug, feeds on the roots of many shrubs and trees.

Control. Cygon, malathion, or carbaryl (Sevin) sprays applied to the leaves and stems will control the Comstock mealy-bug. A dilute solution of Diazinon applied to the soil around the base of the boxwood should control the ground mealybug.

SCALES. Five species of scales, California red, cottony maple, cottony-cushion, lesser snow, and oystershell, may infest boxwood.

Control. Spray with a dormant oil to control overwintering scales. Where infestations are heavy, follow with a Meta-Systox R, malathion, or carbaryl (Sevin) spray when the young are crawling about in May and June.

Other Pests

BOXWOOD MITE. *Eurytetranychus buxi.* A light mottling followed by brownish discoloration of the leaves is caused by infestations of 8-legged mites, about $1/64$ inch long when full grown. Winter is passed in the egg stage. The eggs hatch in April, and the young mites begin to suck out the leaf juices. By June or July, considerable injury may occur on infested plants. As many as six generations of mites may develop in a single season.

Control. The dormant oil spray recommended for scales will destroy many overwintering mites. Cygon, Diazinon, Kelthane, or Tedion applied during May and June will also control mites.

NEMAS. *Pratylenchus pratensis.* Leaf-bronzing, stunted growth, and general decline of boxwood may result from invasion by meadow nemas. These are tiny, eel-like worms visible only through a microscope. They enter the roots, usually near the tips, and move through the cortical tissue. Invaded portions soon die and the plant forms lateral roots above the invaded area. These laterals in turn are infested. Repeated infestations and lateral root production result in a stunted root system resembling a witches' broom. Even heavy rains may fail to wet such densely woven root-bundles. Boxwoods are also subject to several other parasitic nemas, including the southern root-knot nema *Meloidogyne incognita*; various ring nemas, *Criconema, Criconemoides,* and *Procriconema*; and the spiral nema *Helicotylenchus.*

Control. Several chemicals are available for controlling ectoparasitic nemas such as *Pratylenchus pratensis,* which live outside the roots. One of these is Nemagon, which is used as a soil drench around old, infested boxwood. The treatment must be repeated each year for several years before good control is achieved. It must be supplemented by shearing and fertilization to stimulate root activity.

Endoparasitic nemas such as the root-knot nema *Meloidogyne incognita,* which live inside the roots of boxwood, have been controlled with Dasanit or Mocap.

The life of infested but untreated plants may be prolonged by providing good care and by soaking the soil thoroughly during dry spells. Before boxwood is replaced in infested soil, the planting site should be fumigated with any one of several materials available for that purpose. Plant pathologists at state experiment stations will advise on selection and use of fumigants.

CAJEPUT (*Melaleuca*)

This tree has escaped from cultivation and has become naturalized in the Florida Everglades.

Insects

At least 14 species of scale as well as the citrus mealybug have been found on this host in Florida.

Control. Malathion or carbaryl (Sevin) sprays will control the crawler stage of the scales and the mealybug. Summer oil emulsion is also effective.

CAMPHOR-TREE (*Cinnamomum*)

This tree has escaped from cultivation from Florida to Louisiana and has become naturalized in Florida.

Sixteen species of scale insects infest camphor-trees in Florida. The most destructive one, which can be fatal to this host, is the camphor scale *Pseudaonidia duplex*. It is circular in shape, convex, dark blackish brown, and $^{1}/_{10}$ inch across.

Other pests of the camphor-tree are three species of mites—avocado red, plantanus, and southern red—and camphor thrips, *Liriothrips floridensis*.

Control. Summer oil emulsion, applied in February in the deep South and repeated in 30 days, will control the scale insects. Mites are controlled with Kelthane. Malathion will control the camphor thirps.

CEDAR (*Cedrus*)*

This genus contains several very beautiful evergreen trees like the Atlas cedar (*C. atlantica*) and the cedar of Lebanon (*C. libani*). Cedars are relatively free of pests and diseases.

Diseases

TIP BLIGHT. The fungus *Diplodia pinea*, formerly called *Sphaeropsis ellisii*, occasionally causes canker and dieback of branch tips in the South.

Control. The same as for tip blight of pine (p. 530).

* Plants commonly called cedar belong to several genera. See *Juniperus* (juniper), *Thuja* (arborvitae), *Chamaecyparis* (white cedar), and *Libocedrus* (incense cedar).

ROOT ROT. Several fungi, including *Armillaria mellea, Clitocybe tabescens,* and *Phymatotrichum omnivorum,* are associated with root and trunk decay. The last attacks a great variety of trees, shrubs, ornamental and food plants in the South.

Control. No effective, practicable control measures are known.

Insects

BLACK SCALE. *Saissetia oleae.* This dark brown to black scale is primarily a pest of citrus on the West Coast. It attacks a wide variety of trees and shrubs in the South and West, including the Deodar cedar (*C. deodara*). Besides extracting juice from the plant, it secretes on the leaves and stems a substance on which the sooty mold fungus grows.

Control. Carbaryl (Sevin) or malathion sprays when the young are crawling about in May and June are effective.

DEODAR WEEVIL. *Pissodes nemorensis.* This brownish snouted weevil feeds on the cambium of leader and side branches of Deodar, Atlas, and Lebanon cedars. It deposits eggs in the bark, and the ⅓-inch-long white grubs which hatch from the eggs burrow into the wood. Eventually the leaders and terminal twigs turn brown and die. Small trees may be killed by this pest.

Control. A methoxychlor spray applied in April, when the beetles are feeding, will control this insect.

CEDAR, INCENSE (*Libocedrus*)

This handsome columnar or narrow, pyramidal tree grows mainly in the northwestern United States, although it can be grown in warmer parts of the country.

Diseases

The bacterial crown gall caused by *Agrobacterium tumefaciens,* blight by the fungus *Herpotrichia nigra,* branch canker by *Coryneum cardinale,* needle cast by *Lophodermium juniperinum,* root rot by *Phymatotrichum omnivorum,* and rust by *Gymnosporangium libocedri* are recorded on incense cedar.

Control. Control measures are rarely needed.

Insects

The cypress bark beetle, cypress mealybug, and four species of scales—cypress, juniper, pine needle, and Putnam—infest incense cedar.

Control. Effective controls for the cypress bark beetle have not been developed. Mealybug and scales can be controlled with carbaryl (Sevin) or malathion sprays.

Other Pests

The mistletoe *Phoradendron juniperinum* f. *libocedri* infests incense cedar in the western states.

Control. No control is known.

CEDAR, WHITE (*Chamaecyparis*)

Diseases

BLIGHT. *Phomopsis juniperovora.* The leaves of white cedar may be attacked by this fungus. (See twig blight, under Juniper.)

WITCHES' BROOM. *Gymnosporangium ellisii.* This fungus enters the leaves of white cedar and travels down into the living bark of the twigs. The presence of the fungus stimulates the formation of a large number of buds which develop to form characteristic witches' brooms, shown in Figure 17-2. Eventually the branch with its broom dies. During the early

Fig. 17-2. Witches' broom on white cedar.

spring (in April) brown telial horns grow out from infected branches; they are about ¼ inch long and threadlike. Spores from these horns are carried in the wind to the bayberry, *Myrica*, which in turn becomes infected; a light orange-colored rust appears on the leaves and does considerable damage. The rust occasionally affects sweet-fern, *Comptonia*. When the seedlings of white cedar are attacked, the trees become dwarfed; trees 15 to 20 years old, if they live, may not be over a foot or two high. When young trees are infected at the growing point, the main trunk is prevented from developing normally and the tree is stunted. The fungus is deep-seated; sometimes it is even found in the pith region. Heavily broomed trees may die.

Control. No effective control has been proposed other than separating the two hosts. The fungus acts slowly, and thus removal of the brooms prevents the spread of the parasite to the bayberry, which otherwise endangers the evergreens.

SPINDLE BURL GALL. *Gymnosporangium biseptatum.* This rust fungus is more or less local in its infection, probably first infecting the leaves and then penetrating into the young branches. It stimulates an excessive growth of wood into long burls, which may be several inches in diameter. The branches which bear these burls eventually die. When infection occurs at the base of a young tree, the burl may continue to grow with the tree without doing particular damage. Burls a foot across have been seen at the bases of trees of about the same diameter. Occasionally two species of rust attack the trees at the same point, and a combination of burl and witches' broom results. The alternate host of the rust which causes the latter abnormality is the common *Amelanchier* or serviceberry. Ornamental cedars grown individually are rarely infected.

Another species of rust, *Gymnosporangium fraternum*, attacks the leaves of white cedar. It is of little consequence on this host but does some damage to chokeberry (*Aronia*), its alternate host.

Control. Control measures are unavailable.

ROOT ROT. *Phytophthora lateralis.* This highly destructive disease affects native white cedar in the Pacific Northwest. It is especially serious on Port Orford cedar, or Lawson cypress (*C. lawsoniana*). The fungus infects leaves, stems, and trunk in addition to the roots. Another species, *P. cinnamomi*, causes root rot of Lawson cypress seedlings in Louisiana.

Control. No satisfactory controls have been developed.

Insects

Among the pests which attack white cedar are the larvae of the imperial moth *Eacles imperialis*, the bagworm *Thyridopteryx ephemeraeformis* (Fig. 17-3), and the juniper scale *Diaspis carueli*. Details on control of the bagworm are given under Arborvitae.

CRYPTOMERIA (Cryptomeria)

This tree is practically free of fungus parasites and has no important insect pests.

Diseases

LEAF BLIGHT. Leaves and twigs may be blighted by a species of *Phomopsis* during rainy seasons.

Control. Pruning out affected leaves and twigs is usually sufficient. Copper fungicides can be used on valuable specimens. Dormant oil sprays, which may cause serious damage, should never be used on this host.

LEAF SPOT. Two fungi, *Pestalotia cryptomeriae* and *P. funerea*, are frequently associated with a leaf spotting of this host. Infection probably follows winter injury or some other agent.

Control. Same as for leaf blight.

CYPRESS*(Cupressus)

Diseases

CANKER. Twigs and branches be girdled by cankers, and the entire tree may be killed. Cypress, particularly the Monterey cypress, junipers, and Oriental arborvitae are all subject to this disease.

Cause. The fungus *Coryneum cardinale* forms spores in branch and twig cankers. The sexual stage of this fungus is said to be a species of *Leptosphaeria*.

Control. Because the fungus spores are spread by wind-splashed rain, by pruning tools, and perhaps by insects and birds, control is difficult. Remove and destroy severely infected trees. Drastically prune mildly infected ones and spray periodically with a copper fungicide, starting at the beginning of the rainy period.

CYTOSPORA CANKER. The columnar form of Italian cypress, *C. sempervirens*, along the California coast is most subject to this disease. Occasionally it also affects the horizontal form of Italian cypress and the smooth cypress.

Symptoms. Smooth reddish-brown cankers, from which resin flows, develop on young branches. Diseased bark on older branches becomes cracked and distorted with a more abundant flow of resin.

Cause. The fungus *Cytospora cenisia* f. *littoralis* causes this canker.

Control. Prune and destroy dead or dying branches. Trees with cankers on the trunks should be removed and destroyed.

OTHER DISEASES. Cypresses are subject to several other diseases: needle

* Certain species of *Chamaecyparis* and *Taxodium* are also called cypress.

Fig. 17-3. Bags of the bagworm on white cedar twigs.

blight caused by *Cercospora thujina,* crown gall by the bacterium *Agrobacterium tumefaciens,* and monochaetia canker by *Monochaetia unicornis.*

   Control. Control measures are rarely adopted.

   TWIG BLIGHT. *Phomopsis juniperovora.* See under Juniper.

Insects

   CYPRESS APHID. *Siphonatrophia cupressi.* This large green aphid infests blue and Monterey cypress.

   Control. Spray with malathion or carbaryl (Sevin) when the young begin to feed.

   CYPRESS MEALYBUG. *Pseudococcus ryani.* Primarily a pest of Monterey cypress in California, this species also infests arborvitae, redwood, and other species of cypress.

   Control. Control measures have not been developed.

   CATERPILLARS. The caterpillars of the following moths feed on cypress: tip moth, *Argyresthia cupressella*; webber, *Epinotia subviridis*; imperial, *Eacles imperialis*; and white-marked tussock moth, *Hemerocampa leucostigma.*

   Control. Spray with carbaryl (Sevin) when the caterpillars are small.

   BARK SCALE. *Ehrhornia cupressi.* This pink scale covered with loose white wax infests Monterey cypress primarily. It occasionally attacks Guadalupe and Arizona cypress and incense cedar. Leaves of heavily infested trees turn yellow, then red or brown.

Control. Malathion sprays applied to the trunk and branches are said to be effective in combating this scale.

OTHER SCALES. Several other scales, including the cottony-cushion and the juniper, occasionally infest cypresses. These are controlled with malathion sprays.

DOUGLAS-FIR (*Pseudotsuga taxifolia*)

Diseases

GALL DISEASE. *Agrobacterium pseudotsugae.* Galls are formed on the twigs of Douglas-fir and big-cone spruce in California. Young trees (up to 15 years in age) are most susceptible. When galls develop on the main stem, girdling and death of the upper portion follow.

Control. Control measures have not been developed.

CANKERS. *Cytospora* sp., *Dasyscypha ellisiana, D. pseudotsugae, Phacidiopycnis pseudotsugae,* and *Phomopsis lokoyae.* A number of fungi cause cankers on this host, most of them being prevalent in the Pacific Northwest.

Control. Control measures are rarely practiced except on important ornamental specimens.

LEAF CAST. *Rhabdocline pseudotsugae.* Yellow spots first appear near the needle tips in fall. The spots enlarge in spring, then turn reddish-brown, contrasting sharply with adjacent green tissues. With continued moist weather, the discoloration spreads until the entire needle turns brown. When many groups of needles are so affected, the trees have a brown, scorched aspect when viewed from a distance.

Two other fungi produce leaf cast of Douglas-fir: *Adelopus gaumanni* and *Rhabdogloeum hypophyllum.* The former produces symptoms closely resembling those of *Rhabdocline pseudotsugae,* and both may be present in the same tree.

Control. No control measures for large trees have been reported. Severe outbreaks in nurseries or on small trees can probably be prevented by spraying with copper fungicides at the time the spores are being discharged.

OTHER DISEASES. Douglas-fir is susceptible to a leaf and twig blight caused by the fungus *Botrytis cinerea,* which is serious in wet springs; rust by the fungus *Melampsora albertensis,* the alternate stage of which occurs on poplar; needle blight by *Rosellinia herpotrichioides;* and witches' broom by the mistletoe *Arceuthobium.* The fungus *Dermea pseudotsugae* causes a dieback and death of young Douglas-firs in northern California. Controls have not been developed.

Insects

APHIDS. *Chermes cooleyi* and *Essigella californica*. The former, the Cooley spruce gall aphid, is more common on spruce; the latter, the Monterey pine aphid, infests Monterey and ponderosa pines on the West Coast.

Control. The Cooley spruce gall aphid is controlled by a dormant oil spray applied in April when the trees are still dormant, or with a carbaryl (Sevin) spray in May. Nurserymen use either Endosulfan or Baygon sprays to control this pest. The Monterey pine aphid can be controlled with carbaryl (Sevin) or malathion sprays in April and May.

SCALES. Two scale insects, hemlock and pine needle, infest Douglas-fir. Malathion or carbaryl (Sevin) sprays are very effective against the young crawling stage of these pests.

OTHER INSECTS. This host is also subject to the spruce budworm, the pine butterfly, the Zimmerman pine moth, and the strawberry root weevil. The controls for these pests are discussed under more common hosts such as pine, spruce, and yew.

EUCALYPTUS—See Gum-Tree.

FIR (*Abies*)

Several parasitic microorganisms and insects attack firs but rarely produce extensive damage in ornamental plantings. Unthriftiness in many trees is more likely caused by an unfavorable environment.

Firs thrive best in light, porous, acid soils which are well drained and yet are continually moist. They also require full sunlight but appear to grow more vigorously in valleys or protected places than near hilltops or in exposed situations.

Diseases

NEEDLE AND TWIG BLIGHT. In the northeastern United States, needle and twig blight occurs quite commonly on balsam fir and to a lesser extent on Colorado and Alpine firs. Noble and Fraser firs are also susceptible, but are attacked infrequently.

Symptoms. The needles of the current season's growth turn red and shrivel, and the new twigs are blackened and stunted. Severely infected trees appear as though scorched by fire or damaged by frost. The lower branches are most heavily infected. Needles infected in previous years remain attached to the twigs.

Cause. The fungus *Rehmiellopsis balsameae* causes needle and twig blight. It overwinters on diseased needles and twigs. In spring, fruiting bodies mature on these parts and release spores, which infect the newly developing needles. The fungus *Cenangium abietis* occasionally attacks firs but is more common on pine.

Control. In ornamental plantings, control is possible by pruning and destroying infected twigs and by applying a copper fungicide 3 times at 12-day intervals, starting when the new growth begins to emerge from the buds.

LEAF CAST. *Bifusella abietis, B. faullii, Hypodermella mirabilis, H. nervata, Lophodermium autumnale*, and *L. lacerum*. When attacked by any one of these fungi, needles turn yellow, then brown, and drop prematurely. Elongated black bodies appear along the middle vein of the lower leaf surface. Spores shot from black fruiting bodies in summer to young leaves germinate and penetrate the new growth.

Control. Copper sprays applied as for needle and twig blight will control leaf cast.

CANKERS. *Cylindrocarpon* sp., *Cytospora pinastri, Cryptosporium macrospermum, Scoleconectria balsamea*, and *S. scolecospora*. Occasionally sunken dead areas on the trunk and branches of firs in ornamental plantings result from infection by one of the several fungi listed. On balsam fir, the fungus *Aleurodiscus amorphus* forms narrowly elliptical cankers with a raised border on the main trunk of young trees and centering around a dead branch.

Control. Sanitation, avoidance of bark injuries, and fertilization to maintain the trees in good vigor are suggested.

SHOESTRING ROOT ROT and WOOD DECAY are caused, respectively, by the fungus *Armillaria mellea* and by fungi belonging to the genera *Fomes, Polyporus, Lenzites*, and *Stereum*.

Control. No completely effective control is known. Avoid bark injuries and keep the trees in good vigor by watering and fertilization when needed.

RUSTS. *Milesia fructuosa, Hyalopsora aspidiotus, Uredinopsis mirabilis, U. osmundae, U. phegopteris, Pucciniastrum pustulatum, P. goeppertianum, Melampsora abieti-capraearum, Caeoma faulliana, Peridermium ornamentale*, and *Melampsora cerastii*. Most of these rust fungi attack forest firs but are seldom found on ornamental specimens.

Control. Measures to control rusts are rarely adopted because the fungi do not cause much damage. Most of the rusts listed above have alternate hosts which are needed to complete the life cycles of the fungi. The elimination of the alternate host will result in nearly complete disappearance of the fungus. A rust expert must be consulted for the name of the alternate host before any eradicatory steps are taken. Periodic applications of sulfur sprays during summer will also control rusts, but these are not practical for large trees.

SOOTY MOLD. Needles of firs are covered more frequently than those of most other species of evergreens by black sootlike material. This substance consists of fungus tissues that exist on the secretions of aphids and other insects. The black mold will usually disappear if the insects are kept under control.

Insects

BALSAM TWIG APHID. *Mindarus abietinus*. The leaves and shoots of white and balsam firs, as well as spruce, are attacked by this green aphid, which is covered with white waxy secretions. Affected shoots are roughened and curled.

Control. Spray with malathion or Meta-Systox R in late April and repeat in mid-May if necessary.

BALSAM GALL MIDGE. *Dasineura balsamicola*. Small, subglobular swellings at the base of the leaves are caused by this midge.

Control. Spray the newly developing leaves in late April with malathion.

BARK BEETLE. *Pityokteines sparsus*. Seepage of balsam from the trunk, reddening of the needles, and death of the upper parts of the tree result from infestations of the balsam bark beetle, a pest $1/10$ inch long. Vigorous trees are attacked.

Control. Prune and destroy infested parts.

CATERPILLARS. Several caterpillars feed on the needles of firs. These are the larval stage of the hemlock looper moth, the spotted tussock moth, the balsam fir sawfly, the Zimmerman pine moth, and the pine butterfly.

Control. Spray with carbaryl (Sevin) when the caterpillars are young.

SPRUCE SPIDER MITE. *Oligonychus ununguis*. This is one of the most important pests of evergreen trees. The tiny $1/64$ inch long) sap-sucking pest turns the leaves of firs and junipers yellow, those of arborvitae brown, spruce gray, and hemlock nearly white. In very severe infestations it produces a fine silken webbing over the leaf surfaces. The young are pale green; the adult female is greenish-black (Fig. 17-19). Winter is passed in the egg stage on the twigs and needles. Depending on the locality and the weather, eggs hatch in April or May and complete a generation in 4 or 5 weeks. Spider mites cause most damage in hot, dry seasons.

Control. Spray with 1 part concentrated lime sulfur in 10 parts of water or with 'superior'* type dormant oil before growth begins in spring. Or spray in mid- or late May with Aramite, Dimite, Kelthane, Chlorobenzilate, or Tedion to kill the young mites of the first generation. Repeat later in the season if necessary. Because of their staining properties, lime sulfur sprays should not be used on trees near white-painted objects.

* See footnote page 249.

SCALE. Several kinds of scale insects, including the oystershell and pine needle scale, infest firs.

Control. Spray with lime sulfur as for spider mite, or with malathion or carbaryl (Sevin) during May and June to control the young crawling stages.

BALSAM WOOLLY APHID. *Adelges piceae.* This introduced aphid is becoming increasingly prevalent in the Northeast. It attacks twigs and buds and causes dieback of twigs and treetops.

Control. Spray with malathion when aphids become numerous.

BAGWORM. See under Arborvitae.

SPRUCE BUDWORM. See under Spruce.

CEDAR TREE BORER. See under Arborvitae.

Other Pests

DWARF MISTLETOE. *Arceuthobium campylopodium.* In California this mistletoe is a widespread serious pest of red fir (*Abies magnifica*) and white fir (*A. concolor*).

Control. In valuable trees, remove dwarf mistletoe by pruning.

GUM-TREE (*Eucalyptus*)

Gum-trees, also called eucalyptus, are largely natives of Australia. They are widely grown in California and some other parts of the southwestern United States.

Diseases

LEAF SPOTS. *Hendersonia* spp., *Monochaetia monochaeta, Mycosphorella moelleriana,* and *Phyllosticta extensa.* Several species of fungi cause leaf spots of *Eucalyptus.* They are rarely serious enough to justify control measures.

CROWN GALL. The bacterium *Agrobacterium tumefaciens* and many wood-decaying fungi also occur on this host.

OTHER FUNGUS DISEASES. Among other diseases of this host are canker and twig blight caused by *Botryosphaeria dothidea,* shoestring root rot by *Armillaria mellea* in California, root rot by *Clitocybe tabescens* in Florida and by *Phymatotrichum omnivorum* in Texas.

Control. Control measures for crown gall and shoestring root rot are given in Chapter 14.The other diseases are not serious enough to warrant control practices.

EDEMA. Several species of *Eucalyptus* grown in greenhouses as ornamentals are subject to a physiological disease which is manifested by intumescences or blisterlike galls on the leaves. Sections of these galls show several layers of cells formed one above the other. These growths usually crack open and become rust-colored. The disease is difficult to diagnose because it looks so much like the work of a blister-mite or a rust fungus. It is not caused by a parasite, but results from the accumulation of too much water through poor ventilation of the greenhouse or through overwatering of the plants.

Insects and Related Pests

A goodly number of insects attack gum-trees. Among the more common ones are the cowpea aphid; three species of borers—California prionus, nautical, and Pacific flatheaded; the lygus bug; three kinds of caterpillars—California oakworm, omnivorous looper, and orange tortrix; long-tailed mealybug; 17 species of scales; greenhouse thrips; and three species of mites—avocado red, platanus, and southern red.

Control. Aphids, mealybugs, and scales can be controlled with malathion or Meta-Systox R, borers with methoxychlor, caterpillars with carbaryl (Sevin), and mites with Kelthane.

HEMLOCK (*Tsuga*)

Hemlocks are among our most graceful and highly prized evergreens. They grow best in a fairly damp soil where their roots may be cool. The soil must be well drained, however, and moderately acid. Hemlocks are among the few evergreens that thrive near the trunks of large deciduous trees. Like many other conifers, they do not adapt to city conditions and rarely prosper in small front yards of suburban homes.

Hemlocks are less susceptible to diseases and most insect pests than are other conifers, such as firs, pines, and spruces.

Diseases

BLISTER RUST. *Pucciniastrum vaccinii* and *P. hydrangeae.* Young hemlocks and the lower leaves of older trees have yellowish blisters or pustules, from which the spores sift out during June and July. Rhododendron is an alternate host of *P. vaccinii,* which causes a rusty-brown leaf spot, more or less injurious in nurseries. Wild and cultivated hydrangeas are alternate hosts of *P. hydrangeae.*

Control. The only control known for these rusts is to be sure that neither of the alternate hosts is thereafter planted in any given region. Spraying with ferbam may help.

CANKERS. At least 5 species of fungi, *Botryosphaeria tsugae, Cytospora* sp.,

Dermatea balsamea, Hymenochaete agglutinans, and *Phacidiopycnis pseudotsugae,* are known to cause cankers on hemlocks.

Control. Prune affected branches and spray with a copper fungicide if affected trees are particularly valuable.

LEAF BLIGHT. *Fabrella tsugae.* In late summer, leaves of Eastern hemlock turn brown and drop prematurely when attacked by this fungus. Small, black fruiting bodies of the fungus occur on the fallen leaves. These produce spores the following spring, which initiate new infections.

Control. Leaf blight rarely damages the trees sufficently to necessitate measures other than gathering and destroying fallen infected leaves in autumn.

NEEDLE RUST. *Melampsora farlowii.* Eastern hemlock and, to a lesser extent, Carolina hemlock are attacked by this fungus. In late May or early June some of the new leaves turn yellow. Within 2 weeks the shoots to which these leaves are attached turn yellow, become flaccid, and droop. Most of the needles then drop from the affected shoots. Severely rusted trees appear as though their branch tips had been scorched by fire. Red, waxy, linear fungus bodies occur on the lower leaf surfaces, on the shoots, and on the cones.

Control. A spray consisting of 4 pounds of dry lime sulfur in 50 gallons of water applied at weekly intervals in May has given good control of the disease on small trees in nursery plantings. The use of this material for large trees may be justified in unusual circumstances.

SAPWOOD ROT. *Ganoderma lucidum* and *Coniophora puteana.* These fungi frequently cause decay of the tissues immediately beneath the bark at the base of the trunk; this results in the death of the tree.

Control. No effective control measures are known. Avoid wounding the bark, and feed and water trees to keep them in good vigor.

Physiological Disease

SUNSCORCH (nonparasitic). Ornamental hemlocks are frequently subject to severe burning or scorching when the temperature reaches 95°F (35°C). The ends of the branches may be killed for several inches back so that the affected tops may appear as if injured by a strong solution of nicotine sulfate.

DROUGHT INJURY. Hemlocks are more sensitive to prolonged periods of drought than most other narrow-leaved evergreens. The damage is most severe on sites with southern exposures or on rocky slopes where the roots cannot penetrate deeply into the soil. Thousands of hemlocks died in the northeastern United States as a result of severe droughts in the years 1960-66.

Insects and Related Pests

HEMLOCK WOOLLY APHID. *Adelges tsugae.* This pest appears as white tufts on the bark and needles. It is capable of killing young ornamental hemlocks.

Control. When the pest becomes prevalent, spray with malathion, Dylox, Diazinon, or Meta-Systox R.

HEMLOCK BORER. *Melanophila fulvoguttata.* Wide, shallow galleries in the inner bark and sapwood result from boring by a white larva ½ inch long. The adult, a flat, metallic-colored beetle with three circular reddish-yellow spots on each wing cover, deposits eggs in bark crevices.

Control. Prune and destroy severely infested branches. Keep the tree in good vigor by fertilizing and watering.

HEMLOCK FIORINIA SCALE. *Fiorinia externa.* This scale may infest hemlock leaves, and occasionally those of spruce, causing them to turn yellow and drop prematurely. Both male and female scales are elongated. The females are pale yellow to brown and are almost completely covered with their own cast skins. There are two generations a year in the New England states.

Control. Dimethoate (Cygon) sprays are very effective against this scale. In the northeastern United States, a foliar spray in mid-May, using one quart of the 23.4 per cent emulsifiable concentrate in 100 gallons of water, gives adequate control of this pest. An additional application in July is necessary for complete control.

HEMLOCK LOOPER. *Lambdina fiscellaria.* Hemlocks may be completely defoliated by a pale yellow caterpillar with a double row of small black dots along the body, which is more than an inch long at maturity. The adult moth has tan to gray wings, which expand to more than 1 inch. Another species, *L. athasaria athasaria,* occurs less frequently but also defoliates hemlocks.

Control. Spray with carbaryl (Sevin) and a miticide when the larvae are small.

HEMLOCK SCALE. *Aspidiotus ithacae.* The adult female, circular and nearly black, infests the lower surfaces of hemlock leaves, causing premature leaf fall. In heavy infestations it may move to the twigs and branches. Another hemlock scale, *A. pini,* also circular and black, infests hemlock, Douglas-fir, and many species of pine.

Yet another species of scale, *Tsugaspidiotus tsugae,* closely resembles *Aspidiotus ithacae.* It is also circular, somewhat darker brown-black, and nippled at the center. The heaviest infestations of this scale at present is in Fairfield County, Connecticut.

Control. Spray with a 'superior'* type dormant oil, or a combination of

* See footnote page 249.

the oil and ethion, in April before new growth emerges. A dimethoate (Cygon) spray during the growing season is also effective.

GRAPE SCALE. *Aspidiotus uvae.* Hemlock hedges can be destroyed by infestations of this small, dingy-white scale, which has yellowish nipples or exuviae.

Control. Malathion or carbaryl (Sevin) sprays applied from mid- to late June provide good control.

SPRUCE LEAF MINER. *Taniva albolineana.* This species, more common on spruce, occasionally mines the leaves of hemlock.

Control. Spray with malathion when the pests begin to feed in late May.

HEMLOCK ERIOPHYED MITE. *Nalepella tsugifoliae.* The unthrifty look of some hemlocks may be due to infestations of this mite.

Control. Kelthane or Meta-Systox R sprays applied in early April will control this pest.

SPIDER MITES. Hemlocks in ornamental plantings are extremely susceptible to several other species of mites. The spruce spider mite, *Oligonychus ununguis,* is prevalent on spruces and junipers in addition to hemlock. The two-spotted mite *Tetranychus urticae* feeds on the undersides of the needles, sucking the juice from the cells; the needles turn pale and become spotted. Eggs and mites are usually covered with delicate webs.

Control. Mites can be controlled on this host by spraying with chlorobenzilate, Kelthane, Meta-Systox R, or Tedion. These should not be applied to tender foliage during the hottest part of the day, for the susceptibility of hemlock foliage to intense heat is aggravated by spraying.

OTHER PESTS. Hemlocks are also subject to the bagworm, cypress moth, fir flatheaded borer, spruce budworm, gypsy moth, and hemlock sawfly.

Control. Control measures are rarely used.

HOLLY (*Ilex*)

The American holly, *Ilex opaca,* is relatively free of insect and fungus pests. Most of the troubles experienced with trees in ornamental plantings result from improper transplanting practices or unfavorable soil conditions. In localities where it can withstand the winters, holly will thrive in almost any type of soil that is well drained and contains considerable amounts of humus. Incorporating several bushels of well-rotted oak leaf mold into the soil at transplanting time will help to provide the conditions favored by this tree. When the tree is established in its new site, cottonseed meal should be occasionally worked into the soil to supply nitrogen.

Many other species of holly, both of native and Asiatic origin, are also grown. Unless specifically noted, the diseases and insects described here affect primarily the American holly.

Diseases

BACTERIAL BLIGHT. *Corynebacterium ilicis.* This disease was first found in a holly orchard on Nantucket Island in 1957. Leaves and shoots of the primary growth appear scorched in June and July. Diseased shoots wilt, droop, and dry but persist. The infection progresses into the woody shoots of the previous year's growth, where the leaves turn black (Fig. 17-4).

Control. Copper fungicides will probably control this disease. Excessive use of nitrogenous fertilizers and cultivation of soil beneath the trees increase the trees' susceptibility to bacterial blight.

CANKER. *Diaporthe eres, Nectria coccinea, Physalospora ilicis, Phomopsis crustosa,* and *Diplodia* sp. Sunken areas on the twigs and stems may be caused by these fungi.

Control. Prune diseased branches and spray with copper fungicides several times in late spring.

ANTHRACNOSE. *Colletotrichum* sp. Native holly (*Ilex opaca*) leaves develop dead blotches which look like winter scorch symptoms but with a prominent black line margin.

Control. Pick off and destroy affected leaves. New foliage can be protected with either a copper fungicide or ferbam spray applied twice at 2-week intervals, starting when the leaves reach full size.

LEAF ROT, DROP. *Pellicularia filamentosa.* As a result of invasion by the

Fig. 17-4. Blight of American holly caused by the bacterium *Corynebacterium ilicis.*

Rhizoctonia stage of the causal fungus, the leaves of American holly cuttings may decay and drop about two weeks after the cuttings are inserted into the rooting medium. The disease first appears as a cobwebby coating, a combination of the fungus threads and grains of sand adhering to the undersides of the leaves which touch the sand.

Control. Insert cuttings in clean, fresh sand or in pasteurized old sand. Do not use cuttings taken from holly branches that touch the ground.

LEAF SPOTS. *Cercospora ilicis, C. pulvinula, Englerulaster orbicularis, Gloeosporium aquifolii, Macrophoma phacidiella, Microthyriella cuticulosa, Phyllosticta concomitans, P. terminalis, Rhytisma ilicinicolum, R. velatum,* and *Septoria ilicifolia.* Many fungi cause brown spots of the leaves.

Control. Infected leaves should be picked off and destroyed, and the vigor of the trees improved by incorporating oak-leaf mold or cotton-seed meal into the soil. In addition, water should be provided during dry spells. Applications of bordeaux mixture or any other copper spray in late summer and in early fall will largely prevent the formation of the spots. More lasting results are obtained, however, by improving the soil conditions. Copper fungicides may cause some injury, especially to leaves that have been punctured by the holly leaf miner. They also leave an unsightly residue which persists for some time. Benlate, ferbam, or Fore sprays should be used where copper sprays are likely to cause injury.

POWDERY MILDEWS. *Microsphaera alni* and *Phyllactinia corylea.* In the South, holly leaves may be affected by these mildew fungi.

Control. Where the disease becomes prevalent, spray with Benlate, Karathane, or wettable sulfur.

SPOT ANTHRACNOSE. *Elsinoë ilicis.* Leaves of Chinese holly (*Ilex cornuta*) in the South are occasionally affected by this disease. Two types of lesions occur on the leaves: numerous tiny black spots and a large leaf-distorting spot more than an inch in length, which is confined to half of the leaf blade. Lesions on the shoots and berries may also occur.

Control. Periodic applications of copper fungicides will provide control.

TAR SPOT. Native holly and the English holly. (*I. aquifolium*) are subject to the tar spot disease.

Symptoms. Yellow spots appear on the leaves during late May. These turn reddish-brown and finally black by fall. A narrow border of yellow tissue remains around the darkened spots. The efficiency of the leaf is reduced when a large number of spots develop. Premature defoliation seldom occurs.

Cause. Tar spot is caused by the fungus *Phacidium curtisii.* Spores produced in the blackened areas initiate new infections in early spring.

Control. Gather and destroy badly spotted leaves. Spray with a copper fungicide several times at 2-week intervals starting in late spring. Such sprays may cause slight injury if the season is cool.

TWIG DIEBACK. Black stem cankers and black spots on the leaves of English holly grown in the Pacific Northwest are typical of this relatively new fungus disease. During cool rainy weather, complete defoliation and severe twig blighting of the lowermost branches are common.

Cause. The fungus *Phytophthora ilicis* causes this disease. Earlier it was thought that the fungi *Boydia insculpta* and *Phomopsis crustosa* were causes.

Control. Although no control measures have been developed, it is highly probable that periodic applications of copper fungicides will provide control.

OTHER DISEASES. The inflorescence of American holly is blighted by a species of *Botrytis;* a red leaf spot is caused by a species of *Sclerophoma;* and several species of nemas cause root-knot.

Control. Control measures are usually unnecessary.

Nonparasitic Diseases

SPINE SPOT. Small gray spots with purple halos are caused by the puncturing of the leaves by the spines of adjacent holly leaves. A careful examination with a hand lens will reveal tiny, circular holes or an irregular tear at the center of each spot.

Spine spot is often confused with slits made by the holly leaf miner. The latter have neither a gray center nor a purple halo.

LEAF SCORCH. A browning or scorching of the leaves, common on holly in late winter or early spring, is of nonparasitic origin. Occasionally it is caused by the presence of water or ice on the leaves at the time the sun is shining brightly. This causes a scalding, followed by invasion by secondary organisms and finally by scorching.

Hollies planted in wind-swept areas are also more susceptible to so-called winter drying. The leaves in late winter or early spring lose water faster than it can be replaced through the roots. As a result the leaf edges wilt and turn brown. In exposed situations, newly transplanted holly should be protected with some sort of windbreak or sprayed with an anti-desiccant such as Wilt-Pruf NCF.

Insects

BEETLES. The black blister beetle, the Japanese beetle, and the potato flea beetle occasionally infest hollies.

Control. Spray with a carbaryl (Sevin)-Kelthane mixture when the beetles first appear.

BERRY MIDGE. *Asphondylia ilicicola.* The larvae of this pest infest holly berries and prevent them from turning red in fall.

Control. Where only a few trees are involved, hand picking and destruction of infested berries should keep this pest under control.

Diazinon spray applied in early June will control the midge where many trees are being grown.

BUD MOTH. *Rhopobota naevana ilicifoliana.* Holly in the Pacific Northwest is subject to this pest, the larval stage of which feeds on the buds and terminal growth inside a web.

Control. Spray with methoxychlor or carbaryl (Sevin) between the opening of the leaf bud and the time of blossoming.

HOLLY LEAF MINER. *Phytomyza ilicis.* Yellow or brown serpentine mines or blotches in leaves are produced by the leaf miner, a small yellowish-white maggot, $1/6$ inch long, that feeds between the leaf surfaces (Fig. 17-5). The adult is a small black fly that emerges about May 1 and makes slits in the lower leaf surfaces, where it deposits eggs.

Another species, the native leaf miner, *P. ilicicola,* produces very slender mines and may occur on the same tree.

Control. Diazinon, Meta-Systox R, or Dylox sprays applied when the pests are first observed in mid-May and again in early June provide effective control.

HOLLY SCALE. *Aspidiotus britannicus.* Circular, flat, $1/16$-inch scales infest the berries, leaves, and twigs of holly in the West.

Fig. 17-5. Blotch on holly leaf caused by the leaf miner *Phytomyza ilicis.*

Control. Malathion or carbaryl (Sevin) sprays applied to the young crawling stage give excellent control.

PIT-MAKING SCALE. *Asterolecanium puteanum.* This scale is becoming more prevalent on American holly and Yaupon (*I. vomitoria*) in the southern states. Oval, $^1/_{16}$ inch in diameter when mature, and pale yellow in color, this insect imbeds itself in the bark and causes a pitted and swollen condition of the stems somewhat resembling that produced by the golden oak scale (p. 445). Branches are distorted, the leaves take on an abnormal color, and at times there is considerable dieback from the branch tips.

Control. The same as for holly scale.

OTHER SCALES. Nine other species of scale insects attack hollies: black, California red, greedy, lecanium, oleander, oystershell, peach, soft, and tea.

Control. Most of these scales can be controlled with malathion or carbaryl (Sevin) sprays applied when the young are crawling about in spring, the application being repeated several times at 10-day intervals.

JAPANESE WEEVIL. *Pseudocneorrhinus bifasciatus.* The leaves of ash, elm, hemlock, and oak, as well as of holly, are occasionally attacked by this pest. The beetles are about ¼ inch in length, varying from light to dark brown, with striations on the wing covers.

Control. Carbaryl (Sevin) sprays will control this pest.

WHITEFLIES. *Dialeurodes citri* and *Tetraleurodes mori.* The citrus and mulberry whiteflies also occur on this host.

Control. Malathion and Cygon sprays are very effective against the nymphal stages of these pests. Sprays containing the synthetic pyrethroid Resmethrin are also very effective.

Other Pests

SOUTHERN RED MITE. *Oligonychus ilicis.* This mite has become a serious pest of holly.

Control. Apply a dormant oil spray in March or April just before new growth starts, then spray with Meta-Systox R or Kelthane* about mid-May and repeat in 10 days.

JUNIPER (*Juniperus*)

Because of their evergreen habit, diversity of form, and other desirable qualities, the species and varieties in the genus *Juniperus,* known commonly as cedars and junipers, are extensively used in ornamental plantings.

---

* Kelthane may injure Chinese holly (*Ilex cornuta.*)

Diseases

CEDAR RUSTS. The several species of rust fungi that attack various species of *Juniperus* occasionally produce material damage. These rusts require hosts other than cedar for the completion of their life cycles, inasmuch as the spores produced on one host are unable to reinfect the plant upon which they are formed. The fungi cannot survive, therefore, if either of the alternate hosts is removed. For this reason, several important apple-growing states prohibit the planting of susceptible cedars in the vicinity of apple orchards.

The rust fungi all belong to the genus *Gymnosporangium*. The cedar hosts are *Juniperus virginiana* and many of its varieties, *J. sabina, J. scopulorum, J. communis,* and *J. sibirica.* The alternate hosts for these rusts belong to the order *Rosales,* including the cultivated apple, pear, and ornamental crab; *Crataegus; Amelanchier; Cydonia; Sorbus; Aronia;* and others of less importance.

Although at least seven different species of rust fungi attack *Juniperus,* only three are important in the East. These are known as the cedar-apple rust, the cedar-quince rust, and the cedar-hawthorn rust.

The cedar-apple rust, caused by the fungus *Gymnosporangium juniperivirginianae,* attacks junipers, apple, and hawthorn. On juniper twigs it produces large, globose galls, ranging up to 1½ inches in diameter. Long gelatinous orange tendrils or spore horns protrude from these galls during rainy weather in spring (Fig. 17-6). The spores formed on the orange tendrils are carried by wind and insects to developing

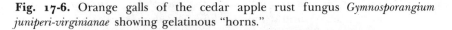

Fig. 17-6. Orange galls of the cedar apple rust fungus *Gymnosporangium juniperi-virginianae* showing gelatinous "horns."

apple and hawthorn leaves and fruits. Yellow or orange lesions are then produced on the leaves or fruits as a result of infection by these spores. This stage of the disease is most destructive, inasmuch as severe defoliation may occur, especially on apple.

Control of Cedar-Apple Rust. On apple, hawthorn, and other rosaceous hosts, as many as 6 applications, at 10-day intervals, of a wettable sulfur or a mixture of wettable sulfur and ferbam may be needed for good control. The initial application should be made just before an expected rainy spell and as soon as the leaves emerge in spring. On junipers, when the horns begin to emerge in spring and are $1/16$ inch long, spray the cedar galls thoroughly with 1 oz. (3 tablespoonfuls) of Actidione in 3 gallons of water.

The cedar-quince rust, caused by the fungus *G. clavipes,* attacks junipers, quince, and the fruit of the hawthorn, the juneberry, and the apple. It appears later in the season and differs somewhat in appearance from the cedar-apple rust. On juniper, it produces slight fusiform swellings on the twigs, branches, and occasionally the trunk. During wet weather, reddish orange spore masses break through the bark. Of the three rusts discussed, quince rust is the most destructive on the evergreen hosts. On the fruits of the rosaceous hosts, quince rust produces slightly swollen areas covered with tiny deep-red dots. Long, white tubelike structures eventually emerge, open, and expose orange-brown spore masses. These spores then reinfect the *Juniperus* hosts.

Control of Cedar-Quince Rust. On quince, hawthorn, and other rosaceous hosts, 3 applications, at 10-day intervals, of the sprays recommended for cedar-apple rust will give control. The first application should be made when the blossom buds are opening. On *Juniperus* hosts, the Actidione spray should be applied, as suggested above, when the galls have formed but before the gelatinous horns emerge.

The cedar-hawthorn rust, caused by the fungus *G. globosum,* attacks junipers, hawthorn, and to a lesser extent, apple. On junipers, it produces small irregularly shaped galls, less than an inch in diameter, with wedge-shaped, gelatinous, orange spore masses. The symptoms on hawthorn and apple are similar to those produced by the cedar-apple rust.

Control of Cedar-Hawthorn Rust. The spray schedule suggested for the control of cedar-apple rust is also recommended for the control of cedar-hawthorn rust, except that the spray on junipers should be applied about August 1 rather than in mid-July.

TWIG BLIGHT. Although primarily a disease of seedlings and nursery stock, twig blight may appear on 8- to 10-foot trees in ornamental plantings, and on larger native red cedars in some parts of the country. The disease becomes progressively less serious, however, as the trees become older, and little damage occurs on trees over 5 years old.

Though primarily a disease of the common red cedar (*Juniperus virginiana*) and its horticultural varieties, twig blight has been found on more than a dozen other groups, among which are arborvitae, cypresses, retinosporas, white cedar, and other species of *Juniperus*.

Symptoms. The tips of branches first turn brown, followed by progressive dying back until an entire branch or even the entire young tree is killed.

Cause. Twig blight is caused by the fungus *Phomopsis juniperovora*. Older trees in the vicinity of an evergreen nursery may harbor the fungus on diseased twigs. The fungus may also be carried on small, diseased branch tips that accompany purchased seed.

In spring and summer, large numbers of spores are produced in fruiting bodies on infected twigs and branches. During rainy periods the spores ooze out from the bodies and are spread to other plants by wind, rain, and laborers.

Control. Where practicable, prune out and destroy infected branch tips. Spray with Benlate plus a spreader-sticker once in the fall and 3 or 4 times at 2-week intervals in spring, starting when warm weather begins.

The use of resistant varieties offers considerable promise as a means of avoiding twig blight. The spiny Greek juniper (*J. excelsa* var. *stricta*), the Keteleer red cedar (*J. virginiana* var. *Keteleeri*), and the Hill Juniper (*J. virginiana* var. *pyramidiformis hillii*) are reported resistant to attacks.

The following cultivars, all of *Chamaecyparis pisifera*, are reported to be resistant: *filifera aureovariegata, plumosa aurea, plumososa argentea, plumosa lutescens,* and *squarrosa sulfurea*.

ROOT ROT. *Phytophthora cinnamomi*. Although junipers are considered to be resistant to this fungus, two trees in an Oregon nursery were found to be infected with it in 1957.

Control. Infected plants cannot be saved. Pasteurize infested soil and replant with healthy specimens.

WOOD DECAY. Several species of wood-decay fungi are occasionally found on junipers but rarely become destructive enough to warrant special treatments. The fungi usually enter through injuries at the base of the tree. Prevention and treatment of wounds, and fertilization to maintain the tree in good vigor are recommended.

Nonparasitic Diseases

Hybrid junipers are among evergreens that may be seriously injured and even killed by coatings of ice which last for several days. Individual branches or whole trees may die from the aftereffects.

Insects and Related Pests

ROCKY MOUNTAIN JUNIPER APHID. *Cinara sabinae*. Twig growth may be checked and the entire tree weakened by heavy infestations of the Rocky Mountain aphid, a reddish-brown insect ⅛ inch long. The so-called honeydew that it secretes is a good medium for the sooty mold fungus, which may completely coat the leaves and further weaken the tree.

Control. Spray with malathion or carbaryl (Sevin) when the aphids are visible.

RED CEDAR BARK BEETLE. *Phloeosinus dentatus.* The adult beetle is about $^{1}/_{16}$ inch long. It lays its eggs in narrow excavations about 1 or 2 inches long. As the young grubs hatch, they bore out sidewise, making galleries of a characteristic pattern which resembles the markings made in elms by the elm bark beetle.

Control. The cedar bark beetle is more apt to attack trees recently transplanted or those that are suffering from lack of water. Spraying with methoxychlor will probably help.

BAGWORM. *Thyridopteryx ephemeraeformis.* Red cedars are among the most susceptible of ornamentals to the attacks of bagworms. The presence of these feeding insects is apt to be overlooked because of the protecting bags made of green leaves.

Control. Pick off the bags by hand or cut them with a pruning pole in late summer, or in fall or winter and destroy them. If this is not done, spray with carbaryl (Sevin) or Diazinon in late spring when the young caterpillars begin to feed.

JUNIPER MIDGE. *Contarinia juniperina.* Blisters at the bases of the needles and death of leaf tips are produced by small yellow maggots, the adult stage of which is a small fly.

Control. Spray the leaves in mid- to late April with dimethoate or malathion.

JUNIPER SCALE. *Carulaspis carueli.* The needles, particularly of the Pfitzer juniper, turn yellow as a result of sucking by tiny circular scales, which are at first snow-white, then turn gray or black (Fig. 17-7). The pest overwinters in the female adult stage.

Control. Spray with 1 part of concentrated lime sulfur solution in 10 parts of water, or a dormant oil plus ethion, before growth starts in spring, or 1 pound of 25 per cent wettable malathion powder in 25 gallons of water during warm weather in May. A second malathion spray should be applied about the middle of June for best results. Carbaryl (Sevin) will also control the crawler stage.

JUNIPER WEBWORM. *Dichomeris marginella.* The twigs and needles are webbed together, and some turn brown and die when infested by the juniper webworm, a small, ½-inch-long, brown larva with longitudinal reddish-brown stripes. The adult female, a moth with a wingspread of $^{3}/_{5}$ inch, appears in June and deposits eggs that hatch in 2 weeks. The winter is passed in the immature larval stage. This pest also attacks the creeping juniper (*J. horizontalis*).

Control. Spray with Diazinon, Dylox, or carbaryl (Sevin) plus Kelthane in late July and again in mid-August.

Fig. 17-7. Juniper scale *Carulaspis carueli*.

JUNIPER MEALYBUG. *Pseudococcus juniperi*. This dark red mealybug infests junipers in the Middle West.

Control. Spray with Cygon, malathion, or carbaryl (Sevin) when the pests appear.

TWO-SPOTTED MITE. *Tetranychus urticae*. The leaves assume a gray or yellow cast when severely infested by tiny green, yellow, or red mites $1/50$ inch long. Infested leaves and twigs are occasionally covered with fine silken webs. Winter is passed primarily in the egg stage.

SPRUCE SPIDER MITE. *Oligonychus ununguis* is also a serious pest of juniper. Both species of mites also infest the creeping juniper (*J. horizontalis*).

Control. To control both species of mites, spray with 1 part concentrated lime sulfur in 10 parts of water or with 'superior'* type dormant oil before growth begins in spring, and with a good miticide such as chlorobenzilate, Dimite, Kelthane, or Tedion during the growing season.

TAXUS MEALYBUG. See under Yew.

* See footnote page 249.

NORFOLK ISLAND PINE (*Araucaria*)

This beautiful evergreen tree does well outdoors in the warmer parts of the United States.

Diseases

BLIGHT. *Cryptospora longispora*. The lower branches are attacked first, and the disease gradually spreads upward. As the entire branch becomes infected, the tip end becomes bent. The limbs die and then break off at the tip ends. Plants 5 or 6 years old are soon killed by this disease.

Control. The infected branches should be pruned off and destroyed as soon as discovered. Seeds of *Araucaria excelsa* imported from Norfolk Island Territory frequently harbor the causal fungus. Hence they are dipped in sulfuric acid by plant quarantine inspectors before being released to nurserymen.

CROWN GALL. *Agrobacterium tumefaciens*. This host has been proved experimentally to be susceptible. A typical gall is smooth and up to 1 inch in diameter.

Control. Prune infected branches.

BLEEDING CANKER. *Botryodiplodia theobromae* and *Dothiorella* sp. Two fungi are associated with this disease in Hawaii, where the Norfolk Island pine is grown for Christmas trees and is used as windbreaks and as an ornamental.

Control. Control measures have not been developed.

Insects

MEALYBUG. *Pseudococcus aurilanatus, Planococcus citri*, and *Pseudococcus ryani*. The first species listed is the golden mealybug; the second, the citrus mealybug; and the third, the cypress mealybug. All are serious pests of Norfolk Island pine in California.

Control. Spray with malathion, Meta-Systox R, or carbaryl (Sevin) whenever mealybugs are seen.

SCALES. Five species of scales are known to attack this host: araucaria (*Eriococcus araucariae*), pure white, feltlike, oval sacs enclosing bodies and eggs of females; black araucaria (*Chrysomphalus rossi*), an almost black species resembling the Florida red scale; chaff (*Parlatoria pergandii*), a circular to elongate, smooth, semitranparent, brownish-gray kind; Florida red (*Chrysomphalus aonidum*), an armored, small, $1/12$ inch, circular, reddish-brown to nearly black scale; and soft (*Coccus hesperidum*), a flat, soft, oval, yellowish-brown, $1/8$-inch-long species.

Control. Repeated applications of malathion or carbaryl (Sevin) will control scales. These are especially effective against the crawling stages.

PALMS (*Palmaceae*)

Diseases

BACTERIAL WILT. *Xanthomonas* sp. A wilt and trunk rot of coconut and Cuban royal palm is caused by this bacterium. At first the lower leaves turn gray and wilt. This is followed by gummosis of the trunk, discoloration of the vascular tissues, and finally collapse of the crown.

Control. No control measures are known.

LETHAL YELLOWING. Mycoplasma-like organism. This highly fatal disease, first observed in Jamaica nearly a century ago, in recent times has been responsible for the death of 300,000 coconut palms (*Cocos nucifera*) in southern Florida. First observed in the Key West area in 1955, it has now spread as far north as Palm Beach County.

An early symptom is the appearance of dead tips of the inflorescences when they emerge from the spathes. Leaf yellowing of the lower fronds follows. Another symptom is 'shelling,' that is, premature dropping of coconuts, regardless of size. The disease progresses until the bud becomes necrotic and the tree dies.

In Florida lethal yellowing has also resulted in death of *Veitchia, Arikuryroba, Washingtonia,* and *Pritchardia* palms.

Control. No practical control is presently available, although cessation of symptom development and resumption of normal growth has been obtained by injecting affected coconut palm trees with oxytetracycline HCL (Terramycin) antibiotic. The Environmental Protection Agency has recently approved the use of this antibiotic as an aid in the control of lethal yellowing.

In large-scale field tests in Florida, Dr. R. E. McEvoy and associates found that oxytetracycline HCL (OTC) protected apparently healthy coconut palms in areas where the lethal yellowing was advancing. The rate of spread decreased three to five times in trees injected with OTC at 4-month intervals, as compared with untreated trees. The treatment may be economically viable for coconut palms grown primarily for ornamental purposes.

One promising method of coping with lethal yellowing is to use resistant varieties. Seed nuts of resistant palms have been imported from Jamaica to be used as replacements. 'Malayan Dwarf' coconut palm is one of the more resistant kinds presently available. Actually, it is not a true dwarf because it will reach a height of 40 to 60 feet in Florida. It begins to flower and produce nuts when four or five years old.

BUTT ROT. *Ganoderma sulcatus.* This is one of the most serious fungus diseases of palms in Florida. The spores of the fungus enter through wounds at the base of the tree made by lawn mowers or other instruments. The lower leaves die and new leaves are stunted. Typical fruiting bodies of the fungus appear at the base of the infected tree near the soil line.

Control. Control measures have not been developed. Affected trees should be removed and destroyed. Clean or steam-pasteurized soil should replace soil in the vicinity of the diseased tree.

FALSE SMUT, LEAF SCAB. *Graphiola phoenicis.* Palms belonging to the genera *Arecastrum, Arenga, Howea, Phoenix, Roystonea,* and *Washingtonia* suffer from a parasite that causes a yellow spotting of the leaves and the formation of numerous small black scabs or warts. The outer parts of these fruiting bodies are dark, hard, and horny. From the inner parts protrude many long, flexuous, sterile hyphae. Within the inner membrane of the structure, powdery yellow or light brown masses of spores arise. The exact place of this unique fungus in the system of classification is not known. Severely infected leaves soon die.

In an experimental planting of date palms in Texas, the variety Kustawy from Iraq developed only light infections from this fungus. In Texas this disease is most troublesome in areas with consistently high humidities.

Control. Cut out and destroy infected leaves or leaf parts at the first sign of the disease, and spray with a copper fungicide. On greenhouse palms, control insects with insecticides rather than by syringing, a practice that helps to spread false smut.

LEAF BLIGHTS. *Pestalotia palmarum* and *P. palmicola.* The first of these fungi infects *Cocos romanzoffiana (plumosus)* and other palms in the axils of the leaves and where leaflets are attached to the leaf stalk. The fungus penetrates into the deeper tissues, causing a brown discoloration. Gray-brown spots develop on the leaf blades and run together to form large blotches. Brown septate spores with characteristic appendages develop in black masses on the upper parts of the leaves.

Blight caused by *P. palmicola* is reported to be very destructive in Florida to *Phoenix, Cocos,* and *Washingtonia.* The blight begins at the tips and works toward the leaf stalk, killing the tissues, which turn brown.

Control. Copper fungicides will probably control these diseases.

Still another serious leaf blight of *Washingtonia* is caused by the fungus *Cylindrocladium macrosporium.* Numerous small dark brown spots with light-colored margins disfigure the leaves.

Along the Pacific coast in southern California the fungus *Penicullium vermoeseni* causes three diseases which result in a great loss of ornamental palms; leaf base rot of *Phoenix,* bud rot of *Washingtonia,* and trunk canker of *Cocos romanzoffiana.* Among the effects are a successive decay of the leaf bases from the oldest to the youngest of the tightly folded bud leaves, and the weakening and breaking of the trunk.

Control. Control measures have not been developed.

LEAF SPOT. *Exosporium palmivorum.* This leaf spot is especially serious in greenhouses where insufficient light is provided. The spots are small, round, yellowish, and transparent. They often run together to form large irregular gray-brown blotches, which may result in death of the leaf. The spores are long, club-shaped, many-celled, and brown. They are formed on tufts of short basal cells.

Control. The same as for false smut.

STEM AND ROOT ROTS. Species of several genera of fungi, among them *Pythium, Fusarium, Phymatotrichum*, and *Armillaria*, have been reported as causing root disease of palms in Florida and several western states.

The *Pythium* root rot is accompanied by yellowing and wilting of the leaves one after another, until the bud falls from the top of the plant. *Fusarium* has been associated with stem and root rot of the royal palm (*Roystonea*). *Armillaria mellea* has been thought to cause root rot of the date palm (*Phoenix*) in California.

In certain palm houses numerous fruiting bodies of *Xylaria schweinitzii* has been found growing from roots of *Howea* and other palms. Since another species of *Xylaria* is known to cause root rot of apple, the poor condition of some greenhouse palms possibly may be due to this fungus. No control has been suggested. As a precautionary measure, however, all black, club-shaped fruiting bodies about 2 inches long should be removed.

In Florida a stem rot of *Chamaedorea seifrizii* is caused by *Gliocladium vermoeseni*. Controls for this rot have not been developed.

BUD ROT and WILT. *Phytophthora* spp. Wilting and bud rot of the coconut palm have been at various times referred to different species of *Phytophthora*, such as *P. palmivora, P. arecae, P. faveri*.

Control. When this disease occurs in ornamental plantings, it is controlled by cutting out the crown of the infected plant.

BLACK SCORCH and HEART ROT. *Ceratocystis paradoxa*. This disease may be destructive to date palms of plantations and ornamental gardens in California. It is found in all structures of the plant except the roots and stems. Lesions are dark brown or black, hard carbonaceous, having the appearance of a black scorch. The fungus gains entrance even in the absence of wounds. The disease is most serious as a terminal bud rot.

Control. All infected fronds, leaf bases, and flower parts should be pruned out and destroyed and the cuts disinfested. Copper sprays give promise of control.

Insects and Related Pests

PALM APHID. *Cerataphis variabilis*. In its wingless form this aphid is often mistaken for a whitefly because it is dark and disclike with a white fringe. The green peach aphid, *Myzus persicae*, also infests palms.

Control. Spray with malathion or carbaryl (Sevin) when the aphids appear.

PALM LEAF SKELETONIZER. *Homaledra sabalella*. In Florida this is a major pest, feeding on the leaves of many species of palms under a protective web of silk. Leaves are blotched, then shrivel and die.

Control. Cut out and destroy infested fronds, or spray with carbaryl (Sevin).

MEALYBUGS. Four species of mealybugs infest palms: citrus, ground, long-tailed, and palm.

Control. All but the ground mealybug can be controlled with malathion or carbaryl (Sevin) sprays. The ground mealybug can be destroyed by drenching the soil around the roots it infests with Diazinon solution.

SCALES. Palms are extremely susceptible to many species of scale insects. At least 23 species of scales have been recorded on this plant family, particularly those grown outdoors.

Control. Carbaryl (Sevin) or malathion sprays will control the crawler stage of scales.

THRIPS. *Heliothrips haemorrhoidalis, H. dracaenae,* and *Hercinothrips femoralis.* Although these species have been reported on palms, they are not considered serious pests. They are not troublesome where scale insects and mealybugs are controlled.

MITES. Three species of mites—banksgrass, privet, and tumid spider—infest palms.

Control. Aramite, chlorobenzilate, or Kelthane sprays will control these pests.

PEPPER-TREE (*Schinus molle*)

Diseases

Heart rot caused by the fungi *Fomes applanatus, Polyporus dryophilus, P. farlowii, P. sulphureus,* and *P. versicolor* have been reported from California. These fungi are difficult to control.

Root rot caused by *Armillaria mellea* and wilt by *Verticillium albo-atrum* also affect pepper-tree. The controls for these fungus diseases are discussed in Chapter 14.

Insects

The omnivorous looper caterpillar, citrophilus mealybug, citrus thrips, and 13 species of scales infest the pepper-tree.

Control. Caterpillars are controlled with carbaryl (Sevin) sprays; mealybugs, scales, and thrips with malathion.

PINES (*Pinus*)

Although pines fare better than hemlock, fir, or spruce in the environment of larger cities, they grow best in small towns and in the country. Among the species most commonly used in ornamental plantings are Austrian pine, mugho pine, Scots pine, and white pine. Each is subject to a number of fungus diseases and insect pests.

Fungus Diseases

CANKERS. A large number of canker diseases occur on all pines. These are more common on trees in forests than in ornamental plantings.

The fungus *Scleroderris lagerbergii* has caused serious losses of red and Scots pines in the northeastern states and southeastern Canada in the past several years.

Infection usually starts in the lower branches and then moves upward. Cankers develop along the main stem, eventually girdling the stem and causing death of the entire tree. Scolytid beetles are suspected of being vectors of the fungus. Control measures suggested for the dieback, tip blight of pines (see below) might be helpful in combating this disease.

The fungus *Tympanis pinastri* attacks red pine and, to a lesser extent, white pine. It produces elongated stem cankers with or without definite margins and with depressed centers that become roughened and open after 2 or 3 years. Each canker centers at a node, indicating that the fungus enters the branch at the base of the lateral branch. Trees in weakened condition are most susceptible.

Other cankers on pines are associated with the fungi *Dasyscypha pini, Atropellis pinicola, A. tingens, Caliciopsis pinea, Fusarium lateritium* f. *pini, Sphaeropsis* sp., *Phomopsis* sp., and *Cytospora (Valsa) kunzei.*

Control. Removal of dead and weak branches, avoidance of bark injuries, and fertilization to increase the vigor of the trees are suggested. Surgical treatment of cankers should be attempted only on valuable specimens.

CENANGIUM TWIG BLIGHT. *Cenangium abietis.* The twigs of exotic species of pine and white pine may be killed by this fungus. Early symptoms are the dying of terminal buds and reddening of the needles. Infection rarely spreads beyond the current season's growth.

Control. Affected twigs should be pruned to sound wood and destroyed. Because twig blight is usually severe only on weakened trees, fertilization and watering are suggested for valuable pines.

DIEBACK, TIP BLIGHT. Within the past 40 years, dieback or tip blight has become a disease of major importance on several of the most desirable pines for ornamental plantings. Austrian pine is, without question, most susceptible to the disease. Scots, red, mugho, Western yellow, and white pines are decreasingly susceptible in the order named. Douglas-fir and blue spruces are occasionally attacked.

Symptoms. The most prominent symptoms are stunting of the new growth and browning of the needles. The lower branches are most heavily infected, although in wet springs the branches over the entire tree may show browned tips.

Tip blight is often confused with troubles caused by low temperatures, drought, winter drying, and pineshoot moth injury. It can be differentiated from these by the presence of small, black, pin-point fungus bodies, which break through the epidermis at the base of the needle (Fig. 17-8). These bodies also occur on affected twigs and cone scales, but are less readily discernible than on needles, especially if the examination is made soon after the needles turn yellow and wilt. Placing such material in a moist atmosphere for a day or so will induce the black bodies to break through the epidermis and thus make them visible.

Fig. 17-8. Single needle cluster of Austrian pine greatly magnified to show fruiting bodies of causal fungus, *Diplodia pinea*.

Cause. The fungus *Diplodia pinea*, formerly called *Sphaeropsis ellisii*, causes tip blight. The generic name is used to distinguish this disease from twig blights caused by other microorganisms. The pest overwinters in infected needles, twigs, and cones. In spring, the small fruiting bodies release egg-shaped, light brown spores, which are splashed by rain and wind to the newly developing needles. The fungus grows down through the needles and into the twigs, where it destroys tissues as far as the first node.

Diplodia pinea has also been associated with a root and root-collar rot of red pine in nurseries, where such trees were completely destroyed. By inserting bits of the fungus into wounded bark near the root collar, the author has induced the same disease on Austrian, mugho, Scots, and white pines, on Douglas-fir, and on Norway spruce. Canadian scientists recently reported that the fungus may follow an infestation of the spittle bug (p. 540).

The fungus *Sirococcus strobilinus* causes a shoot blight of red pine (*Pinus resinosa*) in the Lake States.

Control. No cure is possible for plants that are infested at the base. The use of steam-pasteurized soil is suggested for avoiding root and stem base infections.

Control is possible for the tip blight phase of the disease on older trees. As soon as the blight is noticed, the infected needles, twigs, and cones should be pruned to sound tissues and destroyed. Pruning should be done when the branches are dry, because there is less danger of spreading the spores by contact with the operator and with tools. Where infection has been particularly severe, preventive fungicides are also recommended. Benlate sprays should be applied very early in spring, starting when the buds open and continuing twice at 10-day intervals. In rainy springs, a fourth application about 10 days after the third may be necessary. As a supplementary treatment, fertilization of the trees in fall or early spring is suggested.

LATE DAMPING-OFF AND ROOT ROT. *Pythium debaryanum, Fusarium discolor, Pellicularia filamentosa*, and *Phomopsis juniperovora*. In nurseries, coniferous seedlings too old to be susceptible to ordinary damping-off of very young seedlings are subject to a root rot and a top damping-off by these four fungi. Seedlings of *Pinus banksiana* and *P. resinosa* are especially susceptible.

Control. Disinfest seeds and then plant them in steam-pasteurized soil. Under some conditions Arasan or PCNB (Terrachlor) soil drenches give good control of some damping-off fungi and can be substituted for steaming.

LEAF CASTS. *Bifusella linearis, B. striiformis, Cytospora pinastri, Elytroderma deformans, Hypoderma desmazierii, H. hedgecockii, H. pedatum, H. pini, Hypodermella* spp., *Lophodermium nitens, L. pinastri*, and *Systremma acicola*. Many species of fungi cause leaf yellowing and, at times, premature defoliation of pines primarily in nurseries and in forest plantings.

Control. Leaf cast diseases rarely cause sufficient damage to large trees to warrant preventive practices. They can be controlled on small trees and on nursery stock by applying bordeaux mixture, 4-4-50, or any other copper spray, or maneb when the needles are half grown and again about 2 weeks later. Because such sprays do not readily adhere to pine foliage, casein soap or some other material should be added as a spreading agent. Zineb sprays also provide good control.

LITTLE LEAF. *Phytophthora cinnamomi*. This highly destructive disease occurs on shortleaf and loblolly pines in forest plantings of the southeastern United States. The disease is most easily recognized in its advanced stages when the crown is sparse and ragged in appearance, and the branches, lacking the mass of normal foliage, often assume an ascending habit. Leaves are only half their normal length. Trees die prematurely.

Control. Ornamental pines in home plantings appear to escape this disease even in areas where the causal fungus is known to be present in the soil.

NEEDLE BLIGHT. *Dothistroma pini*. This fungus causes slightly swollen, dark spots or bands on 1-year-old Austrian pine needles in late summer. The distal portion of the swollen needle turns light brown and dies. Severely affected trees show sparse foliage as a result of the premature dropping of needles.

Control. Bordeaux mixture or any copper fungicide or Benlate applied first in late April or early May and for a second time 3 weeks later will control this disease.

COMANDRA BLISTER RUST. *Cronartium comandrae.* This rust is widespread on at least 16 species of hard pines in the United States and has recently become severe on lodgepole pine. Spindle-shaped swellings are formed on branches and trunks of young trees, but on older trunks they may be constricted. Trunk cankers seldom exceed 3½ feet in length.

Control. Control measures have not been developed for this rust.

NEEDLE RUST. *Coleosporium asterum.* Needle rust may be more or less serious. This rust is most common on pitch pine (*Pinus rigida*) in the eastern states, but two or three other species are susceptible. The blisters break out as pustules, which open to discharge the bright orange-colored aeciospores of the rust. Infestation may be serious enough to cause defoliation. The pustules are from $1/16$ to $1/8$ inch high. The peridium or bounding layer remains visible after the spores have been discharged. The spores from these pustules infect either aster or goldenrod, on which plants the fungus forms golden or rust-colored pustules during summer. The rust is often able to winter on the crown leaves of goldenrod and asters, so that the rust can perpetuate itself on these hosts; but the rust on pine must first infect goldenrod or aster before it can be carried to the pine again. It is not perennial in the pine, as is blister rust.

Control. The destruction of wild asters and goldenrod near valuable pines, and spraying or dusting the pines with sulfur early in the season will provide control.

SCRUB PINE NEEDLE RUST. *Coleosporium pinicola. Pinus virginiana* and occasionally other species are seriously infected with this rust, which breaks out in spring with reddish pustules on the needles. The pustules, up to ½ inch long, fade and become inconspicuous later on. Defoliation may occur. This is a short-cycle rust, having no alternate host stage; the spores that develop in the pustules germinate there and shed secondary spores (basidiospores) which in spring reinfect the pines in the vicinity.

It is not a serious rust on ornamental pines except on *P. virginiana.* No control measures have been suggested.

STEM BLISTER RUST. *Cronartium quercuum.* This is a gall-forming stem blister rust. *Pinus sylvestris, P. rigida, P. banksiana*, and *P. virginiana* are all very susceptible to it. A characteristic distortion or kink of the trunk is formed 3 or 4 feet from the ground. The rust may cause the growth of a deep canker instead of galls. Since the rust may appear at the base of a tree near the ground, it may be inconspicuous, even though the infected area may be a foot across. More or less spherical galls 1 or 2 inches in diameter appear on the branches; eventually the parts above the galls are killed. These galls may be so numerous on jack pines as to kill the trees. They should not be mistaken for galls caused by insects. The infection of trunks of small trees of scrub pine results in very striking spherical galls which entirely encircle the trunks. Galls 5 or 6 inches in diameter are not unusual.

The rust has species of oak as alternate host. Numerous long horns of brownish or dark brown spores are formed on the infected oak leaves. The basidiospores, developed on these horns, reinfect pines in spring.

Control. No practical control for this rust has been suggested.

WHITE PINE BLISTER RUST. This disease is probably the most important disease of white pine in the northeastern United States. Other pines, such as Western white pine and sugar pine, having five needles in the leaf cluster are also susceptible. Blister rust also attacks both wild and cultivated forms of currants and gooseberries but produces less damage on these than on pines.

Symptoms. On pines, reddish-brown, drooping needles appear on one or more dead branches. Rough, swollen cankers are found at the bases of affected branches or on the trunk. In late spring, orange-yellow blisters filled with powdery spores break through the bark of the cankered areas (Fig. 17-9). These blisters are most conspicuous from April to June and are the most positive sign of the disease. After that time they may be eaten by squirrels or covered with resin. The disease is fatal when trunk cankers or branch cankers completely girdle the affected parts.

The symptoms are less conspicuous on currants and gooseberries, where minute, orange-yellow pustules or brown, curved tendrils appear on the lower surface. Most of the leaves are stunted when the pustules become numerous.

Cause. White pine blister rust is caused by the fungus *Cronartium ribicola*. Winter is passed in cankered bark of living pines. The orange-yellow spores produced in these cankers in late spring are blown to susceptible currant and gooseberry leaves, where they produce infection. A new type of spore is produced on these leaves in fall. This type is blown to pines, where they infect the needles to complete the life cycle. After the fungus enters the needle it penetrates slowly downward into the twig and eventually the trunk. The whole process takes place slowly: several years may elapse from the needle infection stage to the appearance of the orange-yellow blisters on the branch or trunk.

Control. Because currants and gooseberries are absolutely essential for the survival of the fungus, blister rust can be controlled by eradication of these undesirable alternate hosts. Local control of the disease can be accomplished by destroying all currants and gooseberries within 900 feet of the pines. Furthermore, the European or cultivated black currant should not be grown within a mile of pines. This species, which is more susceptible to rust than are other currants and wild gooseberries, has been found to be the chief agent in the extensive spread and establishment of the disease in previously uninfected areas.

Fig. 17-9. Blister rust of white pine caused by the fungus *Cronartium ribicola*.

Many valuable pines showing moderate infection can be saved by prompt surgical treatments. Small branches with cankers should be removed, and cankers on large branches or on the trunk cut out. The latter practice is justified only where the cankers extend around a relatively small part of the trunk or branch but is not practicable where they nearly completely girdle the affected member. *Pinus peuce*, one of the five-needle pines, is said to be resistant to blister rust.

The removal of all alternate hosts within the distances already suggested is, of course, essential to prevent new infections on pines.

Investigators of the United States Department of Agriculture and some state experiment stations, Wisconsin in particular, have selected and bred white pines resistant to blister rust. This work looks very promising, inasmuch as only one strain of the blister rust fungus is believed to exist. In other rust diseases a number of strains of the same fungus occur, which often makes breeding for resistance to such diseases a very unfruitful undertaking.

OTHER RUSTS. Many other rusts, too numerous to mention in this book, also occur on pines. These appear on all the aboveground parts of the tree, producing many and varied types of symptoms. They rarely become important parasites, however, on pines in ornamental plantings.

WOOD DECAY. Because pine wood contains a high percentage of resins, wood decays are not so frequent as in hardwoods and in some other evergreens. Some of the fungi commonly associated with wood decay are *Stereum sanguinolentum, Fomes pini, F. officinalis, F. roseus, Polyporus circinatus,* and *P. schweinitzii.* The first mentioned is commonly associated with improperly treated pruning wounds.

Control. No control is feasible where extensive decay occurs. Wounds should be avoided and the trees kept in good vigor.

Physiological Diseases

WHITE PINE BLIGHT. A needle blight of white pine (*Pinus strobus*) which appears as a browning of entire needles or tips of needles of the current season's growth has been prevalent throughout the northeastern United States for the last 30 years. The primary cause of the trouble is unknown. Some experts have attributed it to a deficiency or an excess of soil moisture, others to a nutrient deficiency and to fungi, and still others to a virus. The disease is not always fatal. Some trees recover without special treatment.

STUNT. Stunting and death of 5- to 40-year-old red pines (*Pinus resinosa*) may be due to poor soil drainage. To avoid injury, select a well-drained planting site at the start.

AIR POLLUTANTS. Several chemicals, including sulfur dioxide and ozone, produce a tip burn or speckling of the leaves of several species of pines in areas where these materials are released into the atmosphere.

SALT. White pines planted within 50 feet of heavily used highways may be severely injured or killed by the salt used to melt snow and ice. Trees growing close to salt water may also suffer. Spraying trees in such locations with an anti-desiccant such as Foli-Guard, Vapor Guard, or Wilt-Pruf NCF on a mild day in December and again in February will reduce injury.

Insects and Other Animal Pests

PINE BARK APHID. *Pineus strobi.* Though commonly called the white pine bark louse, this aphid occasionally attacks balsam fir also. The insects usually work on the undersides of the limbs and on the trunk from the ground up. They may be recognized by the white cottony material (Fig. 17-10) that collects in patches wherever they are present. In the eastern states white pine may be seriously injured. The winter is passed in the egg stage, the eggs being protected by the cottony covering. The eggs hatch in spring, and soon the young insects may be seen crawling about on the trunk and branches. Several generations are developed each summer.

Control. Apply a 'superior'* type dormant oil spray in early spring, and spray toward the end of April with either Cygon or Diazinon. Respray with either of these in mid-May and again in early July if some aphids reappear.

WHITE PINE APHID. *Cinara strobi.* These aphids feed on the smooth bark of the twigs and smaller branches of young trees and cause a winter injury which results from drying out of the twigs. Sometimes several hundred aphids are clustered together. Sooty mold often develops on the honeydew.

Control. The same as for pine bark aphid.

PINE LEAF CHERMID. *Pineus pinifoliae.* This insect infests species of pines and spruces. It winters over on pine and then moves in spring to spruces, on which it causes terminal galls. In summer the aphids move to white pine, on which they give birth to nymphs. These then suck out the sap from the new shoots, causing either the development of undersized leaves or the death of the new shoots.

Control. Spray the white pines with malathion just after the first galls open on the spruces in June.

PINE WEBWORM. *Tetralopha robustella.* Masses of brown frass at the ends of terminal twigs result from infestations of the webworm, a yellowish-brown larva with a black stripe on each side of the body, which is $^4/_5$ inch long.

Control. Spray with Dylox, methoxychlor, or carbaryl (Sevin) in mid-June when the leaves are young and before the needles are webbed. A second application in early August may be necessary.

BARK BEETLES. *Scolytidae.* Trees in weakened or dying condition are subject to infestation by bark beetle larvae, small worms that mine the bark and engrave the sapwood. On the bark surface where beetles emerge, tiny 'shot-holes' varying from $^1/_{20}$ to $^1/_3$ inch in size (depending on the species) are present.

Control. No effective control measure is known. Trees should be kept in vigorous condition by feeding and watering. Severely infested trees should be cut down and destroyed or, if left standing, should be debarked.

EUROPEAN PINE SHOOT MOTH. *Rhyacionia buoliana.* This is a very serious pest of mugho pines and red pines in ornamental plantings. Austrian,

* See footnote page 249.

Fig. 17-10. Pine bark aphid secretions on trunk and branches of white pine.

Scots, and Japanese black pines also may be badly damaged. The caterpillars, by attacking the tips ends of young shoots, cause them to turn over and become deformed and killed or the lateral buds to be blasted. The caterpillars can be found working in the tip ends in May or the early part of June. Their presence is usually indicated by quantities of resin. The moths that are the adult stage of this caterpillar emerge about June 15 and lay their eggs in August on the new buds.

Control. For small plantings and low trees, hand-picking of infested shoots and buds is probably the most satisfactory method. An early spring (mid-April) spraying with Cygon, Diazinon, Dylox, or carbaryl (Sevin), followed by a late June spraying, gives good control. In states where its use is permitted, carbofuran applied to the soil in granular form in late May or mid-June will also control this pest. Carbofuran sprays applied at the peak of the moth flight are also effective.

NANTUCKET PINE MOTH. *Rhyacionia frustrana.* This species attacks two- and three-needled pines in the eastern United States.

Control. Spray in mid-June with Cygon, Meta-Systox R, or carbaryl (Sevin).

SAWFLIES. *Diprion similis.* The caterpillars of the introduced pine sawflies are about 1 inch long and have black heads and greenish-yellow bodies with double brown stripes down the middle of the back. They feed on the leaves of various species of pine during May and June and later again during September. Four other species of sawflies attack pines: the balsam-fir, *Neodiprion abietis*; the red-headed, *N. lecontei*; the European pine, *N. sertifer* (Fig. 17-11); and the jack-pine sawfly, *N. pratti banksianae.* In severe infestations the tree may be entirely defoliated.

Control. As soon as an infestation is observed, spray the trees with either methoxychlor or carbaryl (Sevin). The red-headed sawfly has broods through the season and hence may require spray applications in June, July, and August. The European pine sawfly in forest plantings has been controlled by airplane spraying of a virus suspension capable of infecting the larvae.

PINE FALSE WEBWORM. *Acantholyda erythrocephala.* The larvae of this pest are about ¾ inch long, greenish to yellowish-brown. They feed on the leaves and tie the masses of excreta and leaf pieces together into loose balls. The damage is illustrated in Figure 17-12.

Control. The same as for pine webworm.

PINE ROOT COLLAR WEEVIL. *Hylobius radicis.* Austrian, mugho, red, and Scots pines on Long Island and in southeastern New York may be

Fig. 17-11. Larvae of the sawfly *Neodiprion sertifer*.

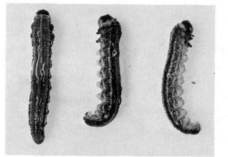

Fig. 17-12. Work of the pine false webworm (*Acantholyda erythrocephala*) in a branch of pitch pine (*Pinus rigida*); infested branch at the left.

severely damaged by this borer. The symptoms on infested trees are sickly and dead foliage and masses of pitch around the base of the trunk 3 or 4 inches below the soil surface.

Control. No effective control is available.

PINE NEEDLE SCALE. *Phenacaspis pinifoliae.* Pine needles may appear nearly white (Fig. 17-13) when heavily infested with this scale, an elongated insect $^1/_{10}$ inch long, white with a yellow spot at one end. The pest overwinters in the egg state under female scales. The eggs hatch in May. The black pine needle scale, *Aspidiotus californicus*, occasionally infests some species of pine.

Control. Spray with dormant oil in April, or with Cygon or Meta-Systox R in mid-May and again in mid-August.

PINE NEEDLE MINER. *Exotelia pinifoliella.* Needles of ornamental pines turn yellow and dry up as a result of mining by a $^1/_5$-inch-long larva.

Control. Spray with methoxychlor in early June. A second application in summer when the yellow-brown moths are flying about is suggested where this pest is particularly prevalent.

PINE TORTOISE SCALE. *Toumeyella numismaticum.* This cherry-red or reddish-brown scale, about $^1/_8$ inch long, attacks jack pine in reforested

Fig. 17-13. Pine needle scale on white pine.

areas, at times destroying 50 per cent of the trees. It is closely related to *T. pini*, which occurs on Scots and mugho pines in some eastern states.

Control. A dormant lime sulfur spray will kill this scale. The crawling stage may be killed in late spring with Diazinon, malathion, or carbaryl (Sevin).

PINE SPITTLEBUGS. *Aphrophora parallela.* These insects are perhaps most common on Scots pine, but white pine also is rather seriously attacked at times. They cause injury to smaller twigs by drawing the sap from them. They form a foamy matter about the young insects, which gives the branches a whitish appearance (Fig. 17-14). The adult insects are sometimes ½ inch long, grayish-brown in color, and resemble small frogs. Another species, the Saratoga spittlebug, *A. saratogensis*, seriously damages jack and red pines.

Control. Spray with malathion, methoxychlor, or carbaryl (Sevin) in mid-May and again in mid-July, directing the spray forcefully so as to hit the little masses of spittle that cover the insect.

WHITE PINE SHOOT BORER. *Eucosma gloriola.* The whitish caterpillars are about ½ inch long. They burrow down the centers of the lateral shoots, causing them to wilt and to die back several inches. The insect spends the winter in the soil and appears as a moth in spring.

Control. Cut off and destroy infested branches as soon as they are discovered. This, of course, is practical only for young trees.

WHITE PINE TUBE MOTH. *Argyrotaenia pinatubana.* Greenish-yellow larvae make tubes by tying the needles together side by side and squarely eating off the free end. White pines in the East and lodgepole and whitebark pines in the Rocky Mountain region are susceptible.

Control. Spray with Diazinon or Imidan in early May and again in mid-July.

PALES WEEVIL. *Hylobius pales.* The bark of young white, red, and Scots pines may be chewed by a night-feeding reddish-brown to black weevil ⅓ inch long. Young trees may be girdled completely.

Control. Spray the bark of seedlings and other conifers and the twigs of larger conifers with methoxychlor in April.

RED PINE SCALE. *Matsucoccus resinosae.* This species now infests red pines in the area of southeastern New York and southwestern Connecticut. The current season's growth on infested trees consists of yellowed needles, which turn brick-red; later the tree dies. The young and adult

Fig. 17-14. Spittlebug on Austrian pine.

stages, very difficult to detect, are yellow to brown in color and are hidden in the bark or inside the needle clusters.

Control. Severely infested trees should be cut down and destroyed. Spray less severely infested ones with Cygon early in June and repeat in early September.

WHITE PINE WEEVIL. *Pissodes strobi.* This weevil is a very common pest of white pine in estates and lawns where trees are planted as ornamentals. It is also injurious in forests of white pine. The larvae feed on the inner bark and the sapwood of the leading branches and terminal shoots of the main trunks. The leader is girdled and killed, and the branches that grow out to replace the leader are more or less distorted. The beetles begin to emerge in July, leaving characteristic holes in the bark. They are about ¼ inch long, reddish-brown and somewhat white-mottled. The larvae are pale yellowish grubs about ⅓ inch long. This insect also attacks spruce, as shown in Figure 17-21.

Control. Cut out and destroy all infested branches so as to kill the insects before they emerge as beetles. Spray valuable trees with a mixture of methoxychlor and Kelthane in early May and repeat in 2 weeks. The methoxychlor kills the adults, which deposit eggs in the bark in May, and also kills the young larvae which hatch out of the eggs. The Kelthane helps to keep down mites, which may become numerous if methoxychlor alone is used. Recent research has revealed that Meta-Systox R can be substituted for the methoxychlor-Kelthane mixture.

Where the central leader is destroyed, a new leader may be encouraged to develop by tying the next lower lateral shoot in an erect position with a small stick and a soft rope. Pruning the dead leader branch at a 45 degree angle, rather than straight across, will encourage the development of a new leader.

ZIMMERMAN PINE MOTH. *Dioryctria zimmermani.* The bark of twigs and branches on many species of pines is invaded by white to reddish-yellow or green ¾-inch larvae. The adult moth is reddish-gray in color and has a wingspread of 1 to 1½ inches. Branch tips turn brown, and the entire tops of trees may break off as a result of boring by the larvae.

Control. Dylox or Thiodan spray applied just before the larvae emerge from hibernation in spring and another application in early August will provide control.

BLACK TURPENTINE BEETLE. *Dendroctonus terebrans.* This pest has caused the death of Austrian pine (*Pinus nigra austriaca*), Japanese black pine (*P. thunbergii*), and pitch pine (*P. rigida*) in recent years on Long Island, New York, and in Massachusetts. Once considered a secondary invader which attacked pines weakened by some other agent, it is capable of infesting apparently healthy pines and killing them.

The beetles are ⅕ to ⅜ inches long, robust, reddish-brown to black. (Fig. 17-15). They bore into the lower 4 feet of the trunk, making

LARVA PUPA ADULT

Fig. 17-15. Pitch tubes of the black turpentine beetle at the base of a pine tree. **(Inset).** Life cycle of the beetle. Actual size is approximately one-quarter inch.

½-to-1-inch-broad galleries which extend downward for several inches to several feet. Resin flows out of the injured area forming so-called 'pitch tubes' which are readily visible on the bark surface (Fig. 17-15). Destruction of the inner bark and wood by the larval stage eventually results in the death of the infested tree.

Control. Maintaining susceptible pine species in good vigor by feeding and watering is one way of warding off attacks by this beetle. Application of lindane to the lower tree trunk has provided protection in the past, but the use of this insecticide is now banned in most states. Methoxychlor sprays may be an effective substitute.

REDWOOD (*Sequoiadendron*)

Diseases

CANKER. *Dermatea livida.* Cankers develop on the bark, in which brown to black fruiting bodies develop. These contain one-celled colorless spores. Another canker is caused by the fungus *Botryosphaeria dothidea.*

Control. No satisfactory control measures have been developed.

NEEDLE BLIGHT. *Chloroscypha chloramela* and *Mycosphaerella sequoiae.* Redwood leaves may be blighted by these fungi. The giant sequoia (*Sequoiadendron giganteum*) is susceptible to two other leaf-blighting fungi, *Cercospora sequoiae* and *Pestalotia funerea*, and to twig blight by *Phomopsis juniperovora.*

Control. Small, importantly placed trees infected with these fungi should be sprayed with a copper or a dithiocarbamate fungicide.

SHOESTRING ROOT ROT. See Chapter 14.

Insects

CEDAR TREE BORER. *Semanotus ligneus.* The larvae of this beetle make winding burrows in the inner bark and sapwood of redwood, cedars, arborvitae, Douglas-fir, and Monterey pine, occasionally girdling and killing the trees. The adult beetle is ½ inch long, black with orange and red markings on its wing covers.

Control. Young trees should be kept in good vigor by feeding and watering when necessary. Sprays containing methoxychlor applied to the trunk and branches when the adult beetles emerge should provide control.

SEQUOIA PITCH MOTH. *Vespamima sequoiae.* The cambial region of redwoods and many other conifers in the West is mined by an opaque, dirty-white larva. The adult moth resembles a yellow-jacket wasp because it is black and has a bright yellow segment at its lower abdomen.

Control. This pest is rarely abundant enough to warrant control measures.

MEALYBUGS. Three species of mealybugs may infest redwoods: citrus, *Planococcus citri*; cypress, *Pseudococcus ryani*; and yucca, *Puto yuccae*.

Control. Spray young, valuable trees with malathion. Repeat in a few weeks if the first spray does not provide good control.

SCALES. Two scale insects have been reported on this host: greedy, *Aspidiotus camelliae*, and oleander, *A. hederae*.

Control. Spray with malathion or carbaryl (Sevin) when the young scales are crawling about.

SCREW-PINE (Pandanus)

Diseases

LEAF BLOTCH. *Melanconium pandani*. Large leaf spots up to 2 inches wide and 3 or 4 inches long may develop from the leaf margin inward. Black fruiting pustules develop in a light gray zone along the inner margin of the spot. Similar spots may develop along the leaf blade at any point.

Control. Prune off infected leaves and spray with a copper fungicide. Badly infected plants should be destroyed.

LEAF SPOTS. *Heterosporium iridis, Melanconium pandani, Phomopsis* sp., and *Volutella mellea* have been reported on screw-pine.

Control. Leaf spots are rarely serious enough to warrant control measures.

Insects

The long-tailed mealybug, *Pseudococcus adonidum*, and 13 species of scales attack screw-pine.

Control. Spray with carbaryl (Sevin) or malathion whenever these pests appear.

SILK-OAK (Grevillea)

Silk-oak, a native of Australia, has become naturalized in southern Florida.

Diseases

Few diseases have been recorded for this tree. These include dieback, said to be caused by a species of *Diplodia*, leaf spot by the alga *Cephaleuros virescens*, root-knot by the nema *Meloidogyne* sp., and root rot by *Phymatotrichum omnivorum*.

Control. Measures are rarely taken to control the diseases on this host.

Insects and Related Pests

Leaf-eating insects on silk-oak include the tobacco budworm (*Heliothis virescens*) and the omnivorous looper (*Sabulodes caberata*); sucking insects include the citrophilus and grape mealybugs, at least 19 species of scales, and two species of mites—avocado red and Grevillea.

Control. Leaf-eating insects can be controlled with carbaryl (Sevin) sprays; mealybugs and scales with malathion; mites with Kelthane.

SPRUCE (*Picea*)

Besides being valuable forest trees, the spruces are highly prized as ornamentals. They thrive best in moist, sandy loam soil and can tolerate more shade than most other conifers. The varieties most commonly used in ornamental plantings are Norway spruce, Colorado blue spruce, and Koster's blue spruce. They are subject to a number of destructive fungus diseases and insect pests.

Diseases

CYTOSPORA CANKER. The most prevalent disease on Norway spruce and Colorado blue spruce is known as Cytospora canker. Koster's blue spruce and Douglas-fir are also subject to it, but to a lesser extent. Although the disease occurs on young trees, those over 15 years old appear to be most susceptible.

Symptoms. The most striking symptoms is the browning and death of the branches, usually starting with those nearest the ground and slowly progressing upward. Occasionally branches high in the tree are attacked, even though the lower ones are healthy.

The needles may drop immediately from infected branches or may persist for nearly a year, eventually leaving dry brittle twigs that contrast sharply with unaffected branches (Fig. 17-16). White patches of pitch or resin may appear along the bark of dead or dying branches (Fig. 17-17). Cankers occur in the vicinity of these exudations. They are not readily discernible but can be found by cutting back the bark in the area that separates diseased from healthy tissues. In the cankered area, tiny, black, pin-point fruiting bodies of the causal fungus are a positive sign of the disease.

Cause. The fungus *Cytospora* (*Valsa*)* *kunzei* f. *piceae* causes this disease. The fruiting structures protrude slightly during wet weather, but are concealed beneath the bark scales during dry spells (Fig 17-18). Under the former conditions they release long, curled, yellow tendrils, which contain millions of spores. Wind and rain splash the spores to bark

---

* *Valsa* is the sexual stage of this fungus.

Fig. 17-16. Left: Blue spruce affected by *Cytospora* canker disease. Note the dead, leafless branches which contrast with unaffected branches.

Fig. 17-17. Right: Close-up of *Cytospora*-infected branch showing white, resinous exudation.

wounds on branches, where infection takes place. When the infection spreads completely around the branch, the distal portions die as a result of the girdling.

Many other trees weakened by adverse growing conditions such as drought, winter injury, insects, fire, and mechanical injuries are subject to different species of *Cytospora*. The following are the most common, in addition to *C. kunzei* f. *piceae* mentioned above and *C. chrysosperma* discussed in other parts of this book: *C. acerina* on Japanese maple; *C. ambiens* on American elm; *C. annularis* on black and red ash; *C. corni* on dogwood; *C. leucostoma* on Norway spruce; *C. microspora* on American mountain-ash and hawthorn; *C. mollissima* on Chinese chestnut; *C. pinastri* on balsam fir; *C. rubescens* on American and European

Fig. 17-18. Fruiting bodies of the canker fungus *Cytospora (Valsa) Kunzei* f. *piceae*.

mountain-ash; and an undetermined species on walnut and white mulberry.

Control. Infected branches cannot be saved. They should be cut off a few inches below the dead or infected parts, or at the point of attachment to the main stem. Because of the danger of spreading spores to uninfected branches, pruning should never be undertaken while the branches are wet. Inasmuch as the available evidence indicates that the fungi enter the branches only through wounds, bark injuries by lawn mowers and other tools should be avoided. Some plant pathologists believe, however, that there is no way of preventing infections. Others report that spraying the lower branches and the trunk 3 or 4 times in spring with a copper fungicide will help to prevent starting further spread. The applications should be spaced at 2- to 3-week intervals, starting about mid-April. The disease appears to be most prevalent on trees in poor vigor. Consequently, trees should be fertilized at least every few years, watered during dry spells, and the soil improved to increase or maintain their vigor.

NEEDLE CASTS. *Lophodermium filiforme*, *L. piceae*, and *Rhizosphaera kal-khoffi*. The lower branches of red, black, and Sitka spruces may be defoliated by one of these fungi. The leaves are spotted and turn yellow before they drop.

Control. Spray valuable ornamental specimens with a copper fungicide, Benlate, or Bravo in June and July.

RUSTS. *Chrysomyxa ledi* f. *cassandrae, C. empetri, C. ledicola, C. chiogenis, C. piperiana, C. roanenis,* and *C. weirii.* Several species of rust fungi occur on spruce needles. Each requires an alternate host to complete its life cycle. On the spruce, the fungi appear as whitish blisters on the lower leaf surface. Affected needles turn yellow and may drop prematurely. The names of the alternate hosts for each of the fungi listed can be obtained from state or federal plant pathologists.

Control. Removal of the alternate hosts in the vicinity of valuable spruces is suggested. Protective sprays containing sulfur or ferbam are rarely justified.

WOOD DECAY. Spruces are subject to a number of wood decays caused by various fungi. Among those most commonly associated with various types of decay are *Trametes pini, Polyporus schweinitzii, P. sulphureus,* and *Fomes pinicola.*

Control. Little can be done once these decays become extensive. Avoidance of wounds, and fertilization to increase vigor are suggested preventive measures.

Insects and Other Animal Pests

SPRUCE GALL APHID. *Chermes abietis.* Elongated, many-celled, cone-shaped galls, less than 1 inch long (Fig. 17-19), result from feeding and irritation by this pest. Trees are weakened and distorted when large numbers of these galls are formed. Norway spruce is most seriously infested; white, black, and red spruces are less so. In spring the adult wingless females deposit eggs near where the galls later develop. Immature females hibernate in the bud-scales.

Control. Spray the tips of twigs and bases of buds with a 60- or 70-second oil in April when the trees are still dormant, or with carbaryl (Sevin) or Meta-Systox R in May.

COOLEY SPRUCE GALL APHID. *Chermes cooleyi.* Galls ranging from ½ to 2½ inches in length on the terminal shoots of blue, Englemann, and Sitka spruces and Douglas-fir are produced by feeding and irritation by an aphid closely related to that which infests the Norway spruce. The adult female overwinters on the bark near the twig terminals and deposits eggs in that vicinity in spring.

Control. Because Douglas-fir is an alternate host for this pest, avoid planting that species near spruces. Spray with malathion or carbaryl (Sevin) in spring just before new growth emerges.

OTHER APHIDS. The spruce aphid, *Aphis abietina,* and the pine leaf

Fig. 17-19. Galls of spruce gall aphid *Chermes abietis* on Norway spruce.

chermid, *Pineus pinifoliae*, also infest spruce leaves. The balsam twig aphid, discussed under Fir, at times attacks this host.

Control. Carbaryl (Sevin) and malathion sprays are very effective against these species.

SPRUCE BUD SCALE. *Physokermes piceae*. Globular red scales, about ⅛ inch in diameter, may occasionally infest the twigs of Norway spruce. The young crawl about in late July, and the winter is passed in the partly grown adult stage.

Control. Before growth starts in spring, spray most spruces with a 'superior'* type dormant oil. For blue spruce, which is sensitive to this type of spray, use malathion or Cygon.

SPRUCE BUDWORM. *Choristoneura fumeriferana*. One of the most destructive pests of forest and ornamental evergreens, this pest attacks spruce and balsam firs in forest plantations and also infests ornamental spruce,

* See footnote page 249.

balsam fir, Douglas-fir, pine, larch, and hemlock. The opening buds and needles are chewed by the caterpillar, which is dark, reddish-brown with a yellow stripe along the side. The adult female moths, dull gray, marked with brown bands and spots, emerge in late June and early July.

WESTERN SPRUCE BUDWORM. *C. occidentalis*. This pest defoliates various conifers in Western North America.

JACK PINE BUDWORM. *C. pinus*. This causes considerable damage to jack pine and to a lesser extent to red and white pine in the Lake States.

Control. Forest areas can be protected from these budworms with airplane applications of Sevimol. Ornamental spruces, pines, firs, hemlocks, and larches can be sprayed with carbaryl (Sevin) just as the buds burst in spring.

SPRUCE EPIZEUXIS. *Epizeuxis aemula*. Ornamental spruces in the Northeast may be attacked by small brown larvae with black tubercles which web needles together and fill them with excrement.

Control. Spray with carbaryl (Sevin) or Diazinon when the larvae begin to feed in late summer.

SPRUCE NEEDLE MINER. *Taniva albolineana*. The light greenish larvae web the leaves together and mine the inner tissues. They enter through small holes at the bases of the leaves, and as they feed inside, the leaves turn brown. The adult is a small grayish moth.

Another species, the spruce leaf miner (*Recurvaria piceaella*), also mines the leaves of spruce.

Control. Spray with malathion in mid-May and again in mid-June.

PINE NEEDLE SCALE. *Phenacaspis pinifoliae*. Although this pest infests pines primarily, it will attack spruces, especially those that are in poor vigor.

Control. Spray with lime sulfur or with dormant oil-ethion in spring just before growth starts.

SAWFLIES. *Pikonema alaskensis* and *Diprion hercyniae*. The former, known as the yellow-headed sawfly, may sometimes defoliate trees completely. Ordinarily, however, infestation results merely in a ragged appearance. The latter, the European spruce sawfly, feeds on the old foliage, and consequently the trees are not killed although the growth may be stunted. The larvae overwinter in cocoons on the ground, where they are subject to attack by mice.

Control. Spray the trees with carbaryl (Sevin) as soon as the caterpillars are noticed.

SPRUCE SPIDER MITE. *Oligonychus ununguis*. Yellow, sickly needles, many of which are covered with a fine silken webbing, indicate a severe infestation of the spider mite, a tiny pest only $1/64$ inch long (Fig. 17-20). The young are pale green; the adult female is greenish-black. Winter is passed in the egg stage on the twigs and the needles. In addition to spruces, arborvitae, junipers, and hemlock are also attacked.

Control. Spray with lime sulfur or with 'superior' type dormant oil in early spring just before new growth emerges. Or spray in mid-May with chlorobenzilate, Kelthane, Meta-Systox R, or Tedion to kill the young mites of the first generation. Repeat in September if necessary. Blue spruces should not be sprayed with dormant oils.

WHITE PINE WEEVIL. *Pissodes strobi.* Oriental spruce and occasionally other kinds may suffer from attacks of this beetle, which feeds on the terminal shoots and causes a heavy flow of sap. The larvae cause much injury by boring within the terminal shoots, tunneling downward and inward, as shown in Figure 17-21. Their work is manifested in July by the brown dying ends of the 'leaders.' The leader is usually killed and the tree stunted. The work of the weevil is easily distinguished from that of the pine shoot moth by the greater length of the shoots killed and by the holes in the bark from which the beetles have emerged (Fig. 17-21).

Control. See under Pine.

BAGWORM. See under Arborvitae.

YEW *(Taxus)*

Yews are among the most useful evergreens for ornamental purposes. They withstand city conditions better than most other evergreens. The English yew, the Japanese yew, and a large number of other species and varities are now planted extensively.

Diseases

NEEDLE BLIGHT. *Herpotrichia nigra* and *Sphaerulinia taxi.* Blighting of needles of the host in the western United States may be caused by these fungi.

Control. This disease is rarely destructive enough to warrant control measures.

TWIG BLIGHT. Several fungi are associated with a twig blight of yew during rainy seasons. One of the most common is *Phyllostictina hysterella,* whose perfect stage is *Physalospora gregaria.* Others are *Pestalotia funerea* and a species of *Sphaeropsis.*

Control. Prune out diseased twigs and destroy them. Spray with a copper fungicide several times at 2-week intervals during rainy springs.

ROOT ROT. *Armillaria mellea.* This disease appears in soil formerly occupied by apple or oak trees. Affected plants wilt and die; white wefts of fungus mycelium are present beneath the bark at the base of the plant.

Control. Diseased plants cannot be saved. Remove and replace them with narrow-leaved evergreens other than yews, or replace the soil to a depth of 12 inches before replanting yews.

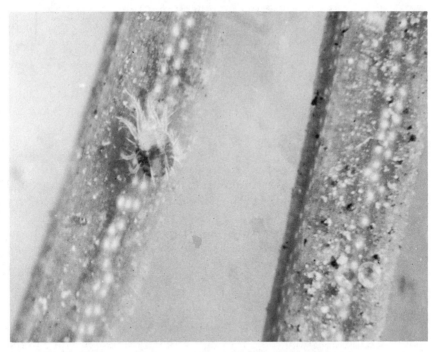

Fig. 17-20. Spruce spider mite *Oligonychus ununguis*.

Fig. 17-21. Work of the white pine weevil (*Pissodes strobi*) in a spruce branch. On the top may be seen the small holes through which the adults emerged; on the bottom is a twig split to show their work inside.

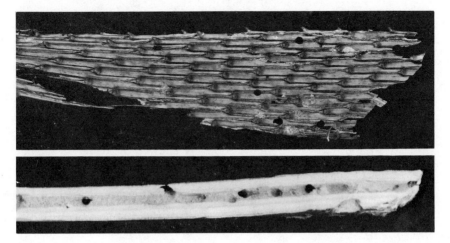

OTHER FUNGUS DISEASES. Among other fungus diseases of yews are a dieback and root rot caused by *Phytophthora cinnamomi*, a root rot by *Pythium* sp., and premature leaf drop in which a species of *Alternaria* is implicated.

Control. Control measures have not been developed.

Physiological Diseases

The most prevalent trouble on yews is dieback. The plants first turn yellow at the growing tips; this is followed by general yellowing, wilting, and death. Several months may elapse from the time the first symptoms appear to the complete wilting and death of the plant. The belowground symptoms are a decay of the bark on the deeper roots; the affected bark sloughs off readily.

This trouble is not caused by parasitic organisms. Studies by the author showed that it is associated with unfavorable soil conditions. In nearly every case investigated, the soil was very acid, pH 4.7 to 5.4, in addition to being heavy and poorly drained. Research at Rutgers University revealed that yews could be killed by immersing their roots in water for 32 to 64 hours and then drying out the soil.

Control. Improve drainage by embedding tile in the soil, or move plants to a more favorable area. Add ground limestone, according to the recommendation of a soil specialist, to increase the pH to about 6.5.

TWIG BROWNING. This condition is not caused by fungus parasites but is due to snow and winter damage. The combined effect of heavy snow cover and low temperatures causes many small twigs at the ends of branches to turn brown in late winter and early spring.

Control. Shake of heavy snow covers with a bamboo rake as soon as the snowfall stops. Prune browned branches in late spring.

Insects and Other Animal Pests

BLACK VINE WEEVIL. *Otiorhynchus sulcatus*. This pest, also known as the taxus weevil, is by far the most serious one on yews. It is so named because of its color and because it attacks grapes in Europe. In the United States, it also attacks retinospora, hemlocks, and such broad-leaved plants as rhododendrons and azaleas. See Figures 17-22, 17-23, and 17-24. The leaves of yew turn yellow, and whole branches or even the entire plant may die when the roots are chewed by the larval stage, a white-bodied, brown-headed pest, ⅜ inch long. As few as eight larvae are capable of killing a large-sized yew. The adult, a snout beetle, ⅜ inch long, feeds on the foliage of yews and other hosts at night. The edges of such leaves are scalloped. Eggs deposited in the soil during July and August hatch into larvae which feed on the roots of susceptible hosts.

Fig. 17-22. Black vine weevil adults.

Fig. 17-23. The larval stage of the black vine weevil causes severe injury to and even death of yews.

Control. See under strawberry root weevil, below.

STRAWBERRY ROOT WEEVIL. *Otiorhynchus ovatus.* This insect is related to the black vine weevil and has similar habits but is smaller, measuring $1/5$ to $1/4$ inch in length. It feeds on hemlock, spruce, and arborvitae in addition to yews. It often wanders into homes in search of hibernating quarters and thus may become a nuisance.

Control. At present no effective control is known. Chlordane and Dieldrin are effective but their use is now banned. Some preliminary tests indicate that spraying the lower parts of susceptible plants and the soil surface beneath them in mid-June and again in early July with

Fig. 17-24. Rhododendron leaves chewed by adult black vine weevils.

Diazinon, will provide control. In states where its use is permitted, Furadan, as a soil drench, will control black vine and strawberry weevils.

TAXUS MEALYBUG. *Dysmicoccus wistariae.* First reported from a New Jersey nursery in 1915, this pest has become increasingly prevalent in the northern United States. The ⅜-inch-long bug, covered with white wax, may completely cover the trunk and branches of yews (Fig. 17-25). Young mealybugs overwinter in bark crevices and mature in June. Although all species of *Taxus* are susceptible, those with dense foliage such as *Taxus cuspidata nana* and *T. wardii* are preferred hosts. This pest has also been seen on apple, basswood, and rhododendron, but probably does not breed on these plants.

Control. Good control is obtainable by spraying with malathion, carbaryl (Sevin), or dimethoate (Cygon) when the young stage is crawling about. In the area of Long Island and Connecticut, the latter part of May is the proper time; in cooler regions the application should be made a week or two later.

GRAPE MEALYBUG. *Pseudococcus maritimus.* This pest occasionally infests the Japanese yew.

Control. Where it infests aboveground parts of yews, spray with malathion.

SCALES. Five species of scale insects infest yews: cottony taxus, California red, Fletcher (Fig. 17-26), oleander, and purple. The first-

Fig. 17-25. Mealybug *Dysimicoccus wistariae* on yew.

Fig. 17-26. The scale *Lecanium fletcheri* on yew. Some of the scales have been opened to show eggs.

mentioned, *Pulvinaria floccifera*, is ⅛ inch long, light brown, and hemispherical. In spring it produces long, narrow, fluted, cottony egg masses.

Control. Apply a 'superior'* type dormant oil spray while the plants are dormant in early spring, when the temperature is well above freezing. In July and again in September, spray with Cygon, Diazinon, Meta-Systox R, or carbaryl (Sevin).

TAXUS BUD MITE. *Cecidophyopsis psilaspis.* The growing tips of yews is enlarged and may be killed. New growth is distorted. As many as a thousand mites can be found in a single infested bud.

Control. Spray with Kelthane in early May and repeat within 2 weeks if necessary.

ANTS AND TERMITES. The black carpenter ant, *Camponotus pennsylvanicus*, and the eastern subterranean termite, *Reticulitermes flavipes*, occasionally infest the trunks of older yews. Both are capable of excavating the trunk and making their nests therein.

Control. Apply Diazinon or Dursban in liquid form around the trunk base and soil surface.

NEMAS. *Criconemoides* and *Rotylenchus* spp. Several species of nemas attack the roots of *Taxus*.

Control. See under Boxwood.

Selected Bibliography

Anderson, G. W. 1963. *Sweetfern rust on hard pines*. USDA Forest Service Pest Leaflet 79. 7 p.

Bachelder, Stephen and E. R. Orton. 1962. 'Botrytis inflorescence blight on American holly in New Jersey.' *Plant Disease Reptr.* Vol. 46 (No. 5). p. 320.

Barras, S. J., D. F. Clower and R. G. Merrifield. 1967. 'Control of Nantucket pine tip moth on loblolly pine with systemic insecticides in Louisiana.' *Jour. Econ. Ent.* Vol. 60 (No. 11). p. 185-90.

Bean, J. L. 1956. *Red pine scale*. USDA Forest Service Pest Leaflet 10. 4 p.

Bean, J. L. and W. E. Waters. 1961 *Spruce budworm in eastern United States*. USDA Forest Service Leaflet 58. 8 p.

Berry, C. R. 1961. *White pine emergence tipburn, a physiogenic disturbance*. USDA Forest Service, Southeastern For. Exp. Sta. Paper No. 130. 8 p.

Brown, J. G. and M. M. Evans. 1933. 'Crown gall on a conifer.' *Phytopathology*. Vol. 23 (No. 1). 97-101.

Campbell, W. A. and A. F. Verrall. 1963. '*Phytophthora cinnamomi* associated with Lawson cypress mortality in Louisiana.' *Plant Disease Reptr.* Vol. 47 (No. 9). p. 808.

Cromwell, I. H. 1934. 'The hosts, life history, and control of the cedar-apple rust fungus.' *Jour. Arnold Arboretum.* Vol. 15. p. 163-232.

Davis, W. C., E. Wright and C. Hartley. 1942. 'Diseases of forest-tree nursery stock.' *Civ. Conserv. Corps Forestry Publ.* 9. p. 1-79.

* See footnote page 249.

Davis, S. H. Jr. and L. M. Vasvary. 1969. *Troubles with yew (Taxus).* Co-op. Ext. Ser., N. J. Col. Agr. and Envir. Sci. Leaflet 240-A. 3 p.

Davison, A. D. 1969. 'Needle rust of grand fir.' *Proc. Forty-fifth International Shade Tree Conference.* p. 257-58.

Doane, C. C. 1965. *The red pine scale.* Conn. Agr. Exp. Sta. Circ. 207. Rev. 7 p.

Duda, E. J. 1962. 'The genus *Matsucoccus* with special reference to *M. resinosae.*' *Scientific Tree Topics* 2 (No. 9) Bartlett Tree Expert Co. p. 1-10.

Epstein, A. H. 1970. 'Fungicidal control of *Dothistroma* needle blight of Austrian pine.' *Plant Disease Reptr.* Vol. 54 (No. 8). p. 679-70.

Ewan, H. G. 1957. *Jack-pine sawfly.* USDA Forest Service Pest Leaflet 17. 4 p.

————. 1961. *The Saratoga spittlebug, a destructive pest in red pine plantations.* USDA Forest Service Tech. Bul. 1250. 52 p.

Felt, E. P. and W. H. Rankin. 1932. *Insects and diseases of ornamental trees and shrubs.* Macmillan, New York. 507 p.

Gambrell, F. L. 1932. 'Studies on some insects of evergreens.' *Proc. Eighth National Shade Tree Conference.* p. 89-93.

Gambrell, F. L. and F. Z. Hartzell. 1939. 'Dormant spray mixtures on conifers.' *Jour. Econ. Ent.* Vol. 32. p. 206-9.

Garriss, H. R. 1959. *Hemlock twig rust.* North Carolina Ext. Serv. Ext. Folder No. 172. 7 p.

Gilgut, C. J. 1936. 'Cytospora canker of spruces.' *Proc. Twelfth National Shade Tree Conference.* p. 113-20.

Guba, E. F. and J. A. Stevenson. 1963. *Fungus and nematode inhabitants and diseases of holly (Ilex).* Mass. Agr. Exp. Sta. Bul. 530. 43 p.

Haasis, F. A. 1961. '*Phytophthora parasitica,* the cause of root rot, canker, and blight of boxwood.' *Phytopathology.* Vol. 51 (No. 10). p. 734-36.

Haasis, F. A. and J. N. Sasser. 1962. 'Control of plant-parasitic nematodes and weeds in holly nurseries.' *Plant Disease Reptr.* Vol. 46 (No. 5). p. 328-32.

Haddow, W. R. and F. S. Newman. 1942. 'A disease of Scots pine caused by *Diplodia pinea* associated with the pine spittlebug.' *Trans. Royal Can. Inst.* 24 (pt. 1). p. 1-19.

Hahn, G. G. and T. T. Ayers. 1934. '*Dasyscypha* on conifers in North America.' *Mycologia.* Vol. 26. p. 73-101, 167-80, 479-501.

Hamilton, C. C. 1926. *Insect pests of boxwood.* N. J. Agr. Exp. Sta. Circ. 179. 14 p.

Hansell, Dorothy. (ed.) 1970. *Handbook of hollies.* Am. Hort. Mag. Vol. 49 (No. 4). 336p.

Heald, C. M. and R. L. Self. 1967. 'Control of root-knot nematodes on dwarf Japanese holly and Japanese boxwood with phosphorate nematocides.' *Plant Disease Reptr.* Vol. 51 (No. 12). p. 1035-38.

Hedgecock, G. G. 1932. 'Notes on the distribution of some fungi associated with diseases of conifers.' *Plant Disease Reptr.* Vol. 16 (No. 4). p. 28-42.

Hepting, G. H. and R. W. Davidson. 1935. 'Some leaf and twig diseases of hemlock in North Carolina.' *Plant Disease Reptr.* Vol. 19. p. 308-9.

Herrick, G. W. 1935. *Insect enemies of shade trees.* Comstock Publishing Co., Ithaca, N.Y. 417 p.

Herridge, E. Anne. 1963. 'Pathological anatomy of leaf spots of holly.' *Phytopathology.* Vol. 53 (No. 4). p. 481-87.

Himelick, E. B. and Dan Neely. 1960. 'Juniper hosts of cedar-apple and cedar-hawthorn rust.' *Plant Disease Reptr.* Vol. 44 (No. 2). p. 109-112.

————. 1963. 'Junipers for resistance to rusts: cedar-apple and cedar-hawthorn. *Trees*. Mar.-Apr. p. 16-17.

Hirt, R. R. 1959. *Pinus strobus: a literature review and discussion of tis fungus diseases in North America*. N.Y. State College of Forestry (Syracuse). Tech. Publ. 82. 90 p.

Houser, J. S. 1940. 'Some troublesome pests of conifers.' *Proc. Sixteenth National Shade Tree Conference*. p. 65-82.

Jackson, L. W. R. 1938. 'Winter injury of *Buxus sempervirens*.' *Phytopathology*. Vol. 28. p. 372-74.

Kimmey, J. W. and W. W. Wagener. 1961. *Spread of white pine blister rust from Ribes to sugarpine in California and Oregon*. USDA Forest Service Tech. Bul. 1251. 71 p.

Luttrell, E. S., T. S. Davis and B. R. Murray. 1962. '*Botryosphaeria* twig blight of Arizona cypress.' *Plant Disease Reptr*. Vol. 46 (No. 4). p. 261-64.

MacAloney, H. J. 1961. *Pine tortoise scale*. USDA Forest Service Leaflet 57. 7 p.

MacAloney, H. J. and D. C. Schmiege. 1962. *Identification of conifer insect by type of tree injury, Lake States*. USDA Lake States For. Exp. Sta. and No. Central Region For. Ser. Paper No. 100. 41 p.

Martin, J. F. 1940. 'The application of surgery to blister rust infected trees of ornamental value.' *Proc. Sixteenth National Shade Tree Conference*. p. 113-20.

Marty, Robert and D. G. Mott. 1964. *Evaluating and scheduling white-pine weevil control in the Northeast*. USDA Forest Service Res. Paper NE-19. 56 p.

Matthews, F. R. 1964. 'Some aspects of the biology and the control of southern cone rust.' *Jour. Forestry*. Vol. 62 (No. 12). p. 881-84.

McCoy, R. E. 1972. 'Remission of lethal yellowing in coconut palm treated with tetracycline antibiotics.' *Phytopathology*. Vol. 56 (No. 12). p. 1019-21.

————. 1975. 'Uptake, translocation, and persistance of Oxytetracycline in coconut palm.' *Phytopathology*. Vol. 66 (No. 8). p. 1038–42.

————. 1976. 'Comparative epidemiology of the lethal yellowing, kaincope, and cadang-cadang diseases of coconut palm.' *Plant Disease Reptr*. Vol. 60 (No. 6). p. 498-502.

McCoy, R. E. et al. 1976. 'Field control of coconut lethal yellowing with oxytetracycline hydrochloride.' *Phytopathology*. Vol. 66 (No. 9). p. 1148-50.

McDaniel, A. T. and C. L. Wilson. 1962. 'A study of symptoms and control of *Phomopsis juniperovora* on Arizona cypress.' *Plant Disease Reptr*. Vol. 46 (No. 5). p. 364-65.

McDaniel, E. I. 1932. *Some chewing insects infesting Michigan evergreens*. Mich. Agr. Exp. Sta. Circ. Bul. 141. 54 p.

Merrill, W. and B. R. Kistler. 1976. 'Seasonal development and control of *Lophodermium pinastri* in Pennsylvania.' *Plant Disease Reptr*. Vol. 60 (No. 8). p. 652-55.

Offord, H. R. 1964. *Diseases of Monterey pine*. USDA Forest Service Res. Paper PSW-14. 37 p.

Parker, A. K. 1959. 'An unexplained decline in vigor of lodgepole pine.' *Forestry Chron*. Vol. 35. p. 298-303.

Peterson, G. W. 1967. '*Dothistroma* needle blight of Austrian and ponderosa pines: Epidemiology and control.' *Phytopathology*. Vol. 57 (No. 4). p. 437-41.

————. 1977. 'Infection, epidemiology, and control of Diplodia blight, of

Austrian, ponderosa, and Scots pines.' *Phytopathology*. Vol. 67 (No. 4). p. 511-14.

Plavsic-Banjac, B., P. Hunt, and K. Maramorosch. 1972. 'Mycoplasma like bodies associated with lethal yellowing disease of coconut palms.' *Phytopathology*. Vol. 62 (No. 2). p. 298-301.

Powers, H. R. and J. S. Boyce, Jr. 1963. *Annosus root rot in eastern pines*. USDA Forest Service Leaflet 76. 7 p.

Sasser, J. N., F. A. Haasis and T. F. Cannon. 1966. 'Pathogenicity of *Meloidogyne* species on Ilex.' *Plant Disease Reptr*. Vol. 50 (No. 9). p. 664-68.

Saunders, J. L. 1970. 'Carbofuran drench for black vine weevil control on container-grown spruce.' *Jour. Econ. Ent*. Vol. 63 (No. 5). p. 1698.

Saunders, J. L. and D. A. Barstow. 1970. '*Adelges cooleyi* control on Douglas-fir Christmas trees.' *Jour. Econ. Ent*. Vol. 63 (No. 2). p. 150-51.

Scharpf, R. F. 1964. *Dwarfmistletoe on true firs in California*. USDA Forest Service Leaflet 89. 7 p.

Scheld, H. W. Jr. and Arthur Kelman. 1963. 'Influence of environmental factors on *Phomopsis juniperovora*.' *Plant Disease Reptr*. Vol. 47 (No. 10). p. 832-35.

Schread, J. C. 1954. *Scale insects and their control*. Conn. Agr. Exp. Sta. Bul. 578. 23 p.

———. 1966. *The black vine weevil*. Conn. Agr. Exp. Sta. Circ. 211. Rev. 8p.

———. 1970. *Boxwood pests and their control*. Conn. Agr. Exp. Sta. Bul. 681. 8 p.

———. 1971. *Leaf miners and their control*. Conn. Agr. Exp. Sta. Bul. 693. (Rev. Jan. 1971).

Schreiber, L. R. and R. J. Green. 1959. 'Dieback and root rot disease of *Taxus* spp. in Indiana.' *Plant Disease Reptr*. Vol. 43 (No. 7). p. 814-17.

Schweitzer, D. J. and W. A. Sinclair. 1976. 'Diplodia tip blight of Austrian pine controlled by benomyl.' *Plant Disease Reptr*. Vol. 60 (No. 3). p. 269-70.

Skilling, D. D. and C. E. Cordell. 1966. *Scleroderris canker*. USDA Forest Service Paper NC-3. 10 p.

Spauldiɪ ɔ, Perley. 1922. *The blister rust of white pine*. USDA Bul. 975. 100 p.

Stevens, R. E. 1959. *Biology and control of the pine needle-sheath miner, Zelleria haimbachi*. USDA Forest Service Tech. Paper 30. 20 p.

Strong, F. C. 1953. 'Spruce branch canker.' *Proc. Twenty-ninth National Shade Tree Conference*. p. 30-36.

Stuckey, Irene H. 1961. 'Leaf drop of *Taxus*.' *Plant Disease Reptr*. Vol. 45 (No. 7). p. 527-29.

Terry, T. A., Treillon, H. B., and E. B. Walker. 1973. '*Scleroderris* canker on red and Scots pine in Vermont.' *Plant Disease Reptr*. Vol. 57 (No. 4). p. 338

Van Arsdel, E. P., A. J. Riker and R. F. Patton. 1956. 'The effects of temperature and moisture on the spread of white pine blister rust.' *Phytopathology*. Vol. 46. p. 307-18.

Waterman, A. M. 1943. '*Diplodia pinea*, the cause of a disease of hard pines.' *Phytopathology*. Vol. 33 (No. 11). p. 1018-31.

White, R. P. 1931. *Diseases of ornamental plants*. N. J. Agr. Exp. Sta. Circ. 226. 97 p.

Wilson, C. L. 1961. 'An undescribed blight disease of Arizona cypress.' *Plant Disease Reptr*. Vol. 45 (No. 21). p. 96-98.

Wilson, L. F. 1962. *Yellow-headed spruce sawfly*. USDA Forest Service Leaflet 69. 4 p.

Zentmeyer, G. A. 1941. 'Cytospora canker of Italian cypress.' *Phytopathology*. Vol. 31 (No. 10). p. 896-906.

Index

563